Ethnic Humor Around the World

Ethnic Humor Around the World

A Comparative Analysis

Christie Davies

Indiana University Press ○ Bloomington and Indianapolis

Manufactured in the United States of America

Library of Congress Cataloging-in-Publication Data

Davies, Christie.
Ethnic humor around the world : a comparative analysis / Christie Davies.
p. cm.
Bibliography: p.
Includes index.
ISBN 0-253-31655-3
1. Ethnic wit and humor—History and criticism. 2. Wit and humor—Social aspects. I. Title.
PN6149.E83D39 1990
809.7′0003—dc20 88–46026
CIP

1 2 3 4 5 94 93 92 91 90

For Gwenda and Janetta and in memory of my father, Christy Davies

CONTENTS

List of Tables

Acknowledgments

In *Ethnic Humor Around the World* I have tried to provide an extensive comparative account of the world's ethnic jokes. The study has its origins in Gujarat in India and in Wales. When lecturing at Sardar Patel University and the M. S. University of Baroda, I became conscious of the close similarity between the ethnic jokes told by Indians and ethnic jokes prevailing in the United States and the United Kingdom, despite the unmistakably local origin of the Gujarati versions. At about the same time, I became curious about the social origins and changing nature of the ethnic jokes that have been told by the English about my own people, the Welsh, for several hundred years past. From these particular concerns grew my interest in the differences and similarities among ethnic jokes throughout the world, an interest which I have pursued in every continent except the Antarctic. Such a study has required the help and cooperation of scholars in many countries, and I am especially conscious of the assistance I have received in the translation of jokes from a diversity of languages. In particular, I thank José Alvarez Junco, Stanislav Andreski, Mahadev Apte, Zyg Baranski, Chris Chevis, Peter Cook, William Coupe, Pete Crofts, Emil Draitser, Alan Dundes, André and Liliane Ghilain, Robin Gwyndaf, J. R. Hawthorn, Melvin Helitzer, John Hobgood, Bengt Holbek, Colin Holmes, Randolph Ivy, Christoph Jaffke, Marjatta Jauhianen, Mark, Janet, and Samuel Jenkinson, Peter K. Jones, Ernest Krausz, Lauri Lehtimaja, Russell Lewis, Richard Lynn, Des MacHale, Geoffrey Matthews, Lawrence Mintz, Don and Aileen Nilsen, Elliott Oring, Charles Preston, Pirkko-Lissa Rausmaa, Walter Redfern, W. M. S. Russell, Barry Schechter, Charles Schutz, Alexander Shtromas, Elene Skondra, Henry D. Spalding, Eugene Trivizas, Magne Velure, the late Alan Wardman, Larry Wilde, and Avner Ziv, for providing me with data, advice, help with translation, and other valuable assistance. None of them is responsible for the use I have made of material they provided, and the opinions expressed in this book are of course entirely my own.

I have also received a great deal of help from colleagues in or from Eastern Europe and I only wish that glasnost was sufficiently well established for me to be able to thank all those East Europeans who provided, translated, and explained their local ethnic and political jokes.

I owe a particular debt to John McDowell and Victor Raskin, who read and commented on the earliest and the penultimate versions of the manuscript respectively; to Robert Mandel, who commissioned the book for Indiana University Press,to my editor, Lauren Bryant, and to my manuscript editor, Nancy Ann Miller, whose skill, judgment and encouragement have been essential to the turning of an idea into a book. I have also relied heavily on the accurate and conscientious word processing of Denise Phillips.

Much of the research for this book has been done in archives and libraries and I would like to express my thanks for their help to the staff of the libraries and folklore archives of the University of California, Berkeley, Indiana University, and the House of Humour and Satire in Gabrovo, and to the staff of the British Library, the Bodleian Library, the library of the London School of Economics, the National Library of Wales, the Polish-American Museum in Chicago, the Schmulowitz Collection in San Francisco Public Library, the libraries of Bombay, Cambridge, Leeds, Punjab, and Reading Universities, and the libraries of the University Colleges of Cork, London, Saint David's Lampeter, and Swansea. I am grateful to the British Council, the Indian University Grants Council, the Institute of Humane Studies, and the research board of the University of Reading for helping to fund the expenses involved in visiting the various libraries and archives.

The editorial staff of the *Christchurch Press*, Christchurch, New Zealand, and of the *Brisbane Courier-Mail*, Brisbane, Queensland, Commonwealth of Australia, presented through their newspapers my requests for material and information. I thank them for their help, which was very useful in broadening my Southern Hemisphere material.

My greatest debt is to my father, Christy Davies, himself a social scientist with a keen sense of humor, whose consistent interest in my work was vital to the research on which this book is based. His close involvement can best be illustrated by an incident from the world's first International Conference on Humour, held in Cardiff, Wales, in 1976. I wrote a paper for the Conference but was unable to go to Cardiff to deliver it. My father agreed to give it in my place and was televised doing so. To this day I am still meeting humor scholars who are unsure whether I am my father or myself. It was a devastating loss to me when my father died suddenly while I was halfway through writing this book. I have dedicated it to him as the person who encouraged me to begin writing it, and to Gwenda and Janetta, whose support enabled me to complete the task.

Ethnic Humor Around the World

CHAPTER ONE
Introduction

Jokes about peoples consist of short narratives or riddles with comic endings which impute a particular ludicrous trait or pattern of behavior to the butts of the joke. Such jokes are a very old phenomenon indeed but they are particularly widespread and popular in the modern world, where they are often known as ethnic jokes. The term *ethnic* tends to be used in a broad way about a group that sees itself and is seen by others as a "people" with a common cultural tradition, a real or imagined common descent, and a distinctive identity.[1] This judgment is usually related to objective factors such as territory or language, though both of these may relate to the group's past, and to the life led by its members' ancestors rather than today's members. Thus, for example, the Poles in Poland constitute a people because they have a distinct territory, language, history, and culture. Neither changes in boundaries, nor partition, nor loss of political independence in the past affected this, though they each might have done, for ethnic groups can and do merge and disappear. The ethnic identity of the Poles in America is loosely linked via their ancestors to a territory that most of them have never seen, to a language that few of them speak,[2] to a nation that had no political existence when their ancestors left it. Yet it is real for all that [see Gordon 1975], though there are clearly major differences between the nature of the ethnic identity of dispersed groups of immigrants and that of territorially based nations and subnations.[3]

Although in essence ethnicity is a primordial characteristic rooted in common descent, an ethnic identity may be chosen or changed either by individuals or by the collective decision of a group, whether suddenly and deliberately or as a gradual result of other decisions [see Horowitz 1975; Smith 1981]. Individuals emigrate, assimilate, intermarry, or "convert," and the members of an ethnic group may collectively choose to assert or neglect the factors that set them apart from others. Using the verb *to choose* very loosely indeed,[4] it could be said that the Americans chose to become a new and separate as well as a politically independent people, that the Newfoundlanders initially at least chose to be "Newfies," not Canadians, that the Jews chose to be the chosen people [cf. Davies 1982A], that the Dutch chose to separate their language from German, that the Belgians chose not to be Dutch, that the Scots chose to retain their own distinctive religious institutions and legal system and their separate ethnic identity when they united politically with England.

If a group is defined and excluded by others in terms of "race," whether or not this is linked to differences in physical appearance, then such choices are blocked. The members of the group are forced to remain a group apart, regardless of their wishes as individuals or as a people making a collective decision. In this special case ancestry becomes an absolute barrier, a form of total exclusion, instead of merely being a usual or preferred criterion for inclusion.[5]

The importance of ethnicity and of ethnic identity varies over time in any particular society, and there even seem to be general cyclical oscillations in the importance of ethnic ties in a range of societies having similar social structures and interconnected cultures [Petersen 1975, 182–83; Smith 1981, 82]. Since people tell jokes about subjects that are salient to them [see Goldstein, Suls, Anthony 1972] a rise in the consciousness and assertion of ethnicity, such as took place in the "ethnic revival" of the 1960s and 1970s,[6] is inevitably accompanied by a boom in ethnic jokes [see Apte 1985, 109]. Such jokes have been generally popular and widespread for a very long time,[7] but the fashion for them fluctuates in line with the overall importance of ethnicity as a social category.

Ethnic identity is often buttressed by religion, as in the case of the Poles, Irish, Scots, Welsh, Dutch, or Greeks, and may even be largely based on religion, as in the case of the Sikhs or the Jews. Jokes about the latter groups or about the religious aspects of any ethnic group's identity have been treated as relevant to this study, but jokes about religions or denominations as such have been excluded. There is a clear sense in which the Jews or the Sikhs, like the Roman Catholic Irish, the Non-Conformist Welsh, the Presbyterian Scots, the Orthodox Greeks, the Shi'ite Persians, the Muslim Pakistanis, the Buddhist Singhalese, constitute a people whereas Roman Catholics, Presbyterians, or Buddhists in general do not and neither do Baptists, Christian Scientists, Mormons, Quakers, Jesuits, Chasidim, or Brahmins, all of whom are the subject of jokes. It is, however, sometimes a difficult distinction to make in practice and it would be futile to try to make a rigorous distinction between ethnic jokes about the religion of a particular people and jokes about religion per se. Similarly, this study in general excludes jokes about the people of a particular town or village or administrative district, but in many cases jokes of this kind, such as those about the peoples of, say, Århus or Laihia, Cardiganshire or Kerry, Ostfriesland or Gabrovo, Monterrey or Aberdeen, are so very similar to the truly ethnic jokes told elsewhere that it would be senseless to omit them. Also jokes told about groups as diverse as Aggies, aristocrats, or apparatchiks, who are defined in completely nonethnic terms, often provide a basis for comparisons which reveal new insights into the nature of unambiguously "ethnic" jokes. Indeed, scholars with a specialized interest in folklore who have studied traditional tales about noodles and numskulls, misers and tricksters may well wish to add yet further dimensions to the comparative analysis employed here.

Jokes about peoples seem at first glance to be of infinite variety and to be easily switched from one group to another. In the English language alone there are jokes about canny Scotsmen, inebriated Irishmen, dumb and dirty Poles, cowardly Italians, boastful Americans, crafty Jews, uptight Englishmen, militaristic Germans, coarse Australians, promiscuous blacks, backward Newfies, and even aggressive, cheese-guzzling Welshmen who later became devious and pious. American jokes about Poles overlap with British jokes about the Irish, French jokes about Belgians, Indian jokes about Sikhs, Greek jokes about Pontians, Brazilian jokes about the Portuguese, and so on all over the world. The purpose of this study is to try to discern the orderly patterns that underlie this apparently chaotic diversity of ethnic jokes, to uncover the implicit cultural "rules" that permit the switching of ethnic jokes between some groups but not others, and to suggest social explanations for these patterns and rules.

It should be stressed at this point that the orderly pattern to be found in a large aggregate of jokes is a spontaneous and self-adjusting and not a planned or corporate order [see Barry 1982; Polanyi 1951, 156, 185]. Jokes are invented and circulated anonymously [cf. Freud 1960, 142] by a very large number of separate individuals who have no common organization or purpose. The orderly pattern that emerges is like that to be found in the marketplace or in conversations and differs from that of a machine or even an organization which is designed for a particular reason by a known and limited number of people. Jokes differ from comedies, cartoons, caricatures, and humorous essays in that, especially when taken in aggregate, they are authorless and it is pointless to look behind them for the kinds of motives, purposes, and feelings that characterize a single author.[8] Jokes also differ from wit in that the humor they convey is not tied to a particular context but is self-contained, thus enabling a joke to be performed successfully on a quite different occasion. Jokes can of course be used to make a particular point, either overtly or covertly [see Emerson 1969], or to manipulate a social situation; but it is impossible to explain the overall patterns of jokes that exist by studying and aggregating the ways in which a given joke is used in particular social contexts, partly because of the sheer variety of different uses which ingenious human beings can find for a joke[9] and partly because most joke-telling is done as a performance which is an end in itself and the joke is a welcome release from the serious telic world of goals and means. Equally, it is not possible to move in the other direction and to deduce from the content alone of a particular joke the motives and feelings of those who share it, for these can only be discovered [cf. Green 1976, 29–30] by a combination of direct observation of the way and the context in which the joke is told and the collection of a good deal of other independent data concerning the individuals involved and the relationships between them. Studies of the latter kind[10] are of great interest and importance, but they operate at a quite different level from the present study.

The basic questions that are addressed in this study relate primarily to the content of the most numerous and widespread ethnic jokes. In general the central theme of these jokes is the pinning of some undesirable quality on a particular ethnic group in a comic way or to a ludicrous extent. This immediately raises two questions: First, why are there so many ethnic jokes about certain paired qualities, notably stupidity and canniness but also cowardice and militarism or aggressiveness, inebriation and teetotalism, snobbishness and vulgarity, boastfulness and understatement? Secondly, why are these qualities pinned onto particular groups in a highly specific way to produce an easily recognizable ethnic script? Why are comic Scotsmen canny or inebriated but not cowardly or snobbish? Why are there jokes that make the shrewd Belgians appear stupid or the well-scrubbed Poles appear dirty?

The answers to these questions will be sought by the use of the comparative method, including a consideration of situations where there is an absence of ethnic jokes even though the (mainly functionalist and conflict) sociological theories of the past suggest that such jokes should proliferate under these particular circumstances. Where similar jokes are told in different places about a variety of groups, an attempt will be made to see what the joke-tellers have in common, what the butts of their jokes have in common, and what the links between pairs of joke-teller and butt have in common. The insights that are gained from these comparisons will then be applied to other cases where there are not enough examples to make such a systematic comparison possible. In each case the jokes will be studied in relation to the broad social and historical situation in which they occur and an attempt will be made to correlate the jokes told about any one group with independent data derived from other studies concerning that group's culture and traditions, rank in a system of social stratification, and social position vis-à-vis the joke-tellers. Similarly the joke-tellers' view of themselves, and their ideological beliefs concerning others, will be examined where relevant. The relative importance of each of these factors will be assessed wherever possible.

Finally, when some kind of basis for the assessment and analysis of ethnic jokes has been established, it should prove possible to make predictions about the significance of ethnic jokes other than those that have formed part of the study and to say whether or not particular types of ethnic jokes can be used as an index of social conditions and relationships.

A further issue that will be dealt with where appropriate concerns the structure of the ethnic jokes themselves. I shall argue that the ethnic identity of the butts of a joke is a necessary part of the construction of certain types of joke. Not only the content but the very form of the jokes depends on conventions regarding comic ethnic traits and on the skilled use of various signals of ethnic identity.

The raw materials of this study are, of course, the ethnic jokes themselves, which have been taken from a variety of sources, both oral and written. Many of the jokes have been recorded by the author in a number of countries and by a variety of scholars, students, and collectors of folklore.[11] Further examples have been taken from printed collections of jokes and anecdotes; these collections have proved particularly useful as a source of the jokes told in past times. In a few cases I have taken jokes from memory or from a brief note of a joke's ending and content that was originally made for use or pleasure rather than study. The latter are in one sense unsatisfactory since they cannot be located firmly in an external source, yet in another respect they are utterly authentic since they were originally memorized or recorded in exactly the same way and for the same reasons that characterize jokes and their tellers in general. In the modern world in particular [see Utley 1971–73] this is how joke-tellers disseminate the jokes they have heard. In almost every case, though, the source (or occasionally the lack of one) of a particular ethnic joke has been recorded and the mode by which a particular joke was acquired can usually be inferred from the notes provided.

In general the jokes taken from different types of source do not differ systematically from one another in content. The only exceptions are those jokes which touch on a taboo subject, such as sexual behavior. There has always been a wealth of spoken jokes about sex, including ethnic ones, but censorship or other, more diffuse social pressures have ensured that many of these never get into print. These pressures are of differing intensity, both between countries and within a given country or culture over time. Indeed, in the nineteenth century in Britain the editors of reprints of the jest-books of an earlier, more permissive age were torn between their duty to reproduce historical documents accurately and their wish to avoid shocking their readers with jokes unsuited to delicate eyes and ears.[12] One consequence of this complication is that it is much more difficult to make a comparative study of jokes about sex than about other subjects, and in this study ethnic jokes about sex are only incidentally referred to.

In most cases the differences between printed and spoken jokes are largely a reflection of the inevitable gap between the way we speak and the way we write. It is an important difference but not one that impinges heavily on the issues raised in this study. Today, at least, jokes shuttle freely between joke-tellers, joke-collectors, and anthologies of jokes. The editors of some of the major contemporary anthologies of jokes do at times omit or water down ethnic jokes that they think might prove ultra-offensive to a section of their potential readers, but these jokes emerge elsewhere in other, more outrageous collections brought out by more daring publishers. In practice most spoken jokes do get into print and there is a reasonable correspondence between the spoken and the written.

One type of ethnic joke that has been deliberately relegated to a minor place in this study is the simple joke in which a member of one ethnic group "puts down" or "scores off" a member of some rival or neighboring ethnic group in an entirely arbitrary way. For example, a member of group X is trying to dissuade a stranger from committing suicide by jumping off a building; he suddenly realizes that he is talking to a member of a rival group, Y, and shouts, "Jump, you Y, jump!"

In such jokes X and Y can change places or be replaced by A and B almost ad infinitum. Precisely for this reason jokes of this type are used by experimenters who want to analyze the differing reactions of individuals to ethnic jokes when everything is held constant except the identity of X and Y. The jokes themselves are regarded as so unimportant that they are often not even reported in accounts of such experiments. If the joke employed in an experiment involves a member of one group urging a member of a rival group to go ahead and commit suicide, it clearly and illicitly biases the experiment by crudely suggesting to the experimentees assessing the jokes the salience and indeed the centrality of interethnic rivalry, conflict, or hostility. If the subjects of the experiment were not given indirect hints and nudges of this kind, they might well assess ethnic jokes in very different ways. The experiments would lose their appearance of formal precision rooted in neatly quantifiable pseudo-variables but they would have far more relevance to social reality.

Jokes of this type differ from most ethnic jokes in that they do not depend on any specified quality being ascribed to an ethnic group. They are usually malleable in that almost any pair of ethnic groups can be fed into them, and the two groups can even change places. Such jokes are atypical of ethnic jokes in general and are largely irrelevant to this study, which is concerned with the content of ethnic jokes that the members of various groups tell about one another. The very aspect of these jokes that makes them so appealing to the experimenter who seeks out ethnic jokes freed from their "irrelevant" social and historical content and context renders them useless for present purposes. The present study is primarily concerned with the origins and reasons for the popularity of specific ethnic scripts [see Raskin 1985, esp. 206], the shared comic images of canny Scots, cowardly Italians, boastful Americans, stupid Newfies, etc., that make ethnic jokes possible. These scripts are conventional, fictional, and mythological [Raskin 1985, 180] and are not seriously held stereotypes, though in certain instances an equivalent stereotype may exist. Where a stereotype exists my explanation of the origins of the ethnic script may also indicate how the corresponding stereotype arose—but this is merely a bonus, for my aim is to avoid the confusion of script and stereotype that has been so common in the past.[13] There are many comic ethnic scripts for which there is no corresponding significant and seriously held stereotype and there are many ethnic stereotypes that have had serious consequences but have not given rise to jokes. Even where there is an apparent match of ethnic script and ethnic stereotype, those who laugh at the jokes do not necessarily subscribe to the stereotype [see Middleton 1959, 180] and indeed may see the joke as a satire on the stereotype, for the ambiguity of humorous statements allows them to be interpreted in radically different ways [see Mulkay 1987].

Ambiguity and incongruity[14] are central to most jokes, for jokes depend on the teller playing with hidden meanings that are suddenly revealed in an unexpected way. Typically a joke consists of a single text which is compatible with two different scripts that are radically opposed to one another [see Raskin 1985, 99]. The skilled joke-teller begins as if he were telling a mundane tale or asking a routine question and the listener, though suspicious, goes along with this until the punch line suddenly switches the joke to a radically different script. First our expectations and interest are aroused by the story, whose purpose we cannot fully discern, and then suddenly all is resolved from a direction we didn't expect. The best accolade the joke-teller can receive is the comment "I didn't see that one coming." As we shall see later, ethnic jokes are especially well constructed, which is one of the factors leading to their popularity.

A further factor that underlies much humor and is brought out particularly well in ethnic jokes is the sense of sudden vicarious superiority felt by those who devise, tell, or share a joke.[15] Ethnic jokes "export" a particular unwanted trait to some other group and we laugh at their folly, perhaps glad or relieved that it is not our own. This possibility is also open to individual members of the ethnic group being ridiculed, for all such groups are internally stratified and differentiated such that a listener from the ethnic group named or implied in the joke can always interpret the joke as referring to a subgroup other than the one to which he or she belongs.[16] Furthermore, individuals are not necessarily simply and unambiguously members of one and only one clearly demarcated ethnic group. In many cases they will have concentric membership in and loyalty to more than one ethnic or national unit [see Smith 1981, 104] and may on occasion identify with and refer or defer to ethnic groups other than the one to which they belong. Far from being trapped in a single, fixed, and predetermined pattern of affiliation, and of reference groups or identification classes, an individual faced with an ethnic joke about what appears to be his or her "own" group can often manipulate the pattern in a creative way so as to become a sharer in the joke rather than a butt of it. Furthermore, jokes are ambiguous and ethnic groups differ in the way they evaluate the particular qualities that are the basis of the scripts of ethnic jokes [see Apte 1985, 142; Arnold 1910, 101]. Reserve is both tact and coldness, cowardice is sensible self-preservation, to be canny may be read as shrewd and thrifty rather than sneaky and stingy [see also Wilson 1979, 146]. Jokes consisting of comic disputes in which the members of one ethnic group win but by dubious means are equally two-edged. The same joke may be easily interpreted and reinterpreted so that both parties to it think that the other "loses" [see Burma 1946, 712]. Thus the "superiority" theory of humor can easily accommodate the fact that those who belong to the group that is the butt of a particular set of ethnic jokes are just as likely to enjoy, tell, and invent such jokes as are outsiders.[17] It should also be remembered that the superiority thesis is only a broad generalization and that there are cases where it may well not apply.

In theory, other things equal, jokers should enjoy more keenly the sense of superiority granted them by a joke when the joke disparages ethnic groups whom they dislike. In practice, however, other things are not equal, and opprobrious scripts are often pinned on ethnic groups toward whom the joke-tellers do not feel hostile, while other situations of intense intergroup resentment or even open ethnic conflict fail to produce any ethnic jokes at all. As soon as the question is approached on a comparative basis the view that ethnic jokes are primarily an expression of ethnic conflicts begins to fall apart. In this study I have outlined my skepticism at length in relation to the analysis of particular types of jokes [see also Oring 1975, 149–50 and 157] and I hope that my criticisms will persuade those who quite validly wish to analyze ethnic jokes in relation to ethnic conflicts to be more precise in their arguments and terminology. I have similar doubts about many of the functional analyses of jokes that portray them as doing wonders for the morale of the jokers at all manner of confused levels from the so-called unconscious mind of the individual to the even more mysterious collective consciousness of a nation, subnation, or ethnic minority of several million people. All too often speculative analyses of the latent functions of ethnic jokes become, in Apte's phrase, "educated guesses at best" [1985, 68]; his choice of adjective is far too generous.

Both functionalist and conflict models misleadingly depict large complex societies as far more integrated and tightly organized than is in fact the case. Societies, except possibly certain small unchanging communities, are not neat consensual assemblages driven by a coherent common set of values, nor are they decisively divided along clear and unchanging lines of cleavage and conflict. Rather, there are shifting, imprecise patterns of consensus, conflict, compromise, contradiction, and anomie. It is particularly dangerous to try to trace clear links between ethnic jokes and the maintenance of a particular order or the furtherance of a particular conflict, for jokes are ambiguous forms of discourse that are created in circumstances and around issues where there is a good deal of uncertainty. While I shall argue that they probably do help briefly to resolve these uncertainties, I would also point out that it is dangerous simply to reduce jokes based on ethnic scripts to what appear to be their serious equivalents or to see them as covert ways of making an accusation. Not only do the joke-tellers deny that this is the case, but if these were in fact their aims they have available to them other and better ways of achieving those aims [see Oring 1975, 149–50].

It is pointless to analyze jokes in terms of their practical consequences, for these consequences are bound to be negligible when compared to the results of other forms of behavior with a direct and clear goal. Yet all too often scholars tend to see ethnic jokes in terms of their supposed consequences, which are then mysteriously recycled to become the causes of the jokes in the first place. This attempt to make jokes appear a more important phenomenon than they really are paradoxically results in the trivialization of humor, for in general jokes neither have consequences nor are they intended to have consequences. Although it is possible to use jokes to further other purposes, and instances of this phenomenon can readily be cited, most joke-telling is done as an end in itself and not as a means to some other end. Thus it is senseless for a sociologist or a student of folklore to conclude an analysis of ethnic jokes or of political jokes in countries with a totalitarian regime by asking a question such as "Are the jokes a safety valve, or do they push the situation toward an explosive confrontation?" [see Burns and Burns 1975, 11–12]. Such a question cannot be answered, and even if an answer were available it would be of little significance.

Jokes are important not because of their consequences but as a phenomenon in their own right, as a favorite pastime of many people and a great source of popular enjoyment and creativity. Also jokes provide insights into how societies work—they are not social thermostats regulating and shaping human behavior, but they are social thermometers that measure, record, and indicate what is going on. To become angry[18] about jokes and to seek to censor[19] them because they impinge on sensitive issues is about as sensible as smashing a thermometer because it reveals how hot it is. Those who do so deserve all the extra derision they then incur for they are fools indeed. Rather, we should collect jokes extensively and examine them intensively, for they can provide us with insights about the societies in which we live that we could not gain in any other way. Indeed, that is one of the key aims of this study. My other main intention is to describe and where possible to explain an activity that takes up a significant part of our lives and provides an even larger portion of our stock of enjoyment.

CHAPTER TWO

The Stupid and the Canny

Although the ethnic jokes told in many societies throughout the world pin a wide range of comic attributes onto a great variety of peoples and ethnic groups, one pair of ethnic jokes seems to be far more widespread, more numerous, and more durable than any other. This pair comprises on the one hand jokes about groups depicted as stupid, inept, and ignorant [see Raskin 1985, 180–88] and on the other, as if in opposition, jokes about groups portrayed as canny, calculating, and craftily stingy. Such jokes far outnumber jokes based on any other comic trait ascribed to any group of people, whether nation, ethnic group, or regional minority. The immense and widespread informal popularity of ethnic jokes about stupidity and canniness [e.g., see Kravitz 1977, 275, 282] has provided joke writers and joke-book publishers with a very large potential market. The huge sales of ethnic joke-books and the diffusion of ethnic jokes through the mass media have made such jokes even more popular [see Wilde 1978A, xi], as has the transfer of new comic ideas, themes, and types from one country to another. Since each country has its own butts for "stupid" and "canny" jokes, ethnic jokes of this kind are easily adapted to fit local circumstances. Such "imports" swell the stock of ethnic jokes available to the people of any country and also stimulate the invention of new jokes, many of which have a very distinctive local flavor. The increased circulation of adaptable cosmopolitan jokes does not result in the destruction of a country's existing tradition of telling ethnic jokes but rather gives a stimulus to it. Old ethnic jokes and themes are revived and revitalized by new ideas and styles in ethnic joking.

Ethnic jokes about "stupid" and "canny" groups are both local and international, both very modern and very ancient. Particularly remarkable is the universality of such jokes. They are especially numerous and popular in industrial societies and in societies in the process of industrialization with a substantial modern sector.

A selection of countries with "stupid" and "canny" jokes is listed in table 2.1. No doubt scholars who have studied jokes in countries other than those cited can add to the list of allegedly stupid and canny groups who are the subject of ethnic jokes. In each of the countries listed in table

TABLE 2.1 **The Stupid and the Canny**

Country where both "stupid" and "canny" jokes are told	Identity of "stupid" group in jokes	Identity of "canny" group in jokes
United States	Poles (and others locally, e.g., Italians, Portuguese)	Jews, Scots, New England Yankees, Iowans
Canada (East and especially Ontario)	Newfies (Newfoundlanders)	Jews, Scots, Nova Scotians
Canada (West)	Ukrainians, Icelanders	Jews, Scots
Mexico	Yucatecos (people from Yucatan	Regiomontanos (citizens of Monterrey)
Colombia	Pastusos (people from Pasto in Nariño)	Paisas (people from Antioquia)
England	Irish	Scots, Jews
Wales	Irish	Cardis (people from Cardiganshire), Scots, Jews
Scotland	Irish	Aberdonians, Jews
Ireland	Kerrymen	Scots, Jews
France	Belgians, Ouin-Ouin (French Swiss)	Auvergnats (people from the Auvergne), Scots, Jews
Netherlands	Belgians, Limburghers	Jews, Scots
Germany	Ostfrieslanders	Swabians, Scots, Jews
Italy	Southern Italians	Milanese, Genovese, Florentines, Scots, Jews, Levantines
Switzerland	Fribourgers	Jews, Genevois, Bâlois (people from Geneva and Bâle/Basel)
Spain	People of Lepe in Andalucia	Aragonese, Catalans
Finland	Karelians	Laihians (people from Laihia)
Bulgaria	Šopi (peasants from rural area outside Sofia)	Gabrovonians (people from Gabrovo), Armenians
Greece	Pontians (Black Sea Greeks)	Armenians

TABLE 2.1 **The Stupid and the Canny**

Country where both "stupid" and "canny" jokes are told	**Identity of "stupid" group in jokes**	**Identity of "canny" group in jokes**
Russia	Ukrainians, Chukchees	Jews
China	Sansui	People from Shansi
India	Sardarjis (Sikhs)	Gujaratis, Sindis
Pakistan	Sardarjis (Sikhs)	Hindus, especially Gujaratis
Iran	Rashtis (Azerbaijanis from Rasht)	Armenians, Isfahanis, Tabrizis (people of Isfahan, Tabriz)
Nigeria	Hausas	Ibos
South Africa	van der Merwe (Afrikaners)	Jews, Scots
Australia	Irish, Tasmanians	Jews, Scots
New Zealand	Irish, Maoris (in the North Island), West Coasters (in the South Island)	Jews, Scots, Dutch

2.1, other types of ethnic jokes are also told. Some of these, such as, say, British-French-Greek-German-American-Czech jokes about "cowardly Italians," occur in more than one country, but none are as numerous or as widespread as the jokes about "stupid" and "canny" groups. These two linked joke types are the dominant ethnic jokes of the modern world, dominant in number, dominant in that they occur in so many countries, and dominant in that they persist over long periods of time.

The sheer variety of ethnic jokes about stupidity and their wide geographical spread are easily illustrated:

A Portuguese (went) to study in England. After some time the man could speak no more. His family, very preoccupied with this fact, took back the man and submitted him to medical exam(ination). The result of medical tests was that the time (the) Portuguese man was in England was not enough for the young man (to) learn English but it was big enough for him to forget (the) Portuguese idiom. [UCBFA Brazil file, James Williams 1965 (1959)]

At the time of the 1982 war in the South Atlantic between Britain and Argentina the Portuguese foreign minister suggested that the dispute between the two countries should be settled by giving the Falkland Islands to Britain and the Malvinas to Argentina. [Brazilian 1980s]

Voice on Irish telephone answering machine: "Speak when you hear the green light." [Chambers 1980, 30]

During the Second World War an Englishman, an Armenian, and a Pontian were hiding from the German army in a derelict house. The Englishman hid in a bamboo chest, the Armenian hid in a tin tub, and the Pontian in a sack. A German soldier came in to look for them and could just about see the chest, the tub, and the sack in the dark room. The soldier kicked the bamboo chest and the Englishman went "miaow miaow." He then kicked the tin tub and the Armenian went "woof! woof!" Finally he kicked the sack and the Pontian said, "Potatoes." [Greek 1980s]

A ship arrived in Athens with no passengers on board. When the ship stopped outside the harbor, all the Pontians got out to push. [Greek 1980s]

Hercules, an intelligent Pontian, and a stupid Pontian are in a room with an apple pie. Which of them gets to eat it?

The stupid Pontian. The other two are imaginary. [Greek 1980s]

Why does a Pontian place a full glass of water and an empty glass next to his bed before he goes to sleep?

One is in case he feels thirsty during the night and the other is in case he doesn't. [Greek 1980s]

Why are Sikhs called Sardars (Surds)?

Because they are the irrational fraction of India. [Indian 1960s]

The house belonging to the Indian Olympic athlete Milka Singh was broken into by thieves who ran away when discovered. Milka Singh ran after them at full speed . . . and overtook them. [Kashmiri 1970s]

Three Sardarjis were standing on a station platform. The train arrived but they didn't notice it until it was about to leave. Then there was a wild rush to get on. Two of them made it but one was left behind. A bystander said, "Never mind, your friends caught the train." "Yes," said the Sardarji, "but they were only here to see me off." [Gujarati 1970s]

Wykowski was arrested for rape. "Don't worry," said the cop, "We'll treat you fair, we'll put you in a line-up with un-uniformed policemen."

They did. They brought the victim in. Wykowski saw the woman, pointed to her and said, "Yeah, that's her." [Wilde 1975A, 26]

Did you hear about the Maori whose library burned down? Not only did the fire destroy his books, but, worse still, he hadn't finished coloring in the second one. [New Zealand 1980s]

Ostfrieslanders visiting Swabia have been forbidden to climb up the Fernsehturm (TV mast). They used to stay up there all day trying to feed the helicopters. [German 1970s]

A Newfie phoned Air Canada and asked the girl how long it took to fly from Newfoundland to Toronto. The girl replied, "One second, Sir."

The Newfie said, "Thank you." [Canadian 1970s]

Why did the Newfie move his house two inches?

He was trying to tighten his clothesline. [Canadian 1970s]

A customer asked a Belgian serving behind a fast-food counter: "Two ham sandwiches please, one of them without mustard."

Belgian: "Which one of them do you want without mustard?" [French 1970s]

These jokes cover many types of stupidity and show the variety of settings in which comic stupidity can be placed. Also they show a range of style, from narratives employing comparisons between the "stupid" group and others, to succinct jokes in the form of riddles. Some of these jokes can easily be switched from one country to another. Thus the joke about the three Sikhs trying to get on a train or a bus is also told about three Poles in America, and the Canadian joke about the Newfie phoning the airport is told about Belgians in France and about the Irish in Britain. There is often little point in trying to discover where a particular joke began, for jokes travel freely and quickly from one place to another and are easily adapted to local circumstances. It would be quite wrong, however, to refer to these ethnic jokes as "floating" jokes [cf. Dundes 1971, 192], since this implies that they could be and are applied to any group whatsoever. The belief that there is a simple antithesis between the "fixed" and the "floating" is as delusory in the study of jokes as in the economics of exchange rates. There are many possible positions between these two extremes which could be recognized and described, though the economists' vocabulary is hardly suited to the study of ethnic jokes. Phrases such as "dirty float," "crawling peg," or "monetary snake" would soon turn into new jokes in their own right. The crucial point is that ethnic jokes about stupidity are frequently and easily told about some groups and rarely about others.

Ethnic jokes about stupidity are easily transferable between different groups all over the world because people in different countries and cultures increasingly seem to have a common view of what constitutes stupidity. There appears to be much less cultural variation regarding the definition of and attitudes toward this admittedly very broad negative human quality than there is in respect to, say, cowardice, impiety, sexual irregularity, boastfulness, or dirtiness. Stupidity is perceived and depicted as a general and universal quality and has come to include and to refer particularly to an inability to understand and cope with those technical aspects of the modern world that are common to most countries rather than simply to a lack of understanding of local customs, practices, or forms of speech.

In the world of jokes the opposite of *stupid* is *canny*,[1] rather than *clever*. The canny person has to have cleverness, but canniness also requires a crafty, calculating, thrifty, measuring disposition. Canniness implies cleverness and rationality, but it is a shrewd cleverness, and a calculating rationality applied in the pursuit of personal advantage [see Junior 1925, 3; Todd 1977, 10; see also Proust vol. I, 304]. Indeed, jokes about "canny" groups often depend not so much on their capacity to be shrewd and calculating (which is taken for granted) but rather on their alleged disposition to use these qualities in ways and in contexts that others find ludicrously inappropriate and excessive.

The comically canny hero of ethnic jokes is represented as "too clever," "too clever by half," "too clever for his own good—or anyone else's, come to that." In ethnic jokes about the canny, calculating carefulness is exaggerated into a pointless and even self-destructive stinginess, rational self-control is made to lead to a dour and joyless existence, and the shrewd pursuit of self-interest is carried much too far and results in crass infringements of social conventions or in sharp practice, the swindling of others, and a general erosion of trust. Good qualities have associated defects and it is those defects that are derived from the canny virtues that form the basis of ethnic jokes about allegedly canny groups.

Ethnic jokes about peoples who have been labeled canny rival in popularity and variety the ethnic jokes about stupidity and are also found in many different countries:

Do you know the best way to stop a riot in Monterrey?
Send in the Red Cross collectors [Mexican 1980s]

A Swabian climbing in Switzerland fell down a crevasse in a glacier. An hour later a rescue team arrived at the edge of the crevasse and peered down at him. "It's the Red Cross," they shouted. "Go away," he replied, "I already gave at the office." [German 1980s]

A test was conducted on the Arctic Circle to see who was more stingy, a Scot or a Laihian. The competitors were shut in a cold room at minus 40 degrees Centigrade with a sack of coal and a box of matches.

When, after a week, the door was opened, the frozen Scot was found warming himself on his second piece of coal. The Laihian was running round the room bathed in sweat with the whole sack of coal on his back. [Jauhianinen 1979. See also 1983]

A person is traveling to the town of Ahmedabad, Gujerat for the first time by train. He is anxious about missing his stop so he descends from the train at each station to ask if he has arrived at Ahmedabad. Finally in answer to his question a man replies "If you give me five paise I'll tell you." The traveler answers "I must be here." [UCBFA Pakistan file]

This is Radio Israel broadcasting on three hundred metres—but for you, two hundred and eighty. [British 1960]

Scotland Yard: 2' 11". [Wilde 1978A, 221]

There on Jumbie Bridge in the old rebel days an old Indian man stopped a bus and enquired after price of fare to Arima. The conductor told him the price was one shilling. Pushing his suitcase on the bus he enquired:

'And how much for this grip?'

'That will go free,' he was assured.

'Ahrl right, carry go grip, me go come waarkin.'

The conductor became insensed [*sic*] and threw the suitcase in the river. At this the Indian started to bawl.

'O Gaard! How you try to drown my little boy?' [Carballo 1977]

Englishman: I hear the price of petrol's coming down.

Scotsman: Och that's great news.

Englishman: But why are you so pleased? You don't own a car do you?

Scotsman: No but I have a lighter. [*The World's Even Worse Worst Jokes Book* 1985]

Three Nigerian clergymen were discussing how they divided up the collection money between themselves and their religion. First the Hausa said "I take my expenses—about 10 percent—and I give the rest to God." Then the Yoruba said "Well, I try to be fair. I divide it up equally, half for me and half for God." Finally the Ibo said "I keep all the money on the collection plate. Then I throw it up into the air, God takes what he wants and I keep the rest." [Nigerian 1980s]

Aberdonian to son stranded on high wall: 'Jump son. Jump, Daddy will catch you.' Son jumps. Father steps aside, saying 'That's your first good lesson. Trust nobody.' [SFGB. Also see Ernst 1927]

A man went into a chemist's shop in Aberdeen and left without his change. As he went down the street the chemist tried to attract his attention by knocking on the window with a sponge. [SFGB]

The popularity and indeed the sheer volume of ethnic jokes about "stupid" and "canny" groups are phenomena that call for an explanation. Why are these jokes so much more common in the modern world than ethnic jokes about other human characteristics and failings? By contrast the jests and anecdotes of the past are said to have dealt more evenly with the "whole gamut of human inadequacies" [Ranke 1972, 13–14]; members of other groups might be characterized as cowardly, belligerent, lazy, gloomy, irreligious, superstitious, gluttonous, untruthful, or dishonest, as well as stupid and canny. Some of these themes are still alive and well while others are moribund, but none of them can compare with ethnic jokes about the stupid and the canny. These latter qualities are admirably suited to the construction of jokes, to the provision of sudden and often bizarre punch lines to end an otherwise plausible tale or of unexpected answers to apparently reasonable questions. Indeed, jokes about numskulls and noodles, tricksters and misers have a long history [e.g., see Shankara 1934]. The idea of pinning comic qualities onto particular groups of people to form ethnic jokes is a very ancient one. The problem to be tackled here is not why such jokes exist but rather what it is about urban, industrial societies, or societies in the process of becoming so, that has led their citizens to create such an enormous stock of ethnic jokes about canniness and stupidity and to take delight in jokes about these themes rather than others.

To answer this question it is necessary to examine how the qualities *stupidity* and *canniness* are regarded in modern societies and the degree to which this attitude differs from the state of affairs to be found in other, more traditional communities. One crucial aspect of the modern world that sets it apart from earlier societies is the extent to which many of its activities and especially work are dependent on the application of a rapidly changing and expanding body of skills, knowledge, and techniques. In a static, traditional society a limited set of skills or amount of learning that is within the capacity of most of its members can last a lifetime, and each new generation needs to acquire only a very slightly modified version of those skills used by its predecessors. Tools and machinery change slowly and their users can understand and repair them without any great difficulty. In such a society it is possible for individuals to make stupid errors in their use of language or to display a lack of practical common sense or understanding, and these mistakes are both a cause of mirth in themselves and the basis on which exaggerated comic narratives or jokes can be constructed. However, the general lack of literacy and numeracy, of any abstract scientific understanding, or of complex machinery requiring and yet also teaching precise and systematic ideas means that there is a relatively limited range of circumstances in which comic stupidity can be displayed.

The lack of formal education and the relative absence of machinery in such a society mean that its people may be deficient in logical and conceptual skills and may have difficulty in thinking in an abstract and general way or in understanding causality, dimensional analysis, or quantitative measurement [see Hallpike 1976, 254–62, and 1979, 30–31, 98–101]. Their failure to appreciate the conservation of quantities, length, etc. [Hallpike 1976, 254, and 1979, 31, 96] means that they cannot appreciate jokes about stupidity involving these subjects, though they may be the butts of them:

An English gentleman travelling from Corke to Waterford met a native of whom he enquired, How many miles it was from Corke to Waterford. The other considering of it a-while at length returned; "Bee Chreesht, Dear Joy, I cannot tell dee how many miles it ish from Corke to Waterford but it ish about eighteen miles from Waterford to Corke." [*Teagueland Jests or Bogg Witticisms* 1690, 104]

[An Irish officer in the British army was showing off his new uniform when an acquaintance noticed] that one of his scarlet stockings was the wrong way outward and told him of the mistake; who replied "I did it on purpose for dat dere wash a hole on de oder shide." [*Teagueland Jests or Bogg Witticisms* 1690, 92]

It is possible that there was a directly corresponding reality behind these jokes about people from a backward peasant society or from the lowest social classes, as Hallpike suggests [1976, 261–62] on the basis of his study of primitive societies today. However, similar ethnic jokes are told today about the Irish or the Poles despite the subtle achievements of Fitzgerald and Sklodowska that demonstrate the limits of notions of strict and inevitable conservation of quantity. The reason these jokes persist lies in the way most, though not all, people have learned about the conservation of quantities in the course of their education or their technical experience and in the errors they therefore ascribe to young children or to the very stupid or ignorant. Modern ethnic jokes on this theme thus indicate what the joke-tellers confidently know rather than the real ignorance of the butts of the jokes:

Six Poles climbed up on one another's shoulders to try and discover the height of a flagpole with a tape measure. Following the predictable collapse of this human pyramid a passerby asked them why they did not simply lower the flagpole to the ground and then measure it. "Don't be silly," said one of the Poles, "we want to measure height not length." [American 1970s]

A Sabena (the Belgian airline) plane was trying to land at Brussels airport. The Belgian pilot signaled to the control tower that the landing strip was too short for him to land on. "Your landing strip," he said in despair, "is only a hundred meters long and several kilometers wide." [French 1980s]

Pat Murphy was riding on a donkey which also had to carry a heavy sack of potatoes and soon got slow and tired. Feeling sorry for the beast, Pat took the sack of potatoes off his back, hoisted it onto his own shoulders, got back in the saddle and rode on. [British]

In ethnic jokes, or in parallel jokes about confrontations between country bumpkins and city slickers, it is noticeable that when those who are normally the butts of jokes about stupidity succeed in winning an argument, it is usually a victory of verbal trickery over logic where the "stupid" one uses language skills to evade the point [cf. Hallpike 1979, 120–21]. It is not a display of verbal reasoning of a universal kind but rather a manipulation of those aspects of language which mirror the idiosyncratic complexity of a primitive preliterate rural social order [cf. Hallpike 1979, v-vi].

The predicaments of rapid social and economic change that are always potentially present in modern industrial societies are not experienced by the peoples of the simpler societies unless novel techniques or artifacts are brought in from outside. The inhabitants of these simpler societies are unlikely to invent or tell the kind of ethnic jokes about stupidity that are so popular in more advanced societies, because as individuals they are unlikely to be confronted with new and baffling technical situations in which their skills prove useless and obsolete and their knowledge inadequate and redundant so that they suddenly and uneasily feel stupid. The introduction of new, sophisticated techniques and machinery from the outside may either provoke crisis and social collapse or else lead to a slow and difficult period of change and adjustment. In the latter case alone are ethnic jokes about stupidity likely to flourish, with those who adjust more slowly and with greater difficulty being the butts of the jokes.

In static societies that are still based on simple technology and relatively isolated from the outside world disaster strikes only too frequently, usually as a result of unpredictable natural forces which nobody in the society understands. The minor mishaps that occur as a result of individual stupidity or error are relatively unimportant compared with the ravages of drought, famine, or plague and what the insurance companies in their wisdom call Acts of God.

The extension of human control over the natural world by means of increased knowledge, whether stored in people's heads, in books, or in computers or built into the design of their machines, means that stupidity becomes a far more threatening quality. Natural disasters recede, but the consequences of human error become relatively and perhaps absolutely more significant. In a society with a complex division of labor everyone is dependent—and knows that they are—on the competence of anonymous specialists, on the operators and builders of impersonal machines [see Helitzer 1984, 30–31; Newall 1985, 150] who exercise skills that are often incomprehensible to the majority of people in that society. If one of these specialized experts makes a stupid error in the designing or fabrication of a bridge, a factory, an automobile, or a satellite, in the manufacture of a drug, an explosive, or a fire extinguisher, in the programming of a computer [see Cane 1984], the funding of a loan, or the siting of a coal tip, the result can be horrendous. People have reason to feel concerned about the consequences not merely of their own blunders but of the blunders of others also. Stupidity is a quality best comically banished to the periphery and located safely in some other group.

Those who travel through the air or space or under the sea can survive only so long as they remain within a special scientifically controlled and constructed environment, and such passengers are placed in dependent, precarious, and artificial situations—an extreme version of the position of the members of a technically advanced society of interdependent specialists. Many ethnic jokes about stupidity have as their setting an airplane, a helicopter, a space rocket, or a submarine. (Submarines are frequently found in French jokes, as Stephane Steeman has noted: "The submarine seems to inspire our French friends and it is with 'chips' the most popular subject of Belgian jokes invented in France" [1977, 95].) In these jokes "stupid" outsiders are placed in positions of control and the result is muddle, chaos, and disaster.

A qualified Belgian pilot was explaining to a new trainee how to fly the plane at night. "You see that red light on the left wing?"

"Yes."

"You see that green light on the right wing?"

"Yes."

"Well night-flying is very easy. You just fly between the two lights." [Van der Boute-Hen Train 1978, 10]

How do you recognize a Belgian in a submarine?

He's the one with a parachute on his back. [Isnard 1979A, 109]

Why are people from Århus not allowed to become sailors in submarines?

Because they like to sleep with the windows open. [Yearhouse 1979]

The pilot of a plane approaching Heathrow airport asked the control tower for a time check. The control tower replied: "If that's Quaint-arse the Australian airline, well the time is now three o'clock. If it's Air France, well the time is now fifteen hundred hours. And if you're Aer Fungus, the Irish airline, well the big hand is on the twelve and the little hand is on the three." [British 1970s]

Aer Fungus, the Irish airline, introduced a completely automatic plane on their flight from Dublin to London. As the plane took off from Dublin airport, a deep voice announced on the loudspeaker: "This is your computer control speaking. You are now traveling in the world's first pilotless completely computerized and automatic aircraft. Everything has been carefully programmed by the very best Irish engineers and you can rest assured that nothing can possibly go wrong, go wrong, go wrong . . . " [British 1960s]

During World War II a German anti-aircraft battery (plane) is flying above, an American plane comes into view. The private aboard the German plane asks his commander what to do. The commander answers, "open fire and Shoot It Down!" This happens also with French, British, Japanese and Russian war planes. They are all shot down by the Germans. When finally the private sees a Mexican plane approaching. The private yells, "Commander! There is a Mexican plane in view. What should we do? Should we open fire?" "No," says the Commander, "just let it fall down by itself." [UCBFA Mexican-American file, Susan Dube 1971 (1963)]

The Swedes sent their first rocket up into outer space with a crew consisting of a chimpanzee and a Norwegian. On the control panel in front of them was a red light and a green light. When the red light flashed it indicated that instructions were about to come through for the Norwegian, and when the green light showed it signaled an imminent instruction for the chimpanzee. Ten minutes after blast-off the green light flashed and the chimpanzee was instructed to alter the course of the rocket slightly, to take infra-red photographs of Sweden, and to repair the radio transmitter. Half an hour later the green light flashed again and the chimpanzee was told to calculate the rate of fuel consumption, adjust the computer, and make observations in connection with the earth's magnetic field.

By this time the Norwegian was getting restless at having nothing to do and resentful of the busy chimpanzee. Then one hour later the red light flashed and the Norwegian eagerly awaited his instructions. A minute later came the order: "Feed the chimpanzee." [Swedish 1970s]

Pokorski got a job as a test pilot. He took a helicopter up to 5,000 feet . . . 10,000 feet . . . 15,000 feet. All of a sudden it crashed.

Pokorski woke up in hospital and his boss was there asking him, "What happened?"

"It got too cold," said the Polish pilot, "so I turned off the fan!" [Wilde 1977, 135]

A Šop astronaut went to the Soviet Union for training. He came back with very red hands. When asked why, he said, "The Russian pilot kept slapping my hands and saying, 'Don't touch that! Don't touch that!' " [Bulgarian 1980s]

Van was a wealthy Free State farmer with his own aeroplane. One day while on holiday in the Cape his friend Van Tonder asked Van if he would like to fly his seaplane. Van gratefully accepted and did a perfect take off from the bay accompanied by Van Tonder as his co-pilot. After flying around for some time, Van began letting down over the aerodrome much to Van Tonder's alarm.

'Hey, Van', he said, 'this is a seaplane, not an aeroplane. You must land on water, not on land'.

Van thanked Van Tonder for his timely advice, pushed forward the throttle and flew off to the bay where he did a graceful landing. He then turned to Van Tonder and said, 'I cannot thank you enough for reminding me not to land on that aerodrome. If you had not pointed it out, it would have been the end of us'.

With these words he stepped out of the plane into the water. [Carver 1980, 39]

The view that modern folklore reflects perceptions of new and incomprehensible technology through, for example, urban legends about disasters in general and crashing airplanes in particular has been expressed by Paul Smith (1983) in *The Book of Nasty Legends*. In relation to the section of his collection on twentieth century technology, Smith comments that "Our dependence on technology and its consequent dangers are encapsulated in tales such as 'The Auto-pilot' and 'Dangers of the Microwave Oven,' " tales that "in the societies in which they are told are considered to be truthful accounts of current situations and events" [1983, 10; see also 63. Helitzer 1984B, 30–31; Newall 1985, 143, 150]. The "sick" jokes that emerge with such rapidity after a disaster also emphasize our potentially precarious dependence on others' expertise in complex societies based on advanced technology, as can be seen from the following jokes about the space shuttle *Challenger*, the Chernobyl reactor, the Aberfan coal tip, the sinking of a car ferry in Zeebrugge, and the fire at the King's Cross subway station:[2]

What does NASA stand for?
Need another seven astronauts. [American 1986]

Why won't they let Ronald Reagan play badminton?
He can't keep a shuttle in the air. [British 1986]

Radio announcement: They've found the black box from *Challenger* and played the tapes back. The pilot's last words to Christa McAuliffe were: "Hey, teacher, why don't you try flying this ship." [American 1986]

What's worse than glass in baby food?
Astronauts in tuna. [Oring 1987]

What is the weather forecast for Chernobyl?
8000 degrees and cloudy. [American 1980s]

What has feathers and glows in the dark?
Chicken Kiev. [American 1980s]

What does U.S.S.R. stand for?
Union of severely scorched Russians. [American 1980s]

What have the *Herald of Free Enterprise* and a condom got in common?

Roll on, roll off, and they are both full of dead seamen/semen. [British 1987]

What's black and goes to school?
A coal tip. [British 1960s]

Have you heard that they are going to rename King's Cross underground station?

They are going to call it Black Friars. [British 1980s]

These jokes are all about well-publicized disasters[3] that have been milked for horror and sympathy by the press, radio, and television, which in a modern society convey to their publics details of distant tragedies that the readers, listeners, and viewers do not and cannot experience directly. What is more, those in control of the news in the mass media tell their audiences how they ought to react and suggest that they are directly involved when in fact they are far away, calm, relatively detached, and often surrounded by the undisturbed routines of their work or domestic life. These incongruities, together with the sandwiching of such news between trivial, banal, and amusing items [e.g., see Ward 1982, 134–35], inspire the rapid production of disaster jokes [see Oring 1987, 277, 282–86].

Jokes about new, strange, and "unnatural" modes of travel change with technology. In the nineteenth century the speed of trains, the ignorance of rustics and others from the periphery regarding trains, and the fear of railroad accidents were all major sources of jokes, even ethnic jokes. Today space travel is new and strange. Even in the late 1950s there were jokes that displayed somewhat ambivalent attitudes to space travel [see Winick, 1961]. As Bob Ward [1982] has documented, the jokes told about space travel by those most closely involved[4] often deal with the hazards of being dependent on others' expertise. When Gus Grissom was asked what he thought would be the most critical part of the Apollo mission he replied, "the part between lift off and splash down" [Ward 1982, 141]. Likewise John Glenn commented, "I looked around me and suddenly realized that everything had been built by the lowest bidder" [Helitzer 1987, 31]. Much of the astronauts' and scientists' joking took an ethnic form, such as the World War II style ethnic jokes about NASA's engineers and space scientists from Germany, including the man nicknamed "the pad fuerher" [Ward 1982, 22, 72, 91, 188]. "Nazi-schmazi," said Wernher von Braun [Lehrer 1981]. There were also the jokes about the fictitious José Jiménez [see Peter and Dana 1982, 63], the "reluctant Hispanic," a terrified Puerto Rican astronaut, which were said by the astronauts to relieve prelaunch jitters [Ward 1982, 39–44]. Likewise, the director of NASA's Marshall Center, the metallurgist William R. Lucas, from West Tennessee, would say of sketchy or inconclusive data, "that's like the East Tennessee method of weighing hogs. You place a log across a fence, put the pig on one end of the log, then pile rocks on the other end until the two loads balance. At that point you guess how much the rocks weigh" [Ward 1982, 82]. These ethnic and regional jokes about German authority, Puerto Rican pusillanimity, and hillbilly stupidity are almost a microcosm of the key ethnic jokes on which this study is based.

Ethnic jokes are, in contrast to "nasty legends," reassuring, for the jokes are usually obviously absurd and the disastrous consequences of stupidity happen to someone else from another group. Ethnic jokes about other peoples' crass errors, misunderstandings, and calamities convey the reassuring message to the joke-tellers that they themselves are competent, their experts are not going to get things wrong, and their machines and organizations are safe.

There are many aspects of modern society that may well tend to erode the individual's sense of his or her own personal competence. Rapid technical changes can quickly and sometimes unpredictably undermine the value of established skills and abilities, confronting their possessors with new situations and problems beyond their capacity and even relegating them to the ranks of the ignorant and the stupid [see Cook 1988, 371–74; Hirszowicz 1981, 30–31, 163–64; Porter, Lawler, and Hackman 1975, 277;

Sabel 1982, 10–15, 92, 159–70]. Another possible source of feelings of frustration and inadequacy is the extent to which people are confronted with sophisticated machines that are difficult to understand and which must not and cannot be tinkered with if they break down [see Kumar 1978, 241]. If the machine does go wrong the person operating it may well refer to it as "that stupid machine" or may even kick it but is left with the uneasy thought that he or she is the more stupid of the two [see Helitzer 1984B, 30–31].

One of the paradoxes of modern society is that the growth of knowledge and formal education has enhanced the general level of competence, understanding, and even in a sense the intelligence of its citizens, but the improved technology and enhanced division of labor that have made this possible have also multiplied stupidity. Increased specialization and the compartmentalization of knowledge mean that the overspecialized cannot understand what other specialists are doing and feel helpless at the thought of being confronted with their strange tasks or machines [see Kumar 1978, 83–88, 227–28, 267–69]. Also the decomposition of skilled tasks and the redistribution of skills as a result of mechanization and an increasing division of labor can create a widening gap between the sophisticated planners and designers of work and those who carry out fragmented and routine tasks requiring little skill or intelligence.[5] Those who perform the least skilled routine tasks experience even less stimulus or challenge in their work than the peasant of an agrarian society [Baechler 1979, 28] and are apt to become, or at least to be perceived as having become, as stupid as it is possible for a normal human being to be [Smith 1902 (1776), 618].

First Paviour: "Bill wat's division of labour as they talks about?"

Second Paviour: "It means you heaves the rammer and brings it down upon the stones with all your might and I stands by to cry out 'Ugh!' " [*The Book of Humour, Wit and Wisdom* 1882, 38]

In a complex and competitive society which values success and indeed prizes ability for its own sake, stupidity is likely to be despised both as a quality that leads to failure in the marketplace, in the education system, and in the ladders of promotion of hierarchical organizations and as a form of failure in itself. An inability to obtain credentials and certificates, to pass examinations, or to score well in I.Q. tests increasingly tends to mean exclusion from many forms of success. To fail in this way can be all the more galling and destructive of a person's self-esteem because it is seen as legitimate failure, a failure that is one's own fault. Also the decay of respect for qualities such as pious simplicity or "character" means that there are fewer well-regarded options open to those who have been labeled stupid. Even if inherited money or status protect the more privileged of the stupid against the full consequences of being or being thought stupid, they too are vulnerable to the ridicule and mockery of others. It is difficult to escape the implications of Wyndham Lewis's harsh modern dictum that "to hate stupidity is really to hate failure, for stupidity is that" [1972, 90].

Once again one of the ways in which the specter of stupidity, together with its dismal concomitant, personal failure, can be exorcised is by telling jokes about it and especially jokes which ascribe this despised quality to members of groups other than one's own. The reassuring humorous message for the joke-tellers is very similar to the one suggested earlier: "The Poles/Irish/Belgians/Newfies—and they alone—are comically stupid. We are not them. Therefore we are not stupid."

As a result of his empirical study of Danes telling jokes about the people of Århus, the Danish scholar Bengt Holbek [1975, 334] has independently concluded that there exists a link of the kind I have suggested between ethnic jokes about stupidity and the distinctive features of modern industrial society outlined above. In his essay "The ethnic joke in Denmark," he writes: "The Århusian (or East Friesian etc.) is a person unable to cope with the complexities of modern life . . . the type of joke discussed here would have been pointless in a simpler society. They express a widespread but not admissible anxiety caused by the rapid development of our society. The anxiety is temporarily relieved by making jokes about dupes too stupid to adapt to progress."

There are many ethnic jokes about stupidity that are well suited to illustrate the point stressed by Holbek. The butts of these jokes are represented as unable to understand or even to operate the most straightforward and familiar technical devices or to carry out the simplest of tasks:

A Toronto woman called a firm which was renowned for its landscaping and interior decorating. A man from the company soon arrived and the lady showed him round the house. Every time she asked what colours he would recommend for a particular room, he used to go to the window, raise it and shout: "Green sides up!" before answering her. This happened several times and the woman's curiosity got the better of her.

"Is this some kind of ritual?" she asked.

"No," he replied, "it's simply that I've got two Newfies next door laying sod." [G. Thomas 1976, 148]

A businessman asked his Belgian secretary to find for him in the phone book the number of the firm 'Zenith'. Two hours later the businessman, having received no reply enquired: "Where is the number I asked you for?"

"Wait a little longer, I've just got to the letter 'R'." [van der Boute-Hen Train 1978, 91]

Why are rest periods never more than ten minutes long in factories in Ostfriesland?

Because if they were longer you would have to retrain the workers. [Krögerson 1977]

A Sardarji (Sikh) working on a building site was trying to knock a nail into the wall head first. Another Sardarji seeing that his efforts were unavailing said to him, "You're using the wrong kind of nail. That nail is meant for the wall opposite." [Kashmiri 1980s]

Then there was the Irish tube [subway] train driver who was sacked for overtaking. [Chambers 1980, 30]

Dabrowski and Bijack met on the street. "Hey," said Dabrowski, "why I no hear from you? How come you no call me on telephone?"

"But you don't have a telephone!" said Bijack.

"I know," said Dabrowski, "but you do!" [Wilde 1977, 152]

Irish secretary to boss: "After I've typed your letter, I'll type the carbon copy and then go to lunch." [Chambers 1981, 33]

Pat was set to work with the circular saw during his first day at the saw mill. The foreman gave careful instructions how to guard against injury but no sooner was his back turned than he heard a howl from the novice, and on turning he saw that Pat had already lost a finger.

'Now how did that happen?' the foreman demanded.

'Sure' was the explanation, 'I was just doin' like this when—bejabers, there's another gone!' [*Jokes for All Occasions* 1922, 95–96]

Irishman standing on ferry boat watching a steam dredger coming up with a ton of mud. Turning to deckhand Mike said: "That's a great invention. What a terrible strain it must be on the pulleys and strain on the chains, but pity the poor man down there filling it up." [Taft 1935, 188]

This guy from Rasht [i.e., a citizen of an Iranian town whose inhabitants are Turks] comes to Teheran and was looking for a place to make a call to Rasht to his family. So he sees a cabinet on the street which was a public rest-room for men and he goes inside and since he hadn't seen a telephone but he had heard about it, he thinks this is a phone-booth. So he puts his head in the toilet and he flushes. He gets all wet and he comes out and he says,

'Well I have to make my call tomorrow, it is raining today in Rasht.' [UCBFA Persian file, A. Hussein Majidi]

Ethnic jokes about stupidity inevitably flourish in modern societies based on competition, rational calculation, and technical innovation, for stupidity means failure and the downfall of self and others alike. However, the canny too have their own modes of failure and destruction which are likewise exaggerated and mocked in jokes. The "canny" virtues of rationality, efficiency, diligence, enterprise, thrift, and hardheaded calculation may lead to material success in the world of work but they also create problems when they are allowed to intrude too forcibly into other areas of life. The members of a society whose way of life is too rational or too calculating can lose their capacity for lighthearted enjoyment, playful humor, spontaneity, unmeasured generosity and affection, and trust in other people [see Sinha 1975 (1966) 317–20]. They may gain the world, but it may not profit them if something more valuable is lost. Also, even in a predominantly secular world there are sacred areas where calculation seems inappropriate or even tasteless. Human life is seen as sacred, and this produces a reluctance, indeed an aversion, to attempts to put a price on it. A similar view is taken of death and of attempts to treat corpses as commodities or to apply canny bookkeeping methods to skimp on funerary memorials such as tombstones or burials. Weddings, like funerals, are sacred *rites de passage*. People in industrial societies may find the order of priorities of, say, an Indian villager who mortgages his land to the moneylender to pay for a lavish wedding incomprehensible and in their terms irrational, but they too would not wish such an occasion to pass without an appropriate display of celebration. The creation and indeed the maintenance of family ties remain a sacred area.

Ethnic jokes about the canny tend to dwell on the intrusion of the canny calculativeness appropriate to the world of work or commerce into areas where it does not belong. Sometimes too we are forcibly reminded that the canny have to pay a price in stress and tedium for their addiction to work and success. The irrational rationality of the canny can be as destructive as stupidity [cf. Wilson 1974B, x-xviii; Winch 1974, 106]. Nor does all the damage fall on the canny persons themselves, for the jokes also represent them as cheating or exploiting others. Once again jokes about the canny seem to be a mirror image of those about the stupid.

Perhaps the most convenient way to arrange jokes from the vast stock of popular ethnic jokes about the canny is to follow the canny through a life cycle but beginning with their general loss of enjoyment in life. The sacrifice of enjoyment directly or indirectly to the demands of canny calculation is the idea that lies at the core of many "canny" jokes. It is a theme that may at times be clearly perceived by the joke-tellers. Thus Professor Dante Zanetti of Pavia, when asked by an American student of folklore why jokes were told in Italy about the "canny Milanese," replied that other Italians, and particularly the inhabitants of the surrounding rural area and nearby small towns, "share an opinion of the Milanese as busy industrious people who have sacrificed a healthy, natural life for the sake of progress and accomplishment while at the same time they have completely sold their personalities to that existence" [UCBFA Italian file, Tanya Gregory. See also Romorantin 1983, 8].

"It's terrible," said a Scotsman, "I never get to drink a cup of coffee the way I really like it. At home, in order to save money, I only take one spoonful of sugar. At friends' houses where it is free I take three. Now what I really like is a cup of coffee with two sugars!" [Guillois and Guillois 1979B, 18]

A well-to-do Gabrovonian travelled third class on the train. It was a very hot summer's day and the train was terribly crowded. 'Chorbadji', a gypsy spoke to him, 'Why should you of all people travel third-class?'

'Because there is no fourth', the rich Gabrovonian replied. [Furtounov and Prodanov 1985]

A group of wealthy southerners, Virginians and Carolinians mostly, were on a train returning from a meeting of the National Fox-hunting Association. Naturally the talk dealt largely with the sport of which they were devotees. A lank Vermonter, who apparently had never done much travelling, was an interested auditor of the conversation.

Presently, when the company in the smoking compartment had thinned out, he turned to one of the party who had stayed on. He wanted to know how many horses the southerner kept for fox-hunting purposes and how large a pack of hounds he maintained and about how many foxes on an average he killed in the course of a season.

The southerner told him. In silence for a minute or two the Vermonter mulled the disclosures over in his mind.

Then he said: "Wall, with fodder fetching such high prices and with dog meat for hounds a costin' what it must cost and with fox pelts as cheap as they are in the open market and taking one thing with another I don't see how you kin expect to clear much money out of this business in the course of a year." [Cobb 1923, 191–92]

Two old Scotsmen sat by the roadside talking and puffing away merrily on their pipes. "There's no muckle pleasure in smoking, Sandy," said Donald.

"Hoo dae ye make that oot?" questioned Sandy.

"Weel," said Donald, "ye see, if ye're smoking yer ain bacca ye're thinkin' o' the awfu' expense and if ye're smokin' some ither body's yer pipe is ramm't sae tight it winna draw." [Lawson 1923, 246]

A Deeside wife listened for a whole evening to the jokes and patter of Billy Connolly without a hint of a smile. Next day she confided to a friend, 'He's a great comic. It was all I could do tae keep from laughing.' [Hodes 1978, 58]

Wee Willie Dougan loved his game of golf but one bright sunny day his friends saw him sitting disconsolately in the club house, his clubs nowhere in sight. 'Why aren't you out playing, Willie?' asked a friend.

'Ach I nae can play agin,' sighed Willie.

'Why not?' asked his friend.

'Ach,' said Willie 'I lost me ball.' [Cerf 1945, 16]

An American businessman visiting in Mexico watched an Indian making pottery vases. He asked the price. Twenty centavos each.

And for 100?

The native thought it over and then answered, 'that will be 40 centavos each.'

The American thought the Indian was making a mistake in his quotation of the price so he tried again. 'And if I bought 1,000 all alike?'

'All alike,' he said. 'One thousand?' Well Senor then they would cost you 60 centavos apiece.'

'Impossible! Why you must be insane!'

'It could be,' replied the Indian. 'But I'd have to make so many and all alike and I wouldn't like that. So you see you would have to pay me for my boredom as well as for my work.' [Braude 1976 (1958), 38–39]

Ethnic jokes about the canny depict them as bringing an overcalculating attitude to marriage also. The shrewd financial assessment of a spouse, the niggardly wedding, the non-honeymoon all fit into the same general pattern.

A young Scotsman, methodical, painstaking and sincere, as so many of his race are, had been a bachelor of long standing. Since coming to this country he had saved his money until now he felt he was qualified properly to support a domestic establishment. One day he went to a friend: "I've about decided to get married," he said. "In fact, I'm looking around for a wife."

"Where are you looking?" asked his friend.

"I'll tell you," said the Scot. "It's my belief that the girls who work as clerks in the big department stores here in New York are mighty fine types. As a rule, they are well dressed and tidy and good-looking and have nice ways. They must be self-reliant or they wouldn't be working. They have to be intelligent or they couldn't hold their jobs. They know how to make a dollar go a long distance, or they couldn't dress as well as they do on the modest wages most of them get. My notion is this: on pretext of wanting to buy something, I am going to tour the big shops until I see a girl behind a counter who seems to fill my requirements. Then I'm going to find out her name and make private inquiries as to her character and disposition, and if she answers all the requirements, I'll secure an introduction to her and if she seems to like me, I'm going to ask her to marry me."

Six months went by. The cautious Scot and the man to whom he had confided his plan of campaign met again. The latter thought his friend looked rather careworn and unhappy.

"How are you getting along?"

"Well," said the Scot, "I'm a married man, if that's what you mean."

"Well, did you follow the scheme you had in mind—I mean the one you told me about the last time I saw you?"

"Yes, I married a girl that worked at Macy's."

"Congratulations. How's everything getting along?"

The Scot fetched a small sigh.

"Sometimes," he said, "I can't help thinking that maybe I might have done better at Gimbel's." [Cobb 1925, 72]

A Scotchman was questioned by a friend: "Mac, I hear ye have fallen in love wi' bonny Kate McAllister."

"Weel, Sanders," Mac replied, "I was near—verra near—doin' it, but the bit lassy has nae siller, so I said to maeself, 'Mac, be a mon.' And I was a mon, and noo I jist pass her by." [*Jokes for All Occasions* 1923, 72]

A Jew married a very wealthy woman. Soon after the ceremony a friend met him. "Congratulations on your wedding," he said, "I hear it was worth about £50,000 to you."

"People vill exaggerate so," said the Jew.

"But I thought it was worth quite that."

"No, no," said the Jew. "Vy, I had to pay sixteen shillings for de ring." [*Further Sunbeams* 1924, 62]

A freak show visited Aberdeen and every bachelor proposed to the fasting woman. [Junior 1928, 17]

Mean? I can still remember his wedding—with everybody tying shoes to the back of the bridal car and him trying them on. [SFGB]

The day an Aberdonian's daughter got married he told all the guests and neighbours that the bridal couple would leave by the back door. In this way his chickens got all the rice. [SFGB]

"Hello there, Pancho, what are you doing here in Acapulco? When did you arrive from Monterrey?"

"I've been here the last two days. I've just got married and I'm here on my honeymoon."

"Congratulations, old man. You must introduce me to your new wife."

"I'm afraid she's still in Monterrey looking after the shop. We couldn't leave the business without someone in charge . . . But when I go back to Monterrey, she will come here to Acapulco for her honeymoon." [Mondragon 1977, 156]

Ethnic jokes about the canny show them as making calculations that no one else would make, calculations that result in worry, pain, or insomnia, or in a failure to escape these undesirable experiences:

At an agricultural exposition in the poultry division there were specimens of hens from Russia, America, Mexico and what have you. The American and Mexican hens were next to each other and as good neighbours they of course crossed the language barrier and had a conversation. The American hen, big and fat, says to the Mexican hen, small and scrawny, 'Let's see what kind of an egg you can lay'. And so she laid an egg and it was a standard "large" size. The American hen says, 'Is that the best you can do? How much would that cost?' 'Three cents'. The American hen says, 'Ha, ha, I'll show you a real egg'. And she lays a 'jumbo' size egg. 'There is an egg!' 'And how much is that', says the Mexican hen. 'Five cents'. 'For two cents I'm not going to tear up my ass like that!' [UCBFA El Salvador File]

An Aberdonian with a rotten molar went to his dentist who said he would charge £5 to pull it out.

Aberdonian: 'Couldn't you loosen it for £1 so that I can pull it out myself?' [SFGB. Also in Lauder 1929, 13–14]

"Hello, Isaac, you vos looking bad this mornink—vat's wrong?"

"Oh, mine goot frient, it vos fear of going to sleep. I must keep awake! I dreamt I found a fortune in London and I'm afraid if I dream again I shall lose it." [Junior 1927, 32]

In bed at night an Aberdonian would always count sheep. First though, he'd always drink a strong black coffee to make sure he didn't miscount. [SFGB]

A Jewish coat-manufacturer who suffered from insomnia was advised by a friend to count sheep to help himself sleep.

The next morning he looked more weary and exhausted than ever.

"What's wrong with you?" asked the friend.

"I've been counting sheep," said the manufacturer. "Last night I counted up to twenty thousand. Then I sheared the sheep, had the wool made into cloth, and made twenty thousand overcoats. Then I spent the rest of the night worrying about where I could get twenty thousand linings." [American 1970s. Also in Crompton 1970E, 43]

Such is the devotion of the comically canny to the calculative pursuit of gain that in the jokes they are even willing to put their lives or those of their spouses at risk. Life itself becomes a commodity, and a cheaply valued one at that. The final absurdity lies in jokes where a decision about life and death is assessed by balancing funeral against medical expenses.

A Scotsman, a Swede and an American were on a ship for a pleasure cruise. They had been out on the water for a long time and were bored, so they decided to make a wager. Whoever could stay under the water the longest would win ten dollars, five from each of the losers. All three of them jumped in the sea. The American was the first to come up, then the Swede but the Scottishman never came up. [UCBFA Swedish file, John Kelly 1968 (1966)]

There was a rich Hindu businessman who became ill. A doctor was called who examined the man and charged him a ten rupee fee and prescribed medicine worth another ten rupees. But the man did not get well with the medicine, so he called his accountant and asked him to figure out how much it would cost him to die. Since Hindus must be cremated, wood and ghee—which is butter—must be used. So the accountant figured the cost would be ten rupees for cremation whereas the doctor would cost the man twenty rupees. So the Hindu businessman said, 'I'd better die so I can save ten rupees.' [UCBFA Pakistan file, Ferial Ava Saeed 1976 (1946)]

Calling on a Jewish patient in a poor quarter of London the doctor found a huge fire blazing in the sick-room and the window tightly closed. "This won't do," he said to the patient's wife, "open the windows and let in some fresh air." "What," said the wife in astonishment. "Open the windows? Do you think Ikey buys coal to warm the street?" [Aye 1931D, 154]

He felt Dollarous.

An old chap and his wife going East from their home in Iowa to visit friends had to halt in Detroit on account of the wife's illness. They went to a hotel and for the first day or two the husband didn't complain of the cost but when his wife grew worse and a doctor was called and a nurse employed he began to hang on to the dollars which were demanded. On the fifth day the doctor looked serious and said the woman would probably die. The husband consulted with the hotel clerk and with a freight agent and going back to his wife he leaned over her and sobbed "Oh! Sarah Jane! you mustn't die here!" "I don't want to leave you Philetus", she replied, "but I fear that my time has come." "Don't Oh! dont die here!" he went on. "If my time has come I must go", she said. "Yes, I suppose so, but if I could only get you back home first I'd save at least forty dollars on funeral expenses and forty dollars don't grow on every bush." [Quad 1872, 134–35]

What's up, Mac . . . anything wrong?

Aye! The wife's had an operation . . . She swallowed half a croon and there's no change yet. [Green 1976, 129]

An Aberdonian sat at the bedside of his friend who was a patient in a nursing home. "Ye seem to be cheerier the day, John," said the visitor.

"Ay man, I thocht I was going to dee but the doctor tells me he can save my life. It's to cost a hunner pounds."

"Eh, that's terrible extravagance! Do ye think it's worth it?" ' [Moffat 1928, 16. See also Aye 1931D, 154]

An undertaker at a Rotary dinner offered a free funeral to the first member of the club to die. Suddenly there was a shot from the back of the room. An Aberdonian had shot himself. [SFGB]

An Aberdonian ran into the road to pick up a penny. He was knocked down by a lorry and killed. The coroner's verdict was 'death from natural causes.' [SFGB]

The jokes about the comic moral career of people in canny societies do not end with death, for in the jokes the surviving canny persons treat the deceased's last wishes, the body, the grave, the tombstone with a crass utilitarian disregard for the sacred or even for conventional propriety.

A Jew wearing a large diamond scarf-pin appeared among his admiring friends. They crowded round him to examine the stone.

'Is it real, Isaac?' they asked.

'Yes,' said Isaac.

'It is fine, Isaac.' 'A splendid stone, Isaac.' 'Where did you get it from, Isaac.' 'How did you get the money, Isaac?' they questioned one after another.

'Vell,' said Isaac, 'you remember Beckstein, ze jeweller?'

'Yes, yes.'

'Vell he left thirty pounds for a memorial stone, and this is ze stone.' [George 1903, 115]

Why do they bury Regiomontanos upright in the ground?

To save a headstone. [Mexican 1980s]

In Monterrey a man killed in a gun fight had six bullets lodged in his body, so instead of burying him they took him to the smelter. [Mexican 1980s]

A Laihian's wife nagged him to buy her a burial plot and tombstone. One year he lashed out and gave them to her for her birthday. The next year he didn't give her anything. When she complained, he said, "You haven't yet used the present I gave you last year." [Finnish 1980s. Jewish version in Wilde 1980A, 51]

An Aberdonian and his wife went to Rothesay for a holiday and went for a sail. Unfortunately the wife fell overboard and was drowned. The Aberdonian asked the pier-master to let him know if her body was found. Two weeks later he received a wire saying, "Body recovered yesterday covered with crabs. Send instructions."

The Aberdonian sent a wire back saying: "Sell crabs, send on money, reset bait." [SFGB]

In jokes canniness, like stupidity, is represented as posing problems, not merely for canny individuals but for those around them who are portrayed as being taken in or exploited in some way:

Customer: If this is an all-wool vest, why has it got a label saying 'cotton' on it?

Aberdeen shopkeeper (confidentially): It's there to deceive the moths. [SFGB]

It is on record that Isaac once went into partnership with an Aberdonian. But they had to dissolve it at the end of a week. Neither of them could sleep for watching the other. [Junior 1927, 8]

An old man on giving advice to his son, said: "Laddie, be honest. Honesty is the best policy. I ken for I've tried them baith." [Taggart 1927, 20]

And then there was the Scotsman who counted his money in front of the mirror so he wouldn't cheat himself. [Ford, Hershfield, and Laurie 1947, 159]

The Yankees are generally supposed to possess more acuteness than any other people on the face of the globe yet the following story will show that some of the Germans possess this faculty to a remarkable degree.

On one occasion a German residing in the country came into Buffalo with hams to sell. Among the rest he sold a dozen or two to a German hotel keeper who afterwards, demonstrating the acuteness of his countrymen over the Yankees, said:

'You may talk 'pout your tam Yankees scheeting but a Dutchman scheeted me much better as a Yankee never was. He prings me some hams—dey vas canvas nice, so better as you never see. I puy one, two dozen all so nice; and if you believe de scheet was so magnificent dat I eat six, seven, eight of dem tam hams pefore I found out dey vas made of wood.' [*The Museum of Mirth* n.d., Part IV, 9]

'Let me have five eggs laid by a black hen,' a Gabrovonian said to the saleswoman. The woman was surprised and just said: 'If you can tell which they are, pick them out for yourself.' The Gabrovonian picked the largest, paid and walked away. [Furtounov and Prodonov 1985]

The proliferation of ethnic jokes about the stupid and the canny is one of the most striking of the humorous responses to the contradictory pressures of a modern industrial society. Modern societies exhort their members to be careful and yet to be carefree, to calculate everything and yet to know the decent limits of material calculation, to compete ruthlessly as individuals and yet to remain social beings. Everyone is a producer engaged in the pursuit of wealth and a consumer engaged in the pursuit of happiness. Both work and pleasure are competed for and this forms a central reality of most people's lives.

In most industrial or industrializing societies there exists a cultural contradiction[6] between two sets of clusters of values and patterns of behavior. This creates a degree of tension and uncertainty of which everyone is aware, although it will be experienced in very different ways depending on an individual's social class, occupation, and other aspects of his or her position in the system. The first of these is the set of values, outlooks, and patterns of behavior that have been variously termed instrumental rationality, economizing, efficiency, i.e., the relentless tendency toward the precise measurement, calculation, and regulation of human activities so as to squeeze more out of less.[7] So far as the individual is concerned this tendency may be experienced as an external pressure, either from the market or from a bureaucratic organization, and one that may intensify unpredictably due to technical or commercial change or as a result of decisions made elsewhere. Yet it is difficult to argue against instrumental rationality or increased efficiency, because these constitute one of the central concerns of industrial societies. Almost regardless of the importance of pursuing a particular set of goals, the efficiency, technique, and economizing employed become an end in themselves [see Wilson 1974, x-xviii] and, for the individual, a duty.

In conflict with this tendency are many others. First there is a residual sense of tradition, continuity, order, stability which is still present in mature industrial societies and was and is particularly strong in the early stages of industrialization. At such a time those whose working lives have been governed by the seasons of nature and the length of daylight and who have fixed ideas about the proper and interpenetrating relationship between work and leisure and between instrumental effort and social celebration have to adjust,[8] often reluctantly and unwillingly, to the mechanical discipline of the factory and the office and their respective clocks. This rise of planned, bounded, and intensive work has been accompanied by the creation of leisure,[9] of demarcated time off when the rewards of work may be spent and enjoyed in ways antithetical to the ethic of the workplace. In time there has also appeared a competing hedonistic "fun morality"[10] which coexists with the work-ethic virtues of diligence, sobriety, self-control, order, and frugality. Work is now portrayed and justified in complementary yet contradictory ways. Work is a duty and even a calling but it is also an unfortunate utilitarian necessity, the means by which the money to finance leisure and pleasure (on top of mere survival) is obtained [see Wilson 1969, 257–59]. In Western societies, in particular, individuals are urged to work hard and yet also to enjoy life, to save hard and to be prudent, thrifty, and self-reliant and yet also to spend hard as befits good consumers [see Bell 1979, xxv, 69].

In the modern West there exists for many people and especially for those in skilled, professional, and intellectual occupations an ideal of work as a source of self-esteem, autonomy, and self-expression as well as of status and survival. There is a clash between this view of work and life and the strong pressures toward instrumental efficiency outlined earlier. The calculative, rationalizing pressures at work can rob the skilled of their autonomy and even their skill and can trap professionals in a bureaucratic spiral of debourgeoisification so that work becomes ever more narrow and constricted, counted and accountable [see Porter, Lawler, and Hackman 1975, 267]. Yet in the same advanced Western societies in which this happens the value of the individual is stressed and satisfaction, creativity, self-actualization, and personal growth in and through work are held up as worthwhile ideals.[11] In modern societies generally there is now no single integrated view of how the individual fits and should fit into the central economic activities of the society. Not only is there a diversity of individual and subcultural views,[12] but at all levels there exists a set of competing pressures and expectations. Faced with these contradictory pressures, each individual has to resolve the problem of how to allocate time, energies, and resources between the competing claims of work, duty, and gain on the one hand and leisure, pleasure, and enjoyment on the other. Both sets of goals are legitimate, and the key problem is how to strike a balance between them. The attainment of any such golden mean is rendered even more difficult by the fact that work in a modern industrial society often demands personal qualities such as rationality, competence, diligence, self-control, punctuality, meticulousness, thrift, and sobriety which are often incompatible with the pursuit of carefree, hedonistic enjoyment.

Many forms of humor have emerged from this contradictory and mal-integrated social world, including ethnic jokes about canny and stupid individuals. The cult of efficiency has been ridiculed in many ways by collections of Murphy's laws [Block 1985; Peers, Booth, and Bennett 1984] that deride and mimic the jargon of technical and organizational rationality [see Minogue 1987] and by mock sociological analyses of the distinctive and supposedly rational ethos and organizations of the modern world,[13] which challenge their most central assumptions in a manner that is part serious criticism and part tongue-in-cheek fun. There are even minor humorous cults of the useless and the ineffective—the Colorado Dull Men's Club, Britain's Wallies [Manning 1983], Mexico's Pendejos [Sofocleto 1980]. These forms of humor [see also Charles 1945; Helitzer 1984B, 30–31] can plausibly be classed alongside many of the ethnic jokes about the canny as a rebellion against rationality while the inane antics of the new clowns of film and television to whom even children can feel superior [Klimmins 1928, 152–53; McCabe 1985, 46, 123] have much in common with ethnic jokes about stupidity.

The linked pair of ethnic jokes about the stupid and the canny reflects the problem everyone faces of attaining a reasonable balance between the requirements of the world of work and money and those of the world of leisure and enjoyment, between making a living and living. These jokes are also perhaps part of the web of informal rules and norms that enable people to maintain some kind of balance in the face of the competing pressures on them that emanate from the large impersonal worlds of the marketplace and of bureaucracy. The jokes, by mocking the excesses of the incompetent and the compulsively acquisitive, seem to convey a pair of linked cultural warnings: Do not take the rational world of work and money too seriously, but do not take it too lightly either. The overall message of the two sets of ethnic jokes is rather like that of the proverb that states:

All play and no work makes Jack a dull boy.
All work and no play makes Jack a dull boy.

The message of the jokes is implicit but in no sense obscure and the Scottish humorist and clergyman David Macrae [1904] has been unable to resist drawing out the moral lesson to be found in the contrast between Scottish and Irish jokes:

> The Irish have long had the reputation of being thriftless and of finding it easier to spend money than to save it. An Englishman, Scotsman and Irishman were jocularly discussing the reason for the shape of coined money. The Englishman said it was made round because it was meant to circulate. The Scot said it was made flat that it might be piled up. "Not a bit," said the Irishman, twirling a half-crown on the table as he spoke. "It's

> made like that, the better to spin." And some of them no doubt make it spin more quickly than wisely. If the English are liberal in giving and enterprising money, and the Scotch keen in acquiring it, the Irish are too often reckless in making it go.
>
> The very generosity of the Irish character probably helps to account for the prevalence of thriftlessness and improvidence. One often sees the money that has been earned by hard toil slipping carelessly away from between their fingers. They quiz the Scotch folk about their excessive carefulness. I remember, at Limerick, an Irish gentleman telling me with great gusto about a company of Scotch artisans who were enjoying a holiday in that city. One wet day, when they were crossing the muddy street one of them was accidentally knocked down and run over by a jaunting car. Another of the party, who was a little way behind came rushing up in great excitement to where his friend was lying stunned by a fall. A gentleman who had already hurried over to help said, seeing this one's excitement, "Is he a relation of yours, sir?" "No," exclaimed the Scot, "he's no relation, but he's got on a pair of my breeks!"
>
> This concern for the safety of the borrowed 'breeks' would certainly not have been the first thought in an Irishman's mind; but the Irish might not be the worse for a little more of the carefulness about which they sometimes joke the Scotch. [Macrae 1904]

Conversely, as the jokes indicate, other people suspect that the Scotch might not be the worse for a little less of the carefulness for which they are comically renowned!

While it is speculative to link the existence of the opposed pair of ethnic jokes about the stupid and the canny to the unresolved pressures of opposed sets of legitimate norms and values as discussed above, there is a very good fit between the two phenomena. Everyone is faced with the possibility that they may fail to strike a correct balance between the complementary yet conflicting goals of economic life and indeed may be unsure as to where the balance lies in an uncertain, changing, and anomic world. Ethnic jokes about the stupid and the canny depict others as comically trapped in absurdly exaggerated versions of one or the other of the two opposed modes of failure that face the joke-tellers. For the duration of the joke the joke-tellers occupy a safe and secure middle ground from which to laugh at those whose failure and imbalance are ludicrously obvious.

CHAPTER THREE

Who Gets Called Stupid?

Ethnic jokes about the "stupid" and the "canny" export these qualities from the joke-tellers' own group and pin them on some other regional, ethnic, or national group. If this were the whole story, then such jokes would presumably be randomly bestowed on other ethnic groups. In practice, however, the jokes are pinned on particular ethnic groups and not others, as is indicated in table 3.1. Ethnic jokes about stupidity and canniness are told about different groups in different countries and, in a world where jokes are international, are easily switched around within each set of groups that are the butt of the "stupid" or the "canny" jokes. However, the jokes are much less likely to be told about groups outside these sets or about a group in the "wrong" set. Thus Americans might have told jokes about "canny Poles" and "stupid Scotsmen" but they didn't, nor do the Belgians tell jokes about "stupid Frenchmen" and there are no French jokes about "canny Belgians." In practice people do not tell ethnic jokes in the manner suggested by Joey Adams's dictum that such jokes "can apply to any minority" [1975, 6; see also 5, 8, 79]. In theory they can, but in practice they don't. It is significant that Joey Adams implicitly excludes the possibility that a majority people could be the butt of such jokes. If the switching around of jokes were completely elastic, then it is difficult to see why majorities should get left out of the game. Clearly ethnic minorities feel inhibited from telling jokes of this type about a majority people. There is also the further question of why some minorities and not others become the butts of ethnic jokes about stupidity or canniness. What are the implicit cultural rules that lead to the attachment of the comic labels *stupid* and *canny* to particular ethnic groups? Since the nature of these "rules" differs between the "stupid" and the "canny" groups it will be convenient to consider them separately.

Who Gets Labelled Stupid in Ethnic Jokes?

Since different ethnic groups feature in ethnic jokes in the various countries where jokes about stupidity are told, it should be possible to infer why the particular peoples listed in table 3.1 are the butts of such jokes by examining on a comparative basis their social position relative to that of the joke-tellers. The next step in this argument is to suggest why such a social position is likely to be regarded as one of inferiority by the joke-tellers so that the attribution of comic stupidity to that particular group seems plausible to them. The purpose of the exercise is not to demonstrate that the butts of the jokes really are lacking in basic mental ability, but simply to show why they are likely to "look stupid" when placed in the joke-tellers' cultural frame. Indeed, the argument can be extended to take in jokes about the stupidity of groups who are not defined in ethnic terms, groups as diverse as aristocrats, apparatchiks, Aggies (from Texas A & M), Hokies (from Virginia Tech), the people of Kentucky, peasants, unskilled workers, militiamen, carabinieri, and East European politicians, to demonstrate (a) that the social forces underlying ethnic and nonethnic jokes about stupidity are often similar and (b) that ethnic jokes about stupidity may be to some extent based on an underlying nonethnic characteristic. Where possible I will indicate the way in which the joke-tellers perceive the relevant social characteristics of the butts of the jokes in practice; this point will also be illustrated by reference to the content of particular ethnic jokes.

The most striking feature of the peoples listed in table 3.1 is how very similar most of the peoples who are the butts of the jokes are to the peoples who tell the jokes about them [see also Apte 1985, 133].[1] Typically each pair of peoples are close neighbors and are, or have been, citizens of the same country; they often share a common language or culture or have languages and cultures that are closely related [see Davies 1987A]. From the joke-tellers' point of view the butts of ethnic jokes about stupidity tend to be the most remote and exotic of provincials, the nearest and most intimate of foreigners, or a group of familiar, well-established, almost assimilated immigrants. In some cases groups may fit uneasily and ambiguously into more than one of these halfway houses. These ambiguities are often recognized by the use of terms that embrace both the joke-teller and the group that is the butt of the jokes and imply the existence of ties of proximity and similarity: Scandinavians, Iberian, the British Isles, the Low Countries, Francophone, etc. Ethnic jokes about stupidity are rarely told about groups that are very different from the joke-tellers or perceived by them as totally alien.[2] Rather, such jokes are kept "within the family" and are told about peoples whose identity relative to the joke-tellers is ambiguous (they are almost like us but not quite the same), people whom the joke-tellers can regard not as mysterious foreigners but as a kind of inferior [i.e., stupid] imitation of themselves.

That ethnic jokes about stupidity are told about closely related groups rather than alien groups who are more likely to be the subject of prejudice and rejection is a fact of which the joke-tellers themselves are often aware. The French joke-collectors Mina and André Guillois have noted:

TABLE 3.1 **Who Gets Called Stupid?**

Country where ethnic jokes about stupidity are told	Group that is the butt of ethnic jokes about stupidity
United States	Poles and locally Italians, Portuguese, etc.
Canada (East and especially Ontario)	Newfoundlanders (Newfies)
Canada (West)	Ukrainians
Mexico	Yucatecos
Colombia	Pastusos
Brazil	Portuguese
Britain	Irish
Ireland	Kerrymen
France	Belgians, Ouin-Ouin (French Swiss)
Netherlands	Belgians, Limburghers
Germany	Ostfrieslanders
Italy	Southern Italians
Austria	Carinthians, Burgenlanders
Switzerland	Fribourgers
Spain	People from Lepe in Andalucia
Denmark	Århusians (Jutes from Århus), Norwegians
Sweden	Norwegians, Finns
Finland	Karelians
Greece	Pontians (Black Sea Greeks)
Jugoslavia	Bosnians, Albanians
Czech Lands	Slovaks
Bulgaria	Šopi
Russia	Ukrainians, Chukchees
Tadzhikistan	Uzbeks
China (South)	Sansui
India	Sikhs (Sardarjis)
Pakistan	Sikhs (Sardarjis)
Iraq	Kurds
Israel	Kurdish Jews
Iran	Rashtis (Azerbaijanis from Rasht)
Turkey	Laz (from around Trebizond)
Nigeria	Hausas
Egypt	Nubians, Sa'idis
South Africa	van der Merwe (Afrikaners)
Australia	Irish, Tasmanians
New Zealand (North Island)	Irish, Maories
New Zealand (South Island)	Irish, West Coasters

> In the United States people mock the Poles and the Italians. In France the Belgians and the Swiss (Ouin-Ouin). In England the Irish etc. . . . In each of these three cases there also exists a large community of immigrant workers who are supposed to be dirty, lazy and stupid and who inspire in women only scorn and revulsion: the Puerto Ricans in the United States, the North Africans in France, the Jamaicans in England.
>
> Why has not one of these groups become the butt of the jokes we call Belgian for convenience? . . . [These alien groups, they conclude,] are not near enough for us to see ourselves in them as in a distorting mirror . . . the Belgians are almost our brothers and thus a suitable group on whom to sharpen our wits. [1979, 15]

The other striking feature of table 3.1 is that most of the countries listed in the first column have their own, local butt of jokes about stupidity. There is a marked contrast here with ethnic jokes about canniness or militarism or cowardice, which are often shared between nations whose cultural and geographical relationship with the butts of the jokes may be quite different.

The common elements among the groups that are the butts of ethnic jokes about stupidity are many and diverse but they can be reduced to two broad categories. The first of these categories may be termed local dominance and is primarily a social and cultural variable, though there may also be a geographical, a political, or even a religious aspect to it. The groups that are the butts of ethnic jokes about stupidity often live either literally or metaphorically at the edge of the culture within which the joke-tellers are the dominant group. The culture of the people who are the butts of the jokes is to a large extent derived from and dependent on that of the joke-tellers, whereas the converse is not the case; the relationship between them is an asymmetrical one, and so in consequence is the pattern of jokes [see also Middleton and Moland 1959; Zenner 1970, 96]. Within any nation the culture of the metropolitan center or centers tends to be dominant over that of the remote periphery. Innovation, modernity, fashion begin at the center and spread outward and not the other way around; thus the people of the periphery appear slow, provincial, old-fashioned, and a fit subject for jokes about stupidity. This is especially likely to happen if the group at the "edge" of the society has a distinctively different ethnic identity; whatever the achievements of the members of the group in their own terms, they may appear to the people at the center as failing to meet the dominant cultural standards. In a similar way the cultures of long-established ethnic groups tend to be dominant over those of more recent immigrants [see Glazer and Moynihan 1975; Klaff 1980, 75–78]. It is clear, for instance, that the way of life, the culture, the identity of, say, Polish-Americans is American, but it is difficult to see how Americans in general could be described as Polonized or as in any real sense Polish. The vast majority of Polish-Americans speak American English and have taken on a largely preexisting American culture, but very few

Americans of non-Polish descent speak Polish or have any knowledge of Polish culture and traditions. This harsh fact undermines the attempt at a reverse ethnic joke told by the Slovak-American writer Michael Novak [1976]:

> Can you speak Polish?
> (No.)
> How does it feel to be dumber than a Polack?

Even if an ethnic group on the periphery secedes or forms a separate state, as in the case of Belgium, Finland, Norway, or Eire, the established pattern of cultural dominance versus dependence often remains. The French tell ethnic jokes about the "stupidity" of the Belgians and the French-speaking Swiss because, although they are politically independent of France, they are culturally dependent on the country that is the home of their language. The Belgians have a double-dependence and are the butts of Dutch as well as French ethnic jokes. The Finns resent Swedish airs of superiority but they continue to defer to Swedish culture and to learn Swedish, whereas the converse is not true. The Swedes tell ethnic jokes about "stupid Finns" but the Finns feel inhibited about retaliating. As the Finnish social scientist Lauri Lehtimaja [1979] put it to the author when asked about this:

> The Finns have special, deep-ingrained hang ups about their long subordination to the Swedish language and culture . . . deep down many Finns still feel inferior to the Swedes and somehow it is not easy to make jokes in such a frame of mind. . . . At one time there was a conscious attempt to spread jokes about the Swedes in Finland but there was not much success.

It is the process of essentially one-way influence that constitutes the very essence of cultural dominance and enables the members of the dominant group to regard the group that is the local butt of jokes about stupidity as (a) similar enough to themselves to be assessed as a mere extension or imitation of themselves, to be judged on the joke-tellers' own terms, and (b) characterized by arbitrary, discordant, and senseless minor deviations from the dominant cultural pattern which make them appear as a marred and distorted version of the joke-tellers' own self-image. Hence "they" can be depicted in jokes as a "stupid" likeness of "us."

Many of the groups listed in table 3.1 as the butts of ethnic jokes about stupidity have been judged by others as inert and unenterprising on the basis of broader criteria derived from the processes of economic and political competition. They are perceived as stupid either because they are thought to have failed economically within an open competitive system or because they have been successful only by creating or maintaining a political monopoly. The social position of ethnic groups labeled comically stupid for these economic and political reasons is the inverse of that occupied by groups that are the butt of canny jokes. The comic label *canny* tends to be attached to ethnic groups whose members are visibly urban, mobile, innovating, entrepreneurial individuals who seek and achieve success in open competition in the marketplace or the examination hall. They are prominent in business, in management, in the professions, in intellectual life. The comic label *stupid*, by contrast, tends to be pinned on ethnic groups whose members are rural peasants with a strong sense of the fixedness of place, tradition, customs, relationships, and even methods of work. When they migrate to the cities of their own or of another nation they become unskilled blue-collar workers, often very visibly so in the construction industry because their old skills cannot be transferred to the new setting. When they form settlements these tend to constitute large visible ethnic neighborhoods where they again seek to create a pattern of life characterized by stability and continuity. In their own terms they may well have been successful, but in societies which value mobility, striving, innovation, and the limitless pursuit of wealth, achievement, or even knowledge, they are apt to be seen as stolid, unenterprising, and thus comically stupid. Such groups usually lack power and influence, but in some cases they are able collectively to exploit a local or even a national political system that incorporates a monopoly element rigged in their favor and which can be used as a source of ethnic patronage and jobbery. Groups that gain power or position in this manner do not escape ethnic jokes about stupidity—power and office are merely incorporated into the jokes.

These portraits of the social positions occupied by "stupid" or "canny" ethnic groups are ideal types that have been extracted from an examination of the whole range of such groups. As such they do not purport to describe in detail the social position of the butts of any particular pair of ethnic jokes, but they do provide a guide to the reasons why the jokes have been pinned on one group rather than another. Groups that are the butt of ethnic jokes about stupidity tend to be or to have been overrepresented in occupations or social strata that are seen as static, unenterprising, unqualified, old-fashioned, or as obstructive rather than in the van of progress.

In practice the two sets of reasons why groups have been labeled comically stupid, the local cultural reasons and the general economic reasons, tend to overlap. Ethnic groups on the cultural periphery often tend also to be cut off from the economic dynamism and opportunities of the central metropolitan areas. However, this is by no means always the case, for economic life may be based on resources and trade routes that spill across national and cultural frontiers. Belgium is culturally at the edge both of France and of the Netherlands but economically it is at the heart of Europe [see Belgium Survey 1980] and was the second nation in the world to industrialize. In any one case there are often overlapping reasons for jokes that attribute comic stupidity to a group. However, for the sake of clarity and convenience the two broad sets of reasons outlined above will be examined in turn.

The local sense of a national and cultural center and periphery has a number of dimensions, geographical, linguistic, and religious, each of which needs to be examined. Ethnic groups or nationalities tend to occupy a particular territory with known boundaries. At the edge or border of their homeland there is a more or less permeable frontier with the territory of another people, or there is the sea. People who live on these geographical margins are especially liable to be the butts of ethnic jokes about stupidity.[3] First let us look at the ethnic jokes of countries that go down to the sea.

The Back of Beyond

Many of the peoples listed in table 3.1 as the butts of ethnic jokes about stupidity live at the physical edge of their society, an offshore island such as Newfoundland, Tasmania, or Sicily, a distant terminal peninsula such as the boot of Southern Italy or Yucatan in Mexico, or a remote coast such as Kerry, Ostfriesland, the west coast of the South Island of New Zealand, or (until recently) Jutland and Norway. Even Ireland, at one time John Bull's "other island," may be classed as an offshore island, albeit a reluctant one. The degree to which these "peoples of the edge" have separate political and ethnic identities varies, though the mere fact of their being cut off from the significantly named "mainland" by a stretch of sea in itself tends to lead to the creation or preservation of a sense of separateness and even to political secession.

It is not surprising, then, that ethnic jokes are told about "peoples over the water" who in the strict sense of the word are not "ethnics"—Newfies in Canada, Tasmanians in Australia, the Jutes of Århus—though the fact of their being the subject of ethnic type jokes should make us remember how arbitrary and subjective ethnic divisions can be.

The people of Newfoundland, who are the butt of Newfie jokes in eastern Canada, differ far less in origin and cultural traditions from other English-speaking Canadians than do the Ukrainian-Canadians who occupy the same position in the ethnic jokes about stupidity told in western Canada. They do, however, have a distinct identity and way of life derived from their insular position which sets them apart from the rest of Canada and which has led to their being the butts of ethnic jokes about stupidity rather than some other remote or economically backward province. It would not be unfair to call the Newfoundlanders reluctant Canadians. They refused to join the Canadian Federation of 1867, and indeed in 1869 there were popular demonstrations in Newfoundland to celebrate the triumph of separateness over "confederation" [see Chadwick 1967, 27; also see Noel 1971]. The Newfoundlanders later voted in a referendum to join Canada, but only by a tiny majority on the second ballot [see Noel 1971, 257–59]. Newfoundland was finally due to join Canada on 1 April 1949, but at the last moment the date of this reluctant union was brought forward by one day "to avoid holding the anniversary of confederation on April Fool's Day" [Noel 1971, 261].

The arguments for preserving an independent Newfie identity and against joining Canada were from a material point of view "stupid" and may well have appeared so to many Canadians, for the Newfoundlanders chose to value the particular, whose value could only be apparent to themselves, and to reject the universal benefits of the larger society. They chose to be an inward-looking folk when they could have been citizens of a greater union. The Newfoundlanders, in the eyes of the Canadians, very nearly missed out on the benefits of being "modernized" and "Canadianized"[4] by preferring the personal, intimate, historic qualities of their local community over the greater opportunities and welfare offered by a more remote and impersonal state [cf. Smith 1981, 195]. All peripheral peoples or ethnic minorities who hold fast to the particular, the familiar, the traditional in a world based on individualism, hedonism, materialism, progress are liable to be seen as comically stupid by dominant groups who are not faced with the same hard choices. "Why do they want to hang on to those old things? Why can't they be modern and progressive . . . like us?" What the dominant joke-tellers fail to see is that they alone have had the privilege of building many particular and familiar aspects of their own ethnicity into "modernity" and "progress." Things are not as universal as they seem and the Californication of the world is a highly particular form of progress.

The relevance of the preceding analysis to the genesis of ethnic jokes about stupidity can be seen from the Welsh-Canadian folklorist Gerald Thomas's comment on his extensive collection of Newfie jokes:

> Newfoundland even today is more socially backward than many other parts of Canada; it is still possible to hear people claim with pride that the Newfoundlander's way of life has hardly changed in over two hundred years. There is enough truth in such an assertion for folklorists and sociologists to view the island as a researcher's paradise.
>
> There is a joke . . . which describes the problems faced by a Newfoundlander when he changes from an axe to a power-saw to cut his daily tally of wood. He manages to keep up to the level of pre-power-saw production but finds it particularly tiring. He complains about the new tool and is frightened out of his life when the vendor presses the starting button. [1976, 144]

Newfie jokes are far older than confederation [G. Thomas 1976, 144], though their widespread popularity is more recent. Within Newfoundland the "Townie" tells Newfie jokes about the "Bayman" or "Outporter" and one "Bayman" may tell the same joke about another [G. Thomas 1976,

144]. In this way the relation of Newfoundland (at the edge) to Canada (at the center) is repeated. At the center (economically as well as numerically) are the "Townies" of the capital, St. Johns. The "Outporters" live in what were, until the second half of the twentieth century, "tiny isolated outports where their way of life was not essentially different from that led by their fore-fathers. The fishery with its antiquated technology and financial structure still remained their basic source of livelihood; such amenities as motor roads and hydro-electric power were practically unknown; while in their homes a simple nineteenth century world of large patriarchal families, Victorian manners and morals, oil lamps and wood stoves remained anachronistically alive" [Noel 1971, 262].

Hence the mainlander jokes about Newfies that relate directly to Newfoundland's sea-girt status and its most famous industry:

Do you know how a Newfie counts his catch? One fish, two fish, another fish, another fish . . . [G. Thomas 1976, 144]

Did you hear about the Newfie who went ice-fishing and caught 150 lbs of ice? [G. Thomas 1976, 144]

The sea has played a similar role in the creation of identities and ethnic jokes in Denmark. Denmark is an unusual country in that it is divided into three (main) parts, the islands of Zealand and Fünen and the peninsula of Jutland, by the sea. The capital, and easily the largest city, is Copenhagen, on the eastern coast of the island of Zealand, facing Sweden. The peninsula of Jutland, and especially north and west Jutland, though on the mainland of Europe is on the periphery both of Denmark and of Scandinavia [see Rokkan and Urwin 1983, 51]. "For centuries jokes and humourous tales have been told about the inhabitants of the outlying regions of Jutland" [Holbek 1975, 327; see also Colleville and de Zepelin 1896; Rockwell 1981, 285] and especially about the alleged stupidity of the Molboer, the people of Mols [e.g., see Thestrup 1981], the southern part of a small peninsula near Århus, the chief town of Jutland. Indeed, in Copenhagen in the nineteenth century the term *Jute* meant "Simpleton," as in the joke of the Copenhagen poet Wessel: "We are all Jutes before the Lord" [Rockwell 1981, 171; see also 339].

The modern jokes about Århus are rooted in the long-established tradition of jokes about nearby Molbo, and Danish cartoons show the Århusians alongside the traditional men of Molbo in their wooden shoes and their hats like nightcaps.

Do you know the difference between Molbo jokes and Århus jokes? Molbo jokes are fictitious. [Yearhouse 1974B]

The three-fold division of Denmark by the sea into Zealand, Fünen, and Jutland has facilitated the telling of classic three-part jokes based on the main towns Copenhagen, Odense, and Århus. In jokes, as in rhetoric, in starting a race, in military orders, in traffic lights, in stories for children, three is a very useful number since it is the shortest possible sequence. In ethnic jokes one sets the scene, two confirms the apparent nature of the sequence, and three starts off as predicted but suddenly produces the unexpected.

Have you heard about the three Danes who were going to be guillotined? One was from Copenhagen, one from Odense, and one from Århus. First the man from Copenhagen lay on the scaffold but the release mechanism stuck fast and the blade refused to fall. According to the ancient custom he was allowed to go free.

The same happy accident occurred for the man from Odense. The blade again stuck fast and he was let free.

Then it was the turn of the man from Århus and as he was lying on the scaffold he pointed up at the release mechanism and said to the executioner, "Hey, don't you think there's something wrong with that thing there." [Yearhouse 1974A. In the original Danish, the last line is written so as to indicate the slow, slurred Danish spoken in Jutland.]

People who live on remote coasts and peninsulas are likely to become the butt of ethnic jokes about stupidity even if they do not differ in ancestry or political status from the people of the center. They live at the end of a country—it is difficult to get there, and, when you do, there is nowhere else to go. Such is the fate of Ostfriesland or Kerry. If you ask the way in Kerry you are likely to be told: "If you want to go there, I wouldn't start from here."

> Why does a Cork man always take his holidays on the Kerry Coast?
> So he can watch it eroding. [Irish 1980s]

In Ostfriesland the local people's amazement at and disapproval of the unfamiliar clothing worn by travelers from the outside world in earlier times gave rise to the proverb "Never wear a brown hat in Friesland" [*Brewer's* 1981, 534], i.e, anything other than the local headgear. Friesland was definitely no place for brown-hatters [cf. Davies 1982A; Paros 1984, 168]. At their other end, the Ostfrieslanders were laughed at for wearing wooden shoes, for Ostfriesland was in the past an inaccessible marshland [see Verbruggen 1977, 103, 150], seen by others as a doubly ambiguous impassable sludge, much like the bogs of Ireland [see *Teagueland Jests or Bogg Witticisms* 1690; Mike G 1985]. Jokes about Ostfrieslanders call them marshmen, just as the Irish are termed bog-trotters. Modern German jokes about Ostfriesland refer directly to the low-lying, Dutch-looking (cf.

Prescott 1978, 14] polder, often below sea level, where the far northwestern corner of Germany merges almost imperceptibly with the sea. Indeed, one book of Ostfriesland jokes takes as its logo a seagull flying upside down.

Why do the seagulls fly upside-down in Ostfriesland?
So that they don't have to see the wretched place. [Krögerson 1977]

Why does the tide go in and out in Ostfriesland?
Because when the Ostfrieslanders settled there the sea was so frightened that it ran away. Now it comes back twice a day to see if they are still there. [Krögerson 1977]

Why is Ostfriesland bounded on the east by the River Weser and on the west by the River Ems?
So that the marshmen cannot destroy the civilisation on the other side of the water. [Krögerson 1977]

Similarly the people of Mexico City who tell jokes about the Yucatecos, the people of the peninsula of Yucatan, see their remoteness as the basis of jokes, and jokes about Yucatecos often refer to the sea, which almost surrounds Yucatan.

A man in Yucatan working on the beach saw a watch lying in the sand. "What kind of fish is this?" he asked. He picked it up and thought he could hear it making a noise so he put it to his ear and listened to it ticking. "Aaargh! It is still alive," he cried, and taking it down to the sea he threw it in the water. [Mexican 1980s]

For the joke-tellers at the center, a remote coast seems an appropriate place to which they can banish all the comic stupidity in the country and dump it in the sea. By the same token they will invent jokes that maroon all morons on an off-shore island.

Language, Identity, Stupidity

Similarities and differences of language between joke-tellers and the butts of their jokes play a crucial role in the creation of ethnic jokes about stupidity. Language is one of the most important factors in determining the identity of both jokers and butts and in defining the relationship between them such that the former are able to regard the latter as comically stupid and to make jokes about them. The content and even the structure of ethnic jokes often hinges on differences in the use of language.

The groups who become the butts of ethnic jokes about stupidity are not strange, esoteric, or alien to those who tell jokes about them; indeed, they are often part of the same linguistic and cultural family, or in the process of becoming so. The most striking feature of each of the peoples listed in table 3.1 as the butts of ethnic jokes about stupidity is that they speak the same language as the joke-tellers, or closely related languages, and the two groups can easily communicate with each other. In table 3.2 a number of pairs of ethnic joke-tellers and the butts of their ethnic jokes have been listed and an attempt has been made to assess the nature of the linguistic relationship between the two groups. The brief description and categorization of these relationships given in the far right-hand column is not intended to be anything more than a rough approximation [see also Davies 1987A]. The key conclusion to be drawn is that for a variety of reasons the joke-tellers are often able to regard the speech of the groups who are the butts of their jokes as a distorted version of their own.

In most of the countries where ethnic jokes about the stupidity of others are told, language is one of the defining characteristics of the nation or its main ethnic group. Those who "belong" speak the language of the country, whereas "outsiders" speak an exotic language of their own. The line between "us" and "them" is one of language, a line between the familiar tongue of home and the incomprehensible babble and jabbering of the foreigner [*Brewer's* 1981, 80] or the baa-baa-barian [see also Apte 1985, 197]. In countries where language and identity are closely related the prevailing myth of national identity [see Petersen 1975] is likely to assert (a) their people's possession of a single homogeneous language rather than a mere set of mutually intelligible dialects, and one that differs significantly from all others [see Smith 1981, 45–49; Rokkan and Urwin 1983, 108]; and (b) the sharp and unmistakable coincidence of national and linguistic boundaries [see Prescott 1978, 20, 47, 109; Rokkan and Urwin 1983, 102].

In practice the myth is often contradicted by experience, for in most of the countries of the joke-tellers listed one or more of the following applies:

(a) There are people outside the frontiers of the society who speak essentially the same language, though perhaps in a distinctive way, but who have a separate national and political identity (the Irish in relation to Britain, the French-speaking Swiss and Belgians in relation to France, the Dutch-speaking Belgians in relation to the Netherlands). In some cases a seceding people may have chosen to stress and even accentuate local differences in speech to the point where they can claim that they have a separate language rather than a mere regional dialect, albeit one that is still largely intelligible to the joke-tellers.

(b) The speech of people who live on the far periphery of a society may differ so much from that of the main metropolitan centers that it is difficult to understand and sounds "almost foreign." People living near a linguistic boundary or interface [see Rokkan and Urwin 1983, 34] are often influ-

TABLE 3.2 **Ethnic Jokes and Language**

Country where jokes are told about allegedly stupid groups	Language of joke-tellers	Group alleged to be stupid in jokes	Language or languages spoken by the butt of the jokes	Nature of the relationship between the language of joke-tellers and that of their butts
Britain	English	Irish	English	Same language spoken. The butts of the jokes who may live in the same or in an adjoining country speak a distinctive and "provincial" version of the joke-tellers' language.
France	French	French Swiss (Ouin-Ouin)	French	
		Belgians	Walloon/French	
Netherlands	Dutch	Belgians	Flemish/Dutch	
Germany	German	Ostfrieslanders	Low German	
Greece	Greek	Pontians (Black Sea Greeks)	("Archaic") Greek	
Italy	Italian	Southerners	Italian Dialects	
Canada (Ontario)	English	Newfies (Newfoundlanders)	English	
Egypt	Arabic	Sa'idis	Arabic	
Denmark	Danish	Jutes of Århus	Danish	
Turkey	Turkish	Laz	Turkish	
Ireland	English	Kerrymen	English	
Colombia	Spanish	Pastusos	Spanish	
Austria	German	Burgenlanders	German (Hungarian influence)	The butt of the joke is a group on a linguistic boundary speaking a version of the joke-tellers' language that shows foreign influence.
		Carinthians	German (Slovene influence)	
Finland	Finnish	Karelians	Finnish (Russian influence)	

Mexico	Spanish	Yucatecos	(a) Maya (b) Spanish	The butt of the jokes is a linguistic minority on the periphery whose members may have only a limited knowledge of the main language of the society.
Iran	Persian (Farsi)	Rashtis	(a) Turkish (b) Persian	
Iraq	Arabic	Kurds	(a) Kurdish (b) Arabic	
South Africa	(a)English (main) (b)Afrikaans	Afrikaners (van der Merwe)	(a) Afrikaans (main) (b) English	The butts of the jokes are in an officially bilingual country. They are in a majority in their own country or area but the joke-tellers' language has a stronger external base.
Sweden	Swedish (only)	Finns	(a) Finnish (main) (b) Swedish Finland is officially bilingual and so is South Africa	
Sweden	Swedish	Norwegians	Norwegian	The butts of the jokes live in an adjoining country and speak a closely related language that is largely intelligible to the joke-tellers.
Denmark	Danish	Norwegians	Norwegian	
Czech lands	Czech	Slovaks	Slovak	
Russia	Russian	Ukrainians	Ukrainian	
Australia	English	Irish	English	The butts of the jokes are immigrants or descendants of immigrants who already spoke a version of the main language of their new country.
New Zealand	English	Irish	English	
Brazil	Portuguese	Portuguese	Portuguese	
United States	English	Poles (and locally Italians, Portuguese, etc.)	English	The butts of the jokes are immigrants or the descendants of immigrants who originally spoke a different language but have learned the main language of their new country.
Canada (West)	English	Ukrainians	English	

enced by the language of the "foreigners" on the other side, so that their speech and their culture constitute a vague zone of transition rather than the sharp line of a political frontier [Prescott 1978, 14, 20, 47]. Indeed, their speech may be described as wavering between one language and another [Goethe 1970, 41].

(c) Linguistic minorities, immigrants, the "other" group in an officially bilingual society may speak the language of the culturally dominant group very imperfectly and as a second language, and even the assimilated descendants of immigrants or former linguistic minorities may preserve strange fragments of their ancestors' language in their speech.

From the point of view of the joke-tellers, all such groups once again have an uncertain and fuzzy identity, for they neither fully belong to the joke-tellers' group nor are they clearly foreign. They each constitute a "Transitional Wavering People and Seemingly Intermediate Nation" and can be designated by the acronym TWPSIN or, for brevity, TWP [for ease of pronunciation the 'w' should be pronounced like the short 'oo' sound in 'took'; see Edwards 1986, 38]. For the joke-tellers the TWPs are anomalous, and ambiguous, a contradiction of the joke-tellers' sense of ethnic and linguistic order and unity, a blurring of the clarity of their boundaries. The joke-tellers are nearly always a culturally and linguistically dominant group vis-à-vis the butt of their jokes. Thus it is the latter who get defined as the ambiguous group on the periphery and not the other way around. French-speaking Belgium and Switzerland are linguistic extensions of France, and while the French-Swiss [see Rousseau 1965 (1781), 77, 98, 110, 280] and especially the Walloons [Hanse et al. 1971; Petersen 1975, 192–93] seek to imitate *le bon usage*, i.e., the cultured French of Paris, the Parisians do not return the compliment [see de Grand'Combe 1933, 218]. The Flemings now call their language Nederlands (Dutch), not Vlaams (Flemish), and study books on how to speak "general cultured Dutch" [Petersen 1975, 204; Rokkan and Urwin 1983, 74], while the Dutch view Flemish as a backward dialect [Geyl 1962, 220–28]. The Irish speak the language of England and not vice versa, and both groups know that this is the case [cf. Joyce 1968 (1916), 192–93]. The speech of the upper middle class of Dublin is closer to that of their English counterparts than is the brogue of the peasants of the periphery:

> What do you call a Kerryman with a Cork accent?
> A social climber. [Irish 1980s]

The culture and language of the TWPs is to a significant extent derived from and dependent upon that of the culturally dominant joke-tellers—indeed, this is the basis of the joke-tellers' dominant position. Individual members of a TWP may be successful within the joke-tellers' culture and using their language but the dominant group still creates and controls the standards of what that language is and how it should be used. The ambiguous TWPs do not constitute a threat to the integrity of the neighboring joke-teller's language and culture. Each TWP is far from the center, a mere eccentric warping of the edges of the dominant group's language and culture. The center holds. Things don't fall apart.

The dominant groups are thus in a position to regard the TWPs as a case of nonthreatening ambiguity, which is a comic situation likely to produce jokes. The TWPs constitute an anomaly that can be dismissed as a joke and through the use of jokes. The TWPs are not important enough to be seen as a dangerous heresy or a form of pollution [see Davies 1982A]. They can be laughed out of existence as a piece of comic stupidity not to be taken seriously:

> Where is the biggest chip-shop in Europe?
> On the border of France and the Netherlands. [Dutch 1970s]
> [Chips (U.K.) = French fries (U.S.)]
>
> What is the thinnest book ever written?
> The history of Polack culture. [Clements 1973, 30]
>
> What is the smallest building in the world?
> The Polish Hall of Fame. [Clements 1973, 30]

This is not a humor of hostility or resentment, it is the humor of superiority and condescension. The joke-tellers see the local TWP not as a powerful alien group that is feared or hated, but as a poor imitation of themselves, a people whose culture or language is an imperfect version of their own. Gifted individual members of the TWP often realize only too well that they belong to a group occupying a subordinate cultural position vis-à-vis the language of the joke-tellers [cf. Joyce 1968 (1916), 192–93].

The central importance of language as a crucial and independent local factor in the genesis of ethnic jokes about stupidity is shown very clearly by the case of French jokes about the Belgians or the Swiss, for the other general factors that can influence these jokes, such as economic inferiority or dependence, immigration or social class, are absent. Belgium and French-speaking Switzerland are on the cultural periphery of France but they are part of the economic core of Western Europe as a whole [see Belgium Survey 1980] and are not economically dependent on France. French jokes about the Belgians or the French-speaking Swiss are an instance par excellence of ethnic jokes about stupidity being rooted in the connection between language and identity. The jokes reflect the fact that French is the dominant language of France and France is the dominant central base of the French language.

Linguistic dominance enables a group to tell ethnic jokes about the stupidity of its neighbors, and the latter find it difficult to reply in kind. The Finnish social scientist Lauri Lehtimaja put this point to the author very clearly:

> Somehow it seems, however, that we have been unable to create a good many jokes about the Scandinavian neighbours. Maybe it is partly due to the language barrier. Most of the Finns never really understood what the Swedes and the Norwegians were saying in their own languages and this is why we could not ridicule them in the same way as the Russian and Karelian salesmen who spoke Finnish but very bad Finnish. [1979]

Only where there is a rough parity between similar languages can an exchange of ethnic jokes about stupidity occur between nations as in the case of Norway and Sweden [Kvideland 1983] and Austria and Switzerland [Burger 1981]. The peoples of both Austria and much of Switzerland speak distinctive forms of the language of their larger neighbor, Germany, so that both are on the edge of the German-speaking world. The Swedes seem to have an edge over the Norwegians both by reason of their overall dominant position in Scandinavia and because their language is more homogeneous and longer established than that of the Norwegians, whose internal linguistic squabbles and attempts to create new words [see Rokkan and Urwin 1983, 81–83, 108; Trudgill 1974] strike the Swedes as absurdly comic [see Ternhag 1975].

How do you get an Austrian's brain to the size of a pea?
Inflate it. [Burger 1981]

The position of immigrants to the United States has been in many ways the most asymmetrical one of all when it comes to making jokes, because it is they who have had to assimilate and learn English. People who were perfectly competent in their own language suddenly became comically dumb Svenskas, Norskies, Polacks, etc. [see Keillor 1986, 8, 79; Lewis 1954 (1923)]. The use of the word *dumb* to mean *stupid*, though it occurs in British English, is distinctively American, as are derivatives such as dumbhead, dumb-dumb, dumbo, dummy which seem to echo the predicament of new arrivals who appear stupid because they cannot yet understand or reply. It is probably also the basis of American mockery of the honorable Polish name Dambrowski,[5] which becomes Dumbrowski in American jokes:

Who wears blue pants, a purple shirt, an orange polka-dot tie and sits on a wall?
Humpty-Dumbrowski. [Clements 1973, 10]

"It's a stupid name enough!" Humpty [Dumbroswki] interrupted impatiently. "What does it mean?" "Must a name mean something?" Alice asked doubtfully.

"Of course it must", Humpty [Dumbrowski] said with a short laugh. "My name means . . . " [Carroll 1965, 171]

As the first generation of immigrants painfully acquired the new language, they became the butts of dialect stories about the inevitable comic errors in their speech [Apte 1985, 201; Esar 1978, 166], not only for old-stock Americans but for their own descendants who had mastered English [Danielson 1975]. The implication was often spelled out in jokes that errors in language also reflected or led to errors in thought or action, i.e., all-round stupidity. It was difficult for the immigrants to retaliate with jokes about the American joke-tellers, for the American joke-tellers were also their linguistic and national reference group [cf. LaFave, Haddad, & Marshall 1974]. The old-stock Americans were, with the possible exception of the Mexican-Americans [see Limón 1977], the only important people in the United States whose linguistic membership group was from the start also their linguistic reference group. For the immigrant not to acquire English was to display a disloyalty to the basic principles of American life [Haugen 1966, 10] and he or she remained an ignoramus, mere raw material for a future American [Haugen 1966, 10]. In time the descendants of these immigrants came to see the language of their ancestors as unrespected by others, and even mother-tongue teachers of those languages [Fishman and Nahirny 1966, 121–22] saw them as useless because they were not recognized by the education system as a valid language qualification for teaching. Indeed, despite the so-called ethnic revival, very few Americans today (other than the Hispanics, who have their own local territorial base) have more than a smattering of their ancestors' language or much real acquaintance with the culture of the country from which their forebears came [see Andreski 1973; Kusielewicz 1969, 97–100; Renkiewicz 1973, 33–39]. Hence the rather sad American joke about Konrad Korseniowski:

Why do Poles learn English?
So they can read Joseph Conrad in the original. [Dundes 1971, 201]

Native speakers of English outside America can and do tell jokes that make fun of the sounds and phrases of standard American English:

American: A lie never passed the lips of George Washington.
Englishman: No, he spoke through his nose like the rest of you. [English twentieth century]

It is easy to see why it is impossible for non-English-speaking immigrants settling in America to crack jokes like this. Not only is it intrinsically difficult for these immigrants to mock the forms of speech which the very fact of immigration demands they acquire, but also there is no alternative standard of English available to them against which American speech can be measured and found comically wanting.

Modern American stupidity jokes are much less likely to depict the butts of the jokes speaking dialect than such jokes did in the past, which is not surprising given that most Polish-Americans have English as their first and usually only language. In consequence there are very few American jokes that actually employ Polish words or phrases:

What was the name of the Polack who invented the mini-skirt?
Seymour Dupa. [Clements 1973, 11]
[Dupa (Polish) = ass (U.S.) = arse (U.K.)]

Not only is there a paucity of American ethnic jokes based on the speech patterns of the Poles but also when Americans tell ethnic jokes about Poles they do not imitate them by putting on an accent or speaking a distinctive kind of distorted English. Nonetheless, the link in people's minds between comic stupidity and broken English is a strong one, as can be seen from the collection of ethnic jokes about Poles compiled and written by the American comedian Larry Wilde. These books sold millions of copies and have probably been the main printed source influencing the dissemination and development of American Polish jokes. In these books Wilde has reversed the original link between language and stupidity by making the Poles in his jokes speak clumsy English to underline their stupidity.

Filipowicz wanted a divorce from his wife.
"Why?" asked the judge.
"Well," replied the Polack, "she be trying to kill me."
"How do you know that?" asked the magistrate.
"Yesterday in the bathroom I find a bottle that say Polish Remover." [Wilde 1978A, 187]

"What you doin?" asked Ladislas
"I write letter to myself," answered Sigismund
"What you tell yourself?"
"How do I know?" snapped Sigismund. "I no get letter until tomorrow!" [Wilde 1973, 120]

Whether Wilde's mock Polish-English is rooted in his childhood memories of the way first-generation immigrants once spoke or whether he has created a new all-purpose ersatz broken English doesn't really matter. What is important is that whereas historically images of comic ethnic stupidity have been rooted in the distortions of language that characterize TWPs, Wilde has made this relationship a reciprocal one by deliberately producing distortions of language in order to make ethnic jokes about stupidity look authentic.

Jokes about stupidity are also told about ethnic groups who live on the interface of two major or prestigious languages whose attempts to speak either one of the languages are likely to contain fragments of the other in a way that those in full command of the "pure" language of the center are likely to find comic. Today's French and Dutch ethnic jokes about "stupid Belgians" are the descendants of dialect stories and satires based on the occurrence of odd bits of Dutch in Walloon French and of French in Flemish [see van Lennep 1894, 289]. Similarly, the alternative butts of Dutch jokes, the Limburghers, live on the edge of the Netherlands in a long, thin province squeezed between Germany and Belgium, which makes the local speech sound comically remote and un-Dutch [see Seipgens 1894; Werner 1894, 231].

> What happens if a Limburgher goes to live in Belgium?
> The average IQ of both Belgium and the Netherlands rises.
> [Dutch 1970s]

The mixing of languages is also one of the factors that has led to the people of the canton of Fribourg being the butt of Swiss jokes about stupidity [see Herdi 1979, 56–57; "Ringo-Ringo" 1978, 86], the other being that it is a strongly Roman Catholic canton [Bonjour, Offler, and Potter 1952, 262–65; *Schweizerische Volkszählung* 1980]. Freiburg oder/ou Fribourg is one of the most linguistically mixed cantons, with the French speakers constituting about two-thirds of the population and the Germans one-third [Bonjour, Offler, and Potter 1952, 304; *Schweizerische Volkszählung* 1980]. There is a blurred rather than a sharp language frontier[6] and the local form of thank-you is the mixed French-German form *Merci vielmal,* which other Swiss find comic.

The symbolic use in Eire of Gaelic words, names, and titles in ordinary English sentences seems an incongruous and muddled "state of chassis" to outsiders and leads to British jokes exploiting double meanings. Thus the renaming of the Irish unit of currency as the Punt practically invited such comic headlines as "Punt sinks again as City punters sell" and the names of the political parties Fine Gael and Fianna Faíl (pronounced Foyle) led to "Fianna Failed again" and "Fianna Foiled again." In the same way Aer Lingus (Irish airlines) becomes Air Fungus and Taoiseach (Prime Minister), the withdrawal symptoms the Irish get when they stop drinking tea.

Cunnilingus is not an Irish airline.
No, it's a tongue twister. [O'Leary and O'Larry 1983]

Car sticker in O'Connell Street, Dublin:
Brush Up Your Erse. [Murtie 1985, p. 47]

The distinctive pronunciation and phraseology of new Irish migrants into Britain and the continued vitality of Irish English have meant that dialect stories told in a mock-Irish brogue have survived better in Britain than have similar tales in America. Even today when most new British ethnic jokes about the Irish, like American jokes about the Poles, are based on material rather than language errors, new jokes based on the distinctively Irish use of English are being invented:

How to speak Irish in one easy lesson.
Say very quickly
Whale
Oil
Beef
Hooked. [*Whitelands Rag* 1985]

Irish graffiti:
I'm a tinker.
Oh! And what are you tinking about? [O'Leary and O'Larry 1983]

Similar jokes exist in French about Belgian speech patterns [Daninos 1955, 126] and Northern Italians tell dialect jokes about backward Southerners [see Cornelisen 1969, 65, 244] but they are difficult to translate. Colombian jokes about Pastusos refer to the people of the department of Nariño, whose capital is Pasto. Nariño lies on the border with Ecuador, with which it has much more in common in terms of landscape, culture, and customs; indeed, it nearly became part of Ecuador when Spain's colonies in South America became independent. Like Ecuador its population is predominantly indigenous and it is by far the most staunchly Conservative department in a country where the Liberals have tended to be the majority party. This sense of Nariño being at the edge of Colombia is conveyed in Pastuso jokes by the use of the high-pitched voice in which Pastusos and Ecuadorians speak Spanish. A Colombian will put on a shrill, innocent voice to tell a Pastuso joke and end sentences with the characteristic phrase "Eh, Ave Maria." As in other ethnic jokes, both material and verbal errors are ascribed to the Pastusos.

Bogotano on phone to Pastuso: Como estas?

["How are you?" but with the alternative meaning "In what position are you?"]

Pastuso: I'm sitting down. [Colombian 1980s]

The speech of peoples who are the butts of ethnic jokes about stupidity is often regarded by the joke-tellers as a slow or old-fashioned version of their own language. By implication the slow of speech are also slow-witted, and out-of-date speech indicates general backwardness, both of which are aspects of the popular view of stupidity. To relate speech to stupidity in this way may be quite unjustified, but the description is one often stressed by the joke-tellers themselves. When I have asked Greeks, and particularly Athenians, why they tell jokes about Pontians (Black Sea Greeks, from "Pontus"), who are neither unpopular nor economically unsuccessful, they have replied that the Pontians speak or used to speak a funny "archaic dialect of Greek" [see also Petropoulos 1987]. Similarly, in a comment on the Dutch joke "Why wasn't Jesus born in Belgium? Because they couldn't find three wise men," Hedy Fixler, a Dutch-speaking American, noted that "the Dutch consider Flemish to be merely 'Old Dutch' and are constantly remarking how backward the Belgians are for not speaking proper modern Dutch" [UCBFA Dutch file, 1975].

If a group's mother language is seen as merely a backward version of one's own and the group is seen as unable to adapt their speech to fit in with "modern" ways of speaking and this becomes the subject of humorous comment, then a situation exists in which the linguistically "backward" group is likely to become the butt of ethnic jokes about its stupid inability to cope with other aspects of the modern world such as technology, and this, as indicated earlier, is the very essence of modern ethnic jokes about stupidity in all countries.

The significance of the Dutch or Greek view of the forms of their language spoken by Belgians or Pontians for the comparative study of ethnic jokes about stupidity is that it suggests the nature of the general link between minor differences of language and a reputation for comic stupidity of a more material kind. A similar point may be made about those groups perceived as speaking slowly who are the butts of ethnic jokes about stupidity. French jokes about the French-speaking Swiss, Danish jokes about Århusians, and Egyptian jokes [see El Shamy 1980, 232–33] about Sa'idis all stress and at times make use of the allegedly slow speech of these butts of ethnic jokes about stupidity. Such jokes are often told as dialect stories, with emphasis on the slow utterance, the long drawn out vowels and slurred consonants, and the needless pauses between words that contain meaningless grunts (Arr) of the "stupid" group. In this respect they are similar to jokes told about the simplicity of rustics in England [e.g., see *East Anglia's Humour* 1976] or parts of the United States.

In the Danish and French jokes, the slow speech of the people of "Aaaarhus" or of the French-Swiss is built into the very structure of ethnic jokes about stupidity:

Do you know the one about the Århusian who had to make a parachute jump?

In the airplane there was also a man from Odense and one from Copenhagen. They had been thoroughly trained and had learned to count up to 3 before they pulled the rip-cord. They jumped and the men from Odense and Copenhagen did as they had been instructed. As they were drifting down, a big black lump fell past them. Rather worried, they landed and ran over to see what had happened to the man from Århus. They discovered a large hole in the ground and when they got there and looked over the top they saw the Århusian lying there saying "T—-W—-O". [Yearhouse 1974A. Also told about the Swiss in French. For other jokes using the Århus drawl see *Humorpiller*, 556 n.d., esp. 62]

French ethnic jokes about the Swiss also rely on slowness, slowness of speech, of articulation, and of action; indeed, slowness is the very essence of these jokes:

On croit généralement que l'inscription S.B.B.–C.F.F. qui figure sur les wagons des trains suisses signifie Chemins de Fer Fédéraux. En réalité cela veut dire: c'est bas bossible, ça fa fite. [Isnard 1979, 19]

Most people think the letters S.B.B.–C.F.F. on Swiss trains stand for Swiss Federal Railroad—Schweizerische Bundesbahn - Chemins de Fer Fédéraux. They actually stand for Shlowly bush bast, coing fast's forbidden. [my translation]

The bell rang at the Swiss home of M. Berthelier and he went to open the door.

—"Ah! It's the plumber! At last! We have been expecting you for the last eight days!"

—"Eight days?" said the plumber in surprise, closing up his toolbox. "I must have come to the wrong apartment. In the place where I'm supposed to be, they called me in two months ago." [Isnard 1977, 17]

The association of slow speech with slow minds also occurs in jokes about dim aristocrats who speak with a drawl, such as the Austrian and German jokes about Graf Bobby or American ethnic jokes about tongue-tied upper-class Englishmen speaking with what is known in Britain as on "old-school-tie-in-the-mouth" voice.

The distinctive speech of a group that is the butt of ethnic jokes about stupidity can also be used as a signal of ethnic identity and stupidity, as a kind of verbal trigger to a joke, and thus as a means of indicating ethnicity indirectly in order to achieve greater surprise:

> An Irishman decided to become a Pole and asked an American surgeon if he could achieve such a difficult transformation. The surgeon said that he could but warned that it would be necessary to cut out a quarter of his brain. The Irishman agreed to this and went to the hospital for the operation. As he was coming round from the anaesthetic he saw that the surgeon was sitting next to his bed holding his head in his hands and looking haggard and distraught. Realizing that his patient was conscious again, the surgeon said: "I'm afraid I've made a terrible mistake; instead of cutting out a quarter of your brain, I cut out three quarters."
>
> "Oh, no," screamed the patient, "Mama mia!" [American 1960s]

The ending of this American joke is an extremely skillful one. Those listening to it suspect that it is an ethnic joke about stupidity and they know what kind of ending to expect, but the punch line still comes as a surprise. "Mama mia" must come as the very last words of the joke, thus rapidly but indirectly switching the focus of the joke between the two most frequent butts of American jokes about stupidity and moving from the Poles to the Italians. For an American audience "Mama Mia" indicates "Italian," and "Italian" indicates "stupid," so the ending springs two traps at once. The joke would not work as well if the two groups were reversed so that a man who wanted to become an Italian became a Pole, since there is no equivalent easily recognized way of signaling Polish ethnic identity indirectly and compactly. The ideal ending produces a pattern of fast–slow–fast: (1) the ending is compact and thus conveys the necessary evidence of ethnic identity suddenly; (2) the ending is indirect so that there is a tiny pause as the audience "translates" the signal; (3) the meaning is then rapidly and correctly understood by everybody.

Thus, as I have shown elsewhere [Davies 1987a], language as a means of defining ethnic identity and misuse of language as an index of an ethnic group's peripheral position are central to the working of ethnic jokes about stupidity. It is those who live at the linguistic edge of a society, whether in space, i.e., geographically, or in time, as in the case of immigrants learning a new language, who are very often the butts of jokes about stupidity.

Religion, Ambiguous Identity, and Comic Stupidity

Religion is, like language, an important means of defining ethnic identity, and since it is often a determinant of whether a people are traditional or enterprising, it is also linked to the question of who gets labeled stupid or canny in jokes. Protestant and especially Calvinist and Unitarian ethnic groups and Jews tend to be the butt of canny jokes and Roman Catholics the butt of jokes about stupidity. Indeed, it is striking how many of the butts of ethnic jokes about stupidity—the Irish in Britain, the Belgians in France and in the Netherlands, the Poles, Italians, and Portuguese in America, the Slovaks in the Czech lands—are from countries where there is a Roman Catholic myth of faith and nation in contrast to the national myths of the joke-tellers, who are Protestant or secular or whose myths contain a strong Protestant or secular element sometimes in rivalry with a Roman Catholic one [Martin 1978, 102]. The striking correlation between Roman Catholicism and stupidity jokes, though less strong than that between Protestantism and jokes about canniness, suggests that the corporate and traditional quality of Roman Catholicism, by damping rather than hyping competitive individualism, leads to relative economic inertia[7] and hence to ethnic jokes about stupidity.

Here, however, I wish to examine a rather different situation, in which religion simultaneously defines an ethnic identity and yet is seen by others as an index of ambiguity and as the badge of a people from the edge of a society and indeed of an entire civilization—a civilization whose key defining characteristic is religion.

The butt of the ethnic jokes about stupidity told in India and Pakistan is a distinctive religious group, the Sikhs (usually referred to in jokes as Sardarjis), who speak the same language, Punjabi, as their immediate Hindu and Muslim neighbors. The Indian subcontinent has long been divided between the followers of two incompatible and conflicting religions, the Hindus, who are three-fourths of India's population, and the Muslims, who constitute almost the entire population of Pakistan and Bangladesh. The Sikhs occupy a peripheral position in India, living on the border with Muslim Pakistan in the frontier state of the Punjab, which was partitioned between India and Pakistan with great loss of life in 1947. The Sikh religion itself reflects their "boundary" position, for though they constitute a separate religion of their own, in many ways they may be regarded as a schismatic Hindu sect formed under the impact of the Muslim invasion, which brought to India Islamic notions of monotheism and the fraternal equality of the faithful [see Kaur 1967]. Thus the Sikhs reject the Hindu caste system, though in practice they continue to observe caste distinctions within their own community [see I. P. Singh 1967]. In the past the ambiguous relationship between Sikh and Hindu has been underlined by the greater willingness of Sikhs to intermarry with Hindus of the same caste as their own than with Sikhs of an inferior caste [see I. P. Singh 1967, 74–76]. The Sikhs are an ambiguous group, part Hindu sect, part independent religion [see Horowitz 1975, 111], poised between the Hindus and the Muslims. The visible outward symbols of their religion, such as the long, unshorn hair and beards of the men, held in place by a turban and a snood, and the wearing of a sword and a metal bracelet, are a proclamation of their distinctive identity yet also an indication of their Hindu origins, for the Sikh symbols are based on an inversion of the symbols and rituals of antinomian Hindu sects [see Uberoi 1967, 91–94]. They demonstrate that the Sikhs wish to repudiate the Hindu world [see Uberoi 1967, 97–98] and yet are a reminder of their historic links with it. The long hair, turbans, and beards of the male Sikhs frequently figure in the jokes told by both Hindus and Muslims about the Sikhs' alleged simplicity.

A Sardarji went into a hotel and ordered that everything (provided for him)—his room, his food, his soap—must be Badshahi (Royal, i.e., fit for a king). And that's how he lost his beard. [Kashmir 1980s]

[Badshahi is also the trade-name of a kind of soap sold in India as a depilatory.]

A Sardarji bought a watch and happened to look at the time at twelve o'clock noon. "I've been cheated," he cried out. "This watch has only got one hand." He immediately took it back to the shop where he had bought it and complained. The shopkeeper told him, "Come back again in five minutes and your watch will be O.K."

The Gujarati ticket-collector who told the author this joke on a local train in Gujarat in 1974 added a joking observation often repeated by other Indians: "Because the Sardarjis don't cut their hair but wrap it up in a turban their heads get too hot at 12 o'clock noon and they become absentminded."

In practical terms it would be just as reasonable—and just as unreasonable—to argue that the Sikhs, like Noel Coward's Englishmen, functioned better than others at noon because their brains were protected from the midday sun by their long hair and turbans acting as solar topees. Far more important is the way in which the joke-tellers link the jokes about Sikh irrationality with the key symbols of their separate, but familiar, and in some ways ambiguous identity.

The odd position of the Sikhs on the penumbra of Hinduism is also indicated in Pakistani jokes:

In the province of East Punjab in India where both Sikhs and Hindus inhabit the place, there was a local election where a Hindu and a Sikh gentleman were campaigning for the position. Both were trying to belittle the others in their campaign speeches. In one of the Hindu communities, the Sikh was delivering a campaign speech. In his zeal to impress the Hindu community about his knowledge of the Hindu religion and the lack of this knowledge by his Hindu opponent he started telling his audience that his opponent, although he is Hindu, does not even know the names of his own gods. "Well, folks," he said, "I am going to tell you the names of all the Hindu gods. There was one named Rama, and there was one named Sita, there was one more and one more and one more and there was one whose name I forgot." [UCBFA Pakistan file, Joy Evans 1966 (1956)]

The nature of the Indian comic image of the Sikhs, and of their related view of the comic potential of the Sikhs' unshorn hair and beards, snoods and turbans, can be emphasized by contrasting it with that of British joke-tellers and cartoonists. The latter use the turban and beard of the Sikh as a symbol of all new and strange immigrants from exotic and alien places [e.g., see *East Anglia's Humour* 1976].

For the Indians the Sardarjis are a very familiar sight and Sikh traders, artisans, and soldiers are a highly visible element throughout the country, an accepted and integral, though today politically controversial, part of Indian society. Penderel Moon noted that in the 1940s "it was customary in the Punjab to laugh at the Sikhs more or less good humouredly for their supposed incapacity for much cerebration" [1961, 82]. The jokes have a long tradition and are now told throughout India—I collected Sardarji jokes in India in the 1970s not only in Gujarat and the Punjab but in big cities such as Bombay, Madras, and Delhi, and in places as remote as Srinagar and Darjeeling. They are also popular in Pakistan and among Indians who have emigrated to Britain and the United States.

Many of these jokes have been pinned on Sikh notables, such as former Indian Minister of Defense Baldev Singh or Indian Olympic athlete Milka Singh.

When India and Pakistan went to war over Kashmir [a landlocked state which is still divided along the cease-fire line] in 1947 the Indian Defence Minister, Baldev Singh, declared "The army will throw the Pakistanis out of Kashmir, if not them then the Air Force, if not the Air Force, the Navy!" [Indian 1970s]

There was a Sikh who was in India when India got partitioned . . . the Sikh was Defence Minister of Armed Forces in India. So what happened was that he was getting out of the aeroplane and there were also other ministers with him, but when you are in the aeroplane in the airport they put stairs so that you can step down to the stairs and walk down from the plane. To get off from the plane you must have these stairs so when the man was putting the stairs, the Sikh started to walk down before the stairs were put and the man said, "Wait, wait," to which the Sikh replied "125 pounds." [UCBFA Pakistan file, Ferial Saeed 1976 (1948)]

It is significant that the same jokes were pinned on this particular Sikh by both Indians and Pakistanis despite the fact that their hopes and expectations regarding the capacities of an Indian Defense Minister must have been very different at a time when there was fighting between the two countries. During the 1980s the Sikhs have become involved in a conflict with the Indian government as a result of a clash between the drive by extreme Sikh reformers to distance their religion from Hinduism and even to gain an autonomous Khalistan, and the strong centralizing tendencies of the Delhi government. This conflict is not the source of the ethnic jokes about Sikhs, but rather both the conflict and the jokes are rooted in the Sikhs' ambiguous situation and history. The jokes interpret the ambiguity while the Sikh reformers seek to resolve it in a particular direction.

Peasants and Plebeians

The members of many of the groups who are the butt of ethnic jokes about stupidity occupy economic positions associated with an absence of skill, education, or entrepreneurial innovation. They are or were peasants in economies where change and modernization, enterprise and progress are associated with the cities and industrial areas. They are not shrewd farmers operating skillfully in the marketplace, but peasants on the periphery, trapped in a relatively unchanging and unthinking world of heavy toil and restrictive tradition. Such people are likely to become the butts of the kind of jokes told by townies and city slickers about the alleged stupidity of rustics, yokels, boobies, leadheads, and country bumpkins, of clods, clodhoppers, clodpolls, clodpates, and clowns, of hayseeds, swedes, and mangel-wurzels, of Rubes and rednecks, of bog-trotters, brier-hoppers, backwoodsmen, hillbillies, mountaineers, and hoosiers,[8] of the people who live in Hicktown, Rubetown, Gophertown, Jaketown, Yokelville, Toonerville, Hiramsville, Silasville, Dogpatch, Podunk, Pumpkin Junction, Hayseed Center [Esar 1978, 188–89, 296, 360–61, 581]. These are just the British and American terms. Thailand has its own genre of Loong Chay (Uncle Yokel) jokes [see UCBFA Thai file] and Singapore its jokes about the Suaku (mountain tortoises), the slow rustics from the outlying rural districts [Chia, Seet, and Wong 1985]. The Japanese comedian Morita Kazuyoshi, known as "Yamori," who tells jokes about the alleged stupidity of the people of Nagoya, a city halfway between the two great metropolitan areas of Tokyo and Osaka, always refers to Nagoya as "a great countryside," i.e., not a proper sophisticated city. The stupid yokel, then, is an almost universal comic image and one which has given rise to innumerable comic nicknames for the allegedly simple country-dwellers.

In many cases the rural people mocked in the jokes may well be skilled and experienced workers within their own sphere, but their skills and know-how are local and limited, not universal and transferable. The comic images formed and disseminated by the literate city-dwellers are the ones that prevail and jokes about the idiocy of rural life proliferate while rural anecdotes about the city slicker getting his comeuppance wither away. If the rural people have a distinctive ethnic or territorial identity this gives an added edge to the jokes. The ethnic jokes told in Germany about Ostfrieslanders, in Britain about the Irish, in Sweden about Norwegians, in Ireland about Kerrymen, in Egypt about Nubians and Sa'idis, in Canada about Newfies, in Denmark about Jutes, in Italy about Southerners, in South Africa about van der Merwe, in Bulgaria about the Šopi, in Yugoslavia about Bosnians, all have a strong element in them of city-dwellers laughing at rural folk[9] and especially at the rustic come to town who has to cope with an unfamiliar world.

Once the image of an ethnic group as comically stupid rustics is established it can often survive subsequent economic changes, particularly if local factors such as geography, language, culture, or religion make that group especially likely to be the butt of ethnic jokes about stupidity. Jokes about the Sikhs probably originally referred to the Jats, "the hard core of the Sikh community—the peasant cultivators of central Punjab" [Moon 1961, 82]. Yet in recent years the Jats have proved to be remarkably enterprising farmers, businessmen, and entrepreneurs, and have even been nicknamed the "Jet-Sikhs." Yet, as Paul Theroux has noted, "For the rest of the Indians, Gujaratis in particular, Sikhs are yokels and jokes are told to illustrate the simplicity of the Sikh mind" [1975, 92].

A parallel point may be made about the jokes told about the alleged stupidity of Texas Aggies or Virginia Hokies, the students and alumni of Texas A & M (Agricultural and Mechanical) University and Virginia Tech respectively, or the "State" jokes told about North Carolina State University at Raleigh, the former State Agricultural and Mechanical College, all of which are very similar to the ethnic jokes about stupidity told elsewhere in the United States.[10] These jokes have their roots in the long-established comic images of agriculturalists and rude mechanicals, and indeed the military, as being ludicrously backward—images enjoyed by those who have attended places of "pure" learning with a higher status such as the University of Texas, the University of Virginia, or the University of North Carolina.

What's the difference between culture and agriculture?

Thirty miles. [Costner 1975, 109]

[the distance between the University of North Carolina and North Carolina State]

How many Virginia Tech Engineering students does it take to change a light-bulb?

One, but you get three credits for it. ["UVa and Tech" 1987]

Virginia Polytechnic Institute and State University has a new title, "Eastern Institute of Enlightenment and Intellectual Outreach" or E-I-E-I-O. ["UVa and Tech" 1987]

Do you know why they had to drop the teaching of drivers' education at Tech this year?

The mule died. ["UVa and Tech" 1987]

T-Sipper: Don't be afraid, It's only a little green snake.

Aggie: Yeah, but it may be just as dangerous as a ripe one. [(Hundred and One) *101 Aggie Jokes* Seventh Generation 1979, 18]

"I come from a small farm, my father isn't rich and I don't own a brand-new sports car like some University of Texas student, but I love you, Rachel Bell" said the Aggie student to his girl friend.

"I love you too," said Rachel Bell, "but tell me more about that Texas student." [Texan 1979]

The NASA space center in Houston was sending samples of moon rocks for the scientists at land grant universities throughout the U.S. to study. By the time they got around to Texas A & M all the moon rocks were gone, so they went to a nearby feedlot, took several well-hardened chips from the ground there and sent them to Texas A & M.

The Aggie scientists just went crazy analyzing those samples. Finally they got together, conferred at length and announced that the cow indeed did jump over the moon. [*Best of 606 Aggie Jokes* 1976, 136]

Peasants who migrate to the towns in search of work are likely to be the butt of jokes about stupidity especially if they are drawn from a distinctive ethnic or territorial group. These ethnic jokes dwell on the ignorance and simplicity of peoples who have had to cope simultaneously with a new and unfamiliar urban and industrial world and with a change of culture, language, or nationality as well.

Underlying Italian jokes about Southerners, Canadian jokes about Newfies, British, Australian, and New Zealand jokes about the Irish, Swedish jokes about Finns, Brazilian jokes about the Portuguese, is the fact that the butts of the jokes have migrated to the joke-teller's country or region in search of work.[11]

A Sicilian went to Milan to get a job. He got the job and at night when he goes home he can't sleep. So he goes to the embalmer, actually it's a what'd-ya-call-it, taxidermist, so he goes there and has a rooster embalmed, then he hangs it up over his bed and he can sleep. [UCBFA Italian file, Michelle Janette 1974]

Mick, who had been working in England, went back to Ireland to find his mates Lenny and Sean were going to Liverpool. 'You'll love England,' he told them. 'Everything's big there—the money's big, the birds are big, the factories are big, and the building sites—Wow!'

Lenny and Sean duly landed in Liverpool, and as they walked down the gangplank, Sean saw an anchor lying on the quayside. 'Bejasus, Lenny, Mick wasn't kidding—look at the size of dat pickaxe dare.' [Hornby 1978, 51]

Ex-peasant immigrants tend to lack skills, education, or capital relevant to an urban or industrial society and are forced into unskilled work in the mines, factories, and construction sites of their new country. Eventually they become upwardly mobile, but the combination of a traditional culture which does not stress entrepreneurship or education together with initial experiences of hardship can delay this process, as indicated in John Bodnar's study of Slavic peasants migrating to America:

> Slavs were carefully establishing working-class worlds in America by integrating Old World traditions with pragmatic innovations necessitated by the constrictions and realities of their socioeconomic status. This process was illustrated in the attitude they assumed toward an industrial society and the results they found in it. Rather than embracing the "American dream" of personal advancement through education and a career, Slavs sought mainly secure employment. Conditions in urban and industrial America only served to strengthen the peasant view of work as an instrument of survival, not success. [Bodnar 1976, 53. See also Greely 1972, 124]

Many ex-peasant ethnic groups, such as the Poles in America, have tended to follow their own distinctive mobility path, seeking advancement within the blue-collar stratum and ownership of a house within an ethnic neighborhood [see Morawska 1977, 79, 100]. In consequence, "as late as the 1960's . . . Polish Americans still clustered in large communities often not far removed from the first neighborhoods of the late nineteenth century, tending to resemble other working-class groups with recent immigrant backgrounds and retained a sense of their Polish identity . . . " [Renkiewicz 1973, vii].

Ethnic jokes about the alleged stupidity of the Poles and other similar groups grew out of this situation and are based on the visible identification of an ethnic group with a social class lacking in status, whose members appeared to lack the ambitions for social and geographical mobility admired in the wider society.[12] Even in the case of much smaller groups, such as the Ukrainians in Alberta or the Portuguese in San Francisco, who have been the butt of local ethnic jokes, the existence of these visible ethnic neighborhoods of blue-collar workers or small-holders is the aspect most apparent to those who tell ethnic jokes about them. It is a point the joke-tellers spontaneously mention when asked about the jokes.

These groups do not seem to be viewed by the joke-tellers as threatening or as present or potential competitors. They are seen by the jokers as static groups, who do not give trouble nor seek political aggrandizement [e.g., see "The Diverse Ethnic Roots of Bay Area Residents" 1985, 4].

However, their very entrenchment in fixed ethnic neighborhoods and their veneration of old customs and traditions seem to others a repudiation of success, change, mobility, innovation. For people who value these latter qualities more highly, the inhabitants of the ethnic neighborhoods appear inert and "stupid." Because their priorities are different, and because the rationale underlying their behavior is not apparent to outsiders, they appear irrational and unenterprising.

The association of ethnicity with low-status occupations is common in ethnic jokes about these groups:

Benito was bragging. "I just got a job promotion. Now I drive the garbage truck and I have two helpers under me."

"That's not so much," sniffed Giovanni. "Take my job! I'm a foreman in a spaghetti factory and I have ten men under me."

A third friend walked up. "I've got a more responsible job than either of you."

"Oh yeah?" they both replied. "What do you do?"

"Well," he said, "I have ten thousand people under me."

Their mouths hung open.

"You betcha," he said, "I cut the grass in the cemetery." [Bonfanti 1976, 166]

An Irishman on a building site was working at a tremendous rate. Every two minutes he dashed up a ladder with an enormous load of bricks. After this had been going on for an hour a friend asked why he was working so hard. 'Oh,' he said. 'Don't tell anyone but I've got them all fooled. I'm not really working hard at all—it's the same load of bricks every time.' [Hornby 1977, 5]

A Šop in America

A group of construction workers in the United States included a Šop immigrant. On a construction project in New York he fell from the fifth floor. He was unhurt. He brushed himself down and was ready to climb the scaffolding again. Then the newspaper reporters showed up on the site followed by representatives of various commercial sporting bodies and they began paying him compliments. They suggested to him that he should take part in a circus act and jump from a high platform. They asked him: "Could you jump from the 10th floor, or the 20th or the 50th?" In answering them the Šop was a bit shy and evasive. At this point the foreman intervened and said: "Oh yes, he can. He'll be perfectly safe, provided he manages to land on his head." [Ogoiski 1975, 70]

What are two Polack professions?

Professional football and professional baseball. [Zewbskewiecz, Kuligowski, and Krulka 1965]

Who was the last Welsh king of the Poles?
John L. Lewis. [Welsh-American 1970s]

What do you call a pit boss in a coal mine?
A Kielbasa. [Wilde 1975A, 76]

There are also indirect references in jokes to the low class position associated with the members of the group that is the butt of ethnic jokes about stupidity. In American ethnic jokes the visible stigmas of the blue-collar worker are the lunch pail, overalls, and the hard hat:

How do you describe a Polack boy with wealthy parents?
He was born with a silver lunch pail in his hands. [Wilde 1975A, 26]

What is the first present a Polish father buys for his baby son?
Booties with cleats. [American 1960s]

Why did the bride think she had the most posh Polish wedding in Poland?
Her veil practically covered her overalls. [Zewbskewiecz, Kuligowski, and Krulka 1965]

British ethnic jokes about the Irish frequently refer indirectly as well as directly to their employment in the construction industry through references to picks, shovels, scaffolding, wheelbarrows, and to the "donkey" jackets and "wellies" worn by building workers. ("Wellies" are Wellington boots, the rubber boots worn by people working in water or mud.)

How do you confuse an Irishman?
Give him twelve shovels and tell him to take his pick. [British photocopy 1970s]

Did you hear about the Irishman who bought his godson a christening shovel? [Chambers 1980, 11]

Have you heard about the expedition of Irishmen who set out to climb Mount Everest?
They ran out of scaffolding thirty feet from the top. [British 1970s]

Wimpey stands for 'We import millions of Paddies every year' [Chambers 1979, 88] and Laing for 'Largely Alcoholic Irish Navvy Gangs' [Marshall 1979, 213]

[Wimpey, Laing, and McAlpine are all large British construction companies.]

How do you tell an Irish solicitor?

Pin-striped donkey-jacket and wellies. [British photocopy 1970s. Also in Hornby 1977, 84]

The captain of an Aer Lingus jet is identified by the three gold rings on his wellies. [Hornby 1977, 84]

An Irishman at work on the roof of a fifteen storey building suddenly dived over with outstretched arms.

"What did you do that for my son?" asked the priest.

"Well," came the reply, "I just got a bit tired of hearing my foreman bragging about how he used to fly Wellingtons during the war." [Murtie 1985, 75]

Footwear has long been an index of social class. In the past it was a mark of poverty not to be able to afford leather shoes but to have to go barefoot or in wooden shoes [Smith 1903 (1776), 691]. To wear clogs, sabots, or other kinds of wooden shoes was a mark of ethnic backwardness [cf. Plumb 1966, 14] as well as individual poverty. Wooden shoes, pattens, cha-kiaks (Chinese clogs) [see Chia, Seet, and Wong 1985, 28], brogues (the old Irish heelless shoe), and clodhoppers (heavy boots for walking through heavy soil) are also the badge of low-status rustics who work out-of-doors in wet or muddy conditions, which is why they are repeatedly mentioned in ethnic jokes about stupidity. Wellies are the badge of the Irish worker on a construction site in contemporary England, but, as might be expected of a society so highly stratified in both jokes and reality, there is a difference between the black wellies worn by construction workers and the wellies of the gentry and would-be gentry who distance themselves from the former by wearing green wellies [e.g., see "Krin" 1981, 3; Sherrin and Shand 1984, 123] when engaged in country sports and pursuits.

Graham Nown, an authority on green wellies, has written that aspiring green wellie wallies should wear "hunters," for "the little half-straps, seldom understood and never used, signal instantly that you do not have a day job at McAlpines. When is a green wellie not a green wellie? When it's a gum boot, sprouting like intensively farmed leeks at point to points, game fairs and in stable yards" [1987A, 27].

Since those who refer to wellies as "gummers" are also the butt of jokes about stupidity, green wellies are as comic as black ones, albeit at a different point in the English class system. Perhaps, in consequence, the English have developed a number of peculiar games, such as wellie-whanging (throwing a wellington boot as far as possible) or running a hundred yards wearing custard-filled wellies [Barwell 1987, 63–64, 109].

We should not be surprised at the importance played by footwear in jokes, for our feet are our link with the ground and influence the way we walk, which in turn is linked to sex, age, occupation, religion, and military or civilian status. The goose-stepping Prussian, the young toddler, the hobbledehoy in clumsy boots, the Chinese woman whose feet were bound to make them small and to inhibit walking, and her successor teetering on high heels, the pile of shoes outside a mosque are all significant indices of social life. So too are the Guardsman who faints, the sinner who stumbles, the fallen woman, the Ulster left-footer, the unclean pig with cloven hooves that does not chew the cud. It is but a short step to John Cleese's ministry of funny walks, banana-skins, and Bergson's *méchanisation de la vie*.

The wellie, whether black or green, is an index of social class, the badge of those members of an industrial society where most people work indoors who either have to work in mud and muck or have the wealth and leisure to wallow in it. Black wellies are to green wellies as a redneck's red neck is to an expensive suntan. Meanwhile the majority of English people located between these two layers of wellies tell jokes about the mutual stupidity of the wellie-wearers.

Afrikaners, Apparatchiks, and Aristocrats

Peoples from the periphery, peoples who are or were peasants and plebeians, are all relatively powerless; indeed, Bengt Holbek [1975, 334] has suggested that this is the key to their being regarded as stupid in ethnic jokes. However, similar jokes are also told about ethnic groups and social classes who are clearly very powerful indeed. One such ethnic group is the Afrikaners, who are the butt of the van der Merwe jokes told in South Africa. The Afrikaners have long enjoyed a near monopoly of political power in South Africa because, until recently, only whites could vote and the Afrikaners were more numerous and united than the English-speaking whites. The Afrikaners used their political power and patronage to ensure that their own people had the lion's share of government jobs, including not only the civil service, the police, and the army, but also the management of socialized industries such as the railroads [see Moodie 1975; Williams and Strydom 1980, 116–29]. However, their rise to power did not destroy the comic image of them as backward rustics, as Boers—as boors. Historically the Afrikaners' rural traditions did not enable them to compete successfully in the marketplace or through modern secular education, and their power was and is based on the manipulation of a rigged franchise.

The Afrikaners used their political power to gain economic power [Moodie 1975]. The legal enforcement of apartheid in jobs, housing, business, and education prevented the black Africans, Coloureds, and Indians from competing with them. The extension of state control over the South African economy enabled the Afrikaner political leaders to reward their own people, to relegate the more entrepreneurial English-speakers to a subordinate role, and to discriminate against the Jews. Although the Afrikaners came to enjoy the fruits of power and success, the jokes about their stupidity remain, for everyone in South Africa knows or suspects that they did not obtain their privileged situation through open competition but by exploiting a political monopoly based on force and fraud.

However, as a result of the growth and development of the South African economy there now exists a sizable Afrikaner urban middle class whose members are shrewd and well-qualified to survive open competition; but in the process they have become bilingual, skilled, and moderately enlightened and are regarded with suspicion by the more rigid, cramped traditionalists who see themselves as the only true Afrikaners. The more sophisticated Afrikaners, as well as the English-speakers, tell van der Merwe jokes about the members of this latter traditional group and especially about those "van der Merwes" who occupy positions of power despite a lack of the relevant skill, knowledge, or proficiency in the use of language.

After years of living in Zambia, Van paid a visit to Pretoria, where he bumped into his old school-friend Nico Diederichs, who had risen to the position of President.

"What are you doing now, Van," asked Dr. Diederichs.

"Oh, I'm working on the railways," said Van.

"I thought you'd make more progress in life than that," said Dr. Diederichs.

"And what about you?" Van asked.

"Oh I'm President of South Africa now."

"Hell," responded Van. "You haven't done much with your life either. Where I come from we have a Black man doing that job." [Koenderman, Langen, and Viljoen 1976, 20]

Van der Merwe was told to take charge of a multiracial bus taking foreign tourists round Pretoria. Before starting he called them together and said "Now I know you all think that in South Africa everything is segregated by color but that will not be the case on my bus. As far as I am concerned you could all be green. Now everybody aboard, dark green at the back, light green at the front." [South African 1980s. Also in Carver 1980]

A traffic officer stopped van der Merwe in his car.

"Where is your third party?" he demanded.

"Look man," said Van. "I'm from the Free State. We haven't even got a second party." [Koenderman, Langen, and Viljoen 1976, 38]

South Africa is an extreme case, but much the same point can be made in relation to American jokes about the Irish in the late nineteenth and the first half of the twentieth century. Americans continued to tell ethnic jokes about "stupid" Irishmen long after the Irish had risen to positions of political power and influence in the major cities. The reason for the persistence of the jokes was not simply the inert survival of an old comic stereotype, nor can it be explained by reference to the parallel British case where the old image of the Irish was kept going by the continual arrival of new generations of naive immigrants. In America the Irish made their initial gains in power and position not in the marketplace or the examination hall but through the politics of patronage. The link between this kind of power and the longevity of American ethnic jokes about the Irish can be inferred from the form that ethnic political conflicts took when other, later immigrant groups sought to challenge them. Ronald Bayor's account of the changing balance of power in New York City in the 1930s is instructive:

> The close ties between the Irish and politics provided a steady flow of civil service jobs into the Irish community. However, the Irish were soon to lose their hold on these valued and relatively stable positions.
>
> The election of Fiorello La Guardia as Mayor in 1933 provided a change in civil service appointments. Before the advent of La Guardia, Jews, Italians, and blacks had been discriminated against when applying for civil service jobs; most of the positions had gone to the Irish. Mayor La Guardia, however, increased the number of jobs in the competitive category. The number of exempt (appointive) and non-competitive jobs (requiring only a qualifying exam) were reduced. . . . Thus La Guardia managed to increase the number of non-Irish, notably the better educated Jews in the City's civil service. . . . The La Guardia administration also made an effort to eliminate political influence and ethnic discrimination for those already in the civil service. Through job ratings and exams, employees were given the opportunity to rise in the civil service more on the basis of their abilities than political connections. [1978, 25]

That the Irish strongly opposed these changes because they rightly feared they would lose out, whereas the Jews strongly supported them, must have given a new lease of life to ethnic jokes about the "stupid Irish" and the "canny Jews." It is not so much the growth of the conflict between the two ethnic groups that is important for an understanding of the jokes but the fact that this conflict which concerned both material interests and cultural values was essentially about Irish patronage versus Jewish confidence in open competition. Bayor has quoted a number of interesting passages from newspapers with a substantial Irish-American readership which indicate the anger and doubt the Irish felt at La Guardia's reforms which favored the better qualified Jews. One writer wondered "whether now a man must be up on his Greek, mathematics, zoology, astronomy and Hebrew before he can become a good cop" [Bayor 1978, 28]. It is easy to see how the writer felt, and he has a point, but when such sentiments are vociferously expressed by the members of a particular ethnic group they invite ethnic jokes about the opposite kind of cop.

In present-day Italy national as well as local politics often operate on the basis of crude political patronage. Italy is a dual economy with a marked contrast between the prosperous, modern, efficient industries of the north and the poor and backward south of the country. The southerners, lacking a business culture [Lutz 1962] or alternative opportunities, are most likely to demand government jobs and sinecures [Nichols 1973, 22], and southern politicians are likely to supply such posts to their supporters regardless of their suitability for them [Nichols 1973, 93]. Also, since there is de facto one-party rule in many parts of southern Italy, the absence of open competition for government jobs is not even mitigated by forceful electoral competition, which can often act as a brake on blatant jobbery [see Nichols 1973, 22, 250]. The elephantiasis of the Italian government bureaucracy to provide jobs for the indigent and unqualified has undermined the efficiency of the public sector, and this is evident to the ordinary citizen as well as to Italian economists. Rather than entrust foreign mail to the vagaries of the Italian post office, people in the north have been known to drive across the border to Switzerland to post their letters, while the senators and people of Rome make use of the independent mailboxes of the Vatican City. A people used to the efficiency of the industries and businesses of the north naturally joke about the stupidity of those who exercise government authority, particularly since many of these are southerners who are the butt of this type of ethnic joke anyway. The Italians are particularly fond of jokes which depict the Carabinieri, a semimilitary, highly bureaucratic armed police force, as absurdly stupid, for these jokes both mock a form of authority which impinges on the individual and are ethnic jokes about the uneducated rural southerners from whom the Carabinieri are predominantly recruited [Medici 1981, 10; Newby 1975, 86; Nichols 1973]. It is clear from the comments made by northern Italian joke-tellers [see UCBFA Italian file] that the southern connection is both explicit and relished.

Why does it say "Carabinieri" on the doors of their cars?

Because a Carabinieri can't fit in the trunk. [UCBFA Italian file, Ellen Gorman 1976]

One Italian cop says to another: "Call me an elevator, please."

The second cop replies: "O.K. Elevator!"

"No, no, with your finger."

The other, putting his finger in his mouth: "Elevator!" [UCBFA Italian file, Jeffrey Howard. For further Carabinieri jokes see Bramieri 1980A and Medici 1981]

Nigeria provides a further case of ethnic jokes about the stupidity of the politically powerful, in this case the Hausas of the backward northern region, who are one of the most politically and militarily powerful tribes in a society of great ethnic diversity.

A Hausa politician was asked on television what he proposed to do about the lack of minerals in the North of Nigeria. "Don't be absurd," he replied. "We have lots of minerals. We have Coke, we have Seven-up, we have Fanta." [Nigerian 1980s]

The existence of these ethnic jokes about the stupidity of the powerful shows that such jokes are not essentially a put-down of the powerless. It is beyond the scope of this book to analyze political jokes in detail as I have done elsewhere [see Davies 1988B and in press), but the fact that ethnic jokes about stupidity can be and are switched to political figures under particular and definable circumstances does provide further comparative evidence relevant to an analysis of this type of ethnic joke. Ethnic jokes about the Afrikaners, southern Italians, and Hausa provide a convenient bridge to the examination of the political jokes told in the socialist countries of Eastern Europe and China which depict the local politicians, apparatchiks, and militia or police as utterly stupid. Individuals as diverse as Khrushchev, Brezhnev, Andropov, Gomulka, Gierek, Ochab, Novotný, Husák, Zhivkov are shown in such jokes as utterly stupid, not just in a political context but in their everyday life in situations only very marginally connected with politics.[13]

The phone rang in the Kremlin one night. Brezhnev woke up, put on the light, put on his glasses, fumbled in his pajama pocket for the appropriate scrap of paper, picked up the phone and read out carefully: "Who is it?" [Bulgarian 1980s]

When Mika Spiljak was on the first official Yugoslav visit to the Pope in Rome the Pope said to him on leaving, 'My special greeting to your wife and children.' To this Spiljak replied, 'My special greeting to yours, too, sir.' [UCBFA Serbian-Yugoslav file, Beverlee Ann French 1970]

The average measure of intelligence in Poland is 50 Ochab. [UCBFA Polish file, Juliana Roth 1969]

[Ochab was formerly chief of the Polish politbureau.]

Politicians in democratic counties, including even those individuals who really are stupid, are not the subject of this type of ritualized joke about overall stupidity. The jokes of the Communist world are rooted not in the qualities of particular individuals but in the system by which they came to power. Once again the key contrast is between monopoly and competition. In a competitive system where the people can always exercise their crucial democratic right to "turn the rascals out," elected politicians, however inept or repellent, exercise legitimate authority because they have won in open competition. If the voters elect someone who turns out to be a fool in office, then in a sense their own judgment and their own representative are at fault and it is difficult to make jokes under those circumstances. By contrast, the political leaders of Eastern Europe are part of a self-perpetuating oligarchy who have attained office within a closed system where there is no open competition and no reason for the effectively voteless mass of the people to feel responsible for their rulers.

A curious fact that reinforces my thesis is that the only major democratic politicians in the English-speaking countries in modern times to have been the butts of ritual jokes about stupidity were the American President Gerald Ford and the British Prime Minister Sir Alec Douglas-Home,[14] both intelligent and experienced politicians with a strong sense of humor, but neither of whom was elected to office by the usual methods. Gerald Ford became President only because of the unprecedented resignation of Vice-President Agnew and later President Nixon. Thus when Ford became President he had never had to run for election as President or as potential President. Lord Home was a member of the House of Lords, as his ancestors had been for umpteen generations, when his predecessor as Prime Minister, Harold Macmillan, became ill. It had long been felt in Britain that it would be undemocratic for a peer to become Prime Minister, and Lords Halifax and Curzon had been excluded from attaining that office on these grounds many years before. Sir Alec got around this objection by resigning his peerage to become a commoner and was then elected to the House of Commons for a safe seat held by his party by means of a specially arranged by-election. As a member of the House of Commons he was then eligible to be Prime Minister.

The result for both men of taking these unusual and indirect routes to office that avoided the usual processes of electoral competition was that they became the subject of jokes about their alleged stupidity.

Only last week Mr. Ford was riding a White House escalator when it broke down—and he was stuck there for three hours. [Brodnick 1976]

Not long ago Mr. Ford met with a delegation of Polish-Americans who had come to the White House to protest the proliferation of Polish jokes.

Said the President: "I know what you mean, fellas. Really I do. . . . " [Brodnick 1976]

Henry Kissinger was studying a photograph of the President in his private office.

Said Mr. Kissinger to one of his aides,
"It's funny—he doesn't look Polish." [Brodnick 1976]

When Sir Alec Douglas-Home resigned his peerage and was elected as a member of Parliament it created a vacancy in the House of Lords—and another in the House of Commons. [British 1960s]

During the British general election of 1964, when the leaders of the two main parties were Harold Wilson and Sir Alec Douglas-Home, a disgruntled elector commented, "What a choice—smart aleck or dull Alec." [British 1960s]

The other monopoly that East European politicians exercise is that brought about by their extension of direct political control over aspects of society such as economic production, education, science, the mass media, and publishing, which in democratic societies enjoy a greater degree of autonomy. In consequence, there is an obvious contrast between the outlook of the technical experts who have attained their positions in a competitive, merit-based system and that of the monopoly politicians who seek to impose arbitrary "stupid" decisions upon them.[15] Even in a democratic society political decisions are inevitably arbitrary and politics cannot be reduced to a species of rational administration [see Robertson 1982]. Politicians hold the ultimate power in a democratic society, though they neither are nor could be chosen according to rules of merit or constrained by requirements of qualifications or by maximum age limits [see Davies 1982C]. Nonetheless, their position of authority is an inevitable and legitimate one, provided they restrict themselves to political matters. If they seek to exercise power way beyond this admittedly uncertain point their decisions are likely to become the subject of jokes, as in the case of those members of the General Assembly of Indiana who in 1897 sought to pass a bill ruling that the value of π (the ratio of the circumference of a circle to its diameter) was 3.2. Had this been enforced all the mathematical and engineering calculations in the state would have gone wrong, pendulum clocks would have gained several minutes every hour, and the absurd anti-surd politicians would have become the most irrational fraction of Indiana.[16] In Eastern Europe and China the existence of a political monopoly with no clear or constitutional limits to the exercise of political power ensures that absurdities such as the above are put into law and enforced, thus generating new themes for jokes about the stupidity of politicians and party officials.

The other link between the political jokes about stupidity of the socialist countries and the essentially similar ethnic jokes lies in the nature of the social classes the East European regimes claim to represent—the proletariat and, rather more uncertainly, the peasantry. These are the very classes who elsewhere have become the subject of jokes because their members are seen as inert, backward, and unable to compete and innovate. In a world of computers and combine harvesters, the hammer and sickle look a bit dated. Indeed, those at the sophisticated end of the engineering industry refer to the unskilled workers at the crude end as the metal-bashers. In humor the hammer is a symbol of the use of crude force instead of skill and knowledge, as when the people of the English Midlands refer to a hammer as a "Birmingham screwdriver." Indeed the use of crude force is the other aspect of socialist regimes treated as stupid in East European jokes. The militia (police) of the cities tend to be recruited from the unskilled and uneducated population of remote rural areas who have no other means of getting work-and-residence permits enabling them to move to the towns [information provided by East European criminologists (anonymously); see also Conquest 1968, 32–33, and 1980, 98]. They are the first line of defense of a policy based on crude force and they behave accordingly. Not surprisingly they are the butts of jokes about stupidity.

Why do Czech militiamen go round in groups of three?

One can read, one can write, and the other is keeping an eye on the two intellectuals. [Czech, also Polish 1980s. See also Tarnóky 1977]

Ignorant leaders or official heroes such as Chapaev [see Draitser 1978], of vaunted peasant or proletarian origin, are often the butt of jokes about stupidity linked to their class background both in Eastern Europe [e.g., see Banc and Dundes 1986, 146–62; Beckmann 1969 and 1980] and in China, where Fox Butterfield has noted:

> The cadres are viewed by the more sophisticated natives of Peking and Shanghai as urban Americans would view hillbillies from Kentucky or Tennessee. Our friends the Wangs liked to tell jokes about the typical cadre. "In a village the county authorities had announced they were going to form the militia and issue rifles," Li began one of his favorite stories. "It was a big event in a place where nothing ever happens and the peasants got very excited. But then days and weeks passed, and the county authorities were having trouble reaching a decision. Finally, after two years, a jeep came down to the village. An important-looking cadre got out and declared there would be a big meeting about forming the militia. At the meeting, he got up and began speaking slowly, 'I am–the–county–Party–secretary,' and with those words the audience burst into thunderous applause. It was a great honor to be visited by such a high cadre. But then the speaker added, 'That is, I was sent by the county Party secretary.' " Li told the story employing the thick dialect of Hunan province, where Mao and many other cadres came from. " 'We have decided, about the guns, that one gun for each person,' and again there was a chorus of applause, 'is absolutely impossible. We have reached the conclusion that one gun for every two people,' and there was still clapping, 'is not right. So I want to announce the final decision of the county Party committee is, one gun for every three people,' which set off more applause. 'But they are wooden guns,' the cadre concluded." [1982, 289]

Another group that has been the butt of jokes (including ethnic jokes) about stupidity is the aristocracy. Aristocrats, like peasants, are viewed by others as tradition-bound and unenterprising, and in addition they often enjoy power and status without having to compete for them. For these reasons aristocrats are the subject of jokes told by the members of other classes who prize merit and achievement.

The English aristocracy has long been the butt of both ethnic and political jokes about stupidity. Such jokes are also told in republics that have had a powerful aristocracy in the past, such as Austria, Germany, or Hungary. Jokes are still told in these countries about Count Bobby and his aristocratic associates and in Hungary about "Arisztid and Tasziló."[17]

Conclusions

1. Ethnic jokes about stupidity are the most widespread of ethnic jokes. Each nation has its own local butt of these jokes. In almost every case the butts of the jokes are very similar people to those who tell the jokes about them. They are not alien strangers but familiar neighbors, provincials, or long-established immigrants, people "almost like us." They tend to live on the geographical, cultural, linguistic, or religious periphery of a society and appear to the dominant people at the center to be backward and provincial, or a comically ambiguous people from the interface between two cultures, whom I have termed the TWPSINs or TWPs. Their culture is a derivative one, and their version of the dominant group's language is a source of mirth. The joke-tellers see them as a comically distorted, "stupid" version of themselves.

2. The people who are the butts of jokes about stupidity have either failed to succeed within an open and competitive system, or exercise monopoly power. They tend to be peoples who value stability, continuity, and community rather than mobility, innovation, entrepreneurship, and individual success. They are often peasants or the descendants of peasants doing unskilled blue-collar work. The butts of ethnic jokes about stupidity can, however, also be powerful, for they may exercise a political monopoly either as hereditary aristocrats or as members of a self-perpetuating elite who use their political patronage to appoint humbler members of the group to positions of minor authority or to gain a high economic position that they could not have achieved in a more competitive system. These generalizations seem to hold true for political as well as ethnic jokes.

3. The pairs of joke-tellers and butts systematically represent many of the most important dichotomies in a modern society (table 3.3).

TABLE 3.3 **The Key Dichotomies**

Joke-tellers	**Butts**
Center	Periphery
Dominant culture	Derivative culture
Urban	Rural
Skilled	Unskilled
White-collar	Blue-collar
Mobile, innovative	Stable, static
Competition	Monopoly
Marketplace success	Party power

CHAPTER FOUR
The Stupid and the Dirty

Modern ethnic jokes about stupidity told in the United States and Canada differ in one important respect from those told in Britain and France in that they routinely mock the butts of their jokes as being dirty as well as stupid [see Apte 1985, 115; Dundes 1971, 199–200; Legman 1982 vol. 2, 961]. By contrast there are very few British jokes about the Irish or French jokes about the Belgians being dirty and no real equivalent of the following American jokes about Poles:

A Pole sent ten thousand septic tanks to Poland as an appreciation of the country of his birth. Two weeks later a message comes back:

"Thank you for your wonderful gift. As soon as we learn how to drive them, we're going to invade Russia." [Katz 1979]

Why won't they let the Poles swim in Lake Michigan?
They'd leave a rim. [American 1960s]

Why did the Polack divorce his wife and marry a garbage can?
The garbage can smelled better and the hole was bigger. [Katz 1979]

Do you know why flies have wings?
To beat the Polacks to the garbage. [Clements 1973, 15]

What did Hitler tell his men before invading Poland?
Don't shit in the street, we're trying to starve them out. [Clements 1973, 16]

How does a Polack take a shower?
(Either) He spits into the wind
(or) He urinates on a fan. [Clements 1973, 38]

Q. How do you say "soap" in Polish?
A. Sorry to disappoint you. There is no such word in the Polish language. [Macklin and Erdman 1976, 63]

Everyone knows that Cortez discovered Mexico and Columbus discovered America, but who discovered Poland?

The Roto-Rooterman. [Wilde 1978A, 181]

The Mayor of New York declared war on the rats. His Honor ordered the health inspectors to send nine Polish exterminators down into the sewers to wipe out the rodents.

A month later only six of the nine Poles came back. "All right," demanded the Mayor, "what happened to the other three men?"

"They defected to the enemy," explained the inspector, "And out of the six that returned, two brought back war brides." [Wilde 1978A, 193]

What do you get if you pour hot water on a Polack?

Instant shit. [Clements 1973, 17]

Despite the strong recent influence of American Polish jokes on British ethnic jokes about stupidity, the British very rarely tell ethnic jokes about the Irish being filthy. Many of Britain's joke-tellers have long been aware of the American jokes about "filthy Poles," and Hornby's book of British ethnic jokes about the Irish (1978) contains a short section (pp. 61–62) of jokes about filthiness crudely adapted from Macklin and Erdman's American joke-book (1976, 23–24) by crossing out Polish or Polack and inserting Irish or Paddies instead.

If it's true that cleanliness is next to Godliness then it's no wonder that so many Polacks/Paddies go to Hell. [Macklin and Erdman 1976, 23; Hornby 1978, 61]

The "Paddies" version has vanished, for it is never told in Britain and it has failed to compete with the local version to be seen everywhere on bumper stickers—"Cleanliness is next to Godliness; only in an Irish dictionary" [Nigel Rees Graffiti, Bumper sticker No. 16].

Hornby's attempt to introduce an American theme that was inconsistent with British cultural assumptions failed, and a Swiss student of mine who initially doubted my view on this point and tried to tell Swiss jokes about filthy Fribourgers to her fellow students at a British university confirmed (to her great surprise) that they didn't find them funny. Sandra McCosh has likewise noted the contrast between ethnic jokes told by children about the Irish in Britain and those told by American children about the Poles. McCosh writes that the comic Irishman "appears as stupid and foolish but also loveable. . . . In contrast the Polish stereotype in the United States is a much nastier image and the Polack is compared to shit and has other dirty habits . . . " [1976, 120].

There is no substantial body of British ethnic jokes about filthiness, merely individual jokes about the incidental uncleanliness of a variety of ethnic groups. Indeed, many British ethnic jokes about the Irish that deal with cleanliness and its artifacts do not make the Irish out to be filthy, merely comically incompetent in their encounters with the means of becoming clean:

Irish baths have a tap at each end so the water will be level. [Chambers 1979, 89]

Not many people know that an Irishman named O'Connor invented the loo seat in 1866. In 1868 it was improved upon when a Scot named MacTollugh cut a hole in the middle. [Cagney 1979A, 33]

An Irishman went into a shop and asked for a bar of soap.
"Certainly, sir," said the shopkeeper. "Do you want it scented?"
"No, I'll take it with me." [British 1980s]

A tourist went into a hotel in Ireland and asked for a room.
"Would you like a shower or a bath?" asked the receptionist.
"What's the difference?" replied the visitor.
"Well for a bath you sit down and for a shower you stand up." [British 1980s]

British ethnic stickers and other artifacts (mugs, plaques, chastity belts, etc.) do not depict the Irish as dirty. There is no British equivalent of the product "Polish, the ultimate room freshener" [Everlasting aroma, can be used in any room, appealing appearance, will not affect the ozone layer, overpowers all foul odors], produced by the Dillon Company of Oklahoma City. Inside the pretty yellow "Polish" box decorated with flowers is a realistic rubber turd labeled "For best results leave exposed in room after guests have gone." Similar items are sold in British jokeshops but they do not carry an ethnic label. Similarly, although the British tell scatological jokes and inscribe them on the walls in the same sorts of places as in America, they do not link these jokes to the Irish. Even those followers of Dr. Spooner who cannot bear to leave a turd unstoned refrain from referring to the Irish as shining wits.

Now if the reductionist argument that ethnic jokes are merely covert serious statements were true, and if the existence and content of such jokes could be treated as an index of aggression and hostility,[1] it would follow that the contrast between the loveable, witty Irishman of British ethnic jokes about stupidity and the dirty, shitty Poles of American ethnic jokes about stupidity must mean that Americans are far more hostile and aggressive toward Poles[2] than the British are toward the Irish. Furthermore, those analysts [see note 1]who show such a tortuous ability to link ethnic jokes to ethnic conflicts should conclude that there is a far greater degree of conflict between Americans and their Polish minority than between the British and the Irish. Indeed, McCosh, who has been influenced by this school of thought, argues: "The Polack is a new immigrant group and is threatening jobs and positions traditionally held by other groups. In England the Irish, although at times immigrants, are considered members of Great Britain and are not a visible ethnic group and therefore are acceptable" [1976, 120].

Unfortunately, for the aggression-hostility-conflict theory, none of her facts are correct, which is hardly surprising given that she cites no independent evidence to support her assertion. The Irish are not and never have been "members of Great Britain," and most of them live in or have emigrated from Eire, a foreign state that in one form or another has been independent of Britain since 1922. Northern Ireland is a constituent part of the United Kingdom but is quite separate from Great Britain. There are nearly a million first-generation Irish immigrants in Britain, and they are a highly visible ethnic group. There is no evidence of excessive Polish upward social mobility[3] threatening other groups, nor that the upward mobility of the Irish in Britain is less in magnitude or perceived as less threatening than that of the Poles in America. Although there has never been very much conflict or hostility within Britain itself between the British and the Irish [see Gilley 1978], nonetheless, because of disputes over the sovereignty of Ireland itself there is and has been in the past far more conflict between the two peoples than between the Polish Americans and their fellow citizens. By contrast, there is, so far as I know, no secessionist movement in Hamtramck. I do not wish to exaggerate the point, for the violence in Ireland, notably in 1916–1922 and during the last two decades,[4] has had relatively little impact on the everyday lives of most citizens of England, Wales, and Scotland. Nonetheless, the realities of British and American life do not in any way coincide with those assumed by McCosh on the basis of her interpretations of the contrast in the content of the two sets of jokes.

The prediction that McCosh made about the quality of intergroup relations, as deduced from the content of the jokes on the basis of the aggression-hostility-conflict theory, has been shown to be false, and the theory is overthrown entirely. To try to rescue the theory by distorting the definition and measurement of conflict or by introducing bogus and untestable concepts such as displaced aggression or latent hostility is merely to render it circular and largely meaningless.[5] While it may well be true that, other things equal, we prefer jokes about groups we dislike to jokes about our affiliates [see Raskin 1985, 36], in the real world other things are not equal. It is not possible to infer the relative degree of conflict or hostility between groups from differences in the content of ethnic jokes about stupidity, and the view that these jokes reveal the hostility or aggressive intent of the joke-tellers vis-à-vis their butts is essentially trivial since you can deduce nothing from it.

If the reader again examines table 3.1, linking those who tell ethnic jokes about stupidity and their butts, they will find that the relationship between them varies between the kind of intense conflict now taking place in the Indian state of Punjab and the generally euxine reception extended by the Greeks to the Pontians, yet there is no correlation between this variable (intensity of conflict) and differences in the content of the jokes told. A diligent search can always uncover *some* kind of past or present conflict because conflicts between neighboring peoples are intrinsically likely due to their proximity; but there is also frequently alliance and sympathy. The Swedes may in the past have resented the secession of Norway, but there is also a high degree of Nordic cooperation between the Scandinavian countries. When the Nazis invaded Norway, the Swedes felt sympathy rather than *schadenfreude* for their neighbor, and their failure to render any real assistance to the Norwegians [see Shirer 1960, 711; Tolstoy 1982, 138–39] was due to this chronic timidity of Sweden's politicians and not to popular malice.

The situational relationships of center/periphery, urban/rural, enterprising classes/inert classes that I have shown to be the source of the ethnic jokes about stupidity may well also give rise to conflicts, which is probably the basis of the erroneous view that the conflicts are the source of the ethnic jokes and the ethnic jokes a tactic in the conflicts. Whether ethnic conflicts break out under the circumstances that I have specified as producing the jokes depends on political and historical factors that do not necessarily correlate with the joking behavior. Furthermore, the joke-tellers inevitably are or have been involved in all manner of *other* ethnic and national conflicts that derive from quite different initial social and political configurations [e.g., see Schoeck 1969, 92], and these do not produce ethnic jokes about the stupidity of their adversaries. The relative social position of joke-tellers and butts is the key to the jokes, not the existence of hostility or conflict per se. The most that can be said about the latter is that it may directly, or indirectly by increasing the salience [see Goldstein, Suls, Anthony 1972] of contrasting ethnic identities in general, act as a booster or damper of the popularity of ethnic jokes that exist anyway for other reasons. The existence of intense conflict may inhibit the telling of such jokes, whereas mild conflict might encourage it, and in the latter case those involved could manipulate the tone with which and the context in which such jokes were told, so as to be able to employ them for particular tactical purposes. This does not help to answer the more central, interesting and difficult questions of why ethnic group A rather than ethnic group B is the butt of jokes about stupidity and why in some cases comic ethnic stupidity is tied to dirt and in others to a capacity for wit.

In the case of the witty Irish[6] I am inclined to accept Vivian Mercier's view [1962] that the importance in Irish culture of wordplay and figurative speech produced among both the native Irish and the Anglo-Irish a remarkable and sustained outburst of humorous genius. No other small country has produced the equivalent of the humor of Swift, Sterne, Goldsmith, Steele, Curran, Wilde, Shaw, Synge, O'Casey, Joyce, St. John Gogarty, and Beckett or been able to rival Ireland's output of popular comedians and entertainers. The reputation of the Irish for wit and humor has long coexisted and interacted with the comic image of the blundering, bull-ridden Irishman. Hence the sterile argument about whether Irishisms in speech are deliberate and witty or accidental and stupid. Both types may well have their origins in the same culture of verbal exuberance and lack of concern with the prosaic tying of words to realities. Rosten, in one and the same study of humor [1973], both praises Irish skill at wordplay [p. 15] and quotes a banner from a parade held in Dublin [pp. 107, 183] that declared "God bless the Holy Trinity." The various ethnic groups who laugh at the Irish see them, without contradiction, both as witty and as a source of wit in others.

Equally it is possible that the Poles in America are or were filthier than the Irish in the British Isles. It is a difficult point to consider, because rejected groups are often regarded as polluted and intrinsically filthy regardless of their actual behavior, and the term *dirty* is used to describe moral and ritual uncleanliness as well as a lack of hygiene. The use of words such as *dirty* or *filthy* to emphasize a variety of outraged moral sentiments, violent ethnic or racial prejudices, or terms of abuse [e.g., see note 2 and Conquest 1971, 562] underlies the difficulty of deciding whether a group is "really" dirty. Indeed, even chimpanzees use the American sign language word for dirty in this metaphorical way [Linden 1981, 8–10].

It is no wonder that sociologists and historians have often shirked the task of deciding whether one ethnic group lives or lived less hygienically than another [Sowell 1981, 295]. Yet there is clear and visible evidence of a reasonably objective kind indicating that there exist significant ethnic, regional, and class differences in both private and, quite separately but more importantly, public [see Bar-Yosef 1980] cleanliness [e.g., see Goethe 1970 (1862–63), 62, 232–33, 319; Rockwell 1981, 140–41], and also that these differences directly give rise to humorous anecdotes [see Cornelisen 1969, Rockwell 1981, 141]. Such differences in degrees of filthiness grow out of more fundamental differences in standards of living, knowledge of the causes of disease, and cultural traditions.

However, there is no evidence to show that the Poles in America are any less hygienic than their fellow citizens. In 1986 (as I had earlier done more casually in other cities in 1966) I deliberately explored the area in Chicago around the Polish-American museum and was struck by how much cleaner and lacking in dilapidation were the houses that bore some form of Polish insignia than were those of other ethnic groups sharing the area [see also Mr. X., Henderson, and Cyr 1979, 239]. It might still be, though, that the original peasant migrants to urban America in the nineteenth century initially brought with them insanitary, indeed dangerous habits, leading first to fear and rejection (this was not irrational, for such behavior led to the spread of epidemic disease [see Sowell 1981, 291]) and, much later, safely later, to ethnic jokes. However, the original Poles were relatively cleaner than other immigrants [see Helmreich 1982, 172–74] and the worst and filthiest slums both in America [see Helmreich 1982, 173; Sowell 1981] and in Britain were those created by the massive Irish immigration of the 1840s into cities ill-equipped to cope with such an influx. Friedrich Engels [1958, 105–107] wrote of the Irish in Britain[7] in 1844–45:

> The Irish have also brought with them filth and intemperance. Dirty habits, which have become second nature to the Irish, do no great harm in the countryside where the population is scattered. On the other hand the dangerous situation which develops when such habits are practised among the crowded population of big cities must arouse feelings of apprehension and disgust. Among the nasty habits which the Irish have brought with them is that of emptying all their filth and refuse out of the front-door and this causes filthy puddles and heaps of garbage to accumulate and so a whole district is rapidly polluted. . . . [1958, 105–106]

If ethnic jokes about filthiness were simply a reflection of the objective past or present social conditions of particular ethnic minorities relative to the majority of the people, then one would expect nineteenth-century British and indeed American ethnic jokes about the Irish to depict them as filthy. However, apart from one or two comic phrases and a few jokes about the squalor of rural Irish cabins shared by the people and their pigs, jokes about the "filthy Irish" were not made or told at the time or later. The Irish were in both countries the butt of jokes about stupidity, but dirtiness was not seen as a comic adjunct of stupidity even in the United States, presumably because cleanliness was not closely tied to rationality in American minds at that time.

In the mid-nineteenth century, the American people do not seem to have been possessed by the fervor for cleanliness that so characterizes them in the late twentieth century. Foreigners visiting America were sometimes struck by the godliness of the people but not as today by their extreme personal cleanliness. Indeed, the persons and cities of America were often seen as rather dirty in comparison with Europe. English visitors disliked the way Americans spat on the floor, and even the more genteel American who expectorated in a cuspidor was seen as a crude colonial figure.[8] In the mid-1980s American attempts to create a market for chewing-tobacco in Britain [Pearce 1985] briefly revived this old image of American crudity [see Bryant 1984]. American nineteenth- and early twentieth-century jokes routinely referred to spitting, bedbugs, grimy eating-places, and insanitary outhouses as an undesirable but unremarkable aspect of life. There were also ethnic jokes about the willingness of German or Irish immigrants to tolerate some of these things—the alleged German lack of disdain for flies was a common theme [e.g., see Landon 1900, 529–

30]—but the jokes did not set these ethnic minorities apart from other Americans as utterly dirty. Dirt was just part of the everyday world for Americans and immigrants alike and it is this view of dirt that is reflected even in ethnic jokes.

"Vell Jake, how you use dot bug poison vot you sold me for a half-a-dollar a box?"

"You catch te pug, Yacop, and opens his mouth and drops it in."

"Ish dot de vay?"

"Yah."

"Vell I yoost cotch dem, tramp dem mit my foot and kill dem dot vay."

"Oh yah, dat's a goot vay too. Dot ish jest as good as the pug powder." [Landon 1900, 533]

Just as a traveller was writing his name in the register of a Leavenworth hotel, a bed-bug appeared and took its way across the page. The man paused and remarked:

"I've been bled by St. Joe fleas, bitten by Kansas City spiders and interviewed by Fort Scott gray backs, but I'll be darned if I was ever in a place before where the bed-bug looked over the hotel register to find out where your room was." [Ernst 1927, 60]

The Japanese are remarkably tidy in the matter of floors. They even remove their shoes at the doorway. A Japanese student in New York was continually distressed by the dirty hall-ways of the building in which he lived. In the autumn, the janitor placed a notice at the entrance which read:

"Please wipe your feet."

The Japanese wrote beneath in pencil:

"On going out." [*Jokes for All Occasions* 1922, 132]

However, the wave of immigrants from Southern and Eastern Europe in the late nineteenth and early twentieth centuries coincided with and reinforced a shift in the American evaluation of hygiene linked with the slow secularization of the American zeal for purity and righteousness, which came to include and even to stress physical cleanliness. Ethnic jokes about the blacks at this time, which contrast metaphysical and physical cleanliness, are very revealing about the changing attitudes of the joke-tellers:

'Yas sah Mr. George,' said an old negro, 'we got ter keep clean. We got ter keep clean sah or dar ain't no hope o' de salvation.'

'Why then don't you go and wash yourself?'

'Whar—whar—what sah? W'y doan I go wash merse'f?'

'Yes, and put on a clean shirt. You are as dirty as can be.'

'Oh now yere I ain't talkin 'bout dat sorter keepin clean. I wuz talkin 'bout keepin' clean in the faif, sah, in de faif. I ain't got no time ter fool erlong wid de waters o' dis yere life. What I means is ter keep yer speret clean washed in the dewdrops o' de New Jerusalem, means as I tell you dat we mus' keep clean in de faif, sah—keep clean in de faif.' [*New Minstrel Jokes* 1913, 28]

She was right.

'Phoebe,' said a mistress in reproof to her colored servant whom she found smoking a short pipe after having repeatedly threatened to discharge her if again caught in the act, 'if you won't stop that filthy act for any other reason, do so because it is right. You are a good church member—and don't you know that smoking makes the breath unpleasant and that nothing unclean can enter Heaven?'

'Deed, missie I does,' said the woman 'but Lord bress yo' heart, when I go to heaben I'll leave my bref behin' me.' [Ernst 1927, 60. Also in Perkins 1901]

The Poles and other immigrants from Eastern and Southern Europe arrived just as established Americans were becoming fervent about cleanliness and more inclined to see the supposed evils of the Old World in terms of physical dirt as well as moral corruption. The immigrants seemed to threaten this new interpretation of an old ideal. Whereas elsewhere improved urban sanitation and public health were gradual utilitarian reforms [see Coulton 1945, 87; Mayhew 1966 (1862), 57; Plumb 1966], in America they became a mark of national identity and superiority, a sign of rationality and affluence, an achievement that combined success and virtue. As America became clean and pure and wholesome, so old corrupt Europe and its teeming refuse of immigrants came to be seen as the antithesis of this [see Gorer 1948; Jones 1960, 224–25].

Thus the explanation of the American (and by extension Canadian) jokes lies in the culture of the joke-tellers and not that of the butts of their jokes; the arrival of the latter coincided with and reinforced the growth of the idea that America alone was the land of rational hygiene. The idea that new immigrants unfamiliar with modern urban hygiene could "stupidly" mistake the nature of garbage collection soon gave rise to the classic joke on this theme which is quoted in Milt Gross's [1927, 24] humorous portrait of a New York immigrant apartment block.

Voice from basement—Garbage?
Chorus—No! Don't Want Any.

This is the prototype of the endless jokes about the "stupid-filthy" that were pinned on the Poles from the early 1960s. The link between comic stupidity and comic filthiness is so close in American culture that any group labeled comically stupid is also automatically the butt of jokes about being filthy. In the jokes not just Poles and Italians, but Texas Aggies and the people of Kentucky were "filthy" because they were "stupid." Any group in America occupying a social position that invites jokes about stupidity is also made to appear comically dirty. The link between the comic image of the members of a group as dirty in the jokes and the real habits of their ancestors is a very tenuous one indeed. The jokes are rather statements about what the joke-tellers are not, and filthiness is pinned on those same familiar but peripheral or low-status American groups who in the United States have been the butts of jokes about stupidity. Canada naturally shares these jokes because it shares so much of American culture anyway.

Why don't they allow Italians to swim in the Hudson River?
They would leave a ring on the shore-line. [Wilde 1978B, 190]

Did you hear about the Italian businessman who went broke?
He imported 200,000 cans of underarm deodorant to Italy—and didn't sell a single one. [Wilde 1975A, 55]

Why is the Roman Colosseum round?
So the Italians wouldn't piss in the corner. [UCBFA Italian file, Paul Fame 1969]

How do they dispose of the garbage in Polish restaurants?
They put it on the menu in Italian restaurants. [Wilde 1975A, 12]

What is the favorite pet in Italian neighborhoods?
A cockroach on a leash. [Wilde 1975A, 17]

Definition of a galloping gourmet: an Aggie running after a garbage truck. [*Best of 606 Aggie Jokes* 1976]

The city of Houston paints a large W on the sides of its old garbage trucks, ships them to A and M and sells them as Winnebagos. [*Best of 606 Aggie Jokes* 1976]

If the Ohio River is full of shit do you know how to tell the difference between the Indiana-Kentucky side?
The Kentucky side will be lined with diving boards. [Katz 1979]

Do you know the definition of air pollution?
The Newfoundland Parachute Brigade. [G. Thomas 1976, 150]

Where do you hide a nickel from a Newfoundlander?
Under a bar of soap. [G. Thomas 1976, 150]

Why does a Newfoundlander color his garbage can orange and black?
To make himself believe he's eating at the A and W. [G. Thomas 1976, 150]

Jokes of this type can be roughly classified in two ways, as indicated in table 4.1. First a distinction can be made between personal dirtiness on the one hand and reveling in public squalor on the other. Private filthiness is shown by members of the ethnic group being covered in, indifferent to, and even liking dirt, dust, oil, or even excreta and by their resolute dislike of water, soap, deodorants, etc. Jokes about the squalid public aspect of the ethnic minority ascribe to them an inappropriate attitude to the elaborate modern sanitary apparatus for dealing with the disposal of filth, refuse, and sewage—the garbage truck, sewers, organized and systematic operations against rodents and insects, the use of chemical septic tanks. In this category of jokes the "dirty" ethnics revel in the public waste that society is trying to disperse, export, hide, and dispose of. The second pair of categories divides dirt into that generated by human beings or, in some cases, animals (feces, spittle, etc.) and manufactured dirt (garbage, oil, coal dust, etc.). The former tends to give rise to scatological (and allied) jokes, which often represent the "dirty" ethnics as coprophile and even coprophagous, and which overlap with other sorts of "dirty" jokes, often of a fairly traditional kind. The latter provide jokes about dirt rather than dirty jokes, for the alleged Polish love of garbage or dislike of soap is reprehensible and incomprehensible but not unmentionable.

Most countries have a long tradition of scatological jokes, but ethnic jokes about artificial dirt and public dirtiness seem to be a recent and distinctively American invention. These jokes are also to be found in Canada but are rare in Britain or France. The latter countries lack a comparable body of jokes about "stupid" minorities who are not merely privately dirty but who also flout the rules of public hygiene. Ethnic jokes about the "filthy-stupid" who display a failure to understand the nature and purpose of the complex mechanisms used for waste disposal and for the maintenance of public cleanliness in all urban industrial societies together with a perverse rejection of the rational hygiene ethic of these societies have flourished best in North America. Modern Americans and Canadians, but not the British or the French, have incorporated cleanliness into their view of what constitutes rationality and intelligence. American ethnic jokes export dirtiness to the periphery of society in the same way that the peoples of most industrial societies export comic stupidity.

By American standards the British appear to be cheerfully grubby, much as the French seem by British standards. Neither comparison has

TABLE 4.1 **Types of Comic Dirt**

	Public dirtiness	Private/personal dirtiness	
Dirt produced by humans and animals	Jokes about sewers, cesspools, septic tanks, Roto-rooter men	Jokes about excretions, expectoration, coprophilia, coprophagy	Dirty jokes
	Scatological jokes		
Artificial dirt and dirty pests	Jokes about garbage cans, trucks, and dumps; rodent control. Presence of flies, cockroaches, etc.	Jokes about an affinity for general dirt, oil, grease, dust. Dislike of water, soap, deodorants. Presence of bugs, fleas, etc.	Jokes about dirt

given rise to many jokes, though the French have invented and feature in the only ethnic jokes I know in which cleanliness is mocked.

A Frenchman and an Englishman were arguing about which of them lived in the more civilized country. The Frenchman held forth for ten minutes about the glories of French cuisine when the Englishman interrupted: "That's all very well," he said, "but what about your dreadful lavatories."

"Alors," said the Frenchman, "in France one eats well, in England one shits well. It's all a question of priorities." [French 1960s]

Englishman to waiter in French restaurant: "Well if your cooking is as French as your lavatories this must be the best restaurant in London." [English 1980s]

Why does a Swiss go on holiday to Paris?
So he can throw a piece of paper on the sidewalk. [French 1980s]

There are also a number of snide or uneasy references in British and indeed in Australian and American humor to the soiled sexual sophistication of the French, who are regarded as too civilized to be dirty and too dirty to be civilized.[9] To some extent this parallels the more general mockery of the French in jokes from Russia to Mexico as sexual gourmets with an unlimited and unsqueamish appetite for new and perverse experiences and sensations. Relative to, say, the ethnic jokes told about the polymorphous perversity of American blacks [e.g., see note 5], sex jokes about the French occur on a more elevated plane and provide an element of fascinated horror for those sharing them. As Shelley Berman has put it, in American English "Every verb modified by French is a Dirty" [1966, 16].

The American obsession with physical cleanliness is a source of humor to the British, though they have not been able to build ethnic jokes round a cleanliness script that would be the counterpart to American jokes about "dirty" Poles, Italians, etc. Although extreme cleanliness can be a threat to health and a corresponding symbolic cleanliness can destroy other, far more important moral values, such as toleration, charity, liberty and mercy, there is a general absence of ethnic scripts mocking the uncommonly clean. The symmetry that can be seen in relation to jokes about the stupid and the canny or militarists and cowards is lacking here. Nonetheless, the humor of the comfortably grubby British does seem to place them, at least in their own regard, in a kind of golden mean between the comic extremes of the casually filthy French and the obsessional Americans [see Atkinson and Searle 1963, 91; Cornelisen 1969, 287; Mikes 1970, 92–93].

The British perception of themselves in contrast to the self-image held by the Americans may be deduced indirectly from a speech made by Lord Strange [1965 col. 615] in the House of Lords on capital punishment which began: "Well, when I got into my bath (Monday is my bath night) I thought, if people can sing in their bath, why cannot they shout and talk to themselves in their bath?" Had that, by British standards, quite unremarkable speech been made in the U.S. Senate the senators would all have shaken their heads and said "That's strange." Nor would an American official body have reported on such a sacred subject with the English understatement of the water softening subcommittee of the British Central Advisory Committee, which declared: "We do suggest with very wide limits (that) washing is a desirable habit" [Dunbar and Webb 1980]. There is further an accepted British humorous tradition of quietly laughing at cleanliness and in favor of mild dirt [e.g., see Barr and York 1983, 72; Samuel Butler in Bentley and Esar 1962, 42; de Witt 1970, 25] that is quite un-American. Even in humor for children, Winnie the Pooh's friend Piglet, in his original British form, was comfortably grubby in contrast to the repellent Pig-pen, whose rugged individualist filth is a bit much even for the tolerant Charlie Brown, or to the Garbage Pail Kids, who provide children with a comically shocking and very American view of dirt, garbage, deformity, and disaster all rolled into one.

The theme of obsessional American cleanliness to be found in British humor has also been taken up by many American humorists, both in relation to the Scandinavian-American fetish of order and cleanliness [e.g., see Keillor 1986, 326–27, 362] and as a general comic statement about an America in which patriotism smells of disinfectant [Keillor 1986, 211; see also pp. 26–27; Berenstain and Berenstain 1970; and Berman 1966, 14].

Allied to this is the humor at the expense of the American love of euphemism and sanitization, expressed in the cleaning up of offensive place-names [Aman 1977], the invention of the "Clirty," or cleaned up "dirty" expletive [Berman 1966, 72], and the American advertisers' search for terms ever more remote from the basic human functions to which they refer [Berman 1966; Tresilian 1968, 54]. Even the traditional, distinctively American chew-and-spit that so offends the British is now marketed as an "innovative smokeless tobacco product" [Bryant 1984]. This may well also be the appropriate place to mention the success of H. L. Mencken's famous bathtub hoax, even after he recanted [Boston 1982, 102–105; MacDougall 1958 (1940), 302–309; Saunders 1980, 80], for his rewrite of the history of the bath fitted the Americans' sense of their own developing refinement. Miner's mock anthropological account of the "body ritual of the Nacirema" [1975 (1956) 10–19], in which the bathroom is a shrine where sacred rituals are performed to ward off disease and debility, provides a link to serious anthropological and historical studies and observations of the Americans that portray them as ultraclean [Botting 1986, 269; Homans 1946, 297–98; Sinha 1975], a quality shared by their Canadian neighbors [Lewis 1978, 172; Wicks 1976, 71], who also consider Europe to be unspeakably dirty. The Indian anthropologist Sinha [1975, 318] explains the peculiar American preoccupation with personal hygiene as part of a general, rational, technological orientation into which the values of cleanliness, punctuality (the proverbial hora Americana), and thrift all fit, thus providing independent confirmation of my general theory.

The greater degree of concern about hygiene that characterizes America and Canada relative to Britain or France can also be deduced from the stress laid on it in advertisements for deodorants, cleansers, and detergents [see Feinburg 1978, 161]. Indeed, to the seedy, grubby, relaxed British and French, the North Americans sometimes seem quite Harpic, or clean round the bend. The joke below is an exclusively American product that wouldn't work elsewhere:

> Q. Have you wondered why you don't hear the popular detergent jingle—Stronger Than Dirt—any more?
> A. They tested it in a Polish neighborhood—and it lost. [Macklin and Erdman 1976, 187]

The market research figures [Heron House Associates 1979, 328–29][10] on the purchase of soap and deodorants in the various countries involved in the ethnic jokes about the stupid and the filthy at the time of the peak of these jokes' popularity are very revealing.

As table 4.2 indicates, it is not the realities of other peoples' lack of cleanliness but the joke-tellers' concern about their own image that is the key to the ethnic jokes. The British do not tell jokes about the soapless

TABLE 4.2 **The Clean and the Sanitized**

	USA	Canada	UK	Ire-land	France	Bel-guim
Percent of households who buy soap (1977)	97	98	99	72	91	91
Percent of men who use a deodorant/antiperspirant regularly	80	85	41	N. A.	29	26
Percent of women who use a deodorant/antiperspirant regularly	90	95	73	N. A.	70	73
Dates of deodorant figures	1974	1974	1976	—	1975	1975

Irish being dirty, whereas Americans and Canadians revel in jokes about "dirty" Poles, Italians, Newfies, or Ukrainians, despite the very low probability of these peoples' being concentrated in the soapless 2–3 percent of the North American population. However, the North Americans' concern with the image of cleanliness, and with an absence of odor, is indicated by the much higher use of deodorants in America and Canada than in Britain, France, or Belgium. The difference is not between the butts of the jokes, i.e., between the Poles, Italians, and Newfies versus the Belgians and the Irish, but between the two sets of joke-tellers.

Americans especially live in a world that is "sanitized." When Americans travel to Britain or France on vacation, they tend to worry about whether the countries they are going to visit, and particularly their hotels, will be sufficiently clean. By contrast British and French visitors to America are amazed by the zeal with which hotel staff remove every speck of dust, and are amused to learn that sensitive areas have been "sanitized for your protection." "Sanitizing" is an essentially American notion and refers to the use of modern technology and techniques to remove or hide all sources of material or moral pollution. Not just dirt, but illness, injury, aging, and even death itself are sanitized in America—cleaned up, hidden, banished to the periphery in a way that appears strange to European eyes. For Europeans America is the country where faces and busts are lifted, where morticians embalm corpses until they appear life-like, where television violence is sanitized so that viewers can have the thrill of violence without the nastiness of injuries, where the sick are banished from retirement suburbs designed for sprightly geriatrics, and where, from 1980 to 1988, red-haired Reagan ruled.

The development of elaborate procedures for embalming corpses in the United States [see Mitford 1963, 16, 70–71; Jones 1977, 2], where custom requires the "presentation of our dead in the semblance of normality . . . unmarred by the ravages of illness, disease or mutilation" [Mitford 1963, 71], is a source of amazement and amusement [see Waugh 1958 (1948)] to the English, who, together with other Europeans, are increasingly likely to favor cremation [see Newall 1985]. The relatives of those English people who are buried usually insist on a traditional, plain, wooden, corpse-shaped coffin and there is no significant market for the elaborate American casket built like a treasure chest [cf. Mitford 1963, 206]. The ritual action that accompanies the words "earth to earth, ashes to ashes, dust to dust" is unchanged and the earth is not, as in America, cast into the grave "with a mere flick of the wrist with the Gordon Leak-Proof Earth Dispenser. No grasping of a handful of dirt, no soiled fingers" [Mitford 1963, 76].

There is no hygienic or religious reason for embalming corpses [Mitford 1963, 67], but it fits the American and Canadian rational, technological orientation and zeal for cleanliness that result in a striving to abolish dirt, decay, decline, and even death, the last enemy of those who seek an endless physical perfection through diet, jogging, orthodontics, and, eventually, embalming. There must be no perishing gap between death and the imperishable spiritual body that is the sure and certain hope of the Resurrection. Christian Americans want to look their best for the end of time, when the day of the Lord comes like a thief in the night and the trumpet will sound.

The British and the French live snaggle-toothed, undeodorized, and unjogged, grow old gracelessly, and seem to know that no college of mortuary science can extract the sting of death or gain a victory over the grave. Hence they are puzzled and at times amused by this aspect of the North American way of life. It is not that the British and the French do not share their North American cousins' fear of their own individual death and dissolution into dust, but simply that they do not seek the answer to this problem in cleanliness or the pursuit of physical perfection.

The difference in American and British attitudes in this respect can be seen from the reaction of an American student to the following British joke, told to her in the dialect of the Black Country, an old smokestack industrial area in the West Midlands of England, by a British colleague:

My mother was pushin' my brother down Crairdlay High Street in his pram. He's an ugly bugger, my brother—he bay a bit like me. Any road up, this bloke comes up and says to her:

'Missis—I have sin some sights in my time—but that's the ugliest babbay I have ever sid in all my born days. He is 'orrible. Vile and disgustin'.'

My mother was shocked and ran all the way to the police station. 'Officer, officer' she said, 'I've just bin accosted and insulted.'

'Doe worry, missis' said the policeman, 'Tek (take) a seat and calm down. I'll get you a nice cup of tea and a banana for the monkey.' [UCBFA English file 1979]

It is significant both that the British graduate student told this joke as if the incident had happened to one of his own family and that the American recording the joke (who fully understood its meaning) felt able to comment:

> Perhaps because the physical atmosphere in the Black Country is stifling and unhealthy, the people and their babies are genuinely unattractive. By American standards most of the English do not seem to be a healthy or handsome or robust people. [UCBFA English file 1979]

The reason for this difference between the outlook of the Americans and that of the British or the French seems to lie in the different ways in which secularization has impinged on their lives [see Luckmann 1969, 149]. With the slow decay of belief in religion in atheist France and agnostic Britain, people have ceased to attend the services of the churches and now pay relatively little heed to their moral teachings [see Wilson 1982, 152, 159–62]. Such attention to religion as remains is kept strictly segregated from the complex rational world of the market, bureaucracy, and technology. The churches are aged anachronisms, propped up by a sentimental aesthetic nostalgia, and the clergy are often but the curators of a museum which the curious occasionally visit on wet Sundays. The United States, however, has perhaps always [see Greeley 1972, 151–52], and certainly since the great awakenings, been a more strongly religious society than Britain or France,[11] a moralistic society whose greatness lies in its goodness, a society founded by Puritans who left Britain because of that country's laxity.

In the United States, as elsewhere, the development of a modern "rational" industrial society has led to a growth of skepticism and a weakening of religious fervor, but the decline in church membership and church attendance has been much less marked than in Europe and nominal adherence to traditional moral views has remained much stronger. The influence of the "moral majority," the strength of fundamentalist churches, the growth of new cults and sects are all indices that the religious spirit is stronger in America than in decadent Western Europe. American mainstream religion has survived and flourished by merging with the new institutions of the industrial society, but at the price of inner secularization. Religion is sold in the marketplace and through the mass media using the techniques of modern advertising, and is often organized with the efficiency of a business corporation. The result of these changes has been that the traditional values and aims of American religion have been transmuted into a more secular and material form [see Lipset 1964, 156; Luckmann 1969, 149; Martin 1978, 7, 28–31; Wilson 1969, 109–10]. Historically Americans prided themselves on their purity, on having souls washed whiter than white, as the last vestige of sin was expelled from them by the water of baptism or the blood of the Lamb, and indeed these beliefs are more strongly held in America than in present-day Western Europe. However, with the arrival of a modern industrial consumer society, part of the American fervor expended on the maintenance of moral purity was infused into the upholding of the ethic of rational hygiene and personal cleanliness. The evil body, once kept pure by abstinence and self-control, now had to be kept clean, scrubbed, and odor-free by soap, shampoo, and showers, by deodorants, depilatories, and after-shave lotion. The body was no longer so strongly repressed for purity but was organized for cleanliness with a puritanical fervor that owed much to a traditional religious zeal that had been merged with the secular world, but lost none of its enthusiasm in the process.[12] Cleanliness was merged with godliness and external dirt with inward sin. In consequence of this merger, there now exists in American thinking an implicit antithesis between the sacred and the physically dirty which emerges in jokes about the sacred rituals and ceremonies of "filthy" ethnic minorities:

Why are there only two pallbearers at a Polish funeral?
There are only two handles on a garbage can. [American 1960s]

How can you recognize an Italian wedding procession?
By the whitewall tires on the garbage truck. [American 1970s]

How does an Italian wedding differ from an Italian funeral?
For the funeral they turn the headlights of the garbage truck on. [American 1970s. Cf. Wilde 1983B, 99]

What's the last thing they do after celebrating an Italian wedding?
Flush the punch bowl. [American 1970s]

The contrast between American/Canadian and British/French jokes about dirtiness makes it possible to suggest plausible cultural explanations for the distinctively North American jokes about the "dirty-stupid." However, it must be stressed that this is a very limited and tentative explanation. A more detailed comparison with a larger range of examples might well produce a different and more general theory that would cover other cases of jokes about the "dirty-stupid" and also cultures where ethnic jokes about the "dirty" and ethnic jokes about the "stupid" are pinned on quite different groups.[13] The nature and intensity of people's attitudes to dirtiness, and indeed their definition of it, though, are much more culture-specific than is the case with stupidity. It may well be that the meaning of "dirtiness" differs so much from one culture to another that it will prove difficult to provide a more general explanation than the limited and local thesis advanced above.

CHAPTER FIVE
Who Gets Called Canny?

The ethnic groups who get called "canny" in jokes are quite different from those who are the butts of jokes about stupidity. Most countries have their own local "stupid" minority or neighbor who is basically similar to the joke-tellers. Although "canny" jokes are equally widespread, they are attached to a much smaller list of ethnic groups. Jokes about the canny tend to be either very local or completely international, as in the case of jokes about the Scots or the Jews. The local butts of "canny" jokes are listed[1] in table 5.1.

Many of the "local" groups listed in table 5.1 are the inhabitants of a town or a district whose people do not differ ethnically from the rest of their countrymen. These butts of "canny" jokes have a civic or regional identity rather than an ethnic one, and their separate identity has not usually been developed to the point where they could be said to constitute a distinct people. The towns and regions where they live are located firmly and unambiguously within the country concerned, though often well away from the center. Ethnic and regional jokes about canniness, like those about stupidity, pin this quality on a particular group, on someone else, but it is not clearly exported to the periphery in the way that stupidity is.

At the other extreme are the ubiquitous jokes about Jews[2] and Scotsmen told throughout the world, often alongside the local "canny" jokes. In part this is because the Jewish diaspora and the massive Scottish emigration in search of economic opportunities have meant that the Jews and the Scots form visible minorities in many countries. However, Scottish jokes are also extremely popular in countries where the people have had very little direct contact with the Scots—in Hungary, France, Italy, Greece, Germany, Scandinavia, and Czechoslovakia, for instance[3]—as well as in all the English-speaking countries where Scots have settled in large numbers. The willingness of European peoples to import and even to invent Scottish jokes rather than to adapt them and fit them to a local group (as is almost always the case in jokes about "stupid" groups) is striking. People want to tell jokes about canny outsiders but it seems that any outsider with the requisite comic reputation will do. Ethnic jokes

TABLE 5.1 **Who Gets Called Canny?**

Country where jokes about local "canny" groups are told	Local "canny" group about whom the jokes are told
United States	New Englanders, Iowans
Canada	Nova Scotians
Mexico	Regiomontanos (people of Monterrey)
Colombia	Paisas (people of Antioquia)
Trinidad	East Indians (from South Asia)
Wales	Cardis (people of Cardiganshire)
Scotland	Aberdonians (people of Aberdeen)
France	Auvergnats (people from the Auvergne)
Belgium	Dutch
Germany	Swabians
Italy	Milanese, Genovese, Florentines
Switzerland	Genevois, Bâlois
Spain	Aragonese, Catalans
Finland	Laihians (people of Laihia)
Bulgaria	Gabrovonians (people of Gabrovo), Armenians
Greece	Armenians
China	People from Shansi
Southeast Asia	Overseas Chinese
India	Gujaratis, Sindis
Pakistan	Hindus (especially Gujaratis)
Iran	Armenians, Isfahanis, Tabrizis
Turkey	Greeks, Armenians
Nigeria	Ibos
East Africa	Asians (South Asians)

about "canny Scots" are not switched to fit a people on the boundaries of the joke-tellers' own ethnic identity in the way that ethnic jokes about stupidity frequently are. The Scots of the jokes are seen as closely related neighbors by the English, Welsh, and Irish, as economically successful immigrants in Canada, the United States, Australia, and New Zealand [Allison 1978, 36; Greenway 1972, 249; Jackson 1968], as occasional visitors or assimilated emigrant entrepreneurs in Northern Europe, and as an exotic faraway people by the inhabitants of the Central European and Mediterranean countries. Even in the countries that have no direct contact with Scotland or the Scots, jokes with a local content have emerged; the basic well-known script about the "canny Scot" has been applied to a local institution:

A Scotsman went into a boulevard cafe and asked the price of a glass of wine. "Four francs," replied the waiter.

"That's a lot," said the Scotsman.

"Well then, don't drink sitting on the terrace. If you stand at the counter it will only cost you two and a half francs."

"Ah," said the Scotsman, "and how much will it cost me to drink at the counter if I stand on one leg?" [French 1970s. Also in Italian in Bramieri 1980B, 277]

The Jews constitute a significant and visible entrepreneurial or trading minority set apart from their host communities by religion, ritual segregation, or social exclusion in most of the countries where jokes about "canny Jews" are told. Jokes are also told about other ethnic groups occupying a similar niche, such as the Armenians in the Middle East or the Balkans, or the Chinese in Southeast Asia. The social position of these peoples is distinctively different from that of the other "canny" groups, and this is reflected in the jokes told about them. Their situation, unlike that of "canny" groups defined as indigenous by the local people, is dangerous and precarious because for a variety of reasons they are perceived as irredeemably alien by the surrounding majority. To be seen as both alien and canny in this way can lead to their being hated and persecuted by those around them [Hagen 1962, 249], who define their own identity in terms of a putatively unchanging space and time into which the "canny" minority are seen as intruders. Consensual ethnic and national rhetoric about the sacred places and history of our ancestors or the importance of roots can easily and nastily be turned against those perceived as rootless cosmopolitans. The ability of a "canny" minority to operate successfully in impersonal and even international markets for goods or finance may be suspect to people with a local outlook [cf. Smith 1902 (1776), 404–410], and especially to those whose finances are part of a network of mutual obligation and who see their products as an extension of themselves. The outsiders who are able to buy and sell such items casually according to supply and demand may be viewed by peoples with a limited local perspective almost as if they, the outsiders, were selling dignity or honor or putting a price on friendship [see Hagen 1962, 60]. The misunderstandings and resentments thus created may well be exploited and amplified into open hostility by fanatical or cynical politicians and can result in pogroms, massacres, and even genocide. Anti-Semitism in particular became an explicit ideology of such obvious force and virulence that any explanation of jokes about "canny Jews" must take account of its existence. The absence of any equivalent anti-Caledonianism means that jokes about "canny Scotsmen" are made and told in a very different social and ideological setting.

The peoples who have been labeled canny in jokes can be conveniently divided into four groups: the prudent provincials, the innovating industrialists, the calculating Calvinists, and the excluded enterprisers. That the peoples of the first three categories rather than some other group have been singled out as the butt of "canny" jokes can be explained largely in terms of visible and distinctive aspects of their behavior which have discernible historical roots.

The Prudent Provincials

The inhabitants of the Auvergne in France, of Laihia in Finland, of Aragon in Spain, and also of Aberdeen in Scotland and Cardiganshire in Wales [see Morgan 1982, 22, 46; Williams 1979A, 95–96] responded to the poverty of the hard, remote areas where they lived by developing habits of thrift, caution, and calculation, which they saw as necessities but which were a source of amusement to those who lived in regions better endowed by nature. It should be stressed that the jokes are not based on behavior directly caused by poverty, for poverty can be associated with fecklessness and fatalism as well as with thrift and prudence. Indeed, the existence of groups such as the Laihians or the Auvergnats casts doubt on the validity of the "culture of poverty" thesis, which argues that material circumstances alone prevent the very poor from acquiring or valuing notions of forward planning or deferred gratification. Rather, it is the particular and visible response of groups such as the Auvergnats and the Laihians to their difficult situation that formed the basis of jokes about their "canny" qualities. Marjatta Jauhiainen's study of Finnish Laihian jokes [1979; see also 1983] clearly indicates their probable origin:

> Much of present-day Laihia is alluvial land on the Gulf of Bothnia and in the period of clearing cultivation it was regarded as unfit for farming. As people gradually settled in meagre Laihia (laiha = meagre) they were forced by natural conditions to live sparingly. When property inventories were made in the 18th century for purposes of taxation the ability of the Laihians to pay tax was found to be considerably greater than in the surrounding more fertile districts. Statistics for individual boroughs compiled at the beginning of the 19th century on luxury goods (pocket watches, etc.) in turn showed that the Laihians had far fewer than their neighbours. To this day every Laihian has more put away in the bank than on average in other similar farming communities.

Humor scholars have not, as far as I know, provided as detailed an assessment of the economic behavior of the peoples of the Auvergne in France or of Iowa in the United States, but both have long been the butt of jokes about tightfistedness:

> Auvergnat give me five sous.
> I haven't got five sous.
> I will give you six in return.
> Here you are then. [Gaidoz and Sébillot 1884, 74; also see pp. 73–75.

For further examples of humor about the Auvergnats see Chrestien 1957, 37; Nègre 1973, vol. I; Paul 1954, 137]

At the end of a church service a preacher in Iowa passed his hat around the congregation for the collection. It came back completely empty. The preacher raised his eyes to heaven and declared "I thank Thee, O Lord, that my hat returned safely." [American 1950s. See also Cerf 1946, 97]

Other, more urban and modern aspects of canniness have often been built on to the earlier comic image of rural stinginess rooted in provincial agrarian reality to produce the full range of canny jokes told in modern industrial societies.

The Innovating Industrialists

Jokes about the people of Gabrovo in Bulgaria, the Regiomontanos of Monterrey in Mexico, and the Paisas of Antioquia in Colombia also have an economic origin, though one of a very different kind, for these towns and regions were the first centers of industrial development in otherwise backward peasant societies. The founders of such towns were men who cast aside the restraints of custom and tradition and applied a rational, calculating, innovative spirit to their work and to social and economic life generally.

The enterprising smiths and artisans of Gabrovo were the first people of their region to use the swift-flowing streams from the mountains to power their machinery, and by the nineteenth century the Gabrovonians were exporting their manufactures all over the Turkish and Austro-Hungarian empires. In 1882 a Gabrovonian entrepreneur set up the first spinning mill in Bulgaria and soon textile machinery was being imported from Western Europe to build up Bulgaria's first industrial enterprises and first industrial town [see Shinov et al. 1981; Stoianovich 1971]. The men who introduced these new methods of production developed a rational, calculating outlook very different from that of the peasant majority, and even when they became rich they continued to live in a modest way. By the 1920s Gabrovo was the second manufacturing town in Bulgaria, after the capital, Sofia. Also it was a self-made town, based on exports rather than government contracts, in contrast to, say, Slieven, which produced goods for local use or for the army. Gabrovonian merchants and salesmen traveled all over Bulgaria and the Balkans in search of new markets, and their diligent and businesslike behavior spread the reputation of "canny Gabrovo" throughout the country. In the latter half of the nineteenth century Gabrovo jokes grew out of the sharp contrast between the ways of these pioneers of industry and those of the more traditional and static majority [Davies 1982D and 1987B; Gergov 1985]. As in the case of Aberdeen in Scotland, fantastic tales about Gabrovo parsimony have flourished. Gabrovo was thus the natural location for Bulgaria's famous House of Humour and Satire. In Gabrovo one can buy scissors for cutting cats' tails and householders' heating bills, for the tailless cats go through doors more quickly thus preventing drafts. The Gabrovonians also sell semi-hexagonal coffee cups so that your guests get only half a cup and spoons with holes in them so that they can't help themselves to your sugar. The Gabrovonian has measured out his life in coffee spoons. Today Gabrovo's biggest industry is jokes:

As he was getting on board a ship a man from Sevlievo asked his friend from Gabrovo: "Please let me have one of your suits."

"But you have your own."

"I can't swim. And if I wear your suit and we're ship-wrecked you'll do your best to save me." [Furtounov and Prodanov 1985]

Mexican jokes about Regiomontanos and Colombian jokes about Paisas have a similar origin. Monterrey is the principal industrial center in the north of Mexico, and is far from the capital, Mexico City. Much of Mexico's recent state-sponsored industrial development has occurred in or around the capital, where the key political decisions about patronage of industry are taken, but Monterrey is a city of independent pioneers whose rise dates from the beginning of the twentieth century when the huge iron and steel complex Compania Fundidora de Fierro y Acero de Monterrey was established. Later it became a major center for textiles, machinery, and glass. Like the Gabrovonians, the Regiomontanos avidly and visibly seized new economic opportunities at a time when this was not usual behavior in Mexico [see Harrison 1985, 102] or in Bulgaria. The Paisas live in what has been jokingly called "Paisalandia," a Scotland-sized region of northwest Colombia containing the department of Antioquia, whose capital, Medellín, is known as the Manchester of the Andes because of its industrial development and the hardheaded commercial outlook of the inhabitants. The Antioqueños have rejected traditional values and status symbols and in contrast to other Colombians rate a business career higher than the position of a military officer, a professional man, or a member of the landed gentry [Hagen 1962, 377–78]. In consequence Antioquia has long provided a large proportion of Colombia's entrepreneurs [Hagen 1962, 365], and in recent years the bulk of the world's illicit trade in cocaine has been controlled by a Medellín cartel.

In both Mexico and Colombia the extraordinary entrepreneurial energy of the Regiomontanos and Antioqueños has given rise to the unsubstantiated myth that these peoples are "new Christians," the descendants of Spanish Jews who pretended to convert to Catholicism to avoid being expelled from Spain [Hagen 1962, 371–72; Harrison 1985, 102] and then later settled in remote cities in the Spanish colonies of the New World to avoid persecution by the Spanish Inquisition. There are many jokes in

Spanish [e.g., see Londoño 1977] about the peoples of these allegedly canny cities:

One day a Paisa businessman comes home early and surprises his wife in bed with another man. He pulls out his revolver and tells his wife's lover: "Get ready to die." The other Paisa replies: "That's a nice revolver you've got there. I suppose you wouldn't care to sell it?" The husband lowers the revolver and says: "I might, what's your offer?" [Colombian 1980s]

Paisa father to son: "Earn money, son. Earn it honestly, but if you can't earn it honestly, earn it." [Colombian 1980s]

In the periodical *Tribuna y El Porvenir* of Monterrey appears the story of a millionaire of that city who died and passed to a better world. At the gates of heaven Saint Peter asked him, "What good deeds have you done?"

"I have given a hundred pesos for the building of the church of the Virgen del Roble."

Saint Peter, not knowing what to do, put the case before the Eternal Father who pronounced this sentence: "Give him back his hundred pesos and then he won't bother us any more." [Peñalosa 1979, 75]

In Italy the inhabitants of many cities that are modern or long-established centers of commerce, banking, or manufacturing are also the butts of "canny" jokes in a country known for local humor based on towns and regions. The citizens of Genoa, Milan, Florence, and Turin are all seen as comically canny and appear in competitive jokes based on the rule of three [see Dundes 1975A and Olrik 1965 (1909)] or in jokes contrasting them with rustics or Southerners.[4]

The Calculating Calvinists

To explain the origins of the worldwide ethnic jokes about "canny Scotsmen" or the more local jokes about "canny Cardis" in Wales, "canny Dutchmen" in Belgium, and "canny New Englanders" in the United States, it is necessary to consider religious as well as economic factors. Each of these peoples are noted for their strong historic adherence to Calvinism or, at a latter date, Unitarianism, and the distinctively severe and calculating attitudes to both moral and economic life that came to be known as the Protestant Ethic [Weber 1930; Eisenstadt 1969]. The Calvinists in time came to place a heavy emphasis on the "canny" calculative virtues of work, duty, diligence, and thrift [Wilson 1969, 41] which others found excessive and even ludicrous. The Calvinists and their rationalist descendants, the Unitarians, produced many of the merchants, entrepreneurs, and capitalists who laid the foundations of the modern industrial and commercial world. The hardheaded calculating spirit, the sense of work as a calling, the ascetic dedication to gaining, saving, investing, and not consuming derived from their religion were conducive to success in the marketplace, but for others there was a grim, joyless, overcompetitive side, which they saw as the unacceptable face of Calvinism [see Weber 1930, 68–69].

After the Reformation the national identity of both Scots and Dutch became inextricably linked with Calvinism [Martin 1978, 102]. In both Scotland and the Netherlands the established church has long been Calvinist, and many emigrants from both countries, whether of the state church or the even stricter break-away sects, have carried their religious principles with them. An old Dutch comic triad neatly places Dutch prudence and foresight between French fecklessness and the obsessive and unnecessary canniness of the Scots:

A hundred Dutchmen, a hundred knives.
A hundred Frenchmen, no knives.
A hundred Scots, two hundred knives. [Werner 1894, 292]

Once again it is others who exemplify the comic unbalanced extremes, while the joke-tellers display moderation and balanced good sense. However, the others in their turn laugh at what they see as the canny Dutch[5] "Tulip-munchers" and "Pfeffer-säcke" (Pepper-sacks, i.e., traders).

George the First, on a journey to Hanover, stopped at a village in Holland and while the horses were getting ready he asked for two or three eggs which were brought him and charged two hundred florins. "How is this," said his majesty, "eggs must be very scarce in this place." "Pardon me," said the host, "eggs are plenty enough, but kings are scarce." [*Wit and Wisdom* 1826, 141]

Similarly, although the inhabitants of Swabia and of Switzerland are of mixed religious affiliation they both contain sizable Calvinist populations. Indeed, the Swiss city of Geneva, at one time the home of and effectively ruled by John Calvin, may be regarded as the center of origin of the Reformed churches generally. Both the Swabians [Brustgi 1978; Reichert 1974] and the inhabitants of the Calvinist Swiss cantons [Herdi 1979] are the butts of jokes about their allegedly canny qualities.

Three Jews make a Bâlois (citizen of Bâle).
Three Bâlois make a Génèvois. [Gaidoz and Sébillot 1884, 299]

After God had created the first Swiss He asked him what he would like to have in his country. "I would like some mountains," said the Swiss, and with a wave of his hand God created the Alps. "I would also like some farmland," said the Swiss, and God promptly created the beautiful meadows of Switzerland. "And now some cows," said the Swiss, and God filled the meadows with the best milkers in the world. "Tell me, God," asked the Swiss, "is there anything I can do for you?" "Yes," said God, tired by His labors, "just bring me some milk to drink from one of your cows." "Certainly," said the Swiss, and went off to milk the cow. Five minutes later he returned and handed God a glass of milk. "Here it is," said the Swiss. "That will be four francs fifty." [French 1980s. Also in Herdi 1979, 8; Isnard 1977; *Pass the Port Again* 1981, 180]

The match between "canny" ethnic jokes and Calvinism is far from perfect, but it is striking nonetheless. The French also tell jokes about the Swiss being slow or even dense, but Ouin-Ouin, the rural butt of these jokes, may well be identified with a different commune or canton, and Switzerland, a country of many languages and religious denominations, is the most decentralized state in Europe [Clinard 1978; Martin 1978, 197–98], with each canton having its own distinctive and treasured local characteristics. The only Calvinists who may definitely be said to be the butt of ethnic jokes about stupidity are the Afrikaners of South Africa, whose particular brand of Calvinism has evolved in a unique, collectivist direction that sets them apart in a category of their own [see Martin 1978, 297; Moodie 1975; Williams and Strydom, 1980]. The butts of ethnic jokes about stupidity are far more likely to be those whose ethnic identity is closely tied to Roman Catholicism and who live on the periphery of a Protestant or strongly secular society. This is hardly unexpected, given that relatively recent empirical studies indicate that even where Protestants and Roman Catholics live in the same society and experience similar economic opportunities and pressures the Protestants are more achievement oriented, more competitive and less communal, more innovative and less traditional than the Roman Catholics.[6]

The Puritans, who were the initial settlers in New England, were in the main Calvinists who emigrated to seek a new world because of their dislike of the episcopal organization and Arminian theology of the Church of England. The New Englanders long retained their severe Protestant outlook, and even the more doubting among their descendants, who retreated from orthodoxy to Deism or Unitarianism [Vidler 1961, 239], were strongly committed to the values of work, frugality, and enterprise. Benjamin Franklin, though a deist, retained a utilitarian version of his father's Calvinistic outlook [Weber 1930, 53] and was himself the subject of jokes about his being canny [e.g., *New Joe Miller* 1801, 16]. In the early nineteenth century Mrs. Trollope [1832, vol. I, 136–37, 280–81 and vol. II, 137–42, 240–41] commented at length on what she saw as both the positive and the negative aspects of the distinctive Yankee view of work and wealth, which she explicitly compared with that of the Scots, the Dutch, and the Jews. In jokes Yankee acuteness[7] is tied directly to its religious origins as well as to its secular payoff:

A Yankee Preacher on Predestination—Let us for argument's sake, grant that I, the Rev. Elder Sprightly, am foreordained to be drowned in the river at Smith's ferry, next Thursday morning, at twenty minutes after ten o'clock; and suppose I know it; and suppose I am a free, moral, voluntary, accountable agent—do you think I am going to be drowned? I should rather guess not! I should stay at home; and you'll never ketch the Rev. Elder Sprightly at Smith's ferry nohow, nor near the river neither. [Dr. Merry n.d., 239]

A 'cute Yankee has invented a nest, in the bottom of which there is a kind of trap door, through which the egg, when laid, immediately drops; and the hen looking round and perceiving none, soon lays another. [Dr. Merry n.d., 152]

The term *Yankee* in such jokes has a varied meaning. In much of the United States it refers to old-stock New Englanders, in Europe it often refers to any American, and in the South it is but half a word. For the joke-tellers the uncertainty doesn't really matter, for the ideals and obsessions of Vermont in time become those of the entire United States [Herburg 1960, 80; Lipset 1964, 94–95], with the possible exception of the "deviant" South.

The Unitarians are a small Protestant denomination whose rationalist secular theology and disbelief in the Trinity is almost the antithesis of *credo quia absurdum* and whose members have long had the reputation of being hardheaded entrepreneurs [Wilson 1969, 184]. This combination of factors has probably contributed to jokes about "canny New Englanders," but the most remarkable case of "canny Unitarians" are the people of Cardiganshire, who have long been the butt of jokes about canniness among the Welsh. The Cardis are in most respects quite indistinguishable from the other inhabitants of West Wales. West Wales is a remote, hilly, infertile rural region with little in the way of natural resources, and all its people, not just the Cardis, have had to struggle against adverse economic circumstances. However, the Cardis alone became Unitarians, and the Teifi Valley of the southeast of the old county of Cardiganshire [Morgan 1982, 16] contained a large district famed for its numerous Unitarian chapels that was known throughout the rest of Wales as the "black spot" because of the heretical beliefs of its inhabitants [D. Elwyn Davies 1980]. As so often elsewhere, the Unitarians were the doubting, rationalist offspring of the Calvinists and Independents [Rees 1883, 182]. They were a group set apart from the impulsive, emotional Protestantism of the rest of Wales and known for their commitment to secular education. Indeed, the other denominations, despite their horror of Cardi heresy, often educated their own clergy at colleges staffed by Unitarian scholars [Rees 1883, 463; Francis-Jones 1984].

Out of this milieu came the Cardi emigrants who set up in business in the drapery and dairy trades in the cities of England [Francis-Jones 1984; Morgan 1982, 6]. As in the case of the Scots, the jokes about the "canny Cardis" are rooted in their visible commercial acumen and "rational parsimony" [Wallis-Jones 1898, 148–49], and in the religious background that was the basis both of that acumen and of their distinctive identity. Dai Lute, the Welsh milkman [Cunningham 1973, 18], was no doubt a Cardi.

The Crafty Cardi

A very important man had died down in Pembrokeshire and he was a wealth man you see. And he had three special friends and he had made his will; all was to be shared between the three: one from Carmarthenshire, one from Pembrokeshire and a Cardi—these were the three. Well, all three had to be present at his funeral and they were supposed to place a hundred pounds each in his hand in the coffin on the morning of the funeral. And so it happened. The men came, all three together. The Pembrokeshire man came forward and placed the hundred pounds in his hand in the coffin. The Carmarthenshire man went forward and placed the same amount in the coffin. That was two hundred pounds then, wasn't it? Well now, this meant that the other one was to place another hundred in after that. Three hundred pounds would have gone to him then, wouldn't they? But the Cardi had come forward now and he took out his wallet from his pocket: there wasn't even a halfpenny in the wallet, he had left everything behind.

'Never mind, though', he said, 'the old man will not be without his due. What shall I do?'

And he took a cheque book from his pocket and wrote a cheque for three hundred pounds. And then, to compensate himself, and also to gain, he took the notes that were already in the dead man's hand and then gave him the cheque to cover everything. [Ranke 1972, Joke 90, 67. For Scots and Jewish versions see Bell 1929, 24, and Rosemarine 1962, 45. There is also a Nigerian version about Ibos.]

The development of the Scottish qualities of frugality, diligence, and calculative rationality so characteristic of mature Calvinism long preceded the development of a modern capitalist economy in Scotland [see Marshall 1980, esp. 107; Smout 1972, 88–91]. The Scots had the requisite ethos, the education [Smith 1902 (1776), 616], and the entrepreneurial motivation, but initially, at least, lacked local economic opportunities [Marshall 1980, 272; Smout 1972, 92]. This combination though was eventually to produce the "Scotsman on the make" of the ethnic jokes, particularly when the Scots began to emigrate in large numbers in search of new openings and to put the disciplined ambition produced by Calvinism to good use in other countries. Nineteenth and early twentieth century jokes about the Scots stress their religious outlook alongside their canny qualities, and they were clearly seen by the joke-tellers as interrelated. Both the business acumen, the ambition and the frugality of the Scots on the one hand and their distinctive religious identity on the other were highly visible, and joke-tellers have long reveled in the connections and also potential contradictions between these two aspects of Scottishness.

It was the Sabbath and the craftsmen of a little Scottish building firm were working overtime to complete a contract on time. Suddenly the boss had a twinge of conscience and of fear of what his neighbors would think. "Stop hammering," he shouted, "use screws." [British 1970s. Also in Kilgarriff 1974A, 25]

A Scotsman loves his specie under pretence of loving his species. [A' Becket 1894, 465–66]

An endless spiral of jokes about the Scots exists, involving not merely the outsiders' comic images of the Scots but the Scots' highly differentiated comic images of the various sections of their own society, the Scots' comic images of outsiders' images of the Scots, the outsiders' comic images of the Scots' images of the various Scottish factions, and so on [cf. Dundes 1971, 188]. Robert Ford's humorous rhyme in the Scottish vernacular [1901] which purports to represent the Englishman's comic image of Scotland illustrates the complexity of these interactions:

Land o' canny, careful' bodies—
Foes to a' ungodly fun;
Those who sum up man's whole duty—
Heaven, hell and number one.

Today it is pointless even to attempt to sift Scottish jokes into exoteric and esoteric versions since most of them are or have become a shared property. Jokes told outside an ethnic group about the group as a whole may well be told from the inside about a particular faction, section, or social class. Thus ethnic jokes about Scots can be told in subtly different ways, depending on who the joke-teller and the audience are, but attempts to build on this fact fail in the face of the fragmented complexity of individual circumstances and interpretations. Scottish jokes have a long history, and so does the interaction of the Scots with a variety of English-speaking neighbors. In such a situation, living joke-tellers can tell us too much, and dead ones not enough. Ultimately one is forced back to a simpler and appropriately parsimonious account of ethnic jokes about "canny Scots" based on the contrast between the distinctive and remarkable national and religious culture [see Marshall 1980, 39–43] which the

Scots have created and those of their neighbors. The history and evolution of these ethnic jokes is discussed in chapter 6, but the future both of the jokes and of the remarkable national culture that gave rise to them, though possibly predestined, is beyond calculation:

> Elder (discussing the new Minister's probation discourse)
> "In my opeenion he wasna justified in dividing folk into the sheep and the goats. I wadna just say, Jamie, that I was among the unco guid, an' I wadna say that you were among the unco bad. So whar do we come in? He'll no do for us, Jamie. We'll no vote for him." [New Punch Library 1933 *Mr. Punch in Scotland*, 182. See also Ramsay 1873, 30–36, 73–75].

In the second half of the twentieth century, Scottish jokes have become increasingly secularized. In a world that routinely demands work, care, and calculation without the backing of any religious imperative [Weber 1930, 181–82; Wilson 1969, 259–61], the Scotsman of the jokes has been gradually stripped of his Calvinism and is a secular and thus less distinctively Scottish canny figure. Nonetheless new "canny" jokes that refer quite specifically to the Scots are continually being created. Often they have their roots in anecdotes based on selectively reported but purportedly real events:

[A Gordon Highlander whose pockets were full of gambling winnings was injured in battle in World War II.] "I've had it, Jock," he said to a friend, "Take my wallet." The friend examined his wound and told him it was only a gash. "Then gie us back my bluidy wallet," replied the wounded one. [Jones 1979, 313]

[Classified ad in] Hamilton (Canada) *Spectator:*
"Lost: Brown wallet at Civic Stadium, Scottish Gathering. Very small reward." [Tempel 1970, 19]

An anthropologist in the United States noted that many members of a particular tribe of Indians had Scottish surnames. Further investigation revealed that Scots "traders finding that their names were much admired and that they were considered by the Indians to be tangible possessions . . . sold them to the tribesmen." [Dunkling 1981, 35]

Jokes about "canny Scots" are learned very early in life by English-speaking children and appear in anthologies of easy jokes that are the child's first jokebooks:

> Englishman: "I hear the price of petrol is coming down."
> Scotsman: "Och, that's great news."

Englishman: "But why are you so pleased, you don't own a car do you?"

Scotsman: "No but I have a lighter." [*The World's Even Worse Worst Jokes Book* 1985]

Modern secular international jokes about the "canny Scotsman" can be treated as a model of the kinds of jokes that are told about the other canny groups discussed thus far. Indeed, it is easy to see how a skilled "switcher" of jokes can slightly adapt a joke about the Scots to fit, say, the Dutch, the Regiomontanos, the Laihians, the Gabrovonians, the Cardis, or any other local group that has somehow acquired the label *canny*. There are, of course, many jokes that hang on a local circumstance, a cultural peculiarity, or a piece of linguistic trickery and thus cannot be "switched" in this way. Jokes about the Calvinist roots of Scots' canniness would make no sense if applied to Gabrovo, and jokes that involve quirks of language are sometimes untranslateable. Nonetheless, the jokes are broadly similar and the three categories of "canny" peoples and jokes dealt with so far can reasonably be treated as a single block for the purpose of contrasting them with the fourth and very different case of the excluded enterprisers.

The Excluded Enterprisers

The situation of the excluded enterprisers is in many respects similar to that of the other "canny" groups. Ethnic minorities such as the Jews, the Armenians, the Asians of East Africa, and the overseas Chinese of South-east Asia have been remarkably and visibly more successful in business and the professions than the people among whom they have settled. In the English-speaking world the rapid upward mobility of the Jewish immigrants from Eastern and Central Europe and their descendants has been a particularly visible and striking phenomenon, as was the combination of ambition, business acumen, and respect for education that produced it.[8] It is not the only case of ethnic success referred to directly in jokes.

What do you call a Patel who doesn't own a post office?
Doctor. [British 1980s. Cf. Martin and Jacobs 1969, 70]

It is not surprising that "canny" jokes should be told about excluded enterprisers which are much the same as those associated with the groups discussed earlier. Many jokes about Jews, for instance, are so similar to those told about the Scots that Seth Kravitz, on the basis of his fieldwork on the ethnic jokes told in London, concluded that Scottish jokes were a "modified sub-set of Jewish jokes" [1977, 287; see also 297]. It would be more accurate to say that there is a high degree of overlap between the ethnic jokes told about Jews and those told about Scots [see also Golden

1959, 268; Wolff, Smith, and Murray 1934, 356, 360]. However, if, instead of stressing the similarity of ethnic jokes about "canny Scots" and those about "canny Jews," we look at some of the contrasts between them, it is clear that there are broadly two kinds of jokes about Jews that do not get told about Scotsmen. The first are distinctively Jewish jokes which stem from a particular cultural tradition. They do not get told about Scotsmen for the same reason that canny tales involving whisky, the kirk, or dour pawkiness are not told about Jews. The second consists of ethnic jokes told about the Jews as "excluded enterprisers" that are not told about the other categories of "canny" groups. Many of these are congruent with the core beliefs of anti-Semites or refer to the social environments in which anti-Semitism flourishes. Jokes of this kind get switched only to other "excluded enterprisers" who are in the same position of being defined as successful urban outsiders in the midst of a decisively separate host population whose resentments and suspicions are apt to lead to paranoia and persecution.

The strength and independence of the Jewish cultural tradition are shown by the unique way in which the standard themes of ethnic jokes are treated in Jewish humor [see, for instance, the Jewish jokes on the theme militarism-cowardice]. Most of the groups who figure in the ethnic jokes discussed in this book are the mere butts of other peoples' jokes, or at best collaborators in the construction of the outsiders' comic image of them. Relatively little is lost by viewing the ethnic jokes about them through the eyes of an outside group telling the jokes. This is not true of the Jews, who have played a very active role in constructing distinctively Jewish jokes that have an individual zest to them, and which have an appeal far beyond the boundaries of the Jewish community. An analysis of the full complexity of Jewish jokes would require another book and indeed a very different kind of book. Here it will simply be noted in passing that the Ashkenazi Jews from Eastern Europe have had an enormous impact on the very vocabulary of jokes about canniness and stupidity by introducing into English (and indeed other languages) words of Yiddish origin, such as schlemiel, schlimazl, nebbish, chutzpah, naches, schnorrer, that had no real equivalent in pre-Yinglish English.[9] That such a plethora of subtle terms existed in Yiddish and were successfully introduced into another language is an indication of a Jewish preoccupation with the themes of canniness/stupidity, success/failure, Yiddisher Kop/Goyisher Kop [see Kumove 1986; Patai 1977, 287; Rosten 1970, 144], which are, of course, themes that lie at the heart of so many ethnic jokes.

Quite apart from jokes about canniness that relate to particular aspects of Jewish or Scottish culture and traditions, there are broad differences between ethnic jokes about "canny Jews" and those about "canny Scots" which relate to the social position of "excluded enterprisers" and that of the more indigenous territorially based "canny" groups. One of the differences that Kravitz noted between British jokes about "canny Scotsmen" and those told about "canny Jews" is that the former are relatively more likely to be placed in a domestic setting and the latter to be set in a business context [see Kravitz 1977, 288]. This ties in with two broader differences between jokes told about groups like the Scots and jokes told about excluded enterprisers such as the Jews.

First, jokes about groups such as the Scots show them as shrewd in avoiding expenditure and obligations but are somewhat less likely to depict them as swindling people. The Scottish joke is indeed widely used to advertise opportunities for the would-be economical purchaser—supermarkets in Germany, motels in the United States, life insurance in Britain. By contrast, jokes about Jewish business malpractice and swindling are common and there are also far more jokes about usury:

After all the films they've made about sharks they're making a new one about loan sharks.
It's called "Jews." [American 1970s. See also Wilde 1979A, 76]

Quel est le vin préféré des juifs?
Le vingt pour cent. [Climent-Galant 1979, 40. Untranslatable pun]

In the standard joke about the shortest book in the world the Jews are represented by "Jewish Business Ethics" and the Scots by "La Dolce Vita in Scotland" [see Dundes 1971, 190–91]. Second, jokes about the excluded enterprisers depict them as using their canny qualities in ways less than loyal to the nation in which they live and suggest that their cleverness is a sneaky substitute for the more heroic or brutal virtues. Jokes of this kind are not told about "canny" groups viewed as securely indigenous, such as stalwart Scots or stubborn Swabians.

Have you heard about the new Scottish regiment for Jews?
It is called the Jordan Highlanders.
Regimental badge: Three brass balls.
First motto: No advance without security.
Second motto: Charge, charge, and charge again.
[British. Interwar period]

There is a notable congruence between the content of these latter jokes and that of anti-Semitic prejudice, ideology, and propaganda [see Davies 1986B]. Indeed, there is a remarkable goodness of fit between the two subjects of joking I have cited and Podhoretz's (1986) view that "the two classic themes of anti-Semitic literature (are) the Jew as alien and the Jew as the conspiratorial manipulator of malign power dangerous to everyone else." Such themes are also to be found, though in a less explicitly developed form, in other cases where an ethnic group has been defined as excluded enterprisers. Anti-Semitism and related beliefs about other excluded enterprisers are qualitatively different from the limited and often casually held beliefs that a people have about various other outsiders, because they are often part of a bizarre system of thought that blames all the political and economic ills of the host society on the allegedly dishonest and conspiratorial behavior of the excluded enterprisers. These hostile fantasies come to have an existence and influence of their own so divorced from everyday reality and experience that the latter are subordinate to the former and are interpreted in terms of it. For this reason I shall henceforth treat anti-Semitic type patterns of belief as social facts in themselves and relate ethnic jokes to these, rather than embark on a lengthy second stage of analysis explaining how and why these beliefs have taken a particular form.

The Jews have not been the only victims of such virulent and crackpot beliefs. In the late 1960s I studied a particular set of excluded enterprisers, the Asians of East Africa, who were seen by many indigenous Africans as dangerous and parasitic or, to use their own term, as "bloodsuckers," siphoning off the wealth of the society or even plotting to take it over. In reality the Asians were a stratum of powerless small traders providing an essential service, on the whole honestly and with small profit margins. Yet they were abused as jackals and swindlers, and one highly educated Ugandan economist told the author: "We think that in the long run with the economic power in their hands, they are capable of ousting us from the cities and the economic areas and industrial centers. . . . I think the Asian population is what I call a Trojan horse. One day they will just come out, you see, and we will get ambushed" [Tape-recorded interview Kampala 1969]. This kind of comment, which represented a widely held view of the Asians in East Africa [see Davies 1972; Theroux 1967], was expressed well before the vicious, crazy, but at times comic [see Coren 1974 and 1975] dictator Idi Amin came to power and persecuted and expelled Uganda's Asian minority. Many other such persecutions of "excluded enterprisers" have taken place in the twentieth century. During World War I perhaps as many as a million Armenians, an industrious minority prominent in trade and industry and deprived of the right to bear arms [Toynbee 1915, 19–34], were murdered by the Turkish government with the approval of their German advisers [Reitlinger 1967; Toynbee 1915]. This was not the first Turkish persecution of the Armenians [cf. sick joke in Graham 1905, 41–42] but it was the most deadly, and three-quarters of Turkey's Armenian minority were killed. Sultan Abdul Hamid declared unambiguously: "The way to get rid of the Armenian question is to get rid of the Armenians" [Toynbee 1915, 12]. At the end of the war the victorious allies did nothing and Hitler later drew his own ominous conclusions from this [Reitlinger 1967, 98].

It is against this very ugly background that jokes told exclusively about excluded enterprisers must be viewed. The first genre of such jokes which I shall consider are the very numerous jokes about Jews burning down their own property in order to defraud an insurance company,[10] which could be taken as a comic metaphor of the anti-Semitic view [Podhoretz 1986] of the "Jew as manipulator of malign power dangerous to everyone else." However, it must be stressed that these jokes are not in and of themselves anti-Semitic, for the nature of the link between the serious and comic is a problematic one. It is easy to postulate, as I have done, that the small comic statements of the jokes reflect the nature of larger seriously held beliefs, but it is difficult to go beyond such imprecise and unsatisfactory terms as *metaphor* or *reflect*. The reader should "reflect" that even in the material world there are many kinds of mirrors producing quite different images by reflection that reveal to us not just a looking-glass world but a shaving mirror and driving mirror world and that the metaphorical use of "reflect" produces yet another level of blurring and uncertainty. Let us also not forget that jokes are first and foremost jokes:

A month after he had taken out his fire-insurance policy, Mottel's store burned to the ground and with it his entire inventory of last season's merchandise. Surprisingly, none of the new merchandise had been damaged. By a strange and fortuitous coincidence he had removed all new shipments to another location. Naturally he notified his agent at once. The agent, in turn, was ordered by his office manager to bring an insurance adjuster with him and, together, they sifted through the charred ruins for a full eight hours. At the end of the day, they returned to their office where the manager, understandably nervous, awaited them.

"Did you find out what caused the fire?" he asked.

"Yes, friction," said the adjuster tersely.

"You mean something rubbed up against something else?"

"Yeah," the adjuster affirmed. "The fire was caused by rubbing a $25,000 insurance policy against a $10,000 dry goods store." [Spalding 1976, 166]

Too previous

Hearing that Isaac had had a fire on his premises, I hailed him with: "How did you get on with the insurance company, Isaac?"

"Hush," he replied, "it is not 'till next week." [Junior 1927, 21]

The cause of the fire

There had been a conflagration at Isaac's tailoring establishment and the usual enquiry was taking place.

"And what do you think was the cause of the fire?" asked the Insurance Inspector. "I think it was the gas light," replied Isaac. The Inspector looked dubious: so Isaac's friend Cohen broke in with: "You vos wrong, Isaac mine frient. I think it vos the electric light." But the Inspector wrote down in his report: "Cause of fire—Israelite." [Robey 1920, 228–29]

Why do Jewish shops in the center of London always catch on fire during the lunch hour?

Because the fire engines can't get down Oxford Street. [Jewish/British 1960s]

Blumenthal asked Schwartz, a clothing store proprietor, "How's business?"

"Not so good," said Schwartz, "It looks like a sure-fire proposition." [Wilde 1980A, 161]

I noticed some bottles on a shelf in Robinski's shop.

"Vot vas dose?" I said.

"They is fire extinguishers," he replied.

"Grashus," I said, "vy do you keep fire extingvishers?"

"Because," he said, "I get 20 per shent off ze premium of insurance."

"And vot was in ze bottles?" I asked.

"I do not know vot vas in zem," he said, "but it is kerosene now!" [Ferguson 1933, 168; MacDonald 1915, 61–62]

"Talking about insurance, Robinski," he said, "Here is a strange letter I got from ze insurance company about a shop of mine in ze Brompton Road—

Sir,—we understand you effected a policy of insurance over premises occupied by you in Brompton Road yesterday forenoon. We are informed that the premises took fire at half-past four the same afternoon when considerable damage was done. Kindly explain the delay.

"It is very funny, Robinski," he said, "and I do not know vot to write in reply." [Ferguson 1933, 168; MacDonald 1915, 62]

A Jew crossing the Brooklyn Bridge met a friend who said: "Abe, I'll bet you ten dollars that I can tell you exactly what you're thinking about." "Vell!" agreed Abe, producing a greasy bill, "I'll have to take dat bet. Put up your money."

The friend produced two fives. "Abe," he said, "You are thinking of going over to Brooklyn, buying a small stock of goods, renting a small store, taking out all the fire insurance that you can possibly get and then burning out. Do I win my bet?"

"Vell," replied Abe, "You don't exactly vin, but the idea is worth de money. Take id." [Patten 1909, 173]

These jokes, far more than most ethnic jokes, vary enormously in impact depending on who is telling them to whom. Many of the jokes cited are from American and British printed sources and it is noticeable that the joke about Robinski and kerosene from James Ferguson's anthology of jokes of 1933 now [Larry Wilde 1980A] appears in print in a very bowdlerized form, presumably because of its congruence with anti-Semitism. Others were told to me by Jewish joke-tellers, sometimes with the caveat "of course there's also an anti-Semitic version of this." The jokes as told were not an expression of self-deprecation nor of deliberate distancing of the teller from his own group, but simply a wry comment[11] on the following:

(A) Such cases of arson for insurance do occur, and members of an ethnic group such as the Jews containing a large number of traders dealing in inflammable dry goods [Jones 1960, 219] are likely to be disproportionately implicated if only because they are more exposed to opportunity and temptation. (B) If the culprit in a case of arson for insurance is Jewish this has tended to be stressed in press reports of the crime [e.g., see Masters 1937], whereas the ethnic or religious affiliations of other insurance arsonists are not. If, for the sake of argument, a Welshman [see Masters 1937], or a Quaker, or a member of Opus Dei were convicted of an insurance fraud involving arson, there would probably be no mention of the group to which he belonged. In this way a grossly inflated image of the Jews as arsonists has been created [cf. Parkes 1945, 89, 102–118]. (C) There exists a seriously held anti-Semitic myth in which arson is regarded as typical Jewish behavior and as an index of a wider and more threatening pattern of Jewish greed and conspiracy [see Robb 1954, 107–109; cf. "The Asian Lightning That Keeps Striking" 1985, 10]. Because urban arson is a threat not only to insurers but to the lives of others working and living in adjoining buildings, it seems to have become a symbol of a more general anti-Semitic belief that the Jews, so that they may prosper, are conspiring to destroy people, economies, and entire societies. Points B and C give significance to point A, which, even were it true, is neither intrinsically important nor obviously visible to others.

The most distinctive attribute of humorous discourse is the use of ambiguity and incongruity so that jokes or other humorous statements cannot be reduced to a single meaning. By their very nature they have to be interpreted in different ways at the same time [Mulkay 1987, 249–52, 255–57]. To treat such jokes as if they were merely and inevitably covert anti-Semitic utterances, as Altman [1971, 14–19], Fuchs [1986, 115], and Greenberg [1972, 145] seem to have done, is crass and simplistic and ignores the crucial distinction [see Levin 1979, 214] between that which is intrinsically anti-Semitic and that which might be exploited by anti-Semites. This conflating of the serious and the comic has also led to the unsubstantiated hypothesis that those Jews who tell and enjoy such jokes must be consumed by masochistic self-hatred.[12] Many observers[13] have reported that it is very common for Jews to tell and enjoy jokes which employ themes of extreme acquisitiveness which, if seriously expressed, would appear anti-Semitic. Furthermore, I can confirm on the basis of the Jewish fire-insurance jokes Barron's suggestion [1950] that the members of the target group invent as well as spread jokes about their own group.

Moreover, the jokes are very similar in content [Bermant 1986, 214, 242; Raskin 1985, 211] and at times even identical in words, though not in spirit, to the jokes ascribed to anti-Semites [Rosenburg and Shapiro 1958, 70]. This indicates that the feelings and sentiments carried by a joke (such as philo-Semitism versus anti-Semitism) are largely a question of tone and of context and cannot be inferred from a content analysis of the jokes. It is possible to make such a judgment about sentiment only at a quite different level of analysis from that adopted here, for it would be necessary to observe how various individuals tell jokes about "canny Jews" in particular situations and to have independent data concerning the joke-tellers' views and intentions and concerning the meaning of the joke to the other people directly involved in the joke-telling.[14] The failure to carry out a series of thorough investigations of this kind has led to the quite unproven view that Jews telling jokes that have been labeled anti-Semitic on the basis of content alone must have accepted and internalized the negative and hostile view of their own people taken by anti-Semites. Such a view exists as a corollary of the assumptions that (A) comic statements are reduceable to their serious equivalents and (B) humor always involves superiority at the expense of others. When the members of a group enjoy jokes at the expense of their own group, assumptions A and B are undermined and so the self-denigration corollary is wheeled in to protect these two central assumptions.

I am much more convinced by the arguments of Ziv [1986A, 55–56] that "self-disparaging" jokes told by Jews in the face of both external hostility and internal division are ways of coping with a harsh reality by making it temporarily appear less threatening. Also, internal differentiation and divisions always allow ethnic jokes to be told about another section of the joke-teller's own group, one to which he or she does not belong [e.g., see Ben-Amos 1973, 123]. However, even if the joke is not redirected in this way, those who laugh at jokes about their own group still have a number of alternative interpretations open to them. In a world where accusation X is seriously made against one's own group, a self-told ethnic joke on theme X is more likely to be a pleasant alternative to and relief from the seriously made accusation than evidence that the accusation is believed by those members of the accused group participating in the joke. Similarly, where such jokes were told by Jews to potentially unsympathetic outsiders they seem to have been a means of appeasing, disarming, and, in a subtle way, mocking hostile others. It is, after all, a technique very widely and successfully used by politicians to undermine particular accusations made against them as individuals. Thus Barry Goldwater, Lyndon B. Johnson, John F. Kennedy, and Adlai Stevenson told jokes about themselves as being, respectively, "reactionary," "a wheeler-dealer," "a Roman Catholic ruled by the Pope," and "overintellectual" [Schutz 1977, 265–72]. They knew what the key negative aspect of their public image was and they sought to dissolve it in jokes. Even though groups cannot be reduced to collective individuals (as the self-hatred thesis demands), the analogy is a reasonable one. Nonetheless, all such views are speculative and we should remain agnostic concerning the meanings and functions of this kind of joking behavior until we have better evidence than is presently available.

There is, though, one useful extra piece of relevant evidence that content analysis can and does provide, namely, the existence of a large number of other, esoteric Jewish scripts for jokes [see Raskin 1985, 221] which show Jewish cleverness in a positive way [see Davies 1986B, 78–82] or which depict anti-Semitism as a malign tragedy and the creed of the stupid and bigoted. If these scripts are placed alongside the "self-critical" ones they provide an overall composite picture of Jewish jokes that is richly varied rather than compulsively masochistic.

A teacher in a German private school was berating her only Jewish pupil.

"You are just like the rest of your race—selfish, greedy, and inconsiderate of others. Here your father pays tuition for only one student, but are you satisfied, Jew? No, you have to learn enough for three!" [Spalding 1969, 195]

A Jew was walking on a street in Berlin when he accidentally brushed against a black-shirted storm-trooper [*sic*].

"Swine!" roared the Nazi.

"Plotnick" said the Jew, bowing. [Wilde 1980A, 115]

An official brought the chief rabbi of a town before the Court of the Inquisition and told him, "We will leave the fate of your people to God. I'm putting two slips of paper in this box. On one is written 'Guilty,' on the other is written 'Innocent.' Draw."

Now this Inquisitor was known to seek the slaughter of all the Jews and he had written Guilty on both pieces of paper.

The rabbi put his hand inside the box, withdrew a slip of paper and swallowed it.

"What are you doing?" cried the Inquisitor. "How will the Court know—"

"That's simple," said the rabbi. "Examine the slip that's in the box. If it reads 'Innocent' then the paper I swallowed obviously must have read 'Guilty.' But if the paper in the box reads 'Guilty' then the one I swallowed must have read 'Innocent.' " [Rosten 1970, 110]

Two Jews were sitting in a crowded tram in Soviet Russia. All around them Russians were grumbling that the Jews had seats while they were standing: "Isn't it typical that these wretched Yids still have all the places that should belong to us Russians." "Ah," said one Jew to the other, "if only we had something to eat, we could imagine we were back in the time of the Tsars." [Soviet Jewish 1980s]

I am also skeptical of the view that jokes based on the canniness script are an important vehicle for expressing anti-Semitic sentiments. During the successive waves of virulent anti-Semitism that have swept through much of the Christian world in the nineteenth and twentieth centuries, and indeed since medieval times, those hostile to the Jews have expressed their aggression with brutal directness through abuse and slander, pogroms and genocide.[15] Any contribution that jokes may have made to this vicious history has been an utterly trivial one by comparison, and indeed anti-Semites seeking to stir up hatred [Crosland 1922, 18; Hitler 1974, 287] have complained that the prevailing comic image of the Jews renders familiar, insignificant, and harmless the very group that they wish to depict as a dangerous menace. Religious and racial anti-Semitic propaganda uses themes such as deicide, sorcery, the poisoning of non-Jews, the ritual murder of children, or the manipulation of malign international power and depicts the Jews as a disease, as bacilli, parasites, lice, maggots, vampires, as a spider or an octopus strangling and consuming the world.[16] With rhetoric and images like these, who needs jokes? Why should those whom we know to have been and who in some countries continue to be overtly aggressive bother to mask their hatred with humor? Such people may well employ jokes and humor as one incidental rhetorical technique, but it is difficult to see that this is of any importance. The only distinguishing characteristic of the "humor" of grossly anti-Semitic people that I can discern is that they derive amusement from the torment and humiliation that they themselves have been able to inflict on individual Jews [e.g., see Feinburg 1978, 38–39]. When I have asked colleagues who have made detailed historical or ethnographic studies of anti-Semitic political movements in Britain about the importance of hostile ethnic joking they have been surprised at the question, for it had never come to their attention as a particularly significant phenomenon.

In the Western world, anti-Semitism, though it still exists, has not been respectable since the Holocaust unleashed by the National Socialists. However, modern contextual studies of non-Jews telling jokes about Jews do not indicate that such jokes are a cloak for a hidden, unrespectable anti-Semitism but rather display a diversity parallel to that found when such jokes are told by Jews. As Lawrence Mintz [1986, 130], in the conclusion of one such study, put it:

> The continuum of the motives and functions of ethnic joking acknowledges that no single theory explains the phenomenon. The meaning of the joke-

> telling is tied to the teller and the audience as well as being in the text, and the effect of the humor can be subtle and complex. In this sense the ethnic joking experience corresponds to the serious relationship of Jews and Gentiles in an urban, mixed religious, mixed ethnic environment, providing a safe, traditionally-licensed opportunity for exploration and expression of sensitive social and cultural needs.

When jokes about "canny Jews" occur without a clearly known context in the mass media or in joke-books they are apt to arouse suspicion or even protest because the real horrors of the past lead people to fear the worst—that the jokes could be a cloak for a serious anti-Semitic statement. Similarly, when subjects are presented with a set of jokes in a formal and even self-consciously scientific setting and asked to fill in questionnaires about them, they are apt to regard the jokes as being closer to serious statements than they would in a context where numerous other cues provide the reassurance that these are jokes and that the aim is laughter for its own sake. Because anti-Semitism is a reality and anti-Caledonianism is not, anthologies of ethnic jokes about Jews, in marked contrast to parallel books about Scots, often contain an explicit reassurance to their readers that no harm, offense, or reference to particular individuals is intended [e.g., see Crompton 1970E, 5; Hicks 1936, 214–15; Junior 1927] and sometimes the jokes are an ethnically bowdlerized version of those in oral circulation [e.g., see Wilde 1979A, 31; 1980A, 34 and 116]. Even where the jokes and the anthologists are obviously of Jewish origin editors have felt obliged to fend off explicitly the criticism [e.g., see Geiger 1923] that the placing of anecdotes about Jewish canniness in general circulation may provide extra ammunition for those who hold a strong, serious, and hostile stereotype of the Jews. But such people already have an ample supply of lethal weapons and are disdainful of jokes. Even today, when direct expressions of anti-Semitism rightly provoke criticism, anti-Semites have other preferred disguises than humor with which to cloak their animosity. Anti-Semitism is currently dressed up as antiracism, anti-Zionism [see Academic Study Group 1985; Eban 1976], the punishment of "economic crime," a campaign against "rootless cosmopolitanism," political denigration of the "Hymies" of "Hymietown," or "historical revisionism," a bland term for denying that the Nazi Holocaust ever occurred. Even as I was writing this chapter, organizations denying the reality of the Holocaust sent me, and a large number of my colleagues, a variety of unsolicited pamphlets on this theme from the anonymity of P. O. Box numbers. It is here that the anti-Semites have taken refuge, not in the world of jokes.

Yet the view is still put forward that the jokes told in Britain about the German hatred and persecution of the Jews during World War II [see Kravitz 1977, 186–87; McCosh 1976] are primarily a means of covertly expressing aggression against the Jews, since otherwise this is not permissible in British society because of the memory of past atrocities. When the meaning of a joke has to be stretched and strained to this extent to make it fit the theory it is a sign that the theory is in trouble. At the very time when the joke-tellers in British society are telling jokes about the atrocities, the anti-Semites are denying that the atrocities ever happened.

A further such point may be made in relation to the contrast between the insignificant practical consequences of jokes about Jewish insurance-arson and the deliberate selection of Jews for execution for "economic crimes" in the Soviet Union, where official discriminatory amplification of alleged ethnic wrongdoing [Parry 1966, 197] has had dire consequences. After the death penalty for economic crimes was reintroduced by the Soviets in 1961, as a matter of policy 60 percent of those put to death were Jews [Parry 1966, 198]. This was both a consequence of anti-Semitism and a means of stirring up further anti-Semitic hatred together with the revival of charges of mass poisoning and ritual murder by Jews [Levin 1979, 48–52].

My point in stressing the nasty realities of anti-Semitism is to indicate how unimportant and impotent ethnic jokes are when compared to the political malice of the powerful and the deliberate propagation of an overtly hostile ideology. In studying and accounting for anti-Semitism it is the latter alone that are important. Once this is clearly established we will at last be able to study even these potentially most tendentious of ethnic jokes as an aspect of humor rather than a twiglet of a branch of the sociology of persecution. Ethnic jokes about "canny" "excluded enterprisers" are not a significant factor in the generation of the bizarre patterns of hostility regarding such peoples. There is inevitably an overlap between the content of the jokes and the content of these hostile ideologies but the jokes are not themselves part of the ideology.

The absence of anti-Caledonianism and of a serious and widely held view of the Scots as alien and threatening accounts for the rare and innocuous character of jokes about Scots and fire insurance, for there is no preexisting set of serious negative images for the joke-inventors to play with. The few jokes that exist about Scotsmen seeking to deceive insurance companies lack the key threatening elements of a premeditated collective conspiracy and the probable destruction of others:

A Scottish farmer put in an insurance claim after one of his barns burned down. The insurance agent who came round to settle the claim took the opportunity to try and sell him some more insurance.

'Why don't you take out insurance against theft,' he asked him, 'or even against floods?'

'Floods?' queried the canny Scot. 'Floods? How do you start a flood?' [Ranke 1972, 119. For Jewish versions lacking a rural setting see *Further Sunbeams* 1924, 124; and Geiger 1923, 11]

This joke is innocuous, partly because it is rural. An isolated farm building burning down does not constitute a sudden menace that could randomly maim or destroy people living nearby. To set one's own barn alight is dishonest and antisocial but such an act cannot be represented as posing a sinister threat to the rest of society.

The setting of the joke is also a reminder of the balanced social image of the Scots, who are thought of and, in consequence, laughed at as crofters, soldiers, caddies, ship's engineers, workers, factors, doctors, ghillies, Presbyterian ministers and missionaries, as well as businessmen. As a result the "canny Scots" of the jokes pursue a great variety of callings, whereas the Jews tend to be shown as traders whose main link with others is through buying and selling. The latter image is one which can be manipulated by the unscrupulous for the benefit of the ignorant so as to depict the Jews as unproductive and parasitic. That the Jews have long been a largely urban people and indeed have often been prohibited from owning land so that they have rarely worked as farmers has often been used to stir up hostility against them among people with rural occupations or a strong sense of local territorial identity. For tradition-bound rural people the city represents a distant source of unpredictable and threatening economic change and modernization, and this view can be exploited along both nonethnic and ethnic lines to produce hostility and violence. Under these circumstances the members of a distinctively urban group defined as alien are particularly vulnerable.

The broad and benign image of groups such as the Scots as farmers, soldiers, engineers, etc., is in marked contrast to the serious and comic images of the Jews and other excluded enterprisers as smart but unheroic urban peddlers lacking in physical toughness and courage. This dichotomy comes across consistently in jokes which pair together and contrast the "canny Scot" and the "canny Jew." George Orwell [1968, vol. 2, 338] wrote of the British music-hall jokes of the 1930s:

> Occasionally a story is told (e.g., the Jew and the Scotsman who went into a pub together and both died of thirst) which puts both races on an equality. But in general the Jew is credited merely with cunning and avarice while the Scotsman is credited with physical hardihood as well. This is seen, for example, in the story of the Jew and the Scotsman who go together to a meeting which has been advertised as free. Unexpectedly there is a collection and to avoid this the Jew faints and the Scotsman carries him out. Here the Scotsman performs the athletic feat of carrying the other. It would seem vaguely wrong if it were the other way about.

Orwell's point may be illustrated by further examples:

An Aberdonian and a Jew had an argument and decided to settle it in the ring. The Jew thought to pull a fast one so he bet the Aberdonian to win. But the Aberdonian, thinking along the same lines, bet the Jew. In the ring the Aberdonian threw a punch, the Jew lay down, the referee started to count. At the count of nine the Aberdonian went over to where the Jew was lying and kicked him. The Aberdonian lost on a disqualification. [SFGB]

The usual trio consisting of an Englishman, a Scotsman and a Jew (the Irishman was ill) had a nine course meal at an expensive restaurant and the waiter presented them with a bill for £42.

'I'll pay that,' offered the Scotsman.

Prominent headlines in the following day's paper said 'JEWISH VENTRILOQUIST FOUND DEAD IN ALLEY.' [Crompton 1970E, 9]

The use of brute force by the Scots to counter the tricks of the Jews appears almost as a virtue in these jokes. Once again in the background is the reputation of the Scots as fierce and reliable defenders of territory on whose prowess their allies can depend. By contrast the second aspect of the pejorative view of the excluded enterprisers often taken by the indigenous host people is that they are intrinsically alien and lacking in national loyalty. Such a view may be quite untrue, but the members of both communities know that it is widely held by the majority and so it is hardly surprising to see it emerge in jokes told by either group.

Who has got the "largest collection of flags" in South-East Asia?

The Chinese—"one for each government that might come into control of the state." [Von der Melden 1976, 218. Cf. joke about Druze, in Zenner 1970, 110]

The head of the Bulgarian secret service desperately needed to obtain some vital documents that were in the possession of the British intelligence service. He sent his two best agents to London to try and get them back, but they failed to return. Finally he called in an Armenian agent from Plovdiv called Kirkov.

"Do you think you can get those papers back for me?" he asked him.

"Of course," replied the Armenian. "My friend Garabet works for British intelligence in London and I'll get him to procure the documents for you."

"But how do you know he will do you such an enormous favor?"

"Why not? He owes me several such favors." [Bulgarian 1980s]

Definition of a patriotic South African—A Jewish doctor who can't sell his house. [South African 1980s]

Two Jews who had not seen each other for several years met by chance in the street in Warsaw and began to exchange news about their families.

"Tell me," said one, "What is your eldest boy, Moishe, doing these days? He always was a bright lad."

"Yes indeed," replied the father, "He's made a brilliant career for himself in Prague. He's been really successful there and everyone says he's helping to build socialism."

"And what about your second boy, Chaim?"

"Well he's working in Moscow now and he's done very well too. He's getting a very good salary and doing really skilled work. And of course he's helping to build socialism there."

"Now didn't you have a third son, Isaac? What has become of him?"

"Oh he's done better than any of them. He emigrated to Israel and he's gone straight to the top of his profession."

"And is he helping to build socialism too?"

"Oh no, he wouldn't do a thing like that—not to his own country." [Polish 1970s]

Two [East] Africans are quarreling; one African points to the sky and says, "That's the sun" while the other, with his foe in a neckhold says, "No, it's the moon!" An Asian shop-keeper walks by and the Africans stop fighting; "Just to settle an argument," says the first African, "Can you tell us whether that's the sun or the moon?" "Sorry," says the Asian, shrugging, "This isn't my country, I can't say." [Theroux 1967, 51]

Theroux cites this latter joke as an instance of the similarity between the self-deprecating quality of the humor of the East African Asians and that of the Jews. Yet this joke, like the others quoted, is particularly funny because it has so many potential meanings depending on which and whose view of the situation is taken.

The only constant element in "canny" jokes about excluded enterprisers is that all parties to the jokes know that behind the joke there is a real world in which the members of these particular "canny" minorities are seen by the self-defined indigenous majority as alien, clever, and untrustworthy. It is a situation that can and does end in real tragedy, but here it is used to construct a make-believe comedy. We cannot fully understand the comedy without having a thorough knowledge of the tragedy, yet the comedy exists in and of itself and is played according to a quite different set of rules. Once ethnic jokes about the "canny" have been calibrated by reference to independent evidence it is then possible to use the content analysis of jokes to infer whether the social situation of the butts of the jokes is a benign one or whether they are likely to experience the hostility leveled against those who have become defined as excluded enterprisers. However, we cannot use content analysis to deduce the feelings and attitudes of the joke-tellers, which can only be discovered by observation of the context and the way in which the joke is told. We can deduce from content alone what the joke-tellers know is believed about the butts of the jokes in their society, for without that knowledge they could neither invent nor appreciate the jokes, but we can say nothing about how they regard what they know, nor whether they have a purpose in telling the joke. The same joke can be used for all manner of conflicting purposes, or none at all. Jokes are ambiguous comic utterances that have a life of their own.

CHAPTER SIX

How Ethnic Jokes Change: The Evolution of the Stupid and the Canny

For much of this study I have treated ethnic jokes as a relatively unchanging phenomenon based on immutable ethnic scripts of stupidity or canniness, drunkenness or consumption of inferior food. Even where I have described the evolution of particular ethnic jokes over time, as in the case of the "cowardly" and "militarist" ethnic scripts, the continuities have been more important than the changes. I now wish to concentrate deliberately on the phenomenon of change in the case of the basic "stupid" and "canny" ethnic scripts. I have by and large limited my analysis to jokes told in the English language, which unfortunately precludes any detailed analysis of changes in jokes involving the Jews. On the other hand, English jokes about the "canny Scots" and the "stupid Irish" can be traced back to the eighteenth and seventeenth centuries respectively, and jokes about the Welsh have an even more ancient and honorable pedigree that stretches back certainly to Tudor England and probably even to medieval times [see Gaidoz and Sébillot 1884, 337]. In the nineteenth and twentieth centuries these slowly evolving jokes are to be found throughout the English-speaking world, and the replacement of the Irish by the Poles in American but not British or Australian jokes about stupidity is a striking phenomenon that must be analyzed.

One problem that does arise in looking at the ethnic jokes of the past is that we are entirely dependent on written and usually printed sources. Also, we cannot be fully sure that these were the ethnic jokes that people told, especially in a world where most people were illiterate. For this reason I have in places cautiously supplemented my examples of ethnic jokes with lines of comic dialogue about the butts of the jokes taken from contemporary plays. So far as I can tell, the writers' main intention in introducing such humor was to gain a laugh by alluding to an ethnic script with which the audience was already familiar. I have, however, done so sparingly, because plays, like cartoons or caricatures but unlike jokes, have an author and therefore an element of deliberation built into them. They do not fit easily into the pattern of "spontaneous order" that characterizes jokes. Nonetheless, such examples do help to establish the reliability of the patterns to be observed in the jokes available from the limited number of early jest-books that have survived. In any case, the censorship and precensorship of the humor of earlier days were concerned more with avoiding blasphemy and obscenity and with preserving the power and dignity of the rulers of church and state than with protecting the susceptibilities of ethnic minorities. There were no media "liberals," in the modern American Tom Lehrer and Phil Ochs sense of the word, available to censor out ethnic jokes on the grounds that they might be construed as degrading and demeaning to the autochthonous Welsh aboriginals. For the same reason, I have not hesitated in places to cite later editions and anthologies of many of these early works. Many of them are facsimiles, and though Victorian editors and anthologists were tempted to bowdlerize sexual or scatological jokes, they did not otherwise tinker with or omit jokes based on ethnic scripts.

In previous chapters ethnic jokes about stupidity and canniness have been treated as essentially modern in order to explain the extraordinary and universal proliferation of such jokes in recent times. However, jokes about the stupid and the canny, though less numerous in the past, do have a long history and the shifts that have taken place, both in the content of these jokes and in the identity of the groups who have been the butts of such jokes, provide further insights into the nature of ethnic joking.

Jokes about stupid or canny individuals have long existed, and a number of studies of traditional tales about noodles and numskulls, blunderers, tricksters, and misers have been made.[1] These terms now have a curiously old-fashioned sound, but people do still tell jokes of this kind without any ethnic or place label attached to them. "Little Moron" jokes, for instance, were popular in the United States during World War II,[2] at a time when many people were taking on new, and to them, strange industrial tasks and skills in settings where the result of stupidity might be disaster.

However, there has also long existed a strong and systematic tendency to fasten such jokes onto a particular group of people. Indeed the jokes told today in Egypt about the simplicity of the Nubians are based on a comic stereotype of the Nubians that is thousands of years old. The Egyptologist Peter Clayton has claimed that such jokes "probably go back to the dawn of time. . . . The Nubians were the butt of Egyptian humour just as the Irish are the victims of modern English jokes."[3] The Nubians then, as now, lived on the southern periphery of Egyptian civilization, a group of distant rustic provincials, neither entirely foreign nor wholly Egyptian.[4] The ancient origin of ethnic jokes of this type was noted at least as long ago as 1622 when Thomas Fuller wrote:

> Men in all ages have made themselves merry with singling out some place, and fixing the staple of stupidity and stolidity therein. Thus the Phrygians were accounted the Fools of all Asia and the anvils of other men's wits to work upon. . . . In Grecia take a single City, and then Abdera in Thracia carried it away for Dullheads. . . . But for a whole Countrey, commend us to the Boeotians for Block-heads; and Boeoticum ingenium is notoriously known. [1811 (1622) vol. II, 206]

The Boeotians, like so many other butts of ethnic jokes about stupidity, were the rustic peasant neighbors of a great urban metropolis [Andrewes 1971, 101]. The ancient jokes of the city-dwellers of Athens about the predominantly pastoral and agricultural Boeotians or about the citizens of Abdera in Thrace survive even today in the mocking terms *Boeotian*, meaning a rude and unlettered dullard, and *Abderite* and *Abderitic* for a simpleton [see *Brewer's* 1981; Grambs 1986, 27; von Wieland 1861].

Many of the jokes of the classical world told about allegedly stupid communities such as Cumae near modern Naples, Abdera, Miletus, and Sidon have been preserved and are known today[5] [see Clouston 1888; Esar 1978, 6, 61–62, 95, 196, 295; Ferguson 1968]. Such cities and regions were often seen as ambiguous; peoples mocked by the Ancient Greeks, for instance, often lived in Greek cities at the edge of Greek civilization or were surrounded and indeed influenced and culturally penetrated by barbarians. Jokes about their stupidity thus have similarities with modern ethnic jokes.

The father of a man of Cumae having died at Alexandria, the son dutifully took the body to the embalmers. When he returned at the appointed time to fetch it away there happened to be a number of bodies in the same place so he was asked if his father had any peculiarity by which his body might be recognized and the wittol replied, 'He had a cough'. [Clouston 1888, 15]

A man of Abdera was trying to hang himself but the rope broke and he cut his head. He went to the doctor to have it patched up and then returned and hanged himself. [Ferguson 1968, 96]

Jokes about foolish communities are later to be found all over Europe.[6] Just as today every country has its own ethnic jokes about stupidity, so in the past every region had a community whose alleged stupidity formed the basis of many jests and anecdotes—Gotham and Austwick in England, Risca and Abercregan in Wales, Gordon and Assynt in Scotland, Domna, Fünsing, Mundinga, Schilde (Laleburg), and Teterow in various parts of Germany, Mols and Agger in Denmark, Kampen in Holland, Dinant in Belgium, Malleghem in Flanders, Cuneo and Cava in Italy, Selpice, Vazec,

Zahorie, Prelouch, and Nová Lhota in Czechoslovakia, Beira in Portugal, Sivri-Hissar in Turkey, Pitsiliá in Cyprus, Saint-Maixent in France, Ràtót in Hungary, Belmont in Switzerland, Nagoya in Japan, to name but a few. In some countries there were a number of such "foolish" communities that became the butt of jokes, indeed as many as fifty have been noted in Britain alone [Briggs 1970, Part A, vol.2, 1–5 and 1977, 51–53]. The reputation of a community for comic stupidity may well last for several hundred years [Stapleton 1900].

Like their modern ethnic equivalents, the "fooltown" jokes render the despised quality of stupidity comic and export it to another group living on the periphery of the joke-teller's social world. In societies where people define who they are in terms of their membership of a local community, they tell jokes about the stupidity of the people of some other local community, that is, they define who they are not in terms of a social unit similar to the one which gives them their basic identity. It is worth noting that in many cases the people of the fooltown are or were originally of an ethnic origin distinctly different from that of those telling jokes about them [see Briggs 1970, Part A, 1–5; 1977, 51; Sobotka 1919]. In ethnically homogeneous communities it was often the people of the next village, township, or parish who were seen as rivals, a local group known to be essentially similar to one's own and yet also held to be inferior, though perhaps only by location. If the sense of superiority to one's rival was buttressed by the recognizable advantages that a community at the center of things has over a more remote community at the periphery, or that an urban center has over its rural hinterland, then jokes about the alleged stupidity of the latter are likely to emerge. The jokes about the villages of Gotham, Tadley, and Abercregan in Britain certainly seem to reflect their position as relatively isolated communities seen in contrast to the busy commercial and manufacturing towns of Nottingham, Reading, and Port Talbot where the jokes were told [see Searing 1984; Stapleton 1900].

The decline of these local jokes and their replacement by Irish jokes in Britain is in part due to the rise of a national network of radio and television and the closing of the local theaters and music halls in which touring comedians performed in the past adapting their material to make use of local comic images. Comedians with a mass audience tell ethnic jokes which latch onto ethnic scripts, images, and joke-conventions which are widely understood and abandon local references which have only a very local and restricted meaning. Similar economies of scale have led to the dwarfing of local joke-books published in small batches by nationally available books of ethnic jokes. The inventors of individual jokes are still spread anonymously throughout the population, and jokes are fed upward from the people to the script-writers and compilers of joke-books, who switch, disperse, and dispense them back again, but the frame within which both groups operate and the scripts they use now tend to be ethnic in character.

A more fundamental and indeed often a much earlier reason for the switch to ethnic jokes is the decay of people's sense of being primarily members of a local community and its replacement by ethnic nationalism as the basis of their identity [see Smith 1981, 69–71]. People's sense of what they are not has also become ethnic to match the change in their perception of themselves. With this change stupidity has to be exported into the domain of another ethnic group rather than dumped on a mere rival local community. Also, the intrusion of the urban world into rural areas has increased to a point where once-remote villages have become part of an integrated economy of increasingly mobile people [see Pahl 1968, 269–77].

One indication that the change from local to ethnic jokes about stupidity has been the result of the rise of national and ethnic loyalties at the expense of local ones is that jokes about "stupid" towns and villages have survived best in countries where national identity is relatively weak and local ties are very strong, such as Italy or Syria and Lebanon [see Longrigg 1958]. Thus in Italy there are jokes about the characteristics of the people of almost every city and province, and it is significant that comic stupidity, when not pinned on Southern Italians, in general is often assigned to the people of Cuneo, a town at the very edge of Italy, almost on the border with France at the foot of the Alpes Maritimes. Local jokes, as distinct from ethnic or national jokes, are even more prevalent in Syria and Lebanon. In both countries many jokes are still told about the stupid quarrels of the inhabitants of two towns, Homs and Hama, on the River Asi (Orentes) [see UCBFA Lebanese file; Clouston 1888, 16; Zenner 1970, 108].

In many countries in which the inhabitants of a town or a district are depicted in jokes as foolish or canny, the small community of the jokes may symbolize or stand for a larger region or a deeper division. Thus Persian jokes about people from the northwestern provincial town of Rasht in Iran refer to the Turkish-speaking minority who live on the borders of Iran with Turkey and Azerbaijan. Similarly, Danish jokes about the people of the town of Århus, which is very close to Mols, a small, once remote rural settlement that was traditionally a butt for Danish jokes about stupidity [see Colleville and de Zepelin 1896, 27, 30–31; Craigie 1898, 220; Rockwell 1981, 285], may well refer to Jutes in general, for Århus is the capital of Jutland, one of the three major sea-girt subdivisions of Denmark [see Holbek 1975]. Guatemalan jokes about Guitecos, the people of the "Indian" town of Guite, east of Guatemala City, are probably ethnic jokes about Indians, as distinct from the people of Spanish descent or culture who live in the capital [see Toledo 1965, 82–85, 93–135].

Two Guitecos arrived at Guatemala City and wanted to take to their town the National Palace because they thought it was beautiful and they did not have an equal in their town. They then put down their suitcases on the ground and began to push the building. After two hours they saw that their suitcases were not there and one said "Already we've gone far, because we cannot see the suitcases." [UCBFA Guatemala file]

Jokes about canny towns have survived better than those about fool-towns, so that jokes are still told and indeed invented about the "canny" citizens of Aberdeen in Scotland, Laihia in Finland, Gabrovo in Bulgaria, Isfahan in Iran, Genoa, Milan, Florence in Italy, Mosul in Iraq, Monterrey in Mexico, and Paphos in Cyprus. However, here too there is a tendency for ethnic jokes about Scotsmen or Jews to oust local "canny" jokes. Today Frenchmen know more jokes about Scots than about Auvergnats, and more Scottish jokes are told in Wales than jokes about canny Cardis. In the United States jokes about canny New England Yankees now sound old-fashioned and almost nostalgic and cannot compete against the tide of Scottish and Jewish jokes. Jokes about Jews and Scotsmen are widespread, partly because these two ethnic groups form visible minorities in so many countries, but jokes about the Scots have become very popular in countries without Scotsmen, such as Hungary, Czechoslovakia, Greece, Italy, France, Sweden, or Yugoslavia. Even in countries such as Bulgaria, Finland, or Germany, with a strong tradition of jokes about a "canny" local group, jokes about the Scots are well known and anthologies of jokes about Scots or Jews may be available in the local language. Jokes are widely told about the "canny" inhabitants of Aberdeen in Scotland, but for most people outside Scotland Aberdonian jokes are simply Scottish jokes. Once again a town stands for an ethnic group.

Although ethnic jokes have tended to replace jokes about smaller communities or groups, the latter often survive locally and indeed the ethnic jokes that prevail across a nation or even internationally may well get adapted for local use. In the United States, for instance, the ubiquitous Polish jokes about stupidity appear locally as ethnic jokes about the Portuguese in San Francisco, the Italians in New Jersey, the Belgians in Wisconsin, etc., and also as jokes about the inhabitants of particular states such as Indiana versus Kentucky or even the students and alumni of a university such as Texas A&M (the Aggies), Virginia Tech (the Hokies), or Carolina State. In Britain the standard pair of ethnic jokes about the stupid and the canny, which are usually told about the Irish and the Scots, have a more restricted equivalent in the north of England where jokes about "canny Yorkshiremen" and "stupid Lancastrians" have a long history[7] and indeed have outlived the county administrative units that gave rise to them. The local inhabitants often still identify themselves with one of the two great northern rivals, Lancashire or Yorkshire [see Spencer 1938, 247–48], and their associated roses, cricket teams, and distinctive patterns of speech, and, in Yorkshire, even with the now obsolete "ridings" into which Yorkshire was divided.

British jokes about "canny Yorkshiremen" can be found as early as the eighteenth century and still survive today, though on nothing like the scale of jokes about the Scots. The English saying "He's too far north for me," meaning "He's too canny, too cunning, a hard bargainer," refers to the people of Yorkshire in the north of England, though it can also apply to the people who live much further north, in Scotland or even Aberdeen [see *Brewer's* 1981, 791], and "To come Yorkshire over any one" meant to cheat him [Grose, 1971]. The strength of Nonconformist Protestantism in the manufacturing towns of what used to be the West Riding of Yorkshire may well underlie the image of the "canny Yorkshireman." In the old East Riding of Yorkshire "canny" jokes were told about the people of the West Riding. Lancashire, by contrast, has long had one of the highest proportions of Roman Catholics (about 1 in 3 compared with about 1 in 10 for England and Wales) of any county in England and Wales. There has always been a high proportion of native English Roman Catholics in West Lancashire [Braxap 1910, 3], but their modern preponderance is largely due to heavy Irish immigration [Walker 1981, 7–10], so there may well be an ethnic element in the jokes. "Manchester" has long been a synonym for capitalism, industrialism, and a commercial and utilitarian view of the world, but the early factories and cotton mills of Lancashire were often larger than those of the Yorkshire woolen industry and employed unskilled and often female labor in contrast to the skilled workers and small entrepreneurs who constituted the "canny tykes" of the West Riding. The male tacklers or overlookers in Lancashire were often the butt of jokes about stupidity told by the weavers, who were mainly women [see Spencer 1938, 265]. Men in families, industries, communities such as Pitsiliá in Cyprus or Penclawdd in Wales (and by extension in counties such as Lancashire) based on female work and earnings are often the butt of jokes that make them out to be generally gormless [see Rockwell 1981, 51].

The "canny" and "stupid" jokes told locally in England about Yorkshire and Lancashire have long been overshadowed by jokes about the Scots and the Irish, and these latter jokes are to be found throughout the English-speaking world and in many other countries besides. To understand how ethnic jokes about the "canny" and the "stupid" have evolved it will be useful to try to uncover something of the history of jokes about the Irish and the Scots in Britain, the United States, and the rest of the English-speaking world. The aim of looking at this data will be to try to find the origins and trace the rise of such jokes and to see how they change over time. Ethnic jokes have no single author and are not part of a purpose or plan: when looked at en masse they exhibit a spontaneous and not a planned order. It is futile, therefore, to seek in them an accurate reflection of short-term fluctuations in the general affective sentiments that the joke-tellers hold toward the butts of their jokes. There are other and better indices of conflict, tension, or amity available and it has not been demonstrated that these correlate well with shifts in the content of jokes. Also, at any one time, the stock of ethnic jokes in existence is enormously greater than the rate of creation of new jokes or the slow demise of old ones.

It is even more doubtful that the anonymous inventors of jokes are unconsciously motivated by the need to keep intact those theories of functionalist or conflict sociology which apply the dynamics of small-group cohesion to nations or sizable ethnic entities. Those who are foolish enough to try to read popular sentiments or changes in sentiment into ethnic jokes about the Irish, Scots, and Welsh [e.g., see Curtis 1985] should have learned from the difficulties experienced by J. O. Bartley (1954), in his exhaustive study of stage plays and notably comedies involving stage Celts, and by L. Perry Curtis [1971; see also Kissane 1986, 40–43], in his attempt to explain British and American cartoons and caricatures of the Irish. Since plays and cartoons have, respectively, authors and artists who are trying to please individual theater-managers or editors as well as the public, they are, in principle, more likely to be shaped to fit the prevailing sentiment of the day. Also, we can usually put an exact date on them, corresponding to their first publication or production. Even so, Bartley's assessment of the contemporary reception and perception of stage Celts, though as good as it could be, is necessarily tentative, uncertain, and qualified, for the surviving detailed and unbiased accounts of actual productions and performances are few.

To give an example of the problems Bartley faced I will merely note that during the German military occupation of the British Channel Islands in 1940–45 the Nazis condemned a performance of Shakespeare's *Merchant of Venice* as being too sympathetic to the Jews and banned "Kiss Me Goodnight, Sergeant-Major" as encouraging disrespect for the military [see Wood and Wood 1976, 203]. Given the position and feelings of the islanders, the wretched National Socialists, however repellent their values, may even have been right in their perception of what was going on in the minds of the local people.

In Perry Curtis's work the problem is that he has selected his examples from a political context [Gilley 1978, 97]. Since the very point of political caricature is to provide a savage visual encapsulation of a particular political point of view and humor is a mere means to an end, there is nothing surprising in his findings that cartoon caricatures of the Irish in Britain and America followed the ups and downs of political controversies in which the Irish were involved either as a national or as an ethnic minority. In a free society political caricature is used to ridicule monarchs, politicians, and social classes [see Gombrich and Kris 1940; Krumbhaar 1966], as well as ethnic groups to the extent that they are explicitly involved in a political conflict. Indeed, the image of the Irish MacSimius that haunted Perry Curtis was still alive and well in the United States in the 1970s in the caricatures of Cardinal Cooke, whose "illiberal" views on money-making, abortion, the Vietnam war, birth control, evolution, and the solar system seem to have outraged the cartoonist Edward Sorel [1978]. Equally to the point is that most cartoonists are not concerned about scoring political points but are exercising a talent to amuse. It is perhaps unfortunate that we use the same word *cartoon* to describe both a largely visual political comment, which may or may not be funny or intended to be funny, and a visual or illustrated joke that usually has no political point to make. The latter may with caution be classed with the more anonymous verbal jokes, but as soon as this is done it becomes clear that Perry Curtis's analysis in terms of contemporary politics and ideology no longer works [see Gilley 1978, 82–85].

It is even more true of verbal ethnic jokes that they cannot usually be explained by reference to the chance shifts of political, ideological, and national conflict. There are, of course, links and parallels between ethnic and political jokes, but these tend to refer directly to political events, whereas most of life and most jokes remain in the realm of the social. The pattern of ethnic jokes does change systematically in response to profound social and economic changes, but it does so slowly and often after a marked time-lag.

British jokes about the supposed irrationality of the Irish first began to be common in the seventeenth century, and in the following century there was an enormous increase in their number and popularity. One of the earliest examples, about an Irish servant in England, is to be found in the 1633 joke-book *Banquet of Jests* [see Wardroper 1970, 67]:

An Irish servant was asked by his master to bring him a pint of claret and a pint of sack (sherry). The servant poured both into one pot and said "I prithee, master, drink off the claret first for the sack is all in the bottom."

In the 1680s appeared what was perhaps the first Irish joke-book, entitled *Teagueland Jests or Bogg Witticisms* [1690, and see Bartley 1954, 209]. Teague is the Irish version of Timothy and was a nickname for an Irishman. Walter Jerrold has written of these early jest-books: "I have been struck by the high proportion of blunder-stories included in them and by the rapid increase of such after the second half of the seventeenth century, when the reputation for making blunders appears to have become fastened more particularly upon the Irishman" [1928, 9].

Irish jokes became very popular in the eighteenth century. There are more jokes about Irish blunderers in *Joe Miller's Jests or the WITS Vademecum* of 1739 than about any other ethnic group or any other trait ascribed to an ethnic group. By 1750 *Teagueland Jests or Bogg Witticisms* had reached at least its sixth edition and was renamed *The Irish miscellany* [Bartley 1954, 209]. The growing popularity of jokes about the Irish was stressed in the new introductory address to the reader: "The Welchman and Scots had a long time engrossed all the Table-talk of the Town; and the Jests and Stories that were related concerning them passed instead of a song or a fiddle. But Teague and his country-man have clearly baffled

Saint Taffy [Saint David of Wales] and Saint Andrew for downright Dunstable, Blunder and Punn."

Many of the eighteenth-century British jokes about the Irish, like later British and American jokes about them, can be linked to the migration of unskilled workers. In either case poor people from Ireland left their own country to seek unskilled but better-paid work elsewhere, and many Irish men and women sought employment in England as domestic servants. The English jokes of the early eighteenth century are often based on the verbal and practical blunders ascribed to Irish migrants grappling with the novelties of urban domestic employment [cf. Chesney's comment (1970, 67) about the Victorian Irish] and the unfamiliar speech of the English. On the basis of an extremely thorough analysis of Irish comic parts in English plays of this period, J. O. Bartley [1954, 206] has concluded that "Foreigners tend to blunder. Servants tend to blunder. Their blunders are humorous. A fortiori the blunders of foreign servants are peculiarly frequent and amusing. In the seventeenth century there was a large number of Irish servants in England." In the jokes of the seventeenth and early eighteenth century about Irish blunders, the central character is very often a servant:

A certain Lady of Quality, sending her *Irish* Footman to fetch Home a Pair of new Stays, strictly charged him to take a Coach if it rained, for fear of wetting them: But a great Shower of Rain falling, the Fellow returned with the stays dropping wet, and being severely reprimanded for not doing as he was ordered, he said, he had obey'd his Orders; how then, answered the Lady, could the Stays be wet, if you took them into the Coach with you? *No,* replyed honest Teague, *I knew my Place better, I did not go into the Coach, but rode* behind *as I always used to do.* [*Joe Miller* 1739, 44]

An *Irishman,* who King *Charles* II had some Esteem for, being only an inferior Servant of the household, one Day coming into the King's Presence, his Majesty ask'd him how his Wife did, who had just before been cut for a *Fistula* in her Backside. *I humbly thank your Majesty,* replied Teague, *she's like to do well, but the Surgeon says, it will be an Eye-Sore as long as she lives.* [*Joe Miller* 1739, 58]

An Irishman on board a man of war was desir'd by his mess mates to go down and fetch a cann of small Beer; Teague, knowing that preparations were making to sail, absolutely refus'd. Arrah! by my Soul, says he; and so while I am gone into the Cellar to fetch Beer the Ship will sail and leave me behind. [*The Joker or Merry Companion* 1763, 15]

Some of these jokers are about practical blunders committed by servants, but others depend for their humor on a distinctive error in the use of language which has become known as an "Irish bull." The Irish bull has been defined as a "self-contradictory proposition" or as "an expression containing a manifest contradiction in terms, or involving a ludicrous inconsistency unperceived by the speaker" [Bartley 1954, 207]. The Reverend Sydney Smith [1854, 68], writing in 1803, described the Irish bull as "an apparent congruity and real incongruity, of ideas, suddenly discovered. . . . the very reverse of wit, for as wit discovers real relations that are not apparent, bulls admit apparent relations that are not real." Yet the Irish bull can be wit as in John Mahaffy's definition: "An Irish bull is a male animal that is always pregnant" [Levinson 1963, 116]. Bartley [1954, 208] sees the Irish bull as a form of blunder that originally occurred in the speech of Irish peasants who had changed from being Gaelic-speakers to speaking English and had not learned to express themselves adequately in English. He argues that a failure to understand how their new language worked, together with a tendency to continue to use some of the forms and structures of their ancestors' tongue [see also Mercier 1962, 93–94], led to the making of bulls. The comparative study of ethnic jokes supports Bartley's thesis, for in the nineteenth and early twentieth centuries the English-speaking Lowlanders of Scotland told ethnic jokes about the bulls perpetrated by Gaelic-speaking Highlanders struggling with English [see Ford 1901], and in Wales there were similar anecdotes about Welsh-speakers with a shaky command of English [e.g., Coulton 1945, 173; Macdonald 1915, 89]. Bartley's explanation would certainly fit my generalization that the butts of jokes about stupidity tend to speak a version of the joke-tellers' language that the latter regard as ludicrous.

Jokes based on the Irish bull soon came to be told about Irishmen of acknowledged social standing also and were known in America too, though some of these may have been imported from Britain.

Lord R—— having lost about fifty Pistoles, one Night at the Gaming-Table in *Dublin,* some Friends condoling with him upon his ill luck, Faith, said he, I am very well pleas'd at what I have done, for I have bit them, by G—— there is not one pistole that don't want Six-Pence of Weight. [*Joe Miller* 1963 (1739), 4]

An *Irish* Lawyer of the *Temple,* having occasion to go to Dinner, left these Directions written, and put in the Key-Hole of his Chamber Door, *I am gone to the* Elephant *and* Castle, *where you shall find me*; and if *you can't read this Note, carry it down to the Stationer's and he will read it for you.* [*Joe Miller* 1963 (1739), 13]

An Irishman of the name of Scannel, who wished to get rid of his wife, wrote her a melancholy letter by the last mail from the West Indies in which he stated that he died of the yellow fever after three days illness and recommended her and their children to the care of Providence and his friends. [*The American Jest Book* 1800, 104. See also p.97]

An Irish lawyer had a client of his own country who was a sailor. During his absence at sea his wife had married again and he was resolved to prosecute her: coming to advise with his counsellor he was told that he must have witnesses to prove that he was alive when his wife married again. "Arrah, by my shoul but that will be impossible" said the other, "for my shipmates are all gone to sea again upon a long voyage and will not return this twelvemonth." "Oh then" answered the lawyer, "there can be nothing done in it: and what a pity it is that such a brave cause be lost now, only because you cannot prove yourself to be alive." [*The American Jest Book* 1833, 116]

Jokes involving Irish bulls grew steadily in popularity throughout the eighteenth century. Many of them were ascribed to the Irish politician Sir Boyle Roche, who was a member of the Irish Parliament in Dublin. J. O. Bartley comments:

> The theory of the gravid bull, and the attribution of bulls to the Irish, no doubt gained verisimilitude from the existence of one genuine bull-making Irishman in the late eighteenth century. Sir Boyle Roche—though he certainly never uttered half the remarks attributed to him—was accustomed to enliven the debates in College Green with some remarkable self-contradictions. Here is Barrington's account of one of them, when it was observed "that the House had no just right to load posterity with a weighty debt for what could in no degree operate to their advantage. Sir Boyle, eager to defend the measures of government, immediately rose, and, in a few words, put forward the most unanswerable argument which human ingenuity could possibly devise. 'What, Mr. Speaker!' said he, 'and so we are to beggar ourselves for fear of vexing posterity! Now I would ask the honourable gentlemen, and this *still more* honourable House, why we should put ourselves out of our way to do anything for *posterity*: for what has *posterity* done for us?' Sir Boyle, hearing the roar of laughter which of course followed this sensible blunder, but not being conscious that he had said anything out of the way, was rather puzzled, and conceived that the House had misunderstood him. He therefore begged leave to explain, as he apprehended that gentlemen had entirely mistaken his words: he assured the House 'that by *posterity* he did not at all mean our *ancestors*, but those who were to come *immediately* after *them!*' Upon hearing this *explanation*, it was impossible to do any serious business for half an hour." [1954, 208. See also Harvey 1904, 213–34]

English jokes about "canny Scotsmen" also have their origin in the seventeenth century, though they did not really become common until the late eighteenth century. A humorous ballad of the seventeenth century [see Ashton 1882, 261–62], "The Unfortunate Welchman or the Untimely Death of Scotch Jockey," contrasts the "aggressive Welsh" with the "canny

Scots." "Jockey" is the diminutive of Jock, a nickname for a Scotsman. To jockey also means to swindle. Like the Jews, the Yorkshiremen, and possibly the Welsh, the Scots became a verb.

By the beginning of the nineteenth century, jokes about Scottish and, in America, New England avarice and overrational calculativeness were well established though mainly in the form of comic anecdotes with a very specific setting and often purporting to describe an actual event.

It requires [says Sydney Smith], a surgical operation to get a joke well into a Scotch understanding. . . . They are so imbued with metaphysics that they even make love metaphysically. I overheard a young lady of my acquaintance, at a dance in Edinburgh, exclaim in a sudden pause of the music, "What you say, my Lord, is very true of love in the aibstract, but—." Here the fiddlers began fiddling furiously, and the rest was lost. [Smith 1839–40, vol. 1, 19–20. Also in Lemon 1891, 291 and see also 212]

A New England merchant who had accumulated a vast property by care and industry yet still was as busy as ever in adding vessel to vessel and store to store though considerably advanced in life being asked by a neighbor how much property he supposed would satisfy a human being, after a short pause replied, "A little more." [*American Jest Book* 1833, 91]

In the year 1797, when democratic notions ran high, it may be remembered that the king's coach was attacked as his majesty was going to the House of Peers. A gigantic Hibernian on that occasion was conspicuously loyal in repelling the mob. Soon after, to his no small surprise, he received a message from Mr. Dundas to attend at his office. He went, and met with a gracious reception from the great man, who, after passing a few encomiums on his active loyalty, desired him to point out any way in which he would wish to be advanced. His Majesty, having particularly noticed his courageous conduct, and being desirous to reward it. Pat scratched and scraped for a while, half thunder-struck—"The devil take me if I know what I'm fit for." "Nay, my good fellow," cried Henry, "think a moment, and dinna throw yoursel out o' the way o' fortun." Pat hesitated another moment, then smirking as if some odd idea had taken hold of his noddle, he said—"I'll tell you what mister, make a Scotchman of me, and, by St. Patrick, there'll be no fear of my getting on." The Minister gazed a while at the mal-apropos wit—"Make a Scotchman of you, sir, that's impossible, for I can't give you prudence." [*Wit and Wisdom* 1826, 335–36. Also in Ford 1901, 173–74]

During the eighteenth century the comic scripts of the blundering Irishman and of the canny Scotsman and the jokes associated with them also gradually became established on the English stage. J. O. Bartley notes of the period 1756–1800 that

> The impression he [the Scotsman] was actually making on the English during these years was such as to stress the sober, hard-headed and calculating aspects of character. . . . Though canniness is not always highlighted it is nearly always present in the make-up of the stage Scot of these years. . . . [Jests about Scottish parsimony in plays] only began in the later eighteenth century and there is only one such reference—which may have been added later—in a play of before 1770. The word used is almost always 'oeconomy' and twice it is significantly paired with 'forecast'. 'Ye have nae kind of aiconomy, nae forecast' says Sergeant Trumbull to Sergeant O'Bradley in Pilon's Siege of Gibraltar, 'you dinna heed the proverb—clap your hand twice to your bonnet for once to your pouch; aw gangs oot: naithing gangs in.' . . . In Lady Graven's 'Miniature Picture', (1780) Lord MacGrinnon says, 'I would no more squander my breath than I would my money, unless I were to get cent percent interest for it' to which Eliza replies, 'I dare say not: true Scottish oeconomy.' [1954, 233–35]

Bartley [1954] has traced the rising popularity of both the "irrational Irishman" and the "canny Scot" in English plays of the eighteenth century by calculating the number of plays depending for their humor on Irish bulls or Scottish economy as a proportion of all plays with recognizable Irish or Scots characters for each year of the period 1700–1800. Irish bulls, which are rare in the plays of 1700, grew steadily in number throughout the century so that they occur in half of all the plays with an Irish character by 1800, and this is just a prelude to the stage Irishman of the nineteenth century [see Styan 1981 vol.I, 94–95]. The theme of Scottish economy developed rather later and only became significant after 1760, but even so, by the turn of the century nearly a fifth of all plays containing Scottish characters mentioned it.

The growing popularity of these humorous scripts of the Irish and the Scots in the eighteenth century coincided with the beginning of important social and economic changes in Britain, changes that in the century that followed were to transform not merely British society but that of the United States and much of the rest of the world. One was the expansion of commerce, trade, and manufacturing that was to make Britain the world's first industrial country [see Ashton 1948; Mantoux 1928; Meir and Baldwin 1957, 143–78] and supreme in production until overtaken toward the end of the nineteenth century by the rapidly growing economy of the United States. The other was the early growth of a modern sense of ethnic and national identity [see Hayes 1960, 38–42; Smith 1981, 70–71], which led to the identification and description of other peoples in such terms also. These two factors underlie the rising popularity of ethnic jokes about blundering Irishmen and canny Scots described by Bartley. The late eighteenth century also saw the unleashing of the pent-up methodical and single-minded Scottish pursuit of material gain as industrial and commercial growth provided the descendants of the Reformation Calvinists with new opportunities [see Smout 1972, 92]. It is also significant that the

Scottish political economists, notably Adam Smith [1776] of the late eighteenth century, were the first to describe and understand the growth of large, impersonal markets and the significance of the increased division of labor, just as later it was a Scotsman who extolled the "Smilesian" virtues of work, thrift, self-help [Smiles 1905]. Industrialization meant that traditional views of the balance between toil and idleness or saving and spending were challenged by a new ethos of work, competition, economic change, and delimited and organized leisure time.

In nineteenth-century Britain and the United States canny entrepreneurs continued to be the masters of rapid economic and technical change, though only by subordinating themselves as well as others to the pressures of the new economy. Below them those who lacked property, education, or skills were often stuck in positions of enforced stupidity [see Smith 1903 (1776), 613–14 and 618]. Jokes about the "canny" and the "stupid" referred to the two fateful extremes, the two possible ways of losing out in the new competitive industrial society. In such a society the incentive to tell ethnic jokes about the "canny" and the "stupid" must have risen and the number of possible themes and topics increased. There were more things to be stupid about, more contexts in which to be canny.

In the nineteenth century the train was the setting for jokes that correspond to the ethnic and other jokes of today that are set in an airplane, a submarine, or a space rocket. The nineteenth century comic equivalent was the artificial environment of "the railway juggernaut" [Punch Library 1908 *Mr. Punch's Railway*, 151; see also Phillips n.d., 69], in which passengers travelled at unnatural and previously unknown speeds while entirely dependent on the expertise of others. Doubters claimed that the human frame would not be able to withstand such speeds, much as their later counterparts did not believe in the possibility of heavier-than-air flying machines or the landing of men on the moon. Disaster jokes that are now told about aircraft or spaceships were told about railroad accidents and played on the passengers' very real fear [see Smith 1854, 667–72] of accidents [e.g., see jokes in Phillips, n.d.; Punch Library 1908 *Mr. Punch's Railway Book*; Russell and Bentley 1948, 21]. These fears were no doubt stimulated by the mass media, which thrived then as now on the sale of real horror and synthetic sympathy [Russell and Bentley 1948, 21]. The Reverend Sydney Smith [1854, 671], in campaigning against the excessive speed and lack of adequate safety precautions of the English trains, declared that nothing would be done until some eminent person had been killed in a crash or in the resulting fire. "A burnt bishop," he noted, might console himself that "his death will produce unspeakable benefit to the public. Even Sodor and Man will be better than nothing." The ethnic jokes of the nineteenth and early twentieth centuries often refer to the fate of an immigrant rustic knocked down by the train [Montgomerie and Montgomerie 1948, 121] or in charge of a level crossing gate [Cobb 1923, 130].

There are a number of American jokes about "dumb Svenskas" settled in rural Minnesota who are equally defeated by trains and canny American claim-agents:

> Up in Minnesota a railroad train killed a cow belonging to a Scandinavian homesteader. The tragedy, having been reported at headquarters, a claim-agent was sent to the spot to make a settlement of damages. . . . "Mr. Swanson," he said with a winning smile, "the company wants to be absolutely fair with you in this matter. We deeply regret that your cow should have met her death on our tracks. But, on the other side Mr. Swanson, from our side there are certain things to be considered. In the first place, that cow had no business straying on our right of way and you, as her owner, should not have permitted her to do so. Moreover, it is possible that her presence there might have caused a derailment of the locomotive which struck her and a serious wreck perhaps involving loss of human life. Now, such being the case, and it being conceded that the cow was, in effect, a trespasser on our property, what do you think, as man to man, would be a fair basis of settlement as between you and the railroad company?"
>
> For a space Mr. Swanson pondered on the argument. Then, speaking slowly and weighing his words, he delivered himself of an ultimatum:
>
> "I bane poor Swede farmer," he said. "I shall give you two dollars." [Cobb 1923, 104–105. Also in Copeland and Copeland 1939, 757]
>
> . . . the Swede farm-hand in Minnesota, who on the witness stand was called upon by the attorney for the railroad to furnish details touching on the tragic death of a companion.
>
> "Aye tell you," he answered. "Me and Ole bane walkin' on railroad track. Train come by and Aye yump off track. By and by, when train is gone, Aye done see Ole any more, so Aye walk on and pretty soon Aye see one of Ole's arms on one side of track and one of Ole's legs on other side of track and then pretty soon Aye see Ole's head but Ole's body is not there, so Aye stop and Aye say to myself, 'By Yupiter, something must a' happened to Ole!' " [Cobb 1923, 227. Also in Lang n.d., 48–49; the English editor Lang has managed to misquote the original American version in such a way as to lose half the point of the joke!]

Even the earliest Swedish settlers in Minnesota must have had some familiarity with railroads, but these stories of their alleged stupidity do remind us of the real possibility of peoples unable to grasp the nature of the "new" technology of the train. Herbert Spencer [1969, 88], who, like Vilfredo Pareto, was a nineteenth-century professional railroad expert turned sociologist, noted that when railroads were first introduced in Spain, peasants would venture onto the railroad track and would be run down by the train, to the anger of their relatives, who would blame the engineer "driving" it. People growing up in remote rural communities had no experience or theoretical knowledge that could enable them to envisage a heavy and fast-moving body whose momentum was such that it could not be stopped in time to save the life of a trespassing pedestrian.

Ethnic jokes about real-world blunders, though, had still not decisively overtaken ethnic jokes based on merely verbal error. The very stupidity of the butts of the latter type of joke is often in and of itself ambiguous and questionable. Also jokers may deliberately and cleverly misuse language and exploit error so that we laugh at the cleverness of their pseudo-foolishness. A person who makes a statement with an ambiguous or contradictory meaning may be regarded by his or her listeners as a silly fool who has made a risible mistake or as a subtle wit who has produced a clever joke. Either way, the audience may laugh, but their estimation of the speaker's abilities will differ greatly depending on how they interpret his or her intention or meaning. In many cases they may well be unsure as to whether the speaker is joking or not, uncertain as to whether they are dealing with a wit or a half-wit. Also jokes, repartee, the pretense of error or stupidity can be used as a skillful means of manipulating other people, so as to evade responsibility, to avoid answering a question, to reduce anger to amusement, or simply secretly to mock the other party. To succeed in such a game requires a great deal of shrewd understanding and/or a gift for language. Only the clever can play the fool.

Because eighteenth and early nineteenth century British jokes about the Irish were so often language-based the very varied corpus of jokes as well as many individual examples could be interpreted in two ways—either as an indication of blundering stupidity or as evidence of a quick and eloquent wit marked by an exuberant use of figurative language [Edgeworth and Edgeworth 1802, 111–12]. By contrast recent twentieth century American jokes about Poles tend to be rooted in a confrontation of a stupid individual with brute reality and are not open to this kind of divergent interpretation. For modern Americans, the basic comic script about "Polacks" is stupid, period. In these jokes the unfortunate Poles always lose, whereas in traditional British jokes about the Irish, the Irish often emerge as "winners" through the employment of shrewd misunderstanding and witty irrationality. Just as the Scots of the jokes are often irrationally rational, so the Irish can be rationally irrational: "Milesians are not stupid, no, not they. They merely act as if they were that way" (with apologies to Demodocus). However, the qualities of stupidity and canniness are already much more clearly antithetical than is the case with the older traditional wise fools and erratic tricksters. The jokes have sorted out the Smilesians from the Milesians.

One morning, at the accustomed hour when the lady was getting into her carriage, the old [Irish] woman began—"Agh! my lady; success to your ladyship and success to your honour's honour this morning, of all days in the year; for sure didn't I dream last night that her ladyship gave me a pound of tea and that your honour gave me a pound of tobacco?"

"But, my good woman," said the general, "do you not know, that dreams always go by the rule of contrary?"

"Do they so please your honour," rejoined the old woman. "Then it must be your honour that will give me the tea and her ladyship that will give me the tobacco." [Edgeworth and Edgeworth 1802, 147. Also in *Wit and Wisdom* 1826, 167–68]

The Irish jokes of the later nineteenth and early twentieth century based on an unexpected use of language and argument are as varied and as double-edged as their predecessors, and the Hibernian central character can win as well as lose. Just as the canny Scots of the jokes are portrayed as losing out by being the subordinates of their own rationality, so the comic and often witty [see Mercier 1962, 78–79, 93–95] Irishman succeeds by being a master of the irrational [see Jennings 1976]. And that, as Humpty Dumpty said, is all [Carroll 1965, 174, but see also 44–45 and 232–33].

A Scotchman and an Irishman happened to be journeying together through an almost interminable forest, and losing their way wandered about in a pitiable condition for a while, when fortunately they came to a miserable hovel, which was deserted save by a lone chicken. As this poor biped was the only thing eatable to be obtained, they eagerly despatched and prepared it for supper.

When laid before them, Pat concluded that it was insufficient for both himself and Sandy, and he therefore proposed to his companion that they should save the chicken until the next morning and that the one who had dreamed the pleasantest dream during the night should have the chicken, which was agreed to.

In the morning Sandy told his dream. He thought angels were drawing him up to heaven in a basket, and that he had never before been so happy. Upon hearing the conclusion of the dream, Pat exclaimed:—

"Och, shure, an' be jabers, I saw ye goin' an' thought ye wouldn't come back, so I got up an' ate the chicken meself!" [Howe 1890, 162]

It chanced, one gloomy day in the month of December, that a good-humoured Irishman applied to a merchant to discount a bill of exchange for him at rather a long, though not an unusual date; and the merchant having casually remarked that the bill had a great many days to run, "That's true" replied the Irishman, "but consider how short the days are at this time of the year." [Lemon 1891, 260]

"Now Pat, I've heard some queer stories about your doings lately."

"Och don't you believe 'em sor; shure not more'n half the lies told about me is true." [Jerrold 1928, 37]

An officer of a certain regiment was one morning inspecting his company on parade, when he came to an Irishman who had evidently not shaved for some days.

Halting in front of the man, he said:

"Doyle, how is it that you've not shaved this morning?"

"Oi have, sorr," was the reply.

"How dare you tell me that," said the officer, "with a beard on you like that?"

"Well, sorr," said Paddy, "it's loike this. There's only one shaving glass in our room, and there was noine of us shaving at the same toime, and maybe oi shaved some other chap's face." [*Further Sunbeams* 1924, 118]

An old gentleman was finding fault with an Irishman for trying to find work on a Sunday. "It is very wicked," he said, "to break the Sabbath."

"Faith, sor," answered the Irishman; "it wuz me or the Sabbath. Wan of us had to be broke." [*Further Sunbeams* 1924, 100]

We are still then some way from the kind of uniform modern comic script of the Irish as "thick" discovered by Kravitz [1977, 276] in his empirical study of London jokes, or of the "dumb Poles" who always lose that is revealed by an American catalogue of Polish jokes [Clements 1973].

Nonetheless, by the beginning of the twentieth century there existed in both Britain and America a very large stock of jokes that depend for their humor on the supposed inability of the Irish to comprehend or use recent inventions or to understand and comply with impersonal institutional procedures. It was a stock that, like the stock of "canny" jokes, grew with the growth of new inventions. Robert Graves [1928, 10] was able to look back on this period and claim that the same stock gags had been applied to steam engines in 1840, to telephones in 1870, to motor cars in 1900, to broadcasting in 1920, and predicted that they would also be tagged to future inventions [see also Thompson 1977, 192]. At the turn of the century it was still the telephone, the elevator, and the telescope:

Paddy and the Telephone:

Father O'Halloran had a telephone put into the parsonage in connection with the church, parochial school, etc. Patrick McFee, his reverence's handy man, was instructed in the use of the instrument, and it was only the next day when Pat, dusting out the church, heard the clatter of the telephone. Well, taking down the receiver, he was pleased to hear

Father O'Halloran's familiar voice asking him something or other about his work. Pat, in essaying to answer, remembered that his reverence was a long way off, and consequently halloed into the transmitter at the top of his voice.

"I didn't understand you, Pat," said the telephone.

Pat tried again with no better success. On his third trial he came near splitting the telephone but came again Father O'Halloran's voice:—

"I can't hear what you're saying, Patrick."

Pat had by this time lost some of his patience, and as he stood gathering his breath for his fourth blast, he couldn't refrain from soliloquizing in a low tone:—

"Ah, may the devil fly away with the old fool!"

But Pat dropped the telephone like a hot potatoe and fell on his knees in dismay, when he heard Father O'Halloran's voice again:—

"Now I hear you perfectly, Patrick." [Howe 1890, 159]

Paddy and the Hotel Lift:

The Irishman who went up in the hotel-lift without knowing what it was, did not easily recover from the surprise. He relates the story in this way:

"I wint to the hotel, and says I: 'Is Misther Smith in?'

'Yes,' says the man with the sojer cap: 'Will yez step in?'

So I steps into the closet, and all of a suddint he pulls the rope, and—it's the truth I's telling yez—the walls of the building began runnin' down to the cellar.

'Och, murther!' says I, 'what'll become of Bridget and the children which was left below there?'

Says the sojer-cap man: 'Be aisy, sorr; they'll be all right when yez come down.'

'Come down is it?' says I. 'And it is no closet at all, but a haythenish balloon that yez got me in!'

And wid that the walls stood stock still, and he opened the door, and there I was with the roof just over my head! And, begorra, that's what saved me from goin' up to the hivins intirely!" [Howe 1890, 102]

The Wonders of Science.—The Principal (from the City through the telephone to the foreman at the "Works") "How do you get on, Pat?"

Irish Foreman (in great awe of the instrument) "Very well, sir. The goods is sent off." The Principal (knowing Pat's failing). "What have you got to drink there?" Pat (startled). "Och! look at that now! It's me breath that done it!" [Punch Library 1908 *Mr. Punch's Irish Humor*, 116]

At the observatory they had engaged a new night porter. He was an Irishman. During his first night on duty he watched one of the professors fixing a large telescope on its stand. He was very mystified. Nothing like this had ever been heard of in his remote village. Presently the professor began to focus his telescope and move it about till he got it into position. At that moment a shooting star darted across the sky, falling rapidly. "Begob," said the porter staring at the Professor, "but that's foine shootin', glory be!" [*Further Sunbeams* 1924, 122. Also in Copeland and Copeland 1939, 728]

Whether or not the errors or failures to understand displayed by the Irish in these relatively modern jokes are different in kind from those exhibited by the numskulls who feature in more ancient anecdotes is a matter that can be disputed. However, the number of circumstances in which comic naive misunderstanding of inventions, machines, or procedures vital to everyday life or work had obviously vastly increased. Without telephones, elevators, or telescopes there can be no jokes about them. Perhaps, too, those who habitually made use of such inventions, or in some cases institutions, and indeed were dependent on them but who did not have a very profound understanding of how they worked, enjoyed a sense of humorous superiority from the plight of the even more ignorant comic Irishman of the jokes.

The Irish were the butt of such jokes in America and Australia, no doubt in part because British emigrants who had settled in these countries carried with them an established comic image of the Irish, and of the Scots also. However, ethnic jokes about the stupid and the canny continued to be pinned on the Irish and Scots respectively, not simply because of the presence of an existing tradition of such jokes but also because of the highly visible social and economic position that immigrants from these countries occupied not just in England and Wales but throughout the English-speaking world.

Although many destitute Scotsmen emigrated to escape poverty at home the fact that impressed itself most on others was the visible success of those Scots who proved to be canny entrepreneurs or merchants or who exploited the practical skills in engineering or medicine that they had acquired in Scotland. The distinctive Scottish combination of a long-established Calvinist tradition of work and striving and wide availability of practical secular education [Smith 1902 (1776), 616] was a formidable one [see Jackson 1968; Ward 1966, 48]. Also the ethnic celebrations of Scots living abroad were often occasions of self-gratulation when Scotsmen who had made it praised Scotsmen on the make. 'Here's tae us, fa's like us!' Non-Scots duly took note.

The link between the perceived social position of the Scots in the United States and Canada and the comic Scotsman of the jokes has been forthrightly—indeed, crudely—stated by the historian Ray Ginger [1974, comment on Anecdote 30]:

> Virtually without exception jokes against the Scots in America have focussed on one charge: They are covetous. A few hours reading in the business correspondence of Scottish and Scot-Irish merchants and cotton factors of the eighteenth century might make anybody wonder if this canard did not originate from hard realities.
>
> Persons not American are referred to the practices, mid-twentieth century of Scottish bankers on Bay Street in Toronto or Sherbrooke Street in Montreal.

Ginger's jokes about "canny Scots" are characteristically grotesque [1974, Anecdote 30], with the Scots revering trivial material gains at the expense of life itself:

An advertisement for a funeral parlour in Camden, South Carolina stated: "Bargains in coffins." Fourteen suicides occurred that day.

A Scottish child killed his parents so that he could go free to the annual picnic of the Orphans Society.

Did ye hear about Ramsay? Scalped by the Indians. Poor chap. Just two days since he paid fifty cents for a haircut.

Irish immigrants, lacking the cultural and educational advantages often possessed by even those Scots who came from poor rural homes, provided much of the unskilled labor in Britain, the United States, and other English-speaking countries. The casual British or American observer could only see their lack of skill, of literacy, and of individual competitiveness and not the social forces that lay behind these. In practice it is often difficult to distinguish ignorance from stupidity, and the causes of ignorance are far less apparent than its manifestations. Hence the plausibility of ethnic jokes about stupidity when applied to a group whose members are overrepresented among the unskilled—those who do the aptly named "donkey-work" of the society [see also Mars 1982, 29–31].

The correlation between ethnicity and economic position in the case of the Irish, as in the case of the Scots and indeed of the Irish relative to the Scots, was perceived and commented on by contemporary observers throughout the nineteenth century in the countries where Irish jokes came to be told. In 1829 the Welsh iron-founder Dafydd Wiliams [1830, 122, 129, 135], during his travels through the United States, observed that the Irish were employed everywhere as cheap, unskilled workers, especially in the excavation of canals [see also Trollope 1832 vol.II, 118], while the Scots had better-paid work as skilled masons. In England, in the same era, Cobbett [1912 (1830) vol.I, 84–85] noted that even in agriculture the Irish were employed as unskilled, seasonal labor in hay-making [see also jokes in *New Joe Miller* 1801, 215 and in *Up to Date Wit and Humour* n.d, 20] whereas Scottish "prudence" (Cobbett uses the word in a sour way) enabled them to gain employment as gardeners.

The population crisis and the famines of the 1840s caused even more poor Irish peasants to emigrate to reinforce the large visible stratum of unskilled Irish laborers in both Britain and America, and emigration of this type remained at a high level.[8] During the nineteenth century a further four million people emigrated from rural Ireland to the cities of the United States and large numbers of Irish immigrants also settled in England, Wales, Scotland, Canada, Newfoundland, Australia, and New Zealand. Thomas Sowell [1981, 35–36: see also Jones 1960, 130–31, 168; Montgomery 1980, 208] has stressed that in the United States the "economic rise and social acceptance of the Irish were . . . slow" and that throughout the nineteenth century the Irish were very overrepresented in domestic service and as unskilled laborers and underrepresented in professional and higher white-collar occupations.

The long sojourn of the Irish immigrants at the bottom of the economic ladder in the United States, Australia [see Ward 1966, 48], and elsewhere was one of the key factors that contributed to ethnic jokes about the Irish and stupidity. Many jokes in America, Australia, and New Zealand referred directly or symbolically to their lowly position.

"Why is the wheelbarrow the greatest invention ever made?"

"It taught a few Irishmen to walk on their hind-legs." [Ginger 1974, Anecdote 31]

During the early 1920s a couple of old Irishmen were road-making on the West coast [of New Zealand] road between Greymouth and Westpoint. Their names were Ned and Jim Burke. The method of moving spoil in those days was by wheelbarrow, not the modern type but heavy wooden ones with iron wheels commonly known in those parts as the Irish locomotive. The overseer for what was called the public works department (or P.W.D.) on his periodic visit to pay the men and so on watched Ned wheel a barrow of spoil away and dump it in the required spot, turn his back on the barrow and pull it back. The overseer asked—why do you always pull the barrow back, Ned. The answer was given in Ned's Irish, "I hate the sight of the bloody thing." [Correspondent in Christchurch, New Zealand 1980]

Early twentieth century American ethnic jokes about the Irish tended to mock either the ignorance and simplicity of first-generation immigrants, the newly-arrived "greenhorns" [see Spalding 1978, 8], or the inept behavior of unskilled workers faced with unfamiliar artifacts, tasks, and situations.

A young Irishman whose family was scattered pretty well over the English-speaking portions of the globe emigrated to America. Soon after his arrival in New York he paid a visit to the Bronx Zoo. He halted in front of a cage containing one of the largest kangaroos in captivity. After watching the curious creature for some time in an awed silence, he hailed a keeper.

"What's that thing?" he asked.

"That," said the keeper in his best professional manner, "is a marsupial, a mammal that carries its young in a pouch on its breast, lives on roots and herbs, can jump twenty feet at one leap, is able to knock a human being down with a kick from either hind leg, and is a native of Australia."

"For the love of Hiven!" cried the Irishman, bursting into tears.

"Me sisther's married to wan of thim!" [Cobb 1923, 173–74. Also in Greenway 1972, 280]

Soon after Casey arrived in this country he went to the home of his friend, Mrs. Doyle. While he was there, Mrs. Doyle's parrot came into the room and started pacing up and down the floor screaming: "Mama! Mama! Polly wants a cracker!"

Casey, who had never seen a parrot before, stared at the bird in amazement.

"Mrs. Doyle," he said, "may I ask you a question? Was your daughter born like that with all those feathers?" [Ford, Hershfield, and Laurie 1947, 107]

There was once an Irishman, who sought employment as a diver, bringing with him his native enthusiasm and a certain amount of experience. Although he had never been beneath the water, he had crossed an ocean of one variety and swallowed nearly an ocean of another. But he had the Hibernian smile, which is convincing, and the firm chanced to need a new man. And so on the following Monday morning Pat hid his smile for the first time in a diving helmet.

Now, the job upon which the crew to which Pat had attached himself was working in comparatively shallow water, and Pat was provided with a pick and told to use it on a ledge below in a manner with which he was already familiar.

Down he went with his pick, and for about fifteen minutes nothing was heard from him. Then came a strong, determined deliberate pull on the signal rope, indicating that Pat had a very decided wish to come to the top. The assistants pulled him hastily to the raft and removed his helmet.

"Take off the rest of it." said Pat.

"Take off the rest of it?"

"Yis," said Pat, "Oi'll worruk no longer in a dark place where Oi can't spit on me hands." [Patten 1909 vol.I, 227]

Two Irishmen, newly landed, got jobs as laborers in a small machine shop on the second storey of a loft-building, so-called, on the lower West Side of New York. Under the fire regulations, smoking by the operatives was not permitted while they were on duty. During their first morning in the new place one of the green hands, whose name was Donlan, craved a few comforting whiffs from his pipe. He voiced his desire and a friendly fellow-employee confided to him that in such cases it was customary to ask leave of the foreman to go to the washroom and there to steal a clandestine smoke.

Thus advised, Donlan approached his boss and inquired the whereabouts of the washroom.

"Go down the hall," said the foreman, "and take the first turn to the right, and the second door you come to after that is the door to the lavatory."

Donlan undertook to follow instructions but he made a mistake. In the darkness he took the turn to the left instead of the right-hand turn and, opening the second door, stepped into the elevator shaft and struck with a bump on the ground floor below. Presently he came back upstairs. He was sweeping up rubbish when O'Day, his buddy, asked him where was the washroom. Donlan gave him the direction as he remembered it, and, as O'Day turned to go, he called out to him: "But say, Larry, look out for the top step—it's a son-of-gun!" [Cobb 1923, 200. See also Lawson 1923, 154]

Clancy and Finnegan were working on the building of a new road. The foreman kept warning them to stay away from the dynamite. "There's a charge of dynamite over there," he said. "Keep away from it."

As soon as the foreman left, Clancy started fooling around with the dynamite. Wham! Did he go up in the air!

"Where's Clancy?" said the foreman when he came back.

"He's gone," said Finnegan.

"When will he be back?"

"If he comes back as fast as he went, he should have been here yesterday." [Ford, Hershfield, and Laurie 1947, 159]

The minstrel parade went swinging along where two husky individuals were assaulting the soil beneath the asphalt with picks, three feet below the surface and over on a side of the street. For the sake of novelty, let us respectively refer to these two industrials as Pat and Mike. They straightened their backs to watch the pageant pass. Behind the band in the front file were the two proprietors and two highly paid end-men. Then trailed a large and assorted company, all in showy parade costumes.

Said Patrick to Michael after the music had died away and they had laboriously resumed work:

"Twas a fine body of men."

"It was," commented his friend, "an' it's a pity that prob'ly not one av thim has a thrade." [Cobb 1925, 216]

In time the Irish were to move up into skilled positions in America and this ultimately led to their being replaced in American ethnic jokes about stupidity by later groups of immigrants, notably the Poles. Their initial success, however, lay in local politics rather than through entrepreneurship or education,[9] and this gave a new lease of life to American jokes about them.

From the start the Irish in America had certain advantages not enjoyed by later immigrants from Europe in that they spoke English and already possessed many of the political skills relevant to a democratic country [see Jones 1960, 233]. They realized that American politicians needed their votes, though in American ethnic jokes this too was linked to their low-class position:

George Penn Johnson, one of our most eloquent stump speakers, who loves a good thing too well to let it slip upon any occasion, addressing a meeting where it was a great point to obtain the Irish vote, after alluding to the native American party in no flattering terms, inquired, "Who dig our canals? Irishmen. Who build our railroads? Irishmen. (Great applause). Who build all our gaols? Irishmen. (Still greater applause). Who fill all our gaols? Irishmen!" This clapping climax, if it did not bring down the house, did the Irish in a rush to the stand. Johnson did not wait to receive them. [Cole 1887, 216. Also in Harvey 1904, 351; (Thousand) *1000 Witty Sayings* n.d., 37]

Outraged Irishman—Gentlemen, I w'u'd loike to ashk thim Amerikans wan thing: Who doog the canals ov the coontry but furriners? Who built the railruds ov the coontry but furriners? Who wurruks the mines ov the coontry but furriners? Who does the voting for the coontry but furriners? And who the divil discovered the coontry but furriners? [Kelly 1906, 31.]

In the latter part of the nineteenth century the Irish gained and often retained outright control of municipal politics in a number of great American cities, including New York, Boston, Chicago, Buffalo, Milwaukee, and San Francisco [Sowell 1981, 30; see also Jones 1960, 144]. The Irish political bosses rewarded their political supporters among their fellow countrymen by giving them municipal jobs, which were largely appointive in nineteenth-century America and did not involve formal or any other kind of qualifications. "By the late nineteenth century, the police forces and fire departments of all major American cities were controlled by Irish Americans" [Sowell 1981, 31; see also Jones 1960, 234]. Also, Irishmen who had worked in the building trade became contractors who could rely on political decisions to award them contracts as a reward for loyalty and not have to worry about competitive tendering in the marketplace.

The Irish attainment of municipal political power did not alter the comic image of the Irish in American jokes—it simply created new subjects for the jokes, such as the dumb Irish cop, politician, or municipal contractor. In the nineteenth century as today groups that held political power as a result of a political monopoly were likely to be the target of jokes about stupidity. In the nineteenth century the Irish politicians of America's cities, like, ironically, the members of the British House of Lords, were the subject of jokes or satires about stupidity, much as Afrikaners or Communist politicians in one-party states are today. Similarly, Irish policemen were the butts of jokes like those told today about Southern Italian carabinieri in Italy or about militiamen in Eastern Europe. Established old-stock Americans, and particularly would-be reformers, saw the power and patronage of the city machines based on ethnic voting as the corrupt and illegitimate fruits of local monopoly, not of virtuous competition, and even as rooted in the use of violence or electoral fraud [see Jones 1960, 153, 232–33; Sowell 1981, 31–33]. These latter themes soon entered the repertoire of American jokes about the Irish:

At a closely contested municipal election in New York the Tammany ticket seemed in grave danger. Accordingly steps were taken. Scarcely had the polls opened when a group of trained and experienced repeaters marched into a down-town voting place.

"What name?", inquired the election clerk of the leader of the squad, who was red-haired and freckled and had a black eye. The young gangster glanced down at a slip of paper in his hand to refresh his memory.

"Isadore Mendelheim," he said then.

"That's not your real name, and you know it!", said a suspicious challenger for the reform ticket.

"It is me name," said the repeater, "and I'm goin' to vote under it—see?"

From down the line came a voice:

"Don't let that guy bluff you, Casey. Soitin'ly your name is Mendelheim!" [Cobb 1923, 87. Also in Cerf 1945, 120]

The ease with which pensions were obtained in America is illustrated by the story of the Irishman, who a few days after landing met a compatriot he knew and who offered to help him in securing a job of some sort.

"It isn't at all necessary," said he, "a friend of mine is getting me a pension at Washington."

Asked if he were a Republican or a Democrat, he replied,

"I don't know anything about your politics, but I'm agin the Government whichever it is." [Robey 1920, 50]

The search of the Irishman of the jokes for even a humble but secure job on the municipal payroll or a political pension or sinecure may be contrasted with the commercial ambition humorously imputed to canny New England Yankees:

A political office in a small New Hampshire town was vacant. The office paid $250 a year and there was keen competition for it. One of the candidates, Ezekiel Hicks, was a shrewd old fellow, and a neat campaign fund was turned over to him. To the astonishment of all, however, he was defeated.

"I can't account for it," said one of the leaders of Hicks' party, gloomily.

"With all that money, we should have won. How did you lay it out, Ezekiel?"

"Well," said Ezekiel, slowly milking his chin whiskers, "ye see that office only pays $250 a year salary, an' I didn't see no sense in paying $900 out to get the office, so I bought a little truck farm instead." [Braude 1976 (1958), 166–67]

Even where Irish laborers turned contractor and used their municipal connections to business advantage American jokes were apt to portray them and their spouses as still trapped in their unskilled status and uncouth state:

An Irishman had died and had a lot of floral offerings on his coffin. The deceased had begun his career at street work digging sewers and cellars and so forth but he afterwards became a rich contractor. The widow since her rise to wealth had put on an awful lot of society airs and she walked into the room where the coffin lay with a very haughty mien. The apartment was full of flowers and mourners. A prominent floral piece was an anchor. The widow gazed upon it. The idea that some of her cast-off friends were trying to disconcert her by calling up memories of her former days came into her mind. Turning to the assembled company she asked: "who the divil sint that pick?" [Ernst 1927, 88]

Of the Irish office-holders the most frequent butt of American ethnic jokes was, however, the policeman and a whole genre of American jokes about "dumb Irish cops" was created. The Irish policeman as an ethnically distinctive and unqualified, uneducated, and unskilled political appointee who exercised petty but personal coercive authority was a classic subject for jokes about stupidity [see Esar 1978, 234].

Ireland is the greatest copper-producing country in the world. [Ford, Hirshfield, and Laurie 1947, 210. Also in Braude 1976 (1958), 165]

On Finnegan's first day as a regular on the police force, the Lieutenant told him, "Finnegan, I'm giving you an easy beat to start with—just from the station house to that red light and back."

Finnegan disappeared for two days. "Where the devil were you?" roared the Lieutenant. "Didn't I tell you your beat was just from here to that red light?"

"You did," agreed Finnegan, "but that red light was on the back of a truck." [Ford, Hirshfield, and Laurie 1947, 80]

Officer Doyle was up for inspection in the police station.

"Doyle, how long have you been on the force?" asked the captain.

"Five years."

"Five years? Where're your sleeve marks? You're supposed to have marks on your sleeve for every year."

"I took them off."

"What right did you have to take them off? Why did you take them off?"

"Because it hurt me nose when I wipe it." [Ford, Hirshfield, and Laurie 1947, 132–33]

An Irish-American labor organizer in his sixties who had grown up in an Irish-American working-class community in New York told one of these jokes to Jacqueline Ferrara [UCBFA Irish-American file 1977] in California:

> It's about the cop that found a dead horse on the street. . . . He was called because the horse died. "What's the name of the street?" (And he goes to write it down) "Nefbrahan Ave," he's told. But he couldn't spell it—so he pulled the horse onto Main Street. [The Irish-American raconteur also commented that] this Irish story frequently circulated the neighborhoods and was aimed at the Irish cops who were usually, in those days, political appointees—men who had been hired as soon as they got off the boat from Ireland. These guys were tough but kinda dumb. Most were illiterate with heavy accents that the Irish-American people couldn't understand and they frequently terrorized the people.

In the long run the overall social and economic position of the Irish in America was transformed and they rose from initial poverty to achieve parity with the standards of income and education enjoyed by other Americans [see Greeley 1980, 234–35; Sowell 1981, 42]. One factor which assisted Irish social mobility was the arrival of new waves of poor peasant immigrants from Southern and Eastern Europe who replaced the Irish at the bottom of the economic ladder.[10] These groups soon and for some time appeared as the supporting cast in ethnic jokes about Irish-Americans who were portrayed in the jokes as asserting themselves at the expense of the new arrivals:

In a New York neighborhood dominated by citizens of Italian extraction, it is the annual custom to parade a fine, life-size statue of St. Rosco through the streets. In the midst of one of these celebrations, the procession paused a moment to rest, and an indignant Irish spectator took the opportunity to proclaim to all and sundry that St. Patrick had it all over St. Rosco in every conceivable way, shape, and form.

Several Italians took issue with the Irishman, who finally got so angry he picked up a stone and heaved it, neatly knocking off the head of the statue. "That just goes to show you" he bellowed triumphantly to the stunned Italians. "If that had been St. Patrick, he'd have ducked!" [Cerf 1959, 264–65. See also Golden 1959, 198; Masson 1913, 187]

The Irish moved up, assimilated, intermarried with other ethnic groups [see Sowell 1981, 41–42], and in time became Americanized [Sowell 1981, 42] to the point where only excessive Catholicism and alcohol consumption remained as distinctive traits that could be made the subject of ethnic jokes. As the Irish became both more successful and less visible, American ethnic jokes about their alleged stupidity and low economic position slowly faded away, though some still remain even today. There had of course been other local butts for ethnic jokes about stupidity, such as the Swedes, the Norwegians, and the Finns. The Scandinavian immigrants, who had arrived as peasants and settled often in rural areas in Minnesota, Wisconsin, and the Dakotas [Jones 1960, 209], were the butt of dialect stories about the defective English of "dumb Norskies and Svenskas"[11] in which Pat and Mike became Lars and Ole.

A couple were applying for a marriage license.
"Your name?"
"Ole Olson."
"And yours?"
"Lena Olson."
"Any connection?"
The bride blushed. "Only vunce. He yumped me." [Wilde 1978A, 229. Also in Legman 1986 (1968) vol.1, 164]

Here the Swedes' defective understanding of English is the mechanism by which the joke is switched from a mundane bureaucratic script to a directly sexual one [cf. Raskin 1985, 32, 127]. In general American dialect stories about "dumb Swedes" seem much more likely to have a sexual ending than equivalent tales about the Irish [e.g., see Hall and Passemon 1933, 8, 47, 69–70 and Legman 1986 (1968), 164–66, 703]. Ethnic jokes about Swedes were popular up to and including the 1920s when, according to Sinclair Lewis [1954 (1923), 222 and 224], Minnesota was seen as "these steppes inhabited by a few splendid Yankees—one's own sort of people and by Swedes who always begin sentences with 'Vell,

Aye tank', who are farmhands, kitchen-maids and icemen, and who are invariably humorous'' and when old-stock Americans believed that "the Minnesota Scandinavians are no matter how long they remain here like the characters of that estimable old stock-company play 'Yon Yonson'—a tribe humorous, inferior and unassimilable.''

As in the case of the Irish, upward economic mobility and social and cultural assimilation [see Lewis 1954 (1923), 225] made the older ethnic jokes about Scandinavians largely obsolete, though occasionally some of the new wave of American Polish jokes were applied to them locally [e.g., see Jarvenpa 1976, 90–91]. The groups who succeeded the Irish as the butts of ethnic jokes about stupidity were the descendants of the unskilled and illiterate immigrants [see Fox 1970, 58–60] from the poorest parts of Eastern and Southern Europe who had migrated to America in the decades before World War I [see Haiman 1974, 3, 156] and taken over the harsh manual tasks formerly performed by the Irish [see note 11]. From the early 1960s on it was the Italians, the Portuguese, and especially the Poles who featured in American ethnic jokes about stupidity. The comic image of the "dumb Polack'' was widely known long before and there are earlier references to "Polack jokes''[12] but it was only at the beginning of the 1960s that ethnic jokes about Poles became widespread in America, following the slow fizzling out of American jokes about dim and lowly Irishmen in the years after World War II. It was a belated recognition of the fact that the Poles had replaced the Irish as the unskilled and semiskilled blue-collar workers of America. The decline of the Irish joke and the rise of the Polish joke are a measure of the assimilation of both groups into American society. The Irish have moved from the periphery to the center of society and have become an integral, accepted, and unremarked on part of American life [see Sinha 1975, 310]. The Poles have ceased to be the mysterious and even threatening aliens unable to speak English whose culture and behavior patterns were not merely unfamiliar but incomprehensible. For mainstream Americans the Poles are no longer "people not like us'' but "people almost like us,'' "people more or less like us''—the kind of people who not just in America but all over the world become the butts of jokes about stupidity. They have come into American society from the outside and now occupy the social edge that was once the place of the Irish [see Greeley 1972, 121–22]. The Irish are no longer ambiguous enough to be joked about, the Poles are no longer alien enough to be excluded from jokes. The Irish are now well inside the social frontier of American society, and the Poles are just inside for they are securely though recently American [see Andreski 1973, 83, 114]. Americans, like everyone else, tell jokes that export stupidity to the periphery of their society, and from the 1960s they used the Poles as a safe if somewhat anachronistic marker of the social boundary of American society.

By the 1960s ethnic jokes about stupidity had themselves changed. They were much more likely to portray total stupidity in the face of an inexorable impersonal world of machines and institutions rather than the verbal stupidity mixed with wit and whimsy that arose from the older jokes involving personal encounters. Despite the well-established reputation of the Irish for wit, this was almost as true of the new British jokes about the Irish as of American jokes about Poles. The British continue to tell jokes about the Irish despite the fact that there has been as much upward mobility and assimilation of the Irish in Britain as in America. One reason for this is that the British, like the French, the Dutch, or other citizens of long-established traditionally homogenous nation-states, perceive the periphery of their nation in geographical as well as social terms; the people living in Ireland itself constitute the periphery. Another reason is that new immigrants have continually left Ireland to seek unskilled manual work in Britain (there have never been any attempts by the British to hinder this) even after the formation of the Irish Free State, later the Republic of Ireland [see Lyon 1969, 167]. It is this group, currently close to a million strong with a quarter of a million in London alone [Eric J. Thompson 1976, 30 and 42–43], that is perceived as Irish whereas most of the much larger number of people (over a tenth of the population, an even larger proportion than is the case in America) whose ancestors came from Ireland in the past are regarded as English, Scots, or Welsh depending on their place of residence and the identity of the group to which they have assimilated. The joke told about the former British Prime Minister, James Callaghan, that he was "an Englishman with an Irish name and a Welsh constituency," illustrates the point [but see also Hoggart 1981, 88]. There are as yet relatively few British ethnic jokes involving the interaction of the Irish with the more recent waves of immigrants from the West Indies, India, and Pakistan [but see Onyeama 1977, 33]

A large proportion of the ethnic jokes now told in Britain about the Irish are similar to American jokes about Poles, though the older "bulls" and jokes based on oddities of speech are still much in evidence. Many of these jokes have no doubt been imported from the United States, but even so they have been subtly adapted to fit the local sense of humor and cultural traditions, and certain types of jokes told in the United States about Poles and Italians, such as those that depict these peoples as dirty, have never caught on in Britain or been applied to the Irish. The imported jokes that have taken root and indeed inspired the creation of hundreds of new local jokes are those that deal with that now almost universal concept "stupidity." British ethnic jokes about the Irish have for a long time increasingly depicted them as inept and unable to cope with the inflexible realities of machines and impersonal institutions. The new, blunter American-style jokes about Poles reinforced and accelerated an existing trend.

The coexistence of the traditional British image of the Irish as witty blunderers who made bulls and the transnational ethnic comic script of the utterly stupid can be used to illustrate the kind of changes in society that underlie the new jokes. It is not simply a British or an American phenomenon, for Bengt Holbek [1975] has noted a similar change in Denmark and the basic point can be illustrated by jokes from many countries, as the following traditional Bulgarian joke about the Šopi illustrates:

An old man, Pervo by name, came to town and crossed the street at the red light. A policeman called out to him and said, 'Hey citizen go back right away!' 'But I'm not a citizen, I'm a peasant and I'll be going back tonight on the train', answered Pervo continuing on his way. [Ogoiski 1975, 22]

Presumably a Bulgarian policeman can be mollified by a joke like this. However, the material world and its machines cannot be propitiated in this way, and there is a big contrast between these traditional verbal blunders or tricks and the inexorable results of stupidity in modern jokes. Indeed, even old Pervo might have been knocked down by a truck while going through the red light. You can escape the policeman but not the ambulance. Even in the nineteenth-century world of railways discussed earlier the basis of order and compliance had shifted from sheer obedience to technical expertise [Smith 1981, 113]. English deference could now mean disaster:

Railway Gatesman (opening gate to let horse and coach through): "It's agin the rules my lady, openin' o' the gate like this; but it ain't for the likes o' me to keep yer ladyship a waitin'." Noble Countess: "Why is it against the rules, my good man?" Railway Gatesman: "Well my lady, the 5.17 down express has been doo these ten minutes!" [Punch Library 1908 *Mr. Punch's Railway*, 166]

A more recent humorous anecdote told by the Irish architectural historian Maurice Craig [in Cusack 1980, 30] makes a similar point:

> I recall travelling in Connaught with Louis MacNiece several years ago. We came across a level-crossing the gate of which was neither open nor shut. The keeper sat on the stile relishing a cigarette. When we approached he greeted us cordially. In answer to our query he told us that he was half-expecting a train. [Also in Chambers 1980, 27]. His remark was not entirely without merit for though it was not entirely rational it had at least the appearance of logicality.

As a "remark" the crossing keeper's answer does have merit and is an amusing, albeit by no means original, riposte to the criticism implicit in Craig's query as to why the gate was half open. However, whether this Irish joke is simply an amusing verbal or mathematical bull or a joke about real stupidity depends, as shown in our earlier discussion of railroad jokes, on the speed of the trains and the density of the road traffic. In rural Connaught a half-open gate can presumably be moved into position in time to satisfy engine drivers (engineers) and Maurice Craig alike. However, a half-open gate that both blocked the approach of a high-speed train and obstructed a busy road might lead to a more decisive kind of joke altogether, as in modern American jokes about Poles:

The sound of the crash was shattering and the wreckage scattered all over the place when Wyszynska racing to beat the train to the crossing, hit the twenty-third car. [Wilde 1975A, 40]

None of the individual elements of this modern ethnic joke is new, but there is a sharper, more highly condensed conjunction of ethnicity, total stupidity, and final disaster than in the jokes of the past. Machines, unlike people, cannot be placated by a joke and the rules that govern them are more inexorable than mere human authority. Errors and ambiguity lead to disaster rather than laughter and modern ethnic jokes about stupidity have taken on this ruthless quality. Even minor linguistic blunders are not appreciated by a computer and hence can cause problems for the elaborate machines that it controls [see Cane 1984]. A human being faced with an Irish bull can both enjoy the joke and make sense of a "remark which is illogical in form but forcibly clear in meaning, the force deriving from the intermediate steps being unexpressed" [Craig in Cusack 1980, 30]. A computer can neither laugh nor supply the arbitrarily missing steps.

Ethnic jokes about stupidity can only rarely refer directly to a person's ignorance of new specialized knowledge or techniques in the way that the jokes told by particular groups of professionals, experts, or skilled craftsmen do. The latter kind of jokes also emphasize the cleverness and skill of the members of the group by depicting outsiders and new trainees or apprentices as stupid and ignorant. Part of the point of "occupational" jokes of this type is that people without the necessary specialist expertise usually fail to understand them, but in consequence such jokes can never enjoy a wider popularity. Indeed, the jokes told by one group of specialists often cannot be adapted or modified so as to be told by the members of another, equally skilled group whose expertise lies in a quite different area. Modern ethnic jokes about stupidity by contrast are easily understood by most people because they refer only to those superficial aspects of new techniques and artifacts which everyone understands. Few people know how a submarine or a telephone, a space rocket or a calculator works, but in each case they know that technical changes have occurred which enable human beings to perform otherwise impossible tasks provided they adhere to a new set of rules. Modern ethnic jokes about stupidity, like traditional jokes about the inhabitants of fooltowns, are based on people's shared everyday knowledge. However, that everyday knowledge now includes a broad albeit superficial understanding of a large range of techniques and machines quite unknown to our ancestors. A general awareness of just how shallow our everyday knowledge is when contrasted with the fund of specialized knowledge available leads to ethnic jokes about groups allegedly too stupid to comprehend even that minimal shared understanding of the modern world which everyone else possesses. This point may be illustrated by reference to an ethnic joke that was turned into a physical object and marketed in the late 1970s and the 1980s by the Leicester Game Co. Inc. of Toledo, Ohio, U.S.A. The container is marked "Polish Electric Calculator, Model POL 54681. Five Function and Exclusive features: Slim line design. Easy eraser feature. Needs no batteries. Simple to operate." Inside the box is a pencil with an eraser at one end which is wired up to a two-pin electric plug!

Ethnic jokes about stupidity go back to the beginning of civilization, but this particular joke sums up the essential modernity of the most recent examples. Jokes of this type rooted in the modern world have not replaced older ethnic jokes about the members of a group displaying a lack of common sense in relation to the straightforward unproblematic aspects of the everyday world. Indeed, the flourishing of ethnic jokes that depict crass stupidity in brand-new contexts meant that jokes could be based on stupid behavior in any context whatsoever, even those that are unreal or imagined. The 1960s, 70s, and 80s saw the emergence of large numbers of ethnic jokes about stupidity which in principle could have been invented long before but were not. The ethnic jokes about stupidity of earlier days demonstrate many different kinds of ignorance, stupidity, and misunderstanding in a variety of contexts, but the portraying of a group of people as totally baffled by all manner of simple everyday objects and tasks has come about in a world based on technical complexity. Only in a complex world of people thoroughly used to the ever-changing pattern of the division of labor have joke-tellers grasped the idea that the very simplest of tasks such as putting on one's shoes, brushing one's teeth, or eating with a fork can be analyzed, dissected, and reassembled to produce a "stupid" version for an ethnic joke [see also Kerman 1980, 458]. At an earlier time a clown might have performed any of these operations in an inept way either as a mimic or as a buffoon but the construction of jokes which made comic errors of this type quite explicit did not occur, even though the butts of more traditional ethnic jokes were depicted as just as stupid in other ways.

A large shoe company has just announced that from now on they will manufacture sneakers especially for Polacks. On the toes will be printed the letters: T. G. I. F.

This will mean: Toes Go in First. [Wilde 1975A, 74]

How does a Polack brush his teeth?

He holds the brush and moves his head. [Clements 1973, 26]

Do you know why Århusians have so many scars round their mouths on Mondays?

It is because they have been practising eating with a knife and fork on the Sunday. [Yearhouse 1974]

Modern joke-tellers have seen that any aspect of reality can be reduced to a logical or empirical relationship which can be subtly transformed, inverted, or rearranged to provide yet another instance of comic ethnic stupidity. Once people know the formula there is practically no limit to the number of such jokes that can be created. Literally anything can be made the subject of an ethnic joke about stupidity—the Irish woodworm that was found inside a brick, or the Irish cuckoo that laid other birds' eggs in its own nest. Ethnic labels such as Polish, Irish, or Belgian serve merely as warning signals that a punch line based on stupidity is on the way. Some of these jokes may superficially appear similar to absurd riddles told about rabbits or elephants or shark-infested custard [e.g., see MacHale 1982], but the ethnic jokes differ significantly from absurd riddles in that the punch line of the ethnic joke does relate to the rest of the joke in a systematic way. It is not possible to guess the answer to an absurd riddle, because it bears an almost random relationship to the question. Children like telling these silly riddles to adults because they have memorized the arbitrary ending and the normally apparently omniscient adult can neither work out what it is going to be nor even fit the answer into the adult framework of knowledge and reasoning that the child lacks. These riddles, like many ethnic jokes, are about stupidity and superiority, but it is the person who doesn't know the answer who is "stupid" and the joke-teller who briefly feels superior. In ethnic jokes about stupidity the ending does relate quite clearly to the rest of the joke, albeit in an unexpected way. The jokes do not abandon the world of real relationships but merely distort it to produce a ludicrous but not arbitrary ending that has a real content. A sense of superiority is shared by joke-teller and audience, who show they are bright enough to "get" the joke at the expense of the ethnic group that figures in the joke. The large element of mock reality in ethnic jokes is shown by the ease with which a good joke-teller can treat a simple question-and-answer joke as a do-it-yourself kit and build it up into a narrative joke or even an anecdote told with a straight face as a tall tale about the stupidity of the Poles, the Irish, or the Belgians, etc. It is much more difficult to do this with an absurd riddle, which is presumably why people rarely attempt to turn elephants into shaggy dogs.

Ethnic jokes about stupidity are rooted in reality, not chaos, and the expansion in the number of such jokes stems from the application of a basic formula in and to an almost infinite number of different discrete real-world contexts rather than from merely playing with meaninglessness. The boundless possibilities of creating new jokes about ethnic stupidity were realized in the boom in such jokes that has taken place since the 1960s in so many different countries. Like all booms it eventually peaked and the rate at which people invented new jokes began to decline, not because joke-tellers ran out of ideas but because their audiences became satiated. The flow of new ethnic jokes about stupidity was bound to slow down in time if only because the existing stock of such jokes had become so enormous. Polish or Irish or Belgian jokes have become for the time being a little dated but they will go on being told because there are so many of them stored in people's minds, books, photocopies, audio and video tapes, and floppy discs. In the future new types of ethnic jokes about stupidity with new themes will emerge and new groups will become the butts of old jokes. If we could but know them they might appear as strange to us as our twentieth century ethnic jokes would seem to an ancient Egyptian brought up on jokes about Nubians falling into the Nile, and yet the joke-tellers of the future will be able to look back and see in our ethnic jokes the early prototypes of their own.

Ethnic jokes about the canny have also changed and multiplied as joke-tellers have abstracted a formula for canniness from existing jokes and applied it in new contexts. The kind of change that has taken place in Finnish jokes about "canny Laihians" has been well summed up by Marjatta Jauhiainen [1979; see also 1983] in her study of Laihian jokes and Finnish folklore:

> In the more recent material in particular Laihianism is taken to the point of absurdity. The Laihian is a resourceful opportunist who does not fail to make use of a single chance to be stingy. . . . One of the most characteristic jests in the whole material is a description of neighbours trying to learn stinginess from the Laihians by sitting without trousers so that they don't become worn out. . . . The recent Laihian material contains a large number of unique products that are traditional only in their basic idea, their stereotype. This reflects the productiveness of Laihian humour. A crystallized stereotype puts out individual shoots, proving the viability of the stereotype. Today Laihian humour is still known among the local older generation as a conservative agrarian tradition alongside the urban tradition maintained by younger people and the mass media.
>
> For a long time Laihian humour kept to old themes, some of them appearing almost throughout the research period. Only in the material collected by schoolchildren in 1969 did modern technology appear to affect Laihianism.

In this way the new has supplemented the old. The story first recorded in 1890 of the "Laihian (who) cried when he splits a match in two and both halves get wasted" [Jauhiainen 1979, 2 and 8; see also 1983] is still told in Finland, but by the 1970s it had been supplemented by new jokes about the energy crisis of that decade:

> How do the Laihians save energy?
> They omit the heating-up stage. [Jauhiainen 1979, 8; see also 1983]

How do the Laihians heat their hospital?
They shift fever patients from one room to another. [Jauhiainen 1979, 8; see also 1983]

The Finns, like the French, the Italians, the Germans, and other peoples distant from Scotland, have taken up the internationally popular jokes about "canny Scotsmen," who are often contrasted with the Laihians. Marjatta Jauhiainen has recorded how the Finnish "Central Taxpayers Association presented the members of the finance committee drawing up the national budget with Scottish ties to remind them of the economy necessary in setting the country's affairs in order and noted: 'Homely Laihianism is no longer enough: there is nothing for it but to be miserly Scots' " [Jauhiainen 1979, 3; see also 1983].

Recent jokes about "canny Scots" have changed in the same way as those about Laihians. Just as new Laihian jokes do not relate to their agrarian origin, so too Scots jokes have become detached from their Calvinist roots and local language and setting. In the nineteenth and early twentieth centuries jokes about "canny Scots" often played up these distinctive and particular adjuncts to Scots canniness [see also Celt 1911, 73; Geikie 1904; Ramsay 1873]:

Sandy McPherson, in a moment of abstraction, put half-a-crown in the collection plate last Sunday in mistake for a penny, and has since expended a deal of thought as to the best way of making up for it. "Noo I might stay awa' frae the kirk till the sum was made up; but on the ither han' I wad be payin' pew rent a' the time an' gettin' nae guid o' 't. Losh! but I'm thinkin' this is what the meenister ca's a releegious defficulty!" [Punch Library 1908 *Mr. Punch's Scottish*, 151]

Irate Landlord (and Free-Kirk Elder, after being called in, for the fiftieth time, about some repairs). "The fact is, Mrs. McRacket, ye'll ne'er be content till ye're i' the hoose made wi'out hands."—(Severely)—"See Second Corinthians, fifth chapter, and firrst vairse, Mrs. McRacket!" [Punch Library 1908 *Mr. Punch's Scottish*, 70]

At a missionary meeting in Manchester, when referring to the material advantages of Christianity, he [a Scotsman, the Rev. Peter Mackenzie] said, "Mr. Chairman, when savages get converted they want Manchester calico. They are no longer satisfied to be dressed in sunshine." [Macrae 1904, 28]

A Scottish gentleman in London, who had an uncle (a decent old Free Kirk farmer from Caithness) visiting him in the city, took him on Sunday to St. Paul's where a prayer-book was handed to him when the service was beginning. He had never seen the English prayer-book before, and his nephew observed him peering curiously into it. By and by, as leaf after leaf was turned, he saw a look of anxiety, deepening almost to alarm, gathering in his uncle's face. Next thing he observed was his uncle laying down the book, picking up his hat stealthily, and making his way to the door. Thinking he was ill, his nephew followed him. On getting outside, he said, "What did you come out for? Not ill, I hope?"

"No; but it was enough to mak' me ill to see yon list o' collections."

"Collections? Why, there's only the offertory near the end."

"Weel," said his uncle, "they shouldna mark so mony collections in the book. When I turned ower the leaves, there was naethin' but 'Collect' and bits o'prayers, and then 'Collect' again, and mair prayers, and ower the pages, 'Collect' again! Dod! says I to mysel', if I bide till a' thae collections is ta'en, I'll no' hae a bawbee left in my pooch!" [Macrae 1904, 55–56]

Jokes like these are still in circulation but in a secular world new jokes about "canny Scots" have lost their Calvinistic savor. An obsessive ascetic canniness still prowls about in many Scots jokes like the *Geist* of *Banko*, but the recent proliferation of international jokes about "canny Scots" has been based on the ingenious but mechanical application of the "canny" comic script to a wide range of circumstances. Joke-tellers have cracked the formula for Scots or Aberdonian canniness and produced a flood of new jokes that are the counterpart of the "new" ethnic jokes about stupidity.

Advertisements in Aberdeen:

'Bring your golf ball to be recovered'.

'Pair of boots for sale. Laces in good order'. [SFGB]

The police in Aberdeen were called out to investigate reports of a Peeping Tom with a telescope. When they arrived they found him leaning out of the window and shouting across the street 'Turn the sound up'. [SFGB]

The man who invented slow motion films got the idea from seeing an Aberdonian reach for the bill in a restaurant. [SFGB]

Why do traffic lights have an orange light as well as a red and a green one?

To give Scottish drivers time to start their engines. [SFGB]

Then there was the Aberdonian who invented a windscreen that wouldn't hold parking tickets. [Hodes 1978, 122]

An Aberdonian ran into the road to pick up a penny and was knocked down by a lorry. Coroner's verdict—'Death from natural causes'. [SFGB]

In Scottish jokes the ethnic reference to the Scots is an indirect hint that the joke has a canny and not a stupid, cowardly, or dirty ending. If all reference to Scots or Aberdonians were deleted the jokes would be less funny because there would be too much ambiguity, with too many possible interpretations. If, on the other hand, a phrase such as "cunning person" or "stingy person" were employed instead of "Scot," the joke would become flat and obvious and there would not be enough ambiguity. The value of the terms "Scots" or "Aberdonian" is that they suggest "canniness" to a knowing audience but avoid a crudely explicit statement to that effect. The audience realizes that a joke is on the way and what kind of joke it is going to be but the fact that Scotland is a real place with real people creates just enough doubt to maintain the right level of ambiguity. The "canny Scot" of recent jokes is a wild fantasy built around a conventionalized character but the pretense of reality is still there. Modern ethnic jokes about the "canny" and the "stupid" are generally based on this combination of wild fantasy and pretended reality linked by a particular known convention. Over time joke-tellers have learned how to abstract the convention from the more ponderous ethnic anecdotes of the past [see also Utley 1971–73, and 1965, 12–13] and to employ it to create new structured puzzles and games of half surprise in which real people are made to behave in unreal ways that can be predicted in general terms but where each specific instance comes as a surprise.

Over time the growth of jokes about the Irish and the Scots has led to the development of standard formulas for constructing ethnic jokes about stupidity and canniness that often make but little use of the particular characteristics of these peoples. In the past jokes on these same themes had a distinctly Irish or Scottish flavor about them and the compilers and raconteurs of such jokes were often themselves Irishmen or Scots who used the jokes to project a distinctive national identity. In the era of snappy formula-based ethnic jokes it has become more difficult for the butts of the jokes to use the jokes in this way; the jokes have become more completely the property of those outside looking on but not in.

CHAPTER SEVEN

Militarists and Cowards

Ethnic jokes about cowardice and militarism can usefully be compared with the opposed pair of ethnic jokes about the stupid and the canny discussed at length earlier. Ethnic jokes about allegedly cowardly and militaristic groups are neither as numerous nor as widespread as those about stupidity and canniness, but they express the same ambivalence about the life of the military as the latter do about the moral and material uncertainties and contradictions of economic life.

In many countries in peacetime, but particularly in the Western industrial societies, the armed forces have often seemed to be a relatively peripheral institution whose concerns do not impinge on the day-to-day life of most citizens. Indeed, the army and its preoccupations have been portrayed as archaic, both by its critics and by its romantic defenders, who have stressed the antithesis between the outlook of the military and the way of life of complex modern societies.[1] Yet for much of the twentieth century people's lives have been overshadowed by war or the possibility of war. Military institutions can and do suddenly become of central importance, vital to the maintenance of the power and position of the state and even to the very existence and independence of the society. The pattern of civil life is disrupted and civilians find themselves either part of or highly dependent on their armed forces. Out of this uncertainty ethnic jokes about cowardice and militarism emerge to take their place alongside the perennial jokes about the stupid and the canny.

The butts of ethnic jokes about cowardice and militarism are often but by no means always, the peoples of present or former enemy nations. Sometimes allied nations or ethnic minorities within a nation's own army figure in the jokes, and in many cases the reshuffling of international alliances often means that yesterday's enemy is today's ally. Ethnic jokes are spontaneously generated by ordinary people and they do not necessarily change to fit in with the gyrations of politicians and diplomats. The problem of why certain ethnic groups rather than others are made the subject of jokes about their alleged cowardly or militaristic propensities has to be resolved, as in the case of the stupid and the canny, by examining the relevant social and historical background to the jokes and, where possible, on a comparative basis.

First, though, it is necessary to look in more detail at why these qualities should be singled out at all as a subject for ethnic jokes. At the root of such jokes there lies once again a cultural contradiction between two legitimate but often incompatible sets of values—those stemming from the civilian way of life and those that underpin the prestige and the moral outlook of the military. This contradiction is a permanent feature of the contemporary world, but it appears at its sharpest as a result of a major war when civilians are ordered to become soldiers and the demands of the military also cut across the lives of the rest of the community, albeit nothing like as drastically. Civilians who suddenly find themselves subject to military authority necessarily experience a conflict of values between, on the one hand, the insistence of the military on the qualities of a good soldier, such as physical courage, discipline, and obedience, and, on the other, the persisting legitimate norms of peacetime that stress self-preservation, individual autonomy, and family rather than military loyalty. Even the civilians who do become disciplined and reliable soldiers may well resent being in the army and may resent even more the patriotic rhetoric of those at a safe distance from actual combat.[2]

> Humor . . . by playing upon incongruities between normal values and the transmuted values of the combat situation or between combat actualities and rearward conceptions of combat or by exaggeration, understatement or the singling out of the irrelevant, helped the men to achieve a kind of distance from their threatening experiences. [Stouffer et al. 1949B]

The combat or wartime situation is productive of two kinds of humor [see Ziv 1984, 106]—an official patriotic humor, favored particularly but by no means exclusively by political and military leaders, and a mocking informal humor that derides the military hierarchy and its values and expresses a strong wish to get back to civilian life. The two forms of humor coexist and indeed can overlap.[3]

An awareness of the contradictory nature of military and civilian roles and values is not limited to those who experience it directly but becomes part of the taken-for-granted world of the rest of the population and indeed is transmitted to future generations. People accept with one half of their minds the official version of heroics, duty, and sacrifice, but they are also well aware that reality has another, stronger and nastier side to it.[4] Under these circumstances the linked pair of opposed ethnic jokes about cowardice and militarism express the two kinds of failure that can overtake the individual or the group, forms of failure that are best comically pinned on other people. Since in the modern world wars usually occur between nations or coalitions of nations it is not surprising that wars give rise to ethnic jokes, for it is a time when ethnic groups are visibly mobilized as such. In the marketplace and even in politics the "visible" behavior of the members of an ethnic group that gives rise to ethnic jokes is sometimes rooted in and reducible to the responses of individuals or social classes to particular opportunities and predicaments. Wars between nation-states, on the other hand, are organized on the basis of ethnicity and its salience is unmistakable, even if the war is justified in ideological terms.

Cowardice is laughed at because it is perceived as one of the most natural and yet discreditable forms of failure for a soldier. Most people caught up in a war are thoroughly scared for much of the time, and even if the cause is a popular and legitimate one, no one wants to be the one who gets killed or mutilated for it. It is difficult enough for people simply to keep on going in these degrading and frightening circumstances, and yet armies do manage to keep fighting in a disciplined way, sometimes for years at a time [see Stouffer et al. 1949B, 107]. As a joke of World War I put it: " 'Bill . . . you're in a hell of a funk.' 'Yes, I am. If you were in as big a funk you'd run away.' " [William Moore 1979, 53].

If, for any reason, a large portion of a country's soldiers should fail to go on fighting and give way to fear, then such mass cowardice could lead to the collapse of the army and the defeat of the country. In an uncertain world jokes ascribe this threatening and all too human quality, which can lead to failure and disaster, to another group of people altogether. It is not necessarily an enemy nation that becomes the butt of such jokes; it may equally well be an ally or an ethnic minority in the joke-tellers' own forces. The strong connection between cowardice and military failure is to be seen in the jokes themselves, for those groups who are the butt of jokes about cowardice also feature in ethnic jokes that refer directly to their military failure or to their unsoldierly traits in general.

Since the Second World War, ethnic jokes about cowardice and military failure have been told about the Italians, in France, Britain, the United States, Australia, Greece, Germany, and many other countries. The jokes found in these countries are often very similar and it is probable that they circulate easily from one country to another because of the popularity of the theme and the shared comic view other people have of the Italians. Similar jokes were told in the Middle East and elsewhere about Egyptians following their defeats by the Israelis, and are told in Spain about Galicians, in Pakistan about Kashmiris and Bengalis, and in Iran about Kashanis [see UCBFA files for Iran and Pakistan]. During and after World War I Americans, and particularly Southerners, told jokes about their own black troops. Jokes based on the ethnic cowardice script are both popular and widespread:

One Bengali comes and says, "I want to be recruited." So the recruiting officer tried to persuade him not to join the army because he might get killed. But the Bengali said, "I want a job in the army and I am willing to be killed." The officer said, "Let me give you a test to see how strong and brave you are." He made the Bengali stand at a distance and the officer shot at him. The first bullet passed on one side of his ear. He just stood there very straight, he didn't get very alarmed at that. The second bullet went close by the other ear. The Bengali was still standing straight. The third bullet went over his head, but he was still standing in the same position. The officer was really impressed that he is really a brave person. So officer goes to candidate, shakes his hand and says, "You are really a brave person. You have been taken in the army." The Bengali says, "Thank you sir, but could you give me one pair of slacks?" [UCBFA Pakistan file, Evans 1966. See also Anstey 1897, 121, 198, and Stouffer et al. 1949B, 201]

They recruited some Kashmiris into the armed forces and gave them guns and told them to fire the guns. So, the Kashmiri soldiers put their guns on the ground under the sun since they were afraid to fire the guns themselves, and said to the officer, "When the sun's rays hit the guns, they will fire automatically." [UCBFA Pakistan file, Saeed 1976. See also Knight 1897, 109–110, and Tyndale-Biscoe 1925, 78–79]

Veni, vidi, Vichy.
I came, I saw, I concurred. [Bushell 1984, 186]

The Italian army has a new battle flag—a white cross on a white background. [British 1970s]

Mussolini appeared on a balcony in Rome and addressed a large gathering of Italian soldiers calling for a volunteer for a dangerous mission. No one came forward, so Mussolini announced that he would drop a feather from a traditional Italian military plumed hat from the balcony and the hero on whose head it fell would be the man chosen. He released the feather and retired from the balcony to wait for the crowd to acclaim the man who had been selected. He waited for a quarter of an hour . . . half an hour . . . an entire hour, but there was complete silence. He quietly peeped over the balcony to see what had happened. The feather was still floating in the air and every soldier was puffing it up as hard as he could. [Clément 1945, 47–48. See also Wilde 1973, 50]

It is said that during the Italian-Greek war, you know during the Second World War when the Italians tried to invade Greece, but they aren't very good soldiers, they're bad. Anyway a Greek was captured by an Italian general, and he was dressed in a red uniform, and the general couldn't imagine just why this crackpot was wearing red. And he says 'Well my general, I am bleeding all over, I am very hurt, but I don't want you to see my blood, because I don't want to give an Italian that satisfaction.' And thereupon the guy collapsed and died. And the Italian general just stood up and said, 'Well, that's a wonderful idea! I'll have to order brown uniforms for all my soldiers.' [UCBFA, Greece, Deborah Rossman 1964. Note also Stouffer et al. 1949B, 201]

German military dispatch 1947:

The OKW has made it known that: German forces under the leadership of Field-Marshall Kesselring yesterday occupied the isthmus of Panama. Another force led by Field-Marshall von Manstein is besieging Washington, the capital of the United States. The Führer has named Marshall Göring as Governor of South America.

Italian planes have bombed and clearly damaged the harbour of Valetta in Malta. [Gamm 1979, 124]

The Voice of a Prophet

A company of a division of colored troops were in heavy marching order awaiting the word to start for the front. It was to be their first actual contact with the enemy. One of the privates had somewhere picked up a copy of the Paris edition of the New York *Herald*.

"Does dat air paper say anything about us boys?" inquired a sergeant.

"It sho' do," answered the private, improvising. "It sez yere dat twenty-five thousand cullid troops is goin' over de top to-night, suppo'ted by fifty thousand Frenchmen."

From down the line came a third voice, saying:

"Well, I knows whut to-morrow's number of dat paper's gwine say. It's gwine say, in big black letters, 'Fifty thousand Frenchmen trompled to death by twenty-five thousand niggers.' " [Cobb 1923, 122. See also House 1944, 55]

Under the strain of heavy bombardment and inactivity, a group of negro soldiers headed away from the front in a big hurry and without any such orders: Afterward, at an inquiry one was asked:

"Were you running?"

He answered, "Naw, suh, but I passed several what wuz." [House 1944, 58]

For sale

10,000 genuine Italian army rifles. Cheap. Have never been fired. Have only been used once. [Wilde 1973, 18]

How do you train Italians to be soldiers?

First teach them to raise their hands above their heads. [Wilde 1973, 24]

The other comic mode of failure, which stands in opposition to cowardice, is seen in ethnic jokes about militarism. The ethnic militarists of the jokes are depicted as too warlike, over-obedient, too prone to subordinate their personal interests to the demands of their military leaders, too willing to go on fighting a lost and hopeless war whatever the cost, too ruthless in their pursuit of victory and conquest.

As with jokes about "canny" groups who are seen as financially shrewd but as failing in a broader, human sense, so too the militarist of the jokes is often portrayed as a thorough soldier but also as a loser, as someone whose very drive for success can be comically self-defeating. The jokes make fun of the idea that men could or should lose their individuality altogether and become mere parts of a military machine, without a life and purpose of their own. The joke-tellers' ambivalent view of the military leads them to mock ethnic groups whose members can be portrayed as reveling in militarism or at least submitting to it without doubt, reservation, or resentment. Just as ethnic jokes about the canny may depict them as a threat to others as well as themselves, so too ethnic jokes about militarists portray them as capable of the ruthless and reckless use of force and of inflicting wanton and deliberate atrocities on others. These are traits which people humorously export from their own group and which are then comically pinned on another nation.

A Bavarian immigrant joined a Union regiment and in the third year of the war was sent to Virginia. One night he imbibed too heavily of strong drink and fell asleep in a corn crib. When he awakened he discovered that during the night a negro camp follower had stolen his uniform, leaving behind a ragged civilian outfit. The German clothed himself in these tatters and set out to find his command.

Presently another and even more disagreeable circumstance than the theft of his wardrobe impressed itself upon him. By certain signs he was made aware that the Federal forces had withdrawn from their old positions and the enemy had advanced so that he was now inside the foe's lines. As he limped towards the rear, hoping to overtake the retreating force, a squad of ragged gray troopers came whirling out of a thicket and surrounded him. Quite frankly he told them who and what he was and they made a prisoner out of him.

Presently his captors halted him where a tree limb stretched across the road, and one of the Southerners, unlooping a plow line from his saddle-bow, proceeded to fashion a slip-noose in one end of it. The captive inquired of the lieutenant in command what the purpose of this might be.

"Why" said the lieutenant, "we're going to treat you as we would any Yank caught inside our lines in disguise. Under the laws of war we're going to hang you as a spy."

"Vell," said the German "votever is der rule!" [Cobb 1925, 210. Cobb says the joke was told to him by a survivor of Mosby's cavalry].

I just found a German-Chinese restaurant. The food is delicious. The only problem is an hour later you're hungry for power. [Wilde 1978A, 92]

In 1940, not knowing what to do next in order to invade Britain, Hitler decided to drain the English Channel. He massed a million German soldiers all along the coast of Normandy, each man standing exactly one metre behind the man in front, and on the command of the officers—ein, zwei [*sic*], drei—each line of men stepped forward and swallowed three mouthfuls of sea-water. During the whole of the first day the operation went very well but as the sun set an evening breeze blew across from the English coast a steady chant of "One, two, three—pee!" [Nègre 1973 vol. 1, 84. See also Clément 1945, 17–18]

The German football team had beaten the English team by seventeen goals to nil. After the match a German supporter meeting a disconsolate English fan on his way home said to him triumphantly, "We have beaten you at your national game."

"So what," replied the Englishman, "We beat you at yours twice." [British 1960s. See also The not the nine o'clock news team 1981 January 24th]

As with the jokes about the "stupid" and the "canny" the opposed pair of ethnic jokes about cowardice and militarism carry an implicit balanced[5] pair of messages:

Don't undervalue the world of the military.
Don't overvalue it, either.

The jokes portray the "cowardly" ethnic groups as abandoning the military qualities of courage and discipline altogether, and failing in consequence. By contrast the "militarists" of the jokes subordinate themselves totally to the military, to their own detriment as well as to the detriment of others. The jokes and their messages once again reflect the dilemma caused by a conflict of two sets of moral requirements and social objectives. There is in many, perhaps most, societies a tension between the wishes of the individual and the demands of the state [see Stouffer et al. 1949B, 551], and this is likely to be intensified in wartime when organized defense necessarily leads to bureaucratic demands for orderly obedience to regulations, even in the face of considerable danger, and the subordination of the individual to a disciplined hierarchy [see Stouffer et al. 1949B, 97–98]. The opposed ethnic jokes about cowardice and militarism are part of a diffuse, informal attempt to find some kind of reasonable balance in a world that is often felt to be unbalanced.

It is sometimes suggested that the reason the Germans and the Italians are the nations most frequently made the butts of jokes about militarism and cowardice respectively in so many Western nations is that they were, from the point of view of the joke-tellers, on the "other side," on the "wrong side" in World War II, and they lost. During the war it would have suited the leaders of the Allied powers to belittle their opponents with a charge of cowardice or to undermine their moral credibility by portraying them as militarists, as aggressors committing atrocities, and jokes could be one way of conveying such images of the enemy.

There is no doubt that attempts are made to manipulate images of the enemy as cowards or militarists in wartime propaganda [e.g., see Szarota 1978, 229–54] but these often fail and rebound in the face of experiences that contradict them. The winners of a war, as well as the losers, are likely to feel disillusioned when atrocity stories turn out to be fraudulent or a supposedly cowardly enemy puts up a strong resistance. In World War I British and American propaganda centered on alleged German atrocities, and German propaganda on the alleged cowardice of their enemies, but in neither case did this give rise to a lasting tradition of ethnic jokes. The ethnic jokes told in English about cowardice with a World War I setting do not refer to any of the enemy nations, but rather focus on allies and ethnic minorities within their own ranks. There is no simple link between the efforts of propagandists and the emergence of ethnic jokes. Ethnic jokes about militarism and cowardice have their origins in wartime conflicts but they cannot be reduced to a crude and wishful labeling of one's enemies. Unlike political cartoons, which portray and respond to ethnic and national conflicts in a very rapid and direct way, ethnic jokes are rarely the result of a deliberate and purposive campaign. There is an orderly and explicable pattern to ethnic jokes but it is a spontaneous order [see Polanyi 1951, 156] arising from the sum of the experiences and perceptions of a large number of individuals, not a planned or corporate order resulting from the interlocking decisions of a small number of politicians, editors, and cartoonists.

Ethnic jokes about the Germans and the Italians are both older and younger than World War II and only tangentially related to wartime propaganda, but nonetheless the majority of them stem from that conflict. The key to an understanding of why in recent times the Italians have so frequently been made the butts of ethnic jokes about cowardice and the Germans of jokes about militarism must be sought in the first instance in certain highly visible yet problematic aspects of World War II.

With the Italians, the visible events were the unwillingness of Italian armies and naval forces to take the offensive, and the ease with which numerically inferior enemy forces defeated the Italians, who surrendered or fled in disorder. The contrast between this behavior and the bellicose propaganda of the Italian government was seen as ludicrous by contemporary observers in many countries and, indeed, it is difficult to see how it could have been viewed otherwise. Every nation involved in World War II experienced surprise defeats or sudden panic—what was unusual about the Italians was that it happened again and again and again, in Albania/Greece, in Ethiopia, and in North Africa.[6] This was not a propaganda claim by their opponents but a highly visible fact and one admitted by the Italians (to themselves at least) and by their allies.[7] The unprovoked Italian invasion of Greece, a much weaker country one-sixth of the size of Italy, in 1940, was a total failure and, but for subsequent German intervention on their side, the Italians might well have lost. After six months of war the Italian army was still on the Italian (Albanian) side of the Greek frontier, whereas the successful German invasion and conquest of Greece took two weeks.[8] French and Greek ethnic jokes about the Italians refer to this fiasco, sometimes directly:

In 1940 at Menton, on the French border with Italy, placards were put up saying: "This is French territory, Greeks. Don't pursue the Italians past this point." [Bauer 1972 vol. 12 No. 1., 309. For further examples see Clément 1945]

The performance of the Italian armies in North Africa was no better. In 1940–41 an Italian army of a quarter of a million was destroyed by an Allied force of 30,000 men which took 130,000 Italian prisoners, including many generals.[9] The Italian surrender, and hence the astounding scale of the surrender, was extensively photographed and reported throughout the world and was even shown in newsreel films, which must have popularized the image of the Italians as reluctant soldiers. Contemporary Allied accounts of the North African campaign written for popular consumption were naturally one-sided but they also expressed *surprise* at events such as those attending the fall of the Italian strongpoint, Bardia; the Allied military leaders had initially *overestimated* the Italian fighting capacity [see Barnett 1983, 31]:

> Then followed an extra-ordinary scene, [at Bardia] thousands of Italians waving white flags came out of the dug outs and caves in the cliff side to surrender. On examining the caves later, our men found large stocks of white flags evidently prepared well ahead for this eventuality. [*The Conquest of North Africa* n.d., 17. See also Horrabin 1941, 90–97]

These events gave rise to British, French, Australian, and American ethnic jokes of many kinds, first long, detailed humorous anecdotes purportedly rooted in fact, then narrative jokes, and eventually highly compressed jokes built around a known formula.

Whether the reason was scepticism about their cause, leadership, weaponry, equipment, prospects or some of everything listed, the Italian Army in the Western Desert showed modified enthusiasm for their task as 1940 moved into 1941.

Their artillerymen were much respected by their British, Indian and Australian opponents. The rest had a leaning towards what a later generation would call unilateral disarmament. . . .

A pioneer confronter of a surrender problem was a subaltern of the 11th Hussars, out ahead with a troop of armoured cars. . . .

There was mention of a modest collection of prisoners among the first of his wirelessed reports. He had, he said, taken five.

His next message raised the total to fourteen.

An hour later he had ninety-three and was beginning to wonder what to do with them.

As time passed he became less precise in head count. He passed on successive bulletins of 'about two hundred', 'about five hundred', 'about a thousand'.

By the late afternoon he had switched to a fresh basis of calculation. 'I now have with me', he signalled, 'two and a half acres of prisoners'. [Noonan 1983, 72]

A mini-Olympics had been organised among NATO troops and when the ground and equipment was being inspected by officers of the various nations competing, an Italian colonel objected to the run-up for the high jump being of sand. It should, he insisted rather too heatedly, be of the same consistency as the track, and he continued to argue and beat the air about this, though nobody else objected. A British colonel who sported the Africa Star tried to smooth (?) things over by remarking amiably, 'Oh come, Colonel, I seem to remember your chaps ran pretty well on sand in the desert'. [Dickinson and Hooper n.d., 18]

The latter joke has rightly been classified by its editors as a "clanger," precisely because it doesn't smooth things over in a context (NATO) where former opponents are now allies.

Eventually the jokes about "cowardly Italians" have been boiled down to a simple basic formula by French, British, and American joke-tellers alike:

What is the fastest car in the world on sand?

One with British tires on the back wheels and Italian ones in front. [British 1960s. See also Clément 1945, 93]

When the Italians went to war, the first requisition the quartermaster received was for two million white handkerchiefs. [Wilde 1975A, 79]

Once again the Germans had to come to the rescue and Rommel's Afrika Corps drove the Allied armies back. Rommel took care to distribute "his German troops to 'corset' the Italian units." The Allies in turn sought to counterattack "where the enemy was weakest—where most of the defenders were Italian" [de Guingaud 1980, 238]. Later, when the first untried American army units collapsed against the Germans in North Africa in 1943, British and French officers who had in consequence been captured spoke of the Americans as "our Italians" in the presence of their German captors [see Whiting 1986, 160; see also Irving 1978, 281, 291]. Not only was it not very kind or polite for the Europeans to refer to their ally in this way, it was also unwise; Rommel got the message and selectively attacked American units at Kasserine, causing them to flee in terror shouting "The Krauts are coming!" [Whiting 1986, 160; see also 204, 211]. Fortunately it did not become a habit, the world was spared a new ethnic joke, and subsequent calls for an American surrender at Bastogne were met with a defiant, not a cracking, "Nuts!"

German jokes about the Italians in North Africa also made fun of them as unreliable and cowardly soldiers, from the perspective of an ally who was doing most of the real fighting.[10]

The Italians have invented a new dance—the dance of retreat. The steps are: one step forward, two steps back, look over your shoulder, push your partner forward and once more from the front. [Gamm 1979, 123]

Italian military news: The Italian divisions under General Pompolini have had an outstanding success on the right wing of our western front at Audjila. A British bicycle was surrounded, and the handlebars are firmly within our grasp. There is still bitter fighting over the pedals. The backwheel has come off according to plan and the frame brought to the ground. [Gamm 1979, 134]

The striking difference between the military performance of the Germans and the Italians, which has been the subject of many ethnic jokes, has been systematically studied by the military sociologist Stanislav Andreski, who was also an army officer in World War II:

> I feel on safe ground accepting the view commonly held among the Allied soldiers who regarded the German troops as formidable and the Italians as easy to cope with. I have never come across a contrary opinion, and everything I have read about the history of the operations fits this assessment. . . . Soldiers commonly have an exaggerated opinion of their own collective capacity and unrealistically underestimate the strength of their enemies or the worth of their allies whom they often accuse of not pulling their weight, but I have the impression that they are fairly objective in making judgements about the relative strength of their enemies. . . . [The Italian] soldiers did not want to fight. The behaviour of the prisoners of war provided evidence of this: whereas the Germans (as least until the very end of the war) had to be closely guarded, very few Italians tried to escape and many seemed to be happy to be out of the fighting. [Andreski 1982, 248–49. See also Newby 1975, 37, 56–59, and Reid 1965 (1952), 164]

With the exception of the miniature submarine and torpedo units, the Italian navy in World War II was also reluctant to take action against a numerically weaker enemy and remained in harbor so that its larger ships would not be risked in a major action.[11] Much of the Italian fleet was put out of action in 1940, while anchored at Taranto, in an attack by twenty slow-moving, obsolete Swordfish biplanes launched from a carrier. Italian caution also brought disaster at the battle of Cape Matapan.[12] The unwillingness of the Italian navy to leave harbor, and its destruction by inferior forces because it was incompetently defended, gave rise to ethnic jokes both at the time and subsequently:

British sailor referring to bespectacled colleague:
Yeah, Mediterranean Fleet I should imagine. Shorty strained his sight looking for the Italian navy. [Thomas 1944B, 8]

How do you view the Italian navy?
Through a glass bottom boat. [UCBFA Italy file, Elizabeth Rupiper 1970]

What was the name of Mussolini's flagship?
Chicken of the Sea. [Wilde 1975A, 17]

The reason that the military incompetence of the Italians in World War II led to so many different ethnic jokes about cowardice is that it was highly visible, spectacular, and baffling. People of other similar nations, who observed or knew about the Italians' collapse, considered that their armies would have gone on fighting under the same circumstances. The people of a given culture have in their minds a rough norm as to how long armies should go on fighting and when further resistance would be senseless. The Italian forces stopped fighting a very long way short of the point that the peoples of other Western countries considered reasonable. There are, as we shall see later, sociological explanations for this, but they are complicated and the subject of disagreement. The rapid collapse of Italian fighting capacity was a puzzle, an intellectual problem, an inexplicable oddity, a visible phenomenon without an agreed cause. In such a situation crude, commonsense explanations emerge, based on a shaky syllogism: "The Italians ran away or surrendered; cowardly soldiers behave in this way; therefore the Italians are cowardly soldiers."

That ethnic jokes about cowardice have been pinned on the Italians has nothing to do with the social position of Italian minorities in the United States [cf. Dundes 1971, 192], Britain, France, or Greece, although their social position may be the cause of other kinds of ethnic jokes told about Italians. It is significant that whereas ethnic jokes about Italian cowardice are common to many countries, other types of ethnic jokes about

Italians differ markedly between countries [e.g., contrast the contents of the jokes in Nègre (1973) with those of Wilde (1973)].

The rough Western norm as to when armies should or should not go on fighting was breached in the opposite direction in World War II by the Germans. The collapse of the Italian will to fight in 1940–41, when they were in a reasonably strong position, has its counterpart in the persisting willingness and ability of the Germans to wage war in 1944–45, long after their military position had become hopeless. Despite intensive Allied propaganda that sought to convince the German troops that their situation was desperate and thus induce them to surrender, they kept on fighting to the very end even though their cities had been utterly destroyed by bombing, their country was occupied by foreign armies, and their people were close to starvation.[13] Even young boys and old men were called up in the last weeks of World War II.[14] The dogged resistance of the Germans against very heavy odds in the last months of the war has been seen by social observers as a puzzling problem calling for a sociological explanation (as was the rapid collapse of the Italian army) and has been the subject of considerable investigation and debate [e.g., see Shils and Janowitz 1975, 345–67]. For most outsiders, however, the only visible phenomenon was the Germans' desperate last-ditch defense and their refusal to surrender long after the point that others regarded as reasonable, sensible, even honorable. This aspect of German militarism has itself given rise to ethnic jokes, both at the time and subsequently.

In 1956, off the coast of the Orkney Islands, a fishing trawler was astounded to see a German submarine rise to the surface, the gun on deck swiftly manned and the captain call across to them from the conning tower to surrender.

"But the war's been over for years!" called back the master of the trawler.

"Himmel!" said the German Naval Captain "Who won?"

"We did," was the reply.

"You did? Ach . . . Hoch der Kaiser!" [Kilgarriff 1979, 20. See also *Die Besten Soldatenwitze* 1982, 138]

It was 1944. The world was in a mess. God decided to send Methuselah to see at first hand what mankind was up to. Methuselah obeyed and came back two days later. "What is going on down there?" God asked him.

"Well," said Methuselah, "I had only just arrived in Berlin when I found I was due to leave very soon. They were calling up my age-class." [Bramieri 1980B, 209][15]

The German people themselves were aware that desperate resistance to the bitter end, using boys and old men as combat soldiers, was excessive and irrational [see Koch 1975, 248–49; Shils and Janowitz 1975, 375]. They went on fighting and obeying orders, but they also told mocking jokes about the desperate use of old and young in battle.

Who has gold in his mouth, silver in his hair and lead in his limbs?
A soldier in the Volkssturm [Home Guard]. [Gamm 1979, 117]

At the last stage of World War II the [German] Optimists said, "We're going to lose the war."

And the Pessimists said, "Yes—but when?" [Raskin 1985, 229]

The Germans perceived the tension between the demands of the military and the aspirations of the individual in much the same way as did other nations with a West European culture and traditions, even though the behavior of the German army and government in World War II was far closer to the militarist end of the spectrum than other people thought reasonable. Yet it is the very fact that the Germans shared a common European culture with the Western Allies that led to the Germans, rather than, say, the Japanese, becoming the butts of ethnic jokes about militarism. The Germans were culturally similar enough to their opponents to be treated as an aberrant version of the familiar. At the back of their minds many of the joke-tellers must suspect that the road to Dunkirk ends in Lüneburg and that the Volkssturm was only Dad's army in action.

By contrast, the continued fierce resistance of the Japanese well into 1945, until atomic weapons were used against them (even then sections of the Japanese military leadership wanted to continue fighting and tried to prevent the Emperor's final broadcast announcing surrender), was incomprehensible to their American, Australian, and British opponents. The absolute unwillingness of individual Japanese soldiers to surrender even when overwhelmed by superior forces, the way the wounded and dying would commit suicide rather than be captured, the fanatical dedication of the kamikaze pilots,[16] and the cruel treatment of Allied prisoners of war could not be understood within a framework of conventional Western cultural categories [see Morris 1980, 458–61]. In consequence there are few Western jokes about Japanese militarism, though such jokes may of course exist in the repertoires of the East Asian peoples of China, Korea, and the Philippines, who bore the brunt of Japanese military brutality [see MacArthur 1965, 338–39; O'Conroy 1933, 37–38; Russell 1960] and who possibly have a greater degree of insight into Japanese society, culture, and character, though even this is doubtful given the sharp division between the Japanese and all *gaijin*.

Western jokes about kamikaze pilots employ the concept not to tell ethnic jokes about the Japanese but to give a new twist to familiar "stupid" and "canny" ethnic scripts—The Polish kamikaze pilot who flew 47 missions, the annual reunion of the Irish kamikaze pilots association, the

Jewish kamikaze pilot who crashed in his brother's scrapyard. The discovery of lone Japanese soldiers on Guam in 1973 and on a small island in the Philippines in 1974 still fighting the Second World War nearly thirty years after it had finished [Onoda 1976] was a major news story and still appears in humorous collections of amazing "true" stories [e.g., Pile 1980, 162], but it has not given rise to a new genre of jokes or anecdotes. During and immediately after the Second World War there was intense hostility toward the Japanese [see Dundes 1971, 192–93] in the Western nations and they were uniformly depicted as fanatical militarists who treated prisoners of war with especial cruelty [e.g., see Herbert 1945, 3; Russell 1960]. Also there were many hostile cartoons that ridiculed Japanese militarism from the time that Japanese aggression first impinged on China in the 1930s to the last fierce battles in the Pacific and in Burma.[17] On the west coast of Canada and the United States well over a hundred thousand people of Japanese descent were interned and treated with quite unjustified harshness, and only very recently has the important positive contribution of Nisei volunteers (often straight from the internment camps) to the Allied war effort been properly recognized. But there were and are hardly any ethnic jokes about Japanese militarism, a fact that undermines the simplistic view that such jokes merely grow out of and provide a cloak for the serious hostile rejection of a particularly alien people.

Ethnic jokes are more likely to be told about peoples who are familiar and similar to the joke-tellers, and whose differences from them are comprehensible. Familiarity and similarity have made it possible for Europeans and Americans to invent jokes about the speed and ferocity of the German conquest of Europe in World War II which depend on a knowledge not simply of events but of aspects of the style and language of German National Socialism and its leaders. No one ever sang about Tojo to the tune of Colonel Bogey [see Barker 1980, 29].

What was the German code name for the first stage of their invasion of the Netherlands?

Rötterdämmerung.

And for the last stage?

Der Fliegende Holländer. [British 1970s]

Rötterdämmerung refers to the destruction of Rotterdam by German bombing in 1940 at the very time when the surrender of the city was being negotiated [Shirer 1960, 722]. German military code names were often drawn from the same "Aryan" mythology [Jones 1979, 169–70] that influenced the nationalistic German composer Richard Wagner, writer of the operas *Die Götterdämmerung* (The Twilight of the Gods, the last battle, which will destroy the world) and *Der Fliegende Holländer* (The Flying Dutchman).

Hitler's speeches also provide a framework for ethnic jokes based on the political and rhetorical style of an expansionist German militarism. Many of these jokes, told long after the war, treat the aggressive style and content of Hitler's tirades as a German ethnic trait:

After World War II the German government appointed a Minister for Denazification, whose task it was to weed out ex-Nazis and those with Nazi sympathies who still held government posts. A couple of years after his appointment he spoke to a large political rally telling them about his achievements: "In the first year of the denazification program we eliminated two hundred Nazis; in the second year of the program we eliminated eight thousand Nazis; last year we eliminated one hundred and twenty thousand Nazis; this year we shall eliminate two million Nazis. And, when we have eliminated all the Nazis in Germany we shall go on to eliminate the Nazis in Holland, France, England . . . and the whole world!" [British 1960s]

This joke captures the manic, boundless, aggressive quality of German National Socialism, especially when told with appropriate gestures and changes of voice and facial expression. It is very much rooted in the rhythms of some of Hitler's speeches and tirades in which repetition culminates in a shriek,[18] a trick also employed in the harangues of lesser German officials [e.g., see Wood and Wood 1976, 222–23].

A German fellow gets a job as a holiday courier. But he's warned by the boss, 'We don't want any of that Nazi nonsense!' So he's fine for three weeks. Then, one day, he's waiting on the station platform. A party of holidaymakers arrive.

'Good morning, happy holidaymakers,' he yells. 'Please line up in twos. You will then march to the dining-room. From there you will march to the swimming pool . . . From there you will march to the Dance Hall . . . and from there you will march through Belgium, France and Holland . . . !!!'[Irwin 1972, 106]

The third aspect of German militarism that has been the subject of jokes during and following World War II has been their harsh treatment of prisoners and of the inhabitants of the countries they conquered. The culminating horror was the planned and systematic murder of several million Jews, a deliberate attempt to wipe out an entire people. Even this last occurrence has become the subject of a number of sick and gruesome jokes about Germans and Jews.

A German prison camp. The prisoners are being drilled. This Nazi Sergeant comes out, and yells: 'I want 200 of you to march up to the parachute tower . . . and zen you must all make ze jump without any parachute.'

One little Cockney private says, 'What's the matter with you, mate? Jump without parachutes? We'll all be killed.'

The German says, 'That's nonsense. Only some of you will be killed. It is only a case of mind over matter . . . We do not mind and you do not matter!' [Irwin 1972, 104]

Did you hear about the new German micro-wave oven? It seats twenty-five. [Wilde 1978A, 89]

S. S. Officer: Do you know the difference between a wagon-load of Jews and a wagon-load of billiard balls?

S. S. man: No.

Officer: Good, then you can unload a wagon of billiard balls with a pitch-fork.[19] [Bramieri 1980B, 84; see also similar jokes on 124, 264, 278, 290]

Ethnic jokes about German militarism, like their counterparts about Italian cowardice, are grounded in a series of highly visible events from World War II. It is in principle possible to find social explanations of these events but these are problematic and not readily apparent, whereas the events themselves were glaringly obvious. Once again we find the emergence of the somewhat circular commonsense view of the type "that is what they do because that is the kind of thing they do," which forms the basis of ethnic jokes. A fuller understanding of the origins of these jokes requires an examination of further historical evidence, both to try to explain why the Germans and the Italians behaved in ways that led to the "commonsense" imputation of cowardice and militarism to them and to examine the evolution of the jokes themselves.

Both the Germans and the Italians are peoples with a very ancient consciousness of their national existence, as old as that of England or France and far older than the United States; yet Germany and Italy are new states, patched together out of fragments in the last half of the nineteenth century [Hayes 1960, 38 and Tower 1913, 7–13]. Also, as A. J. P. Taylor [1982, 4] has put it: "A history of the French state would be, by and large, a political history of the French people; a history of the English state would certainly be a history of the English people. But a history of the Reich would not coincide with a political history of the German people." One might add that for Italy there has often been nothing to coincide.

England and France have long been unitary countries, states with roughly the boundaries they have today. The English and French know where their countries begin and end, and have a secure core area, clearly distinguishable from the lands of ambiguous peoples on the fringe. The latter may secede or form separate states such as Ireland or remain as ethnic minorities like the Welsh or the Bretons, but the core area, which contains the bulk of the population and the wealth of these countries, is firm and not fissile. Similarly, the United States has, with the exception of the Civil War, proved to be a united United States. By contrast Italy and Germany, though nations and clearly identified as such by foreigners, are also agglomerates of once independent political units which have long been the focus of strong loyalties. After unification Germans could still identify themselves as Bavarians, Prussians, Saxons, Swabians, etc., and Italians remained citizens of their home cities and regions rather than of the new Italian state.[20] Also, the differences between local dialects and forms of speech are much greater in Germany or Italy than in England or France,[21] and people's affection for and identification with the particular way of speaking of their home area is much more pronounced [see Cesaresco 1892, 26]. One result of this is that even today it is possible to map out a veritable geography of German or Italian jokes, humorous sayings, and *blasons populaires*. Such a task would be much more difficult in, say, contemporary England and the resulting map would appear anachronistic. No one in England today could hope to emulate Herbert Schöffler's 1970 (1941) *Kleine Geographie des Deutschen Witzes* (Little Geography of German Jokes), for English regions and cities on the whole lack a clear identity and have never had an independent political existence. There is no *Weisswurstäquator* to divide Wessex from Mercia, and the Black Country's Enoch and Eli cannot compete with Tünnes and Schäll of Köln.[22] Only Scotland stands where she did.

The continued strong identification of Italians with their home region, town, or city, or even a particular neighborhood, is reflected in the jokes, and highly specific *blasons populaires*, which are more numerous, vivid, and differentiated[23] than is now the case in countries where national patriotism has replaced local loyalty and identification.

A native of Florence was asked in a survey:

Whom do you dislike the most, the French or the Germans?

First the Milanese, then the French, then the Germans. [Italian 1970s]

I found, spray-painted on a wall in the northern Italian city of Brescia in September 1985, a joke in rather bad taste that indicates the strength of local in relation to national Italian loyalties. In May of that year, the Italian football team Juventus of Turin had met the English team Liverpool in the final of the European Cup held at the Heysel Stadium in Belgium. A group of toughs from among the Liverpool supporters at the match launched an unprovoked attack on the Juventus supporters. The latter, faced with an onslaught from a people widely regarded as the thugs of Europe, ran away and were crushed up against one of the stadium walls, which then collapsed, killing thirty-nine Italian fans. The Liverpool hooligans were quite unrepentant, one declaring "I don't care how many

Italians I killed," another saying it was the Italians' fault for running away instead of standing their ground to fight. The vicious Liverpudlians were later identified from video recordings by the British police, who rounded them up in England, and they were, after some delay, extradited to Belgium to be tried for crimes ranging from assault to manslaughter. It was a disgraceful event that featured in hostile cartoons all over Europe [e.g., see Beeldenstorm 1985], and a leading Czech spokesman on sport immediately declared, on a television news program in Prague, that such behavior was only to be expected from a ruthlessly aggressive nation such as the British, who (unlike the Soviets) had a long history of wantonly attacking others. An official delegation from Liverpool went soon afterwards to Turin to apologize to the Italians for the reckless brutality of their own people. Given this background it was amazing to see spray-gun graffiti in the center of Brescia (and in other cities too) that insulted the supporters of both A. C. (Athletic Club) Milan, here referred to as Milano (as distinct from Internationale Milano, who are known as "Inter"), *and* those of Juventus of Turin:

"Milano campioni di merda. Liverpool Grazie."
[Milan champions of shit. Thank you Liverpool.]

Graffitti intended to be offensive to the supporters of rival football teams are common enough in other European countries but the commendation of homicidal foreigners who have slain one's fellow-countrymen would not occur elsewhere. Had the Heysel incident happened the other way round, the kind of English graffiti artist who writes "Arsenal champions of shit" on a wall in York or Canterbury would not have felt able to add "Thank you Juventus."

In both Italy and Germany the strength of particular local identities and loyalties meant that national identity and loyalty to the state were problematic, not something that could be taken for granted. However, differences in the culture, social structure, and history of the two societies were such that this common heritage of strong local loyalties had quite opposite results after the unification of the two countries in the second half of the nineteenth century. The Italians failed to develop a sense of unity or of commitment to their new nation-state, and the poor performance of the Italian army, not just in World War II but earlier at Caporetto in World War I, in the Spanish Civil War, and in Italy's various colonial wars, was a result of this. There is no reason to believe that Italians are, as individuals, cowardly or disordered, but historically they have been reluctant to place their bravery and capacity for organization at the service of the state. The Italian state has been seen by its citizens as neither important nor legitimate and hence cannot easily call upon the courage and loyalty that Italians willingly give to smaller, more local groups or upon the organizational skill with which they have created thriving modern industries.

In Germany, by contrast, the rulers of the state created in 1871 following three successful wars by Prussia against neighboring countries were able to secure a strong sense of national identity that overrode particular local loyalties, but one created by and dependent on military success.[24] The army was seen as a crucial unifying factor in Germany, and any potential decline in its greatness as a crumbling of the cement that held a nation of centrifugal fragments together [see Balfour 1975, 27, 31, 334]. Citizenship meant universal military service, rather than universal and effective political rights. The political structure of the country was such that separatism and disunity could only be overcome by the successful assertion of national power and military strength [see Craig 1964, xiv-xv, 217].

It is as well to remember that prior to unification the political and military history of most of the peoples of Germany had been one of fear and humiliation as stronger neighboring states, partisans of opposed religious views and imperial dynasties, fought their wars on German territory. Between 1524 and 1815 they came from all sides. The Thirty Years War (1618–48) left Germany a shatter belt of hundreds of often tiny states, and in many areas between two-thirds and three-quarters of the German population perished.[25] So great was the loss and consequent shortage of men in many areas that polygamy had to be permitted [see Gerard 1917, 57; Perris 1914, 93, 232]. A further century and a half of military, political, and economic weakness and division was followed by French conquest and rule under Napoleon, initially seen as political emancipation but soon felt as a long-to-be-remembered national humiliation for the Germans and a spur to their war of liberation against the French.[26]

One negative result of this tragic history for the German people was that when, in the late nineteenth century, they became a united, powerful, and wealthy nation they were haunted by the fear that any failure to overcome and dominate their neighbors, any concession to local particularism or to the self-respect of their small Polish, French, and Danish ethnic minorities in the border areas would be a display of weakness that could plunge the entire nation back into chaotic fragments at the mercy of foreigners. Also, whereas elsewhere in Western Europe national feeling had been able to grow slowly out of a commitment to a particular national social order and settled government, in Germany nationalism was a fierce ideological program that could not rest easily on the nation's existing history or institutions. It is here that we may seek part of the explanation for the strident and aggressive quality of German nationalism [see Balfour 1975, 5; Krejci 1976, 189–90] and for their obsession with the idea of race, which could provide a malleable synthetic basis for the pretense that an unseen racial unity had always been there in the past to transcend the well-remembered historic disunity and humiliation of a Reichless German people [see Balfour 1975, 10, 189–90; Henry and Hillel 1976, 22]. Thus people who were pacific Bavarians or Rhinelanders, Saxons or Hamburgers became racial mystics and German militarists, because this was the most important means of being German that was available to them [see Taylor 1982, 135, 165, 171, 249–51]. The liberal, democratic, and peaceful side of citizenship became associated with separatist or oppositional political parties and German nationalism became distinctively military in character.

It is worth exploring further the social factors that lie behind Italian and German attitudes to the nation-state and its army as part of a history of ethnic jokes about the Germans and the Italians and to show how the comic images of these peoples as militarists or cowards have evolved.

Ethnic jokes about "cowardly Italians" are largely a twentieth-century phenomenon and only really became common after World War II. However, the comic image of the Italians as unwarlike is much older, as Roger Pinon has shown in his discussion of "the saying that 'Itali sunt imbelles, the Italians do not fight', meaning that when confronted with a battle they flee at the first opportunity" [1980, 76]. Pinon has found references to Italian cowardice as far back as the medieval period, when French and Germans alike mocked the alleged lack of martial courage of the Lombards [see Pinon 1980, 76–79]. The unwarlike reputation of the Italians only became securely established however, in the sixteenth century, when it was referred to by writers as diverse as Rabelais, Machiavelli, Erasmus, and Montaigne.[27] For Machiavelli it was a political problem calling for a solution, for the others a source of amusement, a kind of ethnic joke. As in the twentieth century, the popular humorous expression of this accusation was often in terms of the alleged personal cowardice of the Italians. Montaigne wrote circa 1580 that an Italian seigneur had told him that

> the subtle intuition and vivid imagination of the Italians were such that they perceive far in advance the dangers and accidents that may befall them in the future. Accordingly we must not find it strange that in wartime they take steps to ensure their personal security well in advance of a particular threat or danger becoming clearly visible; that we French and the Spaniards, being less sensitive, would advance further and had to see the danger with our own eyes and feel it with our hands before we became alarmed and lost our self-control; but the Germans and the Swiss, being coarser and heavier, have not the sense to change their minds even when overtaken by battle. Perhaps he was only joking. [1965 Book 2, 126]

Montaigne thus implicitly anticipated the argument put forward here that ethnic jokes about cowardice and militarism stem from peoples' perception of themselves as occupying a balanced position between the opposed extremes of others. In Montaigne's jokey assessment his own people, the French, are to be found taking a balanced view of the hazards of war, safely between the timorous Italians and the insensitive Teutons.

The explanation for the Italians' unwillingness to fight has often been sought in their historical experience of seeing their country divided up and occupied by foreigners. Croce [1928 (1917), 219–22; see also Pinon 1980, 76, 107] has suggested that the image of the Italians as unwarlike arose in the sixteenth century because of their failure to oppose the invasion and occupation of their country by the French, Spanish, and Germans. Foreign occupation in itself, even if initially unresisted, can, however, have the opposite effect and long foreign domination can stimulate patriotism and bellicosity, as in the case of the Irish or the Poles.

The peculiar historical experience of Italy has been the combination of (a) intermittent foreign domination of parts rather than the whole of the country, (b) the persisting division of the country into small, conflicting, and often unstable states, and (c) the existence in the center of the peninsula of the temporal possessions of the Papacy. The international character of the Roman Catholic church long stood in the way of Italian national aspirations and in the past this led to recurrent invasions of Italy by the armies of foreign powers seeking to dominate the Roman Church, an institution with its headquarters in Italy but exercising power and influence throughout much of the rest of Europe.

This combination of factors produced a situation in which foreigners could play one small Italian state off against another and could always find local agents and collaborators to assist in the establishment and maintenance of foreign domination. The nature of divided Italy was such that foreign invasion and foreign rule, far from uniting the country against an outside enemy, only made the divisions still deeper [see Hale 1972, 15–16].

The prolonged disunity and powerlessness of Italy led to a situation in which the only strong loyalties were local ones—to a city, a community, a district, not to the nation. Foreign rule and the instability of the governments and boundaries of the mosaic of states that made up Italy led to the alienation of the Italian people from those who ruled them. Since there were often no agreed and accepted principles either of election or inheritance to determine who ought to be the ruler of a particular state, the governments of the states lacked legitimacy. Conflicts between the Italian states now tended to be fought neither by a militia raised from the citizens, which in earlier centuries had provided the cities with some of the best infantry in Europe [see Verbruggen 1977, 126–27, 153], nor by a standing army of professional soldiers tied to the service of a particular state. Their armies were neither peoples' armies nor armies rooted in a territorial aristocracy, for "the growing power of the cities where it had not exterminated this order of men had completely changed their habits" [Macaulay 1890 vol.1, 47; see also Smith 1902 (1776), 307–308]. The Italian states employed mercenaries on short-term contracts who developed no loyalty to or identification with the state that employed them. Macaulay, in his essay on Machiavelli, has summed up the problems that this created:

> The richest and most enlightened part of the world was left undefended to the assaults of every barbarous invader, to the brutality of Switzerland, the insolence of France, and the fierce rapacity of Aragon. The moral effects which followed from this state of things were still more remarkable.
>
> Among the rude nations which lay beyond the Alps, valour was absolutely indispensable. Without it none could be eminent; few could be secure. Cowardice was, therefore, naturally considered as the foulest reproach. Among the polished Italians, enriched by commerce, governed by law, and passionately attached to literature, everything was done by superiority of intelligence. Their very wars, more pacific than the peace of their neighbours, required rather civil than military qualifications. Hence while courage was the point of honour in other countries, ingenuity became the point of honour in Italy. . . .
>
> Military courage, the boast of the sottish German, of the frivolous and prating Frenchman, of the romantic and arrogant Spaniard, he [the Italian ruler] neither possesses nor values. He shuns danger, not because he is insensible to shame, but because in the society in which he lives timidity has ceased to be shameful." [Macaulay 1890 vol. I, 49–52. See also Preston and Wise 1979, 95–100]

Such is the political and historical basis of the humor at the expense of "cowardly Italians" which has its roots in the sixteenth century. Rulers and soldiers, who elsewhere were the upholders of the martial virtues and even laid claim to being the bearers of national tradition, did not and could not perform this task in Italy and respect for these values disintegrated. In a world where soldiers were detached from the service of the state and rulers held power as a result of intrigue or the favor of a foreign power the people naturally withheld their regard and loyalty. Also because Italians knew they could not depend on the state for protection, justice, or welfare their loyalty became exclusively attached to those institutions, notably the family, which could and did compensate for the failures of the state. Loyalty to family and kin came to prevail over loyalty to society as a whole, to the state, or to its impersonal institutions, such as the army.[28]

Italians growing up in such a society develop a strong capacity for loyalty to the small group of people known to them personally but may well have a weak attachment to impersonal institutions such as the army or other bureaucratic state organizations. This tendency has been recognized by the Italian military sociologist Guido Sertorio [1982, 26], who, in a paper delivered in Mexico City, said that the Italian armed forces should act as an agency for "cultural homogenization" in view of the strength of "particularisms and cultural discrepancies" and for "the development of a weltanschauung, based on the priority of social and public orientations which take precedence over the familistic vision of life which is still so common in Italian society."

No way has yet been found in which the strong loyalties that Italians owe to smaller groups can be harnessed by state organizations such as the army, and indeed these loyalties may contribute to an organization's disintegration into squabbling groups of rival patrons and clients. The result has been a nation whose members have shown themselves to be courageous and indeed sometimes brutal members of groups of feuding kinsmen or small guerrilla bands but not effective soldiers in a large army. As Peter Nichols [1973, 53] has put it, the Italians are "capable of marvellous feats of personal bravery but reject fighting as the pursuit of fools."

By the nineteenth century both Italians and foreigners assumed that it was a law of nature that the Italians didn't and couldn't fight [see Pinon 1980, 76–79 and Whittam 1977, 13]. The Italian republics set up by Napoleon rapidly collapsed at the first external threat [Geyl 1965, 87] and the armies of most of the new or restored little Italian states that succeeded them were no better. As one Italian kinglet put it to his son, who was studying military uniforms, "Dress them how you like, they will run away all the same" [Trevelyan 1928, 137].

The formation of a united Italy in the nineteenth century did not enable the Italians to overcome the legacy of centuries of fragmentation and divisive foreign domination. Their historical experience had produced a combination of political cynicism and familism that could not be overcome merely by the proclamation of a new Italian state. There was no Prussian core onto which the fragments of Italy could be fastened and Italy remained psychologically disunited after unification. For the army there was no Prussian tradition to appeal to and the politicians and the generals were afraid to make use of local loyalties and sentiments since these were not securely attached to the new Italian polity [see Whittam 1977, 60, 95, 109, 126]. For many Southern Italians the politicians of the new Italian state were initially regarded as scalawags and Northern carpetbaggers whose aim was to loot, exploit, and impoverish the South as if it were a conquered territory [Seward 1986, 38–39]. The central government was forced to maintain a substantial body of troops in the South to prevent and suppress revolts and the Southerners (together with a large part of the Northern peasantry) resented and resisted military service.[29] Also, whereas in Germany the army was respected because it had unified the country by force, in Italy the army could not take any similar credit for having created the country, for Italian unification took place only because the Italian politicians and generals had been able to exploit to their own advantage the clashes of other, stronger combatants in the European wars of 1859, 1866, and 1870 so as to grab part of the spoils. Indeed, during the Risorgimento, Italian forces on both land and sea again often collapsed into disorderly flight, even when faced by inferior opposition [see Preston and Wise 1979, 229; Whittam 1977, 93–97 and 124]. In 1867, when the process of Italian unification was well advanced, the French writer Henri Carion [quoted in Pinon 1980] declared: "the Italians will certainly invent a machine to dig mouse-holes in which to take shelter when they see bullets on the way or flashes of thunder, and they will not come out of them until they realise there is only one enemy left against ten of them."

After unification the Italians tried to use their army to acquire a colonial empire in Africa, but their campaign in Libya was inglorious and that in Ethiopia a humiliating disaster,[30] nor did they enjoy any of the compensating imperial successes celebrated in other countries.

From the start, then, the armed forces of the new Italian state were a subject of satire for their ineffectiveness. The Czech satirist Jaroslav Hašek, best known for his mockery of Germanic militarism in World War I, also made fun of the Italians for running away from the Austrians in the nineteenth century [Hašek 1974, 515–19]. Hašek also wrote a short story before World War I, "Svejk stands against Italy" [1983, 194–98], in which the Good Soldier captured single-handed a newly designed Italian machine gun from its unsoldierly and comatose Milanese minders during peacetime maneuvers along the Austro-Italian border.

During World War I the Italians sustained very heavy casualties fighting against the Austrians in Northern Italy, but were not particularly successful. Then in 1917 the Italian front crumbled at Caporetto and the Italians fell back in disorder. It was not just the scale of the Italian collapse, when nearly 300,000 men were taken prisoner and a further 350,000 threw their guns away,[31] but the enthusiasm with which sections of the Italian army surrendered and cheered their captors that gave new life to ethnic jokes about the Italians. The Italian Second Army became demoralized and the Austrian troops "encountered Italian units in formed bodies marching into captivity calling out: 'Eviva la Austria!' " [Falls 1966, 59]. Rommel, then a captain in the German army, called upon the petrified Italians to surrender and they brushed aside their officers and ran toward him. "In an instant I [Rommel] was surrounded and hoisted on Italian shoulders. 'Eviva Germania' sounded from a thousand throats. An Italian officer who hesitated to surrender was shot down by his own troops" [Falls 1966, 53; see also Irving 1978, 26]. The military failure of the Italians was apparent not only to their enemies, but to their French and British allies, who had to send their own troops in as reinforcements to prop up the Italian front [see Andreski 1982, 252]. "To make matters worse, Cadorna [the Italian commander] unfairly blamed the defeat on his men's cowardice and thousands were executed" [Mack Smith 1983, 35; see also Seton-Watson 1967, 479].

It is easy to see how such an event would have reinforced the image of "cowardly Italians" held by foreigners. However unfair Cadorna's accusation was, the visible spectacle of a general making such a claim about his own troops and backing it up in such a brutal way was bound to have an impact elsewhere. Those who had doubts about Cadorna may well also have had doubts about a country that produced a general who sought to exculpate himself in such a fashion and received the backing of other military and political leaders. At any rate, during World War I it was "widely believed that the Italian soldiers were less willing to fight than the soldiers of other armies" [Andreski 1982, 252], ethnic jokes about "cowardly Italians" were in circulation at the time [see Andreski 1982, 253 and Pinon 1980, 76], and jokes specifically referring to Caporetto were revived before and during World War II [see Dower and Riddell 1938, 51–52 and Lancaster 1941, 31].

Mussolini came to power in Italy in 1922. He did so quite undemocratically. In the only fair postwar election—that of 1919—his Fascist party gained only 5 percent of the votes and no seats.[32] His rhetoric before and after coming to power displayed an obsession with the need to display national toughness, and policies aimed at conciliation or preserving peace were condemned as "national cowardice" [Mack Smith 1983, 49]. The kind of cultural balance that I have suggested lies behind ethnic jokes about cowardice and militarism was anathema to Mussolini and his supporters. As the center of Fascist ideology lay a sharp dichotomy between national glory, military strength, discipline, successful aggression (good) and decadence, cowardice, individualism, concession (bad). For Mussolini, the Italian people (and other peoples) were viewed almost entirely in these terms—outsiders had to be shown that the Italians were truly martial heroes and the task of Fascism was to make them heroes and perhaps even to rewrite the past to show that they always had been heroes anyway. Mussolini, in his autobiography, wrote of the "typically Italian" shock troops of World War I that "They threw themselves into the battle with bombs in hands, with daggers in the teeth, with a supreme contempt for death, singing their magnificent war-hymns" [1928, 65].[33] How they managed to sing with daggers between their teeth is not made clear.

As soon as Mussolini tried to turn the rhetoric of aggression into action there could only be one of two possible consequences—either he would succeed and his victims would come to hate the Italians as ruthless militarists or he would fail and the obvious gap between rhetoric and performance would lead to a new outburst of ethnic jokes about unwarlike Italians. The latter is of course what happened, and the ethnic jokes that emerged not only mock Italian military failure and cowardice but also refer directly to the contrast between reality and official military rhetoric about national glory. In the jokes this is reduced to mere theatrical show, to speeches, gestures, songs, uniforms, medals and decorations, and these aspects of Italian martial display are often rendered ludicrous by being placed in a context of failure and cowardice.

In the so-called Free Zone [Vichy France] German and Italian armistice commissions operated. In a train travelling between Marseilles and Toulon, the chance workings of this dual system for looting (called control) brought together a German officer and an Italian officer. The latter was completely covered in decorations.

The German asked him about each of them in turn.

—'This one?'

—'Ethiopian campaign.'

—'And that onc?'

—'Albania.'

—'And this one?'

—'Libya.'

—'And that one there?'

—'Battle-fatigue medal.'

—'And all the others?' (at least a score)

The Italian replied with a big smile,

—'And those? Oh! Prizes for playing the mandolin.' [Clément 1945, 24. Cf. also Jones and Smith et al. 1983, 89]

During the Third World War the potent countries will be Germany, France, England, and Italy. And Germany is going to give their infantry, France is going to give the marines, England the aviation and Italians the marching songs. [UCBFA Greece file, Rossman 1964. Cf. also Lancaster 1941, 26].

What do you call a Neapolitan with a war medal?
A thief. [American 1970s]

An Italian officer, impatient at his country's deplorable military reputation, leaped out of the trenches and cried to his men: "Avanti! Avanti!" No one moved. Once again he cried valiantly: "Avanti! Avanti!" Again no one moved but someone called out enthusiastically from a safe position behind a sandbag: "Ah, che bella voce!" [British 1970s. Also in *Anekdoty Slunné Itálie* 1978, 13, Chrestien 1957, 132, Clément 1945, 32]

In the course of a visit to Germany, Mussolini made a number of important observations. He wanted his soldiers to be as well-turned-out as Hitler's. He noted the color of the German uniforms: blue-grey like the sky for the airmen, green like the fields for the infantry, black like steel for Panzer divisions. On returning to Rome he summoned the officer responsible for designing uniforms and ordered: Pantalons kakis . . . for everyone! [Clément 1945, 60. Note also Stouffer et al. 1949 vol. 2, 201]

In the 1930s the Italians were involved in two wars and their efforts in both of these gave rise to jokes. In 1936 the Italians invaded and conquered Ethiopia, in part as a way of demonstrating their military glory. The importance of that motive is shown by the Italian government's willingness before the war started to secure the Ethiopian Emperor Haile Selassie's "collusion in staging a mock battle in which the Italians would be allowed to win; following which, the Ethiopians would, by a face-saving agreement, accept a compromise peace" [Mack Smith 1983, 220]. One reason for the war was to avenge[34] Italy's humiliating military defeat by the Ethiopians in 1896, when the Ethiopians castrated captured Italian soldiers before sending them back [see Barker 1968, 20]. A coarse Australian and British comic song recalls the unpleasant details of this earlier defeat in a way that undercuts Mussolini's later Roman triumph after the conquest of Ethiopia in 1936.

Il Duce gave the order
And the organ-grinders go
Off to Ethiopia
To march against the foe
And now they are returning
Their organs left behind
(So now) they are no longer fit
For any sort of grind.

Il Duce mounts the rostrum
Upon the warriors return
With the unknown eunuch's ashes
In a noble Roman urn
"For their splendid deeds of valour
Some recognition calls
What shall we give our heroes?"
And the heroes answered "Balls!"

The pope is inundated
With requests to join his choir
From men whose normal voices
Are now an octave higher.
[Australian 1980s. See also Bold 1979, 108–109; Morgan 1968, 18. Tune: "The British Grenadier"].

The failures of the Italian troops sent by Mussolini to assist General Franco in the Spanish Civil War (1936–39) [see Thomas 1965, 499–501] also gave rise to ethnic jokes about Italians:

Three officers of Franco's army were watching the progress of a battle, one was Italian, the other German and the third Spanish. The German, looking through his field glasses, said in a tone of surprise: 'But they're fleeing, our friends are fleeing, look, look! The Italians are running away!'

'Let me see through the glasses', said the Italian officer, somewhat agitated. As he peered through them, his face, a little troubled before, began to clear, and a large smile broke out. Describing a broad gesture in the air with his free hand he cried, 'Yes they are fleeing, but proudly—like lions!' [Shaw 1939, 11].

The entry of the Italians into World War II was just as inglorious. The Italians waited until the Germans had defeated the French and British armies in 1940 and then declared war shortly before the French were forced to surrender. The Germans were "surprised that his [Mussolini's] army on the French frontier remained strictly on the defensive and German newspapers had to be instructed to make no ironic comments on what Hitler privately ridiculed as sheer cowardice" [Mack Smith 1983, 292; see also note 7 above]. When the Italians did finally attack, a week before the armistice, they made very little progress against the French even though they outnumbered them more than five to one [Shirer 1960, 740], and they became the butt of French jokes:

On the 25th June 1940 a small detachment of French troops on the Italian border learned that they would have to lay down their arms [because the French had been forced to sign an armistice with the Germans and thus also with the other Axis powers such as Italy]. With a heavy heart the captain called his men together and ordered them to march in a disciplined fashion, with shouldered arms to meet the Italians.

The latter were based three hundred yards away and, seeing the French arriving in parade ground fashion, the officer commanding them walked across to meet them.

The French captain clicked his heels and saluted the Italian.

'The armistice is signed', he said.

'Good', replied the Italian fascist officer holding out his sword to him. 'What are your terms?' [Clément 1945, 11].

The spectacular Italian military failures and surrenders of World War II reinforced the ancient ethnic gibes about Italian cowardice to the point where this ethnic script became a fixed feature of the jokes of many countries. It is nonetheless striking that the Australians should still be mocking a particular Italian military failure in Ethiopia nearly a century later and that the French, the Greeks, the Czechs, the Americans, and the British should still be inventing new jokes about Italians decades after Italy last became involved in a war:

Italian officer to his men: "If the enemy attacks from the North we will go to the South, if the enemy attacks from the East we will go to the West. If the enemy does not attack we will hold our ground at all cost" [*Anekdoty Slunné Itálie* 1978, 17].

It must be stressed once again that the failures of Italian armies are not in themselves evidence that Italians as individuals are cowardly. They merely explain why other peoples perceive them as such and make them the butts of ethnic jokes. The collapse of entire armies is spectacular and visible whereas the remarkable courage displayed by Italians fighting in small units, like the crews of the midget submarines and torpedoes that attacked warships in Gibraltar and Alexandria in World War II, or as groups of locally recruited men defending their home territory,[35] has not and perhaps could not have attracted comparable attention. The latter are the "normal" heroics to be found in any country's history, whereas the scale of the failures is peculiar to Italy. The same point can be made about the gibes of the sixteenth century—the collapsing armies were visible to foreigners, the bravery of individuals was not. The situation at that time was described in a striking and indeed prescient comment by Machiavelli [1980 (1532), 214; see also Preston and Wise 1979, 100].

> Look attentively at the duels and hand-to-hand combats, how superior the Italians are in strength, dexterity and subtlety. But when it comes to armies they do not bear comparison . . . during so much fighting in the past twenty years, wherever there has been an army wholly Italian it has always given a poor account of itself; the first witness to this is Il Taro, afterwards Alexandria, Capua, Genoa, Vaila, Bologna, Mestri.

Ethnic jokes about Italians do not in fact attribute a general pusillanimity to them in the manner of, say, Pakistani jokes about Kashmiris. Indeed, there is another genre of American ethnic jokes about Italians in which they are portrayed as tough and ruthless, albeit in the deviant context of organized crime and the Mafia. Ethnic jokes on this theme about Italians are also told in other countries, such as Czechoslovakia [see *Anekdoty Slunné Itálie* 1978, 11–12] or Britain, but the United States is the chief source. Organized crime has long been a greater problem in the United States than in most other industrial countries, in part because of the disorientation experienced by lower-class immigrants without skills, capital, or experience arriving in a society that stresses the value of competition and success [see Bell 1961B; Merton 1957, 145, 193]. Crime seemed to provide the missing (though deviant) ladder to success for many groups, but immigrants from southern Italy and especially Sicily already possessed forms of durable organization for extortion and violence that could be put to use in a new country. Organizations such as the Camorra or the Mafia became notorious in America, not just because they proved successful in displacing other, earlier criminal organizations with a different ethnic base [see Short 1984, 154], but also because they appeared strange and exotic. To some extent this exotic quality may have led the media and American public opinion to exaggerate both the power and the degree of integration and coordination of the Mafia as a force in organized crime in the United States [see Bell 1961B, 138–41]. Nonetheless the sheer scale and influence of the Mafia as a ruthless criminal organization is obvious, visible, and significant in both America and Italy.[36]

The Mafia grew up originally as an alternative organization to the state in Sicily, as a result of the alienation of the people from oppressive and usually foreign government and absentee landlords [see Lewis 1964, 30; Short 1984, 15–21]. The Sicilian Mafiosi became known for their courage, loyalty, ruthlessness, and discipline. Qualities which the state could not command were readily at the service of an organization of this type with its strong local and personal base. Ironically, in view of all the ethnic jokes about cowardly Italians, the organizers of the Mafia in the United States see Americans as lacking the toughness and discipline of the Sicilian "men of honor" and continue to import hit-men from Italy as "soldiers" who can be trusted in dangerous situations. As Vincent Teresa, formerly a leading figure in the Mafia in America, has put it: "These Sicilian Mafiosi will run into a wall, put their head in a bucket of acid for you if they're told to, not because they're hungry but because they're disciplined. They've been brought up from birth over there to show respect and that's what these punks over here don't have" [Teresa and Renner 1973, 373; see also Short 1984, 47 and Willey 1984, 64–65].

The Mafia is still largely organized on an explicitly ethnic basis. Almost in accordance with established comic ethnic scripts, Jewish financial minds such as Meyer Lansky and Welsh specialists in the corrupt fixing of lawyers, judges, and politicians such as Murray Humphries have in the past been co-opted for their particular expertise, but in general the line management stays Italian. Other ethnic groups in America are also involved in systematic crime and rackets but they have not been able to create organizations that are as widespread, cohesive, and exclusive. It is here that the basis of ethnic jokes about tough Italian-Americans must be sought rather than in the general big-city blue-collar Roman Catholic image that they share with the Poles or the Portuguese.

In the United States in particular, jokes about tough and ruthless Italian gangsters rival jokes about unmilitary Italian soldiers. Joe Bonfanti's 1976 collection of *Italian Jokes*, published in New York, has on one cover a picture of an Italian soldier in a rented uniform with the word HERO inscribed on a large medal; on the other cover, in the center of a group of caricature Italians is a gangster with a submachine gun. It is the latter who are the source of jokes about tough Italians:

Why did they give Gino a cement over-coat?
Because the stiff went straight. [Bonfanti 1976, 5]

Why are Italy's national colors green and red?

Because green stands for money and red is the blood of the guy they shoot to get it. [Bonfanti 1976, 6]

Why don't mosquitoes ever bite the Italian godfather?
Because he's so coldblooded that the mosquitoes would die of pneumonia. [Bonfanti 1976, 142]

A farmer in East Anglia has put up a Mafia scarecrow in his fields. Not only do the birds leave his crops alone but they've brought back all the seed they stole last year. ["The Two Ronnies," BBC TV, July 1987]

A demonstration was organised to protest discrimination against Italian-Americans: what shrewd planning that was. The dais alone represented eight-hundred years off for good behaviour. [Adams 1975, 84]

The F. B. I. got information that there were at least three bodies buried in a pit in a grave on Joe Celso's property where he lived and so they came down with warrants and dug it up . . . (he) had quite a bit of trouble with all the authorities. Now I know he had nothing to do with the death of those people they've dug up on his property. His problem is that he was operating a cemetery in a residential zone. [Short 1984, 57–58]

These latter, mainly American [but see also Gianelli 1987, 8–9, 45, 51, 105] jokes about Italians coexist with the jokes about cowardly soldiers and are specifically told about the Italians alone. Such jokes are not transferable to other ethnic groups, such as the Poles who, together with the Italians, have been the butt of American ethnic jokes about stupidity and filthiness. The latter jokes get switched between various ethnic groups occupying a similar position in American society, but the former are only told about Italians. The distinction can be seen from the joke that became famous in the American presidential campaign of 1980 when the winner, Ronald Reagan, regaled a group of reporters with:

"How do you tell the Polish one at a cock-fight?
He's the one with the duck.
How do you tell the Italian?
He's the one who bets on the duck.
How do you tell the Mafia is there?
The duck wins." [Cross 1980, 1. See also Raskin 1985, 202]

Ethnic jokes about militarism do not have as definite a history as the jokes told about the Italians, but even so jokes and satirical accounts of German and especially Prussian militarism and the related qualities of orderliness and obedience were already in circulation in the nineteenth century. In Britain and America jokes about the authoritarianism of the German army and German reverence for rank and rules were common by the turn of the century, long before either of the English-speaking countries became involved in modern European conflicts:

Major (narrating):—But when on the thirteenth of October the Battle of Leipzig was fought—
Lieutenant:—Excuse me, Major, that was on the eighteenth.
Major:—Young man, do you think you know it better than I?
Lieutenant:—I do know it was not, for only lately I read a history of the battle by a famous historian.
Major:—Don't talk to me about any of your scribblers. I—your major tell you it was on the thirteenth.
Lieutenant:—Pardon me, Major, if I doubt it in spite of that.
Major (boiling with rage):—Very well, Lieutenant, then I tell you officially that it was on the thirteenth.
Lieutenant:—Very well, Major, then it was on the thirteenth. [Jacobs 1903, 172]

A Prussian general [was] sitting on a marble bench in a public garden smoking a cigar. A pretty little girl whom he has been noticing says to him, "General, my papa likes you very much." "What is your papa's business, my dear?" "He makes wooden legs." [(Thousand)*1,000 Witty Sayings* n.d., 169]

Sergeant: Recruit Berger, you were ten minutes late again last night; where were you?
Berger:—I—I was with my sweetheart and she lives so far away—that—.
Sergeant:—How many times must you fellows be told that discipline does not bother with love affairs! If you must fall in love, do it near the barracks. [Jacobs 1903, 178]

A man who worked for a German official . . . when he came to call on his chief would . . . knock at the bottom of the door as a symbol of his awe and respect. [Dollard 1957, 187]

The Hohenzollerns' most characteristic product was the Prussian soldier with his blind obedience, the symbol of German militarism. An often-told story is set on the Potsdam drill-ground where an NCO is training a recruit to do the perfect goose-step, yelling his commands at the man. Suddenly the NCO is called away and forgets to shout '*Halt!*' at the soldier. When he returns after a while, the man has disappeared. Thirty-three years later an old soldier with a long grey beard and in a ragged uniform marches into the drill-ground still goose-stepping as well as he can. He has been marching around the globe because he was not commanded to stop. [Larsen 1980, 27. See also Namier 1947, 21–23].

It was presumably jokes like this that led Henri Bergson [1911, 133] to cite the comic institutional rigidity of the Prussian military as a good illustration of his thesis that laughter is triggered by mechanical behavior that reduces a flexible human being to an automaton.

Similarly, the popular English humorist Jerome K. Jerome saw the military orderliness of German society as a benign subject for satire, on a par with the foibles of the English, the French, or the Scots. In particular, Jerome found the well-policed orderliness of German life an inexhaustible subject for heavy mockery, and portrayed German children as models of a quite unnatural obedience:

> In the German parks there are special seats labelled "Only for grown-ups" (*Nur für Erwachsene*), and the German small boy, anxious to sit down, and reading that notice, passes by, and hunts for a seat on which children are permitted to rest; and there he seats himself, careful not to touch the woodwork with his muddy boots. Imagine a seat in Regent's or St. James's Park labelled "Only for grown-ups"! Every child for five miles round would be trying to get on that seat, and hauling other children off who were on. As for any "grown-up," he would never be able to get within half a mile of that seat for the crowd. The German small boy, who has accidentally sat down on such without noticing, rises with a start when his error is pointed out to him, and goes away with down-cast head, blushing to the roots of his hair with shame and regret.
>
> Not that the German child is neglected by a paternal Government. In German parks and public gardens special places (*Spielplätze*) are provided for him, each one supplied with a heap of sand. There he can play to his heart's content at making mud pies and building sand castles. To the German child a pie made of any other mud than this would appear an immoral pie. It would give to him no satisfaction: his soul would revolt against it.
>
> "That pie," he would say to himself, "was not, as it should have been, made of Government mud specially set apart for the purpose; it was not manufactured in the place planned and maintained by the Government for the making of mud pies. It can bring no real blessing with it; it is a lawless pie." [Jerome 1914, 169–70; see also 165, 244–48]

The German emperors, the pinnacle of German militarism, were also a subject for jokes and mockery. The following extract from the articles published in the French periodical *Le Rire* in Paris[37] soon after Kaiser Wilhelm II had visited the Holy Land in 1898 provides a good illustration of the humor of the time:

"The All-Highest Goes to Jerusalem, being the Diary of the German Emperor's Journey to the Holy Land"
October 28th:

"From Cesarea to Jaffa. Continually by carriage. Few people out to see us pass. This evening, as I noticed signs of demoralization in my troop, I organized a dramatic entertainment. They gave charades in the open air, and I gave a lecture not without some success. Subject, Would the Messiah have succeeded more quickly if he had had an army with him?"
And on October 30th:

"We arrived at Jerusalem toward three o'clock. I immediately dismounted from my horse and ordered an ass. I wished to make my entrance like Him!

"I might have put on a white tunic, but my journey would have lost all signification; it was with a helmet on my head that I entered the city of Judea."

Within Germany jokes and satires about "German militarism" were political rather than ethnic—they were either about the groups and classes who were the strongest supporters of militarism in Germany or else quasi-ethnic South German humor directed specifically at the Prussians.[38] For outsiders, however, these internal conflicts between strata and regions regarding the standing and prerogatives of the military were less important; for them militarism in Germany was German militarism and "subversive" political jokes from within Germany with very little modification became in their hands ethnic jokes about Germans. Once again an entire people was identified by foreigners with a particular and peculiar dominant group. To understand the background to both kinds of jokes it is necessary to look in more detail at the social structure of Imperial Germany and its historical roots.

Most parts of Germany have a history characterized by political absolutism rather than liberal democracy and it may be that this was the origin of German orderliness and of the prevalence of relationships of dominance and submission that have been so characteristic of German society. The mechanisms by which such attributes and relationships are reproduced and relate to national differences in style of humor are, however, a different matter and the subject is so broad as to require an entire book to itself [e.g., see Dundes 1984]. Many societies, however, have a passion for orderliness and hierarchy and most countries have been and indeed are politically authoritarian, but their peoples have not become the butt of jokes about these qualities in the way that the Germans have. The further factor that was crucial in Imperial Germany was the marked importance of the military and the direct and indirect influence this had on the way of life of the people.

The distinctive stamp of German authoritarian militarism was derived from the gradual rise to a position of dominance in Germany of Prussia, a state that had its origins at the very edge of the German-speaking world, the eastern frontier where marcher lords sought to subdue alien peoples by force. Just as there is some connection between American democratic individualism and the frontier or between Australian fraternal anarchy and the outback, so this very different kind of frontier helped to create a particular form of military authoritarianism in Prussia [see Nelson 1971, 16]. The advance of the frontier in America was mainly due to the efforts of individuals and small groups seeking land and wealth, and the original inhabitants were too few and too weak to resist the new settlers effectively.

German expansion to the east in Prussia, by contrast, was under the control first of a military-religious order, the Teutonic Knights, who regarded it as a crusade against the pagan Slavs,[39] and later of a military aristocracy of substantial Lutheran landowners. The Junkers of Prussia were not mere rentiers but men whose character was formed by the need to be frugal, rational, working managers of their estates, carefully squeezing an income out of the poor sandy soil.[40] They were gradually organized by the rulers of Brandenburg and Prussia into a coherent military elite at the service of the state. In return for their military services, the king offered "to the sons of families which often possessed more pride than economic means . . . an education, a standard of living higher than they could otherwise expect, an opportunity to rise to positions of great military and political authority and a social position second to none in the state" [Craig 1964, 11]. The aim of the rulers of Prussia was to create a system in which "finance, policy and the army [were] co-ordinated to the same end, the consolidation of the State and the increase of its power" [Craig 1964, 15].

The rulers of Prussia were ambitious, but their state was small and poor and the only method by which they could make it become a great power was by channeling the peculiar talents of their landed classes into the creation of a military and bureaucratic apparatus that could carefully and systematically apply the limited resources available to an overriding goal of national aggrandizement through warfare [see Nelson 1971, 11; Preston and Wise 1979, 206]. Prussia was described by Mirabeau as "not a state with an army but an army with a state" and Napoleon declared that Prussia had been hatched from a cannonball [see Gerard 1917, 44; Nelson 1971, 15; and Rosebury in introduction to de Catt 1929, xvii]. In Prussia, waste, favoritism, and extortion were avoided and the entire state subjected to bureaucratic rationalization and regulation along military lines.[41]

The autocratic local economic and legal powers of the Junkers within their own areas were not challenged, but in all other respects centralized, state power prevailed [see Craig 1964, 15–16]. The Junkers were confirmed in their privileged economic and political position but had to serve in the administration and defense of the state. They constituted an elite officer corps that developed a "sense of honour—a moral compulsion which forced them out of respect for themselves and their calling to bear hardship, danger and death without flinching and without expectation of reward" (Balfour 1975, 11; see also Craig 1964, 16; de Catt 1929 vol.II, 3]. Other classes in society were seen as collections of individuals whose private desires, aspirations, or rights did not require consideration. Yet they were expected to serve the state and its military establishment with complete fidelity [see Craig 1964, 17; Usher 1914, 67]. Later attempts to reform this system were aimed not at overturning these militarist values but at universalizing them by giving the non-aristocrats more opportunity to share in the rewards of glory and dominance. Thus the nineteenth century reformer Stein's aim was "to inculcate a proud warlike national character, to wage wearying distant wars of conquest and to withstand an overwhelming enemy attack with a national war" [Craig 1964, 47].

Prussia gradually expanded to become the dominant state in Germany, and the country as a whole was united as a result of Prussian military success in wars against lesser German states and against her neighbors Denmark, Austria, and France. In this way a modern nation was created, with an efficient, bureaucratic army and administration that still had much of the ethos of the warlike marcher lords of the eastern frontier, their belief in the supremacy and status of the military over civilians, their dislike of liberal democracy, their disdain for foreigners [see Taylor 1982, 21]. Other Germans accepted Prussian hegemony in part because they had to, for these were the terms and conditions of German unification, and in part because of the long tradition of passive submission to authority that existed even in the other, more pacific German states.

The ethnic jokes and satires of the late nineteenth and early twentieth centuries in France, Britain, or America were aimed at what was seen as the arrogance and bullying of the Prussian and German military elite and at the combination of submissiveness, orderliness, and national pride of the German masses. Foreign visitiors to Germany from more liberal countries, many of whom had gone there to acquire technical skills, scholarly qualification, or a knowledge of German institutions [i.e., they wanted to learn from a country that in many respects led the world and was widely respected and admired], found the visible behavior of members and would-be-members of the military elite either objectionable or comic.[42] The ritual drinking and dueling for scars of some of the student Korps, the harshly assertive and arrogant public behavior of military officers toward uppity civilians from Königsberg to Zabern [see Gerard 1917, 48–53] who could be attacked or penalized if they failed to respond with appropriate groveling and servility [see Perris 1914, 456; Tuchman 1967, 359], the excessive regard paid to the peculiarly military virtues and values of honor, duty, order, discipline, patriotism, courage, and manliness [see Balfour 1975, 393] were mocked by foreigners as indicators not just of militarism but of a specifically German militarism.

A similar view was taken by outsiders of the wild rhetoric, praising war and ruthlessness, exhalting the power of the state and those who served it, and denigrating more peaceful and individualistic callings such as commerce, that was employed not only by the Kaiser and the more reactionary politicians and military men but also by otherwise mild middle-class intellectuals.[43] Examples of similar aggressive rhetoric could be found in most countries of this imperial age, but elsewhere it was more likely to be moderated and diluted by competing values and ideas, by honest doubt, and by a degree of concern for what the world outside might think that was partly genuine and partly cant. When German troops left for China to put down the Boxer Rebellion, Kaiser Wilhelm II exhorted them: "Just as the Huns under their King Etzel created for themselves a thousand years ago a name which men still respect, you should give the name of German such cause to be remembered in China for a thousand years that no Chinaman, no matter whether his eyes be slit or not, will dare to look a German in the face" [Balfour 1975, 226; see also Dillon 1914, xxiv; Nelson 1971, 383]. A speech of quite this degree of bigoted and belligerent silliness was a gift not only to future foreign propagandists (the Germans as "Huns") and to internal political opponents but to the creators of both ethnic jokes about militaristic Germans and political jokes about "Herr Lehmann" himself.

The overregulation of German society by the police and other bureaucratic officials, whose rank and uniform produced magical obedience, was seen as yet another ludicrous facet of a militaristic society, and even today it is difficult not to be amused by some of the mundane details of this "world of crack-pot authoritarianism" [Stone 1983, 169–70].

Ethnic jokes about Germans were jokes about a society with a peculiar ruling class—a military aristocracy skilled in the ways of bureaucracy and commanding a state with a powerful modern economy. This was the group that was aped by other social classes of lesser standing. The newly wealthy sought army commissions for their sons, and the latter, in seeking to emulate the members of the traditional officer class, became a parody version of them [see Balfour 1975, 431; Craig 1964, 238; Shirer 1960, 96] and wanted a bigger army and an aggressive foreign policy that would provide them with greater opportunities for a military career [see Teitel 1977, 218]. Below the elite was a minutely stratified hierarchy of state officials whose task it was to obey and enforce. Perhaps the best satire on the latter class was the ludicrously successful hoax perpetrated by the Captain of Köpernick in 1906 which "provoked the wonder of the world and contributed to the gaiety of nations who laughed at the superstitious reverence of the Prussian for the man with the braided coat and the peaked helmet" [Sarolea 1912, 142].[44]

The German lower classes also displayed a gift and affection for discipline and order, as can be seen from the curious tribute paid by the Chancellor Prince Bernhard von Bülow [1914, 181][45] to the qualities of his political opponents, the Social Democrats:

> It is one of the German's greatest political virtues that discipline is bred in his bone. But the Social Democrats make use of this virtue. Only in a state where the people are used to discipline, where they have learnt to obey unquestioningly in the Army and where they feel the rigid regulations of the administrative machinery daily and hourly could a party organization of such size and solidarity as that of the Social Democrats come into being.

These Social Democratic followers of the original "Red Prussian" [Schwarzchild 1948] were also the butt of jokes that were both political jokes and ethnic jokes about Germans:[46]

The German socialists decided to hold a meeting in Leipzig to plan the revolutionary overthrow of the German state. Delegates travelled by train from all over Germany to Leipzig but when they arrived at Leipzig station they found that there was no one there to collect their tickets. Since it was forbidden to leave the station without handing in one's ticket they remained there patiently all day waiting for the ticket collector to return and the revolution had to be postponed.

Why don't they have a revolution in Germany?
The police wouldn't allow it.

Ethnic jokes about German militarism, then, are both old and new. They are old in the sense that most of the basic themes of such jokes were established well before World War I. However, they differ markedly from earlier ethnic jokes about the belligerence of the Welsh [see Davies 1985B] or the Gascons, known for their boastful individual pride and aggressiveness:

Gasconades.—A Gascon officer, who bore a high reputation for bravery, but who freely indulged in all the license of speech so common to the natives of his province, being engaged in a hot skirmish, fired one of his pistols at an officer of the enemy's cavalry, and immediately boasted to one of his comrades that he had just shot one of the enemy's officers. The other looking round him, "How can this be? my friend," said he, "I see nothing down." "Cap de bious," replied the Gascon, "don't you see that I reduced him to powder?" [*The Cambrian*, 14th October 1826. See also Dulac 1925; *The Mixture for Low Spirits* n.d., 77]

These jokes of an earlier age stress the fiery individualism of the warlike Welsh [see Davies 1985B] or the Gascons, a quality that is quite different from German discipline and obedience [see Bourdon 1914, 168], the virtues required by a bureaucratic military hierarchy.

The comic image of German militarism that stressed order, obedience, and discipline, rather than aggression as such, changed remarkably little as a result of World War I. During the war there was an immense output of books[47] and propaganda [e.g., see Darracott and Loftus 1981A] by the Allies claiming that the "German Militarists" had deliberately caused the war and been responsible for all manner of atrocities. Atrocity stories were circulated to the effect that German soldiers had cut off the hands of Belgian children and the breasts of their mothers, had crucified a Canadian soldier, and, for light relief, had rung the bells in a Belgian cathedral using local monks as and like the clappers. Later it was declared that they were taking corpses from the battlefields and boiling them in caustic soda to make soap. Most of these atrocity stories were completely false[48] and some of them were probably invented as Allied propaganda. In France, Belgium, and Britain angry crowds looted German shops and innocuous German clerks, waiters, and brass-bandsmen were maltreated and interned as potential spies. In England popular anti-German prejudice was so strong that dachshunds were stoned in the streets because they were German dogs and the German shepherd dog was renamed the Alsatian [Pickup 1981] after a province the French sought to recover from the Germans. Even the King felt obliged to discard the German name of his dynasty, Saxe-Coburg-Gotha, which he had inherited from his grandfather, Albert the Good. The Kaiser wittily retorted that in Germany Shakespeare's famous comedy would now be renamed "The Merry Wives of Saxe-Coburg" [Brandreth 1981, 81]. The Battenbergs ceased to be a cake and became and have remained Mountbatten (the name of the present Prince Consort). Several thousand humbler British citizens with Germanic sounding names also changed or discarded them because of the widespread prejudiced excitement against Germans. During the war political cartoonists in Britain and America exploited the idea of the "ruthless Hun" [e.g., see Dyson 1915] whose use of submarines as a counterstroke to the Allied blockade that was preventing food from reaching the starving children of Central Europe was an atrocity, and whose use of zeppelins as bombers and of poison gas in the trenches showed an unfairly premature grasp of how to use modern military technology.

Despite the largely mendacious wartime propaganda about atrocities there is little or no mention of this theme in the ethnic jokes about German militarism told after World War I. The atrocity dimension of the comic image of the Germans did not appear until after World War II, though it was then back-dated in newly invented contemporary jokes about World War I.[49] Jokes about the mistreatment of prisoners of war, with a World War I setting, are probably post–World War II in origin. This is not surprising, given that prisoners of war taken by the Germans in World War I were on the whole treated properly and according to international conventions. The contemporary joke below, ascribed to Hindenburg, in effect takes this for granted:

> Before leaving Insterburg in Eastern Prussia—the Franfurt [*sic*] Gazette (October 8th, 1914) gives the incident—the Russians were unable to destroy or carry off everything as they had wished. They had to make everything useless, and so they poured petrol over enormous quantities of bread. When the General heard about this he gave this order—
> One must not dispute over questions of taste, the Russians have their own preferences. This bread will do to support the Russian prisoners until the supply is exhausted.

Nobody would be able to make Hindenburg understand that this joke was wanting in taste; he would reply—

'Wanting in taste? It smacks of petrol!' [Hervier 1916, 95–6].

During World War II, by contrast, the German treatment of prisoners of war was abominable and millions of Russians died in captivity [Carr 1987, 7; Watt 1975, 231]. In general, prisoners of the Western nations were treated according to established conventions, but even so an appreciable number of American, Canadian, and British prisoners were murdered, tortured, or harshly treated.[50] It is this kind of behavior that the purveyors of a modern gallows humor have back-dated to World War I, thus creating or using a dimension of the German militarism ethnic script that is not rooted in this specific political and historical situation.

Two farm lads went off to join the Army in 1914. After training they were immediately sent to France, and some weeks later the family of one of the boys received the following letter:

'Dear Mum and Dad and all the family, Bill and me was taken prisoner by the Germans two weeks ago but I must say the Jerries treat us fine. They are the nicest people in the world when it comes to taking care of prisoners of war. The food is great and there's lots of it. We get new clothing whenever we need it, the camp is very comfortable with hot water and big roaring fires in every hut, and we even get Charlie Chaplin films once a week. So don't worry about me, as I am in good health and good spirits. Your loving son, Jack.

P.S. Would you tell Bill's parents he was shot this morning for complaining. [Kilgarriff 1979, 40]

A tale of the 1st World War

Some time later came that unforgettable Christmas Day that has gone down in history . . .

'Here sarge, . . . I couldn't believe my eyes . . . Nobby Thunderblast suddenly said it was the season of goodwill and peace and started to walk towards the German trenches. Believe it or not, the Germans came out of their trenches and started playing football with him.'

'That's wonderful'.

'Not really . . . they're using him as the ball'. [Brooke-Taylor et al. 1977, 78]

So far as I can tell jokes of this type were not being told in the 1920s. Indeed, it might have been seen as bad taste to send up the unofficial fraternization between British and German troops that took place at Christmas in 1914, for by then the incident had attained the status of a pacific and sentimental myth; it was no longer seen as an odd, isolated occurrence but as a statement that all of mankind—including the Germans—was innately bursting with peace and goodwill [see Harding 1987]. Much of the contemporary humor about German atrocities makes fun of those who had profited from inventing or spreading wartime lies. H. L. Mencken's essay "Star-Spangled Men" [1920, also in 1956], which mocks those egalitarian Americans who had reveled in anti-German bigotry during the war and later in the honors, titles, and medals conferred on them by European monarchs, is a good instance of this humor. Woodrow Wilson's wife had even claimed royal status on the grounds of her descent from Pocahontas and was apparently greeted by the royal houses of Europe as a person worthy to share their regal perch high above mere citizens and commoners.

The 1920s also saw the publication in Czech of Jaroslav Hašek's *The Good Soldier Švejk,* one of the funniest satires on militarism in general and on German militarism in particular ever written. There were not many new jokes in English about German militarism, however, and some of these may well be "ethnic" adaptations of German political jokes like the following, the first of which is said to refer to the secret German armament program [Larsen 1980, 37] under the Weimar Republic:

The wife of a German workman employed in a perambulator factory tried to induce him to steal a perambulator for their baby.

He refused to do this, but agreed to purloin sufficient parts to make a complete machine.

The great day for the assembly of the parts arrived. After five hours the wife went out to their backyard and found her husband in a state of exhaustion.

'It's no good,' he said. 'It always comes out a machine gun.' [Copeland and Copeland 1939, 756, Joke 7239. Also in Ember 1988, 72–73]

With the old stern Prussian discipline and sense of duty, Paul Falck, 27, sergeant in the Reichswehr before committing suicide, reported his own tragedy in the company record book. The entry read:—"At ten minutes after midnight Sergeant Falck committed suicide by shooting himself; Corporal Junker has been instructed to take over the reveille." [Dated 1930 in Ives 1980, 28]

Although jokes about German militarism have a long history they took on their modern form only during and after the period of National Socialist rule, 1933–45, when the brutality, hysteria, atrocities, and anti-Semitism of the Third Reich became the subject of both sick and satirical jokes. These new themes quickly took their place alongside the older style of jokes about hierarchy, order, and obedience. Thus the last phase of ethnic jokes about Germans reflects *both* (a) the revolutionary and totalitarian changes brought about by the National Socialist Party and by the new specialized hierarchies of oppression, such as the S. S. or the Gestapo, under a race-obsessed leader from Austria, Germany's other Eastern march, *and* (b) the continuity with the Prusso-German past which many of the senior military tried to preserve.

In the Weimar Republic the officer corps still saw themselves not as mere narrow professional functionaries but as a social and political elite [see Müller 1987, 23–24] and the army leaders still regarded the army and its traditions as the crucial unifying national institution. Even in an ostensibly democratic republic many senior army officers still held to the old Prussian view that they, as the embodiment of the army, ought to have an independent position distinct from all other institutions of the state and able to take a leading role in the making not only of military strategy but of foreign and much of domestic policy [see Müller 1987, 60–61]. In 1930 the relatively moderate minister for the army, General Groener, could still declare at a time of crisis that "In all times of need in the history of a people, there is one unshakeable rock in the stormy sea; the idea of the state. The Wehrmacht is its necessary and most characteristic expression" [Craig 1964, 43]. When Hitler came to power the army's leaders were willing to collaborate with him provided that their own power, privileges, and prestige were respected [Müller 1987, 29–31, 107–108], but he proved able both to exploit and use traditional military institutions and militarist values and to subvert and transform them.[51]

The army became, sometimes willingly, sometimes reluctantly, sometimes fearfully, just one more instrument for the enforcement of the National Socialist program of tyranny and conquest and the enslavement and extermination of other peoples.[52] New ethnic jokes about atrocities reflected this drastic change in the character of German militarism and took their place alongside new versions of more traditional jokes about the militarists' overvaluation of order and obedience. The events that lay behind the new jokes—the threatening and hysterical displays of solidarity in Nazi rallies, the brutality with which war and conquest were pursued, the disappearance of millions of people into death camps designed for genocide—were so visible, extreme, startling, and frightening [see Horowitz 1977, 18–26, 37–38] that there is little point in asking why they were perceived as significant by the peoples of Europe and America who referred to them in ethnic jokes.

The more important question is why these jokes are ethnic rather than political in their thrust, given that many Germans too were victims of National Socialist persecution, the relative absence of popular hostility to German refugees in Allied countries (though many were unjustly interned), and the attempt in Allied wartime propaganda to distinguish clearly between "Nazi" and "German." The twentieth century has known other organized atrocities committed on the same kind of scale and with the same combination of unspeakable brutality and ideological fanaticism, in such Marxist socialist countries as the Soviet Union, China, and Cambodia,[53] but these peoples do not figure in ethnic jokes about atrocities in the way that the Germans do. The latter crimes against humanity have given rise only to political jokes aimed at regimes or political leaders:

A group of tourists from Heaven went on a trip to Hell to view the sufferings of the damned. When they got to the place reserved for the most wicked people of all time they saw a lake of boiling shit with only two people in it—Stalin in shit up to his waist and Hitler up to his nose. One of the visitors who had been in the Gulag asked indignantly, "Why is Hitler in up to his nose and that vile scoundrel Stalin only up to his waist?" "Oh," replied the guide, "Stalin is standing on Lenin's shoulders." [Soviet Union 1980s. See also Davies in press A; Raskin 1985, 224 and 239–40; Sturman 1984, 220]

The reason that jokes about the Nazis are also ethnic jokes about Germans lies in the way that the Nazis politicized ethnicity and perverted German nationalism into a racial creed which defined other peoples as subhumans to be degraded and enslaved or vermin to be exterminated because they were not merely non-Aryan and non-German but un-German and anti-Aryan.[54] If entire peoples are killed or brutally mistreated or told they have no secure place (not even that of tolerated, respected, or indulged inferiors and subordinates) in the new order because they have been defined as the antithesis of German, it is hardly surprising if the persecutors and the very acts of persecution should themselves come to be perceived in ethnic terms. By contrast, the murder of millions of kulaks in the Soviet Union or city-dwellers in Cambodia, though comparably massive, cruel, and evil crimes, cannot easily be given an ethnic label but only a political one, and jokes referring to them take an almost exclusively political form.

The racial aggression advocated by the German National Socialists was not just a tactic or a means to an end but the very heart of their ideology, more important even than the traditional military objective of victorious war. Nonetheless the National Socialist ideology and classic militarism have much in common. German National Socialism exalted force, courage, discipline, obedience, and physical prowess as the supreme virtues and measures of German superiority and fitness to rule, qualities to be endlessly exercised and displayed in wars and conquest. Victory was marked not only by vindictive acts of frightfulness but by the systematic petty humiliation of the conquered and the exercise of a new kind of "crackpot authoritarianism" rooted in a totally barmy racial theory.[55] Only its tragic consequences prevent us from seeing much of Nazi ideology and practice as merely comic in its banality. It is not surprising that the absurd side of this violent doctrine gave rise to jokes: "There are only two kinds of people left in Germany, non-Aryans and barb-Aryans"; "What is an Aryan? The Arse-end of a Prolet-Aryan" [Gamm 1979, 79].

Ethnic jokes about German militarism have continued long after the extreme and emotion-provoking years of the Second World War to which they owe their origin, though events such as the trial of Klaus Barbie in 1987 and the controversy over the election of Chancellor Kurt Waldheim in Austria [see Urquhart 1987] are a regular reminder both of the horrors of the past [e.g., see Schechter 1986] and that there is still unfinished business left over from the National Socialist era.

What do they call a loss of memory about wartime events? Waldheimer's disease. [British 1988]

Also the period since 1945 has seen a flood of best-selling memoirs, popular histories, and fiction about the war, as well as films and radio and television productions that regularly reinforce the memories and anecdotes which those who lived through the war have handed down to younger generations, who have learned to invent and tell jokes about a time long before they were born [e.g., see McCosh 1976, 238, 250]. The images of that war are better known and more vivid than those of the military operations in which the joke-tellers' countries have subsequently been involved. Most of this output is serious, but there is also a large stock of humorous material, some of which is the direct comic counterpart of the serious material, some a secondary burlesque of the serious stereotypes, while yet other examples operate at many levels.[56]

The main change that has taken place in recent ethnic jokes about German militarism is that the cluster of qualities that make up this comic ethnic script [see Raskin 1985, 197]—order, obedience, brutality, etc.—have been reduced to a formula which can generate "German" ethnic jokes about any subject:

German weather forecast: "Tomorrow it will be fine and sunny. That is an order." [British 1960s]

A group of Germans who were sun-bathing on an Italian beach realised that a three year old German child had got lost. Their leader announced to the Italians around them: "If he is not returned within ten minutes we will lose ten Italian children." [Romorantin 1983, 63–64. See also *Ridere, Ridere . . . Ridere* 1981, 103]

An Italian visiting Frankfurt asked a German how he could get to a particular address. "First, said the German, you go straight, then take the third right, and then the fourth left, then you go straight again for three blocks, then left, then the second right and then you are there." "Thank you very much," said the Italian. "No," screamed the German, "not thank you. Repeat!" [Italian 1980s]

What does a German woman say after sex?
"Harder next time." [British 1970s]

It was one of those post-war marriages—she was a German girl he met during the war when he was negotiating the sale of his trench. And their trouble was that they could never agree how to bring up the children. He wanted them to go into showbiz and she wanted them to attack Poland.

In the end there was a compromise: they marched into Lew Grade. [Mullins 1979, 59, and BBC TV]

Notice in European train:
It is dangerous to lean out of the window.
E pericoloso sporgesi.
Nicht hinauslehnen! [British 1960s. See also Wintle 1968, 252]

A Swiss bought an expensive silent clock for his young daughter which went tick-tick-tick-tick very quietly. When he gave it to her the wretched child howled because she wanted an old fashioned clock that went Tick Tock Tick Tock. In desperation he went back to the shop and tried to change it but they didn't have anything louder. So he got into his car and drove across the border into Germany to the shop of a German watchmaker. He didn't have a noisy clock either, but he offered to adjust the mechanism of the original one. He took it into the back of the shop and five minutes later he brought it back and it went Tick Tock Tick Tock just as the daughter wanted.

"How on earth did you do it," asked the Swiss in amazement.

"Ah," replied the German knowingly—"we have ways of making you tock." [British 1970s]

Three babies, German, Jewish, and Polish, are in a hospital. The nurse says, "Heil Hitler!" The German baby snaps to attention, the Jewish baby shits, and the Polish baby eats it. [Clements 1973, Joke c6.10]

On a Lufthansa flight from Heathrow to Berlin the captain's speech to the passengers went something like this: 'Gut mornink, ladies and jentlemen, ziss iss your captain shpeakink. Ve took off from Heat'row precisely on time at 10.30 hours British Mean Time, unt ve are now flyink at a height of fifteen thousand feet. In two hours and forty-three minutes ve shall descent to ten thousand feet, und sixteen minutes und fifteen seconds later ve shall descent to five thousand feet. Ve shall remain at this height for seven minutes and twenty-eight seconds and then ve shall land at 13.56 precisely. In the event of an emergency you will all follow to the letter the safety regulations printed on the cards in front of you. There need be no panic or any casualties, provided you all do exactly As You Are Told!' [Kilgarriff 1975, 24–25]

Once again the precarious situation of the airline passenger has been pressed into service in an ethnic joke, albeit one about Lufthansa, order, and obedience rather than Sabena and stupidity. As in the case of jokes about "canny Scotsmen," ethnic jokes about Germans have become simply a compact way of telling jokes about order, obedience, or brutality. The use of the word *German*, or a surrogate such as *Lufthansa*, near the beginning of the joke is an indirect hint that renders the ending intelligible without giving it away. Even the use of a mock-German accent and emphasis can achieve the same result:

Lufthansa air-hostess: "Good morning, ladies and gentlemen. You vill enjoy zer flight." [British 1960s]

Achtung! Achtung! No smoking in zer gas chambers. [British 1980s. See also Kelly and Weidman 1979]

The ending may be innocuously authoritarian or a fearful atrocity but its significance is conveyed by an ethnic signal that evokes a well-known set of associations. If the ethnic signal were left out, or if the jokes were told to an audience from another culture who did not know at what the signal was hinting, the jokes would misfire altogether.

Exactly the same point can be made about the following well known ethnic joke about Italians (originally American but now international), which can be told as a two-stage riddle-joke or as a narrative, or as a mixture of both:

Have you heard about the new Italian tank? It's got five gears, one forward and four reverse. The forward gear is there in case the enemy attacks from behind. [American 1960s]

The word *Italian* is both the name of a real people and a verbal clue that the joke is about cowardice rather than stupidity, canniness, or militarism. The joke works because the joke-teller and the audience possess a common set of cultural rules linking particular ethnic groups with particular comic qualities. If joke-tellers were to take Joey Adams's advice [1975, 5–6, 55, 79] and to try to substitute other ethnic groups of their choice for "Italian" so that they told the same joke about, say, a German tank, an Australian tank, an Irish tank, a Scottish tank, a Newfie tank, an American tank, an English tank, or a Belgian tank, the joke would be robbed of much of its humor [see also Raskin 1985, 206] because the audience would have received either no clue at all or a misleading clue which might lead them to see such a tank in terms of the comic images stupid or canny (result: mild amusement only) or the comic images brutal, boastful, coarse, or up-tight (result: utter bafflement). Ethnic jokes depending on a particular comic quality such as cowardice can only be switched successfully to other ethnic groups having the same comic reputation.

The comic reputations of the Italians and the Germans for cowardice and militarism respectively are like cement, for although these comic images existed well before World War II, it was the spectacular and visible events of that particular war that caused them to "set" and take on a fixed form. Since 1945, neither the Germans nor the Italians have been involved in warfare and no new events have occurred to reinforce the existing comic scripts. The Germans, it is true, remain a more orderly, obsessive, and obedient people than their neighbors [see Dundes 1984], but there is no evidence at all that the people, the politicians, or the military of West Germany are likely to support or pursue a policy of violent aggression, expansion, or persecution. If anything, the West Germans of today are less militaristic than most of the peoples who tell ethnic jokes about them [see Grosser 1974, 348–52].

The West German constitution and German military law embody tighter precautions against the misuse of military power than many other democratic countries [see Keijzer 1978, esp. 119–23, 188–94, 256–59; and Krejci 1976, 191] and in European opinion polls only the Italians show less enthusiasm at the prospect of fighting for one's country.[57] Nonetheless, the legacy of German's past can still produce bad dreams as well as good jokes and "for the dreamer bad dreams have a life of their own and do not cease to be frightening, even though they lack concrete reality" [Coupe 1986, 83]. The bad dreams are themselves a source of comic songs [Lehrer 1981, 93–95, 124] and ethnic jokes:

André Malraux: "I am so fond of Germany that I am glad there are two of them." [see Coupe 1986, 182]

The Germans are a very nice people and not at all like they were in the war or the movies. I for one do not believe the Germans will war with us again. Not after last time and last time II. [Mann 1979, 93]

The "cement" of the ethnic scripts has set hard and the comic reputations of the Germans and the Italians have become fixed and conventionalized—a gift to the composers of ethnic jokes, who can build them around a stable formula known to all. Decades after World War II new jokes about German militarism and Italian cowardice are being invented, as can be seen from the following pair of ethnic jokes about, of all things, worms:

British naturalists visiting Italy have brought back some amazing films showing three Italian birds surrendering to a worm. ["The Two Ronnies," BBC TV 1980]

A pupil at a school asked the German biology teacher if it was true that when you cut a worm in half each half turned into another worm.

Teacher (with a strong German accent): "Not if you do it lengthwise!" ["The Bob Monkhouse Show," BBC TV August 1984]

The above examination of the circumstances in which ethnic jokes about Italian cowardice and German militarism emerged and developed leads to the following conclusions:

(a) Such jokes have a long history and are best explained in terms of the political evolution of the German and of the Italian state. The cowardly and militarist scripts used in ethnic jokes about Italians and Germans have also been employed to construct what are essentially political jokes within the home country.

(b) The familiar comic ethnic images of cowardice and militarism have been formed, shaped, and altered by particular visible and remarkable events and experiences, notably those of World War II.

(c) The most recent jokes on these themes have been built around a bizarre range of items, using well-established formulas that exploit these well-known comic ethnic scripts to produce the well-made joke.

It should be stressed that each of these propositions is derived from the study of ethnic jokes about the Germans and the Italians in their historical context. However, circumstances alter cases and a comparative study of other ethnic jokes about cowardice shows that they can emerge in quite different ways.

The most striking post–World War II development of ethnic jokes about cowardice was the rapid emergence of such jokes told about the Egyptians after their humiliating defeat by the Israelis in the Six-Day War in 1967. As in the earlier case of the jokes about the Italians it was the visible, spectacular, and unexpected rout of the Egyptians that led to the jokes. During the first of the Arab-Israeli wars in 1948 the Arab states had "expected a military walkover, an easy mopping-up operation that would last a few days only" [Elon 1972, 250]. Also some of their leaders employed a "genocidal rhetoric" that "threatened the Jews of Palestine with a blood-bath in the manner of Genghis Khan and Tamerlane" [Elon 1972, 250]. The Israelis had only a few, ill-equipped troops but they held their ground successfully. In 1956 war again broke out in Sinai and the Egyptians fell back in disorder. In 1967 the Israelis were outnumbered three to one and Arab leaders in Egypt and Syria again threatened genocide and destruction and were confident of victory [see Gilbert 1974, 67–70]. At the end of the Six-Day War the Israelis were relieved and perhaps surprised to have survived. The rout of Nasser's army, which the Israelis drove back in disorder across Sinai and the Suez Canal, was the key event which gave rise to a boom in ethnic jokes about "cowardly" Egyptians or Arabs. Many of these jokes were adaptations of old European and American jokes about Italians which were now, under the stimulus of contemporary events, switched to the Arabs. The Italian tank joke now emerged in Hebrew as a joke about an Arab tank [see UCBFA Hebrew file]. Many such jokes were adapted then and later by joke-tellers in the Jewish communities of Europe and America [e.g., see UCBFA Argentina file] who had feared that Israel would be defeated and annihilated but who now realized the vast gap between the fierce rhetoric of the Egyptian and Syrian leaders and the performance of their armies.

Have you heard about the Arab soldier who deserted his unit? He stood and fought. [Bermant 1986, 161–62]

The Israeli army ordered some surplus tanks from the Italians. Major Rosenberg, the officer making the purchase, noticed there were 2 different models, one $50 less than the other.

Why two models he asked Russo, the Italian in charge.

For the extra $50 replied Russo, you get back-up lights.

Give us the less expensive brand, said the Israeli and sell the others to the Egyptians. [Wilde 1980A, 134]

The highest speed attained by any wheeled vehicle is 748.637 mph. The Israeli designed vehicle called the 'Silver Schnell' achieved this record during a secret test over a measured course in the Gaza Strip on November 13th 1976. Speculation that the car attained this incredible speed because of a nuclear-powered engine proved to be totally erroneous. The simple truth is that the speed of the 'Silver Schnell' is due to the arrangement of the tires. It has two Arab tires in front and two Israeli tires in the back. [Burns and Weinstein 1978, 103]

The Egyptians' adviser on military strategy is a Russian. He said to them, "When the Israelis attack, do what we have always done when attacked: retreat back into Egypt and let the Israelis come after you. Then retreat again and draw then on deep into your territory. And then wait for three months. And then the freezing cold of winter will come and drive them out again for you." [British 1970s. See also UCBFA Argentina file]

It is important to note that essentially similar jokes were also told in the Arab world at the expense of the Egyptian army and particularly its officers. These jokes appeared in Arab countries very soon after the Six-Day War. The Italian tank joke was already being told about an Egyptian tank in Beirut, in July 1967 [see UCBFA Lebanon file]. A number of such jokes, which refer to local events and circumstances and are almost certainly indigenous inventions, also circulated in Egypt itself [see UCBFA Egypt file]. Thus Lebanese and Egyptians, Jews and Israelis, together with other, less involved ethnic groups all told ethnic jokes based upon a common perception of events. The Arab versions of the jokes were rooted in what they realized had happened, not in what they wanted to happen (the Egyptians and their allies did not want to lose) or in what they had expected to happen (though some Egyptians may have had their doubts).

A Lebanese joke told in Beirut in 1967 said: "Instead of sending Nasser weapons the Russians should send him spikes." A Lebanese who remembered the joke saw it as "making fun of Nasser's and the army's inability to use weapons and that the spikes are put on shoes to enable the army to run faster—to hasten their retreat." He thought that the joke was very funny because it gave a sense of the "bloody Egyptians running." For him it was mainly an ethnic joke about another ethnic group—the Egyptians. Yet he also saw it as a way of coming to terms with the fact that "Everybody's mad (that) the Arabs lost" [UCBFA Lebanon file, Janie Brill 1968], which indicates the complexity of multiple, competing, and concentric ethnic identities in the Lebanon.

Before Assad's [Syrian] pilots take off to attack the Israelis, he gives them all $25 each so that they can take a taxi back. [Lebanese 1970s]

The Egyptian jokes of the time can be classed as political; these jokes too mock the alleged cowardice of any army, and especially its officers. Once again an external joke about a people corresponds to an internal political joke.

A mother had a baby who could only crawl backwards. She took him to a doctor and said, 'What's wrong with my kid—he only crawls backwards.' The doctor said, 'Nothing's wrong—he'll just become an officer.' [UCBFA Egypt file, Maxim Schrogin 1968]

A man ran very fast to catch a bus. He finally caught it between bus stops. So the ticket man gave him half fare. [The military only have to pay half-fare on the buses in Egypt. A man who is good at running (away) must be in the military.] [UCBFA Egypt file, Maxim Schrogin 1968]

These jokes appeared after 1967, but there is a long tradition of Egyptian political jokes about the cowardice and incompetence of the army from the time of the monarchy [see Rameses 1937, 87–91] which was still potent in the 1960s despite Nasser's nationalist propaganda and the supposed revitalization of the Egyptian army under his rule [see Vatikiotis 1961, 231–32, but also Gawrych 1987, 542]. For the joke-tellers it was more to the point that Nasser's army had run away in 1956, in Sinai and Suez alike. In the joke below this comically negative political image of the army has been combined with the standard Egyptian ethnic script about the droll stupidity of the Sa'idi's [see El-Shamy 1980], the people from the southern edge of Egypt:

The scene is of some Arab troops on the way to the Sinai border. A Sa'idi, a man from Southern Egypt, is on the train with the men. He asks 'Tsk, are we at the border yet?' The men answer, 'No, no, not yet.' In a few minutes he asks again, 'Tsk, are we at the border yet.' Again the men answer 'No, No, not yet.' Another five minutes pass and he asks again the same question and receives the same reply. The Sa'idi asks every five or ten minutes many more times until someone finally says 'Why are you so worried about getting to the border?' The Sa'idi replies 'Because I am going to have to run all the way back.' [UCBFA Egypt file, Michael Raleigh 1969]

It might be thought that here the Sa'idi of the joke possessed rather than lacked insight, but the Egyptian telling this joke, which he had originally heard in Cairo in 1963, saw the Sa'idi's attitude as one of "dimwitted resignation" at having to run away. Indeed, the joke-teller seems to have accepted an Egyptian view of the Sa'idis as "rather stupid, backward and quite unsophisticated" and commented that they were "ideally fitted to being soldiers or better (still) officers in the army" [UCBFA Egypt file, Michael Raleigh 1969]. The comments of the Egyptian joke-teller on this joke indicate that he saw it both as an ethnic joke about Sa'idis and as a political joke about the army and its officers, whom he regarded as both backward and apt to move backwards. Military failure, as well as militarism, can be made the subject of political jokes by those who have distanced themselves from their country's army and its defeats [see also Esar 1978, 109].

One further insight into the way militarism and cowardice are balanced can be gained by looking at the way in which Jewish jokes on these themes have changed with the emergence of ethnic jokes about "cowardly and militarily incompetent Arabs," following their defeat by the army of a Jewish state. There is a marked contrast between these new jokes and traditional East European Jewish jokes that derided not merely aggressive militarism but military organizations and behavior as such. For these Jews in exile, often in virulently anti-Semitic nations, a soldier was defined as "a uniform stuffed with a goy" [UCBFA Jewish file, Natasha Doner 1968. Ascribed to Rabbi Joseph Lovenstein, Warsaw 1919].

The Russian officer, on inspection, scolded a Jewish recruit because one of his buttons wasn't shiny enough.

"Mr. Officer," says the soldier, "is that all that's worrying you?" [UCBFA Jewish file, Natasha Doner 1968. From Sertontzk, Poland, World War I]

One doctor on the draft board staff would accept no graft; no influence could persuade him. The only exception he made was if the candidate had an organic heart disease. Complained the father whose son was about to come up to the physical, 'Such good luck is only given to one in a thousand.' [UCBFA Jewish file, Natasha Doner 1968. From Sertotzk, Poland, World War I]

After the battle all the generals were called to give an account. All of them reported heavy casualties, except the Jew, who only had one man wounded because of an accidental fall. "How is that possible?" they asked the Jewish general. "You were right in the midst of this bloody battle."

"As soon as the enemy started shooting, I personally jumped out of the trenches and yelled, 'Stop! Halt! Don't you see there are people here!!' " [UCBFA Jewish file, Natasha Doner 1968. Ascribed to Rabbi Lovenstein, Sertotzk 1915. Also British Jewish 1960s, and Hillel 1978, 246–47]

In the front line trenches a Jewish sentinel, supposedly scanning the enemy lines, was found on the other side of the hill. The commanding officer threatened him with court martial. To which the Jewish soldier replied, "I so hate the enemy I can't look him in the face." [UCBFA Jewish file, Natasha Doner 1968. Ascribed to draftees in Sertotzk, 1912]

The extreme rejection of military institutions expressed in these jokes, which is also to be found in Yiddish folk sayings [see Kumove 1986, 19, 91, 238], was rooted in the Jewish experience of militarist rule in Eastern Europe. Indeed, the Tsarist army had been used to harass the Jews directly, and young Jewish men were deliberately conscripted into the army for long periods in an attempt to break their belief in Judaism and loyalty to the Jewish community [see Goldberg 1967, 71–72]. The Jews were not merely alienated from the army but viewed it as an agent of persecution. War and the army were seen as meaningless by many Jews in Eastern Europe since, whatever the outcome of any war, someone was likely to attack them. Their main role in wartime was likely to be that of victim:

In our town, my father was the only subscriber to the big city newspaper. My mother's brother, who lived with us, refused to look at it, which annoyed my mother. Finally she asked him, "Here is the whole town waiting (collector's note: the paper was shared among the villagers) and you refuse to look at it. Someday a war is going to break out and you won't even know about it."

To which my uncle, sadly shaking his head, responded, "Oy, will I know!" [UCBFA Jewish file, Natasha Doner 1968. Ascribed to Mendle Lovenstein of Sertotzk, 1912–13, at the time of the anti-Semitic Bayliss [*sic*] ritual child murder trial]

Other people's conflicts always tend to appear senseless, but in this group, for whom an outbreak of conflict between nations brought intensified persecution, there "was a general Jewish animosity towards war and its practitioners. The Jews considered military life and its vagaries as the height of stupidity" [UCBFA Jewish file, Natasha Doner 1968].

The significance of the old East European Jewish antimilitary jokes is that they emerged from a people who viewed the balance between military and civilian values not from the center but from a position near the edge, in which self-preservation, family, and autonomy were the only worthwhile values. For a people without a state of their own, who had experienced nothing but persecution from the states in which they lived, the military virtues were irrelevant. Hence the jokes about cowardice told about East European Jews by outsiders [e.g., see Crosland 1922, 75, 112–19; Raskin 1985, 211] were turned inside out and the values, ethos, and behavior of the military in general were derided as mere foolish militarism and nothing more.

Even today something of this old East European tradition of humor survives in Jewish jokes which pit a competitive commercial individualism against the hierarchical collectivism of the military.[58] However, there is now a competing tradition of Jewish jokes, stressing the military success of the Israelis and mocking the failure of their opponents. Sometimes contemporary Jewish jokes combine and contrast both traditions of humor about the military:

A newly arrived Jewish immigrant in Israel was called up for military service and sent for training. An Israeli NCO pointed to a stuffed figure used for bayonet practice and said to him, "Do you know what that is? It's an Arab."

"Really," said the new arrival, "I thought it was a stuffed figure."

"You've got to hate him," said the NCO, "He's evil. He's your enemy."

The sceptical Jewish conscript did his best to get worked up into a suitable emotional frenzy and asked the NCO: "What do I do now?"

"You charge him."

"How much?" [British 1980s. See also Peter and Dana 1982, 136]

The kind of balancing between values, such as those of the military and those of civilian worlds, which I have suggested forms the basis of much ethnic joking, seems to take a particular form in Israel, a country of immigrants from exile. Elliott Oring [1973, 366; see also 1981], in his study of chizbat humor, a body of Israeli jokes, anecdotes, and tall tales, describes the chizbat as "an investigation of the boundaries of identity or self-image. It playfully explores the elements of two images, Sabra and Jew, and finds them both incongruous yet appropriate." Other, longer-settled peoples use humor to indicate the boundaries of their identity by telling ethnic jokes about their neighbors or other similar peoples whose behavior they deride as being extreme or unbalanced. The Israelis explore their identity through the chizbat, which plays on the incongruities of two established images: the sabra image of the native-born and the galut image of the exile personality, the immigrant from abroad. Oring has shown how these images consist of two antithetical complexes of traits which run through most chizbat humor. What is striking about Oring's two columns of fourteen opposed traits [1973, 365 and 1981, 123] is that at least half of them seem to relate to antithetical views of "assertion through force" versus "restraint." Since chizbat humor was first developed in the Palmakh [Oring 1973, 358–59], a voluntary, underground defense force, this is not surprising, but these issues and tensions are, as has been shown, also a key source of the ethnic humor of other nations.

The study of Jewish jokes about the military indicates how humorous traditions change in response to circumstances. The ethnic jokes about Egyptian "cowardice" show how quickly jokes are switched and invented when a striking event makes them appear relevant. However, there is one category of ethnic joke about military cowardice, those about American blacks in World War I, that seems to be rooted in a racial ideology rather than in any unambiguous events that made the same impression on a wide range of different observers.

The ethnic jokes about cowardly soldiers told about the Italians or the Egyptians were the result of the initially unexpected collapse of entire armies and circulated among a variety of peoples whose feelings about the collapse were very different. The ethnic jokes about cowardly American black soldiers in World War I only circulated in the United States, particularly in the South, and they were not linked to any massive and spectacular event that was visible to the other participants in the war. The only events that might have sparked off the jokes were the collapse, failure, and panic of a number of battalions in the 368th regiment of the black American 92nd division in the Argonne offensive in France in September 1918 [see Barbeau and Henri 1974, 149–63]. These were regarded by army critics of the black troops as support for their preexisting view that the blacks would prove useless and cowardly soldiers. The details of what actually happened and why are obscure, but the scale of the collapse was minimal and similar routine failures can be found in the records of all the armies that took part in the war. It was not one of history's memorable defeats or disasters and was neither seen as a threat by America's allies nor counted as an opportunity by her enemies. The behavior of America's black troops did not differ enough from that of other armies to call for an explanation by an outside observer. Far more striking than the actual performance of the black combat units in France, whether good, bad, or indifferent, were the frequency and vehemence with which blacks were described as cowardly and unsuited to being combat soldiers well before American units got to the fighting [see Barbeau and Henri 1974, 19, 42, 161]. This widespread expectation of cowardice is far more remarkable than anything that actually happened. It was a view that affected people's humorous as well as serious perception of the black soldiers, for "The general impression of Americans was that the colored soldier was mainly a comic figure, incapable of undergoing danger over long intervals" [Stallings 1963, 122].

A crucial practical result of the official application of the view that the blacks would make bad soldiers was that 80 percent of the black troops who served overseas in World War I were allocated to laboring rather than fighting duties. The blacks were one-seventh of those who were drafted but one-third of the laborers [see data in Barbeau and Henri 1974, 44, 89, 191]. Such an assignment may in itself have tended to lead to ethnic jokes about cowardice, for the men in these service units were often ridiculed by the front-line soldiers. When the War Department changed the name of the Labor Battalions to the more "dignified" Services of Supply it was at once shortened by the combat men to the derisive "S. O. S." (Help! Help!) and incorporated in the song "Mother, Pull Down Your Service Flag, Your Son's in the S. O. S." [see Barbeau and Henri 1974, 109–110].

For the ethnic jokes about "Italian cowardice" discussed previously the most important sociological problem was to try to explain the behavior on the part of Italian army units that sparked off the jokes—the perception and common-sense interpretation of that behavior by others was neither surprising nor problematic given the taken-for-granted standards of military behavior of those who laughed. It would have added very little to our understanding of how the jokes came about to ask questions about French/Greek/British hopes and expectations regarding the Italians in World War II, particularly since none of these three peoples had significant social contacts with the Italians before the chance shiftings of international power politics made them opponents.

Jokes about "Italian cowardice" are very old, but there is no reason to suppose that this led others to underestimate the Italians' fighting capacity after Italy entered World War II in 1940 or to be unreasonably eager to label Italian military reverses "panic," "rout," or "surrender." Also the Allies had no real way of manipulating the myth of Italian cowardice and military incompetence to induce behavior congruent with it. The survival of the comic image of Italian cowardice depended almost entirely on what happened out there in the real world, and even the serious version of this view of the Italians had little effect on that. Eventually Allied military commanders incorporated the assumption that the Italians were unsoldierly into their battle plans and tried to attack Italian rather than German held sectors, but this was a shrewd and rational calculation based on experience gained earlier in the same war. In World War I it was likewise feared by American military leaders that German military commanders, who understood this form of "ethnic targeting" all too well, would selectively attack black (and therefore feebly) held sections of the line. Colonel E. D. Anderson of the American General Staff wrote:

> The enemy is constantly looking for a weak place in the line and if he can find a part of the line held by troops composed of culls of the colored race, all he has to do is to concentrate on that, break through, and then he will be in rear of high class troops who will be at a terrible disadvantage. An illustration of this is the way the Germans concentrated on the Portuguese at Ypres, broke through the Portuguese and the whole line had to fall back at heavy loss, losing valueable positions and enormous stores because the enemy had found second-rate troops at one spot. [Quoted in Barbeau and Henri 1974, 191–92 from document in U.S. National Archives RG165 item 8142–150]

However, this was written in an advisory and planning document dated May 16, 1918, before any significant number of black American soldiers had been involved in serious fighting [Barbeau and Henri 1974, 116–19]. It was a scenario based on an assumption, not on experience.

It is thus the preexisting assumptions regarding "black cowardice and military incompetence" that are important. Even if the bulk of the black combat troops had in fact wantonly surrendered and gone happily into captivity or deserted en masse and run away, it would still have been necessary to examine the myth and its implementation very carefully to see if it had been the cause as well as the antecedent of such events. Since nothing extraordinary did happen the issue becomes merely one of asking why the myth was so strong and how and why did it shape people's serious and (more to our present purpose) comic perceptions of the military behavior of the blacks.

It is difficult to estimate more than half a century later how the American jokes about "cowardly blacks" originally circulated, but one man who did a great deal to record and disseminate them was the Southern journalist, raconteur, and anthologist Irvin S. Cobb [1923, 1925], who published a number of best-selling collections of jokes in the 1920s. Cobb had been a war correspondent in France and "became an admirer of the black servicemen" [Barbeau and Henri 1974, 103] in the labor and the combat units. As a result of his visit to one of the latter regiments, which had been lent to the French and distinguished itself in action, Cobb [1918, 283–84] wrote that in the future "n-i-g-g-e-r will merely be another way of spelling the word American." It is very unlikely then that Cobb deliberately selected jokes and anecdotes for his anthologies about "cowardly blacks" because he himself seriously believed that the blacks were cowardly. Yet ten of the fifteen comic anecdotes about the American Expeditionary Force collected and published by him are about blacks and in at least five of these the blacks are laughably cowardly, whereas the jokes about white soldiers depict them as still resolute even when weary of the war [see Cobb 1923 and 1925]. Probably this is a fair sample of the jokes and humorous stories told in Cobb's social milieu at the time. Ethnic jokes about black soldiers in World War I proved very popular in the South, for they were repeatedly reprinted in collections of Southern jokes. During

World War II Boyce House [1944, 18–28 and 54–61; 1945, 61–72] compiled a number of books of Texas jokes in which there were sections on "War" about white soldiers in World War II and sections on "Colored Folks" still containing many World War I stories about black soldiers [see also Cerf 1945, 160; Prochnow 1953 (1949), 306, 369]. Being black was clearly a "master status" i.e., a part of a man's identity that overrode everything else about him, and cowardice was just an aspect of blackness.

The colored unit was under fire for the first time and, as the bombardment increased in intensity, one of the soldiers who had been a preacher in civilian life, dropped on his knees and prayed:

"Oh, Lawd! Send You' Son down to save us 'fore we all gits killed! Oh Lawd! Send You' Son down to help us 'fore we's all blowed to pieces; Oh Lawd! Send. . . . ."

A comrade broke in:

"Don't do dat, Lawd. Don't send Yoah Son! Come down Yoahself: dis ain't no boy's job!" [House 1944, 59. See also 55–58 and House 1945]

Sam was being assigned to sentry duty and he was instructed "If you see anything move, you call out 'Halt' and then you shoot. Do you understand?"

"Yas, suh an' vice versa."

"What do you mean: vice versa?" the lieutenant asked.

"Ef anythin' moves Ah shoots; ef anything shoots, Ah moves." [House 1944, 59]

This last ethnic joke, like many of those about blacks cited earlier, is about the expectation of cowardly behavior rather than the behavior itself, and it has at the core of the joke an admission by a black soldier that he is going to run at the first sign of danger. A central theme in many of these ethnic jokes is this admission by a member of the group itself, sometimes seriously, sometimes half-jokingly, that he and his group are cowardly.

The importance of this admission relates not to the war or even the army but to Southern society back home, and here again there is a crucial difference between the position of the American blacks in World War I and that of the Italians in World War II, which is relevant to an explanation of the jokes. In the latter case, everyone went home after the war and the Italians ceased to interact with the peoples telling the jokes. The joke-tellers went on enjoying and inventing ethnic jokes that unloaded "cowardice" onto another group, but it did not really matter to them which group it was; the Italians merely happened to be the butt that got pinched. By contrast the Southern blacks in World War I came out of and returned to a society where they were subordinate to the white Southerners making the jokes about them, and their subordination was maintained by the whites' use of force and intimidation. For the joke-tellers, cowardice was the appropriate and desired response of the subordinate group to this intimidation and may well have been seen as a racial characteristic that would continue to prevail in a military context.

In the heyday of the jokes the South was a region stratified in a quite different way from the rest of the United States. Before the Civil War most blacks in the South would have been slaves, members of a subordinate class and caste dominated by the use of force [see Andreski 1973, 174; Cash 1973 (1941), 102; Dollard 1957 (1937), 59], for whom retreat and submission in the face of threats were expected forms of behavior. Deferential humorous references to this expectation and to the powerlessness of a person who was also a piece of property were for a slave in and of themselves one way of mollifying and manipulating an angry slave-owner or overseer. Jokes about cowardly black soldiers and potential soldiers were certainly told in relation to the American Civil War, but more work remains to be done on the relationship between these jokes and the battles of that war in which black troops were involved or from which they were deliberately excluded. All that can be said here is that they closely resemble the jokes of World War I vintage:

> "How dat, Sambo? You says you was at de battle of Bull Run, when I sees you at New York on de same night!" "Yes Julius, you did for sartin. You see, our colonel says he, 'Boys strike for yer country and yer homes.' Well some struck for der country, but dis chile he struck for home. Dat splains the matter, you see." [(Thousand) *1,000 Witty Sayings* n.d., 31]

> Our military men apprehend no serious consequences from the army of negroes in process of organization by the Abolitionists at Washington. General Rains says the negro cannot fight and will always run away. He tells an anecdote which happened under his own observation. An officer, when going into battle, charged his servant to stay at his tent and take care of his property. In the fluctuations of the battle some of the enemy's shot fell in the vicinity of the tent and the negro, with great white eyes, fled away with all his might. After the fight, and when the officer returned to his tent, he was vexed to learn that his slave had run away; but the boy soon returned, confronting his indignant master who threatened to chastise him for disobedience of orders. "Massa" said Caesar, "you told me to take care of your property and dis property"—placing his hand on his breast—"is worf fifteen hundred dollars." He escaped any punishment. [(Thousand) *1,000 Witty Sayings* n.d., 168]

In the post-Reconstruction period the Southern whites had again reasserted their dominant position by the use of force, using both official ploys and unofficial means, such as lynching or intimidation by the Ku Klux Klan, and these methods, though in decline, were still in use both during and immediately after World War I.[59] Southern ethnic jokes of the time dwell explicitly on the mixture of terror and humiliation that the imposition of law without order, of mob violence, lynching, and the activities of that ghostly inquisition the Klan, induced in the hapless and wretched blacks. The blacks' response to the horrors inflicted on them was depicted in the jokes as one of explicit groveling acceptance of the legitimacy of Southern white supremacy. Boyce House, in his collection of jokes *Tall Talk from Texas*, noted: "If this collector of jokes were asked to name the three stories that are told oftener than any others the answer would be that the three are all negro jokes" [1944, 57: see also 1945, 67, 68]. The second of his three most frequently told stories is:

A negro, about to be hanged, was asked if he had anything he wished to say to the big crowd. He said: "White folks, dis sho' am gwine to be a lesson to me."

There were many other jokes on this theme:

Along in the 1920s the "Invisible Empire" was flourishing and—not saying there was any connection—a wave of whippings and tar-and-feather parties swept over the State.

Two negroes were talking on the street one day and one of them asked:

"Joe, what would you do ef you got a letter from de Ku Klux?"

The other answered:

"I'd finish readin' it on de train." [House 1943, 40]

It befell in the old days that a mob one night took a negro out of a county jail in southern Kentucky and carried him just across the line into Tennessee and there hanged him at the roadside. As he dangled they riddled him with bullets and then kindled a fire under him with intent to destroy the body.

By the light of the mounting flames somebody saw something stirring in a brush pile, close by the scene of execution. He kicked the brush away and dragged out an old colored man, who had been on his way home when he saw the lynchers coming. He had deemed it the part of prudence to take cover immediately. But as luck would have it, he had gone into retirement at the very spot where the mob halted to do its work.

Men poked big guns in his face and swore to take his life if ever he dared reveal what he had that night beheld. The old man protested that the whole thing was purely an affair of the white folks, in which he had no concern nor interest. He was quite sure that by daybreak of the following morning all memories of the night would be gone from his mind.

The leader of the mob felt it incumbent to press the lesson home to the consciousness of the witness. Still casually cocking and uncocking a long pistol, he flirted a thumb over his shoulder toward the gallows-tree and said:

"Well, you know that black scoundrel yonder got what he deserved, don't you?"

The old man craned his neck about and gazed for a moment upon the grisly spectacle.

"Boss," he said fervently, "it looks lak to me he got off mighty light." [Cobb 1923, 57. See also Graves 1928, 55–56]

It may well be that the best way to interpret the World War I jokes about cowardly black soldiers in France is as an extension of these jokes about humble, servile blacks back in the South who would cower before threats and accept the indignities to which they were subjected. Not only was it assumed by the whites that black soldiers would prove cowardly before they got to the war but it was hoped and expected that they would stay that way after they came back so that the experience of military service abroad would not create a returning army of "uppity niggers" [see Barbeau and Henri 1974, 32–35, 175–77]. However, the jokes to this effect are not in and of themselves a part of the Vardaman-style ideology of white supremacy by force. They are equally capable [see Sterling 1965, 200] of being used as a wry comment on the way things are or were:

Following the close of hostilities two members of a colored labor battalion—natives of the same inland Georgia town—were sitting on a dock at Brest. Naturally, their thoughts dwelt on what they would do when they [had] been shipped back to the States and mustered out of the service.

"Me, I done got it figgered out," said one. "I been takin' a lesson from dese yere Frenchmens. Dey ain't got no race-feelin's; dey don't draw no color-line. So, I 'spects to carry on 'en I gits back jest de same ez I'se been doin' over yere—only mebbe mo' so! Things shorely must 'a' changed back home sence we been away. So, ez soon ez I strikes our ole town I'se goin' git me some w'ite clothes, all w'ite frum haid to foot—w'ite suit, w'ite necktie, w'ite straw hat, w'ite shoes, ever'thing w'ite. An' I'm goin' put 'em on an' den I'm goin' invite some w'ite gal to jine me an' wid her on my arm I'm gwine walk slow down de street bound fur de ice-cream parlor. Whut does you aim to do w'en you gits back?"

"Well," said his companion, "I 'spects to act diffe'nt frum you, an' yet, in a way, similar. I'm goin' git me a black suit, black frum haid to foot, and black shoes, an' I is gwine walk slow down de street, jest behine you—bound fur de cemetery!" [Cobb 1925, 57]

Jokes about cowardly black American soldiers differ from those about cowardly Italians in content and meaning in the same way that jokes about canny Jews differ from those about canny Scotsmen. Just as there is no anti-Caledonian ideology that corresponds to anti-Semitism so too there is no ideology of the supremacy of non-Italians (French, British, Greeks, as well as Germans and Americans) that matches the Southern doctrine of white supremacy. In the case of the blacks, as of the Jews, however, the jokes are told against the background of an elaborate and strongly held set of beliefs about race or some other putatively unchanging and unchangeable characteristic.

Ethnic jokes about cowardice and militarism display a remarkable degree of variety, change, and complexity, but certain patterns can be perceived and they may be summed up as follows:

1. Ethnic jokes about cowardice and militarism reflect the confused coexistence in modern societies of military and civilian values. This pair of jokes represents the two opposed ways in which individuals and groups can fail in war, just as jokes about the stupid and the canny represent failure in general. Jokes about militarists, like jokes about the canny, sometimes depict them as a threat to others also. Ethnic jokes pin these twin undesirable extremes onto other ethnic groups and nations.

2. Particular groups become the butt of ethnic jokes about cowardice or militarism as a result of highly visible wartime events—a spectacular failure or surrender, or a marked display of aggression, brutality, or last-ditch resistance. It is, in general, events themselves that need explaining rather than other peoples' perceptions of them, but there are interesting exceptions to this rule.

3. The explanation of the "extreme" behavior that gives rise to ethnic jokes about cowardice and militarism often lies in the varied nature of peoples' loyalty or indifference to their particular nation-state, which is in turn rooted in their history. Ethnic jokes told about people of a particular nation may well find an alternative expression as political jokes told within that nation. The citizens of fragmented nations, characterized by intensely local loyalties and local jokes about this, may end up the butts of ethnic jokes about cowardice or of ethnic jokes about militarism, depending on the visible results of their attempts to create and sustain national unity, which other peoples contrast with their own self-defined "normal" experience and expectations.

4. In the case of the Germans/Prussians, where the ethnic/political jokes told refer to militarism, the jokes originally reflected the power and standing in that society of an aristocracy whose position was based on military service to the state. The jokes stressed order and discipline rather than the belligerent individualism found in earlier ethnic jokes about the Welsh gentry or the Gascons. After the events and experiences of World War II, brutality and a capacity for committing atrocities were also incorporated into the comic image of German militarism.

5. In certain instances it is necessary to explain a particular ethnic group's perception of militarism or cowardice, such as the antimilitarist Jewish jokes from Eastern Europe told by a group without a state of its own for whom the army meant persecution. For the jokes about the supposed cowardice of black American soldiers told in World War I, it is the perceptions of the white Southerners of the time that call for an explanation, and the nature of that explanation is probably rooted in the relationship of those two groups in a caste-like system of stratification based on force and intimidation.

6. Ethnic jokes about cowardice and militarism eventually become conventionalized, and anecdotes rooted in real events give way to jokes based on a formula in which ethnicity is merely a shared signal that tells the audience the nature and subject of a compact joke ending in a surprise punch line. Ethnicity has once again become a device for telling efficient and effective jokes on particular themes.

CHAPTER EIGHT

Anglo-Saxon Attitudes

The Anglo-Saxon countries, to use a curious and inaccurate collective term imposed on them by the French, are probably seen by outsiders more in terms of their similarities than of their differences. The English-speaking democracies of Australia, Canada, England, New Zealand, and the United States have not only a common language but remarkably similar social and political structures and legal, constitutional, and cultural traditions. Indeed, just how similar these countries are can be seen by contrasting each of them with countries that have a markedly different social order, culture, and values [see Lipset 1964, 248], such as Mexico, France, Japan, Greece, or Romania. However, it is the very social and cultural similarities of these countries that inspire their citizens to invent jokes about each other.

The simplest and crudest examples of such jokes involve a straightforward put-down of the members of one of the nations by those of one of the others. Sometimes a citizen of one of the smaller or weaker countries tries to cut a bigger neighbor down to size, or a citizen of one of the stronger, more powerful countries puts a small but uppitty nation firmly in its place and makes it clear what the real pecking order is. The nature of the "put-down joke" in the two cases is quite different and one is left in no doubt as to the relative size, wealth, and power of the two nations involved:

A car-driver in New Zealand ran into a shop and asked for fifty ice-creams for fifty little people sitting on the back seat of his car. The shopkeeper looked at them in amazement and said: "What nationality are they?"

"Oh, they're Australians with the bullshit squeezed out of them." [From correspondent in Christchurch, New Zealand 1980]

Two men were arguing in a New Zealand pub about TV commercials in which chimpanzees pour themselves cups of tea. One man said the films were made in New Zealand and the other that they were made in England. An Australian who was in the pub at the time was asked to settle the argument. "Well," he said, "You're both right. The films were made in England but all the actors are Kiwis." [Australian 1981]

How do you set up a New Zealander in a small business? Buy him a big business and wait. [Ocker 1986]

Australian radio announcement: "The New Zealand navy arrived in Australia today on a good will visit and is anchored in Garden Island. The two canoes will be on display to the public from midday." [Australian 1981]

An American attended a rowing regatta on the Thames, honored by the presence of the royal family and retinue.

Between events the little diving lads entertained the crowds by going to the bottom for the coppers tossed into the river. The American commenced to flip silver dollars into the stream. A Londoner laid a restraining hand on his arm. "My word," he warned, "you'll have the king diving!" [Copeland and Copeland 1939, 687]

What's the capital of Canada? Mainly American.

What's the automotive capital of Canada? Detroit.

What wars did Canada take part in? Oh the same ones.

When will Canada legalize marijuana? The day after.

How do they take the census in Canada? They take the American census and divide by ten.

What do you get when you cross a Canadian and an American? An American. [Kelly and Mann 1978]

Canadian genius is ten per cent imitation and ninety per cent importation. [Mann 1977, 49]

Q. Why is it a bad idea asking Americans what they think of Canada?
A. Because they're afraid they'll be pestered next by some clown from Ecuador. [Mann 1977, 64]

Q. What's the name of the movie they're making about Quebec after separation?
A. Mon Oncle Sam. [Mann 1977, 46]

Q. Name a popular Canadian T. V. serial.
A. Coronation Street. [Mann 1977, 79]

An enormous American car with Illinois plates drove up to a gas station in Banff, Alberta, in the summer. The province of British Columbia

is a half hour's drive farther west. After the tank had been filled, the driver had a question.
Driver: "Is there some place around here where I can change my Canadian money for British pounds? We're going on to British Columbia."
Attendant: "Yes sir, but it'll be a little out of your way. You know that highway you just came off of—the Trans-Canada? Get back on that and head east until you come to Ottawa: that's our capital. You can't miss it. I'm sure they can fix you up."
Driver: "Thanks a lot for your help." [Ginger 1974, Anecdote 55]

These jokes reflect the fact that for any pair of Anglo-Saxon countries one will be larger, wealthier, more powerful, and more influential than the other. Especially New Zealanders and Canadians must at times be uneasily aware of their larger and at times rather overwhelming neighbors, Australia and America [see McNaught 1969, 295; Richler 1986, 129, 232], whose humor at the expense of their smaller Anglophone cousins tends to depict them as unimportant, culturally subordinate, and drably provincial.[1] The New Zealanders and Canadians face the further problem that English-speaking outsiders tend, on the basis of a crude identification by speech patterns and appearance, to ask Canadians if they are Americans and New Zealanders if they come from Australia. For the person who wrongly guesses their identity it is an unimportant error based on the reasonable statistical assumption that most people who sound vaguely North American are from the United States and that most Antipodeans are Australian. In addition, given that British humorists [see Atkinson and Searle 1963, 24] and American social scientists [see Spradley and Rynkiewich 1975, 166–78] alike casually treat Canada as a mere extension of the United States, it is easy to see why Canadians have a humor that stresses uniquely Canadian institutions and ways of speaking English and indeed French [see Orkin 1973] but which is also mildly self-deprecating [Richler 1986, 147].

Mike Pearson, Prime Minister of Canada, went to see L. B. J. in Texas in 1965: "As we mounted a little podium before a battery of TV cameras the President . . . welcomed me very warmly and greatly enlivened the ceremony by ending his remarks . . . 'and we are so happy to have Mr. Wilson with us.' " [Richler 1986, 236–37]

A survey of schoolchildren's knowledge of great Canadians produced the response from one scholar: "Margaret Atwood, Margaret Laurance —never heard of them so they must be Canadian." [Richler 1986, 147]

The best "definition of 'Canajan' is 'Not Mare Can'." [Orkin 1973, 56]

Simple put-down jokes[2] tell us relatively little about the quality of the contrasts and of the relationships between the Anglo-Saxon countries. Indeed, such jokes tend to arise from the relationship between any two linked, friendly, but uneasily unequal countries [e.g., see jokes in UCBFA Scandinavian and Latin American files]. However, other, more complex and interesting aspects arise when we examine jokes that tap culturally specific elements in the contrasts and relationships between the three most distinctive and separate of the Anglo-Saxon countries, America, Australia, and England.

The starting point of the analysis will be the view that two of the most central values of American society are equality and achievement.[3] These values are shared by the Australians and the English [see Heald 1982; Lipset 1964, 211–12; Rokeach 1973, 89–91] but they do not hold them to the same extent nor in exactly the same ways; it is these differences that underpin the jokes that are told in each nation about the others. Americans in general are more competitive, more inclined to strive for individual success, than are the English, who often still perceive society as a settled hierarchy and whose aspirations and patterns of deference are often shaped by the values of a "gentry" rather than a business culture.[4] Even though patterns of social mobility are not very different in the three countries, it is still true that the English respect for the ascribed status of the well-born leads the self-made Englishman to play down his humble antecedents rather than to glory in the height of his own ascent as an American would [see Pearce 1983, 144–45].

Following the rise of Mrs. Thatcher, it can no longer be true that the English are "horrified at the idea of a country where the little grocers' daughters don't look up" to their "betters" [Badeau 1886, 478], but the sentiment lives on in an attenuated form. The Australians share the American regard for the self-made entrepreneur, but their ambition is swamped by the strong Australian ethic of egalitarian collectivism so that they are probably the least individualistic, competitive, and achievement-oriented of the three peoples.[5] The Australians are more egalitarian[6] in their attitude to their fellow citizens than are the Americans, who in turn are more egalitarian than the relatively elitist, hierarchical, and class-conscious people of England. Thus we can put the three countries in a rough rank-order as shown in table 8.1. It should be stressed, however, that this is a relatively crude categorization, for the exact meanings of "achievement" and of "equality" differ subtly between the three countries.

These differences between the three countries have proved remarkably stable over time despite some tendency to converge brought about by parallel economic development and cultural exchange. The observed pattern is not surprising, given the differences in the origins and history of the three societies.

England's aristocracy survived as a culturally dominant group despite their gradual loss of political and economic power with the growth of

TABLE 8.1 **Equality and Achievement**

	Value placed on equality	**Value placed on individual achievement**
1st	Australia	United States
2nd	United States	England
3rd	England	Australia

democracy and the world's first industrial revolution. That they did is a major sociological puzzle, as is Britain's steady economic decline relative to other countries, from being the world's leading industrial power in the mid-nineteenth century to being just one of the also-rans today. Many would link these two puzzling phenomena, and indeed Wiener [1985, 5–6, 12–23, 128–52] has claimed that from the second half of the nineteenth century an aristocratic cultural counter-revolution undermined the competitive business ethos of industrial England that had posed a threat to the way of life of the older established classes [see Spencer 1904, 573 and 1969, 95, 246–51, 286–88]. The acquisition and administration of the largest colonial empire in the world would have reinforced the tendencies Wiener describes and also provided foreign joke-makers with one of their standard comic images of the Englishman abroad.

The distinctive character of American and Australian life has also provided historians and sociologists with a puzzle and a challenge [see for example Conway 1974; Lipset 1964; Ward 1966] and they have sought to look beyond the rather circular popular commonsense views of national character. America was founded to a large extent by dissenting Englishmen and similarly motivated groups of Scots, Welsh, and particularly Ulster Scotch-Irish [Leyburn 1962; Montgomery 1971] who wished to break away from the control of the English secular and religious establishment. The American Constitution, though largely based on the English liberal interpretation of their own political system, was and is a radically anti-aristocratic document drawn up by independent farmers, merchants, and professional men that specifically repudiated monarchy, titles, and entail and thus entrenched egalitarian individualism as the basic "self-evident" philosophy of American life. The arrival of new immigrants after independence, seeking to become Americans, and the flow of settlers westward, exploiting the free land on an ever-moving frontier, later continually re-created those aspects of American society which favored the basic American values [see Turner 1962] of equality and achievement. The waves of immigrants in the nineteenth century provided the expanding American economy with its unskilled labor and enabled those already established as American citizens to experience an unparalleled degree of upward mobility [see Andreski 1973, 40; Herberg 1960, 116; Potter 1954,

94]. It is not surprising that those thus floated up should have continued to proclaim the virtues of competition, mobility, and individual achievement in the manner so amusingly satirized by Sinclair Lewis [for example see 1974, (1922), 39–40, 177–79].

Many of the earliest settlers in Australia did not choose to go there but rather were "chosen by the best judges in England." After the convicts, Australia received a steady flow of lower-class emigrants from Britain and Ireland who mainly ended up in the cities. Whereas in Britain the key classes influencing the culture were the aristocracy and the gentry and in America the independent middle classes, in Australia, in both urban and rural areas, a working-class ethos prevailed [see Davis and Encel 1965, 18–20; Oxley 1978]. Insofar as there was a frontier it was one controlled by large proprietors, and freedom (or more accurately ambition) for the agricultural workers meant not freedom to rise by one's own efforts but freedom to combine against the "big men's" frontier [Ward 1966, 248; see also 224–26; Greenway 1972, 101; and Lipset 1964, 255].

The high stress placed on achievement in American culture, the emphasis on winning at all costs,[7] and the uncertainty about one's individual status [Potter 1954, 55 and 136] in a society that simultaneously stresses equality of status and the need to strive for inequalities of status based on individual achievement are among the factors that have led to one of the world's most popular comic ethnic scripts—that of the "boastful American." Not merely in English or Australian jokes but in Irish, French, German, and Swiss jokes too the American is depicted as bragging that everything in America is bigger and better than anywhere else in the world.[8] The comic image of the American outside America is indeed almost identical with that of the Texan within America who believes that Texas is the biggest and the best.[9] To some extent, the comic American boasters and boosters had the facts on their side, for America became one of the richest and most powerful countries that the world had ever seen. When we add to American wealth and power the American drive for both individual and collective achievement and recognition and the long-established American tradition for exaggeration and telling tall tales[10] we have the recipe for all those jokes that depict the citizens of the United States as irrepressibly boastful. Sometimes, as in Texas jokes too, the sheer size, natural resources, and scenic wonders of America are the subjects of these boasts, but often the material achievements of the American people are the source of American pride. The jokes about boastful Americans, regardless of source, are by no means one-sided, for the Americans and their rivals seem equally likely to win the competition between boasting and deflation that lie at the heart of these anecdotes:

When someone was describing a monster hotel in Switzerland that seated five hundred guests in the dining-room an American said, "We have a bigger hotel with us out west. Yes, sir, the dining-table in that hotel is so long that the waiters have to gallop about doing their work on horseback." When someone on the piazza of the Grand Hotel in Naples was looking at Vesuvius, which was in eruption at the time, he said to some Americans of the party, "That's one big thing you can't show in America," to which one of them replied, "No, sir, but we have a cataract in America that would put out that thing in two minutes." [Macrae 1904, 317]

Very fast travelling

An American was boasting to an Irishman about the fastness of American trains. "Why, Pat," said the American, "we run our trains so fast in America that the telegraph poles look like a continuous fence."

"Do they, now?" said Pat. "Well, sir, I was wan day on a train in Ireland and as we passed first a field of turnips, then wan of carrots, then wan of cabbage, and then a large pond of water, we were goin' that fast I thought it was broth!" [Lawson 1928, 132]

An American and a Scotsman were walking one day near the foot of one of the mountains in Scotland noted for its echoes. The native wishing to impress his visitor gave out with a loud "Halloo!" When the echo returned clearly after several long minutes the proud Scotsman turned to his companion and said, "There, mon, ye canna show anything like that in your country."

"Well, I don't know," countered the American. "In my camp in the Rockies when I go to bed at night I just lean out of the window and call out 'Time to get up. Wake up!'—and eight hours later the echo comes back and wakes me." [Copeland 1940, 636]

Evidently Larger

"Is your Mississippi River very much larger than our Thames?" asked an English lady of a Western visitor.

"Larger?" answered the Westerner. "Why, ma'am, there ain't enough water in the whole of the Thames to make a gargle for the mouth of the Mississippi." [Knox 1938, 62]

They were boasting about radio sets. "You know," said the American, "in America we have radios so powerful that it is possible to hear the announcer's heart beating."

"That's nothing," the Englishman replied. "I tuned in on Egypt last night, and in less than ten minutes the sand was up to my knees." [Copeland 1940, 700]

Robert Q. Lewis boasted that one of his new pals in Dallas was so rich he flew his own plane. "So what," scoffed a Los Angelite. "Lots of people here fly their own planes too." "Inside the house?" asked Robert Q. [Cerf 1959, 454]

Sometimes even an American bites off more than he can chew. The other day in the Strand a tourist sauntered up to a coster's barrow, and picking up a large melon said, "Gee, but do you mean to tell me bo, that's the largest kind of apple you ginks can grow over here."

"Put that blinkin' grape dahn," retorted the coster. [*Further Sunbeams* 1924, 93]

This latter joke, about the size of fruit, is a very common one in many countries [e.g., see Copeland 1940, 184; Macrae 1904, 317] and one set up so that the boastful American is almost bound to lose. However, a recent version of this joke gives it a new twist which enables the American, appropriately enough a Texan, to emerge as the winner.

A Texan visited a Swiss at his home in Switzerland. The Swiss proudly showed him his fine new swimming pool only to hear the Texan comment: "I've got a bathtub about as big as that in my bathroom." Next the Swiss took the Texan on a tour of his farm only to be told: "I guess we could fit about three of these into our kitchen garden." Finally the Swiss in despair took the Texan to see a giant pumpkin that he had grown near his house. "What's that?" asked the Texan, his curiosity aroused at last. "Oh, simply one of our Swiss apples," replied the Swiss, nonchalantly. "Huh," said the Texan. "I always said William Tell wasn't much of a shot." [French 1980s. Told to the author in a plane flying over Texas]

It has often been suggested that American comic boastfulness and the allied American love of tall tales and exaggeration, like American egalitarianism and individualism, have a common root in the sheer boundlessness of land and resources which presented itself to the first settlers from the cramped and poor countries of Europe [see Neider 1977, xvi]. America was the land of plenty and the open frontier, where there were fewer social, economic, or demographic pressures to restrict and restrain what a man might achieve. Out of this setting came the love of preposterous and ludicrous exaggeration which was at the core of so much early American humor, but which also provided an opportunity for others to mock and to laugh at the new democratic American [see Sklar 1970, 9–18]. The connection between America's traditional tall tales and the physical environment and limitless opportunities of the early years of the United States has been well expressed by the Scottish clerical humorist and moralist the Reverend David Macrae:

> [The Americans] tell, for example, of trees on the great Pacific slope, so high that it takes two men and a boy to see to the top of one—the first man looking till he is tired, and the second beginning where the first man left off. They tell about a man so tall that he had to get up a ladder to shave himself: and of a negro so black that charcoal made a chalk mark upon him.

They tell of a horse—an American horse, of course—that ran so fast round the circus that it could see its own tail about a yard ahead. They tell about American gunboats of draught so light that they can float wherever the ground is a little damp. They tell of an artist who painted a snowstorm so naturally, that his friend caught cold by sitting too near it with his hat off. They tell about a hair-restorer of such wonderful strength that when somebody dipped the end of his penholder into it, it grew rapidly into a shaving-brush. They tell about a storm that burst with such terrific fury upon one of their lake steamboats, that four powerful sailors were required to hold on the captain's whiskers. They tell of gas in some western city so very poor, that the man who went round to put out the lights had to carry a lantern with him to find out where the lamp-posts were. They tell of an unguent of such remarkable efficacy, that when a dog's tail was accidentally chopped off and the unguent was applied a fresh tail grew; and when some was next applied to the chopped-off tail a new dog grew.

This sort of humor—so characteristic of the Americans—was probably a comic reflex of the exaggerated features of nature, and the wonderful resources of the New World, that presented themselves so vividly to settlers going out from a small country like ours—especially in the earlier days of the Republic, when the country seemed immeasurable, and its resources absolutely exhaustless.

Even the form of government—with the new and dazzling opportunities it seemed to offer, as compared with countries where the high places were monopolised by, and practically secured to, the hereditary aristocracy—would help to inflame the imagination. A boy, who today brushed boots in the streets of New York, might thirty years later be governor of that great State; and a lad working on a western farm as a rail-splitter, or as a hand aboard a river steamboat, might rise, in after years, to be President of the United States of America—the four years' King of the great Republic. [1904, 307–309]

Possibly the ownership of these vast lands and resources did encourage much of American humorous exaggeration and boasting, but even more important was the American drive for success and achievement which rendered the lands productive and the resources usable. American comic boasting and exaggeration are as likely to dwell on American inventiveness, mechanical ingenuity, frenzied hard work, and dynamic entrepreneurship as on the mere physical dimensions of the country.

They are an inventive people, and they joke about it. They tell about a man who has patented a machine warranted to chase a pig round a ten-acre lot, and turn its flesh into pork sausages, its ears into purses and its tail into first-class shaving brushes, all within the space of forty-five minutes!

Another man claimed to have patented a kind of nest that would revolutionise the egg trade. The nest was of india-rubber, and had a false bottom, so that when the hen laid an egg it passed quietly through. The hen would look down, see no egg, think there had been some mistake, and proceed to lay another, with the same result. The patentee assured dairy farmers that there was a mint of money in it. [Macrae 1904, 335]

Even Lowell Thomas's 1931 collection *Tall Stories, The Rise and Triumph of the Great American Whopper,* which is largely concerned with outdoor anecdotes, contains a good deal of humor about American hustling, striving, and general frenzied business efficiency.

He [Burt Massee] informs us of a big Chicago business executive who works at such a terrific clip that his office catches fire. This occurs so often that the Fire Department keeps an engine stationed right around the corner.

This hustling business man goes right on working with the smoke and flames drifting around his head. And even when the firemen play the hose on the great executive he just keeps on dictating and shouting to his stenographers: "Take another letter!". . . .

In another up-and-coming Chicago business organisation the employees travel around the office on skis. The floors are covered with snow so that the stenographers can ski around with the utmost rapidity. In fact they have a small ski jump so that the office force can land right in front of the executive's desk.

A sad story is told of an aged book-keeper who had worked for many years in an office where the rapid employees approach the executive's desk with the baseball player's hook slide. Unfortunately he was fired for not making that slide with sufficient vim and abandon.

He got a job, however, in another office where the employees got around on skis. One day the great executive pushed the buzzer calling him. The aged book-keeper went ski-ing swiftly along the snowy floor but as he came to the great executive's desk he had a momentary lapse of memory. He thought he was still in the office where they do the hook slide at that point. On the snow of the office floor, skis and all, he hurled himself into a hook slide. He just kept going. He went right through the wall and out into Michigan Boulevard. It was the end of him. Yes, quite sad. [Thomas 1931, 215–17]

This comic image of frenzied competitive business is at the core of many jokes contrasting compulsively hard-working, go-ahead, hustling, boosting Americans with the supposedly more backward, relaxed, leisurely, and inefficient peoples of other countries.

An American teacher undertook the task of convincing an indolent native son of the Philippines that it was his duty to get out and hustle.

"But why should I work?" inquired the guileless Filipino.

"In order to make money," declared the thrifty teacher.

"But what do I want with money?" persisted the brown brother.

"Why when you get plenty of money you will be independent and will not have to work any more," replied the teacher.

"I don't have to work now," said the native—and the teacher gave up in disgust. [Copeland 1940, 761. Also in Cagney 1976, No. 2878; Lewis and Wachs 1976 (1966), 352; Wilde 1978A, 170]

One of a party of American tourists, so impressed by the mountain scenery of North Wales, approached an old inhabitant and said: "Why don't you Welsh people do the same as they do in Switzerland, where the country is just the same as this only they have cows where you have goats? Why don't you turn all these goats into a business proposition? All you have to do is milk 'em and sell the product as a health-giving piece of sustenance!" The old inhabitant replied: "Yiss, sirr! Tha's all verry well; but we can't make the old goats sit on the tins!" [Miles 1926, 19]

The English rhyme leisure with pleasure.
Americans rhyme leisure with seizure. [Esar 1978, 579]

One well-to-do [American] business man, a manufacturer of psychiatrist's sundries, . . . actually keeps his desk calendar a week ahead of everybody else's; "Nobody's going to steal a march on me, Mac," he explained. On one wall of his office there was a sign which read "It's Too Late Already" and he told me that he had started excavations for a deep shelter before the ink was properly dry on Einstein's theory of Relativity. [Atkinson and Searle 1963, 15]

"Why is it, dad, that all Americans say 'I guess'?" demanded little Willie. "Well, my boy, it's like this, they are all so busy they have no time to make certain of anything." [*Further Sunbeams* 1924, 121]

An engineer was trying to put through a railroad project in one of the Latin-American countries and he was seeking some local support for it.

"How long does it take you to get your goods to market on a burro?" he inquired of a native.

"Four days," he was told.

"See there," cried the engineer triumphantly, "with our road you could get your goods to market and be back in one day."

"But, Senor," protested the native "what would we do with the other three days!" [Lewis and Wachs 1976 (1966), 255]

Americans are defined by themselves and by others as a frenziedly hardworking, striving, competitive people whose prime value is individual success and achievement. It is this more than any other trait that sets them apart from the other Anglo-Saxons. The Americans are also noted for their egalitarianism and many jokes contrasting the Americans and the English rely on the clash between the easy, informal democratic manners of the former and the stiff, hierarchical status-conscious approach to life of the English. These jokes rely for their humor on the Americans' ignorance of and often contempt for the rules of etiquette that characterize the more snobbish and formal social life of England. Depending on the values and viewpoint of the observer, the Americans' behavior is either refreshingly informal or crassly vulgar. These jokes are, however, now getting somewhat old-fashioned, and the Americans are tending to be replaced in English jokes by the Australians as the true representatives of a coarse and vital colonial society. Jokes about crude Americans offending British aristocrats are a mainly nineteenth-century phenomenon, as Kowalski [1974, 9] has pointed out:

> At one time America itself was a big joke, especially to the British. Toward the end of the 19th century no British humor magazine worth its salt would be caught without at least one joke about Hiram P. Swackhammer (some name like that), the self-made Yankee money-bags on the loose in Europe.
>
> According to the British funny books, Americans were just naturally loud, vulgar, tasteless, and the more money they had the worse they behaved. They were always offering zillions of dollars to buy the House of Parliament and ship it back stone by stone and set it up again in a suburb of Pittsburgh or St. Louis. They were just as likely to address Her Majesty the Queen as "sweetie" or "toots"; few if any ever got into polite British society.

Kowalski is wrong about their being unable to enter polite British society, which was always, in practice, open to anyone with enough money and determination. The British aristocracy were snobbish but they were also greedy enough and shrewd enough to have a price well within the reach of the average American zillionaire.

A wealthy American girl was attending a weekend party at a country home in England.

'You American girls haven't such healthy complexions as we English women have,' said an English duchess to the girl. 'I always wonder why our noblemen take a fancy to your white faces.'

'It isn't our white faces that attract them,' responded the American girl. 'It's our green backs.' [Braude 1976 (1958), 33. See also Copeland 1940, 184; Graham 1905, 8]

Boston *Globe*: 'We've got fifty Yankettes married into English nobility right now. Some of them are duchesses. Some are countesses. Eleven are baronesses. Only one is a lady.' [Scott 1931, 74]

The problem, rather, and one which in that era gave rise to many jokes, was that the wealthy Americans who had bought their way into the

British elite then behaved in ways that were incompatible with existing aristocratic British notions about social distance and decorum.

Literal

This story illustrates the characteristics of certain American millionaires who make themselves conspicuous on the other side of the water. This particular millionaire was presented at court when King Edward was on the throne. Queen Alexandria [*sic*] was slightly deaf, and the millionaire was cautioned beforehand about her weakness. After he had been presented, she turned to him graciously and said:

'How long have you been over?'

Looking her in the eye, and holding up five fingers, he exclaimed in a loud voice: 'Five weeks!' [Masson 1913, 8]

Al Woods, the American manager, is an autocrat in his own democratic country, but he's a democrat over here. When he was in London recently he told this story to a well-known dramatist:

"Mrs. Pat Campbell wanted to meet me. To impress me, she brought a duchess with her. I lit a cigar and waited. They arrived. They walked across the room in a most stately manner. But before they could open their mouths, I got up and put 'em at ease. 'Hullo, girls!' I said." [*Further Sunbeams* 1924, 150]

An Honoured Guest

When Lord Elphiston was in America a couple of years ago he was entertained at dinner by a family, the head of which was to accompany his lordship on his hunting trip through the wilds of the Northwest. A child of about five years, named Ethel, during the dinner was big-eyed and big-eared with wonderment—in fact, completely overawed by the presence of the distinguished foreigner. Ethel heard her mother and father now and then say:

'My Lord this, and my Lord that,' or, 'Will you have some of this, my Lord, or some of that?' the dinner being a purely informal one. Finally, when the mother was interested in the conversation of another guest Ethel noticed that milord was gazing interestedly at a dish of relish quite out of his reach. The child thought she saw a chance to please Lord Elphiston, and in a firm, clear voice, exclaimed:

'Mama, God wants some pickles.' [Masson 1913, 44]

In recent years jokes that refer directly to clashes between democratic American and aristocratic English manners have waned. Jokes about comic American crassness, freshness, and innocent egalitarian vulgarity now tend rather to depict the Americans as lacking aesthetic sensitivity or an acquaintance with and appreciation of high culture. Thus the comic clash between elitist and egalitarian values is now expressed in broad terms rather than in terms of the gauche encounters of particular groups of people differing in manners and status.

Climbing out of a waggon in an American city a countryman entered a music store and said he wanted to buy a piece of music for his son. 'If your son is not very advanced, perhaps this would do,' said the assistant, handing over a piece of sheet music. 'How much does it cost?' 'Fifty cents.' 'Well, that's too easy for him. The last piece I bought for him cost seventy-five cents. I reckon he knows enough of music to play a piece worth a dollar and a quarter at least.' [Jerrold 1928, 139]

American going round Jesus College Cambridge: 'Er—excuse me—er—can we er see the actual room?' [Rees 1981, 116; see also p. 85]

It was always considered quite the thing for American tourists to inspect the Louvre in Paris, although the knowledge of most of them as far as art was concerned was confined to the Varga girls in *Esquire Magazine*. They tell about one honeymoon couple that pulled up in front of the main entrance. "Tell you what let's do," suggested the husband. "You walk around the inside and I'll walk around the outside and I'll meet you here in twenty minutes."

It is further related that when this couple returned to their home in Chillicothe, somebody asked them, "When you were in Paris, did you see the Mona Lisa?"

"If it was in the Louvre," said the bride firmly, "we seen it." [Cerf 1945, 135. See also New Punch Library *Mr. Punch and the Arts* 1933, 196; New Punch Library *Mr. Punch and His Travels* 1933, 162]

The New Yorker: You'll find shopping in London, one of the world's shopping centers, a completely satisfying experience. The clerks all speak English. [Tempel 1970, 102]

An American millionaire instructed a Paris firm to send a copy of the famous statue, the Venus de Milo, to his home in New York. On its arrival, he noticed that the arms were missing; so he sent in a claim for damages to the shipping company—and the company paid! [Jerrold 1928, 137–38]

When the Yanks captured Bonn, hundreds of them dropped in to rubber at the home of Beethoven, long a museum, and miraculously undamaged by bombardment. A cocky sergeant, who had been a member of a jazz band before the war, caught sight of the piano at which Beethoven composed his Fifth Symphony, jumped over the red ribbon that guarded it, and played "Rum and Coca-Cola" with one finger. "I guess every pianist who comes into this joint plays something on that pianner," he said to the old guide. "Not quite," said the guide. "When Paderewski was here, he said it would be sacrilege if he touched it!" [Cerf 1945, 3]

Even these cracks about American vulgarity now feel slightly old-fashioned, and English joke-tellers in particular seem to find the Australians a more convincingly crass group about whom to tell such jokes. However, American jokes about the allegedly up-tight, snobbish, hierarchical English have held their popularity [e.g., see Wilde 1978A, 62–75] despite the marked shrinkage in the scale of social distance and deference that has occurred in England during the twentieth century.

American jokes about the English portray the complex English system of stratification as consisting of two groups only, (a) an upper-class of aristocrats, retired Empire-builders, and other traditional figures who speak incomprehensible old-school-tie-in-the-mouth English, and (b) a lower class of doubtful occupation who speak Cockney. The great mass of businessmen, managers, professional people, artisans, industrial workers, financiers, scientists, engineers, teachers, or salesmen who make up the productive majority of the English population rarely appear in American jokes about the English. In this way a comic image of the English social structure is produced which makes it appear extremely hierarchical and totally without economic foundation. As a crude caricature of what was wrong with the British economy such jokes ought perhaps to have been required reading for the English, but as jokes they tell us a good deal more about the Americans. Precisely because equality and achievement are the core values of American society, Americans enjoy jokes about the "class-ridden" English [see Stephenson 1951, 573] which show them as totally deficient in both respects. The American comic view of England portrays it as a static society whose members, regardless of which social class they belong to, fail to show a proper enthusiasm for the American values of work, achievement, and success. It is almost the obverse of the English comic view of the Americans as a nation of workaholics.

Gentry

An Englishman in New York said to a Yankee that America was a very great country, but there were some things that the Americans had not got; they had no gentry.

"What are they?" asked the Yankee.

"Well, people who don't do anything, you know," replied the Englishman.

"Oh," said the Yankee, "we have plenty of them in America, but we don't call them gentry; we call 'em tramps." [George 1903, 107. See also Astor 1963, 8]

The English don't work. The lower classes walk out on the job. The upper classes never had a job to walk out on. [Wicks 1976, 95]

A snobbish old major was asked by a firm if he'd recommend a certain man for the job. The major wrote back:

"Mr. Blank is an excellent young man. He is the son of Major Blank, the grandson of General Blank, the cousin of Sir Henry Blank, the nephew of Lord Blank, and he is otherwise well related."

The firm wrote back: "Thank you very much for your letter of recommendation concerning Mr. Blank. But we must point out that we require him for clerical work—not for breeding purposes." [Copeland and Copeland 19[illegible], 685]

Here the jokes bring out clearly the contrast between the American belief in achievement and the obsession with purely ascriptive status supposed to characterize the English.

Within America itself jokes about this kind of fossilized conservatism, with its disdain for the competitive world of work, money, and material achievement, are also made about Boston Brahmins and Southern gentlemen,[11] groups that have supposedly succumbed to the English and un-American error of rating inherited social status higher than personal material achievement.

A Boston spinster, age sixty-nine, lived with her mother, age ninety-one, on Beacon Hill up behind the Statehouse. They lived genteely but penuriously from a small trust fund that had been left to the mother by her great-grand uncle. Most of their hours were spent sitting veiled behind their shabby genteel windows to watch the flow of traffic, both motor and pedestrian.

Mother: "I can't bear to see these strangers around all the time."

Spinster: "But mother, many of them are tourists, and they spend a great deal of money in the shops about. Mr. Wharton at the bank was telling me just the other day that they are really very important to the economy of Beacon Hill."

Mother: "Can't they just send the money?" [Ginger 1974, Anecdote 61; see also anecdotes 58–65]

When the members of an old Southern aristocratic family heard that their daughter Clarabelle who lived up North had become a lady of the evening they were stunned and shocked. 'Imagine!' cried Uncle Stonewall in despair. 'It's a disgrace. To think of one of our kinfolk working for a living.' [Wilde 1975B, 101]

These jokes are, however, about towns, classes, and regions that are regarded as deviating[12] from the general pattern of the American way of life. By contrast American ethnic jokes about the English refer to a class that has, in the recent past at least, enjoyed a dominant position in English society.

The counterpart and apparent antithesis of American tall tales and of ethnic jokes about boastful Americans is the use of understatement as a distinctive feature of English humor[13] and as a serious[14] characteristic of English speech that is made fun of in the ethnic humor about the English enjoyed by Americans.[15] American jokes poke fun not only at English understatement but at such related qualities as stuffy formality, reserve, politeness [see Raskin 1985, 197], and phlegm, at the sangfroid of the cold-blooded bloody Englishman. These can be opposed to the democratic informality and love of boasting and exaggeration at the core of the humorous image of the Americans. Yet English understatement is only a more subtle form of boasting [Davies 1984, 147–48; see also Tuchman 1967, 24], for "it is the proud perpetual boast of the Englishman that he never brags" [Wyndham Lewis in Muir and Brett 1980, 10]. Both self-praise and self-deprecation are used in the same humorous way when speakers have to confer or accept praise in a formal public context while avoiding a display of conceit or flattery. The exaggerated comic self-deprecation on such an occasion is not to be taken literally and comic images are used that are at one and the same time self-praise and self-deprecation [see Mulkay 1987, 251–57]. In humorous discourse, ambiguity and incongruity rule.

A gangster rushed into a saloon, shooting right and left, yelling, "All you dirty skunks get outta here."

The customers fled in a hail of bullets—all except an Englishman, who stood at the bar calmly finishing his drink. "Well?" snapped the gangster, waving his smoking gun.

"Well," remarked the Englishman, "there certainly were a lot of them, weren't there!" [*Funfare* 1949, 307. Also in *Laughs on the Road* n.d., 3]

Report in British Medical Journal: 'Benzedrine leads to a "dangerous degree of disrespectfulness to superior officers on the telephone".' [Dunbar and Webb 1980, 115]

A New Yorker . . . happened to be in Waterloo Station the day that an engineer fell asleep at the throttle of his cab. The engineer's train hurtled into the terminal at sixty miles an hour and scattered death and debris in all directions. Over sixty persons were killed and hundreds seriously injured. The next morning the New Yorker hurried to read the story in the London Times. He found it on page seven under the headline, 'Mishap in Waterloo'. [Pocheptsov 1974, 282]

'the type of imbecile designated in English by the second and sixth letters of our alphabet' [Lawrence 1973, 78]

English repartee: "You know where you can go to. . . . You know what you can do with it. . . . And you." [Lawrence 1973, 78]

But perhaps the professor who went with Shackleton and Mawson to the Antarctic takes the cake for coolness.

"Are you busy, Mawson?" he called out to that famous member of the party one night.

"I am," said Mawson.

"Very busy, really?" came the voice.

"Yes, very busy. Why?"

"Well, if you are not frightfully busy, Mawson, I'm down a crevasse."

The professor was found hanging down a crevasse by the tips of his fingers, a position he could not have maintained many minutes, and the crevasse was of unknown depth. [Lawson 1923, 247]

A chipper young lieutenant with an eye to the future approached a notoriously grouchy brigadier general at his club in London one day.

"Good morning, General," he saluted ingratiatingly.

"Grumpff," responded the general.

"Lovely day, isn't it?"

"Garumph."

"General, I trust you will pardon me for speaking of such a personal matter, but I read in the papers that you buried your wife yesterday, and I want to extend my heartfelt sympathy."

The general adjusted his monocle and stared at the young man for a moment.

"Oh, yes—yes," he replied. "I buried my wife . . . Had to—dead, y'know." [*Funfare* 1949, 306]

An American was explaining to a British visitor the construction of an electrical sign his concern was about to place on Broadway, New York. "It will contain," he said, "20,000 red lights, 17,000 blue lights, 10,000 white lights, and a central sunburst of orange and purple." The Englishman was impressed. "Most extraordinary," he said. "But don't you think, old chap, that it will be just a bit conspicuous?" [Copeland and Copeland 1939, 683]

The English are a phlegmatic race. I was once week-ending with an Englishman and his wife. Entirely by accident, I happened one day on the Englishman's wife in her bath. Making a hurried retreat I immediately sought out my host, who was reading in his room, and proffered an apology. He brought his head up out of his book and regarded me for a moment. "Skinny old thing, isn't she?" he remarked. [Copeland and Copeland 1939, 687. Also in Elgart 1953, 125; Hall 1934, 53; Phillips 1974B, 15]

This English sportsman had been abroad and returned to his home without notice. While walking through the corridor with his butler, he looked into his bedroom and discovered his wife making love to a strange man.

"Fetch my rifle at once," he instructed his butler.

In a matter of minutes his rifle was brought to him and he raised it to his shoulder taking aim, when he was tapped by the butler who whispered, "If I may say so, sir, remember you are a true sportsman. Get him on the rise." [Wilde 1978A, 74. Also in Elgart 1951, 170; Hall and Passemon 1933, *Playboy* 1965, 45]

Butler: "I have to inform your lordship that there's a burglar downstairs."
His Ludship: "Very well, Parkinson; bring my gun and sports suit—the heather mixture." [Copeland and Copeland 1939, 704]

These jokes of various vintages continue to appear in American anthologies, though both the English social classes and the patterns of behavior that gave rise to such jokes have been in decline for some time. Such jokes and anecdotes may well continue to appeal to Americans because of their comic inversion of American cultural patterns and preferences. The same may be said concerning jokes about the qualities of reserve, formality, and coldness by which each member of the English upper classes is supposed to maintain a correct social distance from the English lower orders or from foreigners. In the jokes these very qualities also establish his or her personal status and privacy but at the cost of social and individual isolation.

"You English are just too reserved," said the American.

"Nonsense," said the Englishman. "Why I rowed for Cambridge some years ago and I knew all the other fellows very well—all except one, that is, and of course, he was away up in the bow." [Wilde 1978A, 63. Also in Copeland and Copeland 1939, 701]

Etiquette

The students at Oxford stand much upon punctilio in the matter of making acquaintance; insomuch that one will not hold the least intercourse with another, unless the proper formula of introduction has been gone through. It is told, as a quiz upon them for this peculiarity, that a young gentleman who had recently entered one of the colleges, happening to be seized with cramp while bathing in the Isis, and being on the point of sinking, probably to rise no more, a youth of older standing, who leaned over a bridge near the scene, thus soliloquized: "Good God! what a pity I was not introduced to that freshman—perhaps I might have saved him." [Masson 1913, 211]

And for comparison an American joke about proper Bostonians:

A man who had learned to share taxis in Washington jumped in with another passenger at Boston's South Station, having overheard the first fare give a destination close to his. He sat back with a cheery wave and turning to the other passenger, said pleasantly, "My name's Jennings."

"Mine," said the Bostonian "is not." [*Funfare* 1949, 5]

Many of the jokes Americans tell about the English upper and upper middle classes depend upon minor differences in the way the two groups use the English language. The naive Englishman becomes a figure of fun when he uses an English English word that has a different and even obscene meaning in American English. He may, for instance, wander into an American office and ask the secretary for the loan of a rubber (eraser/condom). These jokes, taken as a whole, are bilateral, since the American in England has the same comic problems in reverse, as does the Australian who asks in a London office for the Durex (brand of Scotch tape/condom). Since the three countries are far apart and in many ways self-contained, no one version of English can prevail overall with the others relegated to peripheral stupidity, though there are particular domains where this happens.

Nonetheless, upper-crust English English does carry in both America and Australia, and indeed in Wales and Scotland, what might be termed resented prestige. The speech of upper-class Australians and upper-class East Coast Americans is closer (especially for women) to that of their English counterparts than is the speech of those who occupy a lower position in the social class hierarchy or come from a more provincial background. However, both America and Australia are egalitarian countries whose citizens are suspicious of any claim for "establishment" status. The Americans, the Scots, and the Welsh mock "would-be-upper" as well as lower-class patterns of speech [see Apte 1985, 197] with phrases such as "cut glass" or "Mayfair Highlander," and Australians will tell a person who talks plummy like a Pom to spit out the plum [see also O'Grady 1965, 68–69]. Also there are many humorous works whose populist authors and readers revel in the use of relatively low-status forms of English such as Wenglish, Geordie, Ulster, Canajan, Strine, red-neck Southern, etc.[16] "It may not be classy but it's ours and we like it."

However, defiance as well as deference point to the status enjoyed by upper-class English style and style of English [see Dundes 1982, 12–13; Lewis 1974 (1922) 196], which, like other features of this class, was and is disliked but imitated[17] in America and Australia:

If you live in Beverly Hills and can't afford a Rolls Royce, what can you do?

Find a good mechanic who can make your car backfire with an English accent. [Mayer 1982, 136]

Because the claims for the superiority of upper-class English forms of speech are half admitted by others, jokes based on the Englishman's use of language tend to deprive him of it. Sometimes this is done by extending his laconic reserve and reticence and his plummy quality of speech to the point where he becomes tongue-tied, a weak, silent man. In American ethnic jokes the Englishman is shown either as naturally lacking in clarity and fluency or as losing his power of speech because an American has placed him in an embarrassing situation.

An elderly gentleman with a walrus mustache, frock coat and bowler hat, jiggled the telephone receiver. "I say, operator," he said, "I want to talk to Sir Reginald Barrett, in Grosvenor Square, London."

"I'm afraid I can't hear you, sir," said the operator.

"Sir Reginald Barrett, Grosvenor Square, London," said the party.

"I still can't hear you," said the operator. "I guess you're English, aren't you?"

"My dear madam," said the gentleman, "if I were any more English I couldn't talk at all." [Wilde 1978A, 65. See also Cerf 1945, 111]

Lord Plushbottom was guest of honor at Miss Vera Butler's social when she lost her necklace down the back of her dress and asked him to retrieve it.

Blushing furiously he reached, reluctantly groping her for the necklace. "Oh - er - aw - i - ah - I say!" he stammered. "Really you - ah - know"- blushing ever redder - "this makes me feel a perfect - I say - er - aw - a perfect - aw say -" [Ernst 1927, 90].

"Try further down," she advised. He did . . . Still no necklace. "Down still further," she ordered . . . the Englishman blushed even deeper and whispered, "I feel a perfect ass." "Never mind that!" she snapped. "Just get the necklace." [*Playboy's Party Jokes* 1965, 99]

Here we see the Englishman reduced by embarrassment to a whispering, stammering ass [see also Legman 1986, vol.2, p.138] who falls afoul of that word's double meaning in American English. The Englishman is also deprived of his command over his own language in jokes that depict him as unable to understand or to repeat correctly a joke told him by an American:[18]

A British visitor was admiring an American canning factory. The superintendent, showing him about, said in jest: 'In spite of everything you've heard, we're really economical here. This plant proves it. We eat all we can and all we can't we can.' The Englishman looked puzzled. But that evening while dining with an American friend he suddenly saw the point and burst out laughing. 'What is it?' asked his friend. 'I'm laughing at the wit of you Americans,' said the Englishman. 'The superintendent of the canning factory I visited this morning said something rather amusing to me. He said: We eat all we're able to, and all we're not we tin.' [Dundes 1982, 11; Esar 1954, 233]

During the early part of the war, Gerry was stationed in England where he became friendly with many natives. One day Gerry and an Englishman were strolling and came to a river. On the river bank sat a very pretty and luscious girl who was fishing. Gerry called out 'What are you fishing for?' The girl replied, 'Men.' 'How come you are sitting on your bait?' asked Gerry.

The two men walked along down the river. An hour later the Englishman began chuckling: 'That was a very amusing remark you made to that young lady. But how did you know she had worms?' [Elgart 1953, 33]

The Englishman has ruined these jokes within jokes by mixing up English English and American English (a tin can is a tin in England, a can in America), by a prosaic inability to go beyond the concrete meanings of words, and by a naive lack of awareness of sexual double entendres. In many other jokes the Englishman is unable accurately to reproduce a mildly off-color limerick or riddle that he has heard, and unintentionally ends up saying something crass or obscene [see Dundes 1982, 12; Hall and Passemon 1933, 36–37].

These jokes imply that the linguistic superiority that the English often claim in the area of high culture by virtue of their long history and elite-dominated social order does not extend to the common man's pastime of joke-telling. In practice upper-class English people do not experience any more difficulty in telling jokes than Americans do, and any failure on their part to appreciate American comic exaggeration is matched by the American failing to see the point of English comic understatement. Indeed, the coaches of American college debating teams have told me on several occasions that the one skill in which their teams find it difficult to match English university debaters touring America is the use of humor. Yet English comedians and comedy shows cannot be easily transferred to America, whereas there is no problem in the reverse direction. The English are content to accept, unmodified, American humor in large doses, but few English comedians can gain a mass as distinct from a minority cult audience in America without Americanizing their material and performance. Jokes and humor seem to be identified as the property of the mass of the (American) population, and thus the image of the dominant classes among the English as an aloof élite proves as much a disadvantage to performers in this domain as it is an advantage to English people involved in the creation and presentation of those cultural items defined as high culture.

The forms of American jokes about the upper-class English[19] cited here are (with the exception of the "marred anecdote" jokes) also told in most European countries[20] and indeed in Britain itself. Most of the British people are either not English or not upper-class and relish jokes about upper-class "prats" and "twits" who speak with an old-school-tie-in-the-mouth accent.[21] Once again an ethnic joke told outside the society about a dominant or typical class is used within the society as a social class joke or even a political joke.

This is equally true of the other type of American jokes about the English, which feature lower-class individuals who avoid work and speak Cockney with a plentiful loss of 'h's.[22] The contrast between these two kinds of English from the opposite extremes of the class system fits in with the American comic image of England as a hierarchical, dichotomous society of functionless aristocrats and idle proles in marked contrast to their seriously held image of America as a classless society where everyone is or claims to be diligently middle-class [see Stephenson 1951; Treudley 1946] even though they are not quite clear what they are in the middle of. Jokes about class divisions, distinctions, and conflict export these theoretically un-American problems to England. The American jokes portray the lower-class English as being just as work-shy as their "betters." As might be expected, the Australian worker, who has been regarded in all seriousness by Americans as inefficient and generally awkward [see James 1975 vol.2, 177], is the butt of similar Anglo-Australian jokes about idle ockers.

Aussies don't clock in for work. They sign the visitor's book. [Ocker 1986]

In Australia most people stop looking for work the minute they find a job. [Ocker 1986]

" 'Allo, Bill! I 'avn't seen you for weeks—." Bill's pal stopped suddenly. "But wot's wrong, man? You're looking might seedy. Been ill, eh?" he asked.

Bill passed a horny hand across his brow.

"No," Bill sighed, "I ain't been ill. It's work wot's doing for me—work from seven in the morning till six at night, and only one hour off. Think of it, mate!"

"Well, well," replied the other. "And 'ow long 'ave you been there?"

"I ain't been there yet," retorted Bill. "I begin tomorrer," he added gloomily. [Copeland and Copeland 1939, 703]

"Poor Old Jim! 'e's so near-sighted 'e's working 'imself to death."

"Wot's 'is near-sight got to do with it?"

"Well, 'e can't see when the boss ain't looking, so 'e 'as to keep on shovelling all the time!" [Copeland and Copeland 1939, 686]

Tuesday May Have Been Worse

Out in Australia two Cockneys were sentenced to die for an atrocious murder. As the date for execution drew nearer the nerves of both of them became more and more shaken. Dawn of the fatal morning found them in a state of terrific funk.

As they sat in the condemned cell waiting the summons to march to the gallows one of the pair said:

"Me mind's all in a whirl. I carn't seem to remember anything. I carn't even remember what dye of the week it is."

"It's a Monday," stated his companion in misfortune.

"Ow!" said the first one, "wot a rotten wye to start the week!" [Cobb 1923, 144]

"Say, doctor," said the brawny scrubwoman, "yer gettin' a perty good thing out of tendin' that rich Smith boy, ain't yer?"

"Well," said the doctor amused, "I get a pretty good fee, yes. Why?"

"Well, Doc. I 'opes yer won't forget that my Willie threw the brick that 'it 'im." [Copeland and Copeland 1939, 684]

"And when Mrs. Gubbins sez you wasn't no lidy, wot did yer say?"

"I sez, 'Two negatives means an infirmary,' and I knocks 'er down. She is now in the 'orspital." [Copeland and Copeland 1939, 699]

The American soldier stood on a London street corner.

A pretty blond from Soho passed by, and a gust of wind lifted her dress higher than was decent.

"A bit airy," remarked the friendly soldier.

" 'Ell yes!" retorted the Cockney girl. "What did you expect—feathers?" [Wilde 1978A, 69. Also in Hall 1934, 58]

On a quiet evening three Englishmen, newly landed from a Melbourne packet, lined up at the bar.

"Well, gents, what's it goin' to be?" inquired Van Cott.

"We're in a bit of a 'urry," stated one of the visitors in a Cockney accent, "and we'd like to 'ave six 'ighballs."

This was in the day when most lovers of hard liquor favored toddies and the national tipple of Britain was unknown along the Pacific slope.

"Excuse me?" said the puzzled Van Cott. "What was it you said you wanted?"

"Six 'ighballs," repeated the customer.

Van Cott hailed Manuel, his Mexican man of all work.

"Mannie," he said, "these gents here are in a kind of a rush and they want six eyeballs right away. I don't know what they want 'em for but you go out and ketch three Chinamen." [Cobb 1925, 34]

American joke-tellers have taken to using Cockney as the English lower-class accent in their jokes, probably because it is to be heard in the capital city, London, and would therefore be regarded by the Americans as the natural national accent for a lower-class group. In the nineteenth century many English writers of class-based jokes and comedies lived in London and used mock Cockney to represent the speech of the local lower-class butts of their jokes and humor [Pearsall 1975, 134]. American jokers are likely to have obtained some of their jokes from this source and in this way to have acquired a convention that could be applied to the writing of dialect stories about the lower-class English generally. A similar point may be made about jokes and anecdotes with an English setting whose humor depends upon a lack of communication or awkwardness between members of different status groups. Even when American jokes depict English society as a rather more finely graded hierarchy of statuses than the more usual crude dichotomous comic model implies, there are still innumerable opportunities for kinds of status conflict and snobbish put-downs that in theory do not occur in egalitarian America [but see the humor of Lewis 1974 (1922), 60, 157–62]. Whether the jokes were originally English social class jokes or not is irrelevant. Americans prefer to enjoy such jokes about class differences and distinctions as ethnic jokes about the English [see Stephenson 1951, 570–74] rather than to switch the details of jokes originating in England so that they refer to local, American class conflicts or to blunt assertions of the superiority of one American status group over another:

A man approached the inquiry desk of the very swanky Claridge's Hotel in London and asked, "Do you have special terms for commercial travellers?" The frock-coated dignitary behind the desk regarded him coldly and retorted, "We certainly have, you blank-blank blighter! Buzz off!" [Cerf 1959, 170]

Lady: "And what sort of person is Mrs. Robinson, Colonel?"
Colonel: "Oh, the sort of person who calls a table napkin a serviette."
Lady: "But I always call it a serviette."
Colonel (undefeated): "Then you know exactly what kind of person she is." [Copeland and Copeland 1939, 693]

The Bishop of London, speaking at a meeting recently, said that when he was in America he had learned to say to his chauffeur, "Step on the gas, George"; but so far he had not summoned sufficient courage to say to the Archbishop of Canterbury, "O.K., Chief." [Copeland and Copeland 1939, 695]

An old ship's carpenter was giving a lecture on technical details to army officers preparing the invasion of France during World War II. He was continually interrupted when he pronounced words like "helm" and "hash" as the names of trees, by a very la-di-dah voice from one of the officers correcting him. "You mean elm, of course, and ash, don't you?"

Finally, exasperated, the old carpenter said, "Now, 'ere we 'ave the hoak."

"You mean oak, of course!"

"O'coss. It is the finest wood to use for pounding piles into piers. And for the benefit of our young friend 'ere, I don't mean pushin' 'emmeroids hup the harses or hanuses of the Haristocracy!" [Wilde 1978A, 70]

The corresponding Australian jokes and humor about the stuffy, plummy, English upper classes and the deferential, sat-upon lower classes are in essence similar to the American ones [see Wannan 1963, Preface and 75–77, 144–47, and 211], though with a sharper and keener but ambivalent mockery of their speech [Lauder 1969; O'Grady 1965, 68–69]. Australian jokes contrast their own workers who move at "koala speed" [Greenway 1972, 102] with the "Yanks" who are seen as "runnin' round like blue-arsed flies" [O'Grady 1965, 95; see also Greenway 1972, 100]. The comic Australian "dole bludger" and "compo king" (who skive off social security and worker's compensation) are so similar to their English counterparts as to leave little room for distinctively ethnic jokes. There is an Australian humor about muddled or discontented lower-class, English emigrants, who are known as "wingeing Poms," or "Chooms" [see Bowles 1986, 38–40; Howcroft 1977, 52–56], but it has not yet produced a significant and distinctive genre of jokes:

How can you tell if a Qantas plane landing in Sydney is full of Pommie migrants?

Wait till they turn the engine off and see if the plane goes on whining. [Australian 1970s. But see also Wannan 1963, 190–91]

For English joke-tellers the Australians have come to provide a more extreme and more entertaining butt for jokes about vulgar egalitarianism[23] than the Americans. Indeed, such is the force of humor about crude male egalitarian Australia that jokes about coarse Australians are to be found in New Zealand and the United States as well. The Australians have skillfully and sportingly played up to this comic image, which has come to constitute Australia's major cultural export [see Bowles 1986; Hudson and

Pickering 1987; Humphries 1982, 1986; Humphries and Garland 1968, 1972, 1988; Patterson (Humphries) 1986].

The two crucial aspects of Australian culture, relative to the cultures of the other Anglo-Saxon countries, that lie behind the international comic image of Australia are (a) an extreme and highly characteristic egalitarianism and (b) the marked separation and segregation of the sexes in Australian society. Australia is a more crudely masculine society than either England or America and it is this combination of masculinity and egalitarianism that has given rise to the comic image of the coarse, uncultivated Australian.

Australian society is in many respects stratified in much the same ways as England, America, or any other democratic and capitalist industrial society [see Davis and Encel 1965, 18–42], but it has by far the most egalitarian culture of the Anglo-Saxon countries. This is well brought out in H. G. Oxley's classic study *Mateship in Local Organization*:

> Australia's egalitarianism is usually presented as being of a kind other than that which we consider to be its main counterpart in America. American myths stress the fair chances of poor office-boys becoming presidents. The Australian idea, it is said, is that poor office-boys are essentially just as good as presidents anyway. . . . In Australia I did not hear nearly so much about Opportunity . . . but I did hear from people who were 'working men and proud of it'. I even heard unregretted the myth of immobility—that one necessarily stays in the order of one's birth and that attempts to move are somehow improper. [Oxley 1978, 25 and 27; see also Lipset 1964, 251–54]

Australian egalitarianism, grounded as it is in a fierce assertion of equality of status regardless of social and economic position and relatively unhampered by any competing cultural stress on individual achievement, is often more radical in its impact on how individuals behave toward one another than American egalitarianism, which has as its core the idea of equality of opportunity. It has given rise to the distinctive Australian myth that

> the 'typical' Australian is a practical man, rough and ready in his manners and quick to decry any appearance of affectation in others. . . . He is a hard-case and sceptical about the value of religion and intellectual and cultural pursuits generally. He believes that Jack is not only as good as his master but at least in principle a good deal better. . . . He is a fiercely independent person who hates officiousness and authority. [Ward 1966, 1–2]

"Egalitarianism in fact is the persistent motif which runs through Australian culture and the people themselves . . . the feeling that one man is as good as another is the most characteristic quality of social relations" [R. McGregor quoted in Oxley 1978, 23–24]. Oxley comments on this Australian myth that "It is basically the same as the myths of low-stratum groups overseas but it is made more attractive here by the supposed national reference; espousers can claim to be not only fine fellows but the best Australians" [1978, 27].

Australian egalitarianism is not based on any set of abstract universal principles but is rather a set of particular sentiments developed among male Australians that does not extend to those outside this community [see Oxley 1978, 52], such as women or foreigners, and the latter may well be denigrated as inferior beings [see Ward 1966, 131–32, 224–25] and abused as Spags, Dagos, Chows, Slant-eyes, Choongs, Slopeheads, Chooms, Poms, Reffos, etc. [see Wannan 1963, preface]. It is an essentially exclusive egalitarianism. The central tenet is simply that all male Australians should treat one another equally regardless of what social class they belong to. It is a belief most strongly upheld in the loose, unstructured all-male groups of leisure and drinking companions that are an important part of Australian society. It is here that the ideals of "mateship" flourish and that the ethic of "fraternal anarchy" [Conway 1974, 77] still reigns supreme. As these terms imply, it is very much a masculine subculture:

> The groups which bring the strata together in interpersonal interaction are, for the most part, men's groups. And the virtues stressed in egalitarian ideologies (such as the 'Australian legend') are the virtues of masculinity. Egalitarianism seems very closely connected with the expression of male solidarity and superiority—of a tie which cuts across strata. Sex separation thus supports such an ideology. [Oxley 1978, 95].

The masculine egalitarian ideology that still pervades Australian life has its roots in Australia's distinctive history. The transported convicts and later the lower-class immigrants from Britain and Ireland both rejected established authority and hierarchy and upheld against them the values of egalitarian collectivism [see Lipset 1964, 255; Pringle 1960, 22, 124]. In the nineteenth century, when these values were being established and consolidated, there were very few women in Australia: "In 1820 men outnumbered women by ten to three in the towns and by five to one in the country. As late as 1842 the overall ratio was still roughly three men to every one woman. Among these female members of the young society only the minority were genteel or obviously possessed of the softer accomplishments of their sex" [Conway 1974, 29]. Australia was a "bachelor" society, a society created by men and for men, and the women who later emigrated or were born there were forced to fit in as best they could to the crude masculine world the men had established.

Thus Australia differs significantly from both England and America in having less segregation of social classes but more segregation of the sexes, weaker boundaries between social strata but stronger boundaries between male and female. These crucial cultural differences between the three societies are summed up in table 8.2.

TABLE 8.2 **Class and Sex Boundaries**

	Strength of boundaries between social classes	**Degree of sexual segregation**
1st	England	Australia
2nd	United States	England
3rd	Australia	United States

We are now in a position to explain both the similarities and the differences in jokes about American and Australian egalitarianism. Jokes about Australians, like the earlier jokes about Americans, stress their dislike of authority, hierarchy, formality, and high culture but to a far greater extent, for the blunt directness of Australian egalitarianism has not been undermined by individual ambition and success nor softened by female influence and status-seeking [but see Oxley 1978, 95, 206–207], as has happened in America. Even more distinctively different is the extreme coarseness of the comic Australian. Jokes about Australians tend to dwell on their crude approach to women and to sexuality, their scatological and vomitary indiscretions, especially after a bout of manly Australian drinking, their intense dislike of effeminacy and homosexuality, and their incessant but skillful use of coarse language. None of these themes has ever predominated to the same extent in jokes about Americans, even in the days when the English saw them as raw colonials. The pervasive presence, influence, and assertiveness of women in American life have tamed and civilized American male behavior and banished the remnants of the old frontier or immigrant bachelor cultures from the respectable core of American society.

The unstructured, exclusive, masculine egalitarianism that is the characteristic feature of Australian society is neatly caricatured in a number of quips much enjoyed in England though possibly of Australian origin.

Definition of Australian society—a rugby match without a ball. [British 1970s]

An Australian loves his beer, his mates, and his wife—and in that order. [British 1970s. See also O'Grady 1965, 97]

Most married men approve of wife swapping in Western Australia. Most of them want to swap theirs for a catamaran and a snorkle. [Cagney 1979C, 28]

The dislike of formality, hierarchy, and intellectualism that was once an important aspect of jokes about American egalitarianism is today to be found in jokes about Australians. Once again it is the English who explicitly or implicitly represent the values and behavior that the Australians of the jokes repudiate.

'Hi there, Maureen, how are you getting along with the new boyfriend, fresh out of dear old England?'

'Well, he likes visiting the museum and the information bureau and playing chess and listening to operatic music, and he reads a lot of thick books. But then again, who's perfect?' [Cagney 1979C, 30]

An Australian tourist visiting the Vatican with his mates declared: "Hey look at all these crummy murals. Did you ever see anything like it?"

At this point an indignant Italian priest popped his head out of a confessional box and said: "This is-a-Sistine chapel. These are da most-a-beautiful paintings in the world. To enable you to appreciate them properly I will personally give-a-you a conducted tour of the chapel."

"That's very good of you, mate," replied the Australian, "but don't let us rush you. We'll hang on here while you finish having your shit." [Australian 1981]

The shortest books in the world:
The Negro's good food guide to Birmingham Alabama
Britain's economic miracle
Cultural Gems of Australia [Crompton 1973, 59]

A famous Australian jewel thief and homosexual was arrested in Sydney today. [Goldstein-Jackson 1980, 76]

Aussie etiquette:
Got a match, Tom?
No, but I got a lighter.
How'm I gonna pick my teeth with a lighter. [Ocker 1986]

The jokes depict Australians showing disdain for conventions and courtesies within dignified institutions such as the legislature and the courts and in their dealings with foreigners of high status from considerably more deferential and hierarchical societies:

An Australian in London thought he recognized an old friend from Oz walking in front of him in the street. He rushed up to him and clapping him familiarly on the back shouted: "How are you, you old bastard?" To his horror he realized he had made a mistake and the man he had greeted was a distant and dignified traditional English City gent who was now looking at him in total disdain. "Ah, jeez I'm sorry, sport," stammered the Australian, "but you see back in Australia we call everybody bastard." "Yes," said the Englishman coldly, "but then you are, aren't you?" [British/Australian 1980s]

[After the Australian Rupert Murdoch took over the ownership of *The Times* a cartoon by Dickenson showed a man reading '*The Times*' saying to his wife who was dressed in mourning:] "Rather a good obituary of your father, dear—'Old Pommie bastard who never did a day's honest graft in his flaming life.' " [*Punch*, 4th Feb. 1981, 169]

Australian journalist interviewing Mrs. Gandhi; "Excuse me, you've got a dirty mark on your forehead." Licks finger and wipes it off. [Australian, 1981]

A Queensland farmer of Irish extraction, who took a pride in being a local JP, was given the opportunity of exercising his authority—and displaying his dignity—when one of his farm hands, Mick by name, appeared before him on a charge of drunkenness.

Assuming an air of grave importance, he addressed the prisoner: 'What is your name, my good man?'

'Damn it, Jim,' said Mick, getting a little bit annoyed, 'you know me name! I work for you.'

This really upset the JP's equilibrium. 'I'll have ye know, Mick,' he bellowed, 'that callin' me Jim is all right on the farm, but whin I sits on the Binch—I'm Yer Bloody Honner!' [*Best Australian Jokes* 1971, 52]

Sometimes, though, reality does seem to catch up with the jokes:

Report in the *Sydney Morning Herald*, 9 October 1975, of debate in the Australian House of Representatives:
Dr. R. J. Gun (Government backbencher) called out: 'Why don't you shut up you great poofter?'
Mr. J. W. Bourchier (opposition whip) responded: 'Come around here you little wop, and I will fix you up.' [Rees 1983, 14. Cf. Pringle 1960, 20]

One of the most frequent settings for jokes about the Australian dislike of formality, authority, and hierarchy is the army. There are essentially two reasons for this. The first is that armies as institutions tend to be the key upholders in society of two sets of values, one of which the Australians accept, the other of which they reject. The army stresses on the one hand the values of toughness and masculinity, which are highly valued in Australia, and on the other hand the values of discipline, hierarchical order, and formality, which Australians reject. This point was well made in an influential letter written by the official Australian historian for World War

I, C. E. W. Bean, to the Australian minister for the army at the beginning of World War II, explaining why Australians and an English style hierarchy were incompatible:

> "The Australian rank and file cannot serve in a unit officered by English officers either (a) contentedly because the strong social distinctions assumed in English life are offensive to them; or (b) efficiently because traditional English discipline based on suppression of individuality discourages the most useful qualities of the Australian soldier." [Horner 1982, 45]

The Australians have proved to be very tough and effective soldiers, a fact respected by their enemies and allies alike [see Foley 1980; Pringle 1960, 116; Ward 1966, 229], but at times they are disrespectful, insubordinate, and impatient of the rituals and restrictions of military life [see Lipset 1964, 268; Ward 1966, 228–33]. This combination easily gives rise to jokes. The second reason for the popularity of jokes about Australians as soldiers is that this is a role in which historically the English and the Americans are likely to have encountered the Australians en masse. During both world wars and at various times since, Australian troops have fought alongside their British and American allies, and their behavior has given rise to many jokes about the distinctively rumbustious, masculine, egalitarian Australian national character.

My grandfather was one of the first settlers when the new colony became popular. He was a distinguished fighting man, as tough as any migrant who staggered ashore. He had fought with Redvers-Buller. He fought with Baden-Powell, with Roberts, with Kitchener . . . I tell you, he couldn't get on with anybody. [Cagney 1979C, 54]

[During a brief truce in the Gallipoli campaign in World War I negotiations between the Allies and the Turks were carried out in a cave behind a position held by Australian troops.] The proceedings were elaborately formal. Representation was from the very top. The Turkish delegation was led by the brilliant young field commander, General Mustapha Kemal Pasha, who was accompanied by his German adviser, General Liman von Sanders. General Sir Archibald Hunter-Weston spoke for the British. All three generals and their supporting staff officers dressed for the occasion as for a ceremonial parade. There was polished leather and swords and orders and decorations.

Introductions were made with cold correctness and to an accompaniment of salutes, bows and heel-clicking. . . .

Before discussions of substance got under way twentieth century warfare in the shape of an Australian soldier obtruded. He was very tall, very sunburned and was casually dressed in a wideawake hat, a pair of boots and nothing else.

He walked into the cave, looked at the gleaming negotiators without surprise, and addressed them, 'Any of you jokers seen my fucking kettle?' [Noonan 1983, 31–33. See also for similar comic incidents in Egypt, Rameses 1937, 136–43]

General Sir William Birdwood had a good many Australian troops under his command towards the end of the First World War. He was on an inspection tour in rather dangerous territory when suddenly an Australian soldier yelled 'Duck yer bloody 'ead, Birdie'. General Birdwood later recounted the incident to a fellow general who asked, 'What did you do, charge him with insubordination?' 'No' said General Birdwood. 'I ducked my bloody head.' [Australian correspondent 1980]

During the first world war Queen Mary expressed a desire to visit a unit of the Australian forces. The Australians, though magnificent fighting men, were known to have scant regard for social or military etiquette, and one of the Queen's equerries thought it best to approach the colonel of the unit in advance in order to ensure that the proper formalities were observed.

'I assume, Colonel,' he said, 'that your men have been—er—suitably prepared for the occasion.'

'Sure,' replied the colonel, 'only this morning I called 'em all together and said, "The Queen's coming, boys, so you've gotta pull your socks up and be on your best behaviour. Don't swear, don't spit, and for Gawd's sake don't call me Alf." ' [Edwards 1978, 68]

The Australian Army in its early days was a fairly ropey bunch. At divine parades even the company chaplain used to go AWOL. [Cagney 1979C, 54]

A World War I veteran and one from World War II were reminiscing. The 1935–45 Digger extolled his mates, 'Talk about strong! If they wanted to open a bottle of beer they simply took the top off with their teeth.'

'Lot of sissies,' snorted the old Anzac. 'In the First World War, if we wanted to open a bottle of beer, we simply pulled up our shirts and opened it on our navels!' [*Best Australian Jokes* 1971, 52]

Puckapunyal Army training camp story:

The company had been on a night exercise and the company commander was analysing their battle strategy.

The exercise was in defending a uranium mine at the top of a hill. The company had been split into two groups—an attacking force and a defending force.

They'd made every mistake in the book. Talking too much, too much movement, defenders had failed to get into position quickly, attackers had shown little stealth.

'And finally,' roared the captain, 'when you Do contact the enemy, you do Not say, "Good on ya mate!" ' [*Best Australian Jokes* 1971, 23]

While on guard duty one day, the most casual, slothful member of a battalion training at Broadmeadows allowed the Sar' major to pass unchallenged. He merely greeted him with 'Hi mate.'

The S. M. exploded. 'If you don't say "Halt, who goes there?" you flaming idiot, I'll kick your ruddy teeth in!'

The slothful one remembered his tongue-lashing later, when the C.O. himself was on an inspection tour.

As the inspecting party approached his post he jabbed his rifle forward and yelled, 'Stay where yus are, you flaming idiots, or the Sar' major will kick yer ruddy teeth in.' [*Best Australian Jokes* 1971, 37]

Australia now has a standing army of 34,000. Tomorrow they intend to organize a sit-down strike. [Cagney 1979C, 31]

There is a remarkable degree of continuity in these jokes, which consistently employ the same comic image of Australian soldiers as larrikins from the First World War down to the present day. In no other social setting could this distinctive comic combination of toughness and bloody-minded insubordination be so well employed. The attempt to imprison Australian muscular egalitarianism within the framework of an institution that necessarily tends to be formal, bureaucratic, disciplined, and hierarchical produced comic consequences. Jokes about the anarchic misbehavior of Australian servicemen when off-duty, in countries as diverse as Egypt, Britain, or the Philippines, provide an inevitable extension of this theme. Americans seem to have been particularly fond of anecdotes alleging outrageous behavior by Australian soldiers in Britain during the Second World War:

A reporter who was doing a feature story on Madam Tussaud's Wax Works in London sought out the laundress who had washed for the exhibition for twenty-five years.

"Tell me," said the journalist. "Do the queens and the duchesses in the wax works wear anything under those gorgeous velvet robes?"

"As a matter of fact, they don't," the laundress admitted. "But I'd rather you didn't make it public. As it is, nobody knows but me and a few Australian soldiers!" [Cerf 1956A vol. 1, 712–13. Also in Cerf 1944]

An Australian infantry division, recalls George Johnston in *Pacific Partner*, was stationed in England during the blitz in 1940. The boys were invited by the city corporation to visit Manchester, and were given a wonderful time.

At the end of their stay, a huge-muscled sergeant respectfully asked the Mayor to attend a little gathering in the City Hall. The Australians, he explained, would like to make a little presentation as a gesture of thanks to the people of Manchester.

The Mayor, touched by the request, attended the function. The sergeant, speaking on behalf of the assembled Australians, made the usual remarks of appreciation and then handed the Mayor a most magnificent collection of Australian curios and native weapons.

The Mayor, stuttering with emotion, pride and gratitude, mumbled his thanks. The Australians marched out of the hall and filed solemnly to the train that would take them back to camp.

It was not until the next day that the Police Department reported the great burglary of the Manchester Museum, a burglary notable for the fact that the theft was confined to the entire Australian aboriginal art collection. [Cerf 1956A vol. 1, 719–20. Also in Cerf 1944]

The Australians themselves still take great delight in the wild adventures of their servicemen abroad, as can be seen from the front-page leading story in the Brisbane *Courier–Mail* of Friday, May 30, 1980, headed "Crocodile, tars and feathers" and summarized as follows: "This is a true story involving a crocodile, some chickens, two Australian sailors, a Filipino barman, the passengers of three jeepneys, a riot, a posse of Philippines constabulary, diplomats and a compensation bill for $A 45,000. . . . "

Two crucial aspects of the comic image of male Australians are the fluent, skillful, and excessive coarseness of their language[24] and their unfastidious attitudes to sex and bodily functions. These are also expressions of the combination of egalitarian classlessness and sexual segregation that characterizes Australian society. Under these circumstances the two main sources of male politeness and refinement, a wish to assert one's superior status and a concern not to offend the feelings of women, are both absent. Many Australians are, it is true, careful not to use coarse language or behavior in front of women [see O'Grady 1965, 40], but the sexually segregated nature of Australian social life means that the restraining influence of female gentility is usually absent; " . . . men habitually desert their women at social gatherings and crowd around the beer keg, swapping yarns, laughing raucously, literally wallowing in the rituals of mateship" [Conway 1974, 141]. In the most crucial of Australian meeting places, the bars and clubs, where women are absent anyway, "Drink, sports-talk, blue-stories and male solidarity prove effective levellers" [Oxley 1978, 111]. In these circumstances there is almost a competition to prove that one is more masculine and more egalitarian than others by using coarser language and telling bluer stories than anyone else in the group. Such behavior is characteristic of similar male groups in many societies, but in Australia it takes on a national ethnic character because the values, outlook, and behavior of such groups are closer to those of the society at large. This is the background to the jokes in which an Australian blatantly violates the norms of conventional decency and propriety held by outsiders—the English, the Americans, and indeed the forgotten female half of the Australian people. The implied shock to the sensibilities of these groups off-stage is an essential aspect of ethnic jokes about Australians:

Down Under, Hestin bras are said to 'Hold Every Size of Tit In'. [Rees 1983, 58]

An Arab Sheik found it impossible to learn to speak English. He hired tutors from the best universities in Britain and America but failed to make any progress. Eventually in desperation he hired an Australian to teach him English and after his first fifteen minute lesson emerged delighted.

"I have learned half the entire English language," he said proudly.

"How is that possible?" asked his courtiers in amazement.

"Very simple," replied the sheik. "I now know that every second word is 'fuck.' " [Australian 1981]

Australian rigmarole: I was walking along this f**king morning, f**king sun, f**king shining away, little country f**king lane and I meets up with this f**king girl, f**king lovely she was, so we gets into f**king conversation and I takes her over a f**king gate into a f**king field and we has sexual intercourse. [Paros 1984, 7]

During the Second World War a group of Australian soldiers stationed in the Pacific miles from any woman were watching an English (or American, it matters little which it was) film. The hero and the heroine of the film had quarreled and the hero said angrily to the heroine: "I'd like to tear you into a thousand little pieces." At this point an Australian voice from the audience shouted: "Good on yer, mate. Throw us the cunt, will yer." [English 1980s but probably Australian 1950s in origin]

Motto of the Royal Australian Navy:
No sea too rough, no muff too tough. [Australian 1981]

Australian foreplay: 1. Nudging his sheila in the ribs: You awake? 2. Brace yourself, Raelene. 3. Make yer a cuppa after. [Ocker 1986. See also Bowles 1986, 87]

Tasmanian to girl at a party: "Do you want a fuck?"
Girl: "No."
Tasmanian: "Well, do you mind lying down and letting me have one." [Australian 1981]

Tasmanian to girl at a party: "Do you want a fuck?"
Girl: "Not really, but you just talked me into it you smooth-talking Tasmanian." [Australian 1981]

These latter stories exaggerate in a direct and crude way the supposed attitude of the members of the all-male Australian drinking group toward women, particularly in those parts of Australia untouched by the softening cosmopolitan influence of England or America. Even the more restrained jokes about upcountry male Australians show this unromantic and instrumental view of women:

Two ancient battlers of the backblocks were sitting in a brown study on the veranda of the local pub when one broke the silence.

'Ya know, Arthur, if they'd had electric blankets and ready-cooked tucker when I was a boy, I'm darn sure I'd never o' got married.' [Howcroft 1977, 31]

For present comparative purposes, however, the general crudity of the language of the Australian, of the jokes, and his complete disregard for the taboos of polite society regarding the control of body boundaries are significant. The flights of gifted crudity of Barry McKenzie or Sir Les Patterson owe a great deal to the individual genius of Barry Humphries [1982 and 1986; Humphries and Garland 1968, 1972, 1988; see also Bowles 1986, 5; Ingrams 1971, 18], but the basic elements are demotic Australian. The extensive use of phrases like "happy as a pig in shit," "a calendar coat," "up shit creek," "a mouth like an abo's armpit," "sparrowfart," "built like a brick shit-house," "pork sword," "to choke a darkie," and the generalized use of the words "bastard" and "bugger" set Australian English apart from its rivals [see Bowles 1986, 12–13; Humphries 1982 and 1986; Humphries and Garland 1968, 1972, and 1988; O'Grady 1965, 13–14, 20–26, 39–41]. However, Newby's description of an Australian ploughing a field continuously shouting "fuck, fuck, fuck" [1975, 143] and the calculations of an English mathematician that an Australian in full spate could use the word "bloody" 18,200 times in a lifetime [see de Witt 1970, 95] indicate that the reality may be a little more tedious than the humor about it provided by international entertainers.

Australian humor and jokes about Australians are not, however, scatological in the sense that, say, German humor is [see Dundes 1984]. German humor is based on the comic violation of a particular taboo, that concerned with excretion, and the hysterical intensity of German joking on this subject indicates the peculiar strength of the prohibition being tested [see Dundes 1984; Logue 1973, 46; Pieper 1987] in a society known for its rigid behavior and boundaries. Male Australians casually disregard body boundary taboos of all kinds and the shocked audience whose implicit presence is part of the joke lies outside the basic unstructured egalitarian male group and consists of women, foreigners, the English, or any local but exclusive, fastidious, thoroughly un-Australian and elitist male person. The contrast is between the disregard for body boundaries held by those within the egalitarian, classless, unbounded, and unstructured world of male Australia and attempts to control the boundaries of the body as metaphor and reminder of the boundaries of the social hierarchy [cf. Douglas 1970, ix, 64, 72] by members of structured and bounded hierarchical societies concerned with preserving the boundaries between different social classes, status groups, or castes.

In the early nineteenth century the hierarchical English were shocked at the unpompous, egalitarian Americans who spat on the floor or, at best, in a cuspidor.[25] The Reverend Sydney Smith, an English clerical wit, wrote: "We are terribly afraid that some Americans spit on the floor even when the floor is covered by good carpets. Now all claims to civilisation are suspended till this secretion is otherwise disposed of. No English gentleman has spat upon the floor since the Heptarchy" [1854 (1824), 402].

Similarly it is genteel, boundary-conscious peoples who are most upset by those who relieve themselves in public or are uninhibited about farting, nose-picking, or puking. The connection between the English sense of belonging to a hierarchical and bounded social order and their wish stringently to control the boundaries and orifices of the body is well brought out in the following American joke:

A drunk on an English train scandalizes the compartment passengers by picking his nose, scraping the hair off his tongue and putting it under the seat, reaching into his fly and elaborately adjusting his genitals, etc. An Englishman has been watching him coldly from the seat facing and finally says, 'Do you suppose, old chap, that you could conclude the entertainment with a rousing good fart?' [Legman 1982 vol. I, 170]

The obverse in jokes of the Englishman's cold repudiation of the drunk's loss of self-control over the boundaries of the body is the comic flaunting of any breach of these taboos by Australians as an affirmation of their unbounded and unstructured male equality.

Why do Australian men piss in the bushes at parties? Because there's always someone chundering in the toilet. [Ocker 1986. See also Morley 1982, 75–78]

Sydney Australia: Bell Telephone of Australia has introduced its first combination public phone and toilet in an effort to boost revenues. Since Australians consume huge quantities of beer it was reasoned they would use the booths regularly. And while urinating they would be tempted to make a phone call said a Bell spokesman. [*National Lampoon,* August 1979, 96]

The nature of such humor is, however, best brought out in the comic cameos used to illustrate contrasts of national character between Australian and English:

[At an Australian wedding the bride's father, Mr. Foster, objects to his new in-laws' snobbish and most un-Australian sneering comments on his family. So] Mr. Foster decides to mix it and there is a shemozzle. He finally gets up on the bridal table, drops his daks and chucks a browneye. [Bowles 1986, 110]

Barry McKenzie (after being sick over an elderly English lady on a cross-channel ferry): "Isn't it funny when you come to think of it. A bastard tucks away a few jars of ice-cold. It's only in his Ned Kelly for a few jiffs and then when he has a decent hurl it comes out all thick and different somehow. Isn't nature bloody marvellous."

Elderly English lady (whom he has 'entombed' in 'tepid chuck'): "I think I'm going to be sick."

Barry McKenzie: "Go on lady, play the whale, but I'll bet youse a greenie it won't look nothin like what youse had for lunch!!!" [Humphries and Garland 1972]

The formless, half-digested food and drink that the comic male Australian regurgitates and then examines occupies an ambiguous position in relation to the person who previously consumed it. It is food that was on its way to becoming part of the eater's own body tissues, part of his own physical self, but it didn't quite make it. It belongs neither to the consumer's self nor to the world external to him, and, by traveling in the wrong direction, it upsets our usual sense of categories ordered in time and space and makes ambiguous the boundary between one's inner self and the outside world. As such, it is a natural metaphor for the formless social world of male Australian drinkers, who are comically envisaged as putting away "piss" or "suds," heaving it up again, and then being doggedly and doggishly fascinated rather than repelled by the ambiguous contents of their own vomit.

There is, however, one strict, strong boundary that Australians do preserve—that between male and female. In consequence [see Davies 1982A] Australians have very strong taboos against any kind of effeminacy or homosexuality [see Conway 1974, 132–33, 145–48; Vaughan 1983] that might threaten that boundary or introduce an insidious sexual element into the diffuse ties that hold together groups of males or comrades [Davies 1975, 110–39]. The sexual segregation and past numerical imbalance of the sexes in Australian society make male homosexuality more likely and in practice have also resulted in an intensification of the degree to which it is forbidden and punished [see Vaughan 1983; Ward 1966, 94–97]. Hence the immense popularity in Australia of jokes about "poofters" and the proliferation of mocking comic terms for them such as shirt-lifter, bum-jumper, pillow-biter, freckle-puncher, kapok-cruncher, or vegemite-driller. The Australian view is summed up in an English account of an Australian Faculty of Philosophy whose rules were:

Rule one.	No poofters.
Rule two.	No member of the faculty is to maltreat the Abos in any way whatsoever if there's anybody watching.
Rule three.	No poofters.
Rule four.	I don't want to catch anyone not drinking in their room after lights out.
Rule five.	No poofters.
Rule six.	There is no rule six
Rule seven.	No poofters. [Monty Python 1983]

One interesting feature of the Australian jokes discussed in this chapter is the major role played by the Australians themselves in inventing and disseminating such jokes even in England and America. Today the comic image of Australia is built into the advertising of Australian beer in England and of short-term jobs for Australians on a working holiday in London. The model used in this study is based on the broad assumption that ethnic jokes told by members of one group about another are a comic way of exporting some undesired quality. The members of the group that is the butt of such jokes deal with this situation in a number of ways. One is to pass the joke on to a subgroup of their own society—a social class (the English upper class), a region (Kerry), a town (Aberdeen), a state (Texas or Prussia), or in the case of the Australians the people of the off-shore island (and state of the Commonwealth) Tasmania. Crudity jokes in particular get pinned on the Tasmanians, the "daft inbred bastards" from Tassie [Bowles 1986, 42], the shape of whose map reveals it to be a "large triangular land mass deep in the Southern hemisphere" [Humphries 1982, 182].

However, the qualities embedded in the jokes can also be reinterpreted by the audience and indeed by the joke-teller so that canniness is thrift and shrewdness rather than miserliness and swindling, deviousness becomes subtlety, a common little man becomes the common man, snobbishness becomes a respect for traditional standards, and vulgarity becomes matehood when the jokes are told by, for, or within the group that is the butt of the ethnic joke. This is particularly likely to happen where, as here, there is a degree of disagreement and uncertainty about the balancing of basic but opposed values such as equality versus legitimate status differences, achievement versus ascription, collective loyalty versus individual ambition, high culture versus common culture not only between (pairs of) the three societies America, Australia, and England but also within each of them [see Lipset 1964, 211–12]. In certain respects it may be more helpful to view these values as ideal (as distinct from material) goods competing in a marketplace of ideas and allegiances, rather than as sources of absolute disagreement. At the margin we "purchase" an increment of one value at the expense of a decrement in another. If we use this model (which captures one aspect of the truth, just as seeing values as an integrated cultural system captures another), then the Americans, the Australians, and the English may be regarded as aggregates of individuals whose median and weighted average "choice" of balanced "quantities" of competing values differs. However, within each society there will be individuals or even social classes whose preferences lie closer to the pattern typical of one of the other societies. There will be egalitarian Englishmen, order- and tradition-loving Americans, or individualistic, competitive Australians, who are open or closet admirers of an alternative pattern of Anglo-Saxon values and who may even end up emigrating in search of them. They enjoy jokes about their membership group because for some purposes their reference group lies elsewhere. Even a person who is satisfied with his or her own "national pattern" is often able to see that it has been "purchased" at the expense of valid alternatives and may also see the point of jokes made from one of these alternative points of view. If the setting, the tone, and the performance are right, people have no difficulty in laughing at other peoples' jokes even at their own expense.

Even if we change our perspective once more and emphasize the extent to which the members of any one of the three Anglo-Saxon societies define themselves against one of the other three so as to stress differences in basic values and to tie a sense of national identity to such differences, the mechanism of reinterpretation still permits people to laugh at themselves. The compressed and ambiguous nature of humor means that a joke is compatible with quite different serious views of the group that is the butt of the jokes. English jokes mocking "vulgar Australians" can be used by Australians as a means of affirming and legitimating differences of identity and of values. To postulate that a group of Australians telling such jokes about themselves and visibly enjoying the experience are in the grip of self-hatred is absurd and rapidly becomes an entirely circular argument. Identity can be established by celebrating the critical views that the members of a group believe that others hold about them, and jokes, which by their very nature are indirect and ambiguous, are the ideal vehicle for doing so.

The jokes exchanged between the Americans, the Australians, and the English are also one way of exploring differences in shared values and a shared language. The problems and uncertainties of balancing equality against status distinctions, achievement against ascription, individual ambition against collective loyalty which are to be found in most democratic industrial societies find expression in the ethnic jokes told by the citizens of the Anglo-Saxon countries about one another and at times even about their own nation. It should also be noted that the jokes analyzed in the chapter have as their serious counterpart a set of social and historical puzzles that have exercised the minds of many sociologists and social historians. The long, steady, relative economic decline of the British economy, the tumble from the "workshop of the world" and "Manchestertum" to the "British disease," and the relationship of this decline to the peculiar class cultures of England constitute one such intellectual puzzle.[26] Debates regarding the origins and development of the distinctive patterns of values and supposed national characters of America and Australia provide two more. It is within these frameworks that we should seek an understanding of the observation made by the Hungarian humorist George Mikes [1977, 14] that the English see the Scots, the Welsh, the Irish, and, more or less, the Australians and the Americans as neither English nor foreigners, "but they are as ludicrous as foreigners." With a minimal degree of rearrangement Mikes's comment applies equally to the Americans and the Australians.

CHAPTER NINE
Food for Thought: Eating Ethnicity and Humor

Eating is one of man's basic, necessary, and most pleasurable activities. We must eat to live, and indeed some people live to eat. Eating is a social as well as an individual and utilitarian activity. What a person eats, and how and in whose company he or she eats, depend on the customs, traditions, wealth, and power of the ethnic group to which he or she belongs. One common way in which the members of a group will describe themselves as set apart from their neighbors is in terms of the food that they eat and their neighbors don't, and vice versa.[1]

Naturally such an obvious, visible, and fundamental difference between the behavior of two ethnic groups as a difference in eating habits can give rise to a large number of ethnic jokes. In such cases the members of any one ethnic group tell jokes at the expense of a neighboring group which is believed, rightly or wrongly, to eat different, tabooed, or inferior food. Indeed, the comic nicknames of ethnic groups are often derived from a forbidden, despised, or even merely characteristic food which that group is believed habitually to consume.

Thus the French are known jokingly as "Froggies" or "Froschesser" (Frog-eaters), the Germans as "Krauts" (Cabbages), "Kolbassnik" (Sausage-guzzlers), and "Patatucchi" (Spud-swallowers), the British as "Limeys," the Dutch as "Tulip-munchers." A Scotsman may in jest be called "Haggis," an Irishman "Spud Murphy," a Bogotano "Papa Choriada" (a local potato dish), a Liverpudlian a " 'Scouse" (from lobscouse, a sailor's stew).[2] Similarly traditional ethnic buffoons had names like Jack Pudding, Jean Potage, Hans Wurst [Esar 1978, 109]. The habit of attaching a comic gastronomic label to neighbors and immigrants is common to most countries, and similar patterns of naming can often be discerned. Thus we find the Italians are called "spags" by the Australians, "makaronās" by the Greeks, and "loksh" (noodles, the nearest equivalent to macaroni in Jewish cuisine) by the Jews [Cagney 1979C, 18; Roback 1944].

Most European and American ethnic jokes about food refer to foreigners as eating peculiar or inferior rather than forbidden food, for the dominant, Christian religious tradition lacks a coherent set of food taboos and indeed specifically repudiates those of its parent religion, Judaism [Acts 10:9–16; 11:1–11. 1 Corinthians 10:25–26]. Only cannibalism is forbidden, and this activity,[3] ascribed usually either to Africans or Pacific Islanders, is a source of humor. The missionary or explorer in the cannibals' cooking pot is a favorite theme for cartoonists, and there are also many ethnic jokes about cannibalism:[4]

Foreign news. Uganda. At the state luncheon to welcome the German delegation today General Amin ate a hamburger, two frankfurters, and a young man from Heidelberg. [British Television 1970s and Vincent 1977A, 28].

What is the African counterpart of a vegetarian?
A humanitarian. [American 1980s].

President Nyerere of Tanzania was flying to the United Nations on a Mumbo-Jumbo jet. He scanned the lunch menu and said, "I don't like any of this. Bring me the passenger list." [British 1970s. See also Abrahams 1961, 246].

[When Bishop Selwyn was about to leave Britain to become the first Anglican Bishop of New Zealand, the Rev. Sydney Smith declared]: "it will make quite a revolution in the dinners of New Zealand—*tête d' Evêque* will be the most recherché dish and your man will add that there is *cold clergyman* on the side-table." It was on the same occasion that Smith also said to Selwyn, "And as for myself, my lord, all I can say is, that when your new parishioners *do* eat you, I sincerely hope you may disagree with them." [Jerrold 1913, 260. See also Bell 1980, 198]

African comment on modern warfare: 'Look, Sambo, how wasteful whitemen are. They have killed hundreds of times more than they can possibly eat.' [Gorer 1945, 209]

There's a great export trade from Golder's Green [a large crematorium in London]. They send ashes out to the Congo as instant people. You just add water. [Newall 1985, 143]

A related but milder genre of ethnic jokes about the breaking of a food taboo refers to the eating of animals such as dogs, cats, or horses that are kept as domestic pets or as working partners [see Goody 1982, 84, 106]. Since domestic pets are to some extent treated like human beings (they have names, they are often regarded as individuals rather than as replaceable generic animals, they are the recipients of human affection, they live in the same house as their owners, and they are sometimes even given burial plots and tombstones) by the pet-loving Europeans and Americans, to eat a member of a species kept as a pet is in a minor way to infringe the taboos against cannibalism.

Ethnic jokes of this kind are often directed at peoples (usually from East Asia—Chinese, Koreans, Vietnamese—but also Australian aborigines, who are said to have a taste for "putjikata" [Greenway 1972, 276]) believed to be pet-eaters. However, a frequent additional butt of these comic tales is the tourist from a pet-obsessed culture on a visit to these lands who, through error or deception, ends up eating a dog or a cat or even his or her own animal traveling companion. Another favorite setting is a wartime siege when starving pet-lovers are forced to eat the animal members of their household to survive. Some of the jokes thus have a sick quality directed back at the mores of the teller's own group, while others simply make fun of those whose eating habits are allegedly governed by an alien and "defective" pattern of squeamishness and concern for quasi-human animals.[5]

Mabel and Ronald Smith of Watford went on a package tour holiday to Hong Kong, taking their pet dog with them. On their free day they decided to explore the back streets of Kowloon and stopped for lunch at a Chinese restaurant. To their dismay no one in the restaurant spoke English and they had to explain in sign language that they wanted a meal for themselves and another for the dog. A smiling Chinese waiter nodded in agreement and took Rover out the back to feed him. Mr. and Mrs. Smith enjoyed a delicious Chinese meal full of subtle, unfamiliar flavors, paid their bill, and prepared to leave. To indicate that they wanted Rover to rejoin them, Mrs. Smith playfully imitated Rover's cheerful bark. The smiling Chinese waiter pointed at their plates. [British 1960s. See also Morley 1982, 104–105]

Yakob Smirnoff: "After I left Russia for the United States I went shopping in a Los Angeles supermarket. There were lots of tins of dogfood. There were none in Russia. There dogs are food. In America there is such a variety of dogs—poodles, chihuahuas, pekinese—but they all taste the same." [British television, 22 August 1984].

What do you call a Vietnamese with a dog?
A vegetarian!
What do you call a Vietnamese with two dogs?
A rancher. [American 1980s]

During the siege of Paris in the Franco-German war when everybody was starving, one aristocratic family had their pet dog served for dinner. The master of the house, when the meal was ended, surveyed the platter through tear-dimmed eyes and spoke sadly: 'How Fido would have enjoyed these bones'. [*Jokes for All Occasions* 1922, 50. See also 194][6]

The more elaborate Western jokes involving food taboos are told by members of ethnic minorities such as the Jews for whom dietary rules are an important part of their religious life and a crucial means of preserving their separate identity. Unlike most of the jokes being considered here, Jewish jokes about breaches of dietary rules are invented and told almost entirely within the group, for Gentiles are unlikely to possess either the knowledge of or involvement with the subject needed to find the jokes funny. Certain basic notions, though, such as the Jewish separation of meat and milk and abhorrence of the meat of the pig, are widely and at times erratically [e.g., see Ernst 1927, 96] recognized and are the basis of jokes told by outsiders about Jews, as well as circulating within the Jewish community.

Jewish jokes about food refer to their elaborate, coherent and detailed system of rules (*kashruth*) governing what may and may not be eaten. These rules divide food into kosher, i.e., ritually clean and fit to eat, and *trayf*, which is unclean and forbidden. It is forbidden to eat or drink the (life) blood of an animal and all meat must come from animals that have been slaughtered in the correct ritual manner, inspected, and have had the blood fully drained from the carcass. Certain nerves and parts of the fat must also be removed. Meat and milk products must not be mixed or eaten at the same meal or even in proximity and, indeed, should be eaten using separate sets of utensils, dishes, and cutlery. The affluent and orthodox may even have separate meat and milk refrigerators and dishwashers. Only animals, birds, and fish that belong fully to their respective spheres of land, air, and water, and that move and feed correctly, may be eaten. Carnivorous animals, birds, and fish are *trayf*. Fish must have fins and scales to swim and birds must have wings and fly if they are to be kosher. Shellfish and ostriches alike are *trayf*. Only four-legged animals that both chew the cud and walk correctly on cloven hoofs are kosher, i.e., ruminants that resemble the basic pastoralist's animals, cattle, sheep, and goats.[7]

The purpose of these rules is to preserve the separate identity of the Jews as a holy people, the chosen people set apart from the heathen.[8] The rules achieve this, partly, simply by making it difficult for a person observing them to eat in the company of the Gentiles or to marry a non-Jewish spouse. Also dietary rules that stress the keeping apart of separate and symbolic categories of food such as meat and milk, or the living—symbolized by the blood which must not be eaten and must be drained from the meat [see Leviticus 17:11–14]—and the dead act as a perpetual metaphor of the need for the Jews to keep themselves apart from the Gentile world. Only those animals which conform perfectly to the specifications of the category to which they belong may be eaten; ambiguous animals such as the pig, which have one of the attributes of the eatable (a cloven hoof) but not the other (the pig does not chew the cud), are strictly forbidden [see Douglas 1966, 51–57, but also Fieldhouse 1986, 132–37]. This again is a daily reminder of the need to preserve a strict boundary between Jews and Gentiles in order to maintain a clear and unambiguous Jewish identity. By adhering to rigid rules of this kind the Jews have managed to survive exile in Babylon, the alien rule of the Greeks and the Romans, and centuries of dispersion in lands far from Israel [see Davies 1982A, 1036–37]. However, the temptation to break the rules must always have been strong, for the Jews have often had to live in exile as minority communities surrounded by peoples routinely enjoying foods that Jews were not allowed to eat. In the modern, liberal, secular societies of the West, which have afforded an increasing degree of social equality to their Jewish citizens, there has been a drastic decline in the strict observance of the dietary laws [see Rosten 1970, 195; also Fieldhouse 1986, 122–23; Williams 1987, 53–54]. Somewhere between the strict obedience to dietary rules of the past and the relative laxity of the present day there was a period of tension when individuals still believed in the rules but were beginning to break them. Out of this tension has sprung an endless stream of Jewish jokes:

Late one rainy afternoon, when he saw no other customers inside, Mr. Finkelstein walked into an elegant but not kosher delicatessen. He bought some tomatoes and, with elaborate insouciance, asked (for the first time in his life) "By the way, eh, how much costs that—bacon?" Came a terrific flash of lightning and clap of thunder. Finkelstein looked up to the heavens, protesting, "I was only asking!" [Rosten 1970, 197. See also Ford, Hershfield, and Laurie 1947, 94; Spalding 1969, 245]

Why do Jewish women wear two-piece bathing suits?
To separate the milk from the meat. [Wilde 1978A, 165]

The ladies of the Bronx chapter of Hadassah were about to hold their annual fish dinner. But this year all the banquet halls had been reserved and they had no place in which to hold the Zionist fund-raising affair.

The parish priest of St. Thomas Aquinas on 183rd and Clinton Avenue heard of their plight and graciously offered the use of his Sunday school auditorium and even the services of the church chef. The ladies were very grateful and they sent the rabbi to the chef so that he might instruct the cook in the art of preparing kosher food.

When the main course was served, however, the women were horrified to see that the scales had not been removed from the baked fish. Immediately they sent for the priest, who in turn demanded an explanation from the chef.

"But, Father I prepared it exactly as the rabbi instructed," he exclaimed, "he told me that Jews are absolutely forbidden to eat any fish that doesn't have scales." [Spalding 1969, 245–46]

A beggar who was not averse to petty thievery when he thought he could steal without detection knocked on a door and pleaded for something to eat. The compassionate housewife set the table for him and served a hearty meal.

The scoundrel, however, instead of feeling gratitude, pocketed a silver spoon and left.

The housewife missed the spoon almost at once. She flew through the kitchen door and ran down the street shouting "Mister, wait a minute, I want to talk to you."

A police officer was on the corner just ahead of the beggar so he thought it prudent to halt.

"What is it?" he asked fearfully, one eye on the curious policeman. "That spoon you took," the woman gasped. "Remember it's milchik." [Spalding 1969, 28]

[*Milchik* are dairy foods which may not be eaten with or after meat foods, or *fleishik*. The housewife is afraid that the beggar in his ignorance may use a spoon set aside for eating dairy produce to eat a meat dish, thus breaking down the separation of *milchik* from *fleishik* by confusing their corresponding separate sets of cutlery and utensils.]

If you find a fly in your soup, the ruling according to the Peruvian Rabbinate is that the soup is Flychik. [Dines 1986, 12]

Rabbi Grossman and Father O'Malley were seated beside each other at a banquet.

"Have some ham," offered the priest.

"I'm afraid not," answered the rabbi.

"C'mon try some," the priest encouraged. "It's real good."

"Thanks, but I don't eat that kind of meat because of my religion."

"It's really delicious!" said Father O'Malley five minutes later. "You oughta try this ham, you'd like it."

"No thank you!" replied Rabbi Grossman. After dinner the two men shook hands.

"Tell me," said the Jewish clergyman, "do you enjoy sex with your wife?"

"Rabbi, you should know, I'm not allowed to be married," said the priest. "I can't have sex."

"You ought to try it," said the rabbi. "It's better than ham!" [Wilde 1974, 114]

The comparison of ham and sex is an apt one. Ham is forbidden to Jews (though no more to rabbis, who are not priests, than to any other Jew, except in the sense that they are expected to set an example), as a means of maintaining a social boundary between the Jews, a holy people, and the Gentiles. One of the reasons that celibacy is imposed on Roman Catholic priests is to set them apart from the laity and to create a clear boundary between priests and others [see Coser 1974 and Davies 1982A, 1044–49].

Many of these jokes have a slightly old-fashioned tone about them and indeed the American anthologist Henry D. Spalding has suggested that Jewish jokes concerning the religious injunctions about food are gradually disappearing. In his collection of American Jewish humor, Spalding [1976, 196] speaks of there now being a "dearth of such stories—at least of those comparable in excellence with the older jokes." What this probably indicates is that many Jews in America and in Britain have now neglected the strict observation of their dietary laws to such an extent and for so long [see Rosten 1970, 195] that they no longer feel anxious or guilty about doing so. Jewish ethnic jokes about food taboos could only flourish so long as people felt ambivalent about them, so long as there were strongly felt rules which were both commonly observed and frequently broken. Both before this period (in some past age when the rules were unchallenged) and after it (today) the Jewish food taboos were and are much less likely to be a source of ethnic joking.

There is one other historic source of Western ethnic jokes about food taboos that should be mentioned—the Roman Catholic religious ban on the eating of meat on Fridays. This now largely obsolete rule [see Fieldhouse 1986, 112] was not devised as a means of establishing a separate religious or ethnic identity, but for many Roman Catholics living in Protestant countries and particularly for the Irish living in Britain or America that is what it became [see Greeley 1972, 230]. Eating fish on Fridays was a symbol of a separate Roman Catholic and Irish identity in two predominantly Protestant countries [see Douglas 1970, 37]. Significantly it was the Irish adherence to this rule that became the subject of jokes, and these ethnic jokes about the Irish survive today, despite changes in the official rules of the Roman Catholic church regarding the eating of meat on Fridays.

Father Moynihan had been sent as a Catholic missionary to a tribe of cannibals in Africa. In a short time he had achieved great success. He convinced the cannibals that on Friday they should only eat fishermen. [Wilde 1974, 109. See also 99][9]

Madigan and O'Skelly were being sentenced for murder. "Do you have anything to say?" asked the judge.

"I'm sorry they caught us!" said Madigan.

"Then you confess now that you killed the man."

"We might've done it," said O'Skelly, "if it don't do no harm to say so now."

"How did you do it?" the judge inquired.

"I struck him with a stone," answered Madigan.

"And O'Skelly hit him with a shillelagh and then we buried him."

"What did you do before you buried him?"

"We searched him!" said O'Skelly.

"And what did you find?"

"Two dollars and a roast beef sandwich!" replied Madigan.

"You kept the money I'm sure, but what did you do with the sandwich?"

"We was hungry," said O'Skelly, "we ate the bread and threw away the meat."

"Why did you throw away the roast beef?"

"Your honor," said Madigan, "it was on a Friday, it'd been a sin to eat the meat!" [Wilde 1974, 102–103][10]

Most European and American ethnic jokes about food are concerned not with the distinction between permitted and forbidden food but with that between prestigious and inferior food. The joke-tellers characteristically depict the butt of their jokes as being unable or unwilling to consume prestigious foods and as subsisting on inferior foods either from choice or from necessity. By implication those who eat comic inferior food are themselves comically inferior. Their meager diet reveals either their lack of economic and other resources or a deficient ability to choose between "good" and "inferior" food. Perhaps the jokes imply both these alternatives, so that the groups mocked by the jokes appear to consist of ludicrous individuals sufficiently coarse-fibered to enjoy the crude diet which their poverty forces upon them.

Although the nature of the inferior food made fun of in jokes varies enormously, within cultures of European and Christian origin there is a good deal of agreement as to the nature of the superior ideal from which the inferior foods depart. A superior meal has at its core a large chunk of good quality meat, and in the English-speaking world in particular it is beef that has been most exalted.[11] This rather unsubtle view has been modified somewhat in nations with a tradition of haute cuisine, but even here it is the variety and exquisiteness of the meat dishes that has always marked the banquets of the powerful [see Barkas 1975, 68]. Only among the self-consciously ascetic and spiritual in monasteries or among urban intellectuals has the connection between meat and status been challenged, and only in India have the priestly castes of Brahmans stood at the top of a status hierarchy and made a vegetarian diet one to be emulated.[12]

To provide a full explanation for the popularity of meat it is necessary to assume that meat is desired because it is prestigious, as well as being prestigious because it is intrinsically desirable. The independent sources of prestige of a meat-filled diet are two-fold. First, meat is expensive, particularly in relation to other foodstuffs. In general only wealthy individuals, classes, or nations can afford to eat large quantities of meat.[13] Under these circumstances meat often becomes an item of "conspicuous consumption" [see Veblen 1899, 73–74]. Ruling elites and even ethnic groups and nations display their wealth and power by eating large and indeed excessive and wasteful quantities of meat [see Barkas 1975, 169; Drummond and Wilbraham 1958, 252]. Until very recently it could still be said with confidence that, in the modern United States, "a sirloin steak each night is still a dietary sign of prosperity" [Barkas 1975, 178].[14]

In the West generally, to be able to eat meat or, better still, steak every day has long been seen as a mark of prosperity and a sign of high status [Walker and Cannon 1985, 72] and when the incomes of individuals fall and they have to give up meat, this has a strong negative effect on their sense of self-esteem [Fieldhouse 1986, 139]. Similarly, in Eastern Europe it is the shortage of meat rather than other foods that is the most popular subject of political jokes about the economic failings of the socialist regimes.

> Why are the meat shops in Poland all built five miles apart?
> So that the queues don't get tangled up. [Polish 1970s]

In the last quarter of the twentieth century many people are, however, increasingly doubtful about the value of an excessively meaty diet as evidence accumulates that a diet high in animal fats and in red meat rather than fish or fowl may be an unhealthy one [see Walker and Cannon 1985, 70–71]. A note of uncertainty has even crept into the once confident advertising of the meat industry. So far this has had no effect on humor, but it will be interesting to see how jokes will change in the long run if there is a major and sustained collapse of meat consumption among the wealthy and powerful.

The link between meat-eating and the display of wealth was well understood by the vegetarian propagandist George Bernard Shaw. In a characteristically Shavian letter to Symon Gould, the founder of the American vegetarian party, he wrote:

> Today people are brought up to believe they cannot live without eating meat and associate the lack of it with poverty. Henry Salt, a champion vegetarian, said that what was needed in London were vegetarian restaurants so expensive that only the very rich could afford to dine in them habitually and people of moderate means only once a year as a very special treat.
>
> What you have to rub in is that it is never cheap to live otherwise than

as everybody else does: and that the so-called simple life is beyond the means of the poor. [Quoted in Barkas 1975, 96–97]

There is a second link between the eating of meat and the assertion of power and status—the belief that eating meat makes men strong, virile, aggressive, and warlike. In societies ruled by warriors, the dominant group will tend to see meat-eating as a source and a symbol of its power and its martial virtues. Nomadic or pastoral conquerors of settled agricultural peoples may well ascribe their superiority to their meat-filled diet, as may a feudal aristocracy lording it over the meek and meatless serfs and peasants [see Drummond and Wilbraham 1958, 49 and 79]. The view that there is a positive link between meat-eating, belligerence, and fitness for war has persisted into the era of the nation-state and has long been found in both laudatory and critical national propaganda.

In the modern industrial capitalist world, which is concerned primarily with economic matters, a belief in the virtue and utility of crude size, strength, and violence might appear obsolete, but this is not the case. The popularity of sport of all kinds and of hunting among the wealthy, the American insistence on a citizen's right to bear arms, the high prestige enjoyed by officers in the armed forces in Europe, the high status everywhere of distinctively aggressive male roles relative to female ones, the obsession with violence that exudes from films and television programs all indicate that the aggressive virtues are alive and well in the modern West. Nor are they just a chance survival from a feudal, frontier, or belligerently nationalistic past as Veblen [1899, 246–48] suggests. Force is not the central social reality of modern capitalist societies, as it was and is of a feudal, fascist, or socialist social order, but it has certainly not been banished to the periphery, and in wartime or crisis capitalist societies can rapidly divert their resources and energies to the need for armed struggle. In Western societies, too, meat-eating continues to be seen as the right diet for nourishing fighting ability and bellicosity, and meat-eaters are popularly regarded as making the best potential warriors.[15]

We are now in a position to understand the implicit (and indeed, sometimes explicit) messages that lurk in English jokes about the Welsh eating cheese, the Scots eating porridge, or the Irish eating potatoes, American jokes about Poles eating potatoes, blacks eating watermelon, or Mexicans eating beans, Canadian jokes about Newfies eating cod, Australian jokes about Italians eating spaghetti, French and Dutch jokes about Belgians eating *frites* (U.S. = french fries; U. K. =chips; Dutch = *frieten*), Jewish jokes about Litwaks eating herrings, or the comic ethnic nicknames based on food listed earlier. These jokes are not primarily about gluttony but reflect a situation in which the joke-tellers can mockingly say: "We are meat-eaters. You are not. We are wealthier and stronger than you."

Among the earliest examples of these kinds of jokes are the English jokes about the Welsh love of cheese, which were very popular in the Tudor period [see Thomas 1977, 77] and which originally date from at least as far back as the fourteenth century [see Hartley 1979, 492].

Of Saint Peter that cried "Caws Pob"

I find written among old jests how God made Saint Peter porter of heaven and that God of His goodness, soon after His Passion, suffered many men to come to the Kingdom of Heaven with small deserving; at which time there was in heaven a great company of Welshmen which, with their cracking [bragging] and babbling, troubled all the others. Wherefore God said to Saint Peter that He was weary of them and that He would fain have them out of heaven. To whom Saint Peter said, "Good Lord, I warrant you, that shall be done." Wherefore Saint Peter went out of heaven-gates and cried with a loud voice, "Caws Pob!" that is as much as to say "roasted cheese" which thing the Welshmen hearing ran out of heaven at a great pace. And when Saint Peter saw them all out he suddenly went into heaven and locked the door, and so sparred all the Welshmen out. [Rastell 1526 in Wardroper 1970, 119].[16]

The playwrights of Tudor and Jacobean England made frequent use of the popular contemporary ethnic jokes about the Welsh love of cheese. Shakespeare's comedy *The Merry Wives of Windsor* contains several ethnic jokes and quips about cheese aimed at the Welsh parson, Sir Hugh Evans.[17] Jokes about the Welsh addiction to cheese are also to be found in many English jokebooks of the seventeenth century [see Aston 1883, 63–64, 72, 85, 298] and the joke immediately below appears in the first edition of *Joe Miller's Jests* [1739, 37].[18]

An *Englishman* and a *Welchman* disputing in whose country was the best Living, said the *Welchman*, there is such noble Housekeeping in *Wales*, that I have known above a Dozen cooks employ'd at one Wedding Dinner; Ay, answered the *Englishman*, that was because every Man *toasted his own Cheese*.

The Welch are said to be so remarkably fond of cheese that in cases of difficulty their midwives apply a piece of toasted cheese to the *janua vitae* to attract and entice the young Taffy who on smelling it makes most vigorous efforts to come forth. [Grose 1971, 'Welch rabbit']

The social reality behind these jokes was that the Welsh were a poor pastoral people, living in a barren and mountainous country [see Colyer 1976, 1–8], who consumed their own dairy produce but who could not afford to eat much meat.[19] Indeed it was customary for the Welsh to send their cattle to neighboring England for fattening, and much of the meat thus raised was consumed by the richer inhabitants of that country after the cattle had been driven across the border [see Colyer 1976, 4, 42–49]. Thus the Welsh ate cheese at a time when people of an equivalent relative social status [see Owen 1964, 12; Williams 1967, 169–77] in England would have eaten meat and would have regarded dairy produce such as cheese as "food appertinent onelie to the inferiour sort" [Drummond and Wilbraham 1958, 49; see also 53, 105, 171–74].

The jokes about the Welsh love for cheese were jokes about the backwardness of the Welsh economy and the poverty of the Welsh people. They did not, as it happens, carry the additional implication that the Welsh were regarded as an unsoldierly people, for the general image of the Welsh in other sixteenth and seventeenth century English jokes is of an excessively proud, aggressive, and belligerent people [see Davies 1977 and 1985B]. As a result of the Industrial Revolution economic conditions in Wales and England became more similar, and although income levels in England are still higher and the Welsh have retained their taste for dairy products and cheese dishes [see Allen 1968, 97–99], the Welsh are no longer regarded as a meatless people. By the twentieth century both the English and the Welsh had forgotten the original social meaning of the jokes about cheese-eating Welshmen. Indeed, at the first International Humour Conference in Cardiff in 1976, the Welsh humorist Gwyn Thomas suggested that these jokes of an earlier day must have reflected the hallucinogenic properties of cheese.

In consequence, jokes about the Welsh and cheese have become archaic. No new jokes are being invented and the old jokes, though still reproduced (often in works of an antiquarian nature or in historical satire), are frozen in their original wording and setting.[20] The use of the garbled and humorless [Bierce 1971, 262] phrase "Welsh rarebit" for toasted cheese instead of the authentic "Welsh rabbit" [Murray et al. 1888; see also "Scotch woodcock" and "Scotch rabbit"] is an indication of how everyone has forgotten the original basis of the joke about the Welsh and their cheese. The original term, "Welsh rabbit," carried with it the implication that the poverty-stricken Welsh were forced to substitute cheese even for rabbit meat. A "Welsh rarebit," by contrast, is simply a Cardiff virgin [Davies 1978; Wilde 1978A, 71].

The English soon extended this basic joke about food and poverty to cover the Scots and the Irish, their other poverty-stricken neighbors on the northern and western periphery of the British Isles.[21] Already in the eighteenth century dramatists knew that they could raise an easy laugh by referring to the Irish and potatoes [see Bartley 1954] and the jests of Dr. Johnson and the Reverend Sydney Smith about oats and the Scots are well known.[22] Jokes about the Irish and potatoes (which are often referred to as "Irish apricots," "Munster plums," or just "Murphies") [see Grose 1971; Roback 1944, 41, 54] and about the Scots and porridge proliferated during the eighteenth and nineteenth centuries and are still popular today.[23]

Have you heard about the new Irish cookbook?
It's called 120 ways to cook a potato. [British 1980s]

Give me the Emerald Isle, avick
With murphies for to ate
An' as many pigs and childer
As the fingers on me fate. [Graham 1905, 148. See also 13, and Cole 1887, 215].

The only one

The story is that one of the clansmen died and presented himself at the gate of heaven.

"What name," asked St. Peter.

"M' Nab," said the Scot.

"Then you cannot come in here."

"What for no?" said the Scot. "I've led a guid, sober and righteous life."

"That may be," retorted the saint, "but we cannot afford to make porridge for one." [Knox 1926, 13]

A lawyer, examining a Scotch farmer, said: "You'll affirm that when this happened you were going home to a meal. Let us be quite certain on this point because it is a very important one and be good enough to tell me sir, with as little prevarication as possible, what meal it was that you were going home to."

"You would like to know what meal it was?" said the Scotchman.

"Yes, sir; I should like to know," replied the counsel, sternly and impressively; "and be sure you tell the truth."

"Well then," said the Scotchman, "it was just oatmeal." [Copeland and Copeland 1939, 709].

In countries as diverse as the United States, France, Australia, Canada, and the Netherlands exactly the same pattern of ethnic jokes can be found. These jokes mock an ethnic group because its real or supposed poverty forces it to eschew meat and to subsist on cheaper foodstuffs.

Lorenzo was extolling the virtues of his newly adopted homeland. "This isa greata country," he declared. "Looka at Sinatra. Where elsea could a piece of spaghetti end up with so mucha gravy?" [Wilde 1973, 53]

Then there was the Italian girl who ran out of wool while knitting a sweater so she finished it with spaghetti.

The first time she wore it, two meat balls followed her home. [Wilde 1973, 58]

Italian slum—spaghetto. [Wilde 1978A, 91]

How do you make a Polish cocktail?
Drop a boiled potato in a glass of beer. [Wilde 1975A, 28–9]

A Southern man tells of a conversation he overheard between his cook and his maid, both negroes, with reference to a recent funeral of a member of their race, at which there had been a profusion of floral tributes.

Said the cook: "That's all very well, Mandy; but when I dies I don't want flowers on my grave. Jes' plant a good old water-melon vine; an' when she gits ripe you come dar and don't you eat it but just bust it on de grave an' let de good ole juice dribble down through de ground." [Lawson 1923, 197–98]

A Northern visitor to Texas going on a hunting trip was surprised to learn from the Texan sportsman who accompanied him that they regarded the local blacks as just one more quarry to hunt and shoot. As he and his Southern friends were returning after a successful day's shooting he suddenly saw a group of negroes sitting eating in a field of watermelons. He immediately opened fire on them and was rebuked by one of the Texans: "Hey that's not allowed." "But," said the Northerner, "you said it was O. K. to shoot niggers in Texas." "Yup," replied the Texan, "but not in a baited field." [Texas 1970s]

The immigrant Spags in Australia eat so much spaghetti their forks are more like roll-ons. [Cagney 1979C, 124]

A Spag went into a delicatessen joint and asked the bluff Aussie owner for a salami. The owner saluted him obligingly and then pushed his face into a dish of sauerkraut. [Cagney 1979C, 96]

How do you make a sauerkraut?
Pour some vinegar in his beer. [British 1950s]

How do you get ten Newfies in a Volkswagen?
Throw in a codfish. [Tulk 1971, 80]

What is the dirtiest fight ever fought?
An Icelander and a seagull fighting on the beach over a rotten fish. [Klymasz 1970, 168. See also Instad 1966, 293]

Why are the rubber teats on Belgian babies' feeding bottles square?
To train the children from a young age to eat 'frites'. [Guillois and Guillois 1979A, 18]

[Frites = french fries (U.S.) = chips (U.K.)]

How do you drive a Belgian completely mad?
Put him in a completely circular room and tell him you have hidden a 'frite' in one of the corners. [Steeman 1977, 95]

Why do Belgians want to be buried in Germany when they die?
Because the Germans will bury them in the 'Frite'-hof. [Dutch 1970s. See also Van den Broeck 1976, 21, 34–35]

Where is the biggest chip shop in Europe?
On the border between France and the Netherlands. [Dutch 1970s]

The common factor in all these jokes is that the members of the ethnic groups mocked in them are portrayed as eating and liking cheap, rustic, or plebeian food. The implication is that the peoples who are the butt of the jokes are plebes and rustics. Jokes of this kind can be found very far back in history, for the ancient Athenians made fun of the coarse, rustic diet of the Boeotians and the people of Byzantium mocked the Bulgarians in exactly the same way [see Lang 1976, 146]. In general, the basis of such jokes is economic. The members of the ethnic groups who are the butt of such jokes are mocked as being unable to afford to eat anything else and, in addition, as being foolish enough to enjoy and hunger after the cheap foods that fill their diet. Occasionally, as in the Southern jokes about blacks eating watermelon or in the Australian's aggressive behavior towards "Spags," another aspect of the power relationships between ethnic groups intrudes and there is a hint of the direct coercion to which the members of some of the meatless minorities may be subjected.

These latter jokes lead naturally to the cruder version of the comic contrast between the dominant meat-eaters and the butts of their ethnic jokes. It is best seen in English eighteenth-century caricatures which show a brawny beef-fed Englishman drubbing his meager, skinny, meatless French opponent [see Ashton 1888, 58, 267–68, 285; Gombrich and Kris 1940, viii and 29]. The burly warrior, the prosperous merchant or mandarin with a comfortable paunch, have earned their shape by eating large quantities of the meat the wizened peasant or laborer cannot afford [see Andreski 1973, 84–85; Golden 1967, 16], though the girth of the former classes can be a subject of ridicule as well as envy (e.g., see Chia, Seet, and Wong 1985, 66–67; Grose 1971, 'Munster heifer'; Kimmins 1928, 3] if other standards of shape are applied or if the fat and fat-headed are treated as the comic counterpart of the lean and lean-witted [see McCabe 1985, 133–35]. The meat-eaters' jokes indeed may refer directly and derisively to the shape and size of less beefy ethnic groups nourished on a less beefy diet. Thus there are jokes about ethnic groups being small [see also Grose 1971, 'Norfolk Dumplin'; Llewelyn 1986, 55; Thompson and Berkman 1986, 7, 10] but not about taller peoples. Tallness (especially in men), like fairness of skin (especially in women, though today modified to mean suntanned fairness!), is a very widespread, taken-for-granted attribute of individual, class, and ethnic dominance. Even where a physically smaller people hold power they do not seem to mock the "superior" height of their ethnic subordinates (e.g., see Julius Caesar, *Commentarii de Bello Gallico* II, 4 & IV, 1). Ethnic jokes about height work in one direction only.

Last week there was a huge procession in New York of all the Welsh people in America. It was five miles long and five feet high. [American 1950s. See also Davies 1978, 30]

How many Welshmen does it take to change a light bulb?
Six, provided they stand on each other's shoulders, or . . .
Between six and twelve, depending on the height of the ceiling. [British 1980s]

How many Welsh people does it take to screw in a light bulb?
Two, provided they wear breathing apparatus. [British 1980s]

Have you heard about the man from Appenzell [a Swiss canton] who broke his leg? He fell off a ladder while picking strawberries. [Swiss 1980s. See also Inauen 1979]

Beans are another food regarded since ancient times as fit only for rustics and the lower orders, and there is the added comic touch that beans make people fart. "Beanz Meanz Heinz" and "Beanz Meanz Fartz."

Farting is funny because it is a sudden, involuntary breach of social decorum. In a mannered and hierarchical society which stresses the orderly control of bodily functions and body boundaries [see Douglas 1970, 71–72], the farter is a source of embarrassment to himself and of offense to others. In some societies (for example, seventeenth-century Ireland) [see Bartley 1954, 31], people may have regarded it as a great insult if someone were to have farted in their presence, but in general the involuntary nature of flatulence means that it is regarded as a comic and vulgar rather than an insulting breach of social convention. Farting is comic because it is mildly subversive of civilization and the social hierarchy. Every fart is a tiny revolution.

The fart is a rude reminder of our animal nature and of the limits that exist to the degree of social and personal control that can be exercised over the body [see Eco 1983, 477]. When persons of high status fart in public it puts them in a position of crude equality with their social inferiors. No one can remain dignified while farting. Perhaps for this reason there are many jokes about attempts by persons of high status or persons in authority or by others on their behalf to foist their farts on other people. When a person of low status farts in the presence of someone in authority it may well be an expression of resentment and a form of subversion of that authority, yet the person in authority can do little about it, at any rate in a society where farting is recognized as something not entirely under a person's control.

Arabs, Africans, and Japanese as well as Westerners seem to enjoy jokes about farting [e.g., see Hallpike 1979, 461; Levy 1973, 35–46 and Levy 1974, 8], though the nature of the jokes may vary greatly in line with cultural differences in attitudes to breaches of social decorum and beliefs about the extent to which farting is involuntary or controllable. The humor of farting also has a place in more studied exercises in literary humor.[24]

The foods that cause these moments of embarrassment are naturally a source of mirth also, and there are many jokes which link the allegedly excessive and uncontrolled farting of supposedly vulgar and uncivilized ethnic minorities to their rustic or plebeian diet of rhubarb, cabbage [see Ramsay 1873, 250–51], radishes, yams, and especially beans. These humble vegetables are often considered to be a joke in themselves.

Why does a Polack eat beans for dinner on Saturday night?
So he can take a bubble bath Sunday morning. [Wilde 1973, 29 and 1978A, 181]

And there was the Polack parrot who wouldn't eat anything but beans because—in his heart of hearts—he wanted to be a thunderbird. [Macklin and Erdman 1976, 167]

Automotive News Flash

Italy has produced a new car called the 'Fiasco'. It uses no fuel. You just put lasagne in the tank. Then linguini with clam sauce and then some ravioli alla marinara. By the time it gets to the engine it's pure gas. [Wilde 1975A, 56]

Teacher: No, Manuela, second wind is not something a Mexican gets by eating refried beans. [Wilde 1978A, 171]

Why don't Mexicans have barbecues?
How can you keep beans on a grill? [Wilde 1978A, 167]

The last joke brings us back to our central theme, that these jokes are a means of meting out scorn to the meatless. The Mexican eating beans is comic precisely because he can't afford the American summer ritual [Fieldhouse 1986, 55] of a steak barbecue. Once again the jokes are at the expense of a group's low economic position relative to the joke-tellers'.

By contrast, jokes based on the fact that a group eats good quality meat are rare. Such a group may well be envied and resented but only because everyone else would like to be able to afford or have access to such a diet, and such few jokes as there are about meat-eating hinge on this fact.

Woman's logic

At dinner the other evening a pretty woman, very well dressed and with all the evidences of wealth about her, distinguished herself as a specimen of the individuals who comprise the half of the world that does not know how the other half lives. American beef was being discussed and her contribution to the discussion was the observation, "I can't see what the advantages of low prices will be. If meat was only a penny a pound, I should not eat a morsel more than I do now." [(Thousand) *1000 Witty Sayings* n.d., 80. On the economic background see Critchell and Raymond 1969, 1–18, 313–35, 393–402]

Australian child: "Were there pigs in the war?"

Father: "Yes. They didn't take part in the fighting. They were grown so their meat could be given to American soldiers. Their meat is called pork." [Campbell 1963, 92]

Husák is one day walking incognito in Prague. He wants to know what people really think about him and the Communist Party. He is of course accompanied at a discreet distance by one of his secret police. Husák comes upon a queue in Wenceslas Square. To his shadow Husák asks "Why are they queueing?"

The shadow replies. "Comrade Secretary, they are queueing for meat. There are always long queues."

Husák is amazed. "We don't have enough meat in our country?"

The shadow: "Of course we have enough, but the people don't have enough." [Czech 1980s]

What is two hundred yards long and eats cabbage?

A Czech meat queue. [Czech 1980s]

Even the jokes which express resentment at the rich, at American soldiers in Australia or the party bosses in Eastern Europe getting more than their fair share of the meat, merely express once again the supremacy of meat as an index, a symbol of wealth, luxury, privilege, and power. A lack of meat, by contrast, signifies the poverty and failure of an individual, an ethnic group, a nation, or an economic system (such as East European agriculture).

The assumption that there is a real and also a symbolic connection between the possession of political and economic power and the consumption of meat also helps to explain the popularity of the jokes told by white American Southerners about blacks stealing chickens. There are a truly remarkable variety of Southern jokes about black chicken-thieves.

This classic example is widely known outside the South, and indeed outside the United States:

A farmer, awakened one night by a noise in the hen house, grabbed his gun, ran to the back porch and yelled: "Who's there?"

"Nobody but us chickens, boss," came the answer. [House 1944, 57][25]

Boyce House [1944, 57], a Texan, wrote of this joke: "If this collector of jokes were asked to name the three stories that are told oftener than any others the answer would be that all three are negro stories." The first of the three stories he quotes is the one ending "Nobody but us chickens, boss." There are very many other jokes on this theme:

Recently a man had some work that he wanted done around his country place and to that end he sought out an elderly colored man called Rastus. Not being able to find Rastus he left a message with a colored deacon.

"Rastus," said the deacon later in the day, "yo' am to go round an' clean out dat hen house of Judge Johnson's tomorrow mo'ning."

"What am dat?" responded Rastus with a wondering expression. "Did yo' say, hen house?"

"Dat's what I said," repeated the deacon. "Yo' am to clean out dat hen house tomorrow mo'ning."

"Must be some mistake," said Rastus doubtfully shaking his head. "Who ebah heard of cleaning out a hen house in day-time?" [Lawson 1923, 196. See also 195]

"Dear Frien's," the colored deacon said as he whetted the carving knife, "let us thank Providence fo' dis yere meal. Dis yere capon belonged to Jedge Sharp, mah neighbor, an' Ah prayed dat de bird might fly into mah garden. But it never, never came. Den Ah prayed, dear frien's, dat Ah might go over into his yard an' fetch it. An' de very first time ob askin', dear frien's, Providence granted mah request." [Lawson 1923, 199. See also House 1943, 41]

Rastus: "Don't let dem chickens out, Mirandy."
Mirandy: "Why not? Won't dey come home?"
Rastus: "Deed dey won't; dey'll go home!"
[Lawson 1923, 200. See also Cobb 1940, 171–73]

The reputed affinity between the southern negro and unguarded poultry is the subject of a story told by Senator Bacon of Georgia. An old colored man notorious for his evil ways, after attending a revival meeting desired to lead a better life. At a later meeting he was called up to be questioned.

"Well, Rastus," said the revivalist. "I hope you are now trying to live a Christian life in accordance with the rules of the church. Have you been stealing any chickens lately?"

"No, sah! I ain't stole no chicken of late."

"Any turkeys or pigs?"

Rastus, grieved, replied: "No sah!"

"I am very glad to hear that you have been doing better lately," replied the evangelist. "Continue to lead a holy and Christian life, Rastus."

After the meeting was over, Rastus drew a long breath of relief and turning to his wife exclaimed: "Mandy, if he'd said ducks I'd been a lost nigger suah!" [Patten 1909, 207. See also 255–56 and House 1943, 40]

These jokes[26] all indicate very clearly the relationship between meat, power, and color that existed until the latter half of the twentieth century in the traditional society of the southern states of the United States. The dominant Southern whites had almost a monopoly of political, legal, economic, and social power and took on many of the qualities of a ruling caste.[27] This powerful group alone contained people who could legitimately enjoy a plentiful diet of meat, and particularly the more expensive and prestigious meat such as beef. The blacks were restricted to chicken and the less desirable parts of the pig—trotters, chitlins (chitterlings), jowls. The height of their ambition was to live "high on the hog," and for many blacks a stolen chicken might have been the only meat they would get to eat. It may well be true that blacks are or were very fond of chicken [see Davis, Gardner, and Gardner 1941, 528], and in small communities where poor blacks lived on familiar terms with and in rough proximity to the local white notables [see Cash 1973 (1941), 104, 319–20] blacks probably did raid local chicken houses at night (see Davis, Gardner, and Gardner 1941, 502]. However, it is difficult to see why such an essentially trivial crime should in and of itself give rise to so many jokes; the most plausible though admittedly speculative explanation is one couched in terms of its symbolic relationship to the fact and ideology of white supremacy.

The jokes portray even the most supposedly respectable blacks, notably ministers of religion, or deacons [see Cash 1973 (1941), 324–25], as having to stoop to the undignified pursuit of chicken-stealing to get access even to low-status meat, as being forced stealthily to enter a dark and dirty chicken house at night (sometimes with the added indignity of getting caught) to steal a weak and harmless chicken. The full meaning of the joke can only be comprehended if one tries to substitute alternatives for any of its key elements. It is difficult to imagine Southerners telling jokes about a white minister of religion raiding a hen roost, or about a black deacon stealing and eating a bull, the latter a task that would demand courage and organization rather than stealth and deceit and would gain the thief access to the most rather than one of the least honorific forms of meat.

The Negro's lack of meat then was a symbol of his lack of status and power, and the jokes that show him in the comically dishonorable role of chicken thief underline his powerlessness. The Southern legal processes by which white meatmanship was upheld also produced many jokes making essentially the same point. Furthermore, they may be related to a curious reverse link between black powerlessness and chicken-stealing. In Virginia, in 1875–76, as part of a general campaign to disfranchise the blacks and reestablish white supremacy after the Reconstruction era, a law was passed depriving anyone convicted of petty larceny of the right to vote. At a Negro political convention in Richmond in 1875 this caused one of the delegates to lament: "It is hard that a poor Negro can't take a few chickens without losing his right to vote" [Key 1949, 536]. The link between chickens and power could not have been made more explicit.

Sambo was on trial and the judge said: "You are accused of stealing chickens. Do you have any witnesses?"

"Naw suh, jedge," the prisoner responded, "when I steals chickens, I don't have no witnesses." [House 1945, 70]

The colored defendant was accused of chicken-stealing and the evidence was overwhelming. After the jury had brought in the verdict of "Guilty," the judge said to the prisoner: "George, there's one thing about this case that I don't understand. How could you go into that backyard where there was a bulldog, force open the chicken-house door and go right past the window where the owner was asleep, climb back over the fence and get away without arousing anyone?"

The negro said, "Jedge, ain't no use me 'splainin' to you; you couldn't do it." [House 1945, 59. See also Masson 1913, 184]

As in the case of the equally numerous jokes about Jewish arson discussed earlier, the Southern jokes about black chicken-stealing should be seen not as an ethnic puzzle for the criminologist but in relation to a seriously and strongly held set of ideological beliefs about the blacks and their proper place in society. The jokes are not in and of themselves part of the Southern ideology of white supremacy and black subordination (though they could of course be used to further such beliefs if employed in a particular way and in a relevant context), but it is nonetheless the case that only the existence of such an ideology makes the jokes possible. The jokes are a comic reflection of or on a particular set of serious beliefs and institutions whose existence was well known to all Southerners, both white and black. Even though their feelings about this everyday situation might well differ very markedly, both blacks and whites had to acknowledge the reality of institutionalized white supremacy and of the intensely held view of the blacks that lay at the core of the supporting ideology. It is the knowledge and acknowledgment of this social reality that is the necessary underpinning of the jokes, not enthusiasm for it. Blacks [see Burma 1946, 711; Kimmins 1928, 170; Middleton 1959, 177] and whites alike were thus both able to laugh at jokes about blacks stealing chickens. One and the same joke might well be the occasion for a laugh of superiority, a wry comment on the way the world is or was, or both.

There are two instructive exceptions to the rule that there are few jokes directed against meat eating because it is the honorable food of the powerful and the prosperous, whereas the cheap foods of the underdog are the subject of innumerable jokes and gibes. The two exceptions are sausage and bread. There exists an extremely large number of ethnic and other jokes about sausage despite the fact that it is a meat product, whereas there are hardly any bread jokes even though bread is the staple food of many poor groups of people. Sausages are comic while bread is dignified. There are essentially two reasons for this paradox: the first is that bread, though the predominant food of the poor, is also a universal food eaten by all classes and all ethnic groups. Whereas, for instance, spaghetti or macaroni can be portrayed as a distinctively Italian food or porridge as a distinctively Scottish one, thus allowing these foods to be used as vehicles for ethnic jokes, it is much more difficult to use bread as a distinguishing mark of ethnicity or ethnic poverty. Nonetheless, it should be noted that items of equally universal consumption, such as cheese or potatoes, have been used as the basis of ethnic jokes about the Welsh, the Irish, and the Belgians. An item of poor peoples' diets is more easily incorporated in ethnic jokes if the food concerned is highly specific to the group, but this is by no means a necessary condition. The dichotomy between general foods that everyone eats and specific foods regarded as characteristic of a particular ethnic group also helps to explain why sausages are comic. Everyone eats meat, but sausage is particularly associated with certain ethnic groups, such as the Germans and the Poles, and such "characteristic" foods are more likely to be made the subject of ethnic jokes.

Within the sausage-eating groups that are the butt of ethnic jokes, there are many different kinds of sausage, and these are used to mark local ethnic or regional boundaries in a comic way. The line of the River Main that divides Northern from Southern Germany is called the *Weisswurstäquator*, the "white sausage divide."

However, there is a second and more subtle reason for the paradoxically comic status of sausages and the dignified status of bread; it lies in the nature of the processes which transform meat into sausages and grain into bread. The process of sausage-making necessarily destroys the natural form and structure of the meat that is used and converts it into a shapeless mass of sausage-meat [see Gerrard 1969, 2], which has no clear animal identity. Such shape as a sausage has is arbitrarily determined by the nozzle of the sausage-maker or the constraint imposed on the sausage by a sausage skin. Sausage is meat deprived of its origins and, therefore, also of the dignity attached to these origins. It is a formless, ambiguous, identityless, and therefore comic form of meat. It is meat without meatness. By contrast, the process of baking bread transforms a formless mass of flour, a sludge of dough, into a loaf that has a coherent form and a definite structure. Bread, unlike, say, porridge, is thus set at a distance from its humble origins in cheap grain. The process of baking has given bread a dignity and standing which prevent us from making jokes about bread or bread-eaters.

The shapelessness of sausage deprives it of the image of being real meat. This point is instructively brought out in an ethnic joke about the Irish Catholic taboo concerning the eating of meat on Fridays.

'Twas Friday. The village priest went on his rounds, when lo! he finds Tim Doolan licking his lips over a smoking dish of beef sausages.

"Timothy Doolan," quoth the priest accusingly, "is it on a blissid Friday ye'd sin yer sowl for a dish of mate?"

"Taint mate, yer riverince," whined Tim, "sure it's only a troifle of sausage."

"It's mate," retorted the priest, "and ye'll do a pinance!"

"A loight wan, thin plaze, father!"

"Ye'll bring a load of wood to me house tomorrow," commanded the priest.

Tim concurred.

The next morning, as the priest stepped from his house, he discovered Tim in the act of tipping a cart-load of sawdust into the woodshed.

"Tut, tut Timothy!" he exclaimed, "what's all this?"

"It's the pinance, sure," said Tim.

"But I said wood; that's not wood."

"Well," rejoined the imperturbable Tim, "if sausage is mate, that's wood." [Macdonald 1915, 29–30]

Clearly, in the mind of Tim Doolan, sausage has ceased to be meat because it has lost the form of meat, just as sawdust has ceased to be wood, for wood has a form and a shape. Since in the popular mind (as represented by Tim Doolan) the essence of a thing lies in its shape and structure, sausage has ceased to be meat. The priest takes the contrary view that the essence of a thing lies in its content [see also the joke in Goethe 1970 (1862–63), 202]—until he gets a load of sawdust.

Not only has sausage lost the shape and dignity of meat, it also may be composed of inferior offal or adulterated with tabooed meat or with things that are not meat at all [see Gerrard 1969, 2, 40, and, re haggis, 159]. This is why sausage appears in ethnic jokes as a comic food and can be used to mock its consumers, such as the Poles, the Germans, and the Scots (haggis).

A Haggis looks like a football. You don't know whether to eat it or kick it. After you've eaten it, you wish you'd kicked it. [Hodes 1978, 61]

In the year 2001 the inhabitants of the moon begged the United States not to send any more Polish astronauts. Said the senior Moon Man "We thought green cheese smelled bad until we smelled Polish sausage." [Macklin and Erdman 1976, 20. See also 101, 113, 134, 165, 169, 183]

A German went into a restaurant in London and ordered sausage. Half an hour later his meal had not arrived, so he called the waiter over and demanded indignantly: "So! When do I become a sausage?" [British 1950s. See also Edwards 1978, 25]

[In German *bekommen* means to *get*, not to *become*.]

How do you make a frankfurter laugh?

Tell it a Polish sausage joke. [Pines 1976]

Schultz was working in a sewer all day. When he finished work he went to a very smoky saloon and filled himself up with beer. Then he went to the free lunch counter and ate some garlicky sausage and triple strength Limburger cheese. He enjoyed the food so much he put some in his pocket. Then he started for home. The elevator of his apartment house was crowded with women, but Schultz squeezed in. He was only in his apartment a few minutes when the superintendent called him up.

"The women you went up with in the elevator complained about you," he said.

"Complained?" said the amazed Schultz. "I took off my hat!" [Ford, Hershfield, and Laurie 1947, 41]

An English statistician lecturing about demography wished to warn his audience not to draw broad generalizations on the basis of what might be merely a chance correlation. "For instance," he said, "just because the Scots love bagpipes and haggis we would be quite wrong in concluding that there is any general connection between cacophony and offal." [British 1970s]

Sausage often has much in common with the other "foods of poverty" discussed earlier. It is meat but often inferior meat, like tripe or offal [Boyd 1978, 129–30], fit only for those who cannot afford the real thing and who must eat 'umble umble pie. Sausage is depicted in the jokes as a heavy, smelly, coarse food fit only for heavy, smelly, coarse people. Good quality sausages may of course be made entirely of good quality meat, but one cannot tell simply from a sausage's enigmatic appearance what it is or what it contains. Hence, since the time of Aristophanes [see Schutz 1977, 52–59] there have been many jokes about sausages that contain tabooed meat, such as that of domestic pets or working animals. A "hot dog" may be just that. [See *America, the Golden Age of Comedy* 1973, 127; Pines 1976].

"Smith," said the restaurant manager to a waiter, "why did that man at table five leave so abruptly?" "I don't know," replied the waiter. "He asked for sausages and I told him we were all out of them but if he could wait a few minutes I'd get the cook to make some. I went to the kitchen and as I set down a tray of dishes I stepped on the dog's tail and he let out a wild yelp. Then when I went back into the dining-room, the man was on his way out the front door." [Braude 1976, 45]

Provincial tourist (to Kellner who offers him sausages):
"I say old feller, any 'osses died about 'ere lately! Chevals morts, you know!!" [Punch Library 1908 *Mr. Punch on the Continong,* 111]

A man who recently invested in some sausages says that when he got them home he cut them apart and left them. In the morning he visited them. Three of them were twined up together and were sleeping sweetly. Two had crawled to the milk-bowl and were lapping the milk and one, a black and white one, was on the garden wall trying to catch a sparrow. He drowned the lot . . . . . . Speaking of sausages, Mr. Smith passed a pork shop the other day. Mr. Smith whistled. The moment he did this every sausage "wagged its tail". [Cole 1887, 161]

The various manufacturers of sausages are all also the subject of jokes about the uncertain contents of the sausage. Ethnic jokes about sausage manufacturers often depict them as belonging to a group alleged to be canny, such as the Scots or the Jews.

Wimpy = We Include More Potato Yearly. [Marshall 1979, 212]

This is the way the world of sausage ends
Not with a banger but with a Wimpy. [British 1960s. Cf. Eliot, *The Hollow Men* 1925, v, 30–31 in Eliot 1948, 78].

A well-known and greatly respected manufacturer of the best sausages in the West of Scotland and also a theorist in golf was playing a round with one of the canny Fifers, the wise golfers of the East come into the West for its good.

"K—! What is the matter with my putting tonight?" he said. "What am I doing wrong? I can't make it out at all!"

Our old and well-known professional with the familiar glint in his eye answered: "Well, Mr. W—, putting is like eating sausages. It requires confidence!" [Ferguson 1933, 150. See also 'Unspeakable Scot' 1937, 34]

A Jew started a sausage factory in Aberdeen and advertised chicken sausages at one shilling per pound.

"My word! Ikey, how can you do it?"

"Vell," he answered, "I am always fair wid my customers. I give them fifty-fifty—we put a little horse flesh in you know, just fifty-fifty—one chicken and one horse." [Ferguson 1933, 166. See also Ford, Hershfield, and Laurie 1947, 47; Macdonald 1915, 143–44]

The arbitrary shape of the sausage, which the sausage-machine often extrudes in a comic turdlike or phallic form, has also given rise to a number of extremely crude jokes which take the sausage even further away from the category of honored and dignified food.

The butcher lived in an apartment over his shop. One night he was awakened by strange noises coming from below. He tiptoed downstairs and observed that his 19-year-old daughter was sitting on the chopping block and masturbating with a liverwurst. He sighed and tiptoed back to bed.

The next morning one of his customers came and asked for some liverwurst. The butcher explained he didn't have any.

The lady was annoyed. She pointed and said, "No liverwurst, eh? Well, What's that hanging on the hook right over there?"

The butcher frowned at her, and replied, "That, lady, is my son-in-law." [Mr. J. 1980, 40. See also Hall 1934]

The process of sausage-making converts an honorable food into a comic one. Meat is certain, sausage is uncertain. Meat is expensive, sausage may well be cheap and nasty and contain tabooed as well as low-status ingredients. Meat has form and structure, sausage is arbitrary and formless. Sausage-eaters thus suffer the gibes of poverty and sausage-makers comic accusations of fraud and deception. Sausage-eaters, like other eaters of cheap food, may themselves be seen as comically shapeless of body. Dominant meat-eaters see themselves as tall, slim, aristocratic, elegant, in contrast to the coarse, stocky, bulky, shapeless peasant outline of the butts of their jokes whom they see as made that way by a diet of cheap, coarse, bulky, shapeless calories. This image has inspired the illustrators of modern joke-books about the beer-and-potato-fed Belgians, Poles, and Irish. As in the traditional portrait of Cousin Michel, the sausage-German,[28] the idea conveyed is that of grossness and coarseness of shape resulting from grossness and coarseness of appetite. Perhaps this explains the tendency of anthropologists and folklorists to categorize this type of ethnic joke about eating as being primarily about greed and gluttony [see Apte 1985, 148]. However, this is less than half the truth, for it is only the greed of the poor and unrefined that is mocked and not that of those who are wealthy gluttons for fillet steak and who are bred on a high protein diet to be big and beefy [see Walker and Cannon 1985, 70–71], but not bulky. The jokes about the bulky are merely expressing a somewhat more sophisticated version of the old warrior beliefs about size and shape.

In contrast to the many sausage jokes there are hardly any mocking jokes about bread, despite the fact that bread is often the characteristic food of the very poor. Bread may even be a Giffen good, for those in very poor circumstances are forced to eat more of it if its price should rise. As individuals or nations get wealthier they tend to eat less and less bread [see Collins 1976, 27–28]. Bread, like potatoes, oatmeal, or cod, is very much a food of poverty, but it does not attract the same kind of jokes as these other foods. The absence of mocking jokes about bread-eaters is a strange phenomenon that calls for an explanation.

Indeed, such few jokes as there are about bread treat it rather favorably as a food. The loaf is a coherent, solid object, it is grain transformed by milling and baking into something quite different. It lacks the low status of formless grain-based slops, such as porridge or mameligge, or of the amorphous, tangled spaghetti or macaroni. Shapeless foods of this kind tend to be classed as comic along with the slops that form the diet of infants, invalids, or the toothless aged, all of whom lack the full status of active adults able to discharge an adult's tasks and eat an adult's diet. Shapeless food is comic, marginal food because it is the diet of comic, incapacitated, marginal individuals. Those who have hands to work have teeth to chew with. It should be noted here too how often shapeless foods of mixed ingredients are used as a metaphor for stupidity, muddle, disorder, and worthlessness—a farrago of nonsense, making a hash of things, a hodgepodge or hotchpotch, macaronic Latin, a mess of pottage, stew, tripe, tsimmes [see Brewer's 1981].

Bread owes its high status to its clear and coherent shape, which makes it quite unlike its cheap, incoherent, and messy ingredients. By contrast jokes about porridge stress its shapeless resemblance to vomit or half-digested food.

No Scot.

An amateur traveller hurrying down to the saloon of a liner very late for breakfast and seeing a plate of porridge in his place shouted to the steward, "I say, steward, who's been sick in my plate?" [Ike nsmile lettslaff 1937, 45].

Similar jokes are told against vegetarians by meat-eaters who wish to mock their diet for being formless and incoherent.

Sir James Barrie used to pull Bernard Shaw's leg about being a vegetarian. He and Shaw were once staying in the same house and Barrie saw Shaw being given a concoction of salads, green mayonnaise and oils for lunch, while the rest of the party were eating what Barrie considered more wholesome fare. As Shaw was about to lift the first forkful to his mouth Barrie asked him: "Tell me, Shaw, have you eaten that or are you just about to?" [Rossiter 1981, 31. See also Esar 1954, 30–32]

Unlike certain other species, man does not return to his vomit, and half-digested food which has been regurgitated is regarded with some disgust. It is food which has had its shape and coherence destroyed and which has crossed the boundary between one's physical self and the outside world, in the wrong direction. The entire process of cooking, eating, digestion, and absorption, by which what we eat becomes what we are, forms a cycle of successive transformations between the coherent and the incoherent. The coherent points in the cycle are regarded as normal, admirable, and even potentially sacred, while the points of incoherence are regarded with disdain, disgust, or amusement, since they are neither one thing nor the other. They are neither solid nor liquid, neither food nor tissue. Incoherent food is comic because it resembles semidigested food in transition, food that is about to become part of us but has not yet quite made it.

It is now possible to explain why bread has become a holy food, a symbol of the human body and of the God who took on human form. Bread and not other grain-based foods is incorporated into Jewish and Christian prayers and ceremonies not just because it is the basic food of the peoples of the Mediterranean and Middle East, but also because it is coherent. If "Give us this day our daily bread" were changed to "Give us this day our daily porridge" or "Give us this day our daily spaghetti" to give it local "relevance," an important aspect of its meaning would be destroyed. This can be seen indirectly from the following ethnic joke about a canny American:

An American businessman went to see the Pope and offered to donate one billion dollars to the Roman Catholic Church. The Pope refused his offer angrily. Afterwards one of the Pope's aides asked him why he had been so abrupt with the generous Mr. Bouncer. "Well," said the Pope, "in return for the money, he wanted me to alter the Lord's Prayer to 'Give us this day our Bouncer's cornflakes.' " [British? 1950s]

Also significant is the use of unleavened bread by the Jews to celebrate the Passover [see Rosten 1970, 68–69], and the use of bread by Christian churches to commemorate the Last Supper.

And as they were eating, Jesus took bread, and blessed it, and brake it, and gave it to the disciples, and said, "Take, eat; this is my body." [Matthew 26:26, The Bible, King James Version]

And he took bread, and gave thanks, and brake it, and gave unto them, saying, "This is my body which is given for you: this do in remembrance of me." [Luke 22:19, The Bible, King James Version]

Bread thus became for Christians a holy food, a symbol of the body of Christ, and such a symbol must necessarily have a clear, solid outline. The body, which above all has shape and structure, could not be represented by a food which was in any way amorphous or incoherent. The comic effect of substituting something banal and unsuitable for bread in this context can be seen from the following ethnic joke about a linguistic misunderstanding:

The bosun from a British ship went ashore in France to buy some cheese for the officer's mess. To the cheese-monger he explained "C'est pour la Messe." The French shop-keeper replied in amazement, "Quelle réligion!" [Thomas 1944B, 27]

[C'est pour la Messe = It is for the Mass. Quelle réligion = What a religion!]

At a more serious level we may also note the contrast between the bread distributed to the disciples as the body of Christ and the ambiguous, formless, soggy sop that was given to the traitor Judas Iscariot.

Jesus answered, "He it is [the betrayer], to whom I shall give a sop, when I have dipped it." And when he had dipped the sop, he gave it to Judas Iscariot, the son of Simon.

And after the sop Satan entered into him. [John 13:26–27, The Bible, King James Version]

The disciples partook of God Himself,[29] the God who in another person had separated the land from the sea and created order from chaos [Genesis 1:1–19], but as Judas Iscariot swallowed his sop, Satan entered him, the very spirit of evil, disorder, and confusion.

Thus bread became a holy food, not to be mocked, and it has retained something of this significance even in a secular age. Because bread in a religious context signified flesh, it took on the same high status as meat, even among wealthy people whose diet might contain little bread or among people living far from Israel who had no real tradition of baking. Bread spread to Northern Europe from the Mediterranean as a result of the conquests of the Roman Empire and the subsequent conversions of these peoples to Christianity. Bread symbolized status in an aristocratic and clerical civilization. A parallel historical process explains bread's presence and standing today in areas such as West Africa [Goody 1982, 180]. Bread is little suited to either region, but it has taken hold because it is a symbol of cultural advance and the adoption of Christianity [Allen 1968, 23–24; Goody 1982, 145, 236].

Bread has also become a secular symbol of all food, the staff of life, a word to be chanted by peoples made radical by hunger and ready to start a "bread riot." It may be unwise to offer them cake, porridge, or potatoes, however nutritious these are. A further mark of the special symbolic standing of bread is the reluctance of the peoples of Mediterranean Europe to throw it away even when it is stale and unpalatable [see Fieldhouse 1986, 56]. This understandable traditional sentiment and possible superstition has a far more irrational counterpart among some of the affluent in Northern Europe who are capable of feeling guilty about wasting bread even though they unthinkingly waste far more resources in other ways [see Schoeck 1969, 317–19]. If someone else should wantonly waste bread, they are apt to become irrationally, indeed comically angry, out of all proportion to the event, even though there is no way in which these particular discarded crusts and crumbs could be conveyed to the underfed. It is the angry rather than the hungry who are the butts of the periodic waves of sick jokes that sweep through the Western industrial world about the Ethiopian/Eritrean, Biafran, Ukrainian, or other famines. It is not the misfortune of distant peoples that is seen as funny but the foolish nagging and moralizing of folk much closer to home [cf. Oring 1987].

Russian mother to children: "Starve! Starve! There are children in America who are eating." [Yacob Smirnoff. British Television, 22 August 1984]

That bread owed its status to the manufacturing process which transformed its humble shapeless ingredients into an honored product had the disadvantage that the status of bread was greatest when it was furthest removed from its source. Thus white bread, made of bleached and refined flour, came to be more highly regarded than the coarser, darker wholemeal loaf [see Drummond and Wilbraham 1958, 174, 186, 295, 299]. Ultimately people were prepared to eat white bread because of its appearance and because of the prestige attached to the ultra-refined product, even though it tasted like cardboard. Such ethnic jokes about bread as exist tend to hinge on the greater prestige of white bread made from wheat relative to its coarser and darker rivals or to the beige bread of wartime Britain [see Sillince 1943, 38]. White bread was historically regarded as the food of the genteel, and the darker, coarser breads were regarded as fit only for peasants. Only now in the industrial societies, where there are but few peasants and everyone has access to refined foods, do we find this process being reversed. Today it is a prosperous minority who eat the coarser breads and thus distance themselves from the idiocy of urban life.

The sociology of the ethnic humor of eating is necessarily as complex as the diverse eating habits and jokes of the peoples it seeks to study. However, it can be reduced to a small number of basic principles. First, food is one of the means by which an ethnic group asserts that it is different from its neighbors. The more radically a group seeks to set itself apart, the more elaborate will its food taboos be and the more these will be a subject of jokes, especially in a time of social change when the food taboos are upheld and yet evaded. Even where there are no real food taboos a group may well still maintain the superiority of its own food preferences by mocking some food, such as frogs' legs, spaghetti, or sausage, that it regards as an odd and characteristic part of the diet of one of its neighbors. Food that is highly local, specific, and characteristic of a particular group is especially likely to be the butt of ethnic jokes. Such jokes are one of the ways in which the group is defined as different, not so much by itself as by outsiders. Secondly, food is one of the means by which an ethnic group displays its power, wealth, and status, usually by eating excessive quantities of expensive meat. A corollary of this is that the members of the group will enjoy telling jokes about the inferior, cheap, and meatless diets of cheese, porridge, praties, chips, beans, or cod which characterize other groups "inferior" to their own. Finally there is a general tendency to see foodstuffs that have a clear, coherent shape and structure as superior to shapeless, indeterminate, ambiguous items, such as sausage or toasted cheese, and the consumers of the latter kind of food are often the butt of ethnic jokes. Ultimately all jokes about ethnic groups and food are a reflection of the attempts on the part of ethnic groups either to maintain and reinforce social boundaries and identity or to display wealth and power, or both.

CHAPTER TEN
Conclusion

Many of the conclusions derived from the comparative study of particular types of jokes about peoples have already been formulated at the end of earlier chapters, so that this formal concluding chapter is more in the nature of a summing up and an attempt to see how far the questions posed at the beginning of the study have been answered. It is time to assess overall the content of the most common ethnic jokes and the reasons why a particular type of ethnic joke is pinned on one group rather than another. The answers to the latter question are complex and are related to the joke-tellers' sense of their own identity and its boundaries, to the ways in which the societies of both joke-tellers and butts are stratified, and to puzzles of historical sociology that have baffled scholars as well as joke-tellers. There are limits to what can be achieved by general comparisons of ethnic jokes and of large-scale social structures, but it has proved possible to establish fruitful generalizations which enable us to use jokes about peoples as a means of attaining a greater understanding of the joke-tellers, of the butts of their jokes, and of the links between the two groups.

The Content of Jokes about Peoples and the Balancing of Values

The basic assumption that underlies much of the analysis of ethnic jokes presented in this study is that the jokes are a means by which the joke-tellers ascribe human deficiencies to other ethnic groups in an excessive or ludicrous fashion. However, it is not the case that all manner of errors and vices are comically exported in an indiscriminate fashion. On the basis of an extensive examination of the content of ethnic jokes I have argued that the defects which are most frequently mocked can be arranged in pairs that relate to commonly experienced ambiguous and indeed contradictory situations, to dilemmas which seem likely to generate uncertainty and ambivalence. Ethnic jokes express and for the time being resolve the uncertain situations that gave rise to them by mocking excess and corresponding failure in either of two directions and ascribing them to some other group. Someone else gets it wrong. Thus, in the modern world of rational, calculative work which impinges heavily on leisure, human relations, and sacred tradition, there is an enormous number of ethnic jokes about "stupid" and "canny" groups in almost every country. Warfare, too, has produced a widespread crop of ethnic jokes about "cowardly" and "bellicose" or "militarist" groups. In either case the inevitably contradictory values and pressures of a complex society mean that the individual has to steer his or her way uncertainly between pairs of competing and contrary demands knowing that an error in either direction could bring failure or the derision of others. Jokes are the balance in an unbalanced world. Ethnic jokes at the expense of other groups depict them as located at one extreme or the other, with all the failure and discomfort that this brings. Within the English-speaking countries, notably America, Australia, and England, a further kind of ethnic joke can be seen as rooted in the balancing of equality and hierarchy that is an important but varied component of the culture of these societies. The tension between the values of an ordered hierarchy and of egalitarianism is for English-speakers a source of ethnic jokes in which the English are pushed to one stuffily hierarchical extreme and the Australians, the Welsh, and to some extent the Americans to the crassly egalitarian opposite pole. The butts of such jokes might well be termed the "pompous" and the "vulgar."

The framework of ambiguous and even contradictory values postulated here helps to make sense of most of the more common types of ethnic jokes, but it also has its limitations. Ethnic jokes about religion or sex or uncleanliness for instance have only been dealt with on an ad hoc basis as and when these topics have impinged on other basic themes. It may well be possible to analyze these ethnic jokes also in terms of a similar antithetical framework of the "zealots" and the "irreligious," the "oversexed" and the "under-sexed" [cf. Zijderveld 1983], the "clean" and the "filthy," the "pure" and the "polluted," but there are considerable problems in doing so, due to the sheer diversity of cultural beliefs about religion, sexuality, and cleanliness. There is a fair degree of agreement in the modern world as to what constitutes comic stupidity, and likewise the "canny Scot" is as much a figure of fun in Slovakia or Italy as he is in Sweden or Australia. There is no corresponding uniformity of ethnic jokes about religion or sex, which seem to differ from culture to culture as widely as the beliefs, mores, and taboos that have given rise to them. In America ethnic jokes about dirt have been attached to jokes about stupidity, but this seems to be no more universal than the American ethic of "rational" (or obsessional) hygiene. The comparative analyses which elsewhere have revealed remarkable similarities in the patterns of ethnic jokes relating to work or warfare here serve to emphasize the diversity of human morals.

The view that virtue can be seen as a golden mean flanked by the vices of excess and deficiency is an old and also an arbitrary one dating back at least to the time of Aristotle [see *Ethics* Book 2 1104a32 and

1107a28 to 1108b9] and one that underlies the theses of many theorists of humor. Bergson's comically mechanical role players [1911, 46, 122, 134–35] are ludicrous because of their rigid and inappropriate virtues that turn them into misers or militarists. The same may be said of Olson's view of the ridiculous stock characters in comedy [1968, 20], whom he sees as inferior and of no account rather than wicked and who comprise both fools and ignoramuses deficient in rationality itself and misers and cowards who allow their passions to run away with their reason. I would add to this that the fate of the unbalanced is particularly likely to be seen as comic in the large, diverse, heterogenous, and thus necessarily malintegrated societies of the modern world, which are characterized by compatible but competing and conflicting values [e.g., see Lipset 1964, 123]. No single, clear, normative pattern prevails and each individual has at times to be a consumer of ideals, balancing marginal quantities of one value against another as if they were commodities. There are, however, rough collective boundaries to what is seen as reasonable, and ethnic outsiders may be laughed at for supposedly exhibiting either too much or too little of a particular in-group virtue [cf. Merton 1957, 430].

The assertion and maintenance of ethnic identity are themselves values, and each individual is expected to strike a reasonably happy mean between the anomie and paralysis that would result from total cultural relativism and the crass ethnocentrism that automatically negates the cultural values of others. At the extremes, both bigots and ultraliberal cultural onanists are figures of fun. For the members of an ethnic minority faced with the temptations of assimilation there are jokes both[1] about those too eager to discard their origins and traditions and about those who fail to master the skills and particularly the language of the wider society [see Ben-Amos 1973]. The latter jokes often coincide with the ethnic jokes told about the group from the outside. Within the ethnic minority there is often a counterpart to these in the form of a humor which ridicules those among their members who hasten to adopt the speech, manners, way of life, and even the identity of the dominant majority—the bananas, coco-nuts, Mayfair Highlanders, lace-curtain Irish, cut-glass Welsh, bootsies, agringados [see Baxter and Mitchell 1985; Limón 1977]. In general this humor tends to be situational and does not give rise to a plethora of formula-based jokes which become known outside the group. One notable exception are the ingenious Jewish jokes about the fate of apostates who abandon traditional ways, intermarry, convert, change their names, or even deny their ancestry. Jewish jokes are unique in the way in which they refer explicitly to the problematic nature of the boundaries of a people and focus on the blurring of this boundary not by similar or related outsiders but by assimilating insiders. The Jewish jokes that mock in turn both those who neglect or break boundary-related rules and rituals, such as the food taboos, and the ultrarigorous who obsessively obey and extend such rules can be regarded as a subset of the enormous wealth of Jewish jokes that proceed from the tension between the allurements of integration and the wish to preserve an ancient and distinctive ethnic and religious identity.

The exoteric-esoteric distinction [Jansen 1965] may well be less important than that between the jokes favored by assimilators and separatists respectively. However, most of the members of an ethnic minority will be at neither extreme and, in their struggle to maintain a balance between two opposed sets of pressures and between opportunities and "roots" [see Rokkan and Urwin 1983, 115], are able to appreciate both kinds of joke. This is one aspect of a more general problem of balance between "universal" and "particular" values, between, for example, efficiency, rights, and utility on the one hand and loyalty, tradition, and preference for the familiar on the other, between allegiance to a remote, impersonal, and technical "scientific state" and a personal, intimate, and historically rooted ethnic nationalism [see Smith 1981, 187–90, 195]. Both extremes are ludicrous, though the nonrational quality of the latter lends itself more to humor, as in Petersen's description of the shaping of road-safety policy in Belgium:

> A law was proposed to set a speed limit of ninety kilometres [per hour] on ordinary two-lane roads, retaining the prior absence of any limitations only on the major four-lane highways with limited access and other safety features. But one Walloon member of parliament pointed out that most of these better roads are in Flanders, whose inhabitants would thus enjoy the right to drive faster than French-speaking motorists. Some of the older roads of Wallonia were, therefore, exempted from the speed limit in order to extend the privilege over an equal distance in both sections of the country even though this would presumably mean a higher death toll among Walloon drivers and their families. [1975, 203]

In this account of an actual event may be seen the roots of the numerous jokes about the stupidity both of ethnic groups and of politicians.

Jokes Outside and Inside

The ethnic jokes with which this study has been concerned are those jokes told about a people from the outside, which impute an undesirable quality to them in a ludicrous way. The members of ethnic groups who are the butt of such jokes often in turn pass the jokes on to a smaller group, often living on the geographical periphery of their nation, that then becomes the butt of what are essentially the same jokes. Jokes about stupid Irishmen, canny Scotsmen, coarse Australians, boastful Americans, militaristic Germans, devious Welshmen, are told within each of these countries as jokes about the peoples of Kerry, Aberdeen, Tasmania, Texas, Prussia, and Cardiganshire, respectively. Similarly, many of the jokes told about a people from the outside are told from within as political or class-based jokes. American ethnic jokes about the stuffiness or inane pomposity of the English are applied by the English themselves to their own upper crust, "the crumbs held together by dough," "the cream of the country—rich and thick." Ethnic jokes about German militarism or Italian or Egyptian cowardice exist within those countries as political jokes about the over or under enthusiasm of the military. All peoples are divided internally into competing and at times conflicting groups and strata. These internal divisions may be unimportant to or even unperceived by the outsider telling ethnic jokes about the people as a whole, but they are of vital significance to the people themselves and are the social basis of those "same" jokes when told from within. In principle it is always possible for a member of a group that is the butt of a particular genre of ethnic jokes to stand outside the joke and apply it to some other segment of his or her own people [e.g., see Hauser 1962, 102–103; Middleton 1959, 180–81; Wilson 1979, 217]. In the case of immigrants who are in the process of assimilating themselves into the ways of a new country, ethnic jokes told about their people as a whole are often passed on to newly arrived greenhorns or to fractions of the group who have failed or refused to make the transition from immigrant to full member of the new society. Some members of such a minority resist jokes about "their own people," but others may well enjoy such jokes as a celebration of their own successful adaptation to a new world and see them as jokes at the expense of that section of their people who seek to uphold or retain the strictness of those traditional mores that underpin a sometimes restrictive older identity. For those who enjoy the ethnic jokes about the group to which they are linked by ancestry, such jokes are an appropriate response to yet another ambiguous and uncertain situation—that of their ethnic identity itself.

It is often difficult to tell whether particular jokes began outside as ethnic jokes and were adapted for internal use or are the jokes of a people that have become jokes about a people. Welsh jokes about devious preachers and politicians [see Davies 1985B], or Scottish jokes about tippling elders or severe ministers are told outside these countries as ethnic jokes about these peoples as a whole with the preachers, elders, and politicians being regarded as nationally typical groups. I have categorized and analyzed such jokes as ethnic jokes from the outside merely as a simplifying assumption, not as an attempt to resolve the more subtle problems of the origins and adaptations of jokes that cross and recross frontiers.

The very fact that so many ethnic jokes hinge on ambiguous values and ambivalent attitudes often enables the members of an ethnic group that is the butt of jokes from the outside to use these jokes as a means of asserting their distinctive identity, albeit within a framework not of their own choosing. Indeed, in many cases the most ingenious jokes told about a people not only circulate but probably originated within the group, as with many of the jokes that exist about, say, canny Scots, devious Welshmen, hard-drinking Irishmen, or coarse Australians which are often revelled in by the "butts," who use them as a means of asserting a distinctive and gloriously shocking native identity. Also the qualities imputed to these groups in the jokes are not unambiguously derogatory and can be interpreted and evaluated in many ways so that external and internal joke-tellers can enjoy the "same" ethnic jokes but use them for quite different purposes [see Apte 1985, 142; Arnold 1910, 101; Wilson 1979, 146].

This brief account of the uses and meanings of ethnic jokes told within the group that is the butt of these jokes is intended to be no more than an indication of the complexity of the issues involved. It is possible and indeed necessary to analyze ethnic jokes told about another group as if the butt of the jokes were a homogenous entity and were regarded as such by the joke-tellers. It is a simplification but a reasonable one provided it is understood that the purpose of the analysis is to delineate the broad framework within which the jokes are told and not to pursue the diverse aims, motives, and feelings of individuals using ethnic jokes in a variety of contexts. However, it would be misleading to analyze in the same way the ethnic jokes that members of an ethnic group tell about "their own people." Attempts to do so have led to the nonsensical attribution of "self-hatred" or "bad faith" to the joke-tellers because they are seen as attacking themselves, or what the observers see as their essential selves. Once it is realized that a "people" also constitutes an elaborately differentiated society or subsociety in which its individual members occupy very different positions and have a range of choices of identity, it is clear that the largely unsupported explanations of such jokes that invoke self-hatred or bad faith [cf. Ben-Amos 1973] are utterly crass, for this is but one of many possibilities and by no means the most probable. It has also to be accepted that the analysis of ethnic jokes told from within about the joke-teller's "own group" often involves issues quite different from those raised in this or other studies of jokes told "from the outside."

Ethnic Jokes and the Boundaries of Peoples' Identity

There is a sense in which all ethnic jokes mocking another group are assertions of the joke-tellers' perceptions of themselves and their own merits—the "others" are comically stupid/cowardly/canny; we are not. Indeed, this is an underlying assumption in much of the analysis of ethnic jokes not only in this study but in those focusing more directly on the idea that humor and laughter are rooted in a sudden sense of vicarious superiority; all jokes about others, therefore, must contribute to a people's sense of their own identity and character. However, this aspect of ethnic jokes seems stronger in cases where the butts of the jokes closely resemble those who tell jokes about them in culture or language. Here the jokes are focused on the very boundaries of the joke-tellers' identity, on ambiguous peoples who are not quite separate yet not quite members of the joke-teller's group. Ethnic jokes about stupidity nearly always arise from a relationship of this kind and are an almost universal instance of the kind of jokes that are told about groups on the joke-tellers' social, geographical, or linguistic boundaries. A rather different instance of this phenomenon is to be found in the ethnic jokes that the various English-speaking peoples, notably the Americans, the Australians, and the English, tell about one another—the joke that they are "divided by a common language" itself indicates the ambiguous position that each people occupies vis-à-vis the others. The jokes told by the members of each group about the others emphasize and magnify differences of language, culture, behavior, and values, but they are only told and can only be told because of the basic similarities between all of them.

The butts of ethnic jokes about stupidity tend to live on the social, geographical, linguistic, or religious periphery of the joke-tellers' society, and their culture depends on or is derived from that of the dominant group at the center. They are distant provincials, familiar and related neighbors, or all but assimilated immigrants. In consequence the joke-tellers tend to regard them as comic anomalies, as ambiguous, transitional, wavering peoples (TWPs) who are a suitable subject for humor. They are seen not as a clearly separate, alien people in their own right, but as possessing an imperfect, "stupid" version of the joke-teller's own culture. Their culture is seen as imperfect and hence comically inferior because, being at the edge of things, it is out-of-date, unrefined, provincial, or even flawed by fragments of other traditions or languages. As is often the case, the humor of those at the center at the expense of the butts on the periphery is both an expression of superiority and a response to ambiguity. The ambiguous ethnic groups who blur the boundaries of the joke-tellers' identity are dismissed as a piece of comic stupidity in jokes that literally impute stupidity to them. Every national culture has a blurred boundary, an area of ethnic ambiguity far from the dominant center, whose people provide a ready-made butt for ethnic jokes about stupidity.

In some degree this is also the fate suffered by Canadians in American jokes and New Zealanders in Australian jokes. These peoples have a sufficient degree of strength and autonomy to avoid being labeled comically stupid; there are other local groups who have better social qualifications for the role. Nonetheless, ethnic jokes about these similar and smaller neighbors (who do not feature at all in British jokes) tend to deride them as mere backward and powerless imitations of America and Australia respectively.

America, Australia, and England are countries whose similarities are the result of history rather than geography, whose differences seem more important to the peoples themselves than they appear to outsiders. While it is true that the French enjoy jokes about boastful Americans, that the Czechs relish jokes about stuffy, hierarchy-conscious Englishmen, and that the people of Singapore like jokes about coarse Australians, it is nonetheless the case that these jokes generally originate and circulate most freely among those English-speaking peoples for whom the jokes illuminate differences of identity. All three countries share the same basic values of liberal individualism, but the jokes focus on those differences of emphasis and interpretation which set them apart. The comic contrast to American or Australian egalitarianism is the "stuffy and class-conscious" behavior of the English, who, precisely because they are similar enough to be ambiguous, are a much better butt for these jokes than the far more rigidly hierarchical Indians, Russians, Japanese, or Spaniards. The reverse of these jokes are the English jokes about crass, crude colonials which stress the former cultural dependence and provincialism of the now wealthy and powerful nations of America and Australia. American jokes about the static, indolent traditionalism of the English are matched by English jokes about boastful, striving, workaholic Americans. There are other peoples in the world whom these comic images fit better than the English or the Americans, but for the joke-tellers it is once again a similar group that is chosen as the butt of the jokes. Other, more alien groups may deviate more strikingly from the joke-tellers' standards of behavior, but that is beside the point—it is the incongruity of people like us behaving not like us that is funny, and comic superiority over similar or comparable groups that is most enjoyed [see also Wilson 1979, 138–41].

In each of the cases discussed the butts of the jokes are seen by the joke-tellers as a comic, distorted reflection of themselves, not as alien, unfamiliar, and inscrutable but as ambiguous, eccentric, and thus amusing peoples. The social boundaries of a people rarely correspond to the sharp lines of national frontiers, legal definitions of citizenship, or patriotic myth, and there are always individuals and indeed entire peoples who cannot easily be fitted into the crude categories of "insiders" and "outsiders," "us" and "them." It is they who are most likely to become the butts of ethnic jokes.

Ethnic Jokes and Stratification

The explanations of ethnic jokes about particular groups inevitably involve a consideration both of the relative position of joke-tellers and the butts of their jokes within a given social order and, where the butts constitute a nation of their own, of those local peculiarities of their system of stratification which have led to forms of behavior that are mocked by others.

The ethnic jokes about "stupid" and "canny" groups are closely linked to the performance of their members within competitive and changing societies. Those peoples who are the butt of jokes about stupidity tend to dwell on the backward periphery of a given society and to be (or to have been in the past) unskilled immigrants moving to new industrial centers. They are peasants or blue-collar workers who value security and stability of domicile and occupation and as such are seen by the joke-tellers as immobile and unenterprising, i.e., as comically stupid. In general, such peoples are relatively powerless, but both ethnic and nonethnic jokes about stupidity are also pinned on groups whose members exercise considerable political power, especially if it is based on a political monopoly rooted in inheritance, manipulation of a franchise, or a one-party state. English aristocrats, Afrikaners benefiting from apartheid, the Irish-American clients of urban political machines, Communist politicians and functionaries in Eastern Europe have all enjoyed power by excluding competition and in consequence have become the butt of jokes about stupidity.

The members of "canny" groups by contrast have lacked the privileges of monopoly but have produced a large proportion of mobile, enterprising, calculating individuals who have secured advancement in the most rapidly changing and competitive sectors of society, such as business, management, or the professions.

Thus the ethnic jokes about both the stupid and the canny reflect the differential placing of ethnic groups within modern industrial societies. The contrast is best seen in capitalist societies based on competition in the marketplace, but the basic model used to explain the ethnic jokes of the capitalist world can be extended in ways that also illuminate the political jokes of the socialist countries of Eastern Europe.

The jokes that the English-speaking peoples tell about each other can also be related to a similar model of stratification in which the English are identified with two static classes, a traditional aristocracy and a stratum of stolid, work-shy blue-collar workers, the Americans with a ruthlessly competitive and enterprising business class, and the Australians with a coarse and bloody-minded "rough rather than respectable" English working-class transported to a new and affluent setting. Once again the ethnic jokes are also jokes about social classes, though this does not mean that they can be crudely reduced to or regarded as jokes about class.

The same point may be made in relation to ethnic jokes about food. Ethnic jokes about eating are not, as has often been suggested, jokes about gluttony or excessive appetite. The extent of a person's eating is not treated as a moral issue in the jokes. The traditional religious condemnation of gluttony and use of fasting as a spiritual discipline lost their force long ago, and the modern obsession with dieting has given rise to jokes between the sexes rather than between ethnic groups. It is the urge to eat cheap, low-status food that is comic, not excessive eating in itself. These foods are often fattening, however, and this may contribute indirectly to the comic image of the low-status ethnic group, for members of high-status groups have traditionally been depicted as long and lean and those of low status as short, squat and gross. This is a very old comic antithesis but it is still a potent one. A former resident of a Polish district in Chicago, when asked by the author about the rise of ethnic jokes about the Poles in America, said, "They didn't seem to me to have the shape of elegant middle-class Americans. They were, how shall I say, . . . bulky." The bulkiness of the Poles or, in Britain, of the Irish is mocked in ethnic jokes and even more in cartoons, but the link with ethnic jokes about appetite is a tenuous one. Rather, both choice of food and ungainly appearance are independent aspects of ethnic jokes about the low position in the class system and status order of the butts of these jokes in their respective societies. Poor, low-status peoples are mocked for eating poor, low-status, shapeless, bulky, unsophisticated foods such as potatoes, spaghetti, porridge, or sausages, and for becoming in turn poor, low-status, shapeless, bulky, and unsophisticated in their physical appearance.

In America joke-tellers have tended to pin a broad range of lower-class traits, including crudity and dirtiness, on those groups who are the butt of ethnic jokes about stupidity. There is a contrast here with British ethnic jokes about the Irish, even though the latter jokes often refer more directly to occupation and social class. However, in both countries there exists a further genre of jokes based on other characteristics which are pinned on groups occupying the lowest rung of the stratification system who may be subjected to forms of racial exclusion or denigration which do not apply to the butts of the "stupid" jokes. Whereas the jokes about the "stupid" groups mock only their alleged failure within the familiar world of work and family, ethnic jokes about American blacks, Mexicans, Puerto Ricans, or West Indians often place them outside this framework altogether.

Ethnic jokes about militarism, belligerence, or cowardice are also indirectly related to the system of stratification of the peoples who are the butts of these jokes. The ethnic jokes of the sixteenth and early seventeenth centuries about the belligerent Welsh were based on the outlook of a class of impoverished small gentry who dominated the then backward and poor rural society of Wales and whose excessive pride in ancestry and martial tradition was seen by the English not only as ludicrous but as typical of Welsh people in general [see Davies 1985B]. Similarly the earliest ethnic jokes about German militarism refer to the territorial aristocracy of Prussia, a group dedicated to the service of state and army who became the dominant force in a late and shakily united country. It was the Prussian belief in order, discipline, obedience, and the planned use of force that became the basis of jokes about the German nation as a whole. As power shifted to the political elite of the National Socialist movement and the traditional values of the old class were intensified and distorted, so too new and harsher jokes about German militarism emerged.

In Italy there was no sizable equivalent class with a tradition of military service and loyalty to the state to act as the backbone of the army after unification. The fragmentation of the nation and the legacy of long and divisive foreign rule could not be overcome, and for most people their most important identity remained a local one. The state was there to be opposed, evaded, or milked, not to be served. When the Italian army failed in battle, other peoples, who had achieved a greater unity of army and people, revived an old tradition of jokes about Italian cowardice.

It is hardly surprising that there is such a close relationship between ethnic jokes and social stratification. Within any one society some ethnic groups have more power, wealth, and prestige than others, or at least their members are more likely to enjoy these privileges, and the pecking order of peoples is reflected in the ethnic jokes of that society. Within a given society it is noticeable too that the members of the dominant ethnic group tell jokes only about others and not about their own group. By contrast, members of subordinate ethnic groups, lower in the social scale or occupying a socially marginal position, regularly tell, invent, and enjoy jokes that mock the ethnic group to which they belong as well as or even more than jokes about those above them in the hierarchy. There is a striking asymmetry[2] here and, as is often the case, it is the phenomenon of the jokes that could be told but are not that calls for an explanation. The answer lies in the way that the members of a dominant ethnic majority unthinkingly and effortlessly regard their own way of life as normal, reasonable, a pattern for others to imitate, whereas the members of a subordinate or marginal ethnic group must, at the very least, take serious account of the mores of the dominant group. Indeed, this real asymmetry is almost a definition of the nature of dominance. The members of subordinate and marginal groups may perceive the dominant position of others as legitimate or may resent it but they feel relatively powerless and forced to accept it. Either way, they are regularly and routinely confronted with a gap between the dominant mores of the society and their own ways, whereas, even in an anomic and plural society characterized by the kinds of cultural contradiction outlined earlier, it is still possible for the members of a dominant nation or ethnic group to view the morality and traditions on which their own identity depends as a unique and consistent whole. Hence the members of the dominant group never come to see themselves as a people about whom ethnic jokes could be told.

The power and privilege enjoyed by the members of a particular people or by an elite may be based on inherited wealth and status, on performance in the marketplace, or on control of the state and its armed forces, or on various blends of all three, and the nature of the ethnic (and non-ethnic) jokes told about them closely reflects particular patterns of stratification. In particular the division between those classes, peoples, and nations who are the dynamic masters of change and competition and those who hold to stability, tradition, or frozen ideological doctrine is a central source of ethnic and political jokes throughout the modern world.

Ethnic Jokes and the Puzzles of Reality

When ethnic jokes are examined against their social and historical background, it is striking that many of them relate to social "puzzles" that have attracted the attention of sociologists, historians, and other observers who have expended a great deal of time and effort trying to resolve them. The "canny" outlook of neo-Calvinists obsessed by the Protestant Ethic, the repeated displays of panic and incompetence by Italian armies, the entrepreneurial enterprise of trading minorities, the emphatic egalitarianism of the Australians, the American drive for achievement, the decline of the British industrial spirit, the dogged obedience and frightening ferocity of Germans in uniform, the hard drinking of Irish-Americans are all past or present puzzles that seem to call for an explanation. In each case a substantial proportion of the members of a particular people have visibly behaved or still do behave in ways that are markedly different from those thought reasonable and appropriate by other roughly similar peoples. The curious observer asks why, but the tellers of ethnic jokes are content to treat these anomalies as a subject for humor and even mockery. Puzzling oddities are a standard subject for jokes, a common source of laughter. The inventors and tellers of ethnic jokes merely stretch and exaggerate the odd until it becomes the ludicrous.

Sometimes the jokes embody shrewd social observations, such as the importance of the all-male drinking group to the Irish or the Australians, the inner contradictions of canny Calvinism, the shrieking intensity of Hitler's speeches. Other contemporary jokes can be traced back to humorous anecdotes rooted in actual events—the Italian military debacles in North Africa or the savage destruction of Rotterdam are historical facts that have been incorporated in the jokes.

One of the most striking demonstrations of the responsiveness of ethnic jokes to social reality is the way they slowly change not in response to the popularity or unpopularity of the butt of the jokes but as a result of visible changes in the position and qualities of that group. As I have shown elsewhere [see Davies 1985B], the decline of English ethnic jokes about belligerent Welshmen and the rise of a new devious comic image were not based on any shift in the feelings of the English about their nearest neighbor, but reflected profound changes in Welsh society whose symptoms were visible to all. The nature of the (from the English point of view) puzzling oddities of their neighbors' behavior changed and so did the jokes, though after a marked time-lag. A similar point may be made about the response of American ethnic jokes to the upward mobility of the members of various immigrant groups—the changes in jokes about the Irish, and their replacement by jokes about the Poles are good examples of this. The gradual secularization of ethnic jokes about the Scots, and the incorporation of atrocity jokes into the corpus of ethnic jokes told about the

Germans not as a result of the hysterical anti-German propaganda of World War I but as a recognition of the horrific events of World War II provide further evidence of the way many ethnic jokes are rooted in social reality.

However, the perceptions of joke-tellers, like those of everybody else, are not merely selective and partial but are apt to be distorted by hopes, fears, expectations, and beliefs about others rooted in ideology, in dislikes that are not incidental but an integral part of a broad and intensely held view of how the world is and how it ought to be. Under such circumstances jokes are apt to flourish almost regardless of reality, as shown by the analysis of American World War I jokes about cowardly black soldiers. These jokes tell us far more about what the joke-tellers expected and perhaps hoped to see than about the real behavior of the butts of the jokes.

Nowhere is this phenomenon seen more clearly than in the case of ethnic jokes about the dishonesty, disloyalty, and perfidious conspiring of "excluded enterprisers" such as the Jews, the Armenians, overseas Chinese, or East African Asians. The "social puzzle" in this case is not the behavior of the butts of the jokes but the paranoid hostility of the surrounding peoples, who have proved all too willing to indulge in the persecution, expulsion, and even mass murder of hapless and helpless minorities. When one is confronted with the bizarre fantasies of *The Protocols of the Meetings of the Learned Elders of Zion* or *Mein Kampf* there is little point in examining the behavior of the Jews to see what provoked them. Anti-Semitism and other related beliefs were and are social facts in themselves that are far more powerful shapers of the perceptions of the joke-tellers than is the behavior of the excluded enterprisers, which on its own would probably only give rise to the kind of canny jokes told about Gabrovo or the Scots. Despite the congruence between the content of the jokes and the beliefs of the committed haters, it would be a mistake to regard those canny jokes that are told only about the excluded enterprisers as an extension of a hostile ideology directed against these groups. The most that can be said with certainty is that ethnic jokes of this kind are only coined in situations where anti-Semitic type ideologies or beliefs exist. The jokes are an acknowledgment of the existence of these views but cannot be said to be an endorsement of them.

The attempt to decide whether a particular type of ethnic joke grew out of a series of real events and experiences or out of a hostile fantasy produces results which are of necessity somewhat arbitrary and subject to revision. It is not just a simple question of deciding between truth and falsehood, but of (a) trying to discover whether the comic image on which the joke is based is a plausible one given the evidence available to the joke-tellers and (b) looking to see whether there is a serious counterpart to the comic image which forms part of a broad set of beliefs to which a significant proportion of the members of the joke-telling group are strongly attached and which can be shown to influence their behavior. On the basis of these two kinds of evidence it is sometimes possible to reach a reasonable though tentative conclusion as to why the members of a particular ethnic group have become the butt of jokes that ascribe a specific negative quality to them.

The Structure of Ethnic Jokes

Ethnic jokes in general are funnier than similar nonethnic jokes, in part because their internal structure is superior. America's most expert practitioner, Larry Wilde, once advised an aspiring joke-teller, "Now that joke would be 18% funnier if you said it was a [Puerto Rican] stealing shoes from K-mart" [quoted in Nilsen and Nilsen 1984, 33]. The size of the % may be questioned and alternative, appropriate ethnic groups slotted in, but in general terms Wilde is right.

The reason is that joke-tellers have devised a potent formula for the construction of ethnic jokes based on the convention that the butt of a particular type of joke is labeled stupid, canny, cowardly, etc. Indeed, any direct or indirect mention of a well-known and well-labeled group can act as a hint that the tale being told is a joke on one of these conventional themes. The joke-teller thus has available to him the essential ingredients of a joke—two possible contradictory scripts, one based on events in the life of a real people, the other a wild fantasy based on the comic convention that they possess some unwanted human quality to an absurd degree. The ethnic joke is a misleading tale that begins as a plausible account of a real people and then suddenly switches to an absurd script based on a well-known, established convention. Thus not only the content of the jokes but their very structure depends on the use of ethnicity.

The force of this point can be seen from the failure of attempts to create ethnic jokes around fictitious groups, such as the Smogarians or the Ethnicians [see Adams 1975; Phillips 1976, 73–74]. Their names, like those of the equally fake Wallonians and Pireneans invented by the social psychologists, sound suitably alien but the jokes fail because there is no established conventional script of stupidity, cowardice, etc. to which the audience can relate the jokes. Such a script is essential if a joke is to be understood quickly [see Apte 1985], and in humor speed is essential—a good joke must explode with the punch line as the audience suddenly "gets" the joke [see Freud 1960, 234; Pielko 1984, 101]. A good joke-teller can manipulate the response of the audience by skillfully adjusting his or her delivery and timing [see Wilson 1979, 76], but it nonetheless pays to have jokes that are well-constructed. Jokes about Smogarians are one category of what Raskin [1985, 205–206] has termed pseudo-ethnic jokes which fail because they cannot evoke a specific ethnic script. Indeed Raskin goes so far as to declare that a "joke is truly ethnic if and only if its main opposition or one of its main oppositions involves at least one truly ethnic script. The ethnic scripts are . . . a set of pseudo-encyclopaedic scripts which have to be internalized prior to the production or consumption of ethnic jokes . . . if the joke is truly ethnic the removal of the evoked ethnic script renders it incomprehensible . . . [and] the targeted group may be substituted for only by another group which shares the evoked ethnic script with it" [1985, 207].

Raskin has here accurately indicated why it is not possible randomly to switch the identities of the ethnic groups who are the butts of jokes. Even if the audience were to comprehend a pseudo-ethnic joke by spotting analogies with true script-based ethnic jokes they would do so far too slowly and this would ruin the joke. By contrast, jokes that begin "two misers . . . " or "a pusillanimous poltroon . . . " or "mister garbage lover . . . " or "the little moron . . . " provide too much information too early in the joke and undercut the surprise of the punch line. As indicated earlier, ethnic jokes are very well constructed and are probably rather more than 18% funnier.

Extensions, Predictions, and Confirmations

The core of this study has been (1) the identifying of patterns among the most common scripts used in ethnic jokes and the relating of these patterns to the uncertainty with which the citizens of modern industrial societies regard such basic activities as work and war, and (2) the provision of explanations concerning the pinning of specific comic scripts on particular ethnic groups. One way of testing whether this approach to these problems is a fruitful one is to ask whether it can be applied and extended to other types of jokes and other peoples. I am reasonably sure that it can. Thus in the many societies where alcohol is both the most usual, convivial, and euphoriant drug and a source of erratic conduct and violence there are ethnic jokes both about overenthusiastic drinkers and about the tense and sometimes unsuccessfully teetotal. By contrast, there are few jokes about alcohol [see Raskin 1985, 23] in orthodox Muslim societies that have successfully banned alcohol and few jokes about ethnic groups such as the Jews or the Italians who consume alcohol regularly but in a controlled and moderate way. Once again it is loss of balance in a world of insecure guidelines that provides the basis of ethnic jokes! It may also be that I am being too cautious in not accepting Zijderveld's [1983] extension of my central thesis to ethnic jokes about the over- and under-sexed. If he is right, then another large segment of popular joking fits the same basic pattern.

I am also willing to predict that the butts of ethnic jokes in similar countries whose humor I have not yet examined will be determined by the same forces and with the same result as those I have already described. In particular I believe that when humor scholars examine the jokes of a country or reasonably homogeneous cultural and linguistic domain other than those I have cited they will find jokes about a "stupid" group who dwell on the edge of that nation or domain and who are in consequence perceived as comically ambiguous by the dominant people of the center. I think it likely that they will also be rustics who migrate to the center in search of unskilled manual work. The investigation of jokes about other traits should reveal either a real and visible pattern of behavior by the butts of jokes that makes the script of the jokes plausible (though not necessarily seriously believed) or the existence of an explicit and coherent ideology that contains a strongly held stereotype that is the serious counterpart of the comic script. The particular "canny" script associated with "excluded enterprisers" is likely to have a serious and dangerous ideological counterpart, whereas other scripts are probably rooted in visible, plausible yet puzzling aspects of the way the members of the group that is the butt of the jokes behave or have behaved in the past. However, there are exceptions to this rule and careful empirical investigation of each case is advisable.

What Can Jokes about Peoples Tell Us about Society?

Now that some degree of understanding of the nature and the subjects of ethnic jokes has been established it should prove possible to use them as a means of exploring social conditions. The jokes already analyzed in this study cannot be used for such a purpose, for their significance has only become apparent when they have been examined in their social and historical context and matched against other types of data. It should, however, prove possible to apply some of the generalizations developed in the preceding chapters to "calibrate" jokes so that they can be used as a crude but valid diagnostic tool [see Apte 1985, 16–17]. Such jokes should reveal the areas of moral ambiguity and ambivalence in the society where they are told and illuminate the relationship between the joke-tellers and the butts of their jokes. In regard to this latter point, the ethnic (and indeed, nonethnic) jokes that are likely to prove the most revealing are those told about stupidity. Where jokes of this type occur we can be reasonably sure that the joke-tellers regard the butts of these jokes as a similar people but occupying a peripheral position relative to themselves. The jokes thus indicate who is at the center of a culture and who is at the edge and that the culture of the butts of the jokes is subordinate to and derivative from that of the joke-tellers. Ethnic jokes about stupidity are also jokes told at the expense of groups seen as static and unenterprising by those who see themselves as (and who indeed often are) dynamic and competitive. In an open society the jokes indicate the existence of a known and established cultural and economic pecking order of ethnic groups regardless of official rhetoric about equality or pluralism. The butts of the jokes may be liked or disliked, but they are not esteemed. In more closed societies where the butts of the jokes enjoy political power, jokes about their stupidity are an indication that they lack that particular modern form of legitimacy known as merit. These are the kinds of implicit messages that have been carried by jokes about stupidity in the past and it is reasonable to suppose that such jokes can be interpreted in the same way in the future and in societies other than those that have been examined in detail in this study.

There is also an important negative finding that emerges from this study and which particularly applies to jokes about stupidity, viz. that ethnic jokes in general are not a good indicator of the joke-tellers' feelings toward the butts of their jokes, which may range from dislike and hostility to amity and affection. People do not necessarily dislike those whom they disesteem, and the throwers of custard pies do not regard their targets in the same way that those who hurl rocks or grenades do.[3] Those who seek to use ethnic jokes as a predictor of conflict would be better advised to study more immediate indices of political tension, for there is no point in delving for covert resentments in a world where so much direct evidence is available. Whether a particular ethnic or geographical source of ethnic jokes about stupidity explodes like the Punjab or remains as placid as Newfoundland will depend on the politicians, not the joke-tellers. Similarly, political jokes about the ineptitude of the "People's Dynasties" of Eastern Europe indicate these rulers' lack of legitimacy but hardly their subjects' willingness or ability to move from alienation to revolt.

There is one possible exception to the rule that jokes cannot warn—the case of the two kinds of jokes told about canny groups. Where these jokes relate only to the innocuous, stingy, and crafty behavior imputed to, say, the Scots, then the butts of the jokes are likely to thrive and prosper unmolested. Where canniness is stretched to include dishonesty, disloyalty, and conspiracy, however, there is cause for concern and vigilance even if there seems to be little immediate threat to the butts of the jokes. The jokes in themselves are harmless (like all jokes they are the result, not the cause, of a social situation), but they indicate that the peoples who feature in the jokes are perceived in that society as "excluded enterprisers," a category of peoples which we know is liable to experience sudden attack and persecution.

The analyses of jokes not only about stupidity and canniness but also about militarism, cowardice, food, etc., should prove a guide to the interpretation of similar jokes told in other times and places, provided that no major shift in cultural assumptions is involved. Behind such "new" jokes, as behind those already analyzed, there is likely to lurk the blurred or problematic boundary of a people's identity, a "puzzle of reality," or a facet of the system of stratification. A knowledge of this study should at least enable observers to know where to look for an explanation and to identify the social significance of these as yet unexamined or even unknown jokes about peoples more quickly and certainly than if they restricted their studies to the particular culture in which that type of joke occurs.

There are many ways in which jokes about peoples can be used to illuminate social situations, but it should not be forgotten that jokes are an important social phenomenon in themselves. It seems likely that most people spend a larger portion of their lifetime in telling, reading, or listening to jokes than they do voting, praying, stealing, or rioting. The consequences may not be as significant, but the time spent on such an activity does indicate the importance to the jokers themselves of this form of enjoyment. Jokes about peoples have long been a large and popular part of jokes in general and if the reader now feels that he or she has a greater understanding of them, then my purpose in undertaking this study will have been attained.

Notes

I. Introduction

1. On the nature and definition of ethnicity and other related terms see Barth 1969, 9–11; Glazer and Moynihan 1975, 4; Hayes 1960, 1–4; Krausz n.d.; Krejci and Velinsky 1981; Smith 1981; Weber 1961, 305–06.

2. See Andreski 1973, 114; Fishman; Fishman and Nahirny 1966, 122; Kusielewicz 1969, 97–98, 103; Parsons 1975, 64–65.

3. See Herberg 1960, 21; Petersen 1975; Smith 1981, 154–56; Wirth 1961.

4. I.e., certain key leaders made crucial decisions which a majority of the group concerned accepted or supported.

5. On the difference between race and ethnicity see Gilley 1978, 85–92, 105; Rex 1969, 151. A clear distinction should also be drawn between pressures on an ethnic minority to assimilate, i.e., to adopt the culture, language, and religion of the dominant group [see Andreski 1973, 114; Glazer and Moynihan 1975, 14; Herberg 1960, 21; Schoeck 1969, 57], and pressures to exclude them as part of a racial ideology which may be almost the opposite of assimilationism, i.e., the potential assimilation and adhesion of the minority is seen as a threat to the very integrity of the nation [e.g., see Hitler 1983, 47]. These are two very different situations and give rise to very different ethnic jokes.

6. See Biberaj 1984; Eisenstadt 1980, 1, 3; Glazer and Moynihan 1975, 5–7; Rokkan and Urwin 1983, 118; Smith 1981; Zenner 1970.

7. See Adamson 1974, 17–18; Legman 1982 vol. 2, 14; Middleton and Moland 1959; Schwartz 1973, 75.

8. For further instances and studies of the use of humor and caricature (including references to ethnicity) to sharpen or to disguise an argument see Ashton 1888; Curtis 1971; James 1984; Lancaster 1941; Larsen 1980; Low 1949. I have not rigidly excluded such humor, as it clearly overlaps with the main data of this study, viz. anonymous ethnic jokes, and I have quoted examples of it where relevant, but it is in the main a quite different phenomenon.

9. See Goodrich, Jules, and Goodrich 1954; Martineau 1972; Mintz 1980 and 1986; Wilson 1979, 82; Ziv 1984, 3.

10. On the uses of humor, including jokes, in the course of social interaction see Coser 1959; Emerson 1969; Goffman 1968; Haas 1972, 1974, 1977; MacArthur 1965, 147; Mulkay 1987; Schutz 1977, 41; Sykes 1966.

11. I have drawn heavily on the extensive files of material in the University of California, Berkeley Folklore Archive, in the Folklore Institute at Indiana University, Bloomington, and in the House of Humour and Satire, Gabrovo, Bulgaria.

12. On the difficulties caused by the censorship and bowdlerization of jokes seen as obscene or irreverent especially in the nineteenth century, see Al. Goldstein's foreword to the 1982 edition of Hall 1934 [*Anecdota Americana* series 2]. See also Ashton 1888, 83; Davies 1984, 154; Hatton 1893, 177–78; Lawrence 1973,

28–29, 36–38; Ramsay 1873, 186, 352–53; Seton 1903, xii; Wardroper 1976, 3–5. For more contemporary attempts at censorship see Hewison 1981, 25, 41, 67, 78, 81, 93, and Welsch 1967.

13. On the nature of stereotypes see Ashmore and Del Boca 1981. Comic ethnic scripts and serious ethnic stereotypes are hopelessly confused in Adams 1975 (6, 79); Burma 1946 (714); Klymasz 1970; Schwartz 1973; Welsch 1967; and surprisingly even at times in Feinburg 1978 (72) and Helmreich 1982 (1, 16, 71, 167). It is not necessary to believe in an ethnic script to find the jokes funny, whereas an ethnic stereotype has to be believed in to be of any significance—not simply in a nominal sense but as a crude guide to action. Even those who believe that there is some truth behind the comic allegation of an ethnic script may well not be influenced by this in their daily activities. Particular cases where there are strong parallels between the content of an ethnic script and of a strongly held, indeed ideological stereotype are discussed in the text.

14. See Goodrich, Jules, and Goodrich 1954, 179–80; Kimmins 1928, 34–39; Morreau 1983, 15–19; Mulkay 1987; Raskin 1985, 2, 30–33, 116; Wilson 1979, 12–13, 18–19.

15. On the superiority theory of humor see Aristotle *Poetics* 1449; Carritt 1922–23; Freud 1960, 224; Hobbes *Human Nature* 9 1840, 46; Morreau 1983, 4–14; Pearsall 1975; Plato *Philebus,* 48a to 50a; Raskin 1985, 36; Redfern 1984, 123; Rosten 1973, 12; Wilson 1979, 138–41; Ziv 1984, 104. On the extension of the theory using the concepts of affiliates, reference groups, and identification classes see LaFave, Haddad, and Marshall 1974; LaFave and Mannell 1976; Wolff, Smith, and Murray 1934.

16. For discussion and illustration of some of the complex issues involved when the members of a group invent, tell, and enjoy jokes about a group with which they are associated, see Ben-Amos 1973, 112, 118–19; Danielson 1975; Dunkling 1981, 92; Jarvenpa 1976; Kusielewicz 1969, 100–03; Limón 1977, 35; Middleton 1959, 176; Mindess 1971; Pahl 1984, 189; Raskin 1985, 21; Rosenberg and Shapiro 1958, 70; Wilson 1973, 175–77; Zenner 1970, 96, 111; Ziv 1986A.

17. For critical comments on the various humor-as-aggression theses, see Oring 1975; Schoeck 1969, 9–10; Zijderveld 1983; Zillman and Cantor 1972, 147. My own main criticisms are that those who seek conflict, hostility, and aggression in and behind jokes (a) confuse the element of aggression inherent in many forms of play involving competition, rivalry, etc. with the "real world" aggression of pogroms, riots, wars. The former can spill over into the latter as when a "friendly" football match produces a riot, but this is a deviant case where the rules of playful aggression [see Feinburg 1978, 7–9, 48] have been broken. These rules are not as Kravitz [1977, 295–96; see also Apte 1985, 136] seems to think, a separately generated constraint on aggression, but are an integral part of the game and of the playful activity of joking [e.g., see Whiting 1986, 101, and Wood and Wood 1976 for empirical examples]; (b) use these terms as a ragbag explanation of why jokes exist, without discriminating between types of conflict, reasons why a conflict exists, intensity of conflict, etc. In consequence, they are able to shuttle between the individual, social psychological, and social uses of the terms in a superficial and misleading way and tend to exaggerate the level of conflict and its importance for the joke-tellers [e.g., see Kravitz 1977, 281–82, 286–87].

18. For instances of scholars grossly overreacting to the jokes they have studied, see Bourhis et al. 1977, 261; Burma 1946, 714; Gruner 1978, 17; Klymasz 1970; Schwartz 1973; Welsch 1967. For descriptions of overreaction see Cross 1980; Danielson 1975; Richler 1986, 99; Rosenberg and Shapiro 1958, 72; Thorp 1964.

19. For accounts of real and would-be censorship of jokes see Brown and Bryant 1983, 183; Doyno 1983, 61; Gruner 1978; Hughes 1986; Morreau 1983, 103; Stephenson 1951, 570; Wilson 1979, 192, 198; Ziv 1984, 99.

II. The Stupid and the Canny

1. It is perhaps significant that I have to use a Scots word to convey the uncanny mixture of shrewdness and stinginess comically ascribed to that people [see Carroll 1973; Junior 1925, 3; Todd 1977, 10]. While it is possible to disaggregate this quality into two separate scripts [see Raskin 1985, 180–88], I am inclined to follow Aristotle's view [see *Ethics* Book 6 1004a 11 to 32, 1067a 28 to b18, and 1138b 35 to 1139a 16] that rationality has a calculative as well as a contemplative dimension and that the vice of "illiberality involves both going too far in getting and not going far enough in spending." In the context of a modern industrial society the virtue of a balanced view of work and gain is flanked by the opposed vices of those who take these activities too seriously (the canny) and those who don't or can't take them seriously enough (the stupid). In any small work group the rate-busters, the free-loaders, the chiselers are pushed toward the rough norm for the group by a variety of informal sanctions that include ridicule and joking [see Haas 1972; Hirszowicz 1981, 136–37; Roethlisberger and Dickson 1934; Sabel 1983, 173]. There are other qualities that could be built into this very general antithesis but they are the subject of far fewer jokes. There are ethnic jokes about laziness and lack of punctuality [e.g., see Esar 1978, 427–29, 436–38] as departures from the work ethic but they are fewer than those about stupidity and are not necessarily ascribed to the same groups. Similarly, there are very few jokes about or against people who are overgenerous or too good-natured (there is one in Newman 1974, 76, but I have found no others). It thus seems reasonable to treat the two large sets of ethnic jokes about the stupid and the canny as ridiculing opposed and juxtaposed failings, as mocking opposite extremes from a position felt to be moderate, balanced, equipoised.

2. The space shuttle *Challenger* blew up in 1986 with seven people on board, including Christa McAuliffe, a schoolteacher. The Chernobyl nuclear reactor disaster spewed radioactive material over the Ukraine, some of which blew into other countries. The Aberfan coal-tip slid downhill and engulfed a school, killing the children and their teachers. The *Herald of Free Enterprise* car ferry sank leaving Zeebrugge in Belgium for England. A large number of people died in a fire that began under the escalators at King's Cross subway station. For details of the shuttle disaster see McConnell 1987, and of the Aberfan tip see Levin 1979, 40–43. For comments on these jokes and others like them see Abrahams 1961, Hughes 1986, Lewis 1986, Oring 1987.

3. Most but not all jokes are about technical disasters with an element of human error rather than, say, an earthquake, a hurricane, a volcano, a flood. There are exceptions, such as the Ethiopian famine or the spread of AIDS, but it may be significant that unsubstantiated rumor has tried to make even these natural disasters appear to be of human origin.

4. For further studies of the ways in which jokes, including ethnic jokes and jokes about stupidity, are produced and employed by workers in high-risk occupations, see Haas 1972, 1974, and 1977.

5. See Hirszowicz 1981, 32–33; Marx 1974, 341–42; Porter, Lawler, and Hackman 1975, 282–83; Sabel 1982, 13–15, 32–33; Šik 1967, 139; Smith 1902 (1776), 4–12, 618.

6. See Bell 1979; Kumar 1977; Lipowski 1970, 279; Wight 1972.

7. See Bell 1979, xvi, 11, 269; Herzberg 1968, 1–5, 33, 166–79; Hirszowicz 1981, 73; Porter, Lawler, and Hackman 1975, 267; Weber 1947, 43; Wight 1972, 152.

8. See Arensburg and Niehoff 1975, 369–74; Bell 1979, 147; Cunningham 1980, 45, 178; Dumazedier 1967, 84; Lowerson and Myerscough 1977.

9. See Arensburg and Niehoff 1975, 369; Cunningham 1980, 57, 67–73, 150; Dumazedier 1967, 9, 13; Lowerson and Myerscough 1977.

10. See Bell 1961A, 254–59, and 1979, 69; Dumazedier 1967, x; Lipowski 1970; Mendel 1970B; Wight 1972; Wilson 1969, 263; Wolfenstein 1975, 394.

11. See Bell 1979, 269; Herzburg 1968; Hirszowicz 1981, 32; Porter, Lawler, and Hackman 1975, 47; Wight 1972, 122.

12. See Porter, Lawler, and Hackman 1975, 282–83; Sabel 1982, 13; Taylor Nelson 1984.

13. E.g., Parkinson 1958 and 1971; Peter and Dana 1982; Peter and Hull 1970; Preston 1955. See also Chase and French 1913, 224.

III. Who Gets Called Stupid?

1. The table is based on data in the folklore archives of the University of California, Berkeley and Indiana University, Bloomington, plus a large number of other oral and written sources, including those mentioned in the text and the following: (a) Specific studies of ethnic jokes about stupidity: Clements 1973; Colleville and de Zepelin 1896; Craigie 1898; Dundes 1971 and 1975B; Holbek 1975; Jarvenpa 1976; Klymasz 1970; Raskin 1985; G. Thomas 1976; Verlure 1983; Viera 1980; Zenner 1970; (b) Collections of ethnic jokes centered on stupidity: Cagney 1979A and 1979B; Carver 1980; Chambers 1979, 1980, and 1981; Chitrouflet and Van der Fried 1981; Colombo 1975; *De Gaeve Jyder* n.d.; Guillois and Guillois 1979A; Hornby 1977, 1978; Isnard 1977; Koenderman, Langen, and Viljoen 1975; Kowalski 1974; Krögerson 1977; *Lune Jyder* 1971 and 1973; MacHale 1976, 1977A, 1984; Macklin and Erdman 1976; Ogoiski 1975; Stack 1977; *Ten Best Polish Jokes* 1983; Tulk 1971, 1972, 1973, 1974; van den Broeck 1976; Wilde 1973, 1975A, 1977, 1978A, 1978C; Yearhouse 1974A, 1974B, 1979. Also see Keane 1967; Theroux 1975.

2. This seems to be true more generally even beyond the realm of ethnic jokes; e.g., see Bergson 1911, 23. The principle may even be stretched to explain why human beings at a zoo laugh at the antics of the apes, who of all animals are most like them (cf. Linden 1981) but not at snakes or sharks, whom they find alien, sinister, and threatening.

3. Curiously it is also the case that those living at the edge of national and cultural units as diverse as the British Isles, France, and Spain [Lynn 1979A and 1979B], and Poland [Helitzer 1984B, 168] have lower IQ scores than those living at the center, which might help to account for the jokes about stupidity told by the peoples of the center. However, the mechanism suggested is differential migration of the more intelligent from the edge to the center, which would make the migrants from (who are the visible representatives of) the edge appear highly intelligent. I suspect the phenomenon may rather be similar to that observed in relation to the migrations of Poles to the United States. The original migrants scored very low on the tests, but today their Polish-American descendants score at about the American average. At one time unfamiliarity with the culture made them appear stupid (and hence the jokes), but this was ignorance, not innate lack of intelligence. Today they have caught up, but the earlier comic image remains, probably because of their position in the American class structure.

I doubt if many of those telling jokes about stupidity believe that the butts really are stupid, and indeed there is evidence that they do not hold such beliefs [see McCosh 1976, 119]. However, in the case of aristocrats and of people living in small, isolated communities, and especially on islands, there does seem to be a real belief that inbreeding has made them simpleminded. [Re aristocrats see comments in the UCBFA files on jokes from England, Austria, Hungary. For islanders see Pahl 1984, 189; Wood and Wood 1976, 90.] The response of the islanders is to exploit the myth for their own ends to fool others [Wood and Wood 1976, 90] and it is they rather than outsiders who tell self-deprecating jokes that cover a real pride in their origins [Pahl 1984, 189].

4. See Chadwick 1967, 230; Noel 1971, 264–67. For further data re the marginality of Newfoundland see Cohen 1975; McNaught 1969, 275; Yannopoulos 1985.

5. General Dambrowski was the head of Napoleon's Polish legion who was promised that the French would help him free Poland from Russian, Prussian, and Austrian domination. Hence, the patriotic song "March, March, Dambrowski." The Polish word *Niemiec* for German is derived from *Niemy* 'dumb' (i.e., can't speak Polish) but it does not carry the same implication of stupidity that it would in America. Similar derivations of words for particular foreigners from the indigenous term for 'dumb' are to be found in Afrikaans, Czech, and Russian.

6. For humor concerning remote frontiers and language confusion see also Hašek 1974, 394, 535–42; Lamberts-Hurrellbrinck 1894.

7. See Andreski 1973, 63; Demerath 1969, 333; Golde 1975; Greeley 1972, 89; Herberg 1960, 212–14; Lenski 1961, 320–21; O'Dea 1962, 20, 80, 99, 119–20; Wilson 1969, 134.

8. For collections of jokes about country dwellers and of the comic nicknames they have acquired, and also for the social background to and comments on these jokes, see Adair 1982; Adams 1975, 8; Apte 1985, 120, 197; *Brewer's* 1981; Copeland 1940, 78–105; Cornelisen 1969, 63–64; Cremer 1894; Danielson 1975, 50–52; Dudeney 1917; Dwyer 1975; *East Anglia's Humour* 1976; Esar 1978; *Facetiae of Poggio*; Faure 1979; Feinburg 1978, 61; *Hillbilly Laugh Book* 1972; Limón 1977, 42; New Punch Library 1933 *Mr. Punch's Country Manners*; Owen 1971; Pearsall 1975; Powers and Powers 1975; Rockwell 1981, xxii–xxiii; Runninger and Powers 1971; Schwartz 1973, 10; Sullivan 1903; Welsch 1967, 183; Wilde 1984.

9. E.g., see comments in Cornelisen 1969, 244; Holbek 1975; Koenderman, Lengen, and Viljoen 1975, 4. On the rural background see Lutz 1962, 95; Possony 1976.

10. For more jokes about Aggies, Hokies, etc., and for comments on their social background and basis see *Aggie Games You Can't Lose* 1977, *Best of 606 Aggie Jokes* 1977, and (Hundred and One) *101 Aggie Jokes* (8 volumes); Key 1949, 244; Legman 1982 (1975) vol. 2, 961; Randolph 1952; Stewart 1963, 94–99.

11. On the poor peasant origins and low occupational status on arrival of immigrants who are the butts of these jokes see Andreski 1973, 83; Bodnar 1976; Clark 1962, 76–77, 165–66; Edwards 1975, 132; Fox 1970, 58–60, 73; Haiman 1974, 3; Helmreich 1982, 40–41; Kusielewicz 1969, 102; Lutz 1962, 146–47; Nichols 1973, 28; Sowell 1981.

12. On the lower-class background of the butts of ethnic jokes about stupidity see Andreski 1973, 63, 83; "Diverse Ethnic Roots of Bay Area Residents" 1984; Dundes 1971, 199–201; Greeley 1972, 121–24; Lang 1976; Lutz 1962, 95; Lyon 1969, 167; Morawska 1977; Renkiewicz 1973, vii, 10, 13, 21; Stephenson 1951, 571; Zurawski 1975, 123–25.

For examples of ethnic jokes and other humor directly related to social class in addition to those in the text see Daniells 1965, 148; Dawson 1979; Dudeney 1917, 19; Heywood n.d., 81; Horn 1980, 168; Hornby 1977; Montgomerie and Montgomerie 1948, 121; Orkin 1973, 59; B. Phillips 1976; E. Phillips 1974B, 1975A, 1975B; Robey 1920; Spalding 1978, 78–79; Stackman 1953; Tidy 1969; Wilde 1981, 160.

13. For further examples of such jokes and comments on them see Banc and Dundes 1986; Beckman 1969 and 1980; Davies 1982D, 1988A, and in press; Draitser 1978; Dundes 1971; Kolasky 1972; Leininger 1982; *Pass the Port Again* 1981; Schiff

1975 and 1978; Sturman 1984; Tarnóky 1977; Zinoviev 1985, 213. For parallel cases of jokes from and about more traditional autocracies see Brandes 1977; Ferrer 1978; García 1977; Gossett 1972, 116; Yao 1946, 234.

14. For jokes and humor regarding Ford and Douglas-Home see Brodnick 1976; Ford 1987; *Encyclopaedia of Insulting Behavior* 1981, 44; Horn 1980, 512; Ingrams 1971, 15–16, 90–91; Jones and Smith 1983, 178; *National Lampoon* 1979, 18; Pielko 1984, 55–56; Rees 1982, 19, 47, 71; Sherrin and Shand 1984, 50–51, 96; Sorel 1978; Thomas 1985, 39; Wilson 1979, 189.

On the political background to the jokes see Davidson 1981; Ford 1979.

15. On the nature of the monopolistic social order that generates the problems I have described and on the problems themselves see Botting 1986, 294; Butterfield 1982; Cooper 1975, 197; Conquest 1971, 543, 586, and 1980; Fidelius 1984, 4; Haraszti 1977; Hirszowicz 1980 and 1986, esp. 11–20, 36, 68; Klempski 1981, 84; Krejci 1976, 213–17; Langdon-Davies 1949, 18–21, 57; Parry 1966, 46–57, 71–73; Polanyi 1940; Popovsky 1980; Tame 1984; von Mises 1974, 385; Wesson 1984, 188–96; Zinoviev 1985, 89–91.

16. See Grant 1982, 34; Morgan and Langford 1981; Pile 1980, 30. Some sources say they wanted to make the value of π (pi) equal 4.

17. For stupidity jokes and humor about the English upper class see Barr and York 1982 and 1983; Bentley and Esar 1962, 21, 41; Bradley 1982, 222 notes 79–80; Gilbert 1983, *Iolanthe*, Act 2, 236–37; Hicks 1936, 98–99; Hoggart 1981, 39; Lynn and Jay 1981; Melly and Fawkes 1962, esp. 31; Phillips 1974B, 7, 27.

For jokes about County Bobby, Arisztid and Tasziló, and other inane Central European aristocrats see Böhm 1983, 9–12; Ember 1988, 24–30; Grill 1949; Heinrich and Lothar 1979; and UCBFA Austria and Hungary files.

IV. The Stupid and the Dirty

1. See Greenburg 1972; Gruner 1978, 17, 60; Klymasz 1974; Kravitz 1977; Schwartz 1973. For earlier statements but about a quite different case, see Barron 1950; Burma 1946; Stephenson 1951. For an overview, see Apte 1985; Martineau 1972; Raskin 1985, 36–37. For some telling criticisms, see Apte 1985, 68; Mintz 1980 and 1986; Oring 1975.

2. If the jokes were reducible to covert serious statements then the conclusion would follow. It is worth noting for comparative purposes that German propaganda and abuse of the "filthy Poles" in World War II was an indication of extreme hostility, and both a prelude to and an accompaniment and justification of the most appalling persecution and exploitation of the Poles. See Bethell 1976, 140–55; Goebbels 1982 (1939–41), 16, 36–37, 274; Henry and Hillel 1976, 145–47, 180, 240; Szarota 1978. See also Freud 1960, 49–51, 72, 78–81, and Oring 1984, 42 regarding the view held of the "dirty Ostjude" from Galicia in Austrian Poland by German-speakers before World War I. These jokes rode on top of a serious anti-Semitic stereotype of the Galician Jews [see Hitler 1974] that had genocidal consequences. We may also note that ethnic jokes about "dirty Poles" were once common in German Silesia [see UCBFA Germany file]. It is thus a priori reasonable for McCosh to interpret her jokes in the way she does given her theoretical assumptions. It is the theory itself that is wrong.

3. The same or similar points are asserted without empirical evidence to back them up in Schwartz 1973; Ternhag 1975; Welsch 1967, 183. Their arguments are circular.

4. During the fifteen years 1969–1984, about 750 people lost their lives in Ulster and about 4,000 were injured in a population of 1.5 million to which may be added between 10,000 and 20,000 soldiers (depending on the year) brought in

from Great Britain. In 1984 there were about 9,000 soldiers, 8,000 R.U.C.'s and 4,000 local reservists in action in Ulster. It is a tragic situation for the people in Ulster but it rarely constitutes any real threat to the 50 million people in the main island of Great Britain.

The British have in the past felt that their very national survival was at risk in wars with the Spanish, the French, and the Germans. In the twentieth century alone they have (also) been at war with Transvaal, the Orange Free State, Turkey, Austria, Hungary, Russia, Bulgaria, Italy, Japan, Romania, Egypt, and Argentina, and have fought insurgents in Iraq, India, Palestine, Malaya, Aden, Kenya, and Cyprus. There have also been internal ethnic tensions in Britain due to the arrival of substantial new populations of immigrants from Europe, the West Indies, and South Asia. Despite all these possibilities for conflict-generated jokes, the Irish have consistently remained the butt of British ethnic jokes about stupidity.

5. The idea that people tell jokes about Poles in America or the Irish in Britain as a means of avoiding telling jokes about the blacks [see af Klintberg 1983; Dundes 1971, 202; Helmreich 1982, 169] is absurd [see critique in Oring 1975]. There is no shortage of jokes about blacks in oral circulation in the United States [see Katz 1979; Kimmel 1977; Legman 1986 vol. 2, 960; Welsch 1967, 184] or in joke-books [see Alvin 1983A and B; Cobb 1923 and 1925; Ernst 1927; House 1943, 1944, and 1945; Wilde 1975C and 1984], and America even exports them to Britain (author's observation), to Canada [Lyons 1987, 47–53], to France [Climent-Galant 1979, 75–79], and to Sweden [af Klintberg 1983]. The British and the French also have their own indigenous jokes about the recently acquired ethnic minorities of assorted blacks and Pakistanis in Britain and of Arabs from North Africa in France [see Climent-Galant 1979, 59–71; Kravitz 1977; Midwinter 1979, 188; Onyeama 1977; Williams 1973]. The only evidence in support of the "displaced aggression" thesis is that the standard jokes about Poles are told on American television whereas the typical jokes about blacks are not [see *America, the Golden Age of Comedy* 1973, 52; Legman 1986 vol. 2, 960; Welsch 1967, 184]. This is partly an outcome of the American politics of censorship whereby the members of an ethnic or indeed any other group if they have the organization and motivation [see Kusielewicz 1969 on the Poles' lack of these] can lean on liberal television producers and pusillanimous sponsors to ban jokes they don't like and partly because American jokes about blacks tend to involve gross obscenity or to be violent tales in which something nasty happens to a black. Sambo may be dead but Rastus is alive and well in the jokes of coteries of "good old boys," both American and British. It is also fairly easy to see why such jokes do not appear on television:

> Liza: "Rastus, Rastus, you come away from de edge of dat platform or de train's goin' to come along and suck you off." Rastus: "Come awn train!" [American and, by derivation, British 1980s]

6. For further comments on Irish wit, see Gilley 1978, 82–85; Jennings 1976; LeFanu 1893; Macaulay 1979 (1848–65), 294. For jokes in which it is displayed, see Harvey 1904; Phillips 1975A. For sympathetic albeit sentimental portrayals, see Lover 1907 (1842); Somerville and Ross 1970.

7. See also Chesney 1970, 66–67; Clark 1962, 76–77; Gilley 1978, 99–100; Stanley 1910, 20–21. For later periods, see Fisk 1985, 227–28; McCaffrey 1976, 74.

8. Regarding the "dirty" Americans of the mid-nineteenth century, see Dickens 1902 (1842), 65, 170; Emerson 1856, 271, 296. For both humorous and serious references to the American habit of spitting, see *American Jests and Anecdotes* n.d., 216–17; Atkinson and Searle 1963, 18; Borrow 1955 (1862), 259–60; de

Grand'Combe 1932, 171; Dickens 1902 (1842), 91–92, 99–101; Gross 1927, 158; McPhee 1981, 44; Olsen 1970, 9; Williams 1980, 158.

9. For examples of jokes and humor about the "dirty French" see Derrière 1976; Mikes 1950, 85; Not the nine o'clock news team 1981, December 2; Wintle 1968, 253.

10. Irish readers will perceive the humor implicit in the library rules that were written inside the cover of the book by Heron House Associates 1979 that I obtained from Cork County Library:

> Comhairle Chontae Chorcaighe
>
> This book is the property of Cork County Library. You are responsible for any loss or damage to it while in your possession. You must not lend it to another reader.
>
> Keep Your Book Clean.

11. In answer to the question [Heald 1982] "Independent of whether you go to church or not, would you say you were a religious person?" the various peoples of America and Europe answered:

	USA	Great Britain	France	Europe (Average)
Yes, a religious person	81%	58%	51%	63%
Not a religious person	16%	36%	31%	24%
A convinced atheist	1%	4%	10%	5%

Irrespective of whether these answers are genuine or said for effect, they indicate a significant cultural difference between America and Europe. See also Greeley 1972, 86, 107, 151–52; Luckman 1969, 145.

The crude dichotomies employed in the text do not do justice to the complexity of reality. For a more subtle and detailed view of the varied nature of secularization see Martin 1978, esp. 31–32.

12. There clearly is a relationship but it is a problematic one. There is a correlation [Rokeach 1973, 117] between rating cleanliness relatively high on a scale of values and membership in a denomination that stresses personal salvation (Baptists> Congregationalists> Methodists, Lutherans, Roman Catholics> Episcopalians, Presbyterians, Jews, no religion). Also, the advertising image used for Ivory (soap, detergent, etc.) of "Ivory is 99 and 44/100 percent pure" appealed more to the salvation- and clean-minded in comparison with the views of other groups and of the images used by rivals such as Oxydol, Wisk, etc.

Significantly, the trade-name Ivory came as an inspiration to Harley T. Proctor of Proctor and Gamble while he sat meditating in church as the pastor read from Psalm 45:8 [King James Bible]: "All thy garments smell of myrrh, and aloes, and cassia out of the ivory palaces, whereby they have made thee glad" [Flood 1985, 29].

13. I am reluctant to go further than this as I do not have a large enough sample of oral jokes from other countries and, whereas in the case of ethnic jokes about stupidity alone I am certain that oral and written published jokes are essentially similar, it may well be that this is not the case where jokes about dirt

are concerned. The attempt by Hornby artificially (i.e., in breach of implicit cultural conventions) to introduce such jokes into Britain would have been difficult to detect had I not had a thorough knowledge of the oral jokes in circulation in the two societies concerned. However, my main concern is that such jokes may be in oral circulation in country X but are unpublishable for reason of local prudery.

Ethnic jokes about the stupid-dirty are told about Maories in New Zealand and about Fribourgers in Switzerland. There seems to be a tendency for ethnic jokes about dirtiness [e.g., see Kvideland 1983] to be told throughout the obsessionally clean belt of countries that runs from Scandinavia [see Eidheim 1969, 39] through Holland and Germany [see Almond and Verba 1963, 103–05; Botting 1986] to Austria and Switzerland. The obsession may be a product of the secularization of long-established Protestant traditions, both Lutheran and Calvinist, that tie cleanliness in with frugality, work, and efficiency or it may be a general trait of this broadly Germanic cultural area, including the Roman Catholic south [cf. Dundes 1984, 8–9, 147–48]. Sometimes the ethnic jokes about dirt are tied to stupidity, but in Germany there are only a few rural mainly dung-based jokes about Ostfrieslanders [see Krögerson 1977, 23, 27, 39, 47, 85, 87] and the main butts of a separate genre of ethnic jokes about dirtiness are the Turks, who are also, in some German jokes, apparently earmarked for destruction [see Dundes and Hauschild 1983].

V. Who Gets Called Canny?

1. In addition to sources cited in the text, I have drawn on the Folklore Archives of the University of California in compiling table 5.1. Also, re Chinese jokes see Hucker 1975, 5, and re Spanish jokes see Williams 1979A, 95–96.

2. In addition to those cited in the text there are other collections of Jewish jokes in many languages: e.g., see Ember 1988, 42–69; Geiger 1923 and 1925; Hajdu 1985; Harris and Rabinovich 1986; Landmann 1977 and 1978; Polàček 1933; Radványi 1988; Rocheman 1981; Rosemarine 1962; Stephane 1978; Tailleur 1977. Geiger's 1923 book is to be seen in Henri Matisse's 1924 painting *Histoires Juives* in the Philadelphia Museum of Art.

3. See *Anekdoty Velké Británie* 1979; *Besten Schottenwitze* 1982; Bramieri 1980A, 188, 227, 280, 292, 314, 323; Bramieri 1980B, 51; Chrestien 1957, 23; Ember 1988, 34–37; Guillois and Guillois 1979B; Horecký 1985, 189–93. Nègre 1973 vol. II; Olivieri 1980, 24; Prabhu 1966, 19, 23, 54, 68, 99, 125, 129; Scopelliti 1981, 25, 33–34; *Skotske Skottehistorier fra Scotland* n.d.; Tessier 1955, 97–99.

4. E.g., see Bramieri 1980B, 73; Nichols 1973, 266; Romorantin 1983; Scopelliti 1981, 121, Werner 1892.

5. For examples in addition to those in the text see Graham 1905, 25; Morier 1947 (1824); van den Broeck 1976; Werner 1894.

6. See Golde 1975; Herberg 1960, 212–14; Lenski 1961; Merton 1957, 591–606; O'Dea 1962, 71, 99; Wilson 1969, 134.

7. For more examples of jokes about Yankees see *American Jest Book* 1833, 91; Brisk n.d., 70, 126–30, 166, 201, 246; Copeland 1940; Cruikshank 1832, 31–32; Eastman 1970 (1936), 30–39; Masson 1913, 215–16; Funfare 1949, 86, 147; Kelly 1906, 49; *Pearson's Humorous Reciter and Reader* 1922, 306; (Thousand) *1000 Witty Sayings* n.d.; *Up to date jokes and jests* n.d.

8. See Gould 1984; Herberg 1960, 9, 38, 212–14; Holmes 1979, 129–30; Merton 1957, 430–34; Rinder 1973, 315; Rosten 1970, 501.

9. See Golden 1967, 259; Hillel 1978; Kumove 1986; Naiman 1981, 134–

35; Rosten 1970, 85, 214, 352–57 and 1983, 11, 79, 84, 187, 266, 285–87; Spalding 1976, 118–19.

10. For other examples see 'B' 1928, 66; Hicks 1936, 35–36; Holdcraft 1932, Joke 259; Junior 1927, 8, 25, 32–34; Magniac 1930, 18; May 1914; Werner 1894, 237.

11. This is based only on a subjective assessment of the context in which they were told and of the particular Jewish raconteurs, all of whom were known to the author. For further discussion see Ben-Amos 1973 and Oring 1975.

12. This thesis is frequently referred to, sometimes in agreement, sometimes critically, e.g., Apte 1985, 120–24; Barron 1950; Ben-Amos 1973; Freud 1960; Grotjahn 1970; Oring 1975, 149–50, and 1981, 44; Wilson 1979, 146–47; Zenner 1970, 111. It is perhaps most fully expounded in Reik 1962. I am inclined to agree with Ben-Amos [1973, 119] that "the only validation of the Jewish-masochism thesis is its mass acceptance by Jewish intellectuals for the actual evidence derived from the jokes themselves does not support it."

13. See Barron 1950; Bermant 1986, 214, 242; Cornell 1986; Dundes 1971, 189; Freud 1960, 111; Middleton 1959, 176; Oring 1975, 150; Redfern 1984, 128; Reik 1962; Wilson 1979, 146; Ziv 1986A, 56.

14. See Burns and Burns 1975, 11–12; Green 1979.

15. For data covering a large variety of countries and periods see Cohn 1970; Fisk 1985, 549–50; Friedländer 1976; Garwood 1903, 29–30; Gilbert 1985; Holmes 1979; Katz 1979; Levin 1979; Litvinoff 1974; Oring 1984, 107–09; Parkes 1945; Perris 1914, 320–21; Podhoretz 1986; Pois 1970; Reitlinger 1967; Richler 1986, 99, 225–26; Shirer 1960; Tuchman 1967, 208–12, 230, 383; Weinryb 1970; Weyl 1979, 83–88; Winston 1982, 174, 246.

16. See Cohn 1970, 11–15, 205–06, 225, 280–91; Friedländer 1976, 40, 44–46; Levin 1979, 48–52; Oring 1984, 107–09; Reitlinger 1967, 452, 509; Shirer 1960, 663; Trends in anti-Israel cartoons 1985; Winston 1982, 246. For the imagery of a practitioner see Hitler 1974, 276–81, 295–96 and 1983 (1961) 23–26, 132, 212–13.

VI. How Ethnic Jokes Change

1. See Clouston 1888; Esar 1978, 97, 410, 478; Hazlitt 1890; Shah 1978; Shankara 1934; Thompson 1977, 19, 188–96, 486–95; Uysal and Walker 1974; Weiss 1965, 400–413.

2. See Abrahams 1961, 240; Esar 1978, 455; Gruner 1978, 18; Legman 1986 (1968) vol. 1, 129, 161; Mosessons et al. 1974; Schwartz 1973, 75; Sloan 1975.

3. Quoted in Russell 1982, 4. For other ancient instances and references see Brown and Bryant 1983, 149; Esar 1978, 295, 517–18; Legman 1986 (1968) vol. 1, 123–24; Thompson 1977, 190.

4. See Fairservis 1962, 14, 85, 90, 126, 182; Kees 1961, 39, 142, 308, 332; Possony 1976, 4.

5. See *Brewer's* 1981, 2; Clouston 1888; Esar 1978, 6, 61–62, 95; Feinburg 1978, 49–52; Ferguson 1968.

6. See Briggs 1970 Part A, vol. 2, p. 3 and 1977, 51–53; Burke 1978, 54; *Chambers's Encyclopaedia* 1890 vol. 5, entry on Gothamites; Clouston 1888, 16–17; Colleville and de Zepelin 1896, 1–10; Craigie 1898, 220; Esar 1978, 6, 153, 136–37, 195–96, 295, 498; Feinburg 1978, 49; Gaidoz and Sébillot 1884, v–vii, 296, 380; Gašparíková 1980, 125–62; Rockwell 1981, 285; Rosten 1970, 85; Schwartz 1973, 109; Searing 1984, 10; Shankara 1934, 1–3, Sobotka 1919; Stapleton 1900, 9–11, 47–48; Thompson 1977, 190; Weiss 1965, 400–413; Welsch 1967, 183.

7. See W. B. 1928; Crompton 1970A and 1970D; Howe 1891B, 52–53; *Joe*

Miller's Jests 1962 (1739), 42–43; Joell 1944; Mitchell and Waddell 1971; Punch Library 1908 *Mr. Punch's Country Life*, 45; Spencer 1938, 265; Wright 1935, 155–56; and UCBFA.

8. See Clark 1962, 76–78, 165–66; Edwards 1975, 132; Mayhew 1966 (1862), 79, 142, 197, 291, 300; Sowell 1981.

9. See Fanning 1980, 160–61; Golden 1959, 195–98; Green 1980, 202–03; McCaffrey 1976, 77–79, 146; Sowell 1981, 34–38. For Australia see Davis and Encel 1965, 42. For other relevant jokes see Graham 1905, 7; Hall and Passemon 1933, 169.

10. See Andreski 1973, 40; Herberg 1960, 8; Jones 1960, 218–19; Sowell 1981.

11. See Danielson 1975, 39–58; Keillor 1986, 79. For other jokes see Hall and Passemon 1933, 67–70; Legman 1982 vol. I, 131–32; Stackman 1953, 68.

12. See Cerf 1959, 384; Stackman 1953, 78; Welsch 1967; Wolff, Smith, and Murray 1934, 356; Yao 1946, xxv.

VII. Militarists and Cowards

1. E.g., see Spencer 1969, 29, 45, 286 and 1904, 567–73; Veblen 1899, 246–49.

2. See Johnson 1973, 5, 147; Keijzer 1978, xxiv–xxv; Merton 1957, 234–35; W. Moore 1979, esp. observation by George Washington quoted pp. 157–58; Radine 1977; Stouffer et al. 1949B, 107–111, 143, 150–51, 550–51; von Bernhardi 1914, 118.

3. For examples of both types and comments see Bold 1979; de Guingaud 1980; Hoyt 1985, 58; MacArthur 1965, 147; Morgan 1968; Page 1973; Price 1957, 132; Stouffer et al. 1949B, 190; Wood and Wood 1976, 166–67.

4. See Merton 1957, 251–55; Stouffer et al. 1949B, 150, 169; and in relation to humor see Green 1976, 49–69.

5. See also Aristotle *Ethics* Book 3 1115a30–b19 and 1115b19–1116a6.

6. See Mack Smith 1976, 224, 233 and 1983, 302–11; Sykes 1959, 265–67, 308.

7. See Goebbels 1982, 175, 185, 190–91, 216–17, 253, 267, 275, 297, 307; Hitler 1973, 266, 418, 577, 584; Irving 1978, 103–06, 134, 182, 205–14, 226–28, 248–52, 275–77; Mack Smith 1976, 224 and 1983, 306, 317; Playfair et al. 1954 vol. II, 12; Russell 1954, 113; Shirer 1960, 818, 912.

8. See Mack Smith 1976, 233, 309 and 1983, 306–09.

9. See Barnett 1983, 64; Connell 1980, 105; Manvell and Fraenkel 1978, 164; Shirer 1960, 818.

10. The Axis casualty figures at the crucial battle of El Alamein are revealing [based on data in Irving 1978, 252; see also Chodoff 1983, 572–92]:

	Dead and wounded	Missing
German	5,000	7,900
Italian	2,800	20,000

11. See Mack Smith 1983, 296; Playfair et al. 1954 vol. I, 220, 235.

12. See Browne 1969, 127; Playfair et al. 1954 vol. I, 235–37; Shirer 1960, 818.

13. See Botting 1986, 13, 26–29, 77–83, 135–36, 183; Shils and Janowitz 1975, 345–46, 379–82; Wood and Wood 1976, 290.

14. See Botting 1986, 108; Koch 1975, 248–49; Reid 1965 (1952), 288, 291, 310; Shils and Janowitz 1975, 375.

15. For other jokes on this theme see Beeldenstorm 1985, 105; Biron and Folgoas 1977, Book 3, 44; Wood and Wood 1976, 214.

16. See Baechler 1979, 409–14; Browne 1969, 155–56, 200–04, 213–22; Hoyt 1985; Morris 1980, 176–84, 438–62; Onoda 1976, 34–35.

17. E.g., see *Laugh with S.E.A.C.* [1944], 56, 67–68, 87; Low 1949, 11, 15, 25, 33, 49, 53, 55, 87; *The New Yorker War Album* 1943.

18. See Bullock 1962, 540, 548, 632; Manvell and Fraenkel 1978, 146, 151; Shirer 1960, 571, 600, 658, 779–80.

19. On the directly relevant nasty reality behind this particular joke, see Shirer 1960, 970.

20. See Clark 1984, 30; Nichols 1973, 20; Petersen 1975, 182–83; Trevelyan 1919, 6–7; Willey 1984, 19–20, 121–22, 150.

21. See Cornelisen 1969, 65; Golde 1975, 9; Willey 1984, 20.

22. For relatively recent collections of German local and dialect jokes see Heinold 1978; Paulun 1979; Reichert 1974; Reuter 1965; *Tünnes und Schäl Witze* 1977.

23. See UCBFA Italy files; Willey 1984, 118–22; and for an earlier period see Piozzi 1892 (1789).

24. See Balfour 1975, 393; Geyl 1965, 303–04; Nelson 1971, 338; Perris 1914, 212; Preston and Wise 1979, 240; von Treitschke 1914, 23.

25. See Calleo 1978, 4; Nelson 1971, 33; Perris 1914, 46; Shirer 1960, 91–92; Tower 1913, 13.

26. See Balfour 1975, 14; Nelson 1971, 317; Perris 1914, 255, 266; von Bernhardi 1914, 63.

27. See Pinon 1980, 79 and notes 103 and 140; and Rabelais (*Pantagruel* Book II) 199.

28. See Almond and Verba 1963, 402–03; Banfield 1958; Barzini 1964, 198; Cesaresco 1892, 17; Greeley and McCready 1975, 219; and Willey 1984, 148–53.

29. See Seward 1986, 39; Trevelyan 1928, 138; Whittam 1977, 162.

30. See Mack Smith 1983, 226; Rubenson 1976, 380; Seton-Watson 1967, 181–83, 372–73; Whittam 1977, 137; Willey 1984, 153.

31. See Falls 1966; Irving 1978, 27–30; Seton-Watson 1967, 474; Trevelyan 1919, 164–65.

32. For details of the election results of 1919, 1921 (violent), and 1924 (very violent) see Seton-Watson 1967, 588–89, 648–49; and also see Sturzo 1971, 197–204.

33. The absurdity of the text quoted is not a result of faulty translation (see translator's note by Richard Washburn Child, the former American ambassador to Italy [Mussolini 1928, 7–8]). For a fair and more reasoned tribute to the Arditi see Trevelyan 1919, 83, 86–87.

34. See Mack Smith 1983, 226; Seton-Watson 1967, 182–83; Whittam 1977, 137.

35. See Falls 1966, 3, 157; Jones 1979, 302, 671; Trevelyan 1919, 88; Whittam 1977, 126.

36. See Lewis 1978, 120, 137; Short 1984; Willey 1984, 61–67.

37. I have quoted from F. A. Dearborn's translation *The All Highest Goes to Jerusalem* 1918, 59 and 63.

38. See Arnold 1984; Christ 1978; Coulton 1945, 196; Gombrich and Kris 1940, xiv, 31; Larsen 1980, 25–30; Schütz 1979; Tuchman 1967, 359, 388–89.

39. See Balfour 1975, 15; Chaucer 1988 (circa 1386), 24 (general prologue to *Canterbury Tales*, lines 53–54); Nelson 1971, 33; Perris 1914, 19.

40. See Golde 1975, 12; Shirer 1960, 93; Tower 1913, 78; von Bernhardi 1914, 246–47.

41. See de Catt 1929 vol. I, 58 and vol. II, 9; Nelson 1971, 88; Rosebury in introduction to de Catt 1929, xxx–xxxiii.

42. See for example Coulton 1945, 190, 198; Garwood 1903; Howard 1916, 59–82; Jones 1944, 35–37; Vansittart 1941.

43. See Balfour 1975, 393; Nelson 1971, 11; Shirer 1960, 93; von Bernhardi 1914, 63; von Treitschke (ed. Davis) 1914, 110–13.

44. See also Balfour 1975, 270; Christ 1978, 219; Fernau 1916, 110–11; R. V. Jones 1979, 484–85; MacDougall 1958, 54; Mound 1983, 11–12; Perris 1914, 490–91. This real-life incident became the play by Carl Zuckmayer (1961).

45. See also von Bülow 1914, 180 and Sarolea 1912, 145; Tower 1913, 162, 227.

46. Both the jokes that follow were heard in Britain in the 1980s but their origin is uncertain. For the kind of comic incidents in real life that lay behind such jokes about Germans see Carsten 1972, 215–16; B. Moore 1979, 307–08; Ryder 1967, 201.

47. See for example 'A German' 1915; Claes 1915; Dillon 1914; Fernau 1916; Gerard 1917; Graves 1914; McLaren 1916; Muehlon 1918; Usher 1914.

48. See Bethell 1976, 170, 411; Darracott and Loftus 1981A, 8, 60, 65; Grenfell 1953; Hayes 1960, 122; R. V. Jones 1979, 117; Mencken 1920 and 1956; but also see Balfour 1975, 427 and Muehlon 1918, 31, 63, 191.

49. This phenomenon is the reverse of what happened in 1939 in the sphere of serious belief. By that time the tales of German atrocities put out by Allied propagandists in 1914–18 were so discredited that many people dismissed as being the same kind of hokum the essentially truthful official accounts of German National Socialist tyranny, brutality, and persecution issued by the British and French governments. Many were convinced only when the Allied forces entered the extermination and concentration camps in 1945 and provided irrefutable evidence of mass murder, and some stubborn and perverse doubters quibbled and prevaricated even then. See Bethell 1976, 411; Fisk 1985, 41, 438, 469, 549–50; R. V. Jones 1979, 117; Reitlinger 1967, 524.

50. See Grossmith 1984, 32; Irving 1978, 465; Reid 1965 (1952), 22, 146–48, 166, 304; Russell 1954, 23–31; Shirer 1960, 954–56, 1100; Simpson 1979, 40–42; Wood 1946, 28–30, 97.

51. See Carr 1987, 7–8; Müller 1987, 35–41; Nelson 1971, 460; Shirer 1960, 320, 1081.

52. See Bethell 1976, 140–45; Carr 1987, 7–8; Müller 1987, 43; Reitlinger 1956, 253–88, 348–80 and 1967, 259.

53. See Barron and Paul 1977; Conquest 1971; Horowitz 1977; Tolstoy 1982; Weyl 1979, 148. But also for the ethnic dimension in Marxist atrocities and persecutions see Biberaj 1984; Botting 1986, 223–37; Conquest 1971, 404–05; *Death at Katyn* 1944; Fitzgibbon 1971; Levin 1979, 48–56; Litvinoff 1974; Possony 1976, 28–34; Tame 1984; Tolstoy 1982, 25, 244, 267–70; Weyl 1979.

54. See Bethell 1976, 140–52, 222; Cohn 1970, 205–12, 225–34; Henry and Hillel 1976, 136–47, 180, 240; Hitler 1974, 53–55, 138, 274–81, 294–95, 510–14 and 1973 (Trevor Roper, ed.), 87, 545, 575, 589; Horowitz 1977, 18, 24–26, 34–38; Reitlinger 1957, 202 and 1967, 3–7, 98–99, 257, 452, 509, 533; Russell 1954, 227–30; Watt 1975, 231.

55. See for example Bethell 1976, 151–52; Cooper 1975, 197; Henry and Hillel 1976, 128, 180; Manvell and Fraenkel 1978; Reitlinger 1957 and 1967; Shirer 1960, 250; Wood and Wood 1976.

56. See for example Bonvi's (Franco Bonvicini's) cartoon series *Sturmtrup-*

pen in Italian and *Die Sturmtruppen* in German; see also *The Book of the Goons* 1974, 11, 122, 130; Braben 1974, 115–27; Meyerowitz 1979, 33–36; Morecambe and Wise 1979, 36–39; Stubble 1987; Ward 1982, 22, 90–93, 188.

57. In answer to the question "Of course we all hope there won't be another war but if it were to come to that would you be willing to fight for your country?" the percentages of yes and no answers were as follows [Heald 1982; cf. also Almond and Verba 1963, 102]:

USA		UK		Average		West Germany		Italy	
Yes	No	Yes	No	Yes	No	Yes	No	Yes	No
71%	20%	62%	27%	43%	40%	35%	41%	28%	57%

58. E.g., see Hillel 1978, 245; Hillman 1965; Imbach and Favières 1980, 29; Jacobs and Glazer 1979, 93. See also the jokes and comments in Freud 1960, 56.

59. See Cash 1973, 136–40, 152, 186, 256–60, 309–11, 345–46; Davis, Gardner, and Gardner 1941, 44–45, 393–400, 498–502, 527–38; Dollard 1957 [1937], 56–59, 315–63.

VIII. Anglo-Saxon Attitudes

1. For both humor and reports of seriously held views see Atkinson and Searle 1963, 24; Hewison 1981, 70; Ingrams and Wells 1984, 35; Lipset 1964, 252; Richler 1986, 13.

2. For further examples see Cerf 1945, 128; Cobb 1923, 164–65; Edwards 1978, 20; Robey 1920, 215–16.

3. See Lipset 1964, 110–23 and also Apte 1985, 90; Greeley 1972, 159; Herberg 1960, 79; Potter 1954, 48, 55, 106; Trollope 1832 vol. I, 73–75, 96, 136–40 and vol. II, 142.

4. See Astor 1963, 8; Badeau 1886, 4; Bell 1961A, 228; de Grand'Combe 1933, 150; Farber 1953; Hirszowicz 1981, 137; Horner 1982, 45; Kumar 1977; Sedgewick 1841; Tuchman 1967, 15, 25, 33; Whiting 1986, 42; Wiener 1985, 12–23, 42, 89–91, 118–61.

5. See Greenway 1972, 100–02; James 1975, 114; Lipset 1964, 252–67; Pringle 1960, 101–02; Ward 1966, 105–06. On the basis of this evidence, I have placed Australia lower in column 2 of table 8.1 than did Lipset 1964, 244. For a contrary view see Rokeach 1973, 89–91.

6. See Davis and Encel 1965, 18–20 but also 21; Greenway 1972, 100–09; Horner 1982, 4–5; Lipset 1964, 252–54; Milligan 1981, 103; Pringle 1960, 13–14, 31–32, 96–109; Rokeach 1973, 91; Ward 1966, 99–106, 224–33.

7. See Apte 1985, 90; Corbin 1902, 571; Feinburg 1978, 41; Merton 1957, 136–39.

8. For examples and comments in addition to those in the text see Hicks 1936, 42, 94–95; Jones (Pelidros) n.d., 44–45; Leigh 1920, 61; Muir and Brett 1980, 84–86; Neider 1977, xxi; New Punch Library 1933 *Mr. Punch and the Arts*, 130, 196; Ocker (pseud.) 1986; Phillips n.d., 112; Punch Library 1908 *Mr. Punch in Bohemia*, 191; Thackeray 1879, 85–93.

9. For additional examples see Cerf 1945, 36, 43 and 1959, 452–56; Davis 1968, 52; Esar 1978, 525; House 1945; Jones 1976; Kilgarriff 1975, 60–61; Lauber 1955, 109; Muir and Brett 1980, 84; O'Grady 1965, 80; Perkins 1901; Prochnow 1953, 373–74; Randolph 1952.

10. For additional examples and comments see Davis 1979, 96; Esar 1978, 254–55 and 443; House 1944; Kimmins 1928, 130; Nellis and Graziano 1975, 108; Peter and Dana 1982, 62; Prochnow 1955, 167; Redfern 1984, 158.

11. For additional jokes about and reference to jokes about Bostonians see Cerf 1950, 118; Esar 1960, 43; Hall 1934, 71; Legman (*Ophelia*, vol. 3), 43; Phillips 1974B, 38; Pocheptsov 1974, 259; Stephenson 1951, 571.

For relevant jokes about Southerners see Copeland 1941, 49; Dwyer 1975, 27; Esar 1954, 204; *Jokes for All Occasions* 1923, 59; Masson 1913, 38; Perkins 1901, 242–43; Prochnow 1953, 320.

12. See Andreski 1973, 43–44; Buckle 1980, xii; Jaher 1968, 188–262; Wiener 1985, 201.

13. For additional instances and comments see Bushell 1984, 166–67; Dunbar and Webb 1980, 78; Dundes 1982, 12–15; Eysenck 1944, 51; Helitzer 1984A, 67; Lawrence 1973, 77; Peter and Dana 1982, 62.

14. For comments and reasons see de Grand'Combe 1932, 30–31; Schoeck 1969, 40.

15. See Davis 1979, 99–100; Keillor 1986, 24; Perelman 1949, 45–47; Trudeau 1984. For French instances see Daudet 1890, 11; Goscinny and Uderzo 1976, 34.

16. E.g., see Bowles 1986; Dobson 1976; Dwyer 1975; Edwards 1986; Elliot 1974; Graham 1980A and 1980B; Lauder 1969; Mitchell and Rawls 1976; Mitchell and Waddell 1971; O'Grady 1965; Orkin 1973; Pepper 1977 and 1979; Powers and Powers 1975; Ragaway 1977.

17. See Astor 1963, 7–8; Bethell 1976, 269; Greenway 1972, 108; Herberg 1960, 21; Lewis 1974 (1922), 60, 196.

18. For examples and comment see Dundes 1982, 191–92; Elgart n.d., 126; Esar 1960, 233; Hall and Passemon 1933, 36–37; Howells 1905/09; Phillips 1981, 78.

19. In addition to those in the text see examples and comments in Cerf 1945, 100, 128, 153, 170; 1950, 42; and 1956A vol. I, 250–54. Elgart 1951, 104, 170–71 and 1953, 22, 26; Hicks 1936, 65; Jones 1976; Trollope 1832 vol. 2, 166–71.

20. E.g., Aquisti 1979, 40; *Anekdoty Velké Británie* 1979, 79–95; Goscinny and Uderzo 1976; Guillois and Guillois 1979B; Nègre 1973 vol. I, 77–86; Olivieri 1980, 50, 56; Pocheptsov 1974, 234; Tessier 1955, 94–95; Wicks 1976, 10–16. See also Daninos 1955; Maurois 1940 (1918); Rameses 1937, 67–82, 116–20, 130–35.

21. E.g., see Aspinwall 1983, 105; Barr and York 1983; Bateman 1969, 42, 99–104; Bantley and Esar 1962, 21, 42; Berkeley 1980; Bushell 1984; Collinson 1926, 156–57; Cranfield 1983, 45, 95, 114; Gren 1979; Hicks 1936, 65, 68, 102–03; Hilton 1959; Horner 1957; Ingrams 1971, 15–16, 90–91; Kilgarriff 1975, 58; Krin 1981; Lewis 1974 (1922), 197; Melly and Fawkes 1962, 31–40; Monson and Scott 1984; Punch Library 1908 *Mr. Punch in the Highlands*, 169, 177; Rees 1980B, 70, 73 and 1981, 20; Russell 1940, 39–40; Sherrin and Shand 1984, 80–81.

22. E.g., Cerf 1950, 87; Copeland 1940, 4, 28; Elgart 1951, 28 and n.d., 98, 142; Esar 1954, 63–66; Hall 1934, 22; Hall and Passemon 1933, 151.

23. In addition to the examples of jokes and humor cited in the text see Boston 1982, 62–63; Bromfield and Bromfield 1985, 25, 50; Bryson, Fitzherbert, and Legris 1984, 145; Hills 1979, 13; Hunt 1929, 114; Kilgarriff 1975, 8–9; Leigh 1920, 26; Morley 1982; Phillips 1975B, 15; Swain 1965, 42, 45; Thomas 1979, 185; Tinniswood 1981, 51, 69–71.

24. See Bowles 1986, 12–13; de Witt 1970, 10, 95; Ocker (pseud.) 1986; O'Grady 1965, vii; Rushton 1983, 109–16; Stranks and Grand 1980.

25. For jests and comments on American spitting see *American Jests and Anecdotes* n.d., 216–17; Bryant 1984, 3; de Grand'Combe 1933, 171; Franklin 1983, 55; Lawrence 1973, 36; Olsen 1970, 9; Ward 1966, 135.

26. The reasons are even more problematic given the slow rate of growth of

Australian living standards, which has meant economic decline relative to others. On current American economic difficulties see Büschgen 1987, esp. 65.

IX. Food for Thought

1. See Brillat-Savarin 1874, 1; Fieldhouse 1986, 41; Goody 1982, 82, 107, 145–46.

2. See *Brewer's* 1981; de Grand'Combe 1933, 195, 301; Drummond and Wilbraham 1958, 393; Limón 1977; Paul 1954, 113; Roback 1944.

3. For a discussion of the realities of cannibalism see Fieldhouse 1986, 182–91; Goody 1982, 77, 106; Tannahill 1975.

4. For further ethnic jokes about cannibalism in a variety of languages see Adams 1886, 15; Alvin 1983A, 57–62; Cerf 1956A vol. I, 616–17; Climent-Galant 1979, 69; Davidson 1978, 14, 45, 93–94 and back cover; Eco 1983, 95; Marshall 1979, 177; Mosessons et al. 1974; Scopelliti 1981, 47, 97; Vincent 1977B, 24–25. For a sustained humorous treatment of this theme see Waugh 1932.

5. For additional examples of jokes of this type see *America, the Golden Age of Comedy* 1973, 127; Barlow et al. 1980, 81; Delaney and Delaney 1974, 83; Jacobs 1903, 272; Kimmins 1928, 159. For jokes of Oriental origin see Kaneko 1950, 5; Levy 1974, 148. For a sustained spoof see Janssen 1970.

6. See also Bevan 1911, 79–80; Moglia 1981, 338; Taylor 1906, 238 for jokes about cats and dogs eaten in a variety of wars and sieges. Cf. also Aarne and Thompson 1961, 416, Tale type 1409*.

7. For details of these dietary rules in the Old Testament see Exodus 23:19 and 34:26; Leviticus 7:22–27; 11:1–47; 17:10–16; 19:26; Deuteronomy 14:3–21. See also Douglas 1966, 51–57; Fieldhouse 1986, 132–37; Rosten 1970, 196–97; Soler 1973; Williams 1987.

8. See Exodus 23:20–33; Leviticus 11:44–47; 18:1–5, 20, 22–27. See also Davies 1982A, 1033–35; Douglas 1966, 51–57; Williams 1987, 118–19.

9. Also to be found in Birmingham 1927, 18; Harvey 1904, 318–19, Mosessons 1974; Vincent 1977A, 70. For other jokes about converts see Ernst 1927, 114.

10. Also in Eastman 1970 (1936), 81; Kelly 1906, 81; Perkins 1901, 346–47. See also Royidis/Durrell 1965 (1886), 17, 39, for a protracted satire on this point.

11. See Drummond and Wilbraham 1958, 59 107–08; Moffat 1979, 92–96; Oddy and Miller 1976, 55, 216; Ziegler 1956, 11–16. Note also that as people's incomes rise they tend to consume, more than proportionately, larger quantities of meat and smaller quantities of cheaper foods such as grain products and potatoes.

12. See Barkas 1975, 26–27; Fieldhouse 1986, 126–29; Goody 1982, 115–25.

13. See Drummond and Wilbraham 1958, 48–49, 75, 206, 212, 328; *Meat balances in O.E.C.D. countries* 1981; Moffatt 1979, 94; Ziegler 1956, 11, 15–16.

14. The phrase is appropriately ambiguous and captures two facets of meat-eating reality: (a) when people are prosperous they can afford to eat sirloin steak and consequently we can use their consumption of steak as a sign (i.e., index) of their prosperity; (b) when people are prosperous they signal the fact to themselves and to others by eating large quantities of expensive sirloin steak, i.e., it is a deliberate sign of their prosperity. See also Williams 1976, 52. In hard times people are reluctant to give up meat because to do so is an unambiguous sign of poverty and failure. For jokes on this theme see Edwardes 1956, 32 and Patten 1909, 233.

15. See Critchell and Raymond 1969, 317–18; Drummond and Wilbraham 1958, 353, 420; Ziegler 1956, 11.

16. This joke appeared in *A.C. Mery Talys* (A Hundred Merry Tales) printed

by John Rastell in 1526. It is reprinted in Wardroper 1970, 119, joke number 164. The joke is referred to by Sir Nicholas L' Estrange in his manuscript collection "Merry passages and jests" (M. S. Harl 6395) where he comments: "But I believe our Englishmen would run as fast into hell if one were to cry a pipe of tobacco." See also Powell 1880, who corrects St. Peter's Welsh and claims that it should read "caws wedi ei bobi." Powell adds that "The chief of the apostles had only a rather imperfect knowledge of Welsh, which is not to be wondered at as we know that even his Hebrew was far from giving satisfaction to the priests of the capital" [115–16].

17. See William Shakespeare, *Collected Works* 1964, *The Merry Wives of Windsor*, Act I, Scene 1, line 13; Act IV, Scene 4, line 51; and Act V, Scene 5, lines 83–87. See also Bartley 1954.

18. I have slightly modernized spelling and punctuation. See also Ashton 1882, 292 and 1883, 85. According to Ashton (1883) the earliest known version appears in *Witts recreations* 1640.

19. See Allen 1968, 181; Colyer 1976, 2; Drummond and Wilbraham 1958, 256; Gibbon 1910, 31–32.

20. See A' Becket 1894, 71, 461; Chase and French 1913, 68; Cowan and Cowan 1972, 28–29; 'M' 1945, 61, 76.

21. For the economic background see Adler 1977, 60, and Allen 1968, 23, 208. Note too the strong contrast between the views of William Cobbett and Adam Smith regarding the relative merits of potatoes, bread, and oatmeal porridge.

22. See Bell 1980, 15, 34, 117; Boswell 1890 (1791), 97 (Aet 46), 489 (Aet 67), 588 (Aet 69), 713 (Aet 74). Johnson's *Dictionary*, 'Oats'; McPhee 1981, 93.

For jokes and humorous references to the Scots, oatmeal, and porridge in addition to those in the text, see Braude 1966, 304; Jerrold 1913, 254; Knox 1924, 189; 'M' 1945, 114; Milne n.d., 42; *Wit and wisdon* 1826, 360.

23. For additional jokes and humor about the Irish and potatoes see Bermant 1986, 63; Cruikshank 1832, 17; Mitchell and Rawls 1976; Ripley n.d., 248, 309.

24. For example see Chaucer's 1988 [circa 1396] Miller's and Summoner's Tales; Craik 1964; Rabelais 1955.

25. See also Cobb 1925, 154; Cobb 1940, 201; and *Jokes for all Occasions* 1922, 33.

26. In addition to the jokes and sources about blacks stealing chickens cited in the text, see also *American Wit and Humor* 1900, 216; Ernst 1927, 77; Heywood n.d., 9–10; Holdcroft 1932, joke 100; House 1943, 41; *Jokes for All Occasions* 1923, 63; Kimmins 1928, 170; Landon 1900, 507–10, 574; Masson 1913, 184; Mumford 1905; Perkins 1901, 310, 358; Prochnow 1953, 302, 327, 341; Wilde 1982, 144.

27. See Andreski 1973, 73–74; Cash 1973, 106, 127, 146, 361; Davis, Gardner, and Gardner 1941, 44–49, 392–95; Dollard 1957, 56–59, 175, 323–33; Key 1949, 144, 240, 536–38, 646.

28. In the nineteenth century there were numerous jokes about and humorous references to the Germans and sausage and it is still a source of humor today. In addition to the examples in the text see Arnold 1910, 79; Bermant 1986, 63; Forrest 1968, 50; Jacobs 1903, 164, 169, 223; Landon 1900; Dr. Merry n.d., 135; Meyerowitz 1979, 33–36; Punch Library 1908 *Mr. Punch's Cockney*, 50–52; Pearsall 1975, 200; Ripley n.d., 174; Thackeray 1949, 342, 532; Took 1975; Wannan 1963, 105.

29. It need hardly be stressed that the Christian churches have been strongly divided, not only on the question of the nature of the communion service (e.g., symbolic commemoration or real presence), but on the way in which communion should be administered. My explanation relates to one particular pattern of belief and behavior and is rooted in the King James Version of the Bible.

Conclusion

1. See Limón 1977, 35, 41–42 (for background see Schoeck 1969, 57); Rosenberg and Shapiro 1958, 74; Zenner 1970, 96.

2. See Barron 1950; Middleton 1959, 176; Middleton and Moland 1959; Zenner 1970, 96; Ziv 1986, 104, 109; cf. also Coser 1959; Kusielewicz 1969, 100–03.

3. See Apte 1985, 136; Kravitz 1977; Oring 1975. Aggression is not funny per se. Playful aggression [Feinburg 1978, 7–9] operates within rules as to the type and amount of aggression allowed. The aim of saying "Boo!" to an infant, or of Tigger's game of "bounce," is that the jokee should experience a mild and pleasing fright from an attack known to be a mock one. If the joker gets it wrong the infant will howl instead of laugh; getting it right is an integral and essential part of successful joking behavior. This is equally true (see Kravitz's 1977 empirical observations) of humor at the expense of a third party, which also has built-in restraints that distinguish it from true aggression in a way parallel to the distinction between sport and war.

Sources and Bibliography

Archive Material

Of the archives of humorous material that have been consulted the four main ones are indicated in the text as follows:

1. University of California at Berkeley Folklore Archive, indicated in text as UCBFA, followed by the name of the country under which the material is filed, followed (when available) by the name of the collector and the date of collection.

2. The archives of the Institute of Folk-Lore at Indiana University, Bloomington. The material used from this archive is taken from unpublished dissertations and is cited under the author/collector's name in the text and in the bibliography of theses and printed sources.

3. The archives of the House of Humour and Satire, Gabrovo, Bulgaria. The material cited is all from the Scottish file dating from about 1968 and is indicated in the text as SFGB.

4. The archives of the Finnish Literature Society in Helsinki. Material mainly from period 1900–1940. Indicated in text as FLSH.

Thus,

UCBFA = University of California, Berkeley Folklore Archive.
SFGB = Scottish File, House of Humour, Gabrovo, Bulgaria.
FLSH = Finnish Literature Society, Helsinki.

Bibliography of Theses and Published Works

Aarne, Antti and Thompson, Stith (1961) *The Types of the Folktale*, Helsinki, Suomalainen Tiedeakatemia [F.F. Communications, Vol.75, No.184].

A' Becket, Gilbert Abbott (pseud.) (1894, First pub. 1848) *The Comic History of England*, London, George Routledge.

Aberdeen and Temair, Marquess of (1929) *Jokes Cracked by Lord Aberdeen*, Dundee, Scotland, Valentine.

Abingdon, Alexander (pseud.) (1931) *Still More Boners*, New York, Viking.

Abraham, Abu (1974) *Private View*, New Delhi, Sterling.

Abraham, Abu (1977) *The Games of Emergency*, New Delhi, Vikas.

Abrahams, Roger (1961) "Ghastly commands: the cruel joke revisited," in *Midwest Folklore*, Vol.11, No.4, Winter, pp.235–46.

Abrahams, Roger D. (1962) "Playing the Dozens," in *Journal of American Folklore*, Vol.75, pp.209–20.

A.C. Mery Talys (A Hundred Merry Tales) (1526) London, John Rastell. See also *Shakespeare's Jest Book*; Hazlitt 1864 and 1887; Zall 1977.

Adair, Hunter (1982) *Muck Spreadin'*, Alston, Cumbria, Sun Studio.

Adams, Joey (1975) *Joey Adams' Ethnic Humor*, New York, Manor.

Adams, William Davenport (1886) *The Treasury of Modern Anecdotes*, London, Hamilton Adams.

Adamson, Joe (1974) *Groucho, Harpo, Chico and Sometimes Zeppo*, London, Hodder.

Adler, Bill (1964) *The Wit of President Kennedy*, London, Leslie Frewin.

Adler, Max (1977) *Welsh and the Other Dying Languages in Europe, a Sociolinguistic Study*, Hamburg, Helmut Buske.

af Klintberg, Bengt (1983) "Negervitsar," in *Tradisjon*, Vol.13, pp.23–45.

Aggie Games You Can't Lose (1977) Watertown, Mass., American.

Aggie Jokes, 101 [9 volumes, 1965–1979] Dallas, Gigem.

Ahlberg, Janet and Ahlberg, Allan (1987, First pub. 1976) *The Old Joke Book*, Harmondsworth, Penguin.

Akutagawa, Ryunosuke (1938) *Tales Grotesque and Curious*, Tokyo, Hokuseido.

"Alcohol Problems in Eastern Europe" (1985), in *Soviet Labour Review*, Vol.3, No.2, August.

Alderman, Geoffrey (1972) "The Anti-Jewish Riots of August 1911 in South Wales," in *Welsh History Review*, Vol.6, No.2, pp.190–205.

Alerte au Cafard (1940) Lausanne, Spes.

Alford, R. R. (1969) "Religion and Politics," in Robertson, R. (ed.), pp.321–30.

Allen, David Eliston (1968) *British Tastes, an Enquiry into the Likes and Dislikes of the Regional Consumer*, London, Hutchinson.

Allen, Irving Lewis (1983) *The Language of Ethnic Conflict: Social Organisation and Lexical Culture*, New York, Columbia University Press.

The All Highest Goes to Jerusalem, Being the Diary of the German Emperor's Journey to the Holy Land (1918) New York, Doran.

Allison, Sam (1978) *French Power*, Richmond Hill, Ontario, B.M.G.

Almond, Gabriel A. and Verba, Sydney (1963) *The Civic Culture*, Princeton, N. J., Princeton University Press.

Altman, Sig (1971) *The Comic Image of the Jew, Explorations of a Pop Culture Phenomenon*, Rutherford, N. J., Fairleigh Dickinson University Press.

Alvin, Julius (1983A) *Gross Jokes*, New York, Zebra/Kensington.

Alvin, Julius (1983B) *Totally Gross Jokes*, New York, Zebra/Kensington.

Aman, Reinhold (1977) Editorial Note in *Maledicta*, Vol.1, No.1, Summer.

America, the Golden Age of Comedy (1973) New York, A. F. E.

American Jest Book, The (1800) Baltimore, Bonsal and Niles.

American Jest Book, The (1833) Philadelphia, Hogan and Thompson.

American Jests and Anecdotes (n.d.) Edinburgh, Wm. Paterson.

American Wit and Humor (1900) Philadelphia, George W. Jacobs.

Amis, Kingsley (1953) *Lucky Jim*, London, Victor Gollancz.

Amis, Kingsley (1955) *That Uncertain Feeling*, London, Victor Gollancz.

Amis, Kingsley (1987) *The Old Devils*, Harmondsworth, Penguin.

Amsterdam, Morey (1960) *Keep Laughing*, London, Hammond and Hammond.

Andreski, Stanislav Leonard (1973) *Prospects of a Revolution in the USA*, London, Tom Stacey.

Andreski, Stanislav (1982) "Causes of the Low Morale of the Italian Army in the Two World Wars" and "A Rejoinder," in *Journal of Strategic Studies*, Vol.5, No.2, June, pp.248–56 and pp.276–77.

Andrewes, Anthony (1971) *Greek Society*, Harmondsworth, Penguin.

Anecdota Americana Series 1 (1933) and Series 2 (1934). See Hall.

Anekdoty Slunné Itálie (1978) Prague, Lidové Nakladatelsví.

Anekdoty Velké Británie (1979) Prague, Lidové Nakladatelsví.

Angell, Norman (1914) *The Great Illusion, a Study of the Relation of Military Power to National Advantage*, London, Heinemann.

Anobile, Richard J. (ed.) (1969) *Drat! Being the Encapsulated View of Life by W. C. Fields in His Own Words*, New York, Signet.

Anstey, F. (pseud. of Thomas Anstey Guthrie) (1897) *Baboo Jabberjee B.A.*, London, J. M. Dent.
ap Lewys, Edgar (1977) *Hiwmor o Fro'r Glöwr*, Talybont, Dyfed, Wales, Y. Lolfa.
ap Lewys, Edgar (1986) *Hwyl o Fro'r Glöwr*, Talybont, Dyfed, Wales, Y. Lolfa.
Apte, Mahadev L. (1985) *Humor and Laughter, an Anthropological Approach*, Ithaca, Cornell University Press.
Aquisti, Danilo (1979) *La Barzelletta Pornografica*, Rome, Napoleone.
Aquisti, Danilo (1981A) *La Super Barzelletta Pornografica*, Rome, Napoleone.
Aquisti, Danilo (1981B) *Le Barzellette di Pierino*, Rome, Napoleone.
Ardagh, John (1987) *Germany and the Germans*, London, Hamish Hamilton.
Arensburg, Conrad and Niehoff, Arthur H. (1975) "American cultural values," in Spradley and Rynkiewich (eds.), pp.363–78.
Aristotle, *Ethics [The Nicomachean Ethics*, trans. J. Thomson and H. Tredennich, 1976] Harmondsworth, Penguin.
Aristotle, *The Poetics* (trans. D. S. Margoliouth, 1911), London, Hodder and Stoughton.
Arnold, Fritz (1984) *Simplicissimus and the Weimar Republic*, Munich, Goethe-Institut.
Arnold, Matthew (1910) *On the Study of Celtic Literature and Other Essays*, London, J. M. Dent.
Ashmore, Richard D. and Del Boca, Frances K. (1981) "Conceptual approaches to stereotypes and stereotyping," in Hamilton, David L. (ed.) *Cognitive Processes in Stereotyping and Inter-group Behavior*, Hillside, N. J., Laurence Erlbaum.
Ashton, John (1882) *Chapbooks of the Eighteenth Century*, London, Chatto and Windus.
Ashton, John (1883) *Humour, wit and satire of the seventeenth century*, London, Chatto and Windus.
Ashton, John (1888) *English Caricature and Satire on Napoleon I*, London, Chatto and Windus.
Ashton, Thomas Southcliffe (1948) *The Industrial Revolution*, London, Oxford University Press.
"Asian Lightning That Keeps Striking" (1985) in *Searchlight*, No.125, November, pp.10–11.
Askey, Arthur (1977) *Before Your Very Eyes*, London, Hodder and Stoughton.
Aspinwall, Jack (1983) *Kindly Sit Down!* London, Buchan and Enright.
Asselin, E. Donald (1963) *New England Laughs*, Middlebury, Vermont, Vermont Books.
Astor, Michael (1963) *Tribal Feeling*, London, John Murray.
Athenaeus (1980) [trans. C. B. Gulick] *The Deipnosophists*, Vol.5, *Deipnosophistae*, Book 12, Cambridge, Mass., Harvard University Press and London, Heinemann.
Atkinson, Alex and Searle, Ronald (1963) *USA for Beginners*, Harmondsworth, Penguin.
Aye, John (1931A) *Humour among the Lawyers*, London, Universal.
Aye, John (1931B) *Humour in the Army*, London, Universal.
Aye, John (1931C) *Humour of Parliament and Parliamentary Elections*, London, Universal.
Aye, John (1931D) *Humour among the Doctors*, London, Universal.
Aye, John (1933A) *Humour in Our Streets*, London, Universal.
Aye, John (1933B) *I Am the Joker*, London, Universal.
Aye, John (1934) *Clerical Chuckles*, London, Universal.
B, W ('W. B.') (1928) *Two Five Five Smiles*, Blackpool, Strebor.

Bacon, Selden D. (1962) "Alcohol and Complex Society," in Pittman and Snyder (eds.).

Badeau, Adam (1886) "Aristocracy in England," in Commager (ed.) (1974), pp.477–85.

Baechler, Jean (1979) *Suicides*, Oxford, Basil Blackwell.

Bahadur, K. P. (1980) *Humorist's Hoo's Hoo*, New Delhi, Sterling.

Baker, Sidney, J. (1953) *Australia Speaks*, Sydney, Shakespeare Head Press.

Baker, T. Lindsay (1979) *The First Polish-Americans Silesian Settlements in Texas*, College Station, Texas, Texas A. & M. University Press.

Bales, Robert (1962) "Attitudes towards drinking in the Irish culture," in Pittman and Snyder (eds.).

Balfour, Michael (1975) *The Kaiser and His Times*, Harmondsworth, Penguin.

Banc, C. and Dundes, Alan (1986) *First Prize: Fifteen Years, an Annotated Collection of Romanian Political Jokes*, Cranbury, N. J., Associated University Press.

Banfield, Edward C. (1958) *The Moral Basis of a Backward Society*, New York, Free Press.

Barbeau, Arthur E. and Henri, Florette (1974) *The Unknown Soldiers, Black American Troops in World War I*, Philadelphia, Temple University Press.

Baring, Maurice (ed. Paul Horgan) (1970) *Maurice Baring Restored*, London, Heinemann.

Barkas, Janet (1975) *The Vegetable Passion*, London, Routledge & Kegan Paul.

Barker, A. J. (1968) *The Civilising Mission*, London, Cassell.

Barker, Mark (ed.) (1980) *Could Do Better . . .*, London, John Clare.

Barker, Ronnie (1977) *Sauce*, London, Book Club Associates.

Barker, Ronnie (1979A) *Gentleman's Relish*, London, Hodder and Stoughton.

Barker, Ronnie (1979B) *Fletcher's Book of Rhyming Slang*, London, Pan.

Barlow, David; Christie, Peter; Kington, Miles; Davis, Alan Maryon (1980) *The Instant Sunshine Book*, London, Robson.

Barlow, Patrick (1987) *All the World's a Globe*, London, Methuen.

Barnett, Corelli (1983) *The Desert Generals*, London, Pan.

Barr, Ann and York, Peter (1982) *The Official Sloane Ranger Handbook*, London, Ebury.

Barr, Ann and York, Peter (1983) *The Official Sloane Ranger Diary*, London, Ebury.

Barron, John and Paul, Anthony (1977) *Murder of a Gentle Land, the untold story of Communist genocide in Cambodia*, New York, Readers Digest Press.

Barron, Milton L. (1950) "A content analysis of inter-group humor," in *American Sociological Review*, Vol.15, No.1, February, pp.88–94.

Barry, Norman (1982) "The tradition of spontaneous order," in *Literature of Liberty*, Vol.5, No.2, Summer, pp.7–58.

Barth, Frederick (ed.) (1969) *Ethnic Groups and Boundaries, the social organization of culture differences*, London, Allen and Unwin.

Bartley, James Orr (1954) *Teague, Shenkin and Sawney*, Cork, Ireland, Cork University Press.

Barwell, Mike (1987) *The 1988 Alternative Book of Records*, London, Grafton.

Bar-Yosef, Rivka Weiss (1980) "Desocialization and resocialization: the adjustment process of immigrants," in Krausz (ed.), pp.19–38.

Barzini, Luigi (1964) *The Italians*, New York, Bantam.

Basinful of Fun (many issues 1950s), Leeds, F. Youngman.

Batchelor, Kay and Maylin, Keith (eds.) (1977) *Laughing Matter II*, Great Missenden, Topaz.

Bateman, Michael (1969) *This England*, Harmondsworth, Penguin.

Bauer, Lt. Colonel Eddy (1972) *World War II*, London, Orbis.
Baxter, Stanley and Mitchell, Alex (1985) *Stanley Baxter's Suburban Shocker*, Edinburgh, Waterfront.
Bayor, Ronald H. (1978) *Neighbors in Conflict, the Irish, Germans, Jews and Italians of New York City 1929–41*, Baltimore, John Hopkins University Press.
Beckmann, Petr (1969) *Whispered Anecdotes: Humor from Behind the Iron-Curtain*, Boulder, Colorado, Golem.
Beckmann, Petr (1980) *Hammer and Tickle*, Boulder, Colorado, Golem.
Beeldenstorm, Zak (1985) *België in de politieke karikatuur*, Antwerp, Europalie 80.
Beeston, Richard (1984) "Mondale is frustrated," in *Daily Telegraph*, August 16, p.4.
"Belgium survey" (1980) in *The Economist*, January 19.
Bell, Alan (1980) *Sydney Smith*, Oxford, Oxford University Press.
Bell, Daniel (1961A) "Work and its discontents, the cult of efficiency in America," in Bell (1961C), pp.222–62.
Bell, Daniel (1961B) "Crime as an American way of life: A queer ladder of social mobility," in Bell (1961C), pp.115–36.
Bell, Daniel (1961C) *The End of Ideology*, New York, Free Press.
Bell, Daniel (1979) *The Cultural Contradictions of Capitalism*, London, Heinemann.
Bell, John Joy (1929) *Hoots*, Dundee, Scotland, Valentine.
Bellman, Richard (1970) "Humor and Paradox," in Mendel (ed.) (1970A), pp.31–60.
Belloc, Hilaire (1923) *The bad child's book of beasts together with More beasts for worse children and Cautionary Tales*, London, Duckworth.
Bemmann, Hans (1973) *Der klerikale Witz*, Munich, Deutscher Taschenbuch.
Ben-Amos, Dan (1973) "The myth of Jewish humor," in *Western Folkore*, Vol.32, No.2, April, pp.112–31.
Bentley, E. Clerihew (1983) *The Complete Clerihews of E. Clerihew Bentley*, Oxford, Oxford University Press.
Bentley, Nicholas and Esar, Evan (1962) *The Treasury of Humorous Quotations*, London, J. M. Dent.
Berenstain, Stan and Berenstain, Jan (1970) *Mr Dirty vs Mrs Clean*, New York, Dell.
Bergson, Henri (1911) *Laughter, an essay on the meaning of the comic*, London, Macmillan.
Berkeley, Humphrey (1980) *The Life and Death of Rochester Sneath*, London, Hamish Hamilton.
Berman, Shelley (1966) *Shelley Berman's Cleans and Dirtys*, Los Angeles, Price/Stern/Sloan.
Bermant, Chaim (1986) *What's the Joke?* London, Weidenfeld and Nicolson.
Bernhardi, General Friedrich von (1914) *Germany and the Next War*, London, Edward Arnold.
Best Australian Jokes (1971) London, Wolfe.
Best Cornish jokes (n.d.) Truro, Cornwall, Tor Mark.
Besten Schottenwitze, Die (1982) Munich, Moewig.
Besten Soldatenwitze, Die (1982) Munich, Moewig.
Best of 606 Aggie jokes, The (1976) Dallas, Gigem.
Best of Trudeau, The (1972) Toronto, Modern Canadian Library.
Bethell, Nicholas (1976) *The War Hitler Won*, London, Futura.
Bevan, Rev. James Oliver (1911) *Wits and their humours*, London, George Allen.

Biberaj, Elez (1984) "The Conflict in Kossovo," in *Survey*, Vol.28, No.3 (122), Autumn, pp.39–57.

Bible, King James Version.

Bible, New English (1970) London, Oxford and Cambridge University Presses.

Bierce, Ambrose (1912) *The Collected Works of Ambrose Bierce*, New York, Neale.

Bierce, Ambrose (1971) *The Enlarged Devil's Dictionary*, Harmondsworth, Penguin.

Bingham, Stella (1987) *Great Nursing Disasters*, London, Arthur Barker.

Birch, Therese (1980) *Therese Birch's Jelly Bone Graffiti Book*, London, Hutchinson.

Birmingham, George A. (pseud. of James Owen Hannay) (1927) *Now you tell one, stories of Irish wit and humour*, Dundee, Valentine.

Birnbach, Lisa; Roberts, Jonathan; Wallace, Carel McD.; Wiley, Mason (1980) *The Official Preppy Handbook*, New York, Workman.

Biron, François and Folgoas, George (1977) *Eh Bien Raconte*, Paris, Mengès.

100 Blagues (series), Lyon, Egé.

Blake, Robert (1964) *101 Elephant Jokes*, New York, Scholastic.

Blicher-Hansen, I. and Buchwald, Gunnar (1940) *Asfaltens Cowboys*, Copenhagen, C. A. Reitzels.

Blicher-Hansen, I. and Buchwald, Gunnar (1941) *Pastoren er Morsom*, Copenhagen, C. A. Reitzels.

Bloch, Arthur (1985) *Murphy's Law Complete*, London, Methuen.

Blumenfeld, Gerry (1970) *Rx: Doctor's Orders: Laugh!*, New York, Popular.

Blyth, Reginald Horace (1963) *Japanese Humor*, Tokyo, Japan Travel Bureau.

Bodnar, John (1976) "Immigration and modernization, the case of Slavic peasants in industrial America," in *Journal of Social History*, Vol.10, No.1, Fall, pp.44–72.

Böhm, Max (1983) *Böhm's lachendes lexicon*, Vienna, Kreymayr und Scheriau.

Bokun, Branko (1986) *Humour Therapy*, London, Vita.

Bold, Alan (1979) *The Sphere Book of Improper Verse*, London, Sphere.

Boltinoff, Henry (1957) *Sex Is Better in College*, London, Brown Watson.

Bonfanti, Joe (1976) *Italian Jokes*, New York, Leisure.

Bonjour, E.; Offler, H. S.; and Potter, G. R. (1952) *A Short History of Switzerland*, Oxford, Clarendon.

Bonvi (pseud. Franco Bonvicini) *Sturmtruppen* (series 1970s and 1980s), Milan, Corno. The Italian series has been translated into German as *Die Sturmtruppen*, West Berlin, Beta.

Book of Abstracts of The 5th International Conference on Humour and the First Symposium on Irish Humour (1985) Dublin, Boole.

Book of Anecdotes (n.d.) London, Leopold B. Hill.

Book of Humour, Wit and Wisdom (1882) London, Routledge.

Book of the Goons, The (1974) London, Robson.

Borrow, George (1955, First pub. 1862) *Wild Wales*, London.

Boston, Richard (1982) *The C. O. Jones Compendium of Practical Jokes*, London, Enigma.

Boswell, James (1890, First pub. 1791) *The Life of Samuel Johnson LLD*, London, John Murray.

Botkin, Benjamin A. (1957) *A Treasury of American Anecdotes*, New York, Galahad.

Botting, Douglas (1986) *In the Ruins of the Reich*, London, Collins.

Bouker, Gordon (1966) "Paddy, Taffy and Jock," in *Plays and Players*, Vol.14, No.2, November, pp.62–65.

Bourdon, Georges (1914) *The German Enigma*, Paris, Georges Crès.

Bourhis, Richard Y.; Gadfield, Nicholas J.; Giles, Howard; Tajfel, Henri (1977) "Context and Ethnic Humour in Intergroup Relations," in Chapman and Foot (eds.).

Boute-Hen Train, van der (1978) *Anthologie de l' humeur Belge*, Paris, Garnier Frères.

Bowles, Colin (1986) *G'Day! Teach Yourself Australian*, North Ryde, New South Wales, Angus and Robertson.

Bowman, James and Bianco, Margery (1968) *Who Was Tricked?* London, Frederick Muller.

Boyd, Lizzie (1978) "Thrifty secrets of Scottish cooking," in *Readers Digest*, January, pp.127–31.

Braben, Eddie (1974) *The Best of Morecambe and Wise*, London, Futura.

Bracket, Dame Hilda (1980) *One Little Maid, the Memories of Dame Hilda Bracket*, London, Heinemann.

Bradbury, Malcolm (1960) *Phogey!* London, Max Parrish.

Bradbury, Malcolm (1987) *Why come to Slaka*, London, Arrow.

Bradley, Ian (1982) *The Annotated Gilbert and Sullivan*, Harmondsworth, Penguin.

Bramieri, Gino (1980A) *Io Bramieri ve racconto 400 barzellette*, Milan, De Vecchi.

Bramieri, Gino (1980B) *Il Grande Libro delle barzellette*, Milan, De Vecchi.

Bramieri, Gino (1981A) *La mie nuovissime barzellette*, Milan, De Vecchi.

Bramieri, Gino (1981B) *Io Bramieri ve le racconto in un orecchio*, Milan, De Vecchi.

Bramieri, Gino (1983) *La mie ultimissime barzellette su denaro e ricchezza*, Milan, De Vecchi.

Bramieri, Gino (1985A) *Il libro d'oro delle mie barzellette*, Milan, De Vecchi.

Bramieri, Gino (1985B) *Il mio nuovissimo cocktail di barzellette*, Milan, De Vecchi.

Brandes, Stanley H. (1977) "Peaceful protest, Spanish political humor in a time of crisis," in *Western Folklore*, Vol.36, pp.331–46.

Brandreth, Gyles (1981) *The Amazing Almanac*, London, Pelham.

Braude, Jacob M. (1976, First pub. in U.S. 1958) *Braude's Handbook of Humor for All Occasions*, Bombay, Jaico.

Braun, Aurel (1978) *Romanian Foreign Policy since 1965: The Political and Military Limits of Autonomy*, New York, Praeger.

Braxap, Ernest (1910) *The great civil war in Lancashire*, Manchester, University of Manchester Press.

Breinhorst, Willy (1970; First pub. 1963) *Aegtemandens sode liv*, Copenhagen, Winthers.

Brewer's Dictionary of Phrase and Fable (ed. Ivor H. Evans) (1981), London, Cassell.

Briggs, Katherine M. (1970) *A Dictionary of British Folktales*, London, Routledge & Kegan Paul.

Briggs, Katherine M. (1977) *British Folk Tales and Legends: A Sampler*, London, Granada.

Briggs, Sgt. Robert (1985) *A funny kind of war*, London, Arlington.

Brillat-Savarin, J. A. (1875) *Physiologie du goût*, Paris, Charpentier.

Brisk, Richard (n.d.) *The Railway Book of Fun*, London, W. Nicholson.

Brodnick, Max (1976) *The Jerry Ford Joke Book*, New York, Leisure.

Broeck, Walter van den (1976) *Minder Cola met nog meer rietjes*, The Hague, Manteau.

Bromfield, Ken and Bromfield, Tony (1985) *Old Bore's Almanack*, Horndean, Hants, Milestone.

Brooke-Taylor, Tim; Jinkin, John; Cryer, Barry (1977) Extract from the least worst of "Hello Cheeky," in Batchelor and Maylin (eds.).

Broome, Captain Jack (1974) *Services Wrendered*, London, Wm. Kimber.

Brown, Christy (1972; First pub. 1954) *The Childhood Story of Christy Brown*, London, Pan.

Brown, Dan and Bryant, Jennings (1983) "Humor in the mass media," in McGhee and Goldstein (eds.) Vol.2, pp.143–72.

Brown, Ian and Hendrie, James (1985) *The Cabinet Leaks*, London, Sphere.

Brown, Roy "Chubby" (1986) *Wet Knickers*, London, Arrow.

Brown, Stuart (1987) *Sosban fach*, Talybont, Wales, Y. Lolfa.

Browne, Courtney (1969) *Tojo: The Last Banzai*, London, Transworld.

Brunvand, Jan Harold (1983) *The Vanishing Hitchhiker, American Urban Legends and their Meanings*, London, Picador.

Brustgi, Franz Georg (1978) *Heiteres Schwabenbrevier*, Reutlingen Knödler.

Bryant, Ray (1984) "Put that in your pipe and smoke it," in *Reading Weekend Post*, England, October 13, p.3.

Bryson, Kit; Fitzherbert, Selina; Legris, Jean-Luc (1984) *The Naff Sex-Guide*, London, Arrow.

Buckle, Richard (ed.) (1980) *U and non-U revisited*, London, Debrett's Peerage and Futura.

Bullock, Alan (1962) *Hitler, a Study in Tyranny*, Harmondsworth, Penguin.

Bülow, Prince Bernhard von (1914) *Imperial Germany*, London, Cassell.

Burger, Hannes (1981) "Das Ringelspiel der plumpen Scherze," in *Süddeutsche Zeitung*, 164, 3, July 21.

Burke, Carol and Light, Martin (eds.) (1978) *Back in Those Days: Reminiscenses and Stories of Indiana*, Bloomington, Indiana, Indiana Writers.

Burke, Peter (1978) *Popular Culture in Early Modern Europe*, London, Temple Smith.

Burland, Cottie A. (1969) *The Exotic White Man*, London, Weidenfeld and Nicolson.

Burma, John H. (1946) "Humor as a technique in race conflict," in *American Sociological Review*, Vol.11, pp.710–15.

Burns, Stan and Weinstein, Mel (1978) *The Book of Jewish World Records*, Los Angeles, Pinnacle.

Burns, Thomas A. and Burns, Inger H. (1975) *Doing the Wash: An Expressive Culture and Personality Study of a Joke and Its Tellers*, Norwood, Penn., Norwood.

Busch, Wilhelm (1907) *Die fromme Helene*, Munich, Bafferman.

Busch, Wilhelm (1976) *Max und Moritz*, Munich, Südwest.

Buscha, Annerosa and Buscha, Joachim (1986) *Sprachscherze: Anekdoten für den Ausländerunterricht*, Leipzig V. E. B.

Büschgen, Hans E. (1987) "The U.S. dollar, scenario of a world currency," in *Inter Economics*, Vol.22, No.2, March/April, pp.59–68.

Bushell, Peter (1984) *Great Eccentrics*, London, Allen and Unwin.

Butler, Tony (1968) *Best Irish Jokes*, London, Wolfe.

Butterfield, Fox (1982) *China, Alive in the Bitter Sea*, London, Hodder and Stoughton.

Büttner, Henry (1980) *Gesellschaftsspiele*, Berlin, Eulenspiegel.

By all that's holy, it's a bad taste book (1983) London, Silvey-Jex.

Caesar, Julius (see Julius Caesar).

Cagney, Peter (1976) *The Book of Wit and Humour*, Wellingborough, Northants, A. Thomas.

Cagney, Peter (1979A) *The Official Irish Joke Book No.4*, London, Futura.

Cagney, Peter (1979B) *Positively the Last Official Irish Joke Book*, London, Futura.

Cagney, Peter (1979C) *The Official Aussie Joke-Book*, London, Futura.
Cagney, Peter (1980) *The Official Salesman's Joke Book*, London, Futura.
Calder-Marshall, Arthur (1966) *Wish You Were Here*, London, Hutchinson.
Calleo, David Patrick (1978) *The German Problem Reconsidered, Germany and the World Order 1870 to the Present*, Cambridge, England, Cambridge University Press.
Campbell, Roy (1963) *Daddy, are you married?* Sydney, Angus and Robertson.
Cane, Alan (1984) "Towards systems for fault tolerance," in *Financial Times*, November 21.
Carballo, Louis (1977) *Laughter from Trinidad*, San Fernando, Trinidad, Rilloprint.
Carr, William (1987) *Introduction to Müller* (1987), pp.1–12.
Carrillo, Rafael (1981) *Posada y el grabado mexicano*, Mexico City, Panorama.
Carritt, E. F. (1922–23) "A theory of the ludicrous, a footnote to Croce's aesthetic," in *Hibbert Journal*, Vol.21, pp.552–64.
Carroll, Lewis (1965) *The works of Lewis Carroll*, Feltham, England, Spring.
Carroll, Lewis (1973) "The game of logic," in Fisher, John (ed.) *The Magic of Lewis Carroll*, London, Nelson.
Carsten, F. L. (1972) *Revolution in Central Europe 1918–1919*, London, Temple Smith.
Carver, John (1980) *Ag shame, Van der Merwe*, Hillbrow, Johannesburg, Lorton.
Cash, Wilbur Joseph (1973; First pub. 1941) *The Mind of the South*, Harmondsworth, Penguin.
Castel, Robert (1978) *Robert Castel raconte les meilleures histoires de Kaouito le pied-noir*, Paris, Mengès.
Cecil, Robert and Goodenough, Simon H. (eds.) (1975) *Hitler's War-Machine*, London, Leisure.
'Celt' (1911) *The cynic's autograph book*, London, Gay and Hancock.
Cerf, Bennett Alfred (1944) *Try and Stop Me*, New York, Simon and Schuster.
Cerf, Bennett Alfred (1945) *Laughing Stock*, New York, Grosset and Dunlap.
Cerf, Bennett Alfred (1946) *Anything for a Laugh*, New York, Grosset and Dunlap.
Cerf, Bennett Alfred (1948) *Shake Well Before Using*, New York, Simon and Schuster.
Cerf, Bennett Alfred (1950) *Laughter Incorporated Laughter Unlimited*, Garden City, New York, Garden City Books.
Cerf, Bennett Alfred (1952) *Good for a Laugh*, Garden City, New York, Hanover House.
Cerf, Bennett Alfred (1956A) *Bumper Crop* (2 vols.), Garden City, New York, Garden City Books.
Cerf, Bennett Alfred (1956B) *The Life of the Party*, London, Hammond and Hammond.
Cerf, Bennett Alfred (1959) *The Laugh's on Me*, Garden City, New York, Doubleday.
Cesaresco, Countess Evelyn Martinengo (1892) *Introduction to Piozzi*.
Chadwick, St. John (1967) *Newfoundland, Island into Province*, London, Cambridge University Press.
Chambers, Gary (1979) *The Almost Complete Irish Gag Book*, London, Star.
Chambers, Gary (1980) *The Second Almost Complete Irish Gag Book*, London, Star.
Chambers, Gary (1981) *The Last Almost Complete Irish Gag Book*, London, Star.
Chambers's Encyclopaedia (1890) Gothamites, Vol.5.
Chapman, Antony J. and Foot, Hugh C. (eds.) (1977) *It's a Funny Thing, Humour*, Oxford, Pergamon.
Chappell, Connery (1986) *Island of Barbed Wire*, London, Corgi.

Charles, Lucille Hoerr (1945) "The Clown's Function," in *Journal of American Folklore*, Vol.58, pp.25–34.

Chase, Edithe Lea and French, Captain William Edward Pattison (1913) *Toasts for All Occasions*, Hamilton, Kent, Simpkin Marshall.

Chaucer, Geoffrey (1988) *The Riverside Chaucer*, Oxford, Oxford University Press.

Cheer up Britain (1977) London, Wolfe.

Chen, L. (1980) "Humor during old Mao days," in *Free China Weekly*, Vol.21, No.23, June 15.

Chesney, Kellow (1970) *The Victorian Underworld*, London, Temple Smith.

Chia, Corinne; Seet, K. K.; and Wong, Pat M. (1985) *Made in Singapore*, Singapore, Times Books International.

Child, Richard Washburn (1928) Introduction to Mussolini (1928).

Chitrouflet, J. and Van der Fried, M. (1981) *Encyclopédie pratique des jeux Belges*, Paris, Garnier.

Chodoff, Elliot P. (1983) "Ideology and Primary Groups," in *Armed Forces and Society*, Vol.9, No.4, Summer, pp.569–93.

Chrestien, Michel (1957) *Esprit, es-tu là?* Paris, Gallimard.

Christ, Richard (ed.) (1978) *Simplicissimus 1896–1914*, Berlin, Rütten and Loewing.

Claes, Jules (1915) *The German Mole*, London, Bell.

Clark, G. Kitson (1962) *The Making of Victorian England*, London, Methuen.

Clark, Martin (1984) *Modern Italy 1871–1982*, London, Longman.

'Clay pipe and carbon' (1949) *Humour of the Underground*, Cardiff, Priory Press.

Clément, André (1945) *Les 100 meilleures histoires de l'occupation*, Paris, Lesourd.

Clements, Jonathan (1978) *The Armada Book of Jokes and Riddles*, London, Armada.

Clements, William M. (1973) "The types of the Polish joke," in *Folklore Forum*, Bibliographic and special series 3.

Climent-Galant, Jacquie (1979) *Les meillures de Lui*, Paris, Filipacchi.

Clinard, Marshall Barron (1978) *Cities with Little Crime*, Cambridge, England, Cambridge University Press.

Clouston, William Alexander (1888) *The book of noodles: stories of simpletons and their follies*, London, Elliot Stock.

Clout, Bill and Hooper, Nina (1975) *Best Outer Space Jokes*, London, Wolfe.

Cobb, Irvin Shrewsbury (1918) *The Glory of the Coming*, New York, Doran.

Cobb, Irvin Shrewsbury (1923) *A Laugh a Day Keeps the Doctor Away*, Garden City, New York, Garden City Publishing.

Cobb, Irvin Shrewsbury (1924) *Indiana*, New York, George H. Doran.

Cobb, Irvin Shrewsbury (1925) *Many Laughs for Many Days*, Garden City, New York, Garden City Publishing.

Cobb, Irvin Shrewsbury (1940) *Favourite Humorous Stories of Irvin Cobb*, New York, Triangle.

Cobbett, William (1912; First pub. c.1830) *Rural rides*, London, J. M. Dent.

Cohen, Anthony P. (1975) "The definition of public identity: managing marginality in outport Newfoundland following confederation," in *Sociological Review*, 23, pp.93–119.

Cohen, Bernard and Rosenzweig, Luc (1988) *Waldheim*, London, Robson.

Cohen, John Michael (ed.) (1952) *The Penguin Book of Comic and Curious Verse*, Harmondsworth, Penguin.

Cohn, Norman (1970) *Warrant for Genocide: The Myth of the Jewish World Conspiracy and the Protocols of the Elders of Zion*, Harmondsworth, Penguin.

Cole, Edward William (1887) *Cole's Fun Doctor*, Melbourne, E. W. Cole.

Cole, William (1980) *Knock knocks*, St. Albans, Granada.

Collection de l'art brut (1976) Lausanne, Collection de l'art brut.

Collection of Foreign Jokes, A. (1982) Canton, Fujien Province Publishers.

Colleville, Vicomte de and de Zepelin, Fritz (1896) *Contes grotesques du Danemark*, Paris, Chamuel.

Collins, E. J. T. (1976) "The consumer revolution and the growth of factory foods: changing patterns of bread and cereal, eating in Britain in the twentieth century," in Oddy and Miller (eds.).

Collinson, Clifford Whiteley (1926) *Life and Laughter 'midst the Cannibals*, London, Hutchinson.

Colombo, John Robert (1975) *Colombo's Little Book of Canadian Proverbs, Graffiti, Limericks and Other Vital Matters*, Edmonton, Alberta, Hurtig.

Colyer, Richard J. (1976) *The Welsh Cattle Drovers*, Cardiff, University of Wales Press.

Commager, Henry Steele (ed.) (1974) *Britain through American Eyes*, London, Bodley Head.

Connell, John (1980) "Wavell's 30,000," in Liddell Hart (ed.).

Conquest, Robert (1968) *The Soviet Police System*, London, Bodley Head.

Conquest, Robert (1971) *The Great Terror*, Harmondsworth, Penguin.

Conquest, Robert (1980) *We and They*, London, Temple Smith.

Conquest of North Africa, The. The first complete authoritative account of the entire three years North African campaign from Egypt to Tunisia (n.d.) London, Burke.

Conway, Ronald (1974) *The Great Australian Stupor: An Interpretation of the Australian Way of Life*, Melbourne, Sun.

Cook, Anthony Peter (1988) Skill and skilled workers: a comparative and historical study. PhD Thesis, University of Reading.

Cook, Judith (1979) "Bitter and twisted," in *The Guardian*, July 8.

Cooper, Matthew (1975) "Science and technology—brilliance and confusion," in Cecil and Goodenough (eds.).

Copeland, Lewis (1940) *The World's Best Jokes*, Garden City, New York, Garden City Publishers.

Copeland, Lewis and Copeland, Faye (1939) *10,000 Jokes, Toasts and Stories*, Garden City, New York, Garden City Publishers.

Corbett, Helen (1984) *Come on Laugh*, Coleraine, Northern Ireland, Impact.

Corbin, John (1902) "An American at Oxford," in Commager (ed.) (1974), pp.568–82.

Coren, Alan (1974) *The Collected Bulletins of President Idi Amin*, London, Robson.

Coren, Alan (1975) *The Further Bulletins of President Idi Amin*, London, Robson.

Coren, Alan (ed.) (1979) *Pick of Punch*, London, Hutchinson.

Cornelisen, Ann (1969) *Torregreca*, London, Macmillan.

Cornell, George W. (1986) "Jewish humor," in *Washington Post*, May 31.

Coser, Lewis A. (1974) *Greedy Institutions: Patterns of Undivided Commitment*, New York, Free Press.

Coser, Ruth L. (1959) "Some social functions of laughter: a study of humor in a hospital setting," in *Human Relations*, Vol.12, pp.171–82.

Costner, Sharon (1975) " 'State' jokes on the Carolina campus," in *North Carolina Folklore Journal*, Vol.23, pp.107–11.

Cottle, Basil (1978) *Penguin Dictionary of Surnames*, Harmondsworth, Penguin.

Coulton, George Gordon (1945) *Four-Score Years*, London, Readers Union/Cambridge University Press.

Coupe, William (1986) *Germany through the Looking Glass, a Cartoon Chronicle of the Federal Republic*, Leamington Spa, Berg.

Cowan, Lore and Cowan, Maurice (1972) *The Wit of Medicine*, London, Leslie Frewin.

Craig, Gordon A. (1964) *The Politics of the Prussian Army*, New York, Oxford University Press.

Craigie, William Alexander (1898) "Evald Tang Kristensen a Danish folklorist," in *Folklore*, Vol.9, No.3, p.220.

Craik, Thomas Wallace (1964) *The Comic Tales of Chaucer*, London, Methuen.

Cranfield, Ingrid (1983) *Skiing Down Everest and Other Crazy Adventures*, London, Severn House.

Cremer, J. J. (1894) "Farmer Gerrit's visit to Amsterdam," in Werner (ed.) (1894).

Critchell, Joseph Trowbridge and Raymond, Joseph (1969) *A History of the Frozen Meat Trade*, London, Dawsons.

Croce, Benedetto (1928) "La guerra Italiana l'esercito e il socialismo," in *Pagina sulla Guerra*, Bari; Gius, Laterza, pp.218–26. [First pub. in *Giornale d' Italia*, 24th September 1917].

Crompton, Colin (1970A) *Best Lancashire Jokes*, London, Wolfe.

Crompton, Colin (1970B) *Best Newly-wed Jokes*, London, Wolfe.

Crompton, Colin (1970C) *Best Nursing Jokes*, London, Wolfe.

Crompton, Colin (1970D) *Best Yorkshire Jokes*, London, Wolfe.

Crompton, Colin (1970E) *More Best Jewish Jokes*, London, Wolfe.

Crompton, Colin (1973) *Best Office Jokes*, London, Wolfe.

Crosbie, John S. (1972) *Crosbie's Dictionary of Puns*, Richmond Hill, Ontario, Simon and Schuster.

Crosland, Thomas William Hodgson (1905) *The Wild Irishman*, London, T. Werner Laurie.

Crosland, Thomas William Hodgson (1908) *The unspeakable Scot*, London, Stanley Paul.

Crosland, Thomas William Hodgson (1922) *The fine old Hebrew gentleman*, London, T. Werner Laurie.

Cross, David (1980) "Reagan joke drops him in duck soup," in *The Times*, February 20, p.1.

Cruikshank, Robert (1832) *Cruikshank's Comic Album*, London, Wm. Kidd.

Culotta, Nino (see also O'Grady) (1965) *Gone fishin'*, Dee why west, Australia, Ure Smith.

Cunningham, C. (1971A) *How to Die Laughing*, St. Ives, Cornwall, James Pike.

Cunningham, C. (1971B) *Tell the Best Jokes*, St. Ives, Cornwall, James Pike.

Cunningham, Hugh (1980) *Leisure in the Industrial Revolution 1780–1880*, London, Croom Helm.

Cunningham, S. B. (1973) *Piccolo Book of Riddles*, London, Pan.

Cuppy, Will (1952) *The Decline and Fall of Practically Everybody*, London, Dennis Dobson.

Curtis, Liz (1985) *Nothing but the Same Old Story*, London, Information on Ireland.

Curtis, L. Perry (1971) *Apes and Angels, the Irishman in Victorian Caricature*, Newton Abbot, Devon, David and Charles.

Cusack, Cyril (ed.) (1980) *The Humour Is on Me*, Belfast, Appletree.

Danby, Mary (1979) *The Awful Joke Book*, London, Fontana.

Daniels, Arlene K. and Daniels, Richard R. (1964) "The social function of the career fool," in *Psychiatry*, Vol.27, pp.219–29.

Daniells, Red (1965) *Drivers Wild, Wilder and Wildest*, Harmondsworth, Penguin.

Danielson, Larry (1975) "The dialect trickster among the Kansas Swedes," in *Indiana Folklore*, Vol.8, Nos.1–2, pp.39–58.

Daninos, Pierre (1955) *Major Thompson Lives in France*, London, Jonathan Cape.

Darracott, Joseph and Loftus, Belinda (1981A) *First World War Posters*, London, Imperial War Museum.

Darracott, Joseph and Loftus, Belinda (1981B) *Second World War Posters*, London, Imperial War Museum.

Daudet, Alphonse (1890) *Tartarin of Tarascon and Tartarin on the Alps*, London, J. M. Dent.

David, Edward Illtyd (ed.) (1977) *Inside Asquith's Cabinet, from the Diaries of Charles Hobhouse*, London, John Murray.

Davidson, Ian (1978) *The Two Ronnies in a Packed Programme Tonight*, London, Star.

Davidson, James Dale (1981) "The Last Returns," in *Reason*, Vol.12, No.9, January.

Davies, Christie (1972) "Asians of East Africa," in *Quest*, No.77, July-August, pp.33–39.

Davies, Christie (1975) *Permissive Britain, Social Change in the Sixties and Seventies*, London, Pitman.

Davies, Christie (1977) "The changing stereotype of the Welsh in English jokes," in Chapman and Foot (eds.) pp.311–14.

Davies, Christie (1978) *Welsh Jokes*, Cardiff, John Jones.

Davies, Christie (1979) "What's so funny about business?" in *The Director*, Vol.32, No.6, pp.38–39.

Davies, Christie (1982A) "Sexual taboos and social boundaries," in *American Journal of Sociology*, Vol.87, No.5, March, pp.1032–63.

Davies, Christie (1982B) "The comic Welshman in British literature from Shakespeare to Dylan Thomas," in G. Bennett (ed.) *Papers of The Dylan Thomas Society of Wales*, Swansea, Dylan Thomas Society of Wales.

Davies, Christie (1982C) "Women as rulers in modern times," in *New Quest* 35, Sept-Oct., pp.271–89.

Davies, Christie (1982D) "Ethnic Jokes, moral values and social boundaries," in *British Journal of Sociology*, Vol.33, No.3, pp.383–403.

Davies, Christie (1982E) "Itali Sunt Imbelles," in *Journal of Strategic Studies*, Vol.5, No.2, June, pp.266–69.

Davies, Christie (1983) "Religious boundaries and sexual morality," in *Annual Review of the Social Sciences of Religion*, Vol.6, Fall, pp.45–77.

Davies, Christie (1984) "Commentary on Anton C. Zijderveld's trend report on the sociology of humour and laughter," in *Current Sociology*, Vol.31, No.1, Spring, pp.142–57.

Davies, Christie (1985A) "Wits not half-wits," in *Daily Telegraph*, August 5.

Davies, Christie (1985B) "Ethnic Jokes and Social Change: The Case of the Welsh," in *Immigrants and Minorities*, Vol.4, No.1, March, pp.46–63.

Davies, Christie (1986A)"How the Irish win at Irish Jokes," in *Irish Independent*, March 11.

Davies, Christie (1986B) "Jewish jokes, anti-Semitic jokes and Hebredonian jokes," in Ziv (ed.), pp.59–80.

Davies, Christie (1987A) "Language, identity and ethnic jokes about stupidity," in *International Journal of the Sociology of Language*, Vol.65, pp.39–52.

Davies, Christie (1987B) "Folklor, anekdoti i ikonomicheski progres," in *Smekhut vuv folklora, Problemi na Bulgarskiya Folklor*, Vol.7, Sofia, Izdatelstvo na Bulgarskata/Akademiya na naukite, pp.66–77.

Davies, Christie (1988A) "Stupidity and rationality: jokes from the iron cage," in Powell and Paton (eds.), pp.1–32.

Davies, Christie (1988B) "The Irish joke as a social phenomenon," in Durant, John and Miller, Jonathan (eds.) *Laughing Matters—A Serious Look at Humour*, Harlow, Essex, Longman Scientific and Technical.

Davies, Christie (in press) "Humor for the future and a future for humor," in Shtromas, Alexander and Kaplan, Morton (eds.) *The Soviet Union and the*

Challenge of the Future: Ideology, Culture and Nationality, Vol.3, New York, Paragon.
Davies, Christie and Lewis, Russell (1973) *The Reactionary Joke Book*, London, Wolfe.
Davies, David (1883) *Echoes from the Welsh Hills or Reminiscences of the Preachers and People of Wales*, London, Alexander and Shepheard.
Davies, D. Elwyn (1980) *Y Smotiau Duon*, Llandyssul, Wales, Gwasg Gomer.
Davies, Elwyn and Rees, Alwyn D. (eds.) (1962) *Welsh Rural Communities*, Cardiff, University of Wales Press.
Davies, Rees (1975) "Race Relations in Post-Conquest Wales: Confrontation and Compromise," in *Transactions of the Honourable Society of Cymmrodorion*, Sessions 1974–75, pp.32–56.
Davis, Alan F. and Encel, Solomon (eds.) (1965) *Australian Society*, London, Pall Mall.
Davis, Allison; Gardner, Burleigh B; Gardner, Mary R.; directed by Warner, D. Lloyd (1941) *Deep South, A Social Anthropological Study of Caste and Class*, Chicago, University of Chicago Press.
Davis, Henry William Charles (1914) *The Political Thought of Heinrich von Treitschke*, London, Constable.
Davis, Robert B. (1985) "Alcohol abuse and the Soviet military," in *Armed Forces and Society*, Vol.2, No.3, Spring.
Davis, Stanley (1968) *The Joke Is Wild*, Kansas City, Hallmark.
Davis, William (ed.) (1979) *The Punch Book of Travel*, London, Hodder and Stoughton.
Dawson, Les (1979) *The Cosmo Smallpiece Guide to Male Liberation*, London, W. H. Allen.
Deane, Elisabeth (1971) *Smiles, Chuckles and Chortles*, Mount Vernon, Peter Pauper.
Death at Katyn (1944) New York, National Committee of Americans of Polish descent.
de Catt, Henri (1929) *Frederick the Great, Memoirs of his Reader*, London, Constable.
de Grand'Combe, Félix (pseud.) (1932) *England—This Way!* London, Ivor Nicholson and Watson.
de Guingaud, Major-General Sir Francis (1980) "Alamein, the tide turns," in Liddell Hart (ed.).
Dekker, Thomas (Fredson Bowers, ed.) (1961) *The Dramatic Works of Thomas Dekker*, Cambridge, Cambridge University Press.
Delage, Yves (1919) "Sur la nature du comique," in *Revue du Mois*, April 20, pp.337–54.
Delaney, Bud and Delaney, Lolo (1974) *The Laugh Journal*, New York, Scholastic.
Delaney, Bud and Delaney, Lolo (1977) *The Beastly Gazette*, New York, Scholastic.
Demerath III, N. J. (1969; First pub. 1952) "Religion and social class in America," in Robertson (ed.) (1969), pp.333 *et seq.*
Derrière, Pierre (1976) *Up Yours!* New York, Nordon.
de Witt, Hugh (1970) *Bawdy Barrack-Room Ballads*, London, Universal/Tandem.
Dickens, Charles (1902; First pub. 1842) *American Notes [and Pictures from Italy and a Child's History of England]*, London, Chapman and Hall.
Dickenson, Lt.-Col. Dicky and Hooper, Bill (n.d.) *Clangers in Uniform*, Tunbridge Wells, Midas.
Dickman, Harry (1975) *Best Tramp Jokes*, London, Wolfe.
Digrifwch (1882) Amlwch, Wales, D. Jones.
Digrifwr Cymraeg, Y, The Welsh Jester (1820) Carmarthen, Wales, J. Evans.
Dillon, Emile Joseph (1914) *A Scrap of Paper*, London, Hodder and Stoughton.

Dines, Michael (1986) *The Jewish Joke Book*, London, Futura.
Dingle, A. E. (1976) "Drink and working-class living standards in Britain 1870–1914," in Oddy and Miller (eds.).
Diprose, John (1879) *Diprose's Book of Epitaphs: Humorous Eccentric, Ancient and Remarkable*, London, Diprose and Bateman.
Diserens, Charles M. (1926) "Recent Theories of Laughter," in *Psychological Bulletin*, Vol.23, pp.247–55.
"Diverse Ethnic Roots of Bay Area Residents, The" (1984) in *San Francisco Chronicle*, March 19.
Dobie, J. Frank and Boatright, Mody C. (1966) *Straight Texas*, Hatboro, Penn., Folklore Associates.
Dobson, Scott (1976) *Larn yersel' Geordie*, Newcastle on Tyne, Frank Graham.
Dollard, John (1957; First pub. 1937) *Caste and Class in a Southern Town*, Garden City, New York, Doubleday.
Dorinson, Joseph (1986) "The Jew as comic," in Ziv (ed.) (1986B) pp.29–46.
Douglas, Mary (1966) *Purity and Danger*, London, Routledge & Kegan Paul.
Douglas, Mary (1970) *Natural Symbols*, London, Barrie and Rockliff.
Douglas, Mary (1975) *Implicit Meanings: Essays in Anthropology*, London, Routledge & Kegan Paul.
Douglas, Norman (1962; First pub. 1915) *Old Calabria*, Harmondsworth, Penguin.
Dower and Riddell (1938) *Outside Britain*, London, Heinemann.
Doyle, David Noel and Edwards, Owen Dudley (eds.) (1980) *America and Ireland 1776–1976, the American Identity and the Irish Connection*, Westport, Conn., Greenwood.
Doyno, Victor (ed.) (1983) *Mark Twain, Selected Writings of an American Skeptic*, Buffalo, Prometheus.
Draig, Glas (Blue Dragon, pseud. of Arthur Tysilio Johnson) (1910) *The Perfidious Welshman*, London, Stanley Paul.
Draitser, Emil Abramovitch (1978) *Forbidden Laughter, Soviet Underground Jokes*, Los Angeles, Almanac.
Drozdzynski, Alexander (1978) *Der politsche Witz im Ostblock*, Munich, D.T.V.
Drummond, J. C. and Wilbraham, Anne (1958) *The Englishman's Food*, London, Jonathan Cape.
Dudeney, Henry Ernest (1917) *Amusements in Mathematics*, London, Nelson.
Dulac, Edward (1925) *Histoires Gasconnes*, Paris, Editions de France.
Dumazedier, Joffre (1967) *Toward a Society of Leisure*, New York, Free Press.
Dunbar, Janet and Webb, Clifford (1980) *Laughing Matter*, London, Michael Joseph.
Duncan, Professor I. (n.d.) *The Temperance Speaker and Good Templars Reciter*, Wakefield, Nicholson.
Duncan, Ronald (1983) *Critics' Gaffes*, London, Macdonald.
Dundes, Alan (ed.) (1965) *The Study of Folklore*, Englewood Cliffs, N.J., Prentice Hall.
Dundes, Alan (1971) "A study of ethnic slurs: the Jew and the Polack in the United States," in *Journal of American Folklore*, Vol.84, No.332, pp.186–203.
Dundes, Alan (1975A) "The number three in American culture," in Dundes (ed.) (1975C) pp.206–225.
Dundes, Alan (1975B) "Slurs international: folk comparisons of ethnicity and national character," in *Southern Folklore Quarterly*, Vol.39, pp.15–38.
Dundes, Alan (ed.) (1975C) *Analytical Essays in Folklore*, The Hague, Mouton.
Dundes, Alan (1979) "Polish Pope Jokes," in *Journal of American Folklore*, Vol.92, pp.219–22.
Dundes, Alan (1980) "Misunderstanding Humour: an American Stereotype of the Englishman," in Newall (ed.) (1980), pp.10–15.

Dundes, Alan (1981) "Many hands make light work or caught in the act of screwing in light-bulbs," in *Western Folklore*, Vol.40, No.3, July, pp.261–66.
Dundes, Alan (1984) *Life is Like a Chicken-Coop Ladder*, Princeton, Princeton University Press.
Dundes, Alan and Abrahams, Roger D. (1975) "On elephantasy and elephanticide," in Dundes (ed.) (1975C), pp.192–205.
Dundes, Alan and Hauschild, Thomas (1983) "Auschwitz Jokes," in *Western Folklore*, Vol.42, No.4, October, pp.249–60.
Dunkling, Leslie Alan (1981) *Our Secret Names*, London, Sidgwick and Jackson.
Dunne, Finley Peter (1942) *Mr. Dooley at His Best*, New York, Scribner.
Dunne, Finley Peter (1963; First pub. 1898–1906) *Mr. Dooley on Ivrything and Ivrybody*, New York, Dover.
Durkheim, Emile (1964) *The Division of Labor in Society*, New York, Free Press.
Durkheim, Emile (1970) *Suicide, a Study in Sociology*, London, Routledge & Kegan Paul.
Dwyer, Bil (1975) *Thangs Yankees Don' Know*, Highlands, North Carolina, Merry Mountaineers.
Dyson, Will (1915) *Kultur Cartoons*, London, Stanley Paul.
East Anglia's Humour (1976) Ipswich Suffolk, East Anglia Magazine, n.p.
Eastman, R. (1970) *1936 Jumbo Joke Book* (Facsimile), St. Ives, Cornwall, James Pike.
Eban, Abba (1976) "Israel anti-Semitism and the United Nations,"in *The Jerusalem Quarterly*, No.1, Fall, pp.110–20.
Eco, Umberto (1983) *The Name of the Rose*, New York, Harcourt Brace Jovanovich.
Edgeworth, Richard Lovell and Edgeworth, Maria (1802) *Essay on Irish Bulls*, London, J. Johnson.
Edwardes, Michael (ed.) (1956) *The Reverend Mr. Punch*, London, A. R. Mowbray.
Edwards, H. W. J. (1975) *Sons of the Romans*, Swansea, Christopher Davies.
Edwards, Jimmy (1955) *Take It From Me*, London, Panther.
Edwards, John (1985) *Talk Tidy*, Cowbridge, Wales, D. Brown.
Edwards, John (1986) *More Talk Tidy*, Cowbridge, Wales, D. Brown.
Edwards, Kenneth (1977) *I wish I'd said that too*, London, Abelard.
Edwards, Kenneth (1978) *More things I wish I'd said . . . And some I wish I hadn't*, London, Abelard.
Edwards, Lilian M. (1940) *A Welsh Woman's Work in India*, Edinburgh, McCall Barbour.
Eidheim, Harald (1969) "When ethnic identity is a social stigma," in Barth (ed.), pp.39–57.
Einarsson, Magnus (1975) "Oral tradition and ethnic boundaries: 'West' Icelandic verses and anecdotes," in *Canadian Ethnic Studies*, Vol.7, Part 2, pp.19–32.
Eisenstadt, Shmuel Noah (1969) *The Protestant Ethic Thesis*, in Robertson (ed.), pp.297–330.
Eisenstadt, Shmuel Noah (1980) "Introduction: some reflections on the study of ethnicity," in Krausz (ed.), pp.1–17.
Eldin, Peter (1981) *The Complete Practical Joker*, London, Sparrow/Hutchinson.
Elgart, Jack M. (1951) *Over Sexteen*, New York, Grayson/Elgart.
Elgart, Jack M. (1953) *More Over Sexteen*, New York, Grayson.
Elgart, Jack M. (n.d.) *Still More Over Sexteen*, New York, Grayson.
Eliot, Thomas Stearns (1948) *Selected Poems*, Harmondsworth, Penguin.
Elliot, A. and Elliot, B. (1968) *Best Scottish Jokes*, London, Wolfe.
Elliott, Andrew (1974) *A Geordie Life of Jesus*, Newcastle, Frank Graham.
Elon, Amos (1972) *The Israelis*, New York, Bantam.

El-Shamy, Hasan M. (1980) *Folktales of Egypt*, Chicago, University of Chicago Press.
Ember, Mária (1988) *Viccgyü jtemény*, Budapest, Minerva.
Emerson, Joan P. (1969) "Negotiating the serious import of humor," in *Sociometry*, Vol.32, pp.169–81.
Emerson, Ralph Waldo (1856) "English Traits," in Commager (ed.), pp.268–85.
Encyclopaedia of Insulting Behaviour, The (1981) London, Futura.
Engel, Fritz and Falk, Norbert (1927) *Die Anekdote*, Berlin.
Engels, Friedrich (1958) *The Condition of the Working Class in England in 1844*, Oxford, Basil Blackwell.
English As She is Spoke or a Jest in Sober Earnest (1967) Detroit, Gale Research.
English Caricature 1620 to the Present (1984) London, Victoria and Albert Museum.
'An Englishman' (1911) *The Welshman's Reputation*, London, Stanley Paul.
Ernst, Theodore R. (1927) *Laughter, gems of the world's best humor*, New York, Theodore, R. Ernst.
Esar, Evan (1954) *The Humor of Humor*, London, Phoenix House.
Esar, Evan (1960) *Esar's Comic Dictionary*, New York, Bramhall House.
Esar, Evan (1978) *The Comic Encyclopaedia*, Garden City, New York, Garden City Books.
Evans, Cyril James Oswald (1938) *Glamorgan its History and Topography*, Cardiff, William Lewis.
Evans, Eifion (1969) *The Welsh Revival of 1964*, London, Evangelical.
Evans, Emrys (1979) *Hwyl' Stiniog!*, Caernarfon, Wales, Cyhoeddiadau Mei.
Eysenck, Hans Jurgen (1944) "National differences in sense of humor, three experimental and statistical studies," in *Journal of Personality*, Vol.13, pp.37–54.
Facetiae of Poggio and other medieval story tellers, The [n.d.], London, Routledge.
Fairservis, Walter A. (1962) *The Ancient Kingdoms of the Nile*, New York, Mentor.
Falls, Cyril (1966) *Caporetto 1917*, London, Weidenfeld and Nicolson.
Fanning, Charles (1980) *Mr. Dooley in Chicago: Finley, Peter Dunne as Historian of the Irish in America*, in Doyle and Edwards (eds.), pp.151–64.
Fantoni, Barry (1975) *100 Best Jokes of Barry Fantoni*, London, Private Eye/Andre Deutsch.
Fantoni, Barry (1982) *Colemanballs*, London, Private Eye/Andre Deutsch.
Farber, Maurice J. (1953) "English and Americans: values in the socialization process," in *Journal of Psychology*, Vol.36, Part 2, October, pp.243–50.
Farris, John (1970) *The Silent Majority*, New York, Kanrom.
Faure, J. (1979) *1200 Chistes-Humor y Risa*, Mexico City, Azor.
Fearn-Wannan, William (1970) *A Dictionary of Australian Folklore*, Sydney, Lansdowne.
Fechtner, Leopold (1973) *5000 One and Two Liners for Any and Every Occasion*, West Nyack, New York, Parker.
Feinburg, Leonard (1978) *The Secret of Humor*, Amsterdam, Rodopi.
Ferguson, James (1933) *The Table in a Roar*, London, Methuen.
Ferguson, John (1968) *The Wit of the Greeks and the Romans*, London, Leslie Frewin.
Fernau, Hermann (1916) *Because I am a German*, London, Constable.
Ferrer, Julio (1978) "Vitsar om Franco," in *Tradisjon*, Vol.8, pp.79–109.
'Fidelius, Petr' (1984) "In search of Central Europe: On handling words," in *Salisbury Review*, Spring, pp.3–6.
Fieldhouse, Paul (1986) *Food and Nutrition, Customs and Culture*, London, Croom Helm.

Filip, Ota and Škutina, Vladimír (1979) *Anekdoty za Pendrek*, Zurich, Konfrontation.
Filip, Ota and Steiger, Ivan (1981) *Politischer Witz in Prag*, Berlin, Universitas.
Finley, Moses I. (1971) *The Ancient Greeks*, Harmondsworth, Penguin.
Finnemore, John (1915) *Social Life in Wales*, London, A and C Black.
Fisher, Irving and Brougham, H. Bruce (1928) *Prohibition, still at its worst*, New York, Alcohol Information Committee.
Fishman, Joshua A. et al. (eds.) (1966) *Language Loyality in the United States*, The Hague, Mouton.
Fishman, Joshua A. and Nahirny, Vladimir C. (1966) "The Ethnic Group School and Mother Tongue Maintenance," in Fishman et al. (eds.) pp.92–126.
Fisk, Robert (1985) *In Time of War*, London, Paladin.
Fitzgerald, Patrick (1987) *The Comic Book of M.I.5.*, Dingle Ireland, Brandon.
Fitzgibbon, Louis (1971) *Katyn, a Crime without Parallel*, London, Tom Stacey.
Fletcher, Cyril (1982) *Odes and Ends*, St. Albans, Granada.
Flood, Robert (1985) *The Book of Fascinating Christian Facts*, Denver, Colorado, Accent.
'F.M.' (pseud. of Frederick Muller) (1945) *Here's a Good One*, London, Frederick Muller.
Foley, John (1980) "Tobruk Survives," in Liddell Hart (ed.).
Ford, 'Senator' Ed; Hershfield, Harry; Laurie Jr., Joe (1947) *Cream of the Crop*, New York, Grosset and Dunlap.
Ford, Gerald R. (1979) *A Time to Heal*, New York, Harper and Row.
Ford, Gerald R. (1987) *Humor and the Presidency*, New York, Arbor House.
Ford, Rev. John C. (1959) *Shall I start to Drink?* Dublin, Catholic Truth Society of Ireland.
Ford, Robert (1901) *Thistledown*, Paisley, Scotland, Alexander Gardner.
Forrest, S. J. (1968) *Parson's Play-Pen*, London, Mowbray.
'Fougasse' (pseud. of Cyril Kenneth Bird) (1937) *Drawing the Line Somewhere*, London, Methuen.
'Fougasse' (pseud. of Cyril Kenneth Bird) (1942) *Sorry—No Rubber*, London, Methuen.
'Fougasse' (pseud. of Cyril Kenneth Bird) (1945) *The Luck of the Draw*, London, Methuen.
Fowkes, Edith (ed.) (1976) *Folklore of Canada*, Toronto, McClelland and Stewart.
Fox, Paul (1970) *The Poles in America*, New York, Arno.
Francis-Jones, Gwyneth (1984) *Cows, Cardis and Cockneys*, Borth, Wales, Gwyneth Francis-Jones.
Franklin, Benjamin (1983) *On the Choice of a Mistress and Other Satires and Hoaxes*, White Plains, New York, Peter Pauper.
Freud, Sigmund (1960) *Jokes and Their Relation to the Unconscious* (Vol.8 of Complete Psychological Works), London, Hogarth.
Friedländer, Saul (1976) "The historical significance of the holocaust," in *The Jerusalem Quarterly*, No.1, Fall pp.36–59.
Frost, Max Gilbert (1933) *The Merry Stories Omnibus Book*, London, T. Werner Laurie.
Fuchs, Esther (1986) "Humor and sexism, the case of the Jewish joke," in Ziv (ed.) pp.111–22.
Fucks, Wilhelm (1968) *Nach allen Regeln der Kunst*, Stuttgart, Deutsche Verlagsanstalt.
Fuller, Thomas (ed. John Nichols) (1811; First pub. 1662) *The History of the worthies of England*, London, F. C. and J. Rivington.
Funfare, a Treasury of Reader's Digest Wit and Humor (1949) Pleasantville, Reader's Digest.

Further Sunbeams (1924) London, Stanley Paul.
Furtounov, Stefan and Prodanov, Peter (1985) *Gabrovo Anecdotes*, Sofia, Svyat.
'G-W' (1978; First pub. 1916) *Tübingen Gogen-Witze*, Tübingen, Historischer.
Gaeve Jyder, De (n.d.) Copenhagen, Carit Andersens.
Gaidoz, Henri and Sébillot, Paul (1884) *Blason populaire de la France*, Paris, Leopold Cerf.
Gamm, Hans-Jochen (1979) *Der Flüsterwitz im dritten Reich*, Munich, D.T.V.
García, P. (1977) *Les chistes de Franco*, Madrid, Martínez Campos.
Gargadennec, Roger (1972) *Contes de Cap-Sizun*, Paris, Librairie d'Amérique et d'Orient.
Garwood, Alfred Edward (1903) *40 Years of an Engineer's Life at Home and Abroad*, Newport, Gwent, A. W. Dawson.
Gašparíková, Viera (1980) *Ostrovtipné príbehy i veliké cigánstva a žarty*, Bratislava, Tatran.
Gašparíková, Viera (1986) *Slovenská ludová próza a jej súčasné vývinové tendencie*, Bratislava.
Gawrych, George W. (1987) "The Egyptian High Command in the 1973 War," in *Armed Forces and Society*, Vol.13, No.4, Summer, pp.535–59.
Geiger, Raymond (1923) *Histoires Juives*, Paris, Nouvelle Revue Francaise.
Geiger, Raymond (1925) *Nouvelles Histoires Juives*, Paris, Gallimard.
Geikie, Sir Archibald (1904) *Scottish Reminiscences*, Glasgow, James Maclehose.
George, C. W. (1903) *Keep Smiling, a series of personal reminiscences and humorous stories*, London, Stockwell.
Gerard, James W. (1917) *My Four Years in Germany*, London, Hodder and Stoughton.
Gergov, Spass (1985) Introduction to Furtounov and Prodanov.
'A German' (1915) *J'Accuse*, London, Hodder and Stoughton.
German Wit and Humor (1903) Philadelphia, George W. Jacobs.
Gerrard, Frank (1969) *Sausage and Small Goods Production*, London, Leonard Hill.
Geyl, Pieter (1962) *Debates with Historians*, London, Collins.
Geyl, Pieter (1965) *Napoleon: For and Against*, Harmondsworth, Penguin.
Geyl, Pieter (1967) *Encounters in History*, London, Fontana.
Gianelli, Emilio (1987) *Visti da dietro*, Milan, Arnoldo Mondadori.
Gibbon, Rev. J. Morgan (1910) *Weighed in the Balance*, London, National Council of Evangelical Free Churches.
Gifford, Denis (1978) *The Two Ronnies Comic Book*, London, Transworld.
Gilbert, Martin (1974) *The Arab-Israeli Conflict*, London, Weidenfeld and Nicolson.
Gilbert, Martin (1985) *Jewish History Atlas*, London, Weidenfeld and Nicolson.
Gilbert, Sir William Schwenck (1919) *The Bab Ballads and Songs of a Savoyard*, London, Macmillan.
Gilbert, Sir William Schwenck (1983) *The Savoy Operas*, London, Macmillan.
Gillespie, Very Rev. John (1904) *The Humours of Scottish Life*, Edinburgh, Blackwood.
Gilley, Sheridan (1978) "Attitudes to the Irish in England 1789–1900," in Holmes (ed.) pp.81–110.
Ginger, Ray (1974) *Ray Ginger's Jokebook about American History*, New York, New Viewpoints.
Giraldus Cambrensis (Gerald of Wales 1146?–1220?) (1908) *The Itinerary through Wales* and *The Description of Wales*, London, J. M. Dent.
Glad, Donald Davison (1947) "Attitudes and experiences of American-Jewish and American-Irish male youth as related to differences in adult rates of inebriety," in *Quarterly Journal of Studies on Alcohol*, Vol.8, No.3, Dec. 1947.

Gladstone, William Ewart (1891) Speech in British House of Commons, *Hansard Parliamentary Debates*, 3rd series, Vol.350, column 1265, February 20.
Glatt, M. M. (1973) "Alcoholism and drug dependence amongst Jews," in Shiloh and Selavon (eds.).
Glazer, Nathan and Moynihan, Daniel, P. (eds.) (1975) *Ethnicity, Theory and Experience*, Cambridge, Mass., Harvard University Press.
Goebbels, Josef (ed. and trans. Louis P. Lochner, 1948) *The Goebbels Diaries*, London, Hamish Hamilton.
Goebbels, Josef (ed. Fred Taylor, 1982) *The Goebbels Diaries 1939–41*, London, Sphere.
Goethe, Johann Wolfgang von (1970; First pub. 1862–63) *Italian Journey 1786–1788*, Harmondsworth, Penguin.
Goffman, Erving (1968) *Asylums*, Harmondsworth, Penguin.
Goldberg, Marie Waife (1967) *My Father Sholem Aleichem*, London, Gollancz.
Golde, Günter (1975) *Catholics and Protestants, Agricultural Modernization in Two German Villages*, New York, Academic.
Golden, Harry (1959) *Only in America*, New York, Permabooks.
Golden, Harry (1967) *Ess, Ess, Mein Kindt*, New York, G. P. Putams/Berkley.
Goldhamer, Herbert (1976) *The Soviet Soldier*, New York, Crane Russak.
Goldsmith, John and Powell-Smith, Vincent (1981) *Against the Law*, London, Readers Digest Assoc.
Goldstein, Jeffrey H. and McGhee, Paul E. (eds.) (1972) *The Psychology of Humor, Theoretical Perspectives and Empirical Issues*, New York, Academic.
Goldstein, Jeffrey H.; Suls J. M.; and Anthony S. (1972) "Enjoyment of specific types of humor content: motivation or salience," in Goldstein and McGhee (eds.).
Goldstein-Jackson, Kevin (1980) *Joke After Joke*, Kingswood, Surrey, Elliot Rightway.
Gombrich, Ernst Hans Josef and Kris, Ernest (1940) *Caricature*, Harmondsworth, Penguin.
Gooch, John (1982) "Italian military competence," in *Journal of Strategic Studies*, Vol.5, No.2, June, pp.257–65.
Goodrich, Anne T.; Jules, Henry; Goodrich, D. Wells (1954) "Laughter in psychiatric staff conferences: a sociopsychiatric analysis," in *American Journal of Orthopsychiatry*, Vol.24, pp.175–84.
Goody, Jack (1982) *Cooking, Cuisine and Class*, Cambridge, England, Cambridge University Press.
Gordon, Milton M. (1975) "Towards a general theory of racial and ethnic group relations," in Glazer and Moynihan (eds.) pp.84–110.
Gorer, Geoffrey (1945) *Africa Dances*, Harmondsworth, Penguin.
Gorer, Geoffrey (1948) *The Americans; A Study in National Character*, London, Cresset.
Görlitz, Walter (1953) *The German General Staff, Its History and Structure 1657–1945*, London, Hollis and Carter.
Gorrah, Seamus B. (pseud. of Dave Dutton) (1981) *Ireland Strikes Back*, Feltham, England, Hamlyn.
Goscinny and Uderzo (1976) *Asterix in Britain*, Sevenoaks, Knight/Hodder.
Gosling, William Gilbert (1910) *Labrador: Its Discovery, Exploration and Development*, London.
Gossett, Margaret (1972) *Piccolo Book of Jokes*, London, Pan.
Gould, H. Carruthers (1902) *Froissart's Modern Chronicles*, London, T. Fisher Unwin.
Gould, Julius (1984) *Jewish Commitment, a Study in London*, London, Institute of Jewish Affairs.

Gould, William S. Baring (1970) *The Lure of the Limerick*, St. Albans, Panther.

'Graham' (Alex Graham) (1978) *I do like to be . . . People at leisure*, London, Geoffrey Bles.

Graham, Frank (1980A) *The Geordie Netty*, Newcastle on Tyne, Frank Graham.

Graham, Frank (1980B) *The New Geordie Dictionary*, Newcastle on Tyne, Frank Graham.

Graham, Harry (1905) *Verse and Worse*, London, Edward Arnold.

Grambs, David (1986) *Dimboxes, Epopts and Other Quidams*, New York, Workman.

'Grandee' (1979) *Cheer up, Britain*, London, Wolfe and Bond Clarkson Russell.

Grant, John (1982) *A Book of Numbers*, Bath, Ashgrove.

Graves, Dr. Armgaard Karl (pseud.) (1914) *The Secrets of the German War Office*, London, T. Werner Laurie.

Graves, Robert (1928) *Mrs. Fisher or the Future of Humour*, London, K. Paul Trench Trubner.

Graves, Robert (1970; First pub. 1929) *Goodbye to All That*, Harmondsworth, Penguin.

Greeley, Andrew M. (1972) *The Denominational Society*, Glenview, Illinois, Scott Foresman.

Greeley, Andrew M. (1980) "The American Achievement, a report from Great Ireland," in Doyle and Edwards (eds.).

Greeley, Andrew M. and McGready, William C. (1975) *The Transmission of Cultural Heritages* in Glazer and Moynihan (eds.), pp.209–235.

Greeley, Horace (1851) "Glances at Europe in a series of letters from Great Britain, France, Italy, Switzerland during the summer of 1851," in Commager (ed.) (1974).

Green, Benny (1976) *I've lost my little Willie, a celebration of comic postcards*, London, Elm Tree.

Green, E. R. R. (1980) "The Irish in American Business and Professions," in Doyle and Edwards (eds.) pp.193–205.

Green, Rayna (1979) Introduction to Randolph, pp.i-xxix.

Greenburg, Andrea (1972) "The ethnic joke: form and function," in *Keystone Folklore Quarterly*, Vol.17, No.4, Winter, pp.144–56.

Greenburg, Dan (1975) *How to Be a Jewish Mother*, Los Angeles, Price Stern Sloan.

Greenway, John (1972) *The Last Frontier*, London, Davis-Poynter.

Gregory, Kenneth (ed.) (1984) *The Second Cuckoo, a New Selection of Letters to the Times Since 1900*, London, Unwin.

Gregory, Richard (1979) *Knight Book of Howlers*, London, Hodder and Stoughton.

'Gren' (pseud.) (1973) *More of My Wales*, Llandybie, Wales, Christopher Davies.

'Gren' (pseud.) (1979) *Ponty and Pop, the Aberflyarff Story*, Cardiff, Funfare.

Grenfell, Russell (1953) *Unconditional Hatred*, New York, Devin-Adair.

Grill, Sebastion (1949) *Graf Bobby und Baron Mucki, Geschichten aus dem alten Wien*, Munich, Heimeran.

Grose, Francis (attribution dubious) (1971) *1811 Dictionary of the Vulgar Tongue*, Northfield, Illinois, Digest.

Gross, John (1971) *Joyce*, London, Fontana.

Gross, Milt (1927) *Nize Baby*, London, Alfred A. Knopf.

Grosser, Alfred (1974) *Germany in Our Time*, Harmondsworth, Penguin.

Grossmith, F. T. (1984) *The Cross and the Swastika*, Worthing, Sussex, Henry E. Walter.

Grotjahn, Martin (1970A) "Laughter in psychotherapy," in Mendel (ed.) (1970) pp.61–66.

Grotjahn, Martin (1970B) "Jewish jokes and their relation to masochism," in Mendel (ed.) pp.135–42.

Gruner, Charles R. (1978) *Understanding Laughter, the Workings of Wit and Humor*, Chicago, Nelson Hall.
Guillois, Mina and Guillois, André (1971) *L'Amour en 1000 Histoires Droles*, Paris, Fayard.
Guillois, Mina and Guillois, André (1979A) *Histoires Belges et méchantes*, Paris, Mengès.
Guillois, Mina and Guillois, André (1979B) *Les meilleures Histoires Ecossaises, Anglaises Irlandaises, Galloises*, Paris, Mengès.
Guillois, Mina and Guillois, André (1980) *Encyclopadie de l'Amour en 2000 Histoires Drôles*, Paris, Fayard.
Gurney, John (1986) *The World's Best Catholic Jokes*, North Ryde, New South Wales, Angus and Robertson.
Gusfield, Joseph (1962) "Status Politics and the Changing Ideologies of the American Temperance Movement," in Pittman and Snyder (eds.).
Ha! Ha!! Ha!!! (1953) *Everybody's Book of Humorous Stories and Jokes*, London, Foulsham.
Haas, Jack (1972) " 'Binging', Educational control among high steel iron workers," in *American Behavioral Scientist*, Vol.16, pp.27–34.
Haas, Jack (1974) "The stages of the High-Steel ironworker apprentice career," in *The Sociological Quarterly*, Vol.15, Winter, pp.93–108.
Haas, Jack (1977) "Learning real feelings a study of high steel ironworkers' reactions to fear and danger," in *Sociology of Work and Occupations*, Vol.4, No.2, May, pp.147–70.
Habt Acht! 244 militarische Anekdoten und Witze (1910) Vienna, Moritz Perles.
Hacker, Louis M. (1940) *The Triumph of American Capitalism*, New York, Simon and Schuster.
Hagen, Everett E. (1962) *On the Theory of Social Change—How Economic Growth Begins*, Homewood, Illinois, Dorsey.
Haiman, Miecislaus (1974) *Polish Past in America 1608–1865*, Chicago, Polish Museum of America.
Hajdu, István (1985) *Ostropoli Herschel Ostora*, Budapest, Minerva.
Halbritter, Kurt (1954) *Disziplin ist Alles*, Frankfurt am Main, Bärmeier und Nickel.
Hale, John Rigby (1972) *Machiavelli and Renaissance Italy*, Harmondsworth, Penguin.
Hales, Alfred Greenwood (1910) *McGlusky the Reformer*, London, T. Fisher Unwin.
Hall, J. Mortimer (1934) *Anecdota Americana second series*, Boston, Humphrey Adams.
Hall, J. Mortimer and Passemon, William (1933) *Anecdota Americana*, New York, William Faro.
Hallpike, C. R. (1976) "Is there a primitive mentality?" in *Man*, Vol.11, No.2, June, pp.253–70.
Hallpike, C. R. (1979) *The Foundations of Primitive Thought*, Oxford, Clarendon.
Halsey, Ashley (1962) *The Perfect Squelch*, Greenwich, Conn., Fawcett.
Hanse, Joseph et al. (1971) *Chasse aux Belgicisms*, Brussels, Fondation Charles Plisnier.
Hanson, J. Ivor (1978) *We Also Speak English*, Port Talbot, Wales, Daffodil.
Haraszti Miklós (1977) *A Worker in a Worker's State*, Harmondsworth, Penguin.
Hardcastle, William (1972) "Time, gentlemen please," in *Punch*, August 30, p.270.
Harding, Michael (1987) *Bomber's Moon*, London, Michael Joseph.
Harman, John Keith (n.d.) *Our concert party*, London, Felix McGlennon.
Harries, Frederick J. (1919) *Shakespeare and the Welsh*, London, T. Fisher Unwin.
Harris, David A. and Rabinovich Israil (1986) "On a lighter note?" in *Soviet Jewish Humor*, New York, American Jewish Committee.

Harris, George (1982) *Spare a Copper*, London, Police Review.
Harris, Leon (1965) *The Fine Art of Political Wit*, London, Cassell.
Harrison, G. A. and Peel, John (eds.) (1969) "Biosocial aspects of race," in *Journal of Biosocial Science*, Supplement No.1, Oxford, Basil Blackwell.
Harrison, Lawrence E. (1985) *Under-Development Is a State of Mind: The Latin American Case*, Lanham, Maryland, University Press of America.
Hart, Sir Basil Liddell. See Liddell Hart.
Hartley, Dorothy (1979) *Food in England*, London, Macdonald and Jane's.
Hartston, William (1987) *The Drunken Goldfish, a Celebration of Irrelevant Research*, London, Unwin Hyman.
Harvey, William (Aleph) (1868) *Geographical Fun: being humorous outlines of various countries*, London, Hodder and Stoughton.
Harvey, William (1904) *Irish Life and Humour*, Stirling, Scotland, Eneas Mackay.
Hašek, Jaroslav (1974) *The Good Soldier Švejk*, Harmondsworth, Penguin.
Hašek, Jaroslav (1983) *The Red Commissar*, London, Sphere.
Hatton, Joseph (1893) *In Jest and Earnest*, London, Leadenhall.
Haugen, Einar (1966) Introduction in Fishman et al. (eds.).
Hauser, Richard (1962) *The Homosexual Society*, London, Bodley Head.
Havelund, Hjalmar (1977) *Fynsk Lune*, Copenhagen, Stig.
Haworth, Peter (1928) *Rumours and Hoaxes*, Oxford, Basil Blackwell.
Hayes, Carlton J. H. (1960) *Nationalism: A Religion*, New York, Macmillan.
Hayler, Guy (1911) *Famous Fanatics*, London, Funk and Wagnalls.
Hazlitt, William (1910) *Lectures on the English Comic Writers*, London, Dent.
Hazlitt, William Carew (ed.) (1864) *Shakespeare Jest Books* (3 vols.), London, Willis and Sotheran.
Hazlitt, William Carew (ed.) (1887; First pub. 1526) *A Hundred Merry Tales, the earliest English jest-book*, London.
Hazlitt, William Carew (1890) *Studies in jocular literature*, London, E. Stock.
Heald, Gordon (1982) *A Comparison between American, European and Japanese Values*, Paper given at World Association for Public Opinion Research, Hunt Valley, Maryland.
Heath, Michael (1973) *100 Best Jokes of Michael Heath*, London, Private Eye/Andre Deutsch.
Heath, Michael (1975) *100 Jokes of Heath Again*, London, Private Eye/Andre Deutsch.
Heinold, Ehrhardt (1978) *Sachsen wie es lacht*, Reinbek bei Hamburg, Rowohlt.
Heinrich, R. and Lothar, E. (1979) *Erzähle einen guten Witz*, Vienna, Pechans Perlen-Reihe.
Helitzer, Melvin (ed.) (1984A) *Comedy Techniques for Writers and Performers*, Athens, Ohio, Lawhead.
Helitzer, Melvin (1984B) "The hearts theory: the anatomy of humor," in Helitzer (ed.) pp.23–48.
Helitzer, Melvin (1987) *Comedy Writing Secrets*, Cincinnati, Ohio, Writers Digest Books.
Helmreich, William B. (1982) *The Things They Say Behind Your Back*, New York, Doubleday.
Henry, Clarissa and Hillel, Marc (1976) *Children of the S.S.*, London, Hutchinson.
Herberg, Will (1960) *Protestant, Catholic Jew*, Garden City, New York, Doubleday.
Herbert, A. P. (1935) *Uncommon Law*, London, Methuen.
Herbert, A. P. (1945) *Light the Lights*, London, Methuen.
Herdi, Fritz (1979) *Schweizer Witz*, Munich, Heimeran.
Heron House Associates (1979) *The Book of Numbers*, London, Pelham.
Herrera, Antonio Salgado (n.d.) *Lo mejor del humorismo mexicano*, Mexico City, Editorial Libra.

Hershfield, Harry (1947). See Ford, 'Senator' Ed.
Hervier, Paul-Louis (1916) *The Super-Huns*, London, Eveleigh Nash.
Herzberg, Frederick (1968) *Work and the Nature of Man*, London, Staples.
Hewison, Robert (1981) *Monty Python, the Case Against*, London, Eyre Methuen.
Heywood, Abel (n.d.) *Heywood's Stump Speeches and Nigger Jokes*, Manchester, Abel Heywood.
Hicks, Seymour (1936) *Laugh With Me*, London, Cassell.
Hillbilly Laugh Book (1972) Amarillo, Texas, Baxter Lane.
Hillel, Marc (1978) *O Israël*, Paris, Stock.
Hillier, Bevis (1970) *Cartoons and Caricatures*, London, Studio Vista/Dutton.
Hillman, Fanny (1965) *Memoirs of a Jewish Madam*, London, Neville Spearman.
Hills, Dick (1979) *Delayed by Fog in Timbuctoo*, London, Futura.
Hilton, Audrey (ed.) (1959) *This England*, London, Statesman and Nation.
Hirsch, Phil (1978) *101 Hamburger Jokes*, New York, Scholastic.
Hirsch, Phil(lis) and Larkin, Paul(a) (1976) *Male Chauvinists and Women's Libbers*, New York, Pyramid.
Hirszowicz, Maria (1980) *The Bureaucratic Leviathon: A Study in the Sociology of Communism*, Oxford, Martin Robertson.
Hirszowicz, Maria (1981) *Industrial Sociology*, Oxford, Martin Robertson.
Hirszowicz, Maria (1986) *Coercion and Control in Communist Society*, Brighton, Wheatsheaf.
Hitler, Adolf (1974; 1st English trans. 1933) *Mein Kampf*, London, Hutchinson.
Hitler, Adolf (ed. H. R. Trevor-Roper) (1973) *Hitler's Table Talk 1941–44*, London, Weidenfeld and Nicolson.
Hitler, Adolf (1983) *Hitler's Secret Book*, New York, Grove.
Hoare, Robert (1973) *World War Two*, London, Macdonald.
Hobbes, Thomas (1650) "Human Nature or the fundamental elements of policie," in (1840) *The English Works of Thomas Hobbes*, London, Bohn.
Hobhouse, Charles. See David, Edward Illtyd (ed.).
Hodes, Max (1978) *The Official Scottish Joke Book*, London, Futura.
Hofmann, Fritz (1977) *Bümplizer treffen sich und da Sagt der Eine zum Andem*, Berne, Benteli.
Hofmann, Fritz (1979) *E Hampfell Bärner Witze*, Berne, Benteli.
Hogben, Lancelot (1967) *Whales for the Welsh*, London, Rapp and Carroll.
Hogg, Gary (1958) *Cannibalism and Human Sacrifice*, London, Robert Hale.
Hoggart, Simon (1981) *On the House*, London, Robson.
Holbek, Bergt (1975) "The Ethnic Joke in Denmark," in Nespen, W. van (ed.) *Miscellanea Prof Em. Dr. K. C. Peeters, Door Vrienden en Collega hem aangeboden ter gelegenheid van zyn emeritaat*, Antwerp, Govaerts.
Holdcraft, Paul (1932) *Snappy Stories that Preachers Tell*, Baltimore, Stockton.
Holloway, Stanley (ed. Marshall, Michael) (1979) *The Stanley Holloway Monologues*, London, Elm Tree/E.M.I.
Holmes, Colin (1978A) "J. A. Hobson and the Jews," in Holmes (ed.) (1978B).
Holmes, Colin (ed.) (1978B) *Immigrants and Minorities in British Society*, London, Allen and Unwin.
Holmes, Colin (1979) *Anti-Semitism in British Society 1876–1939*, London, Edward Arnold.
Homans, George C. (1946) "The Small Warship," in *American Sociological Review*, Vol.11, pp.294–300.
Honeysett, Martin (1976) *Honeysett at Home*, London, Dempsey and Squires.
Horecký, Michal (1985) *Humor do vrecka alebo vtipy na každý den*, Košice, Slovakia, Vychodoslovenské vydavatol'stvo.
Horn, Maurice (1980) *The World Encyclopaedia of Cartoons*, New York, Chelsea House.

Hornby, Peter (1977) *The Official Irish Jokebook*, London, Futura.
Hornby, Peter (1978) *The Official Irish Jokebook No.3 (Book 2 to follow)*, London, Futura.
Horner, Arthur (1957) *Colonel Pewter in Ironicus*, London, Pall Mall.
Horner, D. M. (1982) *High Command. Australia and Allied Strategy 1939–45*, Sydney, Allen and Unwin.
Horowitz, David L. (1975) "Ethnic Identity," in Glazer and Moynihan (eds.) pp.29–52.
Horowitz, Irving Louis (1977) *Genocide, State Power and Mass Murder*, New Brunswick, N.J., Transaction.
Horrabin, James Francis (1941) *Horrabin's atlas–history of the second great war vol.3, July 1940 to February 1941*, London, Nelson.
Houmand, Aage V. (1942) *Fridolin Hulkefryds*, Copenhagen, Poul Branner.
House, Boyce (1943) *I give you Texas*, San Antonio, Texas, Naylor.
House, Boyce (1944) *Tall talk from Texas*, San Antonio, Texas, Naylor.
House, Boyce (1945) *Texas proud and loud*, San Antonio, Texas, Naylor.
Howard, Ethel (1916) *Potsdam Princes*, London, Methuen.
Howcraft, Wilbur G. (1977) *Black with White Cockatoos or Mopokes and Mallee Roots*, Melbourne, Hawthorn.
Howe, Walter Henry (1890) *Everybody's Book of Irish Wit and Humour*, London, Saxon.
Howe, Walter Henry (1891A) *Everybody's Book of Scotch Wit and Humour*, London, Saxon.
Howe, Walter Henry (1891B) *Everybody's Book of English Wit and Humour*, London, Saxon.
Howells, William Dean (1905 and 1909) "Takes Some London Films," in Commager (ed.) (1974) pp.617–32.
Hoyt, Edwin P. (1985) *The Kamikazes*, London, Panther.
Hucker, Charles Oscar (1975) *China's Imperial Past*, London, Duckworth.
Hudd, Roy et al. (1980) *The News Huddlines*, London, New English Library.
Hudson, Arthur Palmer (ed.) (1936) *Humor of the Old Deep South*, New York, Macmillan.
Hudson, Bob and Pickering, Larry (1987) *The First Australian Dictionary of Vulgarities and Obscenities*, Newton Abbot, Devon, David and Charles.
Huggett, Richard (1975) *The Wit and Humour of Sex*, London, Quartet.
Hughes, Beth (1986) "Cities consider bar on telling Aids jokes," in *San Francisco Sunday Examiner and Chronicle*, Oct. 12, pp.131 and 138.
Hughes, Harry R. (1979) *Welsh Rarebits*, Caernarfon, Wales, Cyhoeddiadau Mei.
Hughes, Idwal (1980) *Cymeriadau Dyffryn Nantlle*, Caernarfon, Wales, Cyhoeddiadau Mei.
Humorous Recitations and Stories (n.d.) London, Foulsham.
Humorpiller, 556 (n.d.) Aarhus, Mikro.
Humour and Counter Humour (n.d.) Shrewsbury, England, Wilding.
Humphries, Barry (1982) *A Nice Night's Entertainment*, London, Granada.
Humphries, Barry (ed.) (1984) *Punch Down Under*, London, Robson.
Humphries, Barry (1986) See Patterson, Dr. Sir Les.
Humphries, Barry and Garland, Nicholas (1968) *The Wonderful World of Barry McKenzie*, London, Macdonald.
Humphries, Barry and Garland, Nicholas (1972) *Bazza Pulls It Off, More Adventures of Barry McKenzie*, London Private Eye/Andre Deutsch.
Humphries, Barry and Garland, Nicholas (1988) *The Complete Barry McKenzie*, London, Methuen.
(Hundred and One) *101 Aggie Jokes* (8 volumes) Dallas, Gigem.
Hunt, H. Cecil (1928) *Howlers*, London, Ernest Benn.

Hunt, H. Cecil (1929) *Fun with the Famous*, London, Ernest Benn.
Hunt, H. Cecil (1931) *Honoured Sir—from Babujee*, London, P. Allan.
Hunt, H. Cecil (1935) *Babujee Writes Home*, London, P. Allan.
Hurwitz, Nathan (1974) "Blacks and Jews in American Folklore," in *Western Folklore*, 33, pp.301–25.
Hyman, Dick (1978) *It's Against the Law*, Pleasantville, New York, Reader's Digest.
Ike nsmile lettslaff (1937) *Jokes, Jokes, Jokes!* London.
Imbach, Jean Pierre and Favières, Maurice (1980) *366 Histoires Droles*, Paris, R.T.L.
Inauen, August (1979) *Us em Appezöller Witztröckli*, Rorschach, Switzerland, Nebelspalter.
Inglis, Edward (1973) *The Wit of the Civil Service*, London, Leslie Frewin.
Ingrams, Richard (1971) *The Life and Times of Private Eye*, Harmondsworth, Penguin.
Ingrams, Richard and Wells, John (1984) *Bottoms Up! Further Letters of Denis Thatcher*, London, Private Eye/André Deutsch.
Instad, Helge (1966) *Land under the Pole Star*, London, Jonathan Cape.
International Joke Dictionary (1969) London, Wolfe.
Irish wit, a budget of blunders (n.d.) London, T. Hughes.
Irish Wit and Humor (1902) Chicago, F. T. Drake.
Irving, David (1978) *The Trail of the Fox*, London, Futura.
Irwin, Ken (1972) *Laugh with the Comedians*, London, Wolfe/Independent Television Books.
Isnard, Armand (1977) *Les bonnes blagues des petits Suisses*, Paris, Mengès.
Isnard, Armand (1979A) *2000 Histoires Belges*, Boulogne, Détente.
Isnard, Armand (1979B) *L'Anthologie des Histoires Drôles Erotiques*, Boulogne, Détente.
Ives, George (1980) *Man Bites Man, the Scrapbook of an Edwardian Eccentric*, London, Jay Landesman.
'J, Mr' (1976) *The World's Best Dirty Jokes*, New York, Ballantine.
Jackson, W. Turrentine (1968) *The Enterprising Scot, Investors in the American West after 1873*, Edinburgh, Edinburgh University Press.
Jacobs, David (ed. Ella Glazer) (1979) *David Jacobs' Book of Celebrities, Jokes and Anecdotes*, London, Robson.
Jacobs, George W. (1903) *German Wit and Humor*, Philadelphia, George W. Jacobs.
Jaher, Frederic Cople (1968) "The Boston Brahmins in an age of industrial capitalism," in Jaher, F. C. (ed.) *The Age of Industrialism in America*, New York, pp.188–202.
James, D. Clayton (1975) *The Years of MacArthur Vol.II 1941–45*, Boston, Houghton Mifflin.
James, Simon R. (1984) *A Dictionary of Sexist Quotations*, Brighton, Harvester.
Jan (1982) *Ik hou van dit land, zijn leiders en zijn bevolking*, Ghent, Masreelfonds.
Jansen, William Hugh (1965) "The exoteric–esoteric factor in folklore," in Dundes (ed.).
Janssen Christian (pseud. of Christie Davies) (1970) Letter *The Listener*, November 26, p.738.
Jarvenpa, Robert (1976) "Visual expression in Finnish-American ethnic slurs," in *Journal of American Folklore*, Vol.89, No.351, pp.90–91.
Jauhiainen, Marjatta (1979) *Genre, theme and stereotype analysis of the Finnish tradition of the stingy Laihians*. Paper given at the Seventh Congress of the International Society for Folk Narrative. Edinburgh, August 12–18. See also (1983) below.
Jauhiainen, Marjatta (1983) "Laihelaborna - Finlands Skottar, En analys av genrer, stereotyper och teman in laihelahumorn," in *Tradisjon*, 13, pp.47–76.
Jeffrey, Graham (1975) *The Gospel of Barnabas*, New York, Harper and Row.

Jellinek, E. M. (1962) "Cultural differences in the meaning of alcoholism," in Pittman and Snyder (eds.).
Jenkins, David (1962) "Aberporth a study of a coastal village in South Cardiganshire," in Davies and Rees (eds.).
Jenkins, R. T. (1938) *The Moravian Brethren in North Wales*, London, Cymmrodorion.
Jenkins, R. T. and Ramage, Helen (1951) *A History of the Honorable Society of Cymmrodorion*, London, Cymmrodorion.
Jennings, Paul (1976) "Forget about the Irishman, . . . Have you heard about the Pole who . . . ," in *T.V. Times*, 19th–25th June.
Jerome, Jerome Klapka (1914; First pub. 1900) *Three Men on the Bummel*, Bristol, J. W. Arrowsmith.
Jerrold, Walter (1913) *A Book of Famous Wits*, London, Methuen.
Jerrold, Walter (1928) *Bulls Blunders and Howlers*, London, Brentano's.
Jiménez, A. (1979A) *Nueva picardía*, Mexicana, Mexico City, Medicanos Unidos.
Jiménez, A. (1979B) *Primicias letreros dibujos y grafitos groseros de la picardía mexicana*, Mexico City, Posada.
Jiménez, A. (1979C) *Vocabulario prohibido de la picardía Mexicana*, Mexico City, Posada.
Joe Miller's Jests: or, the Wit's Vade-Mecum (1739) London, Read [facsimile 1962, New York, Dover].
Joell (1944) *Laugh with Joell*, Hull, A. Brown.
Johnson, Bryan Stanley (ed.) (1973) *All Bull: The National Serviceman.*
Johnson, Samuel (8th edition 1796; First pub. 1755) *A dictionary of the English Language*, Dublin, Marchbank (?)
Joker or Merry Companion, The (1763) Carmarthen, J. Ross and R. Thomas.
Jokes for All Occasions (1922) London, Brentano's.
Jokes for All Occasions (1923) London, Harold Shaylor.
Jolly Jester Book of Fun (n.d.) Lower Chelston, Devon, Gulliver.
Jon (1978) *Cartoons from the Daily Mail*, London, C and C.
Jones, Abel J. (1944) *From an Inspector's Bag*, Cardiff, Abbrevia.
Jones, Daniel (1977) *My Friend Dylan Thomas*, London, Dent.
Jones, Graham (1985) *The Forked Tongues Annual*, London, Hutchinson.
Jones, Griff Rhys; Smith, Mel; Bell, Simon; Coffman, Hilary; Seymour, David (1983) *The Smith and Jones World Atlas*, London, Mitchell Beazley.
Jones, Maldwynn Allen (1960) *American Immigration*, Chicago, University of Chicago Press.
Jones, Reginald Victor (1979) *Most Secret War*, London, Hodder and Stoughton.
'Jones, Scatterstick' (1976) *The C. B. Joke Book*, New York, Belmont Tower.
Jones, Tegwyn (1987) *Anecdotau Llenyddol*, Talybont, Wales, Y Lolfa.
Jones, W. R. ('Pelidros') (n.d.) *Isaac Lewis: A Humorous Welsh Character*, Ferndale, Wales, D. Davies.
Joyce, James (1968; First pub. 1916) *A Portrait of the Artist as a Young Man*, London, Jonathan Cape.
Julius Caesar, *Comentarii de Bello Gallico* (ed. 1853, London, Whitaker).
Junior, Allan (1925) *Canny Tales fae Aberdeen*, Dundee, Scotland, Valentine.
Junior, Allan (1927) *The Aberdeen Jew*, Dundee, Scotland, Valentine.
Junior, Allan (1928) *Aberdeen Again*, Dundee, Scotland, Valentine.
Junwu, Hua (1984) *Chinese Satire and Humour*, Beijing, New World Press.
Kaneko, Norbert N. (1949) *The Old Japanese Humor*, Tokyo, World Information Service.
Kaneko, Norbert N. (1950) *Modern Japanese Humor*, Tokyo, World Information Service.

Karaka, Dosoo Framjee (n.d.) *Arr Bhai being rephlections on the problems oph Bharat*, Bombay, S. P. Phansikar.

Karaka, Dosoo Framjee (1952) *The Adventures Oph Shri Arre Bhai to abroad*, Bombay, S. P. Phansikar.

Katz, Michael (1979) *The Study of Ethnic Jokes*, unpublished dissertation, Institute of Folklore, Indiana University, Bloomington.

Kaur, Rajinder (1967) "Sikhism as an off-shoot of traditional Hinduism and as a response to the challenge of Islam," in *Sikhism and Indian Society. Transactions of the Indian Institute of Advanced Study*, Vol.4, Simla, Rashtrapati Nivas.

Keane, John B. (1967) *Letters of a Successful T.D.*, Dublin, Mercier.

Kéchlek Arisztid, Budapest, Jenö Gabor.

Kees, Hermann (1961) *Ancient Egypt, a Cultural Topography*, London, Faber and Faber.

Keijzer, Nico (1978) *Military Obedience*, Alphen aan der Rijn, Sijthoff and Noordhoff.

Keillor, Garrison (1986) *Lake Wobegon Days*, Harmondsworth, Penguin.

Keith-Spiegel, Patricia C. (1984) "Eight humor theories," in Helitzer (ed.) (1984A) pp.17–22.

Kelly, H. P. (1906) *Gems of Irish Wit and Humor*, New York, Sully and Kleinteich.

Kelly, Sean and Mann, Ted (1978) *National Lampoon. Slightly Higher in Canada*, New York, National Lampoon.

Kelly, Sean and Weidman, John (1979) *National Lampoon's cartoons even we wouldn't dare print*, New York, Simon and Schuster.

Kendrick, Thomas Downing (1970) *British Antiquity*, New York, Barnes and Noble.

Kerman, Judith B. (1980) "The light bulb jokes, Americans look at social action processes," in *Journal of American Folklore*, Vol.93, pp.454–58.

Kessell, Neil and Walton, Henry (1969) *Alcoholism*, Harmondsworth, Penguin.

Key Jr., Valdimar Orlando (1949) *Southern Politics in State and Nation*, New York, Vintage.

Kilgarriff, Michael (1974A) *Best Boss and Worker Jokes*, London, Wolfe.

Kilgarriff, Michael (1974B) *More Best Religious Jokes*, London, Wolfe.

Kilgarriff, Michael (1975) *Best Foreigner Jokes*, London, Wolfe.

Kilgarriff, Michael (1976) *Best Teenage Jokes*, London, Wolfe.

Kilgarriff, Michael (1979) *Best Service Jokes*, London, Wolfe.

Kilroy, Roger (1979) *Graffiti the Scrawl of the Wild*, London, Corgi.

Kilroy, Roger (1980) *Graffiti 2, The Walls of the World*, London, Corgi.

Kimmel, Tom (1977) *An Analysis of the Black Joke*, unpublished dissertation, Institute of Folklore, Indiana University, Bloomington.

Kimmins, Charles William (1928) *The Springs of Laughter*, London, Methuen.

Kissane, Noel (1986) *The Irish Face*, Dublin, National Library of Ireland.

Kivanç, Halit (1977) *Mikrofonunu Kordonuna Göre Uzat*, Ankara, Meta Yayinlari.

Kivanç, Halit (1978) *Gülmece Güldürmece*, Ankara, Kelebek, Çocuk Kitaplari.

Kivanç, Halit (1981) *333 Fikra*, Ankara, Karacan Yayinlari.

Klaff, Vivian Z. (1980) "Residence and Integration in Israel," in Krausz (ed.) pp.53–71.

Klapp, Orrin E. (1949) "The fool as a social type," in *American Journal of Sociology*, Vol.55, pp.157–62.

Klempski, Tymoteusz (1981) "A letter from Poland, between euphoria and mortal danger," in *Encounter*, July, pp.78–85.

Kliban, B. (1978) *Tiny Footprints*, New York, Workman.

Klymasz, Robert B. (1970) "The ethnic joke in Canada today," in *Kentucky Folklore Quarterly*, Vol.25, pp.167–73.

Knight, Edward Frederick (1897) *Where Three Empires Meet*, London, Longmans Green.

Knowles, Ronald (1979) "The Caretaker and the point of laughter," in *Journal of Beckett Studies*, No.5, pp.83–97.

Knox, David B. (1924) *Quotable Anecdotes for various occasions*, London, T. Fisher Unwin.

Knox, David B. (1926) *More Quotable Anecdotes*, London, Ernest Benn.

Knox, David B. (1938) *Laugh and Grow Fat*, London, James Clarke.

Koch, Hannsjoachim Wolfgang (1975) *The Hitler Youth*, London, Macdonald and Jane.

Kochan, Lionel (ed.) (1970) *The Jews in Soviet Russia Since 1917*, London, Institute of Jewish Affairs, Oxford University Press.

Koenderman, Tony; Langen, Jan; and Viljoen, André (1975) *Van der Merwe*, Hillbrow, South Africa, Lorton.

Kolasky, John (1972) *Look, Comrade, the People Are Laughing*, Toronto, Peter Martin.

Koren, Edward (1981) *Well There's Your Problem*, Harmondsworth, Penguin.

Kowalski, Mike (1974) *The Polish Joke-Book*, New York, Belmont Tower.

Krausz, Ernest (ed.) (1980) *Studies of Israeli Society vol. I, Migration, Ethnicity and Community*, New Brunswick, Transaction.

Krausz, Ernest (n.d.) *The uses of the concepts, 'Edah' and 'Ethnic group' in Israel*, Paper for the Ethnicity Glossary of the Committee on Conceptual and Terminological Analysis of the International Social Science Council.

Kravitz, Seth (1977) "London Jokes and Ethnic Stereotypes," in *Western Folklore*, Vol.36, No.4, October, pp.275–301.

Krejci, Jaroslav (1976) *Social Structure in Divided Germany*, London, Croom Helm.

Krejci, Jaroslav and Velinsky, Viteslav (1981) *Ethnic and Political Nations in Europe*, London, Croom Helm.

'Krin, Sylvie' (1981) *Born to be a Queen*, Harmondsworth, Penguin/Private Eye.

Krögerson, Eibe (1977) *Ostfriesenwitze*, Frankfurt am Main, Fischer.

Krumbhaar, Edward Bell (1966) *Isaac Cruikshank*, Philadelphia, University of Pennsylvania Press.

Kumar, Krishan (1977) "A future in the past?" *New Society*, 42, November 24.

Kumar, Krishan (1978) *Prophecy and Progress, the Sociology of Industrial and Post-Industrial Society*, London, Allen Lane.

Kumove, Shirley (1986) *Words like Arrows, a Treasury of Yiddish Folk Sayings*, New York, Warner.

Kunitz, Stanley Jasspon and Haycroft, Howard (1942) *Twentieth Century Authors, a Biographical Dictionary*, New York, H. W. Wilson.

Kusielewicz, Eugene (1969) "Reflections on the cultural condition of the Polish-American community," in Renkiewicz (ed.) (1973) pp.97–106.

Kvideland, Reimund (1983) "Den Norsk-Svenske Vitsekrigen," in *Tradisjon*, 13, pp.77–91.

Laborde, Claude (1980) *Histoires drôles à s'éclater*, Paris, Best-seller.

LaFave, Lawrence; Haddad, J.; and Marshall, N. (1974) "Humor judgements as a function of identification classes," in *Sociology and Social Research*, Vol.58, pp.184–89.

LaFave, Lawrence and Mannell, Roger (1976) "Ethnic humor as a function of reference groups and identification classes," in Lancy and Tindall (eds.).

Lambert, W. R. (1975) "Drink and work discipline in industrial South Wales circa 1800–1914," in *Welsh History Review*, Vol.7, pp.289–306.

Lamberts-Hurrelbrinck, L. H. J. (1894) *In the little republic*, in Werner (ed.) pp.139–73.

Lancaster, Osbert (1941) *New Pocket Cartoons*, London, John Murray.
Lancaster, Osbert (1949) *The Saracen's Head*, Boston, Houghton Mifflin.
Lancaster, Osbert (1971) *Meaningful Confrontations*, London, John Murray.
Lancaster, Osbert (1973) *The Littlehampton Bequest*, London, Methuen.
Lancaster, Osbert (1979) *Ominous Cracks*, London, John Murray.
Lancy, D. F. and Tindall, B. Allan (1976) *The Anthropological Study of Play: Problems and Prospects*, Cornwall, N.Y., Leisure.
Landmann, Salcia (1977) *Jüdische Witze nachlese 1960–1976*, Munich, D.T.V.
Landmann, Salcia (also see above) (1978) *Joodse Humor*, Amsterdam, H. J. W. Becht.
Landon, Melville DeLancey (1900) *Comical hits by famous wits*, Chicago, Thompson and Thomas.
Lang, David Marshall (1976) *The Bulgarians from Pagan Times to the Ottoman Conquest*, London, Thames and Hudson.
Lang, Gordon (n.d.) *Great Laughter in Court*, London, Foulsham.
Lang, Kurt (1972) *Military Institutions and the Sociology of War*, Beverly Hills, Sage.
Langdon, David (1951) *Let's Face It*, London, Methuen.
Langdon-Davies, John (1949) *Russia Puts the Clock Back*, London, Gollancz.
Larsen, Egon (1980) *Wit as a Weapon*, London, Frederick Muller.
Latham, Edward (1904) *A Dictionary of Names, Nick-names and Surnames*, London, George Routledge.
Lauber, Patricia (1955) *Jokes and More Jokes*, New York, Scholastic.
Lauder, Afferbeck (1969) *Fraffly Strine*, Sydney, Ure Smith.
Lauder, Sir Harry (1929) *My Best Scotch Stories*, Dundee, Scotland, Valentine.
Laugh with SEAC (1944) Calcutta, E.S.S.C.O.
Laughs on the Road (n.d.) London, Gnome.
Laughter Gems of the World's Best Humor (1927). See Ernst.
Laurie Jr., Joe (1947). See Ford, 'Senator' Ed.
Lawrence, Jeremy (1973) *Unmentionables and Other Euphemisms*, London, Gentry.
Lawson, T. Gilchrist (1923) *The world's best humorous anecdotes*, New York, Harper.
'Laxman' [Series 1967–74] *You Said It*, Bombay, Pearl.
'Laxman' (1977) *The Management of Management*, New Delhi, All India Management Assoc.
Leather, Ella Mary (1912) *The Folk-Lore of Herefordshire*, Hereford, England, Jakeman and Carver.
Lee, Elizabeth (ed.) (1893) *The Humour of France*, London, Walter Scott.
LeFanu, William Richard (1893) *Seventy years of Irish life, being anecdotes and reminiscences*, London, Edward Arnold.
Legman, Gershon (1982; First pub. Vol.1 1968 and Vol.2 1975) *No Laughing Matter: An Analysis of Sexual Humor*, Bloomington, Indiana, Indiana University Press.
Legman, Gershon [Series 1971–76] *Ophelia Party Jokes*, New York, Ophelia.
Lehrer, Tom (1981) *Too Many Songs by Tom Lehrer*, London, Eyre Methuen.
Lehtimaja, Lauri (1979) Letter to author, August 26.
Leigh, A. M. (1920) *That's a good story*, London, C. Arthur Pearson.
Leininger, Steve (1981) *The Official Russian Jokebook*, New York, Pinnacle.
Lemon, Mark (1891) *The Jest book, the Choicest Sayings and Anecdotes*, London, Macmillan.
Lennep, van Jacob (1894) "The Village on the Frontier," in Werner (ed.) pp.261–90.

Leno, Dan (pseud. of George Galvin) (1968; First pub. 1899) *Dan Leno Hys Booke*, London, Hugh Evelyn.

Lenski, Gerhard (1961) *The Religious Factor*, Garden City, New York, Doubleday.

Letter from Warsaw (1982) in *Private Eye*, June 18.

Levin, Bernard (1979) *Taking Sides*, London, Jonathan Cape.

Levinson, Leonard Louis (1963) *The Left-Handed Dictionary*, New York, Collier.

Levy, Howard (1973) *Japanese Sex Jokes in Traditional Times*, Washington, D.C., Warm-soft Village Press.

Levy, Howard (1974) *Chinese Sex Jokes in Traditional Times* (Asian folklore and social life monograph 58), Taipei, Formosa R.O.C.

Lewis, David (1882) "The Welshman of English literature," in *Y Cymmrodor*, Vol.5, pp.224–60.

Lewis, Don (1973) *More Reverend Sirs, Ladies and Gentlemen*, London, Mowbray.

Lewis, Don (1979) *My Lords, Ladies and Gentlemen . . . Reverend Sirs*, Swansea, Celtic.

Lewis, George Q. and Wachs, Mark (1976; First pub. 1966, U.S.A.) *The best jokes of all time and how to tell them*, Bombay, Jaico.

Lewis, Norman (1964) *The Honoured Society*, London, Collins.

Lewis, Norman (1978) *Naples '44*, London, Collins.

Lewis, Paul (1986) "Disaster as a laughing matter," in *Chicago Tribune*, March 25, Section 1, p.15.

Lewis, Russell (1980) *The Official Shop-Steward's Jokebook*, London, Futura.

Lewis, Sinclair (1923) "Minnesota the Norse State," in *The Nation*, May 30 [Reprinted in Maule et al. (ed.), see below].

Lewis, Sinclair (ed. Maule, Henry E.; Cane, Melville H.; and Friedman, Philip Allen) (1954) *The man from Main Street: Selected Essays and Other Writings of Sinclair Lewis*, London, Heinemann.

Lewis, Sinclair (1974; First pub. 1922) *Babbitt*, St. Albans, Granada.

Lewis, Wyndham (1972) *The Art of Being Ruled*, New York, Haskell House.

Leyburn, James G. (1962) *The Scotch-Irish, a Social History*, Chapel Hill, N.C., University of North Carolina Press.

Liddell Hart, Sir Basil (ed.) (1980) *History of the Second World War*, New York, Putnam.

Limón, José E. (1977) "Agringado joking in Texas Mexican society: Folklore and differential identity," in *New Scholar*, Vol.6, pp.33–50.

Linden, Eugene (1981) *Apes, Men and Language*, Harmondsworth, Penguin.

Linkletter, Art (1967) *Oops! or Life's Awful Moments*, Garden City, New York, Doubleday.

Linkletter, Art (1968) *I Wish I'd Said That*, Garden City, New York, Doubleday.

Lipovski, Z. J. (1970) "The conflicts of Buridan's ass or some dilemmas of affluence: the theory of stimulus overload," in *American Journal of Psychiatry*, Vol.127, No.3, pp.273–79.

Lipset, Seymour Martin (1964) *The First New Nation, the United States in Historical and Comparative Perspective*, London, Heinemann.

Littlewood, Roland and Lipsedge, Maurice (1982) *Aliens and Alienists*, Harmondsworth, Penguin.

Litvinoff, Emmanuel (1974) *Soviet Anti-Semitism; The Paris Trial*, London, Wildwood House.

Llewelyn, Sam (1986) *Yacky Dar Moy Bewty*, London, Grafton.

Lloyd George's Favourite Dishes (1974) Cardiff, John Jones.

Lloyd, Sir John Edward (1912) *A History of Wales from the Earliest Times to the Edwardian Conquest*, London, Longmans Green.

Locke, William John (1925; First pub. 1912) *The Joyous Adventures of Aristide Pujol*, London, John Lane/Bodley Head.

Logue, Christopher (1973) *Christopher Logue's True Stories from Private Eye*, London, A. P. Rushton.
Lolli, Giorgio (1963) "The cocktail hour: physiological, psychological and social," in Lucia (ed.) pp.183–99.
Londoño, Agustín Jaramillo (1977) *Testamento del Paisa*, Medellín Colombia, Editorial Bedout.
Longrigg, Stephen Hemsley (1958) *Syria and Lebanon under the French Mandate*, London, Oxford University Press.
Lopasic, Alexander (1982) "Italian military performance in the Second World War: some considerations," in *Journal of Strategic Studies*, Vol.5, No.2, June, pp.270–75.
Lover, Samuel (1907; First pub. 1842) *Handy Andy, a tale of Irish life*, London, J. M. Dent.
Low, David (1942) *British cartoonists caricaturists and comic artists*, London, Collins.
Low, David (1949) *Years of Wrath, a Cartoon History 1932–1945*, London, Gollancz.
Lowell, Juliet (1960) *Dear Mr. Congressman*, New York, Dell.
Lowell, Juliet (1961) *Dear Folks*, New York, Permabooks.
Lowerson, John and Myerscough, John (1977) *Time to Spare in Victorian England*, Hassocks, England, Harvester.
Lowney, Paul B. (1962) *Offbeat Humor*, Mount Vernon, New York, Peter Pauper.
Lucia, Salvatore P. (ed.) (1963) *Alcohol and Civilization*, New York, McGraw-Hill.
Luckmann, T. (1969) "The decline of church-oriented religion," in Robertson, R. (ed.) pp.141–62.
Lune Jyder (series 1971–73) Vibe, Denmark.
Lutz, Vera (1962) *Italy a study in Economic Development*, London, Oxford University Press.
Lyon, M. H. (1969) "The role of the settlement area in British race relations," in Harrison and Peel (eds.).
Lyons, Johnny (1987) *Joking off*, Toronto, Paperjacks.
Lynn, Jonathan and Jay, Anthony (1981) *Yes, Minister*, London, B.B.C.
Lynn, Richard (1979A) "The social ecology of intelligence in the British Isles," in *British Journal of Social and Clinical Psychology*, Vol.18, pp.1–12.
Lynn, Richard (1979B) "The social ecology of intelligence in the British Isles, France and Spain," in Morton, M. P. et al., *Intelligence and Learning*, New York, Plenum.
'F.M.' (pseud. of Frederick Muller) (1945) *Here's a good one*, London, Frederick Muller.
MacArthur, Douglas General (1965) *Reminiscences*, Greenwich, Conn., Fawcett.
Macaulay, Thomas Babington, 1st Baron (1890) "Machiavelli," in *Reviews, Essays and Poems*, London, Ward Lock.
Macaulay, Thomas Babington, 1st Baron (ed. H. R. Trevor-Roper) (1979; First pub. 1848–65) *The History of England*, Harmondsworth, Penguin.
MacDonald, W. H. (1915) *Yarns, ancient and modern*, Edinburgh, Hodge.
MacDougall, Curtis Daniell (1958; First pub. 1940) *Hoaxes*, New York, Dover.
MacHale, Des. (1976) *The Book of Kerryman Jokes*, Dublin, Mercier.
MacHale, Des. (1977A) *The Worst Kerryman Jokes*, Dublin, Mercier.
MacHale, Des. (1977B) *Irish Love and Marriage Jokes*, Dublin, Mercier.
MacHale, Des. (1982) *The Book of Elephant Jokes*, Dublin, Mercier.
MacHale, Des. (1984) *More of the World's Best Irish Jokes*, North Ryde, New South Wales, Angus and Robertson.
Machiavelli, Nicolo (1980; First pub. 1532) *The Prince*, London, J. M. Dent.
Mack Smith, Denis (1976) *Mussolini's Roman Empire*, London, Longman.

Mack Smith, Denis (1983) *Mussolini*, London, Grenada.
Macklin, Pat and Erdman, Manny (1976) *Polish Jokes*, New York, Patman.
Macrae, Rev. David (n.d.) *A Pennyworth of Highland Humour*, Glasgow, Morison.
Macrae, Rev. David (1904) *National Humour, Scottish, English, Irish, Welsh, Cockney, American*, Paisley, Scotland, Alexander Gardner.
Magniac, Adam (1930) *Loopy Limericks*, London, Jarrolds.
Mahood (n.d.) *Laugh with Mahood*, Churt, Surrey, Leader.
Mahood, Molly M. (1968) *Shakespeare's Wordplay*, London, Methuen.
Malhotra, Ruth (1988) *Politische Plakate*, Hamburg, Museum für Kunst und Gewerbe.
Maloux, Maurice (1977) *L' esprit à travers l'histoire*, Albin, Michel.
Mann, Bill (1977) *The Retarded Giant*, Montreal, Tundra.
Mann, Ted (1979) "A girl's letters home from Europe," in *National Lampoon*, August, pp.50–52, 83, 87, 93–96.
Manning, Paul (1983) *How to Be a Wally*, London, Futura.
Mansur, Carole (1981) *Cuttings 2*, London, Elm Tree.
Mantoux, Paul (1928) *The Industrial Revolution in the Eighteenth Century*, London, Jonathan Cape.
Manvell, Roger and Fraenkel, Heinrich (1978) *Adolf Hitler, the Man and the Myth*, London, Grafton.
Margolis, Jack (1975) *Impotence Is Always Having to Say that You're Sorry*, Los Angeles, Cliff House.
Mark, Sir Robert (1973) *Minority Verdict*, London, B.B.C.
Mars, Gerald (1982) *Cheats at work*, London, Allen and Unwin.
Marshall, Alan (1963) "Blue Stews," in Wannan (ed.).
Marshall, Arthur (1979) *Never Rub Bottoms with a Porcupine*, London, Allen and Unwin.
Marshall, Gordon (1980) *Presbyteries and Profits; Calvinism and the Development of Capitalism in Scotland 1560–1707*, Oxford, Clarendon.
Martin, David (1978) *A General Theory of Secularization*, Oxford, Basil Blackwell.
Martin, David and Jacobs, Harvey (1969) *Mrs. Portnoy's Retort*, New York, Allograph.
Martineau, W. H. (1972) "A model of the social functions of humor," in Goldstein and McGhee (eds.).
Marx, Karl (1974; First pub. 1867–94) *Capital, a critique of political economy*, London, Lawrence and Wishart.
Marx, Karl and Engels, Friedrich (1972) "The German Ideology," Part I in Tucker, R. C. (ed.) *The Marx-Engels Reader*, New York, W. W. Norton.
Marx, Karl and Engels, Friedrich (n.d.) (1844–1894) *Writings not generally known on race, nationalities, colonialism and war. What Marx and Engels said about the Slavs, Irish, Jews, Blacks and others*, London, Centre for Liberal Studies.
Mason, Phil (1980s) *Christian Crackers* (several vols.), Kettering, England, Norheimsund.
Masson, Thomas Lansing (1913) *The Best Stories in the World*, Garden City, New York, Doubleday Page.
Masters, David (1937) *What Men Will Do For Money*, London, Eyre and Spottiswoode.
Matisse, Henri (1924) *Histoires Juives* [Geiger's 1923 book with the same title is in the foreground of this painting, which is exhibited in the Philadelphia Museum of Art].
Maurois, André (1940; First pub. 1918) *Les silences du Colonel Bramble*, Paris, Nelson.
May, Phil (1914) *Humorous Masterpieces*, London, Gowans and Gray.

Mayer, Huey B. (1982) *The Official Beverly Hills Jokebook*, New York, Pinnacle.
Mayhew, Henry (ed. Peter Quennel) (1966; First pub. 1862) *London's Underworld*, London, Spring.
McCabe, John (1985) *Mr. Laurel and Mr. Hardy*, New York, Plume New American Library.
McCaffrey, Lawrence J. (1976) *The Irish Diaspora in America*, Bloomington, Indiana, Indiana University Press.
McConnell, Malcolm (1987) *Challenger, a Major Malfunction*, New York, Simon and Schuster.
McCorrisken, Walter (1981) *Cream of the Corn*, Edinburgh, Albyn.
McCosh, Sandra (1976) *Children's Humor*, London, Granada.
McDonald, Kenneth (1976) *Ouch! The Max Awards for 1976*, Markham, Ontario, Simon and Schuster.
McDowell, John H. (1981) "Towards a semiotics of nicknaming the Kamsá example," in *Journal of American Folklore*.
McGhee, Paul E. and Chapman, Anthony J. (1980) *Children's Humour*, Chichester, Sussex, John Wiley.
McGhee, Paul E. and Goldstein, Jeffrey, H. (eds.) (1983) *Handbook of Humor Research, Vol.1 Basic Issues, Vol.2 Applied Studies*, New York, Springer.
McGranahan, Donald V. (1946) "A comparison of social attitudes among American and German youth," in *Journal of Abnormal and Social Psychology*, Vol.41, pp.245–57.
McLaren, A. D. (1916) *Germanism from Within*, London, Constable.
McNaught, Kenneth William Kirkpatrick (1969) *The Pelican History of Canada*, Harmondsworth, Penguin.
McNeill, Angus (pseud. of Thomas William Hodgson Crosland) (1903) *The Egregious English*, London, Grant Richards.
McPhee, Nancy (1980) *The Book of Insults Ancient and Modern*, London, André Deutsch.
McPhee, Nancy (1981) *The Second Book of Insults*, London, André Deutsch.
Medici, Sandro (1981) *Barzellette sui Carabinieri*, Milan, Tiger.
Meir, Gerald M. and Baldwin, Robert E. (1957) *Economic Development: Theory, History, Policy*, New York, John Wiley.
Melden, Fred R. von der (1976) "Pariah communities and violence," in Rosenbaum, H. Jon and Sederburg, P. C. (eds.) *Vigilante Politics*, Philadelphia, University of Pennsylvania Press, pp.218–33.
Melegari, Vezio (1981) *Manuale della Barzelletta*, Milan, Arnoldo Mondadori.
Melly, George and Fawkes, Wally (1962) *I. Flook*, London, Macmillan.
Mencken, Henry Louis (1920) "Star Spangled Men," in *New Republic*, September.
Mencken, Henry Louis (1949) *A Mencken Chrestomathy*, New York, Alfred A. Knopf.
Mencken, Henry Louis (1956) *The Vintage Mencken*, New York, Vintage.
Mencken, Henry Louis (ed. James T. Farrell) (1958) *Prejudices, a Selection*, New York, Vintage.
Mencken, Henry Louis (1986; First pub. 1948; 1962) *The American Language*, New York, Alfred A. Knopf.
Mendel, Werner M. (ed.) (1970A) *A Celebration of Laughter*, Los Angeles, Mara.
Mendel, Werner M. (1970B) "The New Laughter," in Mendel (ed.) (1970A).
Mercer, John (1965) *The Squeaking Wheel*, Canada, Rubicon.
Mercier, Vivian (1962) *The Irish Comic Tradition*, Oxford, Oxford University Press.
Dr. 'Merry' (n.d.) *The Merry Companion for all Readers*, London, Wm. Nicholson.
Merton, Robert King (1957) *Social Theory and Social Structure*, Glencoe, Free Press.

Meyer, Antoine and Meyer, Phillippe (1978) *Le communisme est-il soluble dans l'alcool*, Paris, Du Seuil.
Meyerowitz, Rick (1979) "A Paranoid's Progress through Germany: a Jew goes back," in *National Lampoon*, August, pp.33–36.
Meyerson, Abraham (1940) "Alcohol: a study of social ambivalence," in *Quarterly Journal of Studies on Alcohol*, Vol.I, pp.13–20.
Middleton, Russell (1959) "Negro and white reactions to racial humor," in *Sociometry*, Vol.22, pp.175–83.
Middleton, Russell and Moland, J. (1959) "Humor in negro and white subcultures: a study of jokes among university students," in *American Sociological Review*, Vol.24, pp.61–69.
Midwinter, Eric (1979) *Make em Laugh*, London, Allen and Unwin.
'Mike G' (1985) *Graffiti from the Bogs of Ireland*, Dublin, Mercier.
Mikes, George (1946) *How to be an Alien*, London, Wingate.
Mikes, George (1950) *Wisdom for Others*, London, Wingate.
Mikes, George (1970) *The Land of the Rising Yen*, London, André Deutsch.
Mikes, George (1977) *How to be Decadent*, London, André Deutsch.
Mikes, George (1981) *English Humour for Beginners*, London, Unwin.
Mikkelsen, Borge (n.d.) *Skipper Historier*, Copenhagen, Carit Andersens.
Miles, C. W. (1926) *Taffy Tales from Welsh Wales*, Dundee, Scotland, Valentine.
Miller, Walter (1958) "Lower-class culture as a generating milieu of gang delinquency," in *Journal of Social Issues*, Vol.14, No.3.
Milligan, Spike (1981) *Indefinite Articles*, London, Michael Joseph.
Milne, F. Murray (1940) *The Proverbs of Hocus Pocus*, London, C. Arthur Pearson.
Mindess, Harvey (1971) *Laughter and Liberation*, Los Angeles, Nash.
Mindess, Harvey and Turek, Joy (eds.) (1980) *The Study of Humour*, Los Angeles, Antioch.
Miner, Horace (1975; First pub. 1956) "Body ritual among the Nacirema," in Spradley and Rynkiewich (eds.) pp.10–13.
Minogue, Kenneth (1987) "In search of lost stupidity," in *The Times*, February 12, p.12.
Minstrel Gags and End Men's Handbook, 1969 (1845) Upper Saddle River, N.J., Gregg.
Mintz, Lawrence E. (1980) "A continuum description of the motives and functions of racial, ethnic and sexist humor," in Mindess and Turek (eds.) pp.53–54.
Mintz, Lawrence E. (1986) "The Rabbi versus the priest and other Jewish stories," in Ziv (ed.) pp.125–31.
Mises, Ludwig von (1974) *Socialism, an Economic and Sociological Analysis*, London, Jonathan Cape.
Mitchell, Austin and Waddell, Sid (1971) *Teach Thissen Tyke*, Newcastle on Tyne, Frank Graham.
Mitchell, Steve and Rawls, Sam C. (1976) *How to Speak Southern*, New York, Bantam.
Mitchell-Kernan, Claudia (1975) "Signifying and Marking: two Afro-American speech acts," in Spradley and Rynkiewich (eds.) pp.91–103.
Mitford, Jessica (1963) *The American Way of Death*, New York, Simon and Schuster.
Mixture for Low Spirits, The (n.d.) London, Diprose and Bateman.
Mockridge, Norton (1965) *Fractured English*, New York, Curtis.
Moffat, D. J. (1979) "World meat consumption, F.A.O. projections of long-term trends," in *United Kingdom and International Demand for Meat. Proceedings of a symposium held on 24th and 25th Sept. 1979*, London, Meat and Livestock Commission Economic Information Service.
Moffat, Graham (1928) *The Pawky Scot*, Dundee, Scotland, Valentine.

Moglia, Miglietto (1981) *Le 1500 più belle Barzellette*, Milan, De Vecchi.
Möller, Vera (1977) *Kleine Erna, Ganz dumme Hamburger Geschichten*, Frankfurt am Main, Fischer.
Mondragon, Magdalena (1977) *Mexico pelado . . . pero sabroso*, Mexico City, Diana.
Monkhouse, Bob (1981) *The Book of Days*, London, Arrow.
Monson, Nicholas and Scott, Debra (1984) *The Nouveaux Pauvres, a Guide to Downward Mobility*, London, Quartette.
Montaigne, Michel de (1965) *Essais*, Paris, Gallimard.
Montgomerie, Norah and Montgomerie, William (1948) *Sandy Candy and other Scottish Nursery Rhymes*, London, Hogarth.
Montgomery, David (1980) "The Irish and the American labor movement," in Doyle and Edwards (eds.).
Montgomery, Eric (1971) *The Scotch-Irish and Ulster*, Belfast, Ulster Scot Historical Foundation.
Monty Python (1983 [1974]) *Monty Python Live at Drury Lane*, Charisma, Record no. Class 4.
Moodie, T. Dunbar (1975) *The Rise of Afrikanerdom, Power Apartheid and the Afrikaner Civil Religion*, Berkeley, University of California Press.
Moon, Penderel (1961) *Divide and Quit*, London, Chatto and Windus.
Moore Jr, Barrington (1979) *Injustice. The Social Bases of Obedience and Revolt*, London, Macmillan.
Moore, William (1979) *The Thin Yellow Line*, London, Leo Cooper.
Morawska, Eva T. (1977) *The Maintenance of Ethnicity: A Case Study of the Polish-American Community in Greater Boston*, San Francisco, R. and E. Research.
Morecambe, Eric and Wise, Ernie (1979) *The Morecambe and Wise Jokebook*, London, Arthur Barker.
More Sunbeams (1923) London, Stanley Paul.
Morgan, Chris and Langford, David (1981) *Facts and Fallacies. A Book of Definitive Mistakes and Misguided Predictions*, Exeter, Devon, Webb and Bower.
Morgan, Harry (1968) *More Rugby Songs*, London, Sphere.
Morgan, Kenneth O. (1982) *Rebirth of a Nation, Wales 1880–1980*, Oxford, Oxford University Press.
Morgan, W. Pritchard (1891) Speech in House of Commons February 20th, Hansard Parliamentary Debates, 3rd series vol.350, cols. 1245–46.
Morier, James Justinian (1947; First pub. 1824) *The Adventures of Hajji Baba of Ispahan*, New York, Heritage.
Morley, Robert (1980) *Morley Matters*, London, Robson.
Morley, Robert (1982) *Robert Morley's Second Book of Bricks*, London, Hodder and Stoughton.
Morrah, Dave (1955) *Heinrich Schnibble*, New York, Rinehart.
Morreau, John (1983) *Taking Laughter Seriously*, Albany, State University of New York Press.
Morris, Ivan (1980) *The Nobility of Failure, Tragic Heroes in the History of Japan*, Harmondsworth, Penguin.
Morrison, Patrick (1986) *Sick Irish Jokes*, Dublin, Mercier.
Morton, George Alexander and Malloch, D. Macleod (1913) *Law and Laughter*, Edinburgh, T. N. Foulis.
Mosessons, E. and N. and R. and C. and C. (1974) *The Perfect Put Down*, New York, Scholastic.
Mound, Andrew (1983) *Heroic Hoaxes*, London, Macdonald.
Muehlon, Wilhelm (1918) *Dr. Muehlon's Diary*, London, Cassell.
Muir, Frank and Brett, Simon (1980) *The Second Frank Muir Goes Into*, London, W. H. Allen.

Muir, John G. (1984) *Classroom Clangers*, Edinburgh, Gordon Wright.
Mulkay, Michael (1987) "Humour and social structure," in Oathwaite, W. and Mulkay, M. (eds.) *Social Theory and Social Criticism*, Oxford, Blackwell.
Müller, Klaus-Jurgen (1987) *Army, Politics and Society in Germany: Studies in the Army's Relations to Nazism*, Manchester, University of Manchester Press.
Mullins, Spike (1979) *Ronnie in the Chair*, London, W. H. Allen.
Mumford, Ethel Watts (1905) *Joke Book. Note Book*, San Francisco, Paul Elder n.p.
Murphy, Arthur (1792) *An Essay on the Life and Genius of Samuel Johnson LLD*, London, T. Longman.
Murray, Sir James Augustus Henry et al. (eds.) (1888) *A New English Dictionary on Historical Principles*, Oxford, Oxford University Press.
Murtie, Kevin (1985) *At Last! The Official Irish Joke Book No.2*, London, Futura.
Museum of Mirth, The (n.d.) Glasgow, James Cameron.
Mussolini, Benito (1928) *My Autobiography*, London, Hutchinson.
Myagkov, Aleksei (1976) *Inside the K.G.B.*, Richmond Surrey, Foreign Affairs.
Naiman, Arthur (1981) *Every Goy's Guide to Common Jewish Expressions*, New York, Ballantine.
Nakazawa, Keiji (1978) *Barefoot Gen*, Tokyo, Project Gen.
Namier, Sir Lewis (1947) *Facing East: Essays on Germany, the Balkans and Russia*, New York, Harper and Row.
Nash, Ogden (1962) *The Pocket Book of Ogden Nash*, New York, Cardinal.
Nègre, Hervé (1973) *Dictionnaire d'Histoires Drôles* (2 vols), Paris, Fayard.
Neider, Charles (1977) *The Comic Mark Twain Reader*, Garden City, New York, Doubleday.
Nellis, William and Graziano, Craig (1975) "Weaseling in the tube room," in Spradley and Rynkiewich (eds.) pp.103–10.
Nelson, Walter Henry (1971) *The Soldier Kings, the House of Hohenzollern*, London, J. M. Dent.
Nesbit, Jo; Ruda, Lesley; Mackie, Liz (1980) *Sourcream*, London, Sheba.
Nevins, John Birkbeck (1892) *Picture of Wales during the Tudor Period*, Liverpool, Edward Howell.
Newall, Venetia J. (ed.) (1980) *Folklore Studies in the Twentieth Century*, Totowa, N.J., D. S. Brewer, Rowman and Littlefield.
Newall, Venetia J. (1985) "Folklore and cremation," in *Folklore*, Vol.96, No.2, pp.139–55.
Newby, Eric (1975) *Love and War in the Appenines*, Harmondsworth, Penguin.
New English Bible (1970) London, Oxford and Cambridge University Presses.
New Joe Miller or the Tickler (1801) London, James Ridgway.
Newman, A. C. H. (1966) *Newman's Joke and Story Book*, Kingswood, Surrey, Elliot Right Way.
New Minstrel Jokes (1913) Philadelphia, Royal.
New Punch Library (1933) 20 Vols, London, Educational. Vol.1 Mr. Punch's Cavalcade: a Preview of Thirty Years; Vol.2 Mr. Punch in Mayfair; Vol.3 Mr. Punch in the Family Circle; Vol.4 Mr. Punch After Dinner; Vol.5 Mr. Punch's Children's Hour; Vol.6 Mr. Punch and the Arts; Vol.7 Mr. Punch and the Services; Vol.8 Mr. Punch with Horse and Hound; Vol.9 Mr. Punch's Theatricals; Vol.10 Mr. Punch in Scotland; Vol.11 Mr. Punch Goes Motoring; Vol.12 Mr. Punch's Country Manners; Vol.13 Mr. Punch in Holiday Mood; Vol.14 Mr. Punch on the Links; Vol.15 Mr. Punch in London Town; Vol.16 Mr. Punch on his Travels; Vol.17 Mr. Punch and Toby's Friends; Vol.18 Mr. Punch's Sports and Pastimes; Vol.19 Round the Year with Mr. Punch; Vol.20 Mr. Punch in Wartime.

New Yorker War Album, The (1943) London, Hamish Hamilton.
Niccol, Andrew and Woodman, Stephen (1983) *Paying through the Nose and Other English Expressions*, London, Sphere.
Nicholas, Margaret (1982) *The World's Greatest Cranks and Crackpots*, London, Octopus.
Nichols, Peter (1973) *Italia, Italia*, London, Macmillan.
Niemand, Piet (pseud.) (1962) *Jan Domm*, London, Geoffrey Bles.
Nilsen, Alleen Pace and Nilsen, Don L. F. (1984) "Humor and social issues: some contradictions," in *Federation Reports, the Journal of the State Humanities Council*, Vol.7, No.2, March/April, pp.30–33.
Nisard, Charles (1864) *Histoire des livres populaires ou de la litérature du colportage depuis le XV-ième siècle jusqu' a' l'establissement de la commission d'examen des livres du colportage*, Paris, Amyot.
Noel, Sidney John Roderick (1971) *Politics in Newfoundland*, Toronto, University of Toronto Press.
Nohain, Jean (1972) *Gaffes et Gaffeurs*, Paris, Pocket.
Noonan, Miles (1983) *Tales from the Mess: A Military Miscellany*, London, Hutchinson.
Norment, John (1958) *Laugh Time*, New York, Scholastic.
Norment, John (1971) *You've Gotta Be Joking*, New York, Scholastic.
Not the nine o'clock news team, The (1981) *Not 1982*, London, Faber and Faber.
Novak, Michael (1976) "The Sting of Polish Jokes," in *Newsweek*, April 12.
Nown, Graham (1987A) *The Green Wellie Guide*, London, Ward Lock.
Nown, Graham (1987B) *Criminal Records*, London, Futura.
Obrdlik, Antonin J. (1942) "Gallows Humor—a sociological phenomenon," in *American Journal of Sociology*, Vol.47, pp.709–16.
O'Brian, Richard; Kaufman, Bill; O'Brian, Sean (n.d.) *Jaws Jokes*, New York, Pinnacle.
Ocker, A. N. (pseud.) (1986) *The World's Best Aussie Jokes*, North Ryde, New South Wales, Angus and Robertson.
O'Conroy, Taid (1933) *The Menace of Japan*, London, Hutchinson.
Oddy, Derek and Miller, Derek (eds.) (1976) *The Making of the Modern British Diet*, London, Croom Helm.
O'Dea, Thomas F. (1962) *The American Catholic Dilemma*, New York, Mentor Omega.
Ogoiski, Petro (1975) *Sto shila v torba*. Sofia.
O'Grady, John (pseud. of Nino Culotta) (1965) *Aussie English*, Sydney, Ure Smith.
Oh Yeah? (1931) New York, Viking.
O'Leary, Seamus and O'Larry (1983) *Irish Graffiti*, London, Futura n.p.
Oliver, Hugh and MacMillan, Keith (1985) *The Canadian Limerick Book*, Don Mills, Ontario, General.
Olivieri, Laura (1980) *La Sai Ultima?* Milan, De Vecchi.
Olmstead, Frederick Law (1852) "Walks and Talks of an American farmer in England," in Commager (ed.) (1974) pp.293–301.
Olrik, Axel (1965; First pub. 1909) "Epic laws of folk narrative," in Dundes (ed.) pp.129–41.
Olsen, Jack (1970) *The Bridge at Chappaquiddick*, New York, Grosset and Dunlap.
Olson, Elder (1968) *The Theory of Comedy*, Bloomington, Indiana, Indiana University Press.
Ó Muirithe, Diarmid (ed.) (1977) *The English Language in Ireland*, Dublin, R. T. E. and Mercier.
Onoda, Lieutenant Hiroo (1976) *No Surrender, My Thirty Years War*, London, Transworld.
Onyeama, Dillibe (1977) *The Book of Black Man's Humour*, London, Satellite.

Oring, Elliott (1973) "Hey, you've got no character. Chizbat humor and the boundaries of Israeli identity," in *Journal of American Folklore*, Vol.86, No.342, December, pp.358–66.
Oring, Elliott (1975) "Everything is a shade of elephant: an alternative to the psychoanalysis of humor," in *New York Folklore Quarterly*, Vol.51, pp.149–59.
Oring, Elliott (1981) *Israeli Humor: The Content and Structure of the Chizbat of the Palmakh*, Albany, State University of New York Press.
Oring, Elliott (1984) *The Jokes of Sigmund Freud, a Study in Humor and Jewish Identity*, Philadelphia, University of Pennsylvania Press.
Oring, Elliott (1987) "Jokes and the discourse of disaster," in *Journal of American Folklore*, 100 (397) July-Sept. pp.276–86.
Orkin, Mark M. (1973) *Canajan, Eh?* Don Mills, Ontario, General.
Orso, Ethelyn G. (1979) *Modern Greek Humor: A Collection of Jokes and Ribald Tales*, Bloomington, Indiana, Indiana University Press.
Orwell, George (1968) *The Collected Essays, Journalism and Letters of George Orwell*, London, Secker and Warburg.
O'S, Mr. (1982) *The World's Best Irish Jokes*, North Ryde, N.S.W., Angus Robertson.
Overbury, Sir Thomas (1890) "A Bragadacchio Welshman," in *Miscellaneous works of Sir Thomas Overbury*, London, Reeves and Turner.
Owen, G. Dyfnallt (1964) *Elizabethan Wales, the Social Scene*, Cardiff, University of Wales Press.
Owen, Jim M. (1971) *Jim Owen's Hillbilly Humor*, New York, Pocket.
Oxley, H. G. (1978) *Mateship in Local Organization*, St. Lucia, University of Queensland Press.
Page, Martin (1973) *Kiss me goodnight, Sergeant Major. The songs and ballads of World War II*, London, Hart-Davis MacGibbon.
Pahl, Raymond Edward (1968) "The rural-urban continuum," in Pahl, R. E. (ed.) *Readings in Urban Sociology*, Oxford, Pergamon.
Pahl, Raymond Edward (1984) *Divisions of Labour*, Oxford, Basil Blackwell.
Palmer, Myles (1980) *Woody Allen*, London, Proteus.
Parkes, James (1945) *An Enemy of the People: Anti-Semitism*, Harmondsworth, Penguin.
Parkinson, Cyril Northcote (1958) *Parkinson's Law*, London, John Murray.
Parkinson, Cyril Northcote (1971) *The Law of Delay*, London, John Murray.
Paros, Lawrence (1984) *The Erotic Tongue*, Seattle, Madrona.
Parri, Dafydd (1980) *Llyfr Jôcs y Llewod*, Talybont, Wales, Y. Lolfa.
Parry, Albert (1966) *The New Class Divided: Russian Science and Technology Versus Communism*, New York, Macmillan.
Parry, William (1893) *The Old Welsh Evangelist*, Bristol, William F. Mack.
Parry-Jones, Daniel (1973; First pub. 1952) *Welsh Country Characters*, Upton Merseyside, Ffynon.
Parsons, Denys (1960) *Never More True*, London, Macdonald.
Parsons, Denys (1965) *Funny Ha Ha and Funny Peculiar*, London, Pan.
Parsons, Denys (1967) *Funny Ho Ho and Funny Fantastic*, London, Pan.
Parsons, Talcott (1975) "Change of ethnicity," in Glazer and Moynihan (eds.) pp.53–83.
Parsons, Talcott; Shils, Edward; Naegele, Kasper D.; Pitts, Jesse R. (eds.) (1961) *Theories of Society*, New York, Free Press of Glencoe.
Parth, Wolfgang W. and Schiff, Michael (1978) *Neues von Radio Eriwan*, Frankfurt-am-Main, Fischer.
Pass the Port Again (1981) Cirencester, Christian Brann.
Passin, Herbert and Bennett, John, W. (1965) "Changing agricultural magic in Southern Illinois," in Dundes (ed.) pp.314–28.

Patai, Raphael (1977) *The Jewish Mind*, New York, Charles Scribner's Sons.
Patten, William (1909) *Among the Humorists and After-dinner Speakers*, New York, P. F. Collier.
Patterson, Dr. Sir Les [pseud. Barry Humphries] (1986) *The Travellers Tool*, London, Hodder Coronet.
Paul, Elliot (1954) *Understanding the French*, London, Frederick Muller.
Paulun, Dirks (1979) *Die Waterkant wie sie lacht*, Reinbek bei Hamburg, Rowohlt.
Pearce, Edward (1983) *The Senate of Lilliput*, London, Faber and Faber.
Pearce, Fred (1985) "Tobacco suckers risk oral cancer," in *New Scientist*, No.1443, February 14, p.6.
Pearsall, Ronald (1975) *Collapse of Stout Party, Victorian Wit and Humour*, London, Weidenfeld and Nicolson.
Pearson's Humorous Reciter and Reader, 1922 (1904) London, C. Arthur Pearson.
Pearson, Frederick S. (1950) *Fractured French*, Garden City, New York, Doubleday.
Peers, John; Booth, George; Bennett, Gordon (1984) *1,001 Logical Laws*, London, Arrow.
Peñalosa, Joaquín Antonio (1979) *Humor con agua bendita*, Mexico City, Jus.
'Pepito' (n.d.) *Los mejores chistes*, Mexico City, Gómez-Gómez.
Pepper, John (1977) *What a Thing to Say*, Belfast, Blackstaff.
Pepper, John (1979) *A Quare Geg*, Belfast, Blackstaff.
Pereira, Anthony (1977) *Naples, Pompeii and Southern Italy*, London, Batsford.
Perelman, Sidney Joseph (1949) *Westward Ha! or around the world in eighty cliches*, London, Reinhardt and Evans.
Perkins, Eli (pseud. of Melville D. Landon) (1901) *Library of Wit and Humor*, Chicago, Thompson and Thomas.
Perris, George Herbert (1914) *Germany and the German Emperor*, London, Andrew Melrose.
Peter, Laurence J. and Dana, Bill (1982) *The Laughter Prescription*, New York, Ballantine.
Peter, Laurence J. and Hull, Raymond (1970) *The Peter Principle*, London, Pan.
Petersen, William (1964) *The Politics of Population*, London, Gollancz.
Petersen, William (1975) "On the sub-nations of Western Europe," in Glazer and Moynihan (eds.) pp.177–208.
Peterson, Gail (1968) *The Last Laugh*, Kansas City, Hallmark.
Petropoulos, Elias (1987) "Oi Pontioi," in *Scholiastis*, July, pp.46–47.
Phillips, Bob (1976) *The All American Jokebook*, Irvine California, Harvest House.
Phillips, Bob (1981) *The Last of the Good Clean Joke Books*, Eugene Oregon, Harvest House.
Phillips, Edward (1970) *Best Football Jokes*, London, Wolfe.
Phillips, Edward (1974A) *Best Ghost and Monster Jokes*, London, Wolfe.
Phillips, Edward (1974B) *Best Upper Crust Jokes*, London, Wolfe.
Phillips, Edward (1975A) *Best English, Irish and Scots Jokes*, London, Wolfe.
Phillips, Edward (1975B) *Best London Jokes*, London, Wolfe.
Phillips, Harry Irving (1927) *The Foolish Question Book*, New York, Edward J. Clode.
Phillips, Pearson (1984) *YAP's the Complete Guide to Young Aspiring Professionals*, London, Arrow.
Phillips, Thomas (n.d.) *Humours of the Iron Road. Stories from the Train*, Carmarthen, Wales, W. M. Evans.
The Pick of 600 (n.d.) London, George Cohen 600 Group.
Pickup, Madeleine (1981) *The German Shepherd Dog*, London, Pelham.
Piekalkieicz, Jaroslaw A. (1972) *Public Opinion Polling in Czechoslovakia*, New York, Praeger.

Pielko, Robert B. (1984) "Saturday night live: nihilism or ethical absolutism," in Helitzer (ed.) (1984A).

Pieper, Werner (1987) *Das Scheiss Buch*, Löhrbach, Werner Pieper.

Pierce, T. Jones (1972) *Medieval Welsh Society*, Cardiff, University of Wales Press.

Pietsch, Jim (1986) *The New York City Cab Driver's Jokebook*, New York, Warner.

Pile, Stephen (1980) *The Book of Heroic Failures*, London, Futura.

Pines, Leonard (1976) *Hot Dog Jokes*, New York, Grosset and Dunlap.

Pinon, Roger (1980) "From illumination to folksong: the armed snail a motif of topsy-turvy land," in Newall (ed.).

Piozzi, Mrs. Hester Lynch [formerly Miss Salusbury and Mrs. Thrale] (1892; First pub. 1789) *Glimpses of Italian Society in the Eighteenth Century from the 'Journey' of Mrs. Piozzi*, London, Seeley.

Pittman, David J. and Snyder, Charles R. (eds.) (1962) *Society Culture and Drinking Patterns*, New York, Wiley.

Plato (trans. J. C. B. Gosling 1975) *Philebus*, Oxford, Clarendon.

Playboy 1966 Book of Party Jokes (1965) London, Four Square.

Playfair, Major-General Ian Stanley Ord; Stitt, Commander (R.N.) G. M. S.; Moloney, Brigadier C. J. C.; and Toomer, Air Vice-Marshall S. E. (1954) *The Mediterranean and the Middle East [History of the Second World War*, U. K. Military Series], London, H.M.S.O.

Plumb, John Harold (1966) *The First Four Georges*, London, Fontana.

Pocheptsov, G. G. (1974) *Language and Humour*, Kiev, Vysca Skola.

Podhoretz, Norman (1986) "The hate that dare not speak its name," in *Commentary*, Vol.82, No.5, November, pp.21–32.

Pois, Robert (ed.) (1970) *Selected Writings of Alfred Rosenberg*, London, Jonathan Cape.

Poláček, Karel (1933) *Židovské anekdoty*, Prague, Orbis.

Polanyi, Michael (1940) *The contempt for freedom, the Russian experiment and after*, London, Watts.

Polanyi, Michael (1951) *The Logic of Liberty*, London, Routledge & Kegan Paul.

Polhemus, Robert M. (1980) *Comic Faith, the Comic Tradition from Austen to Joyce*, Chicago, University of Chicago Press.

Polk, Dora (1982) *A Book called Hiraeth*, Port Talbot, Wales, Alun.

Ponsonby, Arthur Ponsonby (1928) *Falsehood in wartime*, London, Allen and Unwin.

Popovsky, Mark (1980) *Science in Chains*, London, Collins and Harvill.

Porter, Lyman W.; Lawler, Edward E. III; Hackman, J. Richard (1975) *Behavior in Organisations*, New York, McGraw-Hill.

Possony, Stefan T. (1976) "Ethnomorphosis: invisible catastrophic crime,"in *Plural Societies*, Vol.7, No.3, pp.3–35.

Post Scripts Humor (1978) Indianapolis, Curtiss.

Potter, David Morris (1954) *People of Plenty, Economic Abundance and the American Character*, Chicago.

Powell, Chris and Paton, George, E. C. (eds.) (1988) *Humour in society, Resistance and Control*, London, Macmillan.

Powell, T. (1880) "The Welsh as pictured in old English jest books," in *Y Cymmrodor*, Vol.3, part 1, pp.107–116.

Powers, Nick (1973) *Pill Pedlars Joke Book*, Boogar Hollow, Lindale, Georgia, Country Originals.

Powers, Nick and Powers, Willan (1975) *Speakin' Southern Like it should be Spoke*, Boogar Hollow, Lindale, Georgia, Country Originals.

Prabhu, R. K. (1966) *So this is marriage*, Bombay, Jaico.

Prescott, John Robert Victor (1978) *Boundaries and Frontiers*, London, Croom Helm.

Preston, Charles (ed.) (1955) *The Power of Negative Thinking*, New York, Ballantine.
Preston, Michael J. (1975) "A typescript ethnic joke anthology,"in *New York Folklore Quarterly*, No.1, pp.229–34.
Preston, Richard A. and Wise, Sydney F. (1979) *Men in Arms, A History of Warfare and Its Inter-relationship with Western Society*, New York, Holt Rinehart Winston.
Price, Cecil (1955) "Introduction" to Borrow.
Price, Richard Geoffrey George (1957) *A History of Punch*, London, Collins.
Pringle, John Douglas (1960) *Australian Accent*, London, Chatto and Windus.
Prochnow, Herbert Victor (1953 [1949 U.S.]) *The Toastmaster's Handbook*, Blackpool, England, A. Thomas.
Prochnow, Herbert Victor (1955) *Speaker's Handbook of Epigrams and Witticisms*, Blackpool, England, A. Thomas.
Protocols of the meetings of the learned elders of Zion, The (1978), East Shotton, Clwyd, North Wales, British Patriot.
Proust, Marcel [trans. Scott Moncrieff, C. K. and Kilmartin, Terence] (1981; First pub. in French 1913) *Remembrance of Things Past*, London, Chatto and Windus.
Pryor, Oswald (1962) *Australia's Little Cornwall*, Adelaide, Rigby.
Punch Library (1908) London, Educational. 25 Vols. viz Mr. Punch Afloat; Mr. Punch at Home; Mr. Punch at the Play; Mr. Punch at the Seaside; Mr. Punch awheel; Mr. Punch in Bohemia; Mr. Punch in Society; Mr. Punch in the Highlands; Mr. Punch in the Hunting field; Mr. Punch in wig and gown; Mr. Punch on the Continong; Mr. Punch on the Warpath; Mr. Punch on Tour; Mr. Punch's After-Dinner Stories; Mr. Punch's Book of Love; Mr. Punch's Book of Sports; Mr. Punch's Cockney Humour; Mr. Punch's Country Life; Mr. Punch's Golf Stories; Mr. Punch's Irish Humour; Mr. Punch's Life in London; Mr. Punch's Railway Book; Mr. Punch's Scottish Humour; Mr. Punch with Rod and Gun; Mr. Punch with the Children.
Quad, M. (The Detroit Free Press Man) (pseud. of Charles Bertrand Lewis) (1872) *Sparks of wit and humour*, London, Routledge.
R. W. a mighty lover of Welch travels (pseud. of William, Richard) (1682) *Wallography or the Britton describ'd*, London, Obadiah Blagrave.
Rabelais, François (1955) *Pantagruel roy des dipsodes* (Pantagruel Book 2) in Rabelais, F. *Oeuvres Complètes*, Paris, Gallimard.
Radine, Lawrence B. (1977) *The Taming of the Troops: Social Control in the United States Army*, Westport, Connecticut, Greenwood.
Radványi, Tibor B. (1988) *Zsidó-Viccek*, Budapest, Lapés Könyv.
Ragaway, Martin A. (1977) *Plains English*, Beverly Hills, Laughter Library.
'Rameses' [pseud. of Major Claude Scudamore Jarvis] (1937) *Oriental Spotlight*, London, John Murray.
Ramírez, Armando (1978) *El regreso de Chin-Chin el Teporocho*, Mexico City, Grijalbo.
Ramsay, Edward Bannerman (Dean) (1873; 20th ed.) *Reminiscences of Scottish Life and Character*, Edinburgh, Gall and Inglis.
Randolph, John (1952) *Texas Brags*, Tomball, Texas, John Randolph.
Randolph, Vance (1976) *Pissing in the Snow and Other Ozark Folktales*, Urbana, University of Illinois Press.
Ranke, Kurt (1972) *European Anecdotes and Jests*, Copenhagen, Rosenkilde and Bagger.
Rashmi and Amber (n.d.) *Children's Jokes*, New Delhi, New Light.
Raskin, Victor (1985) *Semantic Mechanisms of Humor*, Dordrecht, D. Reidel.
Redfern, Walter (1984) *Puns*, Oxford, Basil Blackwell.

Reed, Langford (1937) *The New Limerick Book*, London, Herbert Jenkins.
Rees, D. Ben (1975) *Chapels in the Valley*, Upton, Wirral, England, Ffynon.
Rees, Nigel (1979) *Graffiti lives, O.K?*, London, Unwin.
Rees, Nigel (1980A) *Graffiti 2*, London, Unwin.
Rees, Nigel (1980B) *Love, Death and the Universe*, London, Allen and Unwin.
Rees, Nigel (1981) *Eavesdroppings*, London, Unwin.
Rees, Nigel (1982) *Foot in Mouth*, London, Unwin.
Rees, Nigel (1983) *Quote . . . Unquote*, London, Allen and Unwin.
Rees, Thomas (1883) *History of Protestant Nonconformity in Wales*, London, John Snow.
Rees, Rev. T. Mardy (1922) *Hiwmor y Cymro*, Liverpool, Hugh Evans.
Reichert, Willy (1974) *Humor aus Schwaben*, Freiburg im Breisgau, Hyperion.
Reid, Jane (1983) *It Can't be True*, London, St. Michael.
Reid, Jane (1984) *It Takes All Sorts*, London, St. Michael.
Reid, Patrick Robert (1965) (1952) *The Latter Days at Colditz*, London, Coronet/ Hodder.
Reik, Theodore (1962) *Jewish Wit*, New York, Gamut.
Reitlinger, Gerald (1956) *The S.S., Alibi of a Nation 1922–1945*, London, Heinemann.
Reitlinger, Gerald (1967) *The Final Solution*, London, Valentine Mitchell.
Renkiewicz, Frank (ed.) (1973) *The Poles in America 1608–1972*, New York, Oceana.
Report of the Commission on the Church of England and other Religious Bodies in Wales and Monmouthshire (1910) London, H.M.S.O. (Cmnd. 5432).
Reuter, Rudolf (1965) *Tünnes und Schäl: Witz aus Köln*, Cologne, Bachem.
Rex, John (1969) "Race as a social category," in Harrison and Peel (eds.) pp.145–52.
Rezwin, G. Max (1983) *The Complete Book of Sick Jokes*, Secaucus New York, Citadel/Lyle Stuart.
Rhys, John and Brynmor-Jones, David (1909) *The Welsh People*, London, T. Fisher Unwin.
Richler, Mordecai (1986) *Home Sweet Home, My Canadian Album*, London, Grafton.
Richmond, Frank M. (1934) *School Yarns and Howlers*, London, Universal.
Ridere, Ridere . . . Ridere (1981) Milan, Euro.
Rinder, I. R. (1973) "Mental health of American Jewish urbanites, a review of literature and predictions," in Shiloh and Selavon (eds.) pp.310–19.
'Ringo-Ringo' (1978) *Todo empezó en Suiza*, Buenos Aires, Caymi.
Ripley, Robert LeRoy (n.d.) *The Omnibus Believe It or Not*, London, C. Arthur Pearson.
Rivers, Joan (1984) *The Life and Hard Times of Heidi Abramowitz*, New York, Delacorte.
Roback, Abraham Aaron (1944) *A Dictionary of International Slurs*, Cambridge, Mass., Sci-Art.
Robb, James H. (1954) *Working Class Anti-Semite*, London, Tavistock.
Roberts, James S. (1981) "Drink and industrial work discipline in nineteenth century Germany," in *Journal of Social History*, Fall, Vol.15, No.1, pp.25–38.
Roberts, Myron; Haynes, Lincoln; and Gilien, Sasha (1969) *The Begatting of a President*, New York, Ballantine.
Robertson, Kenneth Gordon (1982) *Public Secrets, a Study in the Development of Bureaucracy*, London, Macmillan.
Robertson, Roland (ed.) (1969) *Sociology of Religion*, Harmondsworth, Penguin.
Robey, George (1920) *After-Dinner Stories*, London, Grant Richards.
Robinson, W. Heath (1975) *Absurdities*, London, Duckworth.

Rocheman, Lionel (1981) *Les Contes de Grand-Père Schlomo*, Paris, Stock.
Rockwell, Joan (1981) *Evald Tang Kristensen: a Lifelong Adventure in Folklore*, Aalborg, Denmark, Aalborg University Press.
Roethlisberger, Fritz Jules and Dickson, William J. (1934) *Management and the Worker*, Boston, Harvard University Graduate School of Business Administration.
Rogers, Charles (1867) *Traits and stories of the Scottish People*, London, Houlston.
Röhrich (1977) *Ausgemachte Viechereien*, Freiburg im Breisgau, Herder.
Rokeach, Milton (1973) *The Nature of Human Values*, New York, Free Press.
Rokkan, Stein and Urwin, Derek W. (1982) *The Politics of Territorial Identity: Studies in European Regionalism*, London, Sage.
Rokkan, Stein and Urwin, Derek W. (1983) *Economy, Territory, Identity: Politics of West European Peripheries*, London, Sage.
Romorantin (1983) *Le Ultimissime Barzellette Sul Fine Settimana*, Milan, Omega.
Rose, Marius (1954) *The Intelligent Teacher's Guide to Preferment*, London, Chatto and Windus.
Rosemarine, B. (1962) *Haimishe Laffs and Chaffs*, Altrincham, England, John Sherratt.
Rosenberg, Alfred (ed. Robert Pois, 1970) *Selected Writings*, London, Jonathan Cape.
Rosenberg, Bernard and Shapiro, Gilbert (1958) "Marginality and Jewish humor," in *Midstream*, Vol.4, pp.70–80.
Rossiter, Leonard (1981) *The Lowest Form of Wit*, London, Michael Joseph.
Rosten, Leo Calvin (1970) *The Joys of Yiddish*, London, W. H. Allen.
Rosten, Leo Calvin (1973A) *Leo Rosten's Treasury of Jewish Quotations*, London.
Rosten, Leo Calvin (1973B) *Rome Wasn't Burned in a Day: The Mischief of Language*, London, W. H. Allen.
Rosten, Leo Calvin (1979) *O Kaplan! My Kaplan*, London, Constable.
Rosten, Leo Calvin (1983) *Hooray for Yiddish, a Book about English*, London, Elm Tree.
Rousseau, Jean-Jacques (1965; First pub. 1781) *The Confessions*, Harmondsworth, Penguin.
Royer, Jean-Michel (1977) *Le livre d'or de l' Assiette au Beurre*, Paris, Jean-Claud Simoën.
Royidis, Emmanuel/Durrell, Lawrence (1965; 1886) *Pope Joan*, London, Mayflower/Dell.
Rubenson, Sven (1976) *The Survival of Ethiopian Independence*, London, Heinemann.
Runninger, Jack and Powers, Nick (1971) *Favorite Jokes of Mountain Folks in Boogar Hollow*, Boogar Hollow, Lindale, Georgia, Country Originals.
Rushton, Dorgan (1983) *Brush up Your Pidgin*, London, Willow.
Russell, Leonard (1940) *English Wits*, London, Hutchinson.
Russell, Leonard and Bentley, Nicholas (eds.) (1948) *The English Comic Album*, London, Michael Joseph.
Russell, Lord of Liverpool (1954) *The Scourge of the Swastika*, London, Cassell.
Russell, Lord of Liverpool (1960) *The Knights of Bushido*, London, Transworld.
Russell, William Moy Stratten (1982) "Folk Tales and Science Fiction," in *Folklore*, Vol.93, No.1.
Ryder, Arthur John (1967) *The German Revolution of 1918*, Cambridge, England, Cambridge University Press.
Sabel, Charles F. (1982) *Work and Politics: The Division of Labour in Industry*, Cambridge, Cambridge University Press.
Safian, Louis A. (1966) *2000 Insults for All Occasions*, New York, Simon and Schuster.

'Salami, Swami Rami' (1971) *Help my Guru Died*, Hollywood, Pop Montcalm.
Salomone, Arcangelo William (ed.) (1971) *Italy from the Risorgimento to Fascism*, Newton Abbott, Devon, David and Charles.
Sampson, Alistair (1959) *Tonight and Other Nights*, London, Dennis Dobson.
Sanders, Deirdre; Girling, Dick; Davies, Derek; Sanders, Rick (1977) *'Choelia Ti*, Caernarfon, Wales, Cyhoeddiadau Mei.
Sannio, Mario (1985) *Barzellette per Tutte le Occasioni*, Milan, De Vecchi.
Santini, Nicky (n.d.) *Aprenda a contar chistes*, Mexico City, Chupe.
Sargent, Margaret (1979) *Drinking and Alcoholism in Australia*, Melbourne, Longman, Cheshire.
Sarolea, Charles (1912) *The Anglo-German Problem*, London, Nelson.
Saunders, Donald (1985) "F.A.'s Decision Makes Sense," in *Daily Telegraph*, London, March 30, p.33.
Saunders, Richard (1980) *The World's Greatest Hoaxes*, New York, Playboy.
Schaap, Ted (1956) *Two in a Tub*, London, Michael Joseph.
Schafer, Kermit (1973) *Best of Bloopers*, New York, Avenel.
Schechter, Barry (1986) "The day my father was saved from the Nazis," in *Washington Post*, Sunday June 8.
Schiff, Michael (1975) *Radio Eriwans Auslands Programm*, Frankfurt-am-Main, Fischer.
Schiff, Michael (1978) *Radio Eriwan antwortet*, Frankfurt-am-Main, Fischer.
Schmitt, Erich (1984) *Das dicke Schmitt-Buch*, Berlin, Eulenspiegel.
Schoeck, Helmut (1969) *Envy: A Theory of Social Behaviour*, London, Secker and Warburg.
Schöffler, Herbert (ed. Helmuth Plessner) (1970; First pub. 1941) *Kleine Geographie des Deutschen Witzes*, Göttingen, Vandenhoeck and Ruprecht.
Schorske, Carl Emil (1980) *Fin-de-Siècle Vienna, Politics and Culture*, London, Weidenfeld and Nicolson.
Schutz, Charles E. (1977) *Political Humor from Aristophanes to Sam Ervin*, Cranbury, N.J., Fairleigh Dickinson University Press/Associated University Presses.
Schütz, Hans J. (ed.) (1979) *Der Wahre Jacob, ein halbes Jahrhundert in Faksimiles*, Berlin, J. H. W. Dietz.
Schwartz, Alvin (1973) *Witcracks; Jokes and Jests from American Folklore*, Philadelphia, Lippincott.
Schwarzschild, Leopold (1948) *The Red Prussian*, London, Hamish Hamilton.
Schweizerische Volkszählung (1980) Berne, Swiss Federal Statistical Office.
Scitovsky, Tibor (1976) *The Joyless Economy, an inquiry into human satisfaction and consumer dissatisfaction*, New York, Oxford University Press.
Scopelliti, Franco (1981) *600 Barzellette Irresistibili*, Milan, De Vecchi.
Scott, W. W. (1931) *Breaks*, London, Jonathan Cape.
Searing, Roger (1984) "Tadley—the butt of local wits," in *Reading Chronicle–Midweek*, October 16, p.10.
Secombe, Harry (1977) *Goon for Lunch*, London, Star.
Sedgewick, Catherine (1841) "Letters from Abroad," in Commager (ed.) (1974).
Seipgens, Emile (1894) "How Mathis Knoups turned liberal and then Catholic again," in Werner (ed.) pp.212–231.
Selections of American Humour (1883) London, Cassell.
Sellar, Walter Carruthers and Yeatman, Robert Julian (1932) *And now all this*, London, Methuen.
Sertorio, Guido (1982) *Military, Bureaucracy and Society, a Survey on the Italian Situation*, Paper presented at the Military Sociology section of the 10th World Congress of Sociology, Mexico City, August 1982.
Service, Robert (1978) *The Best of Robert Service*, Toronto, McGraw-Hill, Ryerson.

Seton, George (1903) *A Budget of Anecdotes, Chiefly Relating to the Nineteenth Century*, London, Chapman and Hall.

Seton-Watson, Christopher (1967) *Italy from Liberalism to Fascism 1870–1925*, London, Methuen.

Seuling, Barbara (1976) *You Can't Eat Peanuts in Church and other little known Laws*, Garden City, New York, Doubleday.

Seward, Desmond (ed.) (1986) *Naples, a Traveller's Companion*, London, Constable.

Seymour, Robert (1914) *Humorous Masterpieces*, Glasgow, Gowans and Gray.

Shah, Idries (1972) *The Magic Monastery*, London, Jonathan Cape.

Shah, Idries (1978) *The Exploits of the Incomparable Mulla Nasrudin*, London, Pan.

Shakespeare, William (1964) *The Complete Works of William Shakespeare*, London, Oxford University Press.

Shakespeare's Jest Book, an edition of 'A hundred mery talys' (ed. Herman Oesterley, 1866) (1970), Gainesville Florida, Leonard R. A. Ashley.

Shankara, Pandit Dr. Shyama (1934) *Wit and Wisdom of India*, New York, Roerich Museum.

Shaw, B. D. (1939) *Is Hitler Dead?* New York, Alcaeus House.

Sherrin, Ned and Shand, Neil (1984) *1956 and All That*, London, Michael Joseph.

Shiloh, Ailon and Selavon, Ida Cohen (eds.) (1973) *Ethnic Groups of America: Their Morbidity Mortality and Behavior Disorders*, Vol.I, *The Jews*, Springfield, Illinois, Charles Thomas.

Shils, Edward (1975) *Centre and Periphery, Essays in Macro Sociology*, Chicago, University of Chicago Press.

Shils, Edward and Janowitz, Morris (1975) "Cohesion and disintegration in the Wehrmacht in World War II," in Shils.

Shinov, Chavdar et al. (eds.) (1981) *Gabrovit '81*, Sofia, Reklama.

Shirer, William L. (1960) *The Rise and Fall of the Third Reich*, London, Secker and Warburg.

Short, Martin (1984) *Crime Inc. The Story of Organised Crime*, London, Thames/Methuen.

Shtromas, Alexander and Kaplan, Morton (eds.) (1988) *The Soviet Union and the Challenge of the Future vol. I. The Soviet System: Stasis and Change*, New York, Paragon.

Šik, Ota (1967) "Socialist market relations and planning," in Feinstein, C. H. (ed.) *Socialism, Capitalism and Economic Growth*, Cambridge, Cambridge University Press.

Sillince, W. A. (1943) *United Notions*, London, Collins.

'Simple, Peter' (1963) *Way of the World*, London, Johnson.

'Simple, Peter' (1965) *Peter Simple in Opposition*, London, Johnson.

Simpson, Billy (1979) *The Best of Billy Simpson*, Belfast, Blackstaff.

Sinclair, Kevin (1980) "Crocodile, Tars and Feathers," in *Brisbane Courier Mail*, May 30.

Singer, Isaac Bashevis (1975) *The Fools of Chelm and their History*, London, Abelard.

Singh, Indera Paul (1967) "Caste in a Sikh Village," in *Sikhism and Indian Society, Transactions of the Indian Institute of Advanced Study*, Vol.4, Simla, Rashtrapati Nivas, pp.67–88.

Singh, Kirpal (1967) "Origins of Sikhism, socio-cultural context," in *Sikhism and Indian Society, Transactions of the Indian Institute of Advanced Study*, Vol.4, Simla, Rashtrapati Nivas, pp.102–38.

Sinha, Surajit (1975) "Religion in an affluent society," in Spradley and Rynkiewich (eds.) pp.309–22.

Skeels, Edward Ralph Serocold (1930) *Rhymes for Grown Up Children*, London, Alston Rivers.

Sklar, Robert (1970) "Humor in America," in Mendel (ed.) (1970A) pp.9–30.

Skotske Skottehistorier fra Scotland (n.d.) Copenhagen, Carit Andersens.

Sloan, Larry (1975) *The World's Worst Moron Jokes*, Los Angeles, Price Stern Sloan.

Sloggatt, Art Phyz (1965) *After the Council?* New York, Delphic.

Smiles, Samuel (ed. Thomas Mackay) (1905) *The Autobiography of Samuel Smiles*, London, John Murray.

Smith, Adam (1902; First pub. 1776) *An Inquiry into the nature and causes of the wealth of nations*, London, Routledge.

Smith, Anthony D. (1981) *The Ethnic Revival in the Modern World*, Cambridge, Cambridge University Press.

Smith, Denis Mack (1976) *Mussolini's Roman Empire*, London, Longman.

Smith, Denis Mack (1983) *Mussolini*, London, Grenada.

Smith, Harry Allen (1954) *The Compleat Practical Joker*, London, Arthur Barker.

Smith, Paul (1983) *The Book of Nasty Legends*, London, Routledge & Kegan Paul.

Smith, Paul (1986) *The Book of Nastier Legends*, London, Routledge & Kegan Paul.

Smith, Richard (1980) *The Dieter's Guide to Weight-loss after Sex*, London, Souvenir.

Smith, Rev. Sydney (1839–40) *The works of the Rev. Sydney Smith* [4 volumes], London, Longman Orme.

Smith, Rev. Sydney (1854) *The works of the Rev. Sydney Smith*, London, Longman Brown Green Longmans.

Smollett, Tobias (ed. David Herbert) (1885) *The Works of Tobias Smollett*, Edinburgh. W. P. Nimmo, Hay and Mitchell.

Smout, Thomas Christopher (1972) *A History of the Scottish People 1530–1830*, London, Collins.

Snyder, Charles R. (1962) "Culture and Jewish sobriety: The in-group and outgroup factor," in Pittman and Snyder (eds.).

Sobotka, Primus (1919) *Kratochvilná historie měst a míst státu Československého*, Prague, Jos. R. Vilímek.

'Sofocleto' (1980) *Los pendejos*, Mexico City, Vicova.

Soler, Jean (1973) "Sémiotique de la nourriture dans la Bible," in *Annales, Economies, Sociétés, Civilisations*, Vol.28-II, No.4, Juillet-Aout, pp.943–55.

Somerville, E. and Ross, Martin (1970) *The Irish R.M.*, London, Sphere.

Sorel, Edward (1978) *Superpen*, New York, Random House.

Sowell, Thomas (1981) *Ethnic America, a History*, New York, Basic.

Spalding, Henry D. (1969) *Encyclopaedia of Jewish Humor*, New York, Jonathan David.

Spalding, Henry D. (1976) *A Treasure-trove of American Jewish Humor*, New York, Jonathan David.

Spalding, Henry D. (1978) *The Lilt of the Irish*, New York, Jonathan David.

Speight, Johnny (1974) *The Thoughts of Chairman Alf*, London, Sphere.

Spencer, Frederick Herbert (1938) *An Inspector's Testament*, London, English Universities Press.

Spencer, Herbert (1904) *The Principles of Sociology*, London, Williams and Norgate.

Spencer, Herbert (ed. Donald G. Macrae) (1969) *The Man versus the State*, Harmondsworth, Penguin.

Spice, Paul and Spice, Sue (1987) *Jubilee 1887–1987*, Buckingham, Barracuda.

Spradley, James P. and Rynkiewich, Michael A. (eds.) (1975) *The Nacirema, Readings on American Culture*, Boston, Little Brown.

Spurgeon, Charles Haddon (1888) *Eccentric Preachers*, London, Passmore and Alabaster.
Stack, Laura (1977) *The Book of Kerry Woman Jokes*, Dublin, Mercier.
Stackman, Howard (1953) *Bedside Humour*, London, Elek.
Stallings, Laurence (1963) *The Doughboys*, New York, Harper and Row.
Stanley, Sir Henry Morton (ed. Dorothy Stanley) (1910) *The Autobiography of Sir Henry Morton Stanley*, London, Sampson Low Marston.
Stapleton, Alfred (1900) *All about the Merry Tales of Gotham*, Nottingham, R. N. Pearson.
Steeman, Stephane (1977) *Raconte . . . une fois les vraies histoires Belges*, Paris, Mengès.
Stephane, Bernard (1978) *Popeck raconte, les meilleures histoires de l'humeur Juif*, Paris, Mengès.
Stephenson, R. M. (1951) "Conflict and control functions of humor," in *American Journal of Sociology*, Vol.56, pp.569–74.
Sterling, Philip (1965) *Laughing on the Outside: The Intelligent White Readers Guide to Negro Tales and Humor*, New York, Grosset and Dunlap.
Stewart, Samuel D. (1963) *Campus Humor*, New York, Dell.
Stivers, Richard (1976) *A Hair of the Dog: Irish Drinking and American Stereotype*, University Park, Pennsylvania State University Press.
Stoianovich, Traian (1971) "Material Foundations of Pre-Industrial Civilisation in the Balkans," in *Journal of Social History*, Spring, Vol.4, No.3, pp.205–262.
Stone, Norman (1983) *Europe Transformed 1878–1919*, London, Fontana.
Storey, Tom and Girlroy, Sean (1968) *The World's Worst Jokes*, London, Wolfe.
Stouffer, Samuel Andrew; Suchman, Edward A.; De Vinney, Leonard C.; Star, Shirley A.; Williams, Robin M., Jr. (1949A) *Studies in Social Psychology in World War II* Vol.1, *The American Soldier: Adjustment During Army Life*, Princeton, N.J., Princeton University Press.
Stouffer, Samuel Andrew; Lumsdaine, Arthur A.; Lumsdaine, Marion Harper; Williams, Robin M., Jr.; Smith, M. Brewster; Janis, Irving L.; Star, Shirley A.; Cottrell, Leonard S., Jr. (1949B) *Studies in Social Psychology in World War II* Vol.2, *The American Soldier: Combat and Its Aftermath*, Princeton, N.J., Princeton University Press.
Strange, Lord (1965) Speech in House of Lords, *Hansard* 5th series, vol.268, col.615, July 20.
Stranks, Susan and Grand, Don (1980) *Are You Sitting Comfortably?* London, Macdonald.
Stubble, Monty (1987) *Battle for Britain*, London, Private Eye/André Deutsch.
Sturman, Dora (1984) "Soviet joking matters: six leaders in search of character," in *Survey*, Vol.28, No.3 (122), Autumn, pp.205–220.
Sturzo, Luigi (1971) "How counter-revolutions are made, the coup de main of October 1922," in Salomone (ed.) pp.197–204.
Styan, John Louis (1981) *Modern Drama in Theory and Practice Vol.I Realism and Naturalism*, Cambridge, Cambridge University Press.
Štych, Jiří (1970) *Přímo od čepu*, Prague, Melantrich.
Sullivan, James (1903) *The Hayseed Joker*, Cleveland, Ohio, Arthur Westbrook.
Sunbeams (1922) London, Stanley Paul.
Suomalainen, Kari (1953) *Parhaat; kokoelma valittuja myös ennen julkaisemattomia pilapürroksia*, Sanoma, Pürrosparaati.
Suomalainen, Kari (1977) *Keisarivalssi*, Helsinki, Otava.
Swaffield, D. E. (ed.) (1934) *It's Wonderful*, London, Universal.
Swain, David (1965) *The Cant Be Worried Tales*, Sydney, Ure Smith.
Swift, Jonathan (ed. Herbert Davis, 1935; First pub. 1724/1735) *The Drapier's*

Letters to the People of Ireland against receiving Wood's Halfpence, Oxford, Clarendon.
Sykes, Andrew James Macintyre (1966) "Joking relationships in an industrial setting," in *American Anthropologist* 68, pp.188–93.
Sykes, Christopher (1959) *Orde Wingate*, London, Collins.
Szarota, Tomasz (1978) "Poland and Poles in German eyes during World War II," in *Polish Western Affairs*, No.2, pp.229–54.
Taft, Harry (1935) *All Boloney*, London, Universal.
Taggart, Sir James (1927) *Stories Told by Sir James Taggart*, Dundee, Valentine.
Tailleur, Max (1973) *Met een Mop de Wereld Rond*, Bussum, Netherlands, Van Holkema, and Warendorf.
Tailleur, Max (1977) *Jiddisch Fruit*, Amsterdam, Becht.
Tailleur, Max (1979) *Van Sex-tien tot Sex-tig*, Bussum, Netherlands, Van Holkema and Warendorf.
Tales from Wales (1946) Cardiff, Priory.
Tame, Chris R. (1984) "Bottom Marx," in *Economic Affairs*, Vol.4, No.3, April-June, pp.39–41.
Tandy, Jeanette (1925) *Crackerbox Philosophers: American Humor and Satire*, New York, Columbia University Press.
Tannahill, Reay (1975) *Flesh and Blood, A History of the Cannibal Complex*, London, Hamish Hamilton.
Tarnóky, A. L. (1977) letter in *World Medicine*, Vol.13, June 29.
Taylor, Alan John Percivale (1982) *The Course of German History*, London, Methuen.
Taylor, Frank (1972) *The Wit of the Classroom*, London, Leslie Frewin.
Taylor, Frank (1984) "Latest Reagan gaffe revives the age issue," in *Daily Telegraph*, August 16, p.4.
Taylor, Fred (ed.). See Goebbels.
Taylor Nelson Report: Social Change, Present and Future (1984) Epsom, Surrey, Taylor Nelson Group.
Taylor, Susette M. (1906) *The Humour of Spain*, London, Walter Scott.
Teagueland Jests or Bogg Witticisms (1690) London.
Teitel, G. (1977) *The Genesis of the Professional Officer Corps*, Beverly Hills, Sage.
Tempel, Earle (1970) *Classified Humor*, New York, Simon Schuster.
Teresa, Vincent and Renner, Thomas C. (1973) *My Life in the Mafia*, London, Hart-Davis MacGibbon.
Ternhag, Gunnar (1975) "Nynorsk på Svenska," in *Tradisjon* 5, pp.69–71.
Tessier, Carmen (1955) *Histoires de Marie-Chantal*, Paris, Gallimard.
Thackeray, William Makepeace (1879) *Burlesques*, London, Smith Elder.
Thackeray, William Makepeace (1898) *Thackerayana*, London, Chatto and Windus.
Thackeray, William Makepeace (1908) *Miscellaneous Contributions to Punch 1843–54*, London, Oxford University Press.
Thackeray, William Makepeace (1949) *The English Humourists and The Four Georges*, London, J. M. Dent.
Thelwell, Norman (1967) *Up the Garden Path*, London, Methuen.
Thelwell, Norman (1968) *Thelwell's Book of Leisure*, London, Methuen.
Theroux, Paul (1967) "Hating the Asians," in *Transition*, Vol.7(ii), No.33, October/November, pp.46–51.
Theroux, Paul (1975) *The Great Railway Bazaar*, London, Hamish Hamilton.
Thestrup, Ole (1981) *Spege-Silden og Ålen*, Copenhagen, Apostrof.
Thickett, Maude (Series 4 Vols. 1984–88) *Outrageously Offensive Jokes*, New York, Pocket.

Thomas, Dylan Marlais (1954) *Under Milk Wood: a play for voices*, London, J. M. Dent.
Thomas, Gerald (1976) "Newfie Jokes," in Fowkes (ed.).
Thomas, Gwyn (1985) *High on Hope*, Cowbridge, Wales, D. Brown.
Thomas, Hugh (1965) *The Spanish Civil War*, Harmondsworth, Penguin.
'Thomas, John' (1979) *Best Rugby Jokes*, London, Arthur Barker.
Thomas, Jonathan (1976) *English as She is Fraught*, London, Wolfe.
Thomas, Keith (1977) "The place of laughter in Tudor and Stuart England," in *Times Literary Supplement*, January 21.
Thomas, Lowell Jackson (1931) *Tall Stories, the Rise and Triumph of the Great American Whopper*, London, Hutchinson.
Thomas, Samuel Evelyn (1942) *Laughs with the Home Guard*, London, Harrap.
Thomas, Samuel Evelyn (1944A) *Good Humour*, London, S. Evelyn Thomas.
Thomas, Samuel Evelyn (1944B) *Laughs with the Navy*, St. Albans, S. Evelyn Thomas.
Thomas, Samuel Evelyn (1946) *Laughs with the Workers*, St. Albans, S. Evelyn Thomas.
Thomas, Samuel Evelyn (1947A) *Laughs with the Lovelies*, Northolt, Middlesex, P. J. Press.
Thomas, Samuel Evelyn (1947B) *Laughs around the Land*, Northolt, Middlesex, P. J. Press.
Thomas, Samuel Evelyn (1947C) *More Laughs with the Forces*, St. Albans, S. Evelyn Thomas.
Thomas, Samuel Evelyn (n.d.) *Laughter Awheel*, London, S. Evelyn Thomas.
Thomas, William I. and Znaniecki, Florian (1958) (as 2nd edit.) *The Polish Peasant in Europe and America*, New York, Dover.
Thompson, Barney (1972) *Typogoofs*, Greenwich, Conn., Fawcett.
Thompson, Eric J. (1976) "Patterns of migration," in Harrison, S. A. and Gibson, J. B. (eds.) *Man in Urban Environments*, London, Oxford University Press.
Thompson, Harry et al. (1987) *The News Quiz Book of the News*, London, Robson.
Thompson, Harry and Berkmann, Marcus (1986) *Shorties*, London, Corgi.
Thompson, Roger (ed.) (1976) *Samuel Pepys' Penny Merriments*, London, Constable.
Thompson, Stith (1977) *The Folktale*, Berkeley, University of California Press.
Thorp, Willard (1964) *American Humorists*, Minneapolis, University of Minnesota Press.
Thousand Witty Sayings (n.d.) London, Milner.
Thrid Book of Boobs from Private Eye, The (1985) London, Private Eye/André Deutsch.
Tidy, Bill (1969) *Tidy's World*, London, Hutchinson.
Tidy, Bill and Hillier, Bevis (1974) *Dead Funny*, London, Ash and Grant.
Timpson, John (1983) *The Lighter Side of Today*, London, Allen and Unwin.
Tinniswood, Peter (1981) *Tales from a Long Room*, London, Arrow.
Todd, George (1977) *Todd's Geordie Words and Phrases*, Newcastle on Tyne, Frank Graham.
Took, Barry (1975) *The Max Miller Blue Book*, London, Robson.
Took, Barry (1983) *Took's Eye View*, London, Robson.
Toledo, Monteforte (1965) *Guatemala. Monografìa Sociologica*, Mexico City, Universidad Nacional Antonoma de Mexico.
Tolstoy, Nikolai (1982) *Stalin's Secret War*, London, Pan.
Tóth, Béla (1935) *A Magyar Anekdotakincs*, Budapest, Singer and Wolfner.
Tower, Charles (1913) *Germany of Today*, London, Williams and Norgate.
Toynbee, Arnold J. (1915) *Armenian atrocities, the murder of a nation*, London, Hodder and Stoughton.

Toynbee, Arnold J. (1946) *A Study of History*, London, Oxford University Press.
Train, John (1979) *Remarkable Names of Real People*, London, Futura.
Treitschke, Heinrich von (1914) *Selections from Treitschke's Lectures on Politics*, London, Gowans and Gray.
Treitschke, Heinrich von (see also Davis, Henry William Charles).
'Trends in anti-Israel cartoons' (1985) in *Academic Study Group Bulletin*, No.8, Autumn, pp.4–6.
Tresilian, Liz (1968) *The W. C. Companion*, London, Arlington.
Treudley, Mary Bosworth (1946) "An ethnic group's view of the American middle-class," in *American Sociological Review*, Vol.11, No.6, December, pp.715–24.
Trevelyan, George Macaulay (1919) *Scenes from Italy's war*, London, T. C. and E. C. Jack.
Trevelyan, George Macaulay (1928) *Garibaldi and the Thousand, May 1860*, London, Nelson.
Triverton, Sanford (1981) *Complete Book of Ethnic Jokes*, New York, Galahad/A and W.
Trollope, Mrs. Frances Milton (1832) *Domestic manners of the Americans*, London, Whittaker Treacher.
Trudeau, Garry B. (1973) *Call Me When You Find America*, New York, Holt Rinehart and Winston.
Trudeau, Garry B. (1984) *Doonesbury Dossier*, New York, Holt Rinehart and Winston.
Trudgill, Peter (1974) *Sociolinguistics, an Introduction*, Harmondsworth, Penguin.
Tuchman, Barbara W. (1971; First pub. 1958) *The Zimmerman Telegram*, New York, Bantam.
Tuchman, Barbara W. (1967; First pub. 1966) *The Proud Tower, a portrait of the world before the war 1890–1914*, New York, Bantam.
Tulk, Bob (1971) *Newfie Jokes*, Mount Pearl, Newfoundland.
Tulk, Bob (1972) *New Newfie Jokes*, Mount Pearl, Newfoundland.
Tulk, Bob (1973) *Bob Tulk's Newfie Jokes*, Mount Pearl, Newfoundland.
Tulk, Bob (1974) *Even Funnier Newfie Jokes*, Mount Pearl, Newfoundland.
Tumin, Stephen (1983) *Great Legal Disasters*, London, Arthur Barker.
Tünnes und Schäl Witze (1976) Frankfurt-am-Main, Fischer.
Turner, Frederick Jackson (1962) *The Frontier in American History*, New York, Holt Rinehart Winston.
Twain, Mark (ed. Victor Doyno) (1983) *Selected writings of an American Sceptic*, Buffalo, Prometheus.
Tyndale-Biscoe, Cecil Earle (1925) *Kashmir in sunlight and shade*, London, Seeley Service.
Uberoi, J. P. Singh (1967) "On being unshorn," in *Sikhism and Indian Society. Transactions of the Indian Institute of Advanced Study* Vol.4, Simla, Rashtrapati Nivas, pp.89–100.
'Unspeakable Scot, An' (1937) *Wit, Wisdom and Humour*, Glasgow, Archibald Sinclair.
Up to Date Jokes and Jests (n.d.) London.
Up to Date Wit and Humour (n.d.) London.
Up with Skool (1981) Harmondsworth, Penguin.
Urquhart, Brian (1987) *A Life in Peace and War*, London, Weidenfeld and Nicolson.
Usher, Ronald G. (1914) *Pan-Germanism*, London, Constable.
Utley, Francis Lee (1965) "Folk Literature: an operational definition," in Dundes (ed.) pp.12–13.

Utley, Francis Lee (1971–73) "The Urban and Rural Jest," in *Béaloideas*, Nos. 39–41, pp.344–57.
"UVa and Tech the Jokes on You" (1987), in *The News and Daily Advance*, September 17, Lynchburg, Virginia, pp.C1-C2.
Uysal, Ahmet E. and Walker, Warren S. (1974) "Saintly fools and the Moslem establishment," in *Journal of American Folklore*, 87, pp.357–61.
Van den Broeck, Walter (1976) *Minder Cola met nog meer rietjes*, The Hague, Manteau.
Van der Boute-Hen Train (1978) *Anthologie de l'humeur Belge*, Paris, Garnier Frères.
Van Dyke, Dick (1970) *Faith, Hope, and Hilarity*, Garden City, New York, Doubleday.
Van Lennep, Jacob (1894) "The village on the frontier," in Werner (ed.) pp.261–90.
Vansittart, Robert Gilbert, Baron Vansittart (1941) *Black Record, Germans Past and Present*, London, Hamish Hamilton.
Varga, György N. (1986) *Vicc-magazin*, Budapest, Kossuth.
Varga, György N. (1987) *Vicc-kosár*, Budapest, Kossuth.
Vatikiotis, Panayiotis Jerasimof (1961) *The Egyptian Army in Politics: Pattern for New Nations?* Bloomington, Indiana, Indiana University Press.
Vaughan, W. E. (1983) *Sin, Sheep and Scotsmen*, Belfast, Appletree.
Veblen, Thorstein (1899) *The theory of the leisure class*, New York, Macmillan.
Veitch, Andrew (1981) *Naked Ape, an Anthology of Male Chauvinism*, London, Duckworth.
Velure, Magne (1983) "Djävla Utlänning! Rykte og Vitsar om innvandrarar i Sverige," in *Tradisjon*, 13, pp.3–21.
Verbruggen, J. F. (1977) *The Art of Warfare in Western Europe during the Middle Ages*, Amsterdam, North Holland.
Veszy-Wagner, Lilla (1970) " 'Gay' jocularity of the homosexual," in Mendel (ed.) pp.81–85.
Vidler, Alec (Alexander) Roper (1961) *The Church in an Age of Revolution*, Harmondsworth, Penguin.
Vieria, Nelson H. (1980) "The Luso-Brazilian Joke," in *Western Folklore*, Vol.30, pp.51–56.
Vincent, Peter (1977A) *The Two Ronnies, but first - The News*, London, W. H. Allen.
Vincent, Peter (1977B) *Nice to be with you again, more of the Two Ronnies*, London, Star.
Vishwanath, M. (1976) *Smile a-while*, Bangalore, India, Rajdeep.
Voinovich, Vladimir (1978) *The life and extraordinary adventures of private Ivan Chonkin*, Harmondsworth, Penquin.
von Bernhardi, General Friedrich (1914) *Germany and the Next War*, London, Edward Arnold.
von Bülow, Prince Bernhard (1914) *Imperial Germany*, London, Cassell.
von der Melden, Fred R. (1976) "Pariah Communities and Violence," in Rosenbaum, H. Jon and Sederburg, P. C. (eds.) *Vigilante Politics*, Philadelphia, University of Pennsylvania Press, pp.218–33.
von Mises, Ludwig (1974) *Socialism, an Economic and Sociological Analysis*, London, Jonathan Cape.
von Treitschke, Heinrich (1914) *Selections from Treitschke's Lectures on Politics*, London, Gowans and Gray.
von Treitschke. See Davis, H. W. C.
von Wieland, C. M. (1861) *The Republic of Fools, being the history of the state and people of Abdera in Thrace*, London, W. H. Allen.

'W' (1978). See 'G-W'.
W.B. (1928) *Two Five Five Smiles*, Blackpool, Strebor.
Walker, Caroline and Cannon, Geoffrey (1985) *The Food Scandal*, London, Century.
Walker, P. J. (1981) *Democracy and Sectarianism: A Political and Social History of Liverpool 1868–1938*, Liverpool, Liverpool University Press.
Wallington, Mark (1987) *Destination Lapland*, London, Hutchinson.
Wallis-Jones, W. J. (1898) *Welsh Characteristics*, London, Western Mail.
Wannan, Bill (ed.) (1963) *Modern Australian Humour*, London, Angus and Robertson.
Ward, Bob (1982) *The Light Stuff, Space Humor from Sputnik to Shuttle*, Huntsville, Alabama, Jester.
Ward, Christopher (1980) *Our cheque is in the post*, London, Secker and Warburg.
Ward, Russell (1966) *The Australian Legend*, Melbourne, Oxford University Press.
Wardroper, John (1970) *Jest upon Jest: a selection from the Jest books and collections of Merry Tales published from the reign of Richard II to George III*, London, Routledge & Kegan Paul.
Wardroper, John (ed.) (1976; Facsimile of 1511) *The Demaundes Joyous*, London, Gordon Fraser.
Wardroper, John (1977) *The Caricatures of George Cruikshank*, London, Gordon Fraser.
Watt, Donald Cameron (1975) "Nazi political warfare," in Cecil and Goodenough (eds.).
Waugh, Evelyn (1965; First pub. 1928) *Decline and Fall*, Harmondsworth, Penguin.
Waugh, Evelyn (1932) *Black Mischief*, London, Chapman and Hall.
Waugh, Evelyn (1958; First pub. 1948) *The Loved One, an Anglo-American Tragedy*, London, Chapman and Hall.
Webb, Garrison (1976) *Lost Pages from American History*, Harrisburg, Pennsylvania, Stockpole.
Weber, Max (1930) *The Protestant Ethic and the Spirit of Capitalism*, London, Unwin.
Weber, Max (1947) *The Theory of Social and Economic Organisation*, London, Hodge.
Weber, Max (ed. H. H. Gerth and C. W. Mills) (1948) *From Max Weber, Essays in Sociology*, London, Routledge & Kegan Paul.
Weber, Max (1961) "Ethnic Groups," in Parsons et al. (eds.) Vol.I, pp.305–09.
Wechster, H.; Demone, H. W., Jr.; Thurn, D.; Kasey, E. H. (1973) "Religious-ethnic differences in alcohol consumption," in Shiloh and Selavon (eds.) pp.274–84.
Weinberg, A. A. (1973) "On comparative mental health research of the Jewish people," in Shiloh and Selavon (eds.) pp.320–33.
Weinryb, Bernard N. (1970) "Anti-Semitism in Soviet Russia," in Kochan (ed.).
Weinstein, Sol (1971) *Everything you never wanted to know about sex*, New York, Paperback Library/Rary.
Weiss, Harry B. (1965) "Something about Simple Simon," in Dundes (ed.) pp.400–413.
Weiss, M. (1967) "Rebirth in the airborne," in *Transaction*, 4, May, pp.23–26.
Welland, Colin (1982) *Colin Welland's Anthology of Northern Humour*, Feltham, Middlesex, Hamlyn.
Wells, Herbert George (1928) *A Quartette of Comedies*, London, Ernest Benn.
Welsch, Roger L. (1967) "American numskull tales: the Polack joke," in *Western Folklore*, Vol.26, pp.183–86.
Werner, Alice (ed.) (1892) *The Humour of Italy*, London, Walter Scott.
Werner, Alice (ed.) (1894) *The Humour of Holland*, London, Walter Scott.

Wesson, Robert (1984) "Totalitarian strengths and weaknesses," in *Survey*, Vol.28, No.3 (122), Autumn, pp.186–204.
West, Nathanael (pseud. of Nathan Wallenstein Weinstein) (1965) *The Collected Works of Nathanael West*, Harmondsworth, Penguin.
Weyl, Nathaniel (1979) *Karl Marx: Racist*, New Rochelle, Arlington House.
White, Jean and Morris, Michael (1978) *Post Scripts Humor*, Indianapolis, Curtis.
White, William Allen (1946) Autobiography in Commager (ed.) (1974) pp.658–66.
Whitelands Rag (1985) London, Whitelands College Students Union.
Whiting, Charles (1986) *Kasserine*, New York, Stein and Day.
Whittam, John Richard (1977) *The Politics of the Italian Army 1861–1918*, London, Croom Helm.
Wholly Libel, The (1978) London, Private Eye/André Deutsch.
Wicks, Ben (1976) *Ben Wicks' Canada*, Toronto.
Wieland, von C. M. (1861) *The Republic of Fools, being the history of the state and people of Abdera in Thrace*, London, W. H. Allen.
Wiener, Martin J. (1985) *English Culture and the Decline of the Industrial Spirit 1850–1980*, Harmondsworth, Penguin.
Wight, Robin (1972) *The Day the Pigs Refused to be Driven to Market*, London, Hart-Davis.
Wilde, Larry (1973) *The Official Polish/Italian Jokebook*, New York, Pinnacle.
Wilde, Larry (1974) *The Official Jewish/Irish Jokebook*, Los Angeles, Pinnacle.
Wilde, Larry (1975A) *More the Official Polish/Italian Jokebook*, Los Angeles, Pinnacle.
Wilde, Larry (1975B) *The Official Virgins/Sex Maniacs Jokebook*, New York, Pinnacle.
Wilde, Larry (1975C) *The Official White Folks/Black Folks Joke Book*, New York, Pinnacle.
Wilde, Larry (1976) *The Official Religious/Not So Religious Joke Book*, New York, Pinnacle.
Wilde, Larry (1977) *The Last Official Polish Joke-Book*, Los Angeles, Pinnacle.
Wilde, Larry (1978A) *The Complete Book of Ethnic Humor*, Los Angeles, Corwin.
Wilde, Larry (1978B) *The Official Dirty Joke Book*, Los Angeles, Pinnacle.
Wilde, Larry (1978C) *The Last Official Italian Jokebook*, Los Angeles, Pinnacle.
Wilde, Larry (1979A) *More, The Official Jewish/Irish Joke Book*, Los Angeles, Pinnacle.
Wilde, Larry (1979B) *The Official Book of Sick Jokes*, Los Angeles, Pinnacle.
Wilde, Larry (1980A) *The Last Official Jewish Joke Book*, Los Angeles, Pinnacle.
Wilde, Larry (1980B) *The Official Republican/Democrat Joke Book*, Los Angeles, Pinnacle.
Wilde, Larry (1981) *The Official Doctors Joke Book*, New York, Bantam.
Wilde, Larry (1982) *The Official Lawyers Joke Book*, New York, Bantam.
Wilde, Larry (1983A) *The Absolutely Last Official Polish Joke Book*, New York, Bantam.
Wilde, Larry (1983B) *The Last Official Irish Joke Book*, New York, Bantam.
Wilde, Larry (1984) *The Official Rednecks Joke Book*, New York, Bantam.
Wilde, Larry (1985) *The Official Sports Maniacs Joke Book*, New York, Bantam.
Wilde, Larry (1986A) *The Ultimate Jewish Joke Book*, New York, Bantam.
Wilde, Larry (1986B) *The Official Executive Joke Book*, New York, Bantam.
Wiliams, Dafydd (1830) *Dychweliad D. Wiliams, y cymro o Mexico trwy unol daleithiau America yn 1829*, Swansea, J. Wiliams.
Willans, Geoffrey and Roetter, Charles (1954) *The Wit of Winston Churchill*, London, Max Parrish.
Willey, David (1984) *Italians*, London, B.B.C.
Williams, Charlie (1973) *Ee—I've had some laughs*, London, Wolfe.

Williams, E. F. (1976) "The development of the meat industry," in Oddy and Miller (eds.).

Williams, G. J. and Thomas, Iorwerth (1979) *Hiwmor Dyffryn Nantlle*, Caernarfon, Wales, Cyhoeddiadau Mei.

Williams, Gwyn A. (1979A) *When Was Wales?*, London, B.B.C.

Williams, Gwyn A. (1979B) *Madoc. The Making of a Myth*, London, Eyre Methuen.

Williams, Gwyn A. (1985) *When Was Wales? A History of the Welsh*, London, Black Raven.

Williams, Ivor and Strydom, Hans (1980) *The Super Afrikaners*, Johannesburg, Jonathan Ball.

Williams, Janice (1987) *Conceptual Change and Religious Practice*, Aldershot, Hampshire, Avebury/Gower.

Williams, Kenneth (1980) *Acid Drops*, London, J. M. Dent.

Williams, W. Ogwen (1967) "The social order in Tudor Wales," in *Transactions of the Honorable Society of Cymmrodorion*, Session 1967, Part 2, pp.167–78.

Wilson, Bryan R. (1969) *Religion in Secular Society*, Harmondsworth, Penguin.

Wilson, Bryan R. (ed.) (1974A) *Rationality*, Oxford, Basil Blackwell.

Wilson, Bryan R. (1974B) "A sociologist's introduction," in Wilson (ed.) (1974A) pp.vii-xviii.

Wilson, Bryan R. (1982) *Religion in Sociological Perspective*, Oxford, Oxford University Press.

Wilson, Bryan R. (1985) "Morality in the evolution of the modern social system," in *British Journal of Sociology*, Vol.36, No.3, Sept., pp.315–32.

Wilson, Christopher P. (1979) *Jokes: Form, Content, Use and Function*, London, Academic.

Wilson, Glenn D. (1973) "Conservatism and response to humour," in Wilson, Glenn D. (ed.) *The Psychology of Conservatism*, London, Academic Press.

Wilson, Justin and Jacobs, Howard (1979) *Justin Wilson's Cajun Humor*, Gretna, Louisiana, Pelican.

Wilson, Paul (1980) "Drinking Habits in the United Kingdom," in *Population Trends* 22, Winter, pp.14–28.

Winch, Peter (1974) "Understanding a primitive society," in Wilson (ed.) pp.1–17.

Windsor, Barbara (1979) *Barbara Windsor's Book of Boobs*, London, Hamlyn.

Winick, Charles (1961) "Space jokes as indication of attitudes towards space," in *Journal of Social Issues*, Vol.17, No.2, pp.43–49.

Winston, Richard (1982) *Thomas Mann, the Making of an Artist 1875–1911*, London, Constable.

Wintle, Lt. Col. Alfred Daniel (1968) *The Last Englishman*, London, Michael Joseph.

Wirth, Louis (1961) "The problem of minority groups," in Parsons et al. (eds.).

Wit and wisdom or the world's jest book (1826) London, Joseph Smith.

Wolfenstein, Martha (1975) "The emergence of fun morality," in Spradley and Rynkiewich (eds.) pp.394–402.

Wolff, H. A.; Smith, C. E.; Murray, H. A. (1934) "The psychology of humor, a study of responses to race-disparagement jokes," in *The Journal of Abnormal and Social Psychology*, Vol.28, No.4, Jan-March.

Wood, Alan and Wood, Mary Seaton (1976) *Islands in Danger*, London, New English Library.

Wood, Lieut. I. E. R. (ed.) (1946) *Detour*, London, Falcon.

Wood, Starr (1933) *Cocktail Time*, London, T. Werner Laurie.

The World's Even Worse Worst Jokes Book (1985) Manchester, World International.

Wright, C. Kent (1935) *The Lighter Side of Local Government*, London, Allen and Unwin.

Wright, John Charles (1921) *Children's Humour*, London, George G. Harrap.

'Mr. X'; Henderson, Bruce E.; and Cyr, C. C. (1979) *Double Eagle: The Autobiography of a Polish Spy Who Defected to the West*, New York, Ballantine.

Yannopoulos, George (1985) *Reluctant Province: The History of Newfoundland's Union with Canada in the Light of the Modern Theory of Economic Integration*, University of Reading Graduate School of European and International Studies Discussion Paper, No.5.

Yao, George (ed.) (1946) *Chinese wit and humor*, New York, Coward-McCann.

Yearhouse, H. A. (1974A) *De Forste 59 Aarhus-Historier*, Copenhagen, Chr. Erichsen.

Yearhouse, H. A. (1974B) *60 Nye Aarhus Historier*, Copenhagen, Chr. Erichsen.

Yearhouse, H. A. (1979) *De Bedste Århus Historier*, Copenhagen, Chr. Erichsen.

Youngman, Henry (1966) *400 Traveling Salesmen's Jokes*, Richmond Hill Ontario, Simon and Schuster.

Zajdman, Felix (1979) *Sonria, por Favor*, Mexico City, Diana.

Zall, Paul Maxwell (ed.) (1977) *A Hundred Merry Tales and other English Jestbooks of the Fifteenth and Sixteenth Centuries*, Lincoln, University of Nebraska Press.

Zebrik, Reginald E. (1976) "Russian Rebels: an introduction to the memoirs of the Russian workers Semen Kanatchikov and Matrei Fisher," in *Russian Review*, Vol.35, Part 3, July, pp.249–89.

Zenner, Walter P. (1970) "Joking and ethnic stereotyping," in *Anthropological Quarterly*, Vol.43, pp.93–113.

Zewbskewiecz, E. D.; Kuligowski, Jerome; and Krulka, Harvey (1965) *It's fun to be a Polack*, Glendale Calif. Collectors.

Ziegler, P. Thomas (1956) *The Meat We Eat*, Danville, Illinois, Interstate.

Zijderveld, Anton C. (1968) "Jokes and their relation to social reality," in *Social Research*, 35:2, pp.286–311.

Zijderveld, Anton C. (1983) "Trend report on the sociology of humour and laughter," in *Current Sociology*, Vol.31, No.3, Winter, pp.35–59.

Zillman, Dolf and Bryant, J. (1974) "Retaliatory equity as a factor in humor appreciation," in *Journal of Experimental and Social Psychology*, Vol.10, pp.480–88.

Zillman, Dolf and Cantor, R. J. (1972) "Directionality of transitory dominance as communication variable affecting humor appreciation," in *Journal of Personality and Social Psychology*, Vol.24, pp.191–98.

Zinoviev, Alexander (1985) *The Reality of Communism*, London, Granada.

Ziv, Avner (1984) *Personality and Sense of Humor*, New York, Springer.

Ziv, Avner (1986A) "Psycho-social aspects of Jewish Humor in Israel and in the Diaspora," in Ziv (ed.), pp.47–71.

Ziv, Avner (ed.) (1986B) *Jewish Humor*, Tel Aviv, Papyrus/Tel Aviv University.

Zoltán, Iszlai (1987) *A fehér asztaltól a sárga földig*, Budapest, Editorg.

Zuckmayer, Carl (1961) *Der Hauptmann von Köpernick*, Frankfurt-am-Main, Fischer.

Zurawski, Joseph W. (1975) *Polish American History and Culture, a classified bibliography*, Chicago, Polish Museum of America.

Index